D1682501
9780318650029

TRIAL TECHNIQUE

BY

IRVING GOLDSTEIN

MEMBER OF THE CHICAGO BAR; FORMER ASSISTANT STATE'S ATTORNEY; INSTRUCTOR IN TRIAL TECHNIQUE AT NORTHWESTERN UNIVERSITY SCHOOL OF LAW

FIRST PRINTING, SEPTEMBER 17, 1935
SECOND PRINTING, OCTOBER 4, 1935
THIRD PRINTING, NOVEMBER 2, 1935
FOURTH PRINTING, SEPTEMBER 23, 1936
FIFTH PRINTING, OCTOBER 20, 1937
SIXTH PRINTING, FEBRUARY 4, 1938
SEVENTH PRINTING, APRIL 14, 1938
EIGHTH PRINTING, MAY 1, 1939
NINTH PRINTING, JULY 1, 1940
TENTH PRINTING, JULY 1, 1943

CHICAGO
CALLAGHAN AND COMPANY
1935

Dedicated To

MY WIFE

WHOSE ENCOURAGEMENT
AND INSPIRATION HAVE MADE
THIS EFFORT POSSIBLE

PREFACE

A practical book on trial procedure from the viewpoint of the attorney who must try cases should have: (1) Question and answer illustrations covering the technique involved in making proof of all facts in all types of cases, (2) It should cover all phases of trial tactics and the psychology of the court-room, (3) Citations of authorities to sustain all illustrations and points of law set out, (4) Illustrations and points of law simply indexed for ready and quick reference, (5) It should be in one compact volume so as to be available for use in the court-room during the progress of the trial and (6) It should be plainly and simply written so as to be easily understandable.

It has been my endeavor to cover all of the above requirements in this book. The illustrations have been gathered from more than a thousand records of actual cases tried by leading and successful trial attorneys. Every type of case is represented. Almost every situation that may arise, in either the ordinary or unusual case, has been covered. The personal injury case, the medical or chemical case and the ordinary contract action, in all of their phases, have been considered. Illustrations have been collected and set out to take care of the daily needs of the trial lawyer and of the general practitioner who only occasionally goes into court. As for the novice, it is my hope that it will frequently prove to be a veritable "life-saver."

The many suggestions contained herein as to the right and wrong ways of conducting examinations of both jurors and witnesses—the methods of addressing the Court, as well as the psychological methods of appealing to the jury in an effort to influence a favorable verdict should fully satisfy the desire of both the trial lawyer and the general practitioner for a useful book in the field of trial practice.

It has been prepared with a view to meeting the requirements for a practical trial manual available for instant use during the stress and excitement of a highly contested trial. The simplicity of its literary structure must become apparent at once. It has been written in the plainest and most simple language so as to be easily understandable.

If you want to know how to prove a telephone conversation, the legal foundation necessary, the requirements as to recognizing the voice of the other party, turn to page 269; if you want to introduce an X-ray, see page 391. If you desire to introduce a carbon copy of a letter into evidence, refer to page 302. If you have to prepare a hypothetical question or must cross-examine in reference to a hypothetical question, see Chapter X. If it becomes necessary for you to qualify a medical expert, a psychiatrist, an engineer or real estate appraiser, or to cross-examine any type of expert witness, see Chapter IX. Should you be required to make an important offer of proof, legally sufficient to be of use on appeal, or if you desire to destroy and impeach a witness completely who has given contradictory testimony at some prior hearing or who has signed some prior contradictory statement, or if you want to know how to effectually cross-examine a plaintiff in a personal injury case so as to avoid liability on the grounds of contributory negligence or should you want to know how to prepare an argument to the jury as well as hundreds of other things important for the trial lawyer to know, suggestions as to the procedure to be followed will be found within the pages of this book.

With every phase of proof illustrated, it will be found that trial practice has almost been reduced to a formula, and that most of the formulas are contained herein.

The answers to most questions on trial technique are contained within the succeeding pages. The best possible test is to think of several questions involving the method of proving certain phases of a case, then to turn to the index, and see if the answers are not included in this work.

I wish to acknowledge the many valuable suggestions and helpful assistance of my law partner, Mr. Samuel S. Cohon, in editing and revising some of the text material, also the many valuable suggestions of Mr. James C. Cahill, as well as the assistance of Dr. John H. Carpenter, in reference to the material on X-rays, Mr. Vernon Faxon for the material on Handwriting, etc., Mr. Julius Huffman of the Kaufman Fabry

Co. on Photography, Judge William H. McSurely of the Illinois Appellate Court (First District) for his kind permission to refer to all records of cases, and the kind assistance of Mr. Joseph Morrison, Deputy Appellate Clerk. I also wish to gratefully acknowledge the assistance of Mr. Richard F. Frohman, Mr. Lawrence Bloomenthal, Miss Libbie Shapiro and many others who so willingly aided me at one time or another during the three years of effort necessary to complete this manuscript.

Irving Goldstein

September, 1935

The fourth printing of "Trial Technique" has made possible the opportunity of incorporating numerous suggestions made by judges and lawyers throughout the country, particularly Judges Victor Hemphill, Michael Feinberg, and Joseph B. David, all of which are herewith gratefully acknowledged.

Irving Goldstein

September, 1936

TABLE OF CONTENTS

CHAPTER I

PREPARATION OF THE FACTS

PAGE

§ 1. Confidence ... 1
§ 2. Preparation ... 2
§ 3. Preparation of the facts ... 3
§ 4. — What it includes ... 4
§ 5. (1) Acquisition of knowledge ... 4
§ 6. — In general ... 4
§ 7. — Time of preparation ... 5
§ 8. — Scientific aids ... 5
§ 9. — Ultra-violet rays ... 6
§ 10. — — Alterations and erasures ... 6
§ 11. — — In criminal cases ... 7
§ 12. — — Fluorescence and photography ... 8
§ 13. — Lie detector ... 10
§ 14. — — In divorce cases ... 10
§ 15. — — In personal injury cases ... 11
§ 16. — — Missing merchandise ... 11
§ 17. — — Personnel work ... 12
§ 17a. — — Co-operation ... 12
§ 17b. — — Objections ... 12
§ 18. — — In criminal cases ... 13
§ 19. — Blood tests ... 14
§ 20 — Gun powder tests ... 16
§ 21 — Disputed documents ... 16
§ 22. — — Enlarged photographs ... 17
§ 23. — — Submit all questionable documents to expert ... 17
§ 24. — — Fields of investigation ... 18
§ 25. — — Legal citations ... 18
§ 26. — — Equipment ... 18
§ 27. — — Infra-red rays ... 19
§ 28. — — Standards of comparison ... 19
§ 29. — — General suggestions ... 20
§ 30. — Scientific Crime Detection Laboratory ... 21
§ 31. — Photographs in dark ... 24

		PAGE
§ 32.	—Moving pictures, photograph records and dictographs	24
§ 33.	—Photographs for legal use	25
§ 34.	——How photographs should be made	26
§ 35.	——Kind of film to be used	26
§ 36.	——Color filters	27
§ 37.	——Lighting	27
§ 38.	——Filing of data	27
§ 39.	——Perspective	27
§ 40.	——Retouching	27
§ 41.	—Maps and diagrams	28
§ 42.	—The place of the X-ray in medico-legal cases	28
§ 43.	——Fluoroscope	29
§ 44.	——Radiograph	29
§ 45.	——Distortion	29
§ 46.	——How should be taken	30
§ 47.	——Age of bone injuries	30
§ 48.	——Marking and identifying	31
§ 49.	——Illuminating boxes	31
§ 50.	—Medical facts	31
§ 51.	—Credit agency reports	32
§ 52.	—Telephone, gas and electric records	32
§ 53.	—Ownership of automobiles	32
§ 54.	—Abstracts of records and briefs	32
§ 55.	—Private detectives	33
§ 56.	—Weather reports	33
§ 57.	—Encyclopedias	33
§ 58.	(2) Interviewing client and witnesses	33
§ 59.	—Signed statements	34
§ 60.	——Intimate details	35
§ 61.	——In handwriting of witness	35
§ 62.	——"O.K.'d" statements	35
§ 63.	——General suggestions	36
§ 64.	——Signed confessions	37
§ 65.	—Granting interviews	37
§ 66.	—Corroboration of client's story	37
§ 67.	—Investigating client and his story	38
§ 68.	—Questionnaire	41
§ 69.	—Have story written out by clients and witnesses	45
§ 70.	—Additional facts	46
§ 71.	(3) Anticipating and preparing for opponent's proof	46
§ 72.	—Cross-examine client	46
§ 73.	(4) Outlining elements to be proved	47
§ 74.	—Diagram of case	47
§ 75.	—Aged witnesses	49

Page

§ 76. —Arranging and tabulating documentary evidence.... 49
§ 77. —Debtor who claims another person is obligated.... 50
§ 78. —Notice to city in personal injury cases.... 50
§ 79. —Court reporters 51
§ 80. —Attorney's liens—contingent fee cases.... 51

CHAPTER II

PREPARATION OF THE LAW

§ 81. In general 52
§ 82. (1) The recognition of propositions of law involved.... 52
§ 83. —In personal injury case—The facts.... 53
§ 84. —The method followed.... 56
§ 85. (2) The recognition of the questions involving the method of proof 59
§ 86. —Anticipating objections 60
§ 87. —The method 60
§ 88. (3) Finding of favorable authorities.... 61
§ 89. —Various subject headings.... 61
§ 90. —Local statutes, ordinances, digests and text-books.... 62
§ 91. —Words and Phrases.... 63
§ 92. —Negligence and Compensation Cases Annotated (N.C.C.A.)... 63
§ 93. —Uniform Laws Annotated.... 64
§ 94. — Questioned Documents 64
§ 95. —Cooley's Briefs on Insurance Law and Couch's Cyclopedia of Insurance Law.... 64
§ 96. —Commerce Clearing House current decisions reports.... 65
§ 97. —Index to legal periodicals.... 65
§ 98. —Magazine articles 66
§ 99. —Text-books 66
§ 100. —Annotations and supplements.... 66
§ 101. —Citator 66
§ 102. —National Corporation Reporter and Daily Law Bulletin.... 66
§ 103. —Advance sheets 67
§ 104. —Analyzing citations of authority.... 67
§ 105. (4) The anticipation of all propositions of law relied upon by opponent 68
§ 106. (5) Securing authorities to show opponent's contentions not tenable in law.... 69
§ 107. (6) Outline of all propositions of law involved.... 69
§ 108. (7) The trial brief.... 70
§ 109. —What it should contain.... 70
§ 110. ——(1) Diagram of the case.... 71
§ 111. ——(2) A résumé of the facts in narrative form.... 71

PAGE

§ 112. — — (3) A list of the witnesses.......................... 72
§ 113. — — (4) An abstract of each witness' story in narrative form... 72
§ 114. — — (5) A detailed signed statement from each witness in question and answer form.......................... 72
§ 115. — — (6) An abstract of the pleadings.......................... 72
§ 116. — — (7) Brief on the law.......................... 73
§ 117. — — (8) Instructions 73
§ 118. Presenting trial brief to court.......................... 73
§ 119. Arguing the law.......................... 74
§ 120. Preliminary motions 76
§ 121. Preparation of the pleadings.......................... 77

CHAPTER III

PRELIMINARY MOTIONS

§ 122. In general 79
§ 123. (1) Motions to strike and demurrers.......................... 79
§ 124. (2) Examination of adverse party.......................... 81
§ 125. (3) Discovery before trial.......................... 83
§ 126. — Motion for discovery of documents.......................... 87
§ 127. — Motion to produce listed document for inspection.......... 87
§ 128. — Motion for order requiring affidavit as to possession....... 88
§ 129. — Motion to show cause why document should not be produced.. 88
§ 130. — Motion by defendant to dismiss for refusal to allow inspection of documents.......................... 88
§ 131. — Motion by defendant to dismiss for refusal to obey order to produce document 89
§ 132. — Motion by plaintiff to strike answer for refusal to allow inspection of documents.......................... 89
§ 133. — Motion by plaintiff to strike answer for refusal of defendant to obey order to produce document.......................... 90
§ 134. — List of documents under discovery order.......................... 90
§ 135. — Supplemental list of documents under discovery order....... 91
§ 136. — Motion for discovery.......................... 92
§ 137. — Motion to produce listed document for inspection.......... 92
§ 138. — Notice of motion by defendant to dismiss for refusal to allow inspection of document.......................... 93
§ 139. — Notice of motion by plaintiff to strike answer for refusal to allow inspection of documents.......................... 93
§ 140. — Notice of motion by defendant to dismiss complaint for refusal of plaintiff to obey order to produce.......................... 94
§ 141. — Notice of motion by plaintiff to strike answer for refusal of defendant to obey order to produce.......................... 94
§ 142. — Notice of motion to show cause why document should not be produced 94

PAGE

§ 143. —Notice of motion for order requiring affidavit as to possession of document 95
§ 144. —Legal authorities 95
§ 145. (4) Depositions 97
§ 146. (a) As a means of discovery..... 97
§ 147. —When use indicated..... 98
§ 148. —Early use advisable..... 98
§ 149. —To ascertain proper parties to sue..... 98
§ 150. —Commissioner 98
§ 151. —Compelling attendance of witnesses..... 99
§ 152. —Statutory provisions 99
§ 153. (b) As method of proof..... 99
§ 154. —Procedure 100
§ 155. —Statutory provisions—Chancery cases..... 100
§ 156. —Law cases 101
§ 157. —Oral examination 101
§ 158. —Oral examination—Costs 102
§ 159. —Stipulations for issuance of dedimus..... 102
§ 160. —Attorney should take deposition personally if possible..... 104
§ 161. —Oral interrogatories recommended..... 105
§ 162. —Care should be exercised in taking depositions..... 105
§ 163. —Objections 106
§ 164. —Motions to suppress..... 106
§ 165. —Reading depositions 106
§ 166. (5) Interrogatories 106
§ 166a. —Form of interrogatories..... 107
§ 167. (6) Admissions 111
§ 168. —Value of procedure..... 112
§ 169. —Admission in writing of genuineness of paper or writing..... 113
§ 170. —Notice for admission of facts..... 113
§ 171. —Limitations upon right..... 114
§ 172. —Public records 119
§ 173. —Admission of facts..... 120
§ 174. —Admission of genuineness of document..... 120
§ 175. (7) Bills of particulars..... 120
§ 176. —When indicated 121
§ 177. —Value 121
§ 178. —Code provisions 121
§ 179. —Affidavit in opposition to demand for bill of particulars..... 122
§ 180. —Notice to furnish..... 122
§ 181. —Goods sold 122
§ 182. —Labor and materials..... 123
§ 183. —Notice of motion to make pleading fuller and more particular. 123
§ 184. —Notice of motion to strike pleading because no bill filed..... 124

Page

§ 185. — Notice served with bill of particulars furnished on demand... 124
§ 186. — Motion that demand for bill of particulars be denied........ 125
§ 187. — Form of bill of particulars........ 125
§ 188. — Fraudulent sale of stock........ 125
§ 189. (8) Notice to produce........ 126
§ 190. (9) Subpoena duces tecum........ 128
§ 190a. — Petition for subpoena duces tecum........ 130
§ 191. (10) Change of venue........ 131
§ 192. — Statutory provisions........ 132
§ 193. — Affidavit or verification........ 135
§ 194. — Affidavit opposing........ 135
§ 195. — Petition—Prejudice of judge........ 136
§ 196. — Petition—Undue influence—People prejudiced........ 136
§ 197. (11) Continuances........ 136
§ 198. — Code provisions........ 138
§ 199. — Forms—Absence of witness—Affidavit by defendant........ 139
§ 200. (12) Amendments........ 140
§ 201. — Statutory provisions........ 140
§ 202. — Motions should be accompanied by proposed amendment..... 141
§ 203. — Examine pleadings........ 141
§ 204. Affidavit of amendment........ 142
§ 205. (13) Summary judgments........ 143
§ 206. — Affidavits in proceedings for summary judgments........ 144
§ 207. — Summary judgments—Counterclaims........ 144
§ 208. — Value........ 145
§ 209. — Affidavit for summary judgment—Recovery of money....... 146
§ 210. — Affidavit for summary judgment—Recovery of land....... 146
§ 211. — Affidavit of defense—To all of claim........ 147
§ 212. — Affidavit of defense—To part of claim........ 147
§ 213. — Facts known only to hostile person........ 148
§ 214. — Notice of motion for summary judgment........ 148
§ 215. — Motion for summary judgment........ 149
§ 216. — New York authorities........ 149

CHAPTER IV

SELECTING THE JURY

§ 217. Importance........ 152
§ 218. When jury is to be demanded........ 152
§ 219. New jury........ 153
§ 220. Six-man jury or twelve-man jury........ 153
§ 221. Examining jurors in panels of four or twelve........ 154
§ 222. Diagrams........ 155
§ 223. Types of jurors........ 156
§ 224. Women jurors........ 158

PAGE
§ 225. Prior accidents 158
§ 226. One-man jury 159
§ 227. Study of law or medicine........ 160
§ 228. Fairness 161
§ 229. Embarrassing prospective juror 161
§ 230. Testing juror's knowledge and education........ 162
§ 231. Technical terms 163
§ 232. Manner 163
§ 233. Investigating jury 165
§ 234. Consult with client 165
§ 235. Excusing jurors 166
§ 236. Recognizing prejudices and natural sympathies........ 167
§ 237. Accepting juror without questioning........ 168
§ 238. Brilliancy should not be overly displayed........ 169
§ 239. Use of the word "please"........ 171
§ 240. Stress the law 172
§ 241. Preventing statements on the law........ 174
§ 242. Plaintiff's attorney should talk of damages........ 174
§ 243. Watch number of challenges........ 175
§ 244. Prepare questions in advance........ 176
§ 245. Watch jurors as they take seats........ 177
§ 246. Street-car motormen as jurors........ 177
§ 247. Where judge questions jury........ 178
§ 248. Challenges after tender or acceptance........ 179
§ 249. Do not question all jurors in detail........ 179
§ 250. Objections 180
§ 251. Opening remarks and conclusion........ 181
§ 252. List of questions to jury—For the plaintiff........ 182
§ 253. — For the defendant 186
§ 254. Kinds of challenges 191
§ 254a. Statutory provisions 191
§ 255. Competency and qualifications 194

CHAPTER V

OPENING STATEMENTS

§ 256. In general 201
§ 257. Purpose 201
§ 258. Failure to make good opening statement........ 201
§ 259. Testing opening statement 202
§ 260. Detailed or short opening statement........ 202
§ 261. Directed verdict on opening statement........ 204
§ 262. Administrators, executors, trustees, and next friends........ 205
§ 263. Waiving or reserving opening statement........ 206

PAGE

§ 264. Forcing defendant to make opening statement 207
§ 265. Where secret defense 208
§ 266. Motion to exclude witnesses 209
§ 267. Over-statement and exaggeration 211
§ 268. "We expect to prove" 211
§ 269. Pictures 212
§ 270. Logical sequence 212
§ 271. "As you know" 212
§ 272. — The jury 213
§ 273. — The court 213
§ 274. Demeanor 214
§ 275. Argument 214
§ 276. Anticipating defense 215
§ 277. Objections 216
§ 278. Citing the law 217
§ 279. Harmful evidence 217
§ 280. Plaintiff and defendant 217
§ 281. Admissions 218
§ 282. "We" 219
§ 283. Calling attention to adverse witness' idiosyncrasies 220
§ 284. Framing the opening statement for plaintiff 221
§ 285. (1) Introduction—Personal injury case 221
§ 286. (2) Parties 222
§ 287. (3) Theory of the case 223
§ 288. (4) Scene of the accident 223
§ 289. (5) Word picture of accident 225
§ 290. (6) Injuries sustained 226
§ 291. (7) Medical, surgical, and other care 227
§ 292. (8) Extent of injuries 227
§ 293. (9) Monetary loss 227
§ 294. (10) Conclusion 228
§ 295. The opening statement for defendant should include 228
§ 295a. (1) Introduction 229
§ 296. (2) Establishing the issue 229
§ 297. (3) Party defendant and his agents 230
§ 298. (4) A picture of how accident happened from view-point of defendant 231
§ 299. (5) Theory of the defendant 231
§ 300. (6) Conclusion 232
§ 301. Contract case 232
§ 302. (1) The introduction 233
§ 303. (2) The parties 233
§ 304. (3) Theory of the case 233
§ 305. (4) Picture of cause of action 233

PAGE

§ 306. (5) Damages 234
§ 307. (6) Conclusion 235
§ 308. Opening statement for defendant in contract case 235
§ 309. Opening statement for plaintiff in suit for real estate commission 235
§ 309a. Opening statement for defendant in suit for real estate commission 238
§ 310. Opening statement for plaintiff in suit for damages to real estate 240
§ 311. Opening statement for defendant in suit for damages to real estate 241
§ 312. Opening statement in wrongful death case for plaintiff 242
§ 313. Opening statement in wrongful death case for defendant 245

CHAPTER VI

DIRECT EXAMINATION

§ 314. What is included 247
§ 315. (1) To prove all the elements necessary to merit a favorable verdict 248
§ 316. (2) To present a picture of the cause of action with clarity, understanding and interest 248
§ 317. (3) To present the witnesses to the greatest advantage so as to secure acceptance of their stories as true by court and jury .. 251
§ 318. (4) To present the story and picture by proper questioning according to the rules of evidence 252
§ 319. Have witnesses visit court room 253
§ 320. Interviewing witnesses 253
§ 321. Connectives 253
§ 322. "Tell the Court and jury, please" 255
§ 323. Right to correct testimony 255
§ 324. Refreshing memory 256
§ 325. Leading questions 258
§ 325a. Handling of witnesses 259
§ 325b. General suggestions 265
§ 326. Interview all witnesses 266
§ 327. Exhibits 267
§ 328. Offer of harmful evidence 267
§ 329. Fairness 267
§ 330. Affectation 268
§ 331. Never attack a woman's character 268
§ 331a. General illustrations 268
§ 332. Conversations 269
§ 333. Telephone conversations 269
§ 334. Fixing time 271
§ 335. Stipulations 271
§ 336. Admissions by attorneys 272

Page

§ 337. Depositions 272
§ 338. Identifying persons 273
§ 339. Amendments 274
§ 340. Where witness indicates 275
§ 341. Interpreters 276
§ 342. Witness resuming stand 276
§ 343. Withdrawing witness 277
§ 344. Offering incompetent witnesses 277
§ 345. Absent witnesses 277
§ 346. Proof of distance 278
§ 347. Proving interest 279
§ 348. Forgotten questions 279
§ 349. Custom 279
§ 350. Denial of existence of a custom 281
§ 351. Demonstrations and experiments 282
§ 352. — Use of demonstrative evidence 284
§ 353. — Experiments 285
§ 354. — Preliminary proof 286
§ 355. Speed 287
§ 356. Reading testimony given at previous trial 288
§ 357. Market price and value 291
§ 358. Pain and suffering 291
§ 359. Qualifying child witness 292

CHAPTER VII

EXHIBITS

§ 360. In general 293
§ 361. Exhibits must be material 293
§ 362. Preliminary foundation 294
§ 363. Objections to exhibits 295
§ 364. Identifying exhibits 296
§ 365. "What is it?" 297
§ 366. When exhibits offered 298
§ 366a. Offering exhibits identified by opponent 299
§ 367. Photostatic and certified copies 299
§ 368. Offering both sides of exhibits 300
§ 369. Re-offering exhibits 300
§ 370. Changes, alterations and interlineations 301
§ 370a. Motion to reserve decision on admissibility 301
§ 371. Examine each offered exhibit 302
§ 372. Limiting purpose of exhibit 302
§ 373. Simple foundation 302
§ 374. Carbon copies of letters, etc 302
§ 375. — The notice to produce—Form 303

Page
§ 376. — Original letter produced 304
§ 377. — Proof of carbon copy 304
§ 378. — Proof of preparation of original and carbon copy 305
§ 379. — Proof of mailing 306
§ 380. Books of account 308
§ 381. — In general 308
§ 382. — Ledger 309
§ 383. — Records made by others 310
§ 384. Promissory note 315
§ 385. Contracts 316
§ 386. Check 316
§ 387. Lease 317
§ 388. Weather reports 318
§ 389. Delivery receipts 319
§ 390. Mortgage 320
§ 391. Lost instruments 320
§ 392. — Lost instrument—Proof of copy 321
§ 393. — Proof of lost instrument where there is no copy 322
§ 394. X-rays—Skiagraphs 323
§ 395. Photographs 326
§ 396. — Admissibility 327
§ 396a. — Documents 328
§ 396b. — Insured persons 328
§ 397. — Photographs, proof of 329
§ 398. Notice to city before suit 330
§ 399. Foreign statutes and laws 330
§ 400. Ordinances—Judicial notice 332
§ 401. — Ordinances, proof of 333
§ 402. Records 334
§ 403. Certificates 334
§ 404. — Clerks of County and Circuit Court 334
§ 405. — Notary 334
§ 406. Certified copies 335
§ 407. Mortality tables 336
§ 408. Corporate minutes 336
§ 409. Repair bills 338
§ 410. — Where repair bill is not paid 339
§ 411. Foreign judgment 341
§ 412. Stipulations of facts 342

CHAPTER VIII

OBJECTIONS

§ 413. In general 345
§ 414. Ruling must be obtained 345

PAGE

§ 415. How objections should be made 345
§ 416. Types of objections 346
§ 417. — General objections 346
§ 417a. — Legal requirements 347
§ 418. — Specific objections 347
§ 419. — — When necessary 348
§ 420. Waiver of objections 350
§ 420a. Subject to objection and reserving ruling 351
§ 420b. Legally preserving record 351
§ 421. Improper remarks of counsel 352
§ 421a. Exceptions to court's remarks and conduct 353
§ 422. Few objections should be made 354
§ 423. Subject to objection 358
§ 424. Promise to connect 358
§ 425. "Withdraw the question" 359
§ 426. Offers of proof 359
§ 427. — Requisites and sufficiency of offer of proof 361
§ 428. General illustrations—Leading questions 364
§ 429. — Exhausting recollection 365
§ 430. — Proper direct or leading question 365
§ 431. — Counsel assuming facts in question 365
§ 432. — Not responsive to question 366
§ 433. No foundation for conversation 366
§ 434. — Double questions 367
§ 435. — Hearsay 367
§ 436. — Indefinite term 367
§ 437. — Characterizing conclusion 368
§ 438. — Conclusions 368
§ 439. — Document speaks for itself 368
§ 440. — Best and secondary evidence 369
§ 441. — Parol evidence—Exceptions thereto 369
§ 442. — Vary a written instrument by parol 372
§ 443. — Merged in contract 372
§ 444. — Offers of compromise—In general 372
§ 445. — Voluntary admissions 373
§ 446. — Customary method 374
§ 447. — Making of one specific objection as waiver of all other objections 374
§ 448. — Conjectural 375
§ 449. — Incompetent witness 375
§ 450. — — Statutory provisions 375
§ 451. — Objections must be made in time 376
§ 452. — General objections 377
§ 453. — Variance 377

PAGE

§ 454. — Not bearing on issues 378
§ 455. — Immaterial 378
§ 456. — Alternative questions 378
§ 457. — Privileged communications 379
§ 458. — Self-serving documents 379
§ 459. — Where insurance company defends 380
§ 460. — Cross-examination of or impeaching own witness 381
§ 461. — Arguing with witness 381
§ 462. — "What is the fact?" 382
§ 463. — In some states it is objectionable to introduce exhibits on cross-examination 382

CHAPTER IX

THE EXPERT WITNESS

§ 464. Opinion evidence 383
§ 465. In general 384
§ 466. Sciences and trades 384
§ 467. Questions for court 384
§ 468. Study 384
§ 469. Subjective symptoms—Pain and suffering 385
§ 470. Examination solely for purpose of testifying 385
§ 471. Reasons 386
§ 472. Health and physical condition 386
§ 473. Facts 387
§ 474. Selection of expert 387
§ 475. Qualifying expert 388
§ 476. — Admitting qualifications of expert 389
§ 477. — Qualifying expert by cross-examination of opponent's expert 389
§ 478. The paid expert 390
§ 479. Withdrawing witnesses 390
§ 480. Methods of qualifying expert witnesses in various fields 391
§ 481. Alienist and psychiatrist 399
§ 482. Toxicologist 401
§ 483. Chiropractor 403
§ 484. Handwriting expert 404
§ 485. Engineer 406
§ 486. Real estate appraiser and broker 408
§ 487. Chemist 410
§ 488. Jeweler 411
§ 489. Limit expert to scope of question 412
§ 490. Cross-examination 414
§ 491. — Cross-examination as to qualifications 425
§ 492. — Cross-examination as to subjective symptoms 427

Page
§ 493. — Cross-examination to test recollection 429
§ 494. — Cross-examination where expert relies on some authority.... 433
§ 495. — Cross-examination as to relationship with parties and lawyers 437
§ 496. — Cross-examination of non-expert as to mental condition..... 438
§ 497. — Cross-examination in handwriting cases 445

CHAPTER X

HYPOTHETICAL QUESTIONS

§ 498. In general 452
§ 499. Value 452
§ 500. Preparation of hypothetical question 452
§ 501. — Method of preparation 453
§ 502. Elements 453
§ 503. — Commencement 454
§ 504. — Body 454
§ 505. — Limit use of word "assume"............................... 454
§ 506. — Conclusion 455
§ 507. — Forms of conclusions 455
§ 508. — Several opinions on same hypothesis...................... 456
§ 509. Some requirements 457
§ 510. Objections 459
§ 511. Previous good health 460
§ 512. Improper commencement 460
§ 513. Modifying question 460
§ 514. Note all objections 460
§ 515. Copies of hypothetical questions 461
§ 516. Having question re-read 461
§ 517. Anticipating cross-examination 461
§ 518. Answers to hypothetical question 462
§ 519. — As to temporary or permanent............................ 463
§ 520. — If basis of opinion is desired........................... 463
§ 521. — Motion to strike 463
§ 522. Using opponent's hypothetical question 463
§ 523. Hypothetical question in personal injury case................ 464
§ 524. Defendant's hypothetical question 466
§ 525. Death case 468
§ 526. Mind and memory 468
§ 527. Specific objections—Amending and correcting hypothetical question 471
§ 528. Cross-examination as to hypothetical questions............... 475
§ 529. — Medical books 475
§ 530. — Breaking up question into parts.......................... 476
§ 531. — Show witness prepared question—Testing recollection....... 477

PAGE

§ 532. — Emphasizing hypothetical nature of question 478
§ 533. — Requesting opponent's hypothetical question 478
§ 534. — Admissions 478
§ 535. — Additional facts 478
§ 536. — Using opponent's question 479
§ 537. — Disproved facts 479
§ 538. — Unnecessary elements in question 480
§ 539. — Where expert has not examined injured person 480
§ 540. — Testing recollection 481
§ 541. — Testing each detailed fact—Sanity and testamentary capacity 482
§ 542. — Mind and memory 482
§ 543. — — Another illustration 485

CHAPTER XI

CROSS-EXAMINATION

§ 544. In general 487
§ 545. Objects of cross-examination 487
§ 546. Primary purpose of cross-examination 488
§ 547. Right to cross-examine 488
§ 548. Scope of cross-examination 489
§ 549. Court may ask questions 490
§ 550. Counsel assuming facts in questions 490
§ 551. Contradiction on immaterial fact 490
§ 552. Insulting, etc., questions 490
§ 553. Repetition 491
§ 554. Refreshing memory 491
§ 555. Planning cross-examination in advance 491
§ 556. Preparation for cross-examination 494
§ 557. Listen carefully to direct examination 495
§ 558. Demeanor 495
§ 559. Never cross-examine unless you know what answer will be 496
§ 560. Objective must be hidden 496
§ 561. Determine whether or not to cross-examine at all 497
§ 562. Never cross-examine a truthful witness as to his direct examination 498
§ 563. Do not have story repeated by witness 498
§ 564. Plan your traps 499
§ 565. Avoid broad cross-examining 504
§ 566. Do not over cross-examine 504
§ 567. Make your big points 505
§ 568. Avoid small triumphs 506
§ 569. Evasions by the witness 506

Page
§ 570. Cross-examination of women and children 506
§ 571. Do not allow interruptions by opposing counsel 507
§ 572. "To whom have you talked about this case?" 507
§ 573. "When did you first know you were to be a witness?" 508
§ 574. Assuming facts in questions 508
§ 575. "I don't remember" 508
§ 576. Cross-examination to show story improbable 509
§ 577. — Testing recollection—Delivery of merchandise 512
§ 578. Real estate broker's commission case 512
§ 579. Suit for return of deposit 514
§ 580. "Alibi" witnesses 516
§ 581. Court's witness 517
§ 582. Cross-examination of adverse party 517
§ 583. Cross-examination where signature denied 526
§ 584. Contributory negligence 527
§ 585. Slipping on rugs or polished floors 530
§ 586. Length of time confined to bed 533
§ 587. When case given to attorney 535
§ 588. Discrediting story of one witness by cross-examination of another 536

CHAPTER XII

IMPEACHMENT

§ 589. In general 541
§ 590. Own witnesses generally 542
§ 591. Adverse party 542
§ 592. Refreshing memory 543
§ 593. Immaterial issues 543
§ 594. Must be impeaching evidence 543
§ 595. Impeachment proof available unless direct admission made 544
§ 596. Disinterested witnesses—To prove contrary facts 544
§ 597. When impeachment available 545
§ 598. Keep object hidden 545
§ 599. Impeachment proof necessary 546
§ 600. Objection should be made whenever cross-examination improper 546
§ 601. Former contradictory oral statements 546
§ 602. Former contradictory written statements 550
§ 603. — Direct examination of impeaching witness—Investigator 556
§ 604. — Cross-examination of impeaching witness—Investigator 559
§ 605. Cross-examining opponent's witnesses as to statements signed ... 564
§ 606. Former contradictory sworn statements, pleadings, and affidavits 565
§ 607. — Laying the foundation 567
§ 608. — Use of sworn applications to disprove denial of ownership .. 568

Page

§ 609. — Former contradictory sworn testimony in a previous trial or preliminary hearing 569
§ 610. — Impeaching witness—Court reporter 574
§ 611. — — Qualification and examination of court reporter........ 574
§ 612. Impeachment by proof that the witness' general reputation is bad 577
§ 613. — Good reputation 577
§ 614. — Selection of character witnesses........ 578
§ 615. — Proving reputation 578
§ 616. — Discussing reputation 579
§ 617. — Preparing character witnesses 580
§ 618. — "Would you believe him under oath?"........ 580
§ 619. — Cross-examining adverse character witness........ 582
§ 620. — Using opponent's witness 584
§ 621. Former conviction of infamous crime........ 584
§ 622. — Arrests, indictments, etc. 585
§ 623. — Conviction of felony 585
§ 624. — Proof of conviction where probation granted........ 585
§ 625. — Admission as to conviction........ 586
§ 626. — Cross-examination as to former conviction........ 586
§ 627. — Proof of former conviction........ 587
§ 628. — Old convictions 588
§ 629. Showing relationship to parties or interest in the outcome of case 589
§ 630. Impeachment by public records........ 592

CHAPTER XIII

RE-DIRECT EXAMINATION AND REBUTTAL

§ 631. In general........ 593
§ 632. Signals........ 595
§ 633. Leading question........ 596
§ 634. Cannot repeat direct examination........ 596
§ 635. Let well enough alone........ 597
§ 636. Be careful of traps........ 597
§ 637. Refreshing memory........ 597
§ 638. Opening the door........ 599
§ 639. Planning traps........ 599
§ 640. Forgotten questions........ 600
§ 641. Scope of re-direct examination........ 601
§ 642. Rebuttal 602
§ 643. Direct questions........ 603
§ 644. Witnesses 603
§ 645. Scope of rebuttal........ 604
§ 646. Evidence in chief........ 606
§ 647. Reply or surrebuttal........ 606

CHAPTER XIV

ARGUMENTS TO THE JURY

Page

§ 648. In general.......... 607
§ 649. Preparation for argument.......... 608
§ 650. Adopt a theory of case.......... 609
§ 651. Models or hands.......... 609
§ 652. Word pictures.......... 610
§ 653. Exhibits.......... 612
§ 654. Making speech.......... 612
§ 655. Demeanor and attitude.......... 612
§ 656. Convey thoughts, not words.......... 613
§ 657. Planned argument.......... 613
§ 658. One issue.......... 615
§ 659. Outline.......... 616
§ 660. Improbabilities.......... 616
§ 661. Avoid personalities and epithets.......... 616
§ 662. Misstating evidence.......... 617
§ 663. Objections.......... 617
§ 664. Plaintiff's opening argument—Full or incomplete.......... 617
§ 665. Damages in personal injury cases.......... 619
§ 666. Argument based on instructions.......... 620
§ 667. Negligence, due care and contributory negligence.......... 620
§ 668. Questions for counsel to answer.......... 620
§ 669. Unfavorable instructions.......... 621
§ 670. Evidence answers every argument.......... 621
§ 671. Names rather than parties.......... 622
§ 672. Exaggerated opening statement.......... 622
§ 673. Framing the argument.......... 622
§ 674. (1) The introduction.......... 622
§ 675. (2) The issue.......... 623
§ 676. (3) The picture of the cause of action.......... 623
§ 677. (4) The corroboration and cumulation.......... 624
§ 678. (5) The opponent's contentions.......... 625
§ 679. (6) The refutation.......... 625
§ 680. (7) The appeal and conclusion.......... 625
§ 681. General suggestions.......... 626
§ 682. Right to open and close.......... 631
§ 683. —In criminal cases.......... 631
§ 684. —Determination of right.......... 632
§ 685. —Defendant's right.......... 632
§ 686. —Waiver.......... 633
§ 687. —Discretion of court.......... 633
§ 688. Right to make closing argument.......... 634

PAGE
§ 689. — Purpose of reply to argument 634
§ 690. — Time limit 634
§ 691. — Limitation on number of attorneys 634
§ 692. — Waiver of right 635
§ 693. — Right to interrupt improper argument 635
§ 694. — Scope of arguments—Generally 635
§ 695. — Matters within counsel's personal knowledge 636
§ 696. — Reading authorities 636
§ 697. — Reference to previous trial 637
§ 698. — Reference to instructions 637
§ 699. — Reading of pleadings 637
§ 700. — Objections by opponent 638
§ 701. — Excluded evidence 638
§ 702. — Conduct of parties 638
§ 703. — Vouching for witnesses 638
§ 704. — Failure to produce witnesses 638
§ 705. — Failure to produce evidence 639
§ 706. — Well known facts—History 639
§ 707. — Reference to jurors by name 639
§ 708. — Requesting jurors to make notes prohibited 639
§ 709. — Appeals to passion and prejudice—Violent language 639
§ 710. — — Personal animosity 640
§ 711. — — Prejudice against corporations 640
§ 712. — — Reference to insurance 641
§ 713. — — Appeals to sympathy 641
§ 714. — — Wealth or poverty of parties 641
§ 715. — — Requesting jurors to put themselves in plaintiff's place ... 641
§ 716. — Amount of damages 641
§ 717. — Comments as to the law 642
§ 718. — Retaliatory remarks 642
§ 719. Arguments in suit on insurance policy 642
§ 720. Arguments in suit against husband for jewelry sold to wife as necessaries 656
§ 721. Disputed document case 663
§ 722. — Another illustration 667
§ 723. Personal injury case 669

TABLE OF CASES 693

INDEX 743

TRIAL TECHNIQUE

CHAPTER I

PREPARATION OF THE FACTS

§ 1. Confidence.

Not long ago a certain judge stated, "the greatest need of the lawyer in the trial of cases is confidence." He found, during his service as a judge that the greatest handicap of the trial attorney was the lack of confidence, either in himself or in his case.

He made the further observation that "whether or not confidence could be obtained in any other way than through the repeated trials of many cases is a question."

Let us see whether that question can be answered in the affirmative.

Confidence is an intelligent faith based on fact. It is a self-assurance that comes from knowledge. The essential confidence for the trial lawyer must be built upon, developed, and rounded in a thorough knowledge of what he ought to know, of what he ought to do, and how he ought to do it.

It is not contended that with even all of this knowledge, every trial lawyer will have full confidence and assurance the first or second time he walks into a courtroom.

It cannot be denied, however, that a lawyer walking into a courtroom to try his first case fortified with a thorough knowledge of what he ought to know, what he ought to do and how he ought to do it, will gain and acquire confidence and assurance as during the progress of the trial he comes to a realization that his presentation of the case, his introduction of the evidence, his cross-examination and his presentation of the law have all been permitted to follow a planned procedure and technique in the trial of the case.

When the lawyer prepares his case in accordance with these suggested principles, he will enter the courtroom with the assurance that he is prepared to meet whatever may confront him.

There will always be some nervousness just before the trial commences. Most famous lawyers have confessed to this feeling of nervousness even after many years of trial work. Therefore, the trial lawyer should not allow this feeling of nervousness to discourage him from trying cases. Professor Arthur E. Phillips who wrote "Effective Speaking," claimed that this feeling of nervousness before speaking was merely "the spark of genius that spurs us on to greater and more glorious efforts."

Confidence in trial work is based upon proper preparation and knowledge—planned procedure. Knowledge sufficient for the needs of the average trial lawyer may be obtained by the study and application of the suggestions contained in this book.

Recently an investigation in one large city disclosed the fact that within a period of two weeks, the plaintiffs in fourteen cases were forced to take non-suits in jury cases owing to the lack of preparation and inability to prove a prima facie case.

In another instance, a judge stopped a case during the trial because of the fact that the attorney for the plaintiff had not prepared his case and stated that it would be an injustice to the client to permit the case to proceed. A juror was withdrawn and the case was continued with the admonition to the plaintiff's attorney to prepare the case for trial by that date.

§ 2. Preparation.

Planned procedure includes, among other things, a thorough preparation of the facts. It is to this important phase of the preparation of the trial of cases that this chapter is devoted.

Many lawyers claim that their cases involve such small amounts that it does not pay to put so much time in preparation. They fail to realize that if the case is not worth the effort necessary to win it, it is not worth taking.

A succession of successful trials, even though some or most of them do not involve large amounts of money, is the basis of an increasing and more important clientele. In most instances the little additional work necessary to prepare the case properly spells the difference between success and failure.

Successful trial attorneys have been heard to state that cases are either won or lost in the lawyer's office months before the trial commences. By this they mean that the cases have been won or lost by either adequate or inadequate preparation.

Some time ago, in a suit where a lawyer was suing a former client for attorney's fees, another lawyer was called as a witness to testify as to the value of the legal services rendered. In testifying the lawyer fixed the same rate for preparation as for trial work which seemed to startle the attorneys on both sides as well as the judge. It has always been the theory that a lawyer was entitled to more compensation for trial work than for preparing the case. On cross-examination the opposing lawyer wanted to know why the attorney figured the same rate for preparation. He replied that in many instances after a full and complete preparation, cases have been settled mainly as a result of such preparation and that if the lawyer personally prepared the case and accomplished a favorable result, it was his opinion that he was entitled to the same rate of compensation as though he had tried the case in court. The cross-examiner then asked him if it was not true that there was a greater mental and nervous strain in the trial of cases which should entitle the lawyer to more compensation for trial work. The witness' answer was that if a case was fully and completely prepared, if the trial tactics were duly planned and outlined, and if all the witnesses were properly investigated and prepared, there should be no undue attendant nervous strain and excitement during the trial of cases, except in so much as the trial lawyer unduly and unnecessarily creates such excitement and nervous strain within himself.

This theory seemed to be received as somewhat revolutionary, but is worthy of serious consideration.

The conclusion arrived at therefore is that confidence in trial work is based in a great measure upon proper preparation and knowledge.

§ 3. Preparation of the facts.

Some lawyers permit their preparation to be limited almost entirely to the law of the case. After the law is all prepared they consider that they are ready for trial. They frequently pay little attention to the preparation of the facts and then to their surprise they are not able to prove sufficient facts to make the law they have prepared applicable.

A full and complete preparation of the facts is necessary in order to determine the law applicable to the case. It also enables one to distinguish and differentiate apparently unfavorable cases that may be cited. It is surprising how frequently a thorough detailed knowledge of the facts will make it possible to distinguish apparently unfavorable authorities as well as to apply the law in favorable decisions.

Intensive preparation of the facts gives a better scope for applicable law. The experienced trial lawyer may be better able to cross-examine, and he may be better able to argue to the jury, but if you have all the facts and the law properly prepared, and can legally present them to the court and jury, and if the client is entitled to a verdict, victory will perch on your shoulder.

§ 4. — What it includes.

The proper preparation of the facts includes:

(1) Acquisition of general, special and scientific knowledge.

(2) Collection of the facts through interviewing clients and witnesses, and investigating their stories.

(3) Anticipating and preparing for opponent's proof.

(4) Outlining the elements to be proved.

§ 5. — (1) Acquisition of knowledge.

The ability to prepare the facts properly and fully in a case depends entirely upon the scope and extent of the general knowledge which the trial attorney has acquired. Unless that knowledge is broad enough to enable him to recognize the kind of preparation necessary to be made on all phases of the facts in his case, he must fail in such preparation.

§ 6. — — In general.

A trial attorney who is not familiar with the scope and extent of the assistance that a hand-writing expert can give him in the preparation of the facts of the case will completely pass over the questions which naturally arise whenever disputed documents appear in the case. If he does not know something about photography and distortions in photography, the importance of utilizing photographs or attempting to keep out improper photographs from the evidence is not apparent to him. The same thing is true in the case of x-rays, in the use of ultra-violet rays, automobile repairs and mechanics, moving pictures and all of the various scientific aids now available to the trial lawyer in the preparation and trial of his cases. Therefore, it necessarily follows that the first step in the preparation of the facts of the case is the acquisition of knowledge in every conceivable field of human endeavor. The greater the scope of knowledge the greater will be the ability to make proper preparation of the facts of the case.

Whenever a case involves some unfamiliar field, it is an absolute necessity to seek all possible information in reference to the matter involved. For instance, if the proprietor of a beauty parlor is sued for alleged burns to hair and scalp, it becomes important to learn all about the machine used in the operation, the chemicals employed, as well as the length of time applied and the procedure involved. With this information the defense can then be planned, arrangements can be made for all necessary witnesses as well as preparation made for cross-examinations of opponent's witnesses.

The ability to try cases is augmented according to the knowledge of the subject involved in the law suit.

This thorough preparation, seeking after knowledge and acquiring it, insures a more satisfied client and gives him a greater feeling of confidence as to the trial lawyer's ability to handle the case in question.

§7. Time of preparation.

Some lawyers leave the preparation of the facts until just before the case is called for trial. This is a serious mistake. The facts should be prepared as soon after the happening of the event as it is possible to do so. This is the opinion of all successful personal injury and general trial attorneys.

§8. Scientific aids.

The trial of cases in modern times, in view of the complexity of business relationships, and the advent of the more educated juror who is no longer swayed by oratory alone, makes it necessary for the modern trial lawyer to resort to the science of today for weapons to combat the exigencies of the occasion.

Little do most people realize that in order to be successful trial lawyers today, in order to meet competition, and in order to be able to win cases, it is necessary to take advantage of every scientific aid.

Almost every case, large or small, now requires preparation and knowledge unheard of and undreamed of yesterday.

As business has progressed, the practice of law has become more complex and more specialized. Embezzlers, forgers and murderers have become more clever. Witnesses have become deliberate and clever perjurers. The truth has become harder to discover and to prove.

Winning a case today is quite an achievement and the knowledge of modern scientific methods and the utilization of that knowledge in the preparation and trial of law suits will almost always help to accomplish the seemingly impossible.

§ 9. — Ultra-violet rays.

One of the modern scientific discoveries now utilized by lawyers is the ultra-violet ray light. To most people the ultra-violet ray light is something the doctors use to give sun-tan or to supply deficiencies of Vitamin D. But to the lawyer it has many possibilities hitherto undreamed of, both in Civil and Criminal cases.

It has been discovered that when exposed to the ultra-violet ray light almost everything under the sun has its own peculiar glow or fluorescence. Different substances will show up differently. A diamond will show up in one way, while a piece of glass will show up in another, and so experts have conducted experiments and have classified many thousands of different substances.

§ 10. —— Alterations and erasures.

The ultra-violet light will immediately show up erasures and alterations.

There was an occasion recently to employ the ultra-violet ray machine in a case involving the fraudulent forgery of a waiver of mechanic's lien. The waiver had originally been given by the client on a building at a certain address. When delivered by the client, the waiver had been filled in with pen and ink. Suspicion of other waivers led to an investigation of all outstanding waivers. The forgeries were so cleverly made that certain waivers were suspected as being forgeries only because of the belief that two waivers given on a certain building, one of which was supposed to be the client's and the other a waiver turned in by another contractor, were dated the same day and appeared to be written by the same typewriter, or at least the same make of typewriter. This fact and coincidence coupled with the fact that the other waiver had been turned in by one of the men suspected of being guilty of these forgeries convinced the lawyer that here was a definite lead. The bank that had possession of this waiver ridiculed the idea that something was wrong, but the lawyer finally secured permission of the bank to subject the waiver to examination by a handwriting expert. When placed under the ultra-violet ray machine, one glance was sufficient to show every portion of the waiver that had been tampered with and altered. An ink eradicator had been used to take out all of the ink and then it had been typed over again so as to make it a waiver on an entirely different building on which the client had due him a large sum of money.

In the same investigation two other waivers were discovered with apparently the same typewriting which were subjected to a chemical fuming process. This restored temporarily a great portion of the eradicated ink handwriting. The waivers were photographed in their restored state. These photographs, together with another demonstration of this restoration before a jury, would be sufficient to convince any juror, however skeptical he might be, that a forgery had been committed.

The ultra-violet ray has been successfully used in demonstrating forgeries of wills, labels of perfume bottles, labels of all kinds, fake compositions of chemicals in inks, liquids of all kinds, paper cloth, in fact, almost everything conceivable.

§ 11. — In criminal cases.

The use of the ultra-violet ray light in the detection of crime reads almost like the fiction detective story of yesterday. It is full of romance and thrills. Edwin W. Teale, in the October issue 1931 of Popular Science Monthly, cites a number of instances in which the ultra-violet ray light has been used to good advantage.

Take the solution of the "Bandana Murder" case in the middle west not long ago. Motorists discovered a body lying in a ditch with a bullet in the head. There were signs of a struggle, and a single clue, a red bandana handkerchief, caught on bushes through which the slayer had escaped. The victim proved to be a miser who was foreclosing on farms in the neighborhood. He had many enemies. All who might have had cause for committing the murder were held on suspicion. The handkerchief, into which grayish lines of dust had been caked by perspiration, was examined under ultra-violet rays by an expert. The lines of dust burst into indigo fire. "Feldspar," said the expert.

Samples of dust from the farms of suspected men were next placed under the rays. Most of them showed the presence of feldspar, but none reacted with the exact shade of the bandana particles. Not far from the scene of the murder there was a clay pit from which laborers dug material for pottery. Samples of this clay, placed under the light, burst into the exact sheen of the original dust. A round-up of the laborers resulted in the capture of the culprit, who had shot his victim during an attempted hold-up.

In another case, a milkman in an eastern city, early one morning found a body lying at the side of the street. Near the spot were fragments of broken glass from the headlight of a car. Not far down the street, detectives found a machine in a garage with a broken headlight. The fragments seemed identical with the glass picked up in the street. It was learned that the owner had driven in late the night before. His story was that he had been driving in the country. On a gravel road, he said, a stone thrown up by a passing car had smashed his headlight. Few people believed that explanation until the glass found near the body fluoresced under ultra-violet rays with a greenish tinge that the fragments discovered in the broken headlight lacked. The "black light" of ultra-violet vibrations had removed suspicion from an innocent man.

Erasures in "boosted" checks that are invisible in daylight appear instantly under the ultra-violet rays, and counterfeit bills shine a sickly green in contrast to the snappy blue of genuine currency. In a number of European banks, ultra-violet lamps are installed as part of the regular equipment.

§ 12. — — Fluorescence and photography.

Elbridge W. Stein, in the October 1932 issue of Scientific American Magazine, writes on Ultra-Violet Light and Forgery, in part as follows:

"The effect of filtered ultra-violet light, which is a valuable aid in the detection of forgery, is called fluorescence. Although the rays themselves are invisible, they are capable of generating visible light when they strike certain substances.

Fortunately, a number of these substances are used in documents and give this peculiar fluorescence when flooded in darkness by ultra-violet rays.

"There are three main divisions in a fluorescence study of a document: First: certain kinds of materials can be distinguished from each other although by ordinary observation in daylight they are identical. Second: certain things that are invisible even under the microscope are made visible by filtered ultra-violet light. Third, and perhaps the most valuable phase of the fluorescence study of a document, is the possibility of photographing the peculiar effect of the ultra-violet rays on document materials. It is also a surprising and helpful fact that the sensitized photographic plate records things that cannot be seen by the eye even when the document is exposed to the ultra-violet rays.

"A valuable part of a fluorescence study of a document is making the effects permanent by means of photography. Fluorescence not only can be recorded on the photographic plate but these effects can be enlarged and put into such concrete form that anyone can see them, and when they are properly explained, understand them. An additional and highly important value of photography, as stated above, is the fact that certain details can be recorded on the photographic plate which are not actually visible to the eye even under the ultra-violet rays. This startling result has two main explanations: First, the necessary visible light produced in generating the ultra-violet rays is reduced to the lowest practical point when making a fluorescence study, and this dim light necessarily increases the difficulty of seeing the complete details of fluorescence. The second reason is that the rays themselves, which cause fluorescence, are wholly invisible, but the effect of some of them passes through the lens of the camera and makes an impression on the photographic plate so that things are recorded which are invisible to the eye. No thorough fluorescence study of a document should omit careful photographing of the effect of the rays. Although fluorescence effects on a document are not easily photographed, it can be done with special equipment and a knowledge of the exacting requirements. The photographs illustrating this article were made with specially designed equipment."

§ 13. Lie detector.

Another scientific aid we utilize today is the lie detector, sometimes called the cardio-pneumo-psychograph, also known as the Keeler polygraph. The machine consists of a cuff which is placed about the upper arm of the subject to register blood pressure and a tube about the chest, to measure respiration. These register on a cylinder of paper driven by a synchronized motor. Reactions to key questions are noted and from these guilt or innocence is determined.

Dr. John A. Larson, assistant state criminologist and inventor of the lie detector, in his book "Lying and its Detection," holds that no suspect should be sent to jail and no man should be released from jail solely on the evidence of his invention.

The machine, he states, is accurate, but the human interpretation of its records may be faulty, and there is a constant percentage of error ranging from five to twenty-five per cent. Dr. Larson constructed the first lie detector in 1921, when he was serving as a policeman in Berkeley, Cal., under Chief August Vollmer. He has used it continuously for eleven years in criminal cases. Dr. Larson at one time was known as the "only Ph. D. cop in the world."

In eleven years Dr. Larson reports finding only seven persons who lied without being detected. These seven cases were of mental defectives, psychopaths, and drug addicts. Of hundreds of suspects only seven refused to take the test on advice of counsel and were later found guilty.

The lie detector is now widely used in detection of crime, but there are many cases in which it can be successfully used in Civil Practice.

§ 14. — In divorce cases.

The lie detector can be successfully used in divorce cases both for the purpose of clearing the innocent and effecting reconciliations as well as securing confessions of unfaithfulness. This usually eliminates long drawn out and contested trials.

The principal ground for divorce that is based on circumstantial evidence is, of course, adultery. Further, adultery is the one most unforgivable of marital breaches. Therefore, a suspicion of adultery is the most difficult to remove. It is also the most difficult to establish conclusively. Suspicious circumstances may abound, yet the subject of the suspicion may be perfectly innocent.

It is under conditions such as these that the lie detector can render invaluable service, either in establishing the innocence of the suspected spouse, or in establishing his or her guilt.

As in criminal cases the unjustly suspected spouse will gladly subject himself or herself to the test of the lie detector. The guilty spouse will either object to being subjected to the lie detector with vociferous claims of innocence or in a conceited belief in his or her ability to "beat" the machine, will prove his or her guilt.

§ 15. — In personal injury cases.

The lie detector has been successfully used in personal injury cases to discover whether in reality the claimants are actually injured—and to determine deafness, pains and all classes of injuries. In one case, where the plaintiff claimed to have gone blind in one eye, or at least was losing the sight of the eye so rapidly that he was almost blind, he was subjected to a lie detector and it was conclusively proved that the claim was a fraudulent one. The supposedly normal eye was covered, the lie detector applied and various pictures were displayed in front of the supposedly bad eye. First he was shown a street scene, no emotion was recorded. Then a mountain scene with the same result, then a person dressed and still no response. He was then shown a nude woman. A change was noticed immediately. A few more obscene pictures and in a few seconds the recorder was jumping all over the place. That ended the case.

§ 16. — Missing merchandise.

What did we do in the old days when our clients came to us with the story that someone in their employ had been stealing things? They had suspicion of so and so, but were afraid of damage suits. The lie detector is now being successfully used in those cases in which our clients come to us with the statement that someone of their employees is stealing money, merchandise, etc. When all employees are subjected to the lie detector, success in determining the guilty person is almost assured. The use of this instrument has recovered money and property through confessions. There are no false arrest suits, no damages to be worried about and no publicity and the missing articles are recovered. These are very important considerations in favor of the lie detector as a modern scientific aid in the practice of the law today.

§ 17. — Personnel work.

The lie detector is now being used to check up on all employees of banks and various businesses, not only for old employees but for new ones before they are employed to determine whether their past records show dishonesty. It has proved its efficacy and has been a source of prevention. Modern business will undoubtedly adopt the use of the lie detector almost universally within a short time.

§ 17a. — — Co-operation.

It is relatively easy to elicit the requisite co-operation. The suspect is told that he happens to be under suspicion in regard to an alleged crime and that it is our desire to eliminate him, if possible. The suspect is often glad to have such an opportunity (for in many cases suspicion has been wrongly fastened upon an innocent individual), and if guilty, he does not dare to refuse because he is afraid that such a refusal may appear suspicious.

§ 17b. — — Objections.

The machine has been subjected to criticism, however, and perhaps justly so. The principal objections relate to fear and anger, and the failure of the machine to distinguish the reactions caused by these emotions and the emotions stirred by lying. Fear or anger of the innocent suspect certainly plays an important role in the deception syndrome during the actual investigations. These emotions can be of sufficient intensity to interfere with the elimination of innocent suspects.

The elimination of the factors of fear and anger in an analysis of the record of the lie detector may be procured, however, by the proper conduct of the examination. It has been found that if the proper procedure is followed, the result is that the reaction of the suspect, if guilty, becomes defensive and his fear increases instead of diminishing with the progression of the test, whereas if innocent, he becomes reassured as the test proceeds and fear diminishes, although he may be under considerable tension at first.

It may be readily seen that while the machine itself may be absolutely accurate, the resulting conclusion is dependent upon the analysis and construction of the record of the machine in taking into account all possible factors, which might have caused the various ups and downs in the record.

Deception, if present, will cause changes in the record. Since all changes and comparisons are relative, there are several checks available. These differences may be due to physiological or pathological differences, on the one hand, and, on the other, to differences in tension between an innocent man and one who is guilty. The record of the innocent suspect will usually vary but slightly, if at all, from its normal. The record of the individual who lies, on the other hand, is not only different from that of an innocent person, but shows changes with the attempt at deception.

§ 18. — — In criminal cases.

In one case a young man of twenty-three came to the police with a story of being held, bound, and gagged by two masked men while his employer's money was taken from him. According to routine procedure, he was tested as to the veracity of his story with the result that his record showed disturbances and seemed indicative of deception. He later confessed that he had gambled and lost the money and was afraid to tell the truth.

In another case a murder had been committed in Salt Lake City, and three witnesses were alleged to have seen the murderer. A description of this individual was sent throughout the United States, and some weeks afterwards a tramp was picked up. Upon his being questioned, it developed that he had recently arrived from the vicinity of the murder. His statements seemed so contradictory and his behavior so strange that his picture was sent to Salt Lake City. The picture was identified by the three individuals as that of the murderer. A detective was sent for the suspect. The officers in Richmond, California, where the suspect had been picked up, suggested that he be brought to Berkeley and tested. Aside from the identification of the photograph, the suspect's own words seemed to implicate him. He not only said that he might have been in Salt Lake City but that he might have committed the murder. However, his record on the lie detector when he was asked about the crime, was as clear as that section before it when there were no specific stimuli. As a result of an analysis of his record, he was cleared of the crime on the *assumption* that he was capable of conscious deception. The real murderer was later apprehended in Los Angeles and confessed to the deed.

Newspaper comments on this case, as follows, are of interest:

"Although there was apparently no doubt of the man's guilt, the machine proved him innocent of the crime. Larson (the detective from Salt Lake City) even hestitated about taking him back to Salt Lake.

"Hahn (the suspect) stated finally that he was in jail in Stockton for vagrancy on December 2. Investigation proved his statement correct and he was identified by the Stockton police.

"This was the most convincing case we ever had," said Chief of Police August Vollmer in commenting on the case. "Everything pointed to the man's guilt. The pictures were identified and the descriptions tallied. Now the man's innocence has been proved. He was confined in the Stockton jail on the day of the murder. So far we have never made a mistake with the machine. I will not say it is infallible. But thus far, it has proved so."

In order to be able to expose those papers or documents or things that lie and are not genuine the lawyer of today must avail himself of scientific and technical information pertaining to the matter or thing suspected of being false. He must probe all branches of medicine, wire tapping, dictograph, inks, papers, chemistry, automobile mechanics, photography and x-rays and keep abreast of all scientific discoveries and advances.

§ 19. Blood tests.

Blood tests are now resorted to by the modern trial attorney in various instances.

Laurence H. Snyder in Scientific American writes: "In Illinois a mother contends that she was given the wrong baby to bring home from the hospital. In Connecticut a man denies being the father of an illegitimate child when accused by the mother. . . .

"Such are the cases that offer opportunities to determine parentage by blood group tests. The past few years have seen the discovery of new facts about inheritance, and with the microscope and proper test serums, scientists can now tell to what blood group a person belongs. In 1900 Dr. Karl Landsteiner discovered in Vienna that when he mixed the red blood cells of one person with the serum (clear part of the blood) of another person, a clumping of the red blood cells sometimes occurred. This clumping is due to a substance in the red cells being acted upon by an antibody in the serum. It soon becomes apparent that there are two such substances in human red cells, acting very much alike. It was found that a person might have one of these substances in his blood or he might have the other, or he might have neither or both. A person having substance A is said to belong to group A; a person having substance B belongs to group B; a person having both substances belongs to group AB, and one having neither belongs to group O.

"The first application of the knowledge of blood groups was in transfusions. Before every transfusion a test is made to make sure that the blood given will not have its cells clumped up by the serum of the patient. Shortly after the importance of blood groups in transfusion was recognized, students found that these substances obeyed fixed hereditary laws. Substance A never appeared in the blood of a child unless also present in the blood of at least one parent.

"Recently two mothers went home from the hospital at the same time, each with a new baby. Upon bathing her baby mother No. 1 found the name of mother No. 2 on a tag on the baby's body. A court case resulted, and after various attempts to settle the case, blood tests were made. The parents of family No. 1 were both of group O and the baby they took home was group A. In family No. 2 the father was group O and the mother was group AB; the baby they took home was group O. Tables covering all possible combinations show that a child of these parents could never be of group O. Clearly the babies had been given to the wrong mothers and the court ordered them exchanged. In some instances both babies might be of the same group or both families might be of the combination to produce either child; in such case the blood tests would prove nothing. It has been computed, however, that the tests can solve about one-third of the cases.

"Another legal use to which blood groups may be put is the question of disputed paternity. Suppose a child has substance

A in his blood, and the mother does not. Then we know that the child's father must have substance A. In this way a man in group O or group B would be cleared. In a recent case the mother was group A and the child in group B. Substance B must have been inherited from the child's father. The man in question was group A, like the mother, and could not have been the father of the child."

§ 20. Gun powder tests.

Another instance wherein a knowledge of modern scientific methods may mean the difference between winning and losing is best illustrated in the following case:

Suppose a man was found dead, shot, with a revolver beside him. The dead man was a fairly wealthy business man who a short time before had applied for and received a $50,000 Life Insurance Policy which had a provision invalidating it if the insured committed suicide within one year. Everything about this case seemed to indicate suicide, but the widow, who was designated as beneficiary, could not and would not believe her husband had shot himself, and incidentally, she could not bring herself to the point of giving up the possible collection of the $50,000.

Her attorney immediately caused what is known as a powder nitrate test to be made on the right hand of the dead man to determine whether any powder marks or powder burns, however slight, would be shown. Tests made of the gun and bullet shell in question disclosed that black powder had been used in the bullet fired. No trace of powder marks or burns could be found which definitely established the fact that the insured had not shot himself, or at least, had not used the hand which now appeared to hold the gun in shooting himself.

This proof would help to satisfy the insurance company or at least worthwhile evidence would be had upon which suit could be predicated.

§ 21. —Disputed documents.

Almost all cases today require a knowledge of questioned documents, including handwriting and typewriting. Albert S. Osborn's book on "Questioned Documents" is a worthwhile addition to every lawyer's library; at least a knowledge of its contents and suggestions is almost a necessity today. If lawyers would become acquainted with handwriting experts in their cities they would be amazed to learn of the almost invaluable assistance available to them in every case involving questioned documents.

§22. ——Enlarged photographs.

Enlarged photographs of that portion of the questioned document which the lawyer seeks to disprove, with extra copies for each *two* jurors, should be made so that they can intelligently follow the testimony of the expert.

§23. —Submit all questionable documents to expert.

Some years ago a wealthy manufacturer died leaving an estate which was appraised at several hundred thousand dollars. A woman who was associated with him in his lifetime went to a reputable firm of attorneys to present a claim against the estate. After hearing her story the attorneys concluded she had a legitimate claim and so informed her. She then produced a promissory note, an agreement and several letters all purporting to bear the signature of the deceased, and all either acknowledging or reaffirming the validity of her claim. This seemed to the attorneys too good to be true, and in the careful preparation of the case submitted all the papers to an Examiner of Questioned Documents for his opinion as to the validity of the signatures. The expert quickly demonstrated that the documents had all been forged by the tracing process. In no uncertain terms the lawyers told their client she had a good cause of action and not to jeopardize it by producing any more spurious writings. The case was finally won but had the attorneys not had the foresight to have the documents produced by their client examined, and had based their action upon the forgeries, it is easy to prophesy what the outcome would have been.

The foregoing is but one illustration of the importance of having every document of value examined by an expert. By "every document," of course, is meant those which the lawyer does not personally know to be genuine. Sometimes the language of a paper produced does not harmonize with one's theory of the case; sometimes the manner in which a paper was procured does not seem appropriate; sometimes the signatures themselves look suspicious. The wise procedure is to turn it over to an Examiner of Questioned Documents and ask him for an opinion as to whether or not the paper is genuine. It may develop that the signature is bad, the paper was not manufactured until after the date of the document, it was not continuously written as it purports to have been, or there was a page or words substituted in the body of the document. There are many possibilities which might be developed from a careful study and analysis of a paper.

§ 24. —— **Fields of investigation.**

The field of document investigation has developed until now it covers handwriting, typewriting, inks, paper, pencil marks, printing, and the law pertaining to the identification of documents. It is possible to show identity or lack of identity of handwriting and typewriting. It is possible to tell the make of typewriter and that it was manufactured between certain dates. The establishment of whether two typewritten documents were written on the same machine is not a difficult matter. It can sometimes be told whether ink writing is as old as it purports to be. Ink writing which has been eradicated by ordinary ink eradicater can be reproduced without changing or mutilating the document. The composition of paper can be determined and often the date the paper was first put on the market. Erased pencil writing can sometimes be reproduced. Pen or pencil printing can be identified.

§ 25. —— **Legal citations.**

The well qualified examiner has at his command the legal citations pertaining to any question which will probably arise in the trial of a document case and the lawyer should consult him regarding any legal questions he anticipates will arise in the case. The attorney should have the expert submit to him written questions pertaining to his qualifications and the manner in which he is prepared to develop the case. The attorney and the expert should confer together upon the proposed cross-examination of opposing experts.

§ 26. —— **Equipment.**

For the formation of opinion and development of facts the equipment of the Examiner of Questioned Documents consists of an extensive library on many subjects and a complete modern laboratory. In the laboratory will be found microscopes ranging from low to high power magnification, a comparison microscope, various test plates and protractors for revealing traced signatures, identifying typewriters, measuring angles and curves, and a micrometer caliper for measuring the difference in the width of paper in ten thousandths of an inch. It will also include many kinds and sizes of cameras with a wide selection of lenses for making photographs and photo-micrographs and photographing erased ink and pencil writing. On the shelves of his laboratory will be different chemicals for the determination of the kind of ink used and chemicals for producing gas which will make legible certain ink writing.

§ 27. — — Infra-red rays.

There are two fields of investigation which are comparatively new and are being developed daily which have to do with the spectrum. The ultra-violet ray on the cold end and the infra-red ray on the warm end. Many things can be told by the examination of a document under the ultra-violet ray such as the kind of paper and reading erased ink writing. Very little is known of the possibilities of the infra-red ray, but it has lately been developed that much can be told in regard to pencil writing when photographed under the infrared ray.

§ 28. — — Standards of comparison.

The practicing attorney should consult the code of his state in regard to the proof of handwriting for the laws are many and vary in the different states. In some states it is provided that any document which it is intended to use as a standard of comparison must be described and set forth in a notice served on the opposing counsel within a reasonable time prior to the introduction in evidence, and if the opposing lawyer so desires, he and his expert may be permitted to examine the standards before they are produced in court. Standards of comparison are signatures or writing which may or may not have anything to do with the facts and are used for the purpose of comparing with the questioned writing to determine whether the party sought to be charged with the writing actually did write it. The attorney should select for standards of comparison only writings which can be unquestionably proved and about which there will be no question. It has happened in the past that an attorney has turned over to his expert writings to be used as standards which he was not able to prove in court and then the expert could not use the photographic preparation he had made for trial and his testimony was nullified or greatly weakened because he was not able to present his testimony in the proper manner. This could have been avoided had the attorney used proper care in the selection of standards.

In presenting a question to an examiner it is sometimes impossible to show him the paper in question or some of the standards. If possible always tender the original papers but if that cannot be done, then have good clear photographs made. It is never advisable to use photostats. No careful document examiner will render a positive opinion based upon the examination of photostatic copies. The photostat is merely a black and white likeness, has no intermediate tones or grades of color. A signature might be patched, overwritten, contain many suspicious pen lifts, or be of a tremulous character and none of these qualities show on even the best of photostats.

Every attorney should read "The Problem of Proof" by Albert S. Osborn. This book, as its name implies, will acquaint him with the proper way to try a case involving a disputed document and contains sample cross-examination questions to be used on opposing experts, and will suggest many lines of attack to the thinking lawyer.

§ 29. — — General suggestions.

Finally in submitting your problem to an Examiner of Questioned Documents, do not tell him what you want to prove or what you contend. Merely turn over to him the questioned document and the standards with a request for a detailed opinion as to the facts. You will then get his honest opinion and he will not be swayed, either consciously or unconsciously, by a desire to serve the attorney. No reputable document examiner will testify against what he believes to be the fact in order to help the attorney who employs him or for the collection of an anticipated fee. He should be absolutely neutral and testify to just what he thinks the facts warrant. He should never arrange for a contingent fee or have any financial interest in the outcome of the case. Further, it is not good practice for the document examiner to sit at the counsel table in order to consult with the attorney. Any suggestion the examiner may have can be conveyed to the counsel by a note passed over to him, or at a recess.

§ 30. Scientific Crime Detection Laboratory.

Every modern trial lawyer should become acquainted with the aids offered by the Scientific Crime Detection Laboratories of Northwestern University in Chicago. They are prepared to offer assistance in the following fields:

1. Automobile Tire Prints: Identification of by photography, the making of casts, etc.
2. Blood: Identification of stains made by, and further classification as to whether stain is from blood of human being or other animal.
3. Bombs: Identification of explosive employed, through study of fragments, etc.
4. Bones: Determination as to whether these are from human beings or other animals. Also (in some cases) age, height, and sex of person from whom they came.
5. Bullets: Identification of caliber, type, kind of powder by which fired, and type of weapon used. Also, in case of a suspected weapon, whether or not this actually fired the bullets in evidence.
6. Casts: Of tool marks, teeth marks, or of entire objects reproductions of which might have value as evidence. Casts may be made of wounds of any part of a body and preserved to indicate the nature and extent of such wounds, also of the entire heads of unknown dead persons, and held for purposes of identification, etc.
7. Codes: Letters or messages in code can be deciphered by those familiar with code systems, (as are a number of our associate staff).
8. Deception: See special discussion of this subject.
9. Dust: Analyses of dust from the clothing, from pockets of an automobile, or other sources, may yield valuable information concerning the habits of the person wearing the clothing, using the automobile, etc.
10. Explosions: Examination of premises following explosions may yield evidence which will reveal the cause behind these.
11. Feces: Examination of bowel movements of prisoners (feces) will reveal nature of food recently consumed and may be used to upset alibi statements.

12. Fingernail scrapings: When these are made from the nails of the victim of an attack or those of a suspect, they may show the presence of blood, hair, clothing, fibres, or other materials which will help solve the crime.
13. Firearms: Examination of these will show whether they have been recently fired and if so, with what kind of powder.
14. Fires: Study of premises may reveal evidence indicating the causes at work.
15. Food: Examination of particles of food may reveal presence of poisons, harmful bacteria, etc.
16. Gastric (Stomach) Contents: Examination of these may, as in case of feces, help upset a suspect's alibi.
17. Hair: Strands of hair from clothing, automobile fenders, etc., may be identified as similar to those from the heads of victims or suspects in crimes of various types.
18. Handwriting: Specimens of handwriting may be identified as to the hand that wrote them, erasures and alterations revealed, etc.
19. Inks: Study of the kind of ink used in a document may substantiate its authenticity or prove it a forgery.
20. Invisible Writing: Secret inks may be employed to write messages invisible to the naked eye between the lines of communications innocent in appearance. Such messages can be brought out by proper treatment.
21. Jewels: Identification of fake jewels can be made by employing scientific methods involving chemical tests, microscopic examinations, the use of ultra-violet rays, etc.
22. Metals: Serial numbers stamped in metal, as in firearms, automobiles, etc., and subsequently erased, can be brought back by proper treatment.
23. Money: Counterfeits of both metallic and paper can be identified by simple laboratory methods.
24. Paper: Knowledge of paper making and the history of paper often makes it possible to pronounce a certain document genuine or forged.
25. Parasites: Parasites found on the clothing of a body may be identified as of the same type as others present on the premises where a murder was committed, and so forth.

26. Paternity (Fatherhood): In a certain percentage of cases it is possible to establish paternity of blood-grouping tests made upon parents and child.
27. Poisoning: Chemical analyses of stomach contents, organs, etc., will reveal presence of poisons.
28. Postage Stamps: These are frequently forged, but forgeries can be detected by proper methods.
29. Postmarks: These may be forged in connection with fake alibis. They can be detected without difficulty.
30. Powder Marks: On skin or clothing these may serve to identify the kind of powder used and distance at which shot was fired.
31. Printing: A study of this will reveal its approximate date as the varieties of type used are constantly changing. Thus the age of a printed document may be established.
32. Seals, Embossed: These may be forged but the forgery can be detected.
33. Seals, Wax: These may be forged or removed and replaced. Detection is possible in both cases.
34. Seminal Stains: These may readily be identified on clothing in rape cases.
35. Shells, Empty, Fired: These can be identified as to the particular arm in which they were fired, etc.
36. Shoe Prints: These may be photographed and casts made of them which will show every abnormality present in the soles of the shoes which caused them. Thus the suspect may be convicted by identifying certain prints as having been made by shoes worn by him.
37. Soil: Soil adhering to shoes, clothing, etc., will help identify the locality through which the wearer has recently passed, and thus to confirm or upset an alibi.
38. Spots and Stains: These may be found on materials of all sorts. Analysis will usually reveal their nature, which may have an important bearing in the case.
39. Stamps, Rubber: These may be forged but the forgery can be identified.
40. Teeth Marks: These may be found in food, on human bodies, etc. Molds may be taken of them whereby the teeth of the person causing them can later be identified, as the teeth of no two persons will leave the same marks in an object bitten.

41. Textiles: Fibres of different types of cloth can be identified under the microscope and may prove very important evidence in many kinds of cases.
42. Tool Marks: Marks of jimmies or other tools on doors, etc., can be molded and the casts retained for future use. These will show any defects present in the tool used and may serve to identify the actual tool involved.
43. Typewriting: This can be identified as to the make of machine employed and as to the particular machine of that make which wrote it. Alterations, erasures, etc., can be revealed.
44. Urine: When this contains abnormal constituents it may serve to identify a given individual.
45. Wads (from Guns): These can be identified as to the factory which made them. This may be an important point in shooting cases.

Deception: The psychological department, which is directed by Mr. Leonard Keeler, has perfected the use of the instrument popularly known as the "lie-detector."

§ 31. Photographs in dark.

A new aid of great benefit is the development by the Eastman Research Laboratory connected with the Eastman Kodak Company that will permit the taking of photographs in the dark. This should be quite an aid in criminal prosecutions and divorce proceedings.

§ 32. Moving pictures, phonograph records and dictographs.

Many successful trial attorneys are now making use of moving pictures, sound pictures, and phonograph records, as well as testimony and evidence secured by dictographs. The legal authorities on the use of moving pictures as evidence are collected in 83 A. L. R. 1315. Some courts have held that their use is within the legal discretion of the trial judge.

The value of moving pictures in the preparation of the facts is illustrated in one case which was tried in a large central western city. It was a case where the plaintiff and the defendant attempted to fraudulently secure a large judgment on account of purported injuries claimed to have been sustained by the plaintiff when he was run over by the defendant's automobile. The defendant was insured against public liability.

At the trial the plaintiff took the stand and testified that he had not known the defendant before the accident and had not seen him since the defendant picked him up from the street and took him to his home. The defendant later took the stand and also testified that he was a stranger to the plaintiff. The plaintiff claimed that he knew of no witnesses to the accident but stated that he had been attended by a certain physician for some time. However, the physician did not appear as a witness. The Insurance Company undertook to defend the suit in the name of the defendant. The attorney for the insurance company, in preparing the case for trial, made a searching investigation of both the plaintiff and the defendant in view of the fact that each claimed that there were no witnesses to the accident. The investigation disclosed that instead of being strangers, the plaintiff and the defendant came to this country in the year 1906 from the same town, where they had been neighbors. Moving pictures were taken and displayed in the court room during the trial showing the defendant visiting at the home of the plaintiff since the accident. The judge stopped the trial, ordered the case dismissed and held both the plaintiff and the defendant to the grand jury for possible indictments.

Moving pictures are frequently used in the defense of personal injury cases to show that alleged permanent injuries are in truth and in fact fraudulent ones. Purported cases of permanent injuries to the back as well as to the legs have been defeated through showing the claimants working, playing or attending their usual and customary business or employment or doing some sort of work in and around their homes through the use of moving pictures.

Everyone can well appreciate the effectiveness of this type of evidence.

§ 33. Photographs for legal use.

Most trial lawyers are familiar with the added psychological value of photographs in the trial of personal injury cases. It is always a great deal easier for the jury to keep in mind the scene of an accident when presented to them in the form of photographs rather than a detailed word picture or description. No matter how able the trial lawyer is it will require far greater effort to successfully picture the scene of an accident where he depends entirely upon words rather than photographs.

It is always advisable that the trial lawyer have the photographs made under his supervision rather than to depend upon his opponent's photographs or the taking of such photographs by some stranger to the case. The attorney will know just what particular features of the scene of the accident he wants to bring out and therefore it is sometimes better to have a number of views taken; if possible, they should be taken from all four directions to the point of the accident. The attorney must always be in a position to prove the correctness of the photographs taken, the position of the camera, the type of lens used, as well as the development of the films by the person who developed them.

In those instances where the trial attorney is engaged some time after the accident occurred and conditions have changed so that photographs may not be admissible in evidence, it is possible to find photographs taken shortly after each accident where someone is injured at the Accident Prevention Bureau of the local police department. This Bureau is usually charged with the duty of taking photographs of the scene of all accidents involving personal injuries immediately after the accident and while the scene remains unchanged. In fact the police department insists upon everything remaining in the same condition until the photographs are taken.

§ 34. How photographs should be made.

Following are suggestions to obtain best results with photographs to tell a true story, to be used legally:—The Lens—must be of medium or long focal length to avoid *distortion* of objects which appear nearest in photograph so that they are not distorted out of proportion to objects of the same size appearing farther back in the same view. A short focus lens should never be resorted to unless under conditions where it is impossible to make photograph with a medium focal length lens owing to lack of space in which photograph is to be made.

§ 35. — Kind of film to be used.

Either Orthochromatic or Panchromatic film should be used in legal photography—briefly the difference amounts to this: Orthochromatic film is not sensitive to any object which is *Red* which explains why it can be developed in Red Light. Panchromatic film is sensitive to Red and must be developed in Green Light.

§ 36. — Color filters.

Color filters can be used on either Orthochromatic or Panchromatic films, and are fitted between the Lens and film while the exposure is being made to accentuate certain colors that are being photographed.

§ 37. — Lighting.

Lighting should always be considered whenever the opportunity presents itself, for example—if an exposure is made with what is termed a flat lighting, it is not interesting and very often is misleading and more or less untrue. Let us say we are to make a photograph in deep snow which is to show a deep rut. If this photograph were to be made at a time of the day when the sun was shining directly into the rut, it would hardly show any depth to the rut—but if the same rut were to be photographed several hours earlier or later, the sun at this time would be off to one side or the other and would cast a shadow into the rut which would appear dark in the finished photograph which would bring out in contrast against the white snow the depth of the rut.

§ 38. — Filing of data.

The photographer must never trust his memory concerning the data about which he may be asked to testify. This data is to be filed away so the photographer can refresh his memory if called upon to testify.

§ 39. — Perspective.

Perspective should always be considered by the photographer. For example—an automobile parked in an alley about six feet away from a wall could be photographed from a straight side view to make it appear as though the auto was parked within a few inches of the wall—but if the photographer would place his camera either towards the front or rear of the automobile and photograph from say about a forty-five degree angle, it would readily show in the photograph that the auto was some distance from the wall, or if the camera were placed on a direct line with the wall it would show at once that there was a decided space between the wall and auto.

§ 40. — Retouching.

Retouching on a negative can be identified by examining the film. Retouching is done on the film by applying negative varnish to the film and then retouching with a lead pencil which shows plainly upon examination.

Retouching on the photographic print can be identified by holding the print in a good light and looking for a duller or an opaque color which most always is applied by an artist with an air brush.

§ 41. — Maps and diagrams.

In the event that maps and diagrams are prepared of the scene of the accident the distances should be measured and marked and the person who did the work should be available for testimony in court as to the correctness of such maps and diagrams.

§ 42. The place of the X-ray in medico-legal cases.[1]

Many worthy cases involving medico-legal phases fail to receive a just award through faulty preparation of the case. This is especially true regarding the radiologist. He should have an opportunity to suggest what films he thinks should be taken of the case to determine the full extent of the pathology. He should have the time necessary to prepare his side of the case as carefully as the attorney does his. He should help frame the questions to be asked him and other medical witnesses during the trial, as no one understands better than he does the embarrassment of trying to answer a question worded in such a way as to hurt his side of the case. He is supposed to be an impartial witness and if his answers are to have weight with the jury, they must be strictly confined to the question as asked.

It is generally accepted that a properly taken radiograph is the best evidence of the condition of structures below the surface of the body. In legal procedures this is especially true regarding the condition of the bones, the locating of foreign bodies and the condition of the chest, particularly as regards the diagnosis of pneumonoconiosis and tuberculosis, and no examination is worthy of the name that does not include its use. Radiographic examination is also made to determine the presence of early pregnancy, from a legal standpoint. This determination can be made any time after the fourth month.

The x-ray differs from ordinary light in that it penetrates substances according to their atomic weight, and that it is not

[1] By J. H. Carpenter, M. D., Chicago.

seen because it penetrates the back of the eye without registering any effect. There are many substances that completely obstruct ordinary light that offer little or no resistance to the x-ray. The lighter metals, such as aluminum, obstruct its passage very little, while lead and the heavier metals offer great resistance to its passage. This characteristic action is taken advantage of in examining the human body, the soft parts offering very little resistance to its passage while the bones or the more dense foreign bodies are not penetrated as readily. The normal lung tissue is readily penetrated by the x-ray while the pathological areas are more dense and are readily distinguished.

§ 43. — Fluoroscope.

There are two methods of using the x-ray in making an examination, the fluoroscope and the radiograph. The fluoroscopic examination is conducted in a darkened room. The part to be examined is placed between the source of the x-ray and the fluoroscope which is a specially constructed screen, (which has been) treated with chemicals and becomes luminous when exposed to the x-ray, the difference in the densities of the part being examined being seen on the screen. This method is desirable where it is necessary to examine a part in motion, such as the chest, or in adjusting broken bones in the reduction of fractures, but it has a limited value in medicolegal work.

§ 44. — Radiograph.

A radiograph commonly known as an x-ray or roentgenogram is taken by placing the sensitive photographic film in a light-proof container on one side of the part to be examined and the source of the x-ray on the other, so that the x-rays may pass through the part and their effect be registered on the photographic film. It is essential that the source of the x-ray be placed at right angles to the photographic film and be centered over the part to be examined. If this relationship is not observed there is sure to be a distortion of the image as shown on the film. If the x-ray tube is not properly placed in relation to the part to be examined, one side of the body may seem to have less density than the other.

§ 45. — Distortion.

Films are often presented in court that were not properly taken and consequently do not convey a correct representation of the part. This distortion may simulate a dislocation of a hip or shoulder or indicate a deformed pelvis claimed to be due to an alleged injury. Improperly taken films of the head may, by displacing the normal position of the grooves in the skull, simulate fractures. These misrepresentations are not seen by the jury and need to be pointed out by someone familiar with the taking and interpretation of x-ray films.

§ 46. — How should be taken.

Whenever possible films should be taken at right angles to each other to bring out complete detail of the part. In some instances as the skull, pelvis, some parts of the spine, the hip and shoulder, stereoscopic films give a better interpretation of the part being examined. Stereoscopic films consist of two films so taken that when viewed in a stereoscope it is possible to get the third dimension or depth of the part. Stereoscopic films of the chest should be made with the films at least sixty inches from the tube with short exposures to avoid distortion and blurring. If films are under- or over-exposed, detail will be lost and the examination will be of little or no value. All chest cases should be examined with the fluoroscope to note the movements of the diaphragm and the width of the retrocardiac spaces.

§ 47. — Age of bone injuries.

Often it becomes necessary to determine the age of bone injury. Recent fractures show an uneven edge which smooths off in time. Where a fragment has become detached recently, there will be no dense edge or cortex at that point, while older fractures will show some of this formation. Callus formation depends to some extent upon the location and extent of the injury, the length of time since the fractures, and the age and health of the individual. If there has not been any displacement of the bones at the point of fracture, there will be very little noticeable callus. Callus is more rapid and profuse in the bones of the extremities than in the ribs, skull or vertebrae.

Usually very little callus is formed in vertebral fractures. Callus does not form in the skull as in other parts of the body. The bodies of the vertebrae have very little cortex or hard bone on the surface and are especially subject to compression fractures. These fractures may easily occur without demonstrable change in the intervertebral discs, which are formed of cartilage which usually yields without fracture. A fracture of the spine often shows more deformity two weeks after the injury than it does at the time the injury was sustained. It is generally understood that it requires four months for a fracture of the spine to become fixed. In taking radiographs of fractured bones, it must not be forgotten that good films cannot be obtained through a plaster-paris cast. To get the best results, the cast should be removed, the films taken, and the cast replaced.

§ 48. —Marking and identifying.

It is very important that radiographic films be properly marked at the time they are taken, so that there can be no question at any time regarding their connection with the particular patient. This marking should in some way be a part of the taking of the film and not put on after the film is made, as there is too great a chance for error if it is done at the latter time. It is preferable that this marking be in some person's handwriting so that it can be identified later if need be and that it be made a part of the photographic process. The marking should give not only the name of the patient, and the date, but some mark to show who took the film and for whom it was taken.

§ 49. —Illuminating boxes.

Proper illuminating boxes should be provided in court so that the jury can get a better idea of the nature and extent of the injury than is possible by ordinary light. The physician explaining the films should use both the technical and common names of the parts as far as possible, the one for the records and the other for the jury, being careful that he makes himself understood by the jury.

§ 50. Medical facts.

Preparation of the facts on medical phases of a case can be made by referring to medical text books at the libraries, both general and law libraries. In some localities the libraries will be found to contain complete and up to date medical reference books.

The medical testimony should always be taken up and studied under the guidance of your medical adviser and expert.

It is also advisable to talk over all theories of your case with some other physician who happens to be disinterested. Get his reactions to the theories of your expert. These discussions plus your individual study of the medical authorities should familiarize and prepare you for trial and for possible cross-examination of your opponent's experts.

§ 51. Credit agency reports.

Another important aid in the preparation of cases for trial has been the use of Dun and Bradstreet's financial reports. By resorting to these reports, one can learn who are the proper parties to sue, the parties who might be interested in the business so as to become liable for the debts of that business. In one instance, a client did business with a young man who filed a petition in bankruptcy. Client came to his lawyer with the statement that he had heard that this young man's father-in-law was interested in this particular business but could offer no proof thereof. A report was procured through Dun's and in that report, was a statement that the father-in-law of this young man had claimed that he was interested in the business and that he had put up all of the money and that the business was in reality his. With this information and with the testimony of the investigator, the client was enabled to recover a judgment against the father-in-law.

§ 52. Telephone, gas and electric records.

Information may be secured as to the right parties to sue in many cases from public utility company records—telephone, gas, or electric companies.

§ 53. Ownership of automobiles.

It is frequently necessary to determine the ownership of automobiles in automobile accidents and personal injury cases where only the license number is secured. The method of determining ownership either by letters to the Secretary of State, License Bureaus or the Police Department should become known to the lawyer.

§ 54. Abstracts of records and briefs.

Another valuable assistance in the preparation of cases for trial in large cities where appeal courts are located, is to locate similar cases that have been tried and appealed, and to go to the Appellate Court and read the transcript of the evidence and abstracts of the record and if the judgment has been affirmed, to note the proof offered. This will show the kind of proof necessary. That case can then be used as a guide. It is also advisable to read the briefs on both sides so as to get acquainted with all points of law raised.

In some states abstracts of the records and briefs in all late cases in the courts of appeals are available for preparation purposes at the local bar associations.

§ 55. Private detectives.

Every trial lawyer should become familiar with the assistance that a private detective agency can give him in the investigation and preparation of cases for trial. A knowledge of wire-tapping, under what circumstances a dictograph can be used, how the private detective can help in locating witnesses and also guarding them, of how to investigate prospective jurors and also check up for cross-examination purposes, the opponent and his witnesses, is almost a necessity today.

§ 56. Weather reports.

Where weather conditions are important in trials of cases, a telephone call to the United States Weather Bureau located in your city will give you the desired information in a moment. Copies of the reports can then be easily secured and presented in evidence.

§ 57. Encyclopedias.

General knowledge on various subjects can be obtained by resorting to encyclopedias such as Britannica, New International Nelson Loose Leaf and a host of others. It is surprising in most instances how much information can be found in these encyclopedias on almost every subject.

§ 58. (2) Interviewing client and witnesses.

This is one of the most important factors in the preparation of the facts. Unless the client and the witnesses on both sides and the adverse party are all interviewed as early as possible, the true facts of the case may remain a hidden mystery until the time of trial. Then it is usually too late. An unfavorable verdict is the probable result of the lack of preparation of evidence which might have been secured that would have refuted the surprise testimony.

The interview with the client should, therefore, be very searching and detailed. The client should first be permitted to tell his story in his own way with very little interruption so that we may get a good general idea as to just what the case is about. Then all pertinent questions should be asked to clear up details not clearly understood. Then his entire statement should be taken and signed.

§ 59. Signed statements.

Both the client and all witnesses should be interviewed as soon after receiving the case as possible, and the scene of the occurrence particularly in personal injury cases should be visited by the trial attorney, the client and the witnesses. It is surprising how many worthwhile and additional ideas will occur to the lawyer who visits the scene of an accident soon after its occurrence. It is suggested that statements be taken from both the client and the witnesses in question and answer form rather than in the narrative. This is, of course, subject to the objection that it takes too much time and that the witnesses are too restive. A further objection will probably be that the investigator is not equipped to take that kind of a statement. In spite of all these possible objections the suggestion still holds good. However, in many instances statements have been taken in question and answer form by having a court reporter go with the investigator to take the statements down on a portable typewriter.

When the narrative form of statement is attempted to be used for purposes of impeachment, in many instances, one can realize the ineffectiveness of such form of statement.

Many narrative statements have been nullified before juries in attempting to use them for impeachment purposes where the investigator under cross-examination admits that the story was given him in response to numerous questions and that the answers have been combined in narrative form in the words of the investigator with the investigator's own interpretation placed on the answers of the witness. Frequently the impeaching effect of a written statement is entirely lost by the sworn testimony of the witness that he did not make the statements as alleged and that he signed such statement without reading it.

Some of these troublesome features may be obviated by taking the statement in question and answer form and by resisting all temptation to use any but the witness' words in the answers. As closely as possible the words of the witness should be given especially where the lawyer is interrogating an uneducated witness. Any jury will be able to detect the difference in the words substituted and such a statement will do more harm than good.

§ 60. — Intimate details.

Again, every statement taken should contain several questions and answers by the witness concerning one or two intimate details of his life that the lawyer or investigator could not possibly have known. Greater credence will be given to the statement by the jury on the grounds that that part of the information must have been given by the witness and that, therefore, the balance of the statement must also have been made by the witness. These intimate details might concern the maiden name of the witness, the names of the mother, wife or grandmother, where witness was born, names of parents, addresses if living, when died (if dead), schools attended, dates, etc.

§ 61. — In handwriting of witness.

In taking statements from adverse party or from witnesses both favorable and unfavorable it is always good policy for the investigator to ascertain whether the party signing the statement can read or write. If he can read, the statement should conclude with a sentence indicating and acknowledging that the witness "has read and signed each page of the statement consisting of the above three pages" or acknowledging that "the foregoing statement consisting of three pages which has been signed by me on each page thereof has been read to me and which I acknowledge as being a true and correct statement of how the above accident happened."

If possible the witness should be requested to write out the above suggested sentence or two. This will prevent him from later repudiating the statement or claiming he never made or read the statement.

§ 62. — "O.K.'d" statements.

Many witnesses have been warned by attorneys not to sign statements for anyone in personal injury cases. A method utilized by some trial lawyers is to have a witness read over the statement and then ask him, to mark it O.K. in his own handwriting. After the witness has "O.K.'d" the statement, the trial lawyer usually asks him to put his initials under the O.K. to designate that the statement is all right. It is always a comparatively simple matter to prove that even though the witness did not initial the statement, the letters "O.K." are in his handwriting. If he were to admit that at any later date few jurors would believe that he did not sign it or make the statements attributed to him in the body of the instrument.

It is, of course, fundamental procedure for the trial lawyer to have every witness in the case sign a statement in every instance. The possibility of the witness later forgetting details of his story as well as a precaution against the witness later changing his story, dictates the necessity for such procedure. In addition thereto, some witnesses may later decide that they do not wish to be bothered with attending court and may become hostile and claim that they did not remember anything about the case. Showing such a witness a statement signed by himself will usually eliminate this possibility.

As has been stated, it is always advisable to interview the adverse party at the earliest possible moment. This procedure will eliminate the possibility of the adverse party changing his story and will also give the trial lawyer a knowledge of just what he will have to meet at the trial of the case.

§ 63. — General suggestions.

The taking of statements in question and answer form is also advisable from the standpoint of the young attorney in that it serves as a basis for questions to be used in direct examination on the trial of the case. Each question and answer can be analyzed to determine whether or not it is objectionable and then reframed to obviate the possible objections. The question and answer form of the statement also prepares the witness for his testimony in court.

The statement should be prepared in duplicate so that a copy of it may be handed to the witness just before trial. A re-reading of the statement several times should improve his testimony.

So while this form of statement is more trouble and takes more time at first, it is far more valuable than is the narrative form. Its use in the actual trial, in the preparation of the facts and in the preparation of the witnesses, makes it far more advisable.

It is suggested that all witnesses be interviewed separately for fear of too much concert of ideas and to eliminate words suggestive of the tutored witness.

§ 64. — — Signed confessions.

It might not be amiss to suggest here that all prosecutors and investigators charged with the duty of taking confessions in criminal cases follow the suggestions above in taking statements as to crimes committed. If the person charged with the crime is led into giving details of the happening with the names of all persons with whom he came in contact, where he procured or purchased implements used also and the names and addresses of such persons, it will then be easy to secure the corroboration required by the law to prove the corpus delicti and a conviction can be obtained that will not be based on the confession alone.

These suggestions should also be followed in interviewing the adverse party wherever possible.

§ 65. Granting interviews.

Clients and their witnesses should be cautioned against granting interviews or signing any statements for opponent's investigators or to anyone overly interested in the case unless the attorney is present to determine whether or not such action is advisable.

Clients and witnesses must be made to realize that a great deal of damage and harm may be done even though they do not actually sign a statement as any verbal statement may also be used against them. They should also be told as to the possibility of some investigator deliberately distorting their statements to the point of causing an unfavorable verdict.

§ 66. Corroboration of client's story.

Some lawyers take the facts as given to them by their clients, prepare their law with great intensity upon the basis of those facts and when they appear on trial find that the facts are either insufficient or entirely incorrect. While in order to have confidence in ourselves, we must have confidence in our clients and their cases, still we must never place such implicit faith in their stories so as to blind us to the necessity of proving up their stories in the light of all the other known facts. We must seek for corroboration of the truth of our client's statements. This should be done by interviewing as many disinterested witnesses as possible for verification of the client's story. The best possible proof of a fact is to secure documentary evidence. If the client had documents prepared in the usual course of business at a time when no law suit was contemplated, then you can be fairly certain of your position. Such documentary evidence will have great weight before a court and jury, for as one judge of the Supreme Court of Georgia in the case of Miller v. Cotten in 5 Ga. 341 on page 349 said: "I would sooner trust the smallest slip of paper for truth than the strongest and most retentive memory ever bestowed on mortal man."

Osborn in his Problem of Proof says: "Every lawyer sooner or later learns that the most formidable evidence that appears in the court is the silent evidence of things. A letter, a telegram, a postal card, a signature is that which turns the scale of justice."

§ 67. Investigating client and his story.

In no class of cases is it more important to investigate your own client and the story he tells than in personal injury cases and in all medical and chemical cases where the injuries complained of are of an internal character and where the symptoms are subjective rather than objective.

An able trial lawyer once stated that "the greatest hazard of the legal profession is a lying client." So too is the one who deliberately fails and refuses to make a complete and full disclosure of all the facts to his lawyer. A client claimed to be suffering from carbon tetrachloride poisoning while engaged in the electric arc welding of certain refrigerator parts which had been dipped in carbon tetrachloride to dissolve grit and oil which had accumulated. The doctor who had examined the client made a routine blood test, among many other tests, which showed negative. After a great deal of preparation a prima facie case of occupational disease was proved when to the lawyer's surprise the defendants proved that the client had been suffering from syphilis. They also showed that a year prior to his seeking employment with the defendant he was treated by a doctor to whom he gave a history listing almost the identical symptoms and complaints his lawyer was now seeking to ascribe to carbon tetrachloride poisoning.

In previous questioning of the client, he had denied absolutely ever having been treated for any other serious ailment except the ordinary sicknesses of childhood which, coupled with the negative blood test, completely threw his lawyer off the track. He had accepted his client at face value. The result was a "not guilty" verdict which left his lawyer much sadder and wiser.

We now find that it is of the utmost importance in every case to investigate the client's story and to check up his past life for anything that might prevent a possible recovery in his case.

To guard against a similar experience the following list of questions should be submitted to every client in all personal injury and medical-chemical cases. These questions should be asked casually in order to give the lawyer a complete basis to investigate the client. After all questions are answered it is wise to caution the client against withholding any information on the ground that the other side will investigate his life from the day of his birth and that his lawyer must be in possession of all the facts so that he can prepare for anything that is likely to develop.

(List of Questions)

Name or names............(If married woman, her maiden, last and previous married names)............

Business............Present and for how long, give details of duties............

Present employer ....

Schooling — Names of Schools — Periods of attendance at each; from date to date............

Name of father or mother. If living — .....If deceased—Ages and causes..... ....Their present addresses.......

Name of father or......If deceased—Ages and causes......
mother. If living.........Their present addresses.........

Brothers and sisters............No. and ages of each—Living, dead and causes of death............

Address of living..

Other blood relatives............Any family disease among such, or above?............

Names and address
of employers............Since starting to work and nature of business and duties............

Street addresses
where client has lived
the last 10 years............and cities or towns............

What claims or law suits
started in last five years
and against whom?..

What doctors have treated you in the last 10 years and for what?	....Duration of disease (each).... ....Complications during or following other diseases with no doctor attending............

What hospitals have you
been treated at
and for what?..........At any time. Give dates..........

What examination or
tests made........On blood, urine, etc., also x-rays?........

What companies have examined
you for life insurance or health
insurance and when?
Ever rejected for insurance?..........................

What other physical examinations
have you ever had and with what
results? ....
Previous employment..................................
Army, navy, or other military service: United States; foreign countries.
Schools ....
Gymnasiums ....

Have you ever consulted
any other attorney in this case?..........................

§ 68. — Questionnaire.

A most complete list of questions for use in automobile accident cases is found in Schwartz on "How to Try an Automobile Accident Case" and is as follows:

Questionnaire

GENERAL INFORMATION

Client's name.
Residence. Floor. Apartment. Phone.
Occupation.
Business address. Phone.
Age.
Infant. With whom does infant reside? Name of father, mother. Who is to be guardian? Is proposed guardian competent? Adversely interested? Financially able? Will he consent?
Married or single? Name of husband.
Has client given any interviews or made any admissions?
Was any other attorney consulted?
Who recommended case?
Will proper party be available to sign pleadings?
If client is defendant give date summons was served on him.

THE ACCIDENT

What happened? (Have the client tell his story in his own way and, if possible, take it down verbatim. See that the following points are covered:)
Date of accident. Time of day. Day of week.
Scene of accident. (Draw a diagram showing the streets, indicate thereon the direction in which each party was traveling and the exact spot where collision occurred.)
Width of street or highway.
Condition of street and of pavement. Obstructions. Condition of sidewalk.
Weather conditions.
Extent of traffic: Vehicular. Pedestrian.

FACTS REGARDING PEDESTRIANS

What was pedestrian doing just prior to accident? (Crossing) walking on street, or highway? Alighting from street car? Working in street? Playing in street? Standing still? In safety zone or on sidewalk?
Did he cross at street crossing?

Did he look before crossing? If so, when and how many times, and in what directions? Right or left? Both ways? Straight ahead? Backwards?
Direction in which he walked. Straight or diagonally?
On what part of roadway did he walk?
Distance walked after last look for approaching vehicles.
Did he see the approaching automobile?
Distance from automobile when it was first seen.
His actions upon sighting automobile.
Distance from curb when struck.

FACTS REGARDING AUTOMOBILE, ITS OWNER, OPERATOR
Make, model and age of automobile? Bought new or used? General condition of car? Defective parts?
Name and address of operator of automobile.
Age.
Operator's license number.
Name and address of operator's employer.
Automobile registration plate number. Names and other signs painted on automobile.
How did operator come to have automobile?
Destination and purpose of trip.
Orders and instructions given operator.
Description of automobile.
Was automobile empty or loaded?

PASSENGERS
How many?
Who were they?
Position in automobile?
Relationship between driver and passenger.
Acts of passenger prior to accident. (Did he see danger? Protest against speed? Take any other steps for his own safety?)

NEGLIGENCE
Speed of each automobile.
Signals: Was horn sounded? Hand signals?
Lights: Head lights lit. Rear light.
Was operator blinded by glare of bright lights?
What equipment did automobile have? Mirror?
Were brakes in good condition?
Law of road, any violations?

What were relative positions of automobiles prior to impact?
In what direction was each automobile traveling?
Was each automobile on right side of road?
Which automobile reached intersection first?
Was automobile parked? Backing up?
Did automobile stop or slow up suddenly?
Parts of automobiles which collided.
Did automobile stop after collision? How far away?
Position of automobiles after collision.
What did driver of other automobile do after accident?

Damages

PERSONAL INJURIES: TREATMENT: MEDICAL EXPENSES

Sensations on being struck. Was he rendered unconscious, and if so, for how long did he remain unconscious?
What assistance was given?
Describe injuries.
Was he ever injured prior to the accident?
Details of treatment, pain and suffering.
Length of time confined to bed (to house, or hospital, to wheel chair, or crutches, to splints and bandages).
Present physical condition. (What injuries are permanent? Scars, marks, sores, loss of weight.) (Deformities, anatomical loss of parts, physiological alteration or loss of function.)
(Full) name and address of house doctor.
Length of time under his care.
Number of visits by client to doctor's office.
Number of visits by doctor to client's home.
Was an ambulance called?
Name and address of hospital.
Date brought to hospital. How long there?
(Full) name of ambulance doctor—ambulance chaser.
Name of interne.
Names of nurses.

MEDICAL EXPENSES

Doctors.
Hospital.
Nurses.

Medicines.
Surgical apparatus.
Ambulance.
Were these bills paid? By whom?
Obtain these bills and also medical certificate.

LOSS OF EARNINGS

Name of employer at time of accident.
Kind of work.
Length of time employed there.
Prior employments.
Education and prospects.
Wages.
When he returned to work. How long away?
Total loss of wages.
Were wages paid during absence?
Present employment and earnings.

SAME, IF IN BUSINESS

Duties.
Amount of time devoted to business.
Reasonable value of service.
Length of time absent from business due to accident.
Cost of hiring substitute.
Average income.

PROPERTY DAMAGE

Year of manufacture of automobile.
From whom automobile was purchased.
Cost when purchased.
Condition of automobile before collision.
Value of automobile before collision.
Condition of automobile immediately after the collision.
Was automobile repaired? Wrecked?
Name and address of repairman.
Date automobile was given to be repaired.
Time necessarily taken to make repairs.
What did repairs consist of? Get itemized bill.
If not yet repaired: Estimate of cost.
Towing cost.
Were repairs paid for?
Amount of salary paid chauffeur during repairs.
Was substitute automobile hired or taxi fares paid during repairs?

Amount expended for substitute automobile.
Condition and value of automobile *after repairs.*
Nature and extent of damages to opponent's automobile.

INFORMATION REGARDING WITNESSES

(Persons who actually witnessed the accident. Passengers in the automobile. Other persons injured in the same accident; policemen; repairmen; conductors or motormen of street cars.)
Names and addresses.
Relationship of parties.
Occupation.
Did the witnesses see the accident or come later?
Uniformed man's badge. Precinct.

INSTRUCTIONS

Instruct the client that all negotiations concerning the case are to be conducted by the attorney.
Warn clients not to give any interviews or statements or to make any communications regarding the case without the attorney's knowledge.
Obtain authorization from client for examination of police blotter. Have client sign retainer.

§ 69. Have story written out by clients and witnesses.

In all cases where the client and his witnesses are of the educated, intelligent type, it is a good plan to have such client and each of his witnesses write out, when they return to their offices or homes, the story as they know it with all the names of the various people who could prove each detail of said story or what written memorandum of any kind would corroborate such statement of fact. It is surprising how many things the client and his witnesses will think of when they sit down to write out the story in the privacy of their offices or homes. This procedure has the benefit of impressing upon the client and the witness the story he has to tell from the witness stand; it gives the lawyer the client's and the witnesses' stories for his permanent record and file, so that in final preparation for trial, he has the entire story (unless you have a stenographer take down the client's story when you interview him). While lawyers follow the procedure, in many cases, of having client's story taken down by a stenographer, it is always best to have him write the story to get additional facts. It helps the client in relating the story on the witness stand. It is, of course, a well recognized fact that the more times the witness writes his story and retells it, the better he will deliver it from the witness stand, especially if the lawyer permits him to express the story in his own words. Client and all witnesses should be cautioned against trying to memorize the exact words.

§ 70. Additional facts.

After listening to a client's story the lawyer must then start to prepare the facts of the case by considering what additional facts it will be necessary to prove to constitute a good cause of action, if representing the plaintiff, or a good defense, if representing the defendant, what witnesses will be necessary, are the witnesses interested or disinterested, what corroboration is there, and what documentary evidence is there to prove client's contentions.

§ 71. — (3) Anticipating and preparing for opponent's proof.

The trial lawyer who becomes so immersed in his client's cause that he fails to take into consideration his opponent's case has lost half of the battle before the trial commences. This is a common fault of some young lawyers. They become so imbued with the justice of their client's claim that they completely lose sight of the old saying that "there are two sides to every question." Or else, they quickly arrive at the conclusion that there *are* two sides to the question in this case—"*our* side and the wrong side." This may be due to their eagerness and desire to believe their client. They deliberately shut their eyes to the unfavorable and to the improbable aspects of the client's story until the rude awakening in court under somewhat embarrassing circumstances.

An attorney who can only see his client's side of the case is due for many surprises and discloses at once a failure to prepare his case properly for trial.

§ 72. — Cross-examine client.

In attempting to arrive at the actual facts of a case, it becomes necessary for the lawyer to cross-examine his own client searchingly for the minutest details of the case. Naturally, the client will attempt to cover up any facts or circumstances prejudicial to his interests. It seems that even the most truthful client on first telling his story minimizes or leaves out entirely the other side of the story. The lawyer should question the client closely as to what the other man claims. He should assure the client that it probably is not so but that it is necessary for the lawyer to know everything the opponent may contend no matter how immaterial, so as to prepare against it. When the client finally tells the lawyer the other man's contentions, he should ask client what witnesses or proof the other side could possibly produce. Then he should follow by asking client to produce some witness or evidence that will or can refute opponent's contentions.

If the adverse party is interviewed as suggested above, and an exhaustive analysis made of opponent's pleadings the lawyer is then in a position to see both sides of the case; he should then be able to ascertain the unfavorable facts which he will have to overcome as well as the weaknesses of his side of the case. He is then in a position to seek some proof or testimony which will overcome the defendant's contention.

§ 73. (4) Outlining elements to be proved.

After receiving the facts in the case from the client and briefing the law, the lawyer is then in a position to know just what to prove in order to win. Reading similar cases involving the same sort of facts will usually suggest many items which may have been omitted in taking the original statement of facts from the client.

§ 74. — Diagram of case.

After getting the entire story down, the lawyer must now set out a list of the main facts to be proved. Opposite each fact to be proved, he must list the witnesses who will prove those facts and all documents, letters or records which will corroborate proof of said facts. Listing the facts in this way, with the names of the witnesses is a particularly useful and beneficial method of preparing in advance an outline to be used for opening statements, for the direct examination and for the final arguments. The presentation of the argument to the jury on each fact with a complete showing of corroboration of each fact, either by witnesses, documents or records, tends to convince them of the truth of your particular story. The psychological effect and the value of corroborating proof is a fact emphasized by all successful trial lawyers. The diagram should be planned so as to present the facts in logical sequence and *to an interesting climax.* It should be sufficient under the law to prove not only a prima facie case but a case sufficient to warrant a favorable verdict. This diagram, plus the witnesses' statements, plus the brief on law will constitute a trial brief for the case.

For illustration purposes let us take a simple contract action for a balance due for goods, wares and merchandise sold and delivered.

Diagram of Case

Elements and facts to be proved	Witnesses	Written evidence or corroboratory documents
(1) Legal entity of client: Name Address Individual, partnership or corporation	Client or Salesman	Charter of a corporation
(2) Legal entity of defendant: Name Address Individual, partnership or corporation	Salesman	Certified copy of charter (if corporate entity denied)
(3) Agency of client's representative	Client or Salesman	
(4) Agency of defendant's representative	Salesman	
(5) Order and sale	Salesman	Signed order

(6) Delivery	Deliveryman	Delivery tickets
(7) Account and amount due	Client or Bookkeeper	Books of account
(8) Interest (if any)	Same	
(9) Demand for payment	Client Salesman Bookkeeper	Statements Letters
(10) Possible claims of defendant (Not as per sample)	Salesman	
(11) Refuted by talk with salesman, satisfied, also payments on account	Salesman Bookkeeper Admission by defendant	Books of account Receipts

§ 75. Aged witnesses.

Where a witness is advanced in years and is unable to read without glasses, the attorney should always remind the witness to bring his glasses so that he will be able to read any papers or documents that may be shown him. In a recent case, a failure to take this precaution caused a great deal of harm and embarrassment.

§ 76. — Arranging and tabulating documentary evidence.

When the preparation of the facts has been duly completed, the final step should be the arranging and tabulating of all documentary evidence in the order in which you expect to introduce them in evidence. Many judges and juries become impatient with the lawyer who must go through all of his files in court, keeping both the judge and jury waiting until he can find the paper he intends to use. This is also true in the preparation of arguments on the law. Each book that is intended to be used should contain tabs at the proper place with notations on each tab as to the particular point of law referred to and the page where found so that the judge will not become impatient when the lawyer is called upon to produce the authority for any proposition of law that may be advanced by him.

§ 77. Debtor who claims another person is obligated. In those instances where client has a claim against one person and that person contends that it is really the obligation of another, it is always good policy to sue both and let them fight it out against one another. Suing them one at a time, may cause the loss of both cases.

§ 78. Notice to city in personal injury cases. In suits against a municipal corporation such as a city, preliminary notice must be served on the persons designated therein and as required by the statute. If suit is to be started against the city for personal injuries the notice may be in the following form, and must be filed within the time limited by the statute.

Chicago, Illinois
January 5, 19—

Notice

To: Barnet Hodes, Corporation Counsel
Room 602—City Hall
Peter J. Brady, City Clerk
Room 107—City Hall.

Notice in writing, in pursuance of an act concerning suits at law for personal injuries and against cities, villages and towns, approved May 13, 1905, in force July 1, 1905.

1. The name of the person to whom cause of action has accrued: Thomas Brown.

2. The name and residence of the person injured is: Name, Thomas Brown. Residence, 1040 S. Halsted Street.

3. The date and about the hour of the accident are: Date —January 4, 19—. Hour—At or about 10:20 P. M.

4. The place or location where said accident occurred is: The sidewalk in front of premises known as 4240 W. Madison Street.

5. The name and address of the attending physician is: Dr. John Doe, address 4310 W. Madison Street.

Thomas Brown
By Smith and Green
His Attorneys

Received a statement in writing of which the foregoing is a true and correct copy and the same is filed in my office this 5th day of February, 19—.

Barnet Hodes
Corporation Counsel of the
City of Chicago

By Samuel J. Allen
Assistant Corporation Counsel

Received a statement in writing of which the foregoing is a true and correct copy and the same is filed in my office this 5th day of February, 19—.

Peter J. Brady
City Clerk of the City of
Chicago

§ 79. — Court reporters.

In those states, where the courts do not provide court reporters, experience has taught the trial lawyer that every case that is worth trying requires the services of a court reporter. The court reporter in the trial of cases serves a twofold purpose. The realization that the court reporter is taking down all that is said during the trial of the case causes both the lawyers and the judge to be more careful in what they say and do. In addition the possibility of appeal must lie uppermost in the trial attorney's mind and an appeal without a true and correct transcript of the evidence by a court reporter is almost impossible.

§ 80. Attorney's liens—Contingent fee cases.

It sometimes becomes necessary that attorneys take cases on a contingent fee basis; where provided for by statute, written agreements should always be prepared and the client made to sign them at the earliest possible moment. Where provision is made by statute for an attorney's lien, notice should be prepared in accordance with the statute and particular attention paid to the decisions of the state governing the proper service of notice. The reason for this precaution is that some defendants follow a practice of settling cases unethically direct with the claimant in an effort to reduce the settlement by eliminating the attorney's fee. Proper service of notice of attorney's lien should prevent any such attempt.

CHAPTER II

PREPARATION OF THE LAW

§ 81. In general.

Proper preparation of the law, to the successful trial lawyer, means something entirely different from what it means to the average law school student. To the student, preparation of the law may mean the knowledge of how to look up the law. To the student it may mean using the knowledge of what he learned in a good legal bibliography course such as is taught in our leading law schools. But to the trial lawyer proper preparation of the law consists of:

(1) *The recognition* of the various propositions of law involved in the case; that is, all the elements necessary to prove the cause of action.

(2) *The recognition* of the questions of law involving the method of proof or evidence to be adduced; that is, the law governing the proof and admission of testimony as to the facts.

(3) The finding of favorable authorities which support his position—rather than general statements of the law.

(4) The anticipation of all propositions of law that may be relied upon by his opponent.

(5) The securing of authorities which show that opponent's contentions are not tenable nor well-founded in law.

(6) The preparation of an outline of all questions of law involved.

(7) The preparation of a complete trial brief and two copies of that portion covering all questions of law involved.

§ 82. — (1) The recognition of propositions of law involved.

It is a comparatively simple matter to be able to "look up" a proposition of law when told on just what question legal authorities are wanted, but it is a little more difficult to take facts and pleadings and to ascertain just what propositions of law are involved. The ability to make such proper analysis is by far the more important to the lawyer who wishes to become successful in the trial of cases.

The preparation of the law from the viewpoint of the trial lawyer means the practical application of theoretical knowledge of the law to a searching analysis of the facts in order to determine the legal questions involved and to then apply the knowledge obtained in the bibliography or "How to find the law" courses in obtaining favorable citations of authority.

§ 83. —In personal injury case—The facts.

The following simple personal injury case illustrates the method of preparing the law in the case: On December 11, 1933, Sam Moreen was driving a 3½-ton coal truck east on 51st Street which has two-way street car tracks. He was driving on the right-hand side of the street straddling the outer tracks. He was to deliver two tons of coal which he had on the truck to a garage. To reach this garage it was necessary to make a left-hand turn into an alley which was half-way between Wabash Avenue and Michigan Avenue. As Moreen was about to make this left-hand turn, he noticed a street car approaching from the east on 51st Street just leaving the corner of 51st and Michigan, which was about 200 feet away from the alley. This was a "one-man" operated street car. It was coming along about 25 to 30 miles per hour. Moreen and his helper claimed that they felt that they had plenty of time to make the turn in broad day-light, so they did so. As they started to go up toward the alley, a lady with a small child attempted to cross the alley. Moreen slowed his truck down so that it was hardly moving in order to permit the lady and child to pass. The operator of the "one-man" street car apparently did not see the truck and ran into it striking the right rear end and throwing the truck about five or ten feet towards the curb. One witness who was on the front platform of the street car claims that the conductor was not looking ahead just before the impact, but was collecting fares and giving transfers at the time and that this witness had to call his attention to the danger ahead. The operator tried to stop the car but was unable to do so. Moreen claims that after the impact the operator of the car came down and admitted that it was his fault. Moreen hurt his back by being thrown backward with some force against the rear of the cab of his truck. The right rear wheel and various parts of the truck were damaged. The truck was taken to a regular auto repair shop, repaired, and the bill marked "paid." Moreen was taken home, put to bed suffering from pain. A few days later a doctor was called, who examined him and took a record of the subjective and objective symptoms. He treated Moreen for several months. X-rays were taken by another physician about one week after the accident, but Moreen's doctor was present while the x-rays were being taken. He was also present while the other physician developed the films and he examined the x-rays while still wet. After they were dried they were turned over to Moreen's doctor who has had them in his possession ever since. The physician who actually took the x-rays is seriously ill and unable to come down to court to testify.

During the time the truck was being repaired Moreen had to rent another truck and had another man do his work. Moreen now claims that he still suffers pain when he works.

The street car company claims that Moreen cut across the path of the oncoming street car without notice or warning and that the accident happened as a result of his "own negligence." In other words that Moreen was guilty of contributory negligence.

Suit was started by Moreen's attorney who filed a claim as follows:

Plaintiff's claim is:

(1) That on to-wit: December 11, 1933, he owned, operated, and managed a certain truck, which he then used to haul and transport coal, and was in the exercise of due care, caution, and diligence in his own behalf.

(2) That at the time and date aforesaid, he was driving his truck east on 51st Street, going towards Michigan Avenue, when he turned to the left at or near the middle of the said block, for the purpose of driving into an alley.

(3) That plaintiff's truck, facing the entrance of said alley and moving in a northerly direction after making a left hand turn, was proceeding at an extremely slow rate of speed, with the rear portion of his truck on the west-bound street car track and the front part of his truck at or near the sidewalk line.

(4) That while said truck was in this position, said defendants, engaged in the ownership, management, and operation of one of its street cars, in the City of Chicago, County and State aforesaid, which car is a one-man street car, i. e. in the control of one individual serving as both conductor and motorman, was driving said car in a westerly direction on 51st Street, and after crossing Michigan Avenue, proceeded in the direction of plaintiff's truck in a fast, and rapid rate of speed.

(5) That notwithstanding the plaintiff's position on said car track in clear view of the operator of said defendant's street car the said defendants, by and through the operation of said street car, did then and there carelessly, negligently, and recklessly so manage, control, and operate said street car that it was driven into the right rear of plaintiff's truck, damaging same and injuring plaintiff.

(6) That as a result of the negligence of said defendants, plaintiff sustained injuries to his vertebrae and other portions of his back and spine, and was otherwise seriously injured internally and externally, resulting in severe pain and discomfort, causing headaches, nervousness, insomnia, loss of appetite, and other disorders.

(7) That plaintiff has been prevented from performing and attending to his usual business and affairs as a result of the defendant's said negligence; that plaintiff was compelled to employ a doctor in his care and is now, and will in the future be required to retain the services of a physician in treating his injuries.

(8) Plaintiff's damages to date are as follows:

Medical expenses	$150.00
Rental of truck	90.00
Damage to truck	141.20
Earnings or income loss to date	200.00
Total	$581.20

Plaintiff's claim is for the sum of One Thousand ($1,000.00) Dollars.

The Street Car Company filed an answer as follows:

"(1) That defendants were not guilty of the negligence, carelessness and recklessness charged in plaintiff's statement of claim;

(2) That the collision in question and injuries and damages, if any, arising therefrom, were not caused by any negligence, carelessness, or recklessness on the part of these defendants or their agents or servants, but were due to the negligent manner in which the truck of the plaintiff was managed and driven at the time and place in question;

(3) Defendants deny that the said street car was operated at a fast and rapid rate of speed at the time and place in question;

(4) Reserving the right to object to any insufficiency in plaintiff's statement of claim and any insufficiency of plaintiff's evidence to establish these said defendants' liability."

§ 84. — The method followed.

Then the case was turned over to a trial lawyer, who had to prepare the case for trial. The facts and the pleadings presented all of these questions to his mind:

1. What law governs the operation of the street car?
   (a) City Ordinances.
   (b) State Codes.
   (c) State, Commerce, or Public Utility Commissions.
2. Are there special laws governing the operation of a one-man street car?
3. Is operator permitted to collect fares or give transfers while street car is in motion?
4. Are rules made by the Commerce or Public Utility Commissions?
5. Had Moreen the right to pass in front of an approaching street car and make a left turn into the alley?
6. What duty does law impose on street car operator passing an alley as to degree of watchfulness?
7. Must Moreen wait until street car passes?
8. What would be a reasonable distance?
9. What sort of a signal would Moreen have to give of his intention to turn into alley?
10. Was this contributory negligence?
11. When is contributory negligence not a good defense?
12. Does proof of wanton and wilful conduct overcome the defense of contributory negligence?
13. If it does will the plaintiff's complaint be sufficient?

14. Will it be necessary to amend the complaint?

15. Will an amendment be proper?

16. Will it be stating a new cause of action so as to be barred by the statute of limitations?

17. Can there be a recovery for loss of use of truck?

18. Can one action be brought to recover both personal injury and property damage?

19. When is wanton and wilful conduct a question of fact for jury?

20. Will it require a special interrogatory to be submitted to the jury on the question of wanton and wilful conduct?

After considering all of these questions and collecting the authorities on each point it was decided to file an amended complaint as follows:

"Plaintiff's claim is:[1]

1. That on, to-wit, December 11, 1933, he owned, operated, and managed a certain truck which he then used to haul and transport coal, and was in the exercise of due care, caution, and diligence in his own behalf.

2. That at the time and date aforesaid, he was driving his truck east on 51st Street, going towards Michigan Avenue, when he turned to the left at or near the middle of the said block, for the purpose of driving into an alley.

3. That plaintiff's truck, facing the entrance of said alley and moving in a northerly direction after making a left-hand turn, was proceeding at an extremely slow rate of speed, with the rear portion of his truck on the west-bound street car track and the front part of his truck at or near the sidewalk line.

4. That while said truck was in this position, said defendants, engaged in the ownership, management, and operation of one of its street cars in the City of Chicago, County and State aforesaid, which car is a one-man street car, i. e. in the control of one individual serving as both conductor and motorman, was driving said car in a westerly direction on 51st Street, and after crossing Michigan Avenue, proceeded in the direction of plaintiff's truck at a fast and rapid rate of speed.

5. That notwithstanding plaintiff's position on said car track in clear view of the operator of the said defendants'

---

[1] Refer to local authorities as to right to plead both negligence and wilfulness.

street car, the said defendants, by and through their agents, did then and there wilfully, wantonly, maliciously, carelessly, negligently, and recklessly in utter disregard of the property and person of the plaintiff herein, so manage, control, and operate the said car that it was driven into the right rear of the plaintiff's truck, damaging the said truck of the plaintiff and injuring the plaintiff.

6. That there was then and there in full force, virtue and effect an order made and entered of record by the Illinois Commerce Commission of the State of Illinois, in words and figures following:

'No operator of any one-man street car operated on the street railway system of the Chicago Surface Lines shall collect any fare, make change, accept or issue any transfers, make any entry upon any record, or count transfers, tickets, or money while such vehicle is in motion in, along, or upon any public street or highway in the City of Chicago.'

7. Plaintiff further alleges that notwithstanding the fact that the order hereinabove referred to was in full force, virtue, and effect, the operator of said street car, then and there being the duly authorized agent of the defendants, while the said street car was in motion in, along, and upon the said public street as aforesaid, did make change, and accept or issue transfers in violation of the said order hereinbefore set out, and as a direct and proximate cause of the wilful, wanton carelessness and recklessness of the said agent of the defendants in making such change, accepting or issuing transfers, counting transfers, tickets, or money while the said street car was in motion, and as a direct and proximate cause of the carelessness and negligence of the defendants as hereinabove set forth the plaintiff sustained injuries to his vertebrae and other portions of his back and spine and was otherwise seriously injured, internally and externally, resulting in severe pain and discomfort, causing headaches, nervousness, insomnia, loss of appetite, and other disorders.

8. That plaintiff has been prevented from performing and attending to his usual business and affairs as a result of the defendants' said negligence; that plaintiff was compelled to employ a doctor in his care and is now, and will in the future

be required to retain the services of a physician in treating his injuries.

9. Plaintiff's damages to date are as follows:

Medical expenses	$150.00
Rental of truck	90.00
Damage to truck	141.20
Earnings or income loss to date	200.00
Total	$581.20

Plaintiff's claim is for the sum of One Thousand Dollars ($1000.00)."

The Surface Lines then filed their defense to the amended complaint as follows:

"(1) That defendants were not guilty of the negligence, carelessness, recklessness, wilfulness, wantonness or maliciousness charged in plaintiff's amended statement of claim.

(2) Defendants deny that the said street car was operated at a fast and rapid rate of speed at the time and place in question.

(3) Defendants deny that the operator of the said street car did any of the acts set forth by plaintiff in Par. 7 of the complaint as violations of the alleged order of the Illinois Commerce Commission or any act at all in violation of orders or regulations of the Illinois Commerce Commission.

(4) That the collision in question and injuries and damages, if any, arising therefrom, were not caused by any negligence, carelessness, recklessness, wilfulness, wantonness or maliciousness on the part of these defendants, or their agents or servants, but were due to the negligent manner in which the automobile of the plaintiff was managed and driven at the time and place in question."

§ 85. (2) The recognition of the questions involving the method of proof.

It is always important in the proper preparation of the law of a case to take into consideration the many problems of proof which will confront the attorney upon the trial of the cause. It is quite manifest that even the most intensive preparation as to the facts, the pleadings, and as to the general questions of law will be unavailing if the trial lawyer is unable to present the testimony or the evidence so as to prove his contentions legally. Since there is always a proper and an improper method of making proof, it becomes of the utmost importance that the trial lawyer learn the technique of making such proof and it is almost of equal importance that he have at hand citations of authority showing that he has the right to prove his contentions in the way he is doing and also by the particular type of witness he has produced.

§ 86. — Anticipating objections.

The trial lawyer must be able to recognize and to anticipate the objections which his opponent will probably make to his technique in proving the various points in controversy. It, therefore, becomes necessary to subject the facts and the pleadings in the case to a searching analysis in order to determine the methods to be employed in proving each feature of the cause. The competency and restrictions placed upon each witness must be considered and also as to how far the proof must go as well as what foundation must be shown.

§ 87. — The method.

For illustration, let us further consider the facts and pleadings set out under Point 1, which appears on pages 52 to 59. The following questions will present themselves for consideration to the trial lawyer:

1. Can we prove admission of operator of street car that it was his fault?
2. What witness will be used?
3. Is our doctor competent to make proof as to the x-rays?
4. Must we produce doctor who actually took the x-rays?
5. Can our doctor testify to the history of pain and as to how the accident occurred as related to him by Moreen?
6. Can plaintiff testify to his pain and suffering?
7. Can other members of the family or witnesses to the accident testify to plaintiffs pain and suffering?
8. How must the proof be shown?
9. Will a hypothetical question be necessary?
10. Is a certified copy of Commerce Commission order admissible?
11. The weather conditions may become important—How can proof be made?

12. Will a certified copy be sufficient?

13. May it be advisable to prepare diagrams showing scene of the accident?

14. What proof will be necessary in order to introduce this diagram into evidence?

15. Is the same true as to photographs?

16. Moreen has a paid repair bill for repairs to his truck—Is it admissible in evidence as proof of damages?

17. Will it be necessary to produce an automobile repair man?

18. How can damages resulting from loss of use of truck be shown and proved?

19. Are models of street car and truck permitted to be used to demonstrate how accident happened?

20. How is loss of earnings proved?

21. What medical expenses are recoverable and how proved?

When this procedure is followed, all questions in reference to methods of proof will have been anticipated and preparation made.

§ 88. (3) Finding of favorable authorities.

In some instances failure to make proper preparation of the law is due to the fact that the lawyer is unfamiliar with the working tools of his profession. In other cases his experience in looking up law is so limited that he is frequently unable to locate citations of authorities on the points involved. Therefore, one of the first steps in considering preparation of the law for trial of cases should be to become familiar with the more common legal encyclopedias and digest systems, such as Corpus Juris and Cyc., the American Digest System, National Reporter Systems, such as Federal Reporter, New York Supplement, Atlantic, Northwestern, Northeastern, Southern, Southwestern, Southeastern, and Pacific Reporters, the Lawyers Reports Annotated, both old and new series, Ruling Case Law, American Law Reports, all State Digests and Annotated Statutes and local text-books.

§ 89. —Various subject headings.

One fact to be kept in mind is that the editors of the various digest systems and encyclopedias sometimes have ideas differing from that of the average lawyer as to just where certain authorities shall be placed. In some instances, the attorney may feel that he should look under a certain subject heading and he may be surprised to find that no authorities are listed under that heading. A little more search and consideration of the index will usually disclose just where the editor has placed those particular citations. Narrowing down the search for authorities too much often results in failure.

Some attorneys reach the end of their patience in searching for authorities without really giving themselves a chance to find them. If they do not readily find the authorities they are seeking, they arrive at a conclusion that there are no citations on their particular point and "leave it go at that." This is usually a mistake. A little more perseverance—a closer analysis of the index—will usually be rewarded.

§ 90. Local statutes, ordinances, digests and text-books.

It is a frequent cause for complaint among leading jurists, both in trial and appellate courts, that lawyers fail to properly prepare the law in their cases due to a lack of regard to the controlling value of local statutes, ordinances and decisions. Particularly pronounced complaint is made by appellate justices in the so-called smaller states.

Due to a faulty procedure, it frequently happens that the attorneys fail to locate some local decision which controls the case. Judges point out that many times the lawyers on both sides are guilty of this and as a result neither party cites applicable authorities.

This is especially true where a local statute or ordinance is involved. It is only by reference to local digest systems and local text-books that the attorney is in a position to secure a proper and controlling authority.

One state supreme court justice, in recently voicing this complaint against the attorneys in his jurisdiction claimed that the fault was due to the habit formed by lawyers in recent years of depending entirely upon general legal encyclopedias and digest systems for local authorities.

This is a sad mistake. While the general encyclopedia and general digest system serve a very necessary and admirable purpose and while no office should be without them if possible, yet where purely local statutes, ordinances or peculiarly local legal problems are involved, resort should first be had to local annotated statutes, local digest systems and local text-books.

Local text-books on specific subjects are of particular value to the attorney. The author almost always has selected a somewhat limited subject for a detailed treatment. All local decisions on the subject are considered at great length and in many instances a complete brief on the point involved is available.

A good practice to follow on local problems is to start with your local statute, code, ordinance, annotated statutes, digest and text-books.

It is almost impossible for the general digest or encyclopedia to give all of the decisions construing all statutes in all of the states.

Local works for local problems is a worth-while practice that will pay unusual dividends in winning cases.

§ 91. Words and Phrases.

In all instances where the legal construction of a word or phrase is involved or where the legal definition of any phrase is desired it is always good policy for the lawyer to exhaust the possibilities of the four series of the work known as "Words and Phrases." Not only will this worthwhile work give the legal construction of the word or phrase involved with the cases construing such word or phrase, but frequently it will give the lawyer a lead or even a citation which will be directly in point with his own case. The citations are kept up-to-date, and should be resorted to.

Legal construction of words and phrases may also be found in Corpus Juris, American Digest System and all local digests, but are more conveniently collected in Words and Phrases.

§ 92. Negligence and Compensation Cases Annotated (N. C. C. A.).

Every lawyer about to try any case involving general negligence law, personal injuries, property damage, malpractice, automobile, railroad, street-car or workmen's compensation cases of any kind or description should never fail to make use of this most admirable set of books. There is no set of law books that ever had a more simple, complete, and more easily usable index than Negligence and Compensation Cases Annotated (N. C. C. A.). No matter what point is involved in the question under consideration, a reference to the index will locate the proper citations of authority. Almost any boy with a high school education could use N. C. C. A. No lawyer who has ever once used N. C. C. A. has ever failed to use it continuously ever after. It is always included in the library of all lawyers specializing in negligence and compensation cases.

§ 93. Uniform Laws Annotated.

This is another worthwhile series of books treating a number of subjects that have been enacted almost uniformly by many states in this country. Here will be found conveniently collected all the authorities construing various sections of the so-called uniform statutes and codes such as sales, conditional sales, bills and notes or negotiable instruments, partnership, warehouses, and many others. It is always possible to find an authority construing some section of a local statute which the local courts have not yet passed on.

The distinguishing features of apparently contrary opinions are commented upon as well as the possibly small differences in the wording of the statutes of the states following such apparently contrary opinions.

§ 94. Questioned Documents.

This book written by Albert S. Osborn, together with his outside efforts, was primarily responsible for lifting the position of the so-called "handwriting expert" to that of a much respected assistant in the dispensing of justice. The examiner of disputed documents today is truly an expert. The trial lawyer should become familiar with the various citations of authority contained in "Questioned Documents" as well as the theories and principles treated. It is of invaluable assistance to the attorney who must try cases involving questioned documents.

§ 95. Cooley's Briefs on Insurance Law and Couch's Cyclopedia of Insurance Law.

Every question involving insurance law should be looked up in either Cooley's Briefs on Insurance Law or Couch's

Cyclopedia of Insurance Law or both. While every attorney utilizes the different digests and encyclopedias, it is always advisable to resort to various sets of books dealing with a particular subject. When the author's efforts are limited to only one subject, it is usually found to be much easier to locate the particular citations desired.

On the question of insurance law these two sets of books are strongly recommended for use.

§ 96. Commerce Clearing House current decisions reports.

This is an unusually good series published by the Commerce Clearing House on various subjects of the law, which comprise current decisions from all over the country. These current decisions are within a week or two of the rendition of the opinions in all courts of record from all states of the Union. It is always good policy just prior to going to a trial in any case to make a search of the recent decisions in Commerce Clearing House reports. It is frequently possible to find a favorable decision in point. It is always possible to secure copies of the complete opinions from the Commerce Clearing House long before they appear in any advance sheets.

§ 97. Index to legal periodicals.

Another source of value in the location of favorable authorities will be found in the index to Legal Periodicals. There are now several different series available. One is Jones' Index to Legal Periodicals, another is the Commerce Clearing House Index to Legal Periodicals. There are others also worth while.

In some instances when it seems impossible to locate authorities on a proposition, as a last resort the trial lawyer should seek aid in some good index to legal periodicals. This is especially true where the case involves some new or novel point. It is the policy and practice of writers of law review articles to write up comments annotated with authorities on all new and unusual cases, as well as recent decisions of a radical or new nature. The law review articles are usually written by scholars or specialists in that particular field who have exhausted the subject and have collected authorities which may well serve as the trial lawyer's brief on that point.

§ 98. Magazine articles.

It is frequently possible to locate favorable authorities by making use of magazine articles dealing with special subjects in various fields of endeavor. For questions of insurance law, the Insurance Law Journals and magazines contain a world of information, decisions, and comments. This is also true in the field of criminal law, banking law and procedure, and many others.

§ 99. Text-books.

No preparation of the law can ever be considered as complete without exhausting all text books published on the subject under consideration. Text books are continually being published on almost every conceivable subject. No conscientious trial lawyer will ever go to trial without a search for a text book covering the subject under inquiry. The authors of text books usually exhaust the subject and generally have collected all the authorities on each point.

§ 100. Annotations and supplements.

No proposition of law should be considered as thoroughly briefed until resort has been had to all annotations or supplements to the particular set of books you are using. No case is prepared as to the law unless the last known word on the subject has been investigated and exhausted.

§ 101. Citator.

No case should ever be cited or relied upon until after the citator has been used to determine whether or not that particular authority has ever been overruled or whether that case has been reversed. It is very embarrassing to have opposing counsel point out to the court that you are citing a case which has been reversed by a higher court or that it has been overruled by a later decision. It is not only embarrassing but may sometimes arouse suspicion as to your good faith.

§ 102. National Corporation Reporter and Daily Law Bulletin.

In Chicago, lawyers can keep abreast of the important new decisions by reading digests of cases in both the National

Corporation Reporter and the Chicago Daily Law Bulletin. It is surprising how frequently a newly reported case will help win a law suit as well as keep one up-to-date on the law. The National Corporation Reporter also gives in digest form all recent cases decided in the Illinois Supreme Court and all cases in the First District of the Appellate Court.

§ 103. Advance sheets.

Every lawyer will concede the necessity of constantly reading the advance sheets of both the local courts and Reporter Systems. Yet it is surprising the number of lawyers who never seem to have time enough to do so. Once the habit of reading the "advance sheets" has been acquired over a period a few years, it will repay the trial lawyer a thousandfold in increased knowledge of the law. A new decision may give him the lead towards a solution of his particular legal problem.

§ 104. Analyzing citations of authority.

After locating and finding cases apparently deciding the law applicable to the case, it becomes of the utmost importance to analyze the authorities in the light of the facts involved in such case. The law may be applicable because of the facts set out in the authority, but when considered in the light of the facts in the case at bar, the law may not be applicable at all or at least can be distinguished if the law is apparently unfavorable.

Many lawyers fail to take into consideration the facts upon which the court decided a particular case. If the case cites law favorable to their contentions, they accept it without any further investigation and cite it to the judge. When opposing counsel, who has fully prepared himself, shows the court that the case was decided on facts that are clearly distinguishable from those involved in the case on trial, the lawyer may have a rude awakening when the judge rejects the law he has presented.

It is, therefore, suggested that all citations of authority be thoroughly read, analyzed and digested and briefed both as to the law and the facts before being presented to the court.

§ 105. (4) The anticipation of all propositions of law relied upon by opponent.

Next in importance to the securing of legal authorities supporting the trial lawyer's position is the ability to so detach himself from the case as to be able to view the facts and the pleadings impersonally with the thought in mind of trying to anticipate the position and contentions of his opponent. It usually requires quite a bit of effort to deliberately seek out the weaknesses in one's own case and in addition to try and mentally place oneself in the opponent's position. Trying to figure out all the steps which the trial lawyer would take if he were on the other side of the case will usually make it possible to anticipate all of opponent's contentions. This is especially true where the trial lawyer does not deliberately close his eyes to the weaknesses of his own case.

If he has questioned and cross-examined his own client as suggested in the chapter on "Preparation of the Facts" and has interviewed all witnesses, both favorable and unfavorable, as well as the adverse party, and has made a searching analysis of the pleadings, the trial lawyer should be enabled to anticipate almost every point which the opponent could possibly raise.

The best procedure to follow in an attempt to anticipate opponent's contentions is to list all thoughts on the subject on a sheet of paper. It is surprising how many things will be presented to the mind of the trial lawyer when he resorts to this method.

This worth-while effort when followed in all cases will be found to be of unusual value. The trial lawyer will usually find that he has not only anticipated everything his opponent will present, but in most cases, *he has anticipated a number of things which his opponent has failed to present.* With this type of preparation there should be very few surprises in store for the trial lawyer. Naturally this kind of preparation will enable the attorney to seek for law or evidence with which to meet every point advanced by his opponent.

In the illustrative case of Moreen v. Surface Lines, it is quite apparent that the main defense it will be necessary to overcome is that of contributory negligence. It has already been determined that wanton and wilful conduct will eliminate the defense of contributory negligence. Reference to a complete instruction and the cases on wanton and wilful conduct show that a failure to see or recognize danger to another by the exercise of ordinary care may constitute wanton and wilful conduct. One of the occupants of the "one-man" street car will testify to the effect that the car was in motion while the operator was collecting fares and giving transfers and being thus engaged was unable to keep a "look-out" for danger ahead. As a result he did not see Moreen's truck until too late to avoid the collision.

With this in mind it then becomes important to determine and to support by legal authorities that this constitutes wanton and wilful conduct.

§ 106. (5) Securing authorities to show opponent's contentions not tenable in law.

The anticipation of all propositions of law that may be relied upon by opponent would all be unavailing unless it is followed up by the securing of legal authorities to show that opponent's contentions are not tenable nor well-founded in law.

This would include collecting those authorities which are apparently in favor of opponent's position, subjecting them to a searching analysis, and briefing the facts and the law so as to be able to show that they have no application by reason of the differences between the facts in the case at bar and those in the supposed authorities.

The proper preparation of the law in a case requires a complete search for authorities that may be relied upon by the opponent. Thus it will be seen that the preparation of the law means not only a search for authorities to be utilized by the trial lawyer, but also a complete familiarity with the law to be used by his opponent.

This type of preparation will make it possible to fully anticipate opponent's contentions and will more readily suggest possible theories with which to refute an adversary's contentions.

§ 107. (6) Outline of all propositions of law involved.

It is suggested that the most effective method of analyzing the questions of law involved in the case is to list on paper each and every proposition of law that presents itself. When this method is followed and a searching analysis of the pleadings is made as well as all the known facts it should be a comparatively simple matter to "ferret" out all questions of law that may arise.

An illustration of the method to be followed in listing all questions is found on pages 56 to 61. When this procedure is utilized it is a comparatively simple matter to outline all questions of law involved in the case. It also serves as an aid to anticipating all of opponent's contentions.

§ 108. (7) The trial brief.

There is no doubt that a young lawyer is at a disadvantage in court when he is opposed by an older, more experienced trial attorney. In many instances the older lawyer capitalizes on the young lawyer's inexperience by violating many of the rules of law governing the admission of evidence. This seems to be especially true of some personal injury experts. Some judges place the burden on the young attorney to support his objections by legal authorities. In rare instances, the judge's failure to comprehend aided by the fact that the opposing attorney is recognized as a leader in his specialty prompts such specialist to take advantage of the situation.

The only way of combating this possibility is to prepare complete and exhaustive trial briefs of the law in every case and always to carry into court some recognized local treatise on the law of evidence. By following this procedure it will be possible to present authorities at a moment's notice.

To many lawyers the trial brief remains the most mysterious part of the trial lawyer's equipment. Among attorneys there is a vast difference of opinion as to just what a trial brief should contain. Some are content to gather a few citations of authority following a sentence or two into which they have condensed several propositions of law. Others consider the trial brief as containing only a collection of legal authorities covering the law applicable to their side of the case. Some add authorities to refute their opponent's contentions.

§ 109. — What it should contain.

The true trial brief in its final analysis represents the complete preparation of the case for trial. It includes the preparation of the facts, the law and the pleadings. The trial brief when completely prepared will eliminate any uncertainty as to just what should be done at any stage of the trial. It will also eliminate any fear of overlooking some element of proof necessary.

The true trial brief should include:

(1) A diagram of the case.

(2) A résumé of the facts in narrative form.

(3) A list of the witnesses.

(4) An abstract (in narrative form) of each witness' story.

(5) A detailed signed statement from each witness in question and answer form.

(6) An abstract of the pleadings of both sides, that is, as to

- (a) Allegations made.
- (b) Elements and measure of damages to be proved.
- (c) Admissions in opponent's pleadings.

(7) Brief on the law including:

- (a) Favorable authorities showing right to recover.
- (b) Favorable authorities as to method of proof.
- (c) Authorities refuting opponent's contentions.
- (d) Copy of Statute relied upon (where involved).
- (e) Extra copies of brief on law for judge (and opponent).

(8) Instructions.

§ 110. —— (1) Diagram of the case.

A discussion of the value of the preparation of a diagram of the case as well as an illustration of just how it should be done is contained on pages 47, 48 and 49 on the Preparation of Facts. No trial lawyer should ever proceed to trial without the preparation of some diagram or outline of his case.

§ 111. —— (2) A résumé of the facts in narrative form.

Every trial brief should contain a general statement of the facts involved in the case which should include a paragraph or two in reference to the plaintiff's claims and also a paragraph or two in reference to the facts from the defendant's point of view. When this statement is prepared it will enable the trial lawyer to block out quickly his opening remarks and his opening statement to the jury.

§ 112. ——(3) A list of the witnesses.

Every trial brief should contain a list of the witnesses expected to be used in that particular case. The names of the witnesses should be placed in the order in which it is expected to have the witnesses testify. As each witness is produced a line should be drawn through his name and the next witness in order called. This procedure when followed will prevent the possibility of overlooking or failing to call some particular witness.

§ 113. ——(4) An abstract of each witness' story in narrative form.

It is always advisable to include in the trial brief a short narrative form résumé or statement of what each witness will testify to. Many successful trial lawyers do not resort to question and answer form statements and, therefore, the narrative form statement, whether signed or unsigned, should always be included in the trial brief ready for immediate use during the examination of the witness.

§ 114. ——(5) A detailed signed statement from each witness in question and answer form.

As has been previously suggested in the chapter on the preparation of the facts, most statements should be taken of witnesses in question and answer form. (Page 34.) When this procedure is followed such statements should be included in the trial brief and utilized by the trial lawyer in the examination of such witness.

§ 115. ——(6) An abstract of the pleadings.

It is very important that the trial lawyer acquire the habit of reading and abstracting all the pleadings filed in the case before trial and then including the abstract of such pleadings in the trial brief. It is surprising how many lawyers go to trial in a case without making a searching analysis of the pleadings. When questions arise as to whether or not proof offered is beyond the scope of the pleadings filed, they are astonished to learn that their own pleadings are hardly broad enough to cover the offered proof or that the opponent has made admissions in his pleading which eliminate the necessity for such offered proof.

It is, therefore, good policy to make an abstract of the pleadings to show

(a) Allegations and charges made.
(b) Elements and measure of damages to be proved.
(c) Admissions in opponent's pleadings.
(d) Affirmative defenses set out by opponent.

When this kind of searching analysis is made of the pleadings and the various elements thereof reduced to writing, it will eliminate many embarrassing moments for the trial lawyer.

§ 116. —— (7) Brief on the law.

The trial brief will, of course, include an exhaustive analysis and search for citations of authorities as referred to in this chapter. It will contain:

(a) Favorable authorities showing right to recover.
(b) Favorable authorities as to method of proof.
(c) Authorities reviewing opponent's contentions.
(d) Copy of Statute relied upon (where involved).

§ 117. —— (8) Instructions.

The trial brief should always contain a full and complete copy of all instructions which the trial lawyer wishes to be used in that particular case. In most instances it is possible for the trial lawyer, after a full and complete preparation of his case to determine just which instructions he believes will be necessary to be used. On his own copy of each instruction which he includes in his trial brief he should have thereon a citation of authority showing the propriety and legality of such instruction. This should be done even in the so-called instances of "stock" instructions.

§ 118. Presenting trial brief to court.

Many successful trial lawyers follow the recommended practice of handing to the court a copy of their trial brief at the commencement of the trial. This serves to familiarize the court with the law applicable to the case and tends to smooth the way for the reception of all material evidence. The brief in many instances may change the court's preconceived ideas as to the law. It helps the judge to easily follow a proposed theory of the case. It also serves notice of the fact that the lawyer following this procedure is prepared for trial. Incidentally it helps the court not to commit reversible error and secures the attendant good will on the part of the judge.

The value of this practice was demonstrated recently in one case involving a certain type of health and accident insurance policy. During the explanation to the court as to the issues involved, the judge made the remark that this was the first case in that field he had ever tried. A release was pleaded as a defense. The theory of the plaintiff, supported by a number of authorities, was lack of consideration which on the face of things might be considered absurd in view of the fact that $175.00 had been paid at the time of the execution of the release. Both opposing counsel and the court seemed unable to grasp or understand the theory. An extra copy of the trial brief, if made available at that time for the use of the court, who could have perused it during the course of the trial, would have made a great deal of difference, especially in view of the judge's frank statement that he had never tried that type of case before. As it was, he failed to grasp the theory and as a result progress in the trial became very slow and arduous for the plaintiff.

§ 119. Arguing the law.

At some time during the course of a trial it becomes necessary to argue propositions of law before the court. This will occur on motions for directed verdict, motions for a new trial, and more frequently on questions involving the admissibility of certain evidence.

It is always a pleasure to listen to a well-prepared lawyer arguing various propositions involved in a case. His thorough understanding of his citations is apparent in the confident manner in which he presents them to the court. Just as in all other phases of the trial, the argument on the law must be planned to present the citations in an interesting and understandable manner. The cases and points should be made in a natural sequence so as to arrive at a logical conclusion. Each case should be presented by stating the name of the case, the volume and page, with a brief résumé of the facts involved and then reading verbatim that portion of the case claimed to support the contentions made.

All cases should be arranged in the order they are expected to be read. This will insure an uninterrupted smooth presentation. Each volume should be tabulated by small tabs to be used as book marks. At the top of the tab should be written the subject the case deals with and below it the volume and page. Should the tab become displaced or fall to the floor it can immediately be picked up and the correct page located.

Some lawyers who do not follow this procedure may cause impatience on the part of the court, by the time wasted in trying to locate the volume and page they wish to cite or read from. This breaks up the continuity and interestingness of the argument until it is almost impossible to follow. More important than anything else is the possibility of prejudicing the court to the point that the judge will not be interested in trying to follow with an open mind the attorney's particular legal theory.

If possible all arguments on the law during the progress of the trial should be made *outside* the presence of the jury. It is, in most instances, poor policy to argue the law on the admissibility of certain evidence in the presence of the jury. If the law is argued in the presence of the jury a number of times during the trial and the judge should happen to decide against the lawyer on all or most of the occasions, it tends to place him in a rather bad light before the jury. They may feel that he does not know his business. This is more especially true in those instances where the trial judge is of the caustic, sarcastic, or explosive type. He may harm either side before the jury by his manner or his derisive disagreements with the proponent's contentions or may pass some disparaging remark which may result in creating an unfavorable response on the part of the jury.

The simplest method of securing a hearing on the law outside of the presence of the jury is to request a hearing by the court "in chambers." Most judges will grant the request unless made so frequently as to become obnoxious.

If, after a full and complete hearing, the court should rule adversely, an exception should be taken and the record preserved by making an offer of proof with a subsequent ruling on the offer and an exception.

Once the court has ruled and the record has been legally preserved, prudence dictates quietly abiding by the ruling and not irritating the court by unduly persisting in arguing one's contentions. Should further proceedings clearly indicate that the trial attorney's position was legally correct, a quiet request to the court for a further consideration of the point will invariably be granted by all fair-minded judges.

In those cases where there are questions of law involved of a complicated nature, it is good policy to explain that fact to the court with a request that all questions of law be argued before the trial commences on the theory that it will facilitate the trial and will eliminate the necessity of stopping every few minutes during the course of the trial to argue questions of law.

When this procedure is followed, it results in a saving of time as far as the court is concerned, but with the far greater benefit to the trial lawyer of a smooth, interesting presentation of his case before the jury, as well as eliminating the possibility of a number of adverse rulings on the part of the court.

A great failing of some lawyers seems to be their inability to read the law to the court in an interesting and understandable manner. In one instance a lawyer attempted to read a certain section of a statute to the court and no one in the court room, even those standing almost beside him, could understand what he was reading. He read the section in a mumbling monotone and in a voice that did not seem to carry even as far as the Judge.

Lawyers should realize the importance of a good voice to the trial lawyer. All voices can be greatly improved by proper training and practice. Many successful trial lawyers have benefited by such training.

§ 120. Preliminary motions.

No preliminary motions should ever be argued without having all citations of authority at hand to be read to the court. Many attorneys go into court on preliminary motions without taking this precaution and as a result are unable to prove to the court that their theory is correct. We must not proceed on the assumption that the judge knows all the law. He does not have the time to investigate the law in each particular case as well nor as thoroughly as the lawyer has and if perchance the opponent should happen to talk "louder and faster" it might confuse the judge or make him somewhat doubtful as to the position taken. If the attorney has his authorities ready and presents them to the court it will eliminate any indecision on his part and will insure a favorable ruling. It frequently becomes very important that a proper and favorable ruling be secured on a preliminary motion so that the plan of action and procedure may be carried out to a successful conclusion.

In one instance two lawyers appeared before the court to argue a preliminary motion. The attorney making the motion came into court prepared to argue, supporting his contentions with authorities. His opponent in opposing the motion made his argument in a loud tone of voice, but failed to produce any authorities. Whereupon the other lawyer replied by saying, "If the Court please, if noise is going to decide this motion, all right, I can holler too, but if it is to be decided on the law, let counsel produce some authority to support his position. I am sure that he cannot do so."

The judge then said, "Yes, counsel, if you have any cases on the point let us have them."

Counsel was unable to produce any and the motion made by his opponent was thereupon allowed.

This was a most effective method of silencing the loud, blustering manner of this lawyer.

§ 121. Preparation of the pleadings.

The pleadings in so far as the trial attorney is concerned merit his most serious consideration. The important question uppermost in his mind is—do the pleadings filed state a good cause of action, if representing the plaintiff, and if representing the defendant do the pleadings set up a good defense.

His main concern is to see that the pleadings filed are broad enough to permit the offer of all the proof and testimony he has in the case.

Sometimes certain testimony is objected to on the grounds that the pleadings do not set up any such defense. Many cases have been lost because the pleadings were too limited in their scope. In some personal injury cases, proof is offered as to failure to sound horn, violations of rules of road, etc., without specifically setting them out in the complaint only to have objections sustained to such offered testimony.

All pleadings should be re-examined just before going to trial to see whether they are broad enough to cover all the evidence and testimony it is wished to present. If not, amendments should be prepared at the earliest possible moment. If left for the trial, the court in his discretion may refuse to permit attorney to file the amendment and thus the benefit of important testimony may be lost.

CHAPTER III

PRELIMINARY MOTIONS

§ 122. In general.

It is always important that the trial attorney be familiar with the procedure possible to be utilized in completing his preparation for trial. In some instances he may resort to any one of the steps discussed under the heading of "Preliminary Motions" to make the difference between success and failure. On the other hand, some lawyers make too frequent use of certain preliminary motions only to find that they have harmed themselves thereby. The judicious use of preliminary motions is a subject worthy of earnest consideration and study for the attorney.

Preliminary motions will be considered as embracing the following:

(1) Motions to strike and demurrers.
(2) Examinations of adverse parties.
(3) Discovery before trial.
(4) Depositions.
(5) Interrogatories.
(6) Admissions.
(7) Bills of particulars
(8) Notices to produce.
(9) Subpoena duces tecum.
(10) Change of venue.
(11) Continuances.
(12) Amendments.
(13) Summary Judgments.

§ 123. — (1) Motions to strike and demurrers.

In some states the "demurrer" has been abolished. It has been replaced in codes by the "motion to strike" which now serves the same purpose and is used in place of demurrers.

The discussion under this heading will, therefore, be considered as though only motions to strike were under consideration. However, all suggestions made are equally applicable to demurrers.

It has been found that attorneys are in the habit of making too many motions to strike pleadings. It seems as though their first impulse upon the examination of an opponent's pleading is to rush into court on a motion to strike. In most instances, this is a grave error. Motions to strike should never be made unless the object to be gained far over-shadows the harm that may be done. An impulsive, ill-considered motion to strike will only result in a harmful education of the opponent. He may have improperly or imperfectly pleaded his cause of action or his defense, but an improvident motion to strike will educate him to a realization of the defects and also teach him, as a result of the argument on the motion, just how to remedy the defects. He proceeds to do so by filing an amended pleading. Far greater harm than just a waste of time may result, however. During the argument on the motion before the Court, there is usually some discussion as to the facts involved in the case, the elements to be proved, the method of proof, with the citation of authorities, and an argument on the law involved. In a short while the maker of the motion to strike begins to realize that not only has he educated his opponent on the intricacies of proper pleading, but he has awakened his opponent to the necessity of really preparing his case for trial. In all probabilities, by this time the trial attorney has so displayed his "hand" that the opponent for the first time really realizes just what he must meet. In addition there is the possibility of the argument suggesting a new theory of offense or defense to opponent that he probably would never have thought of before. In other words the "sleeping lion" has been aroused. Where, in most instances, opponent would have gone along satisfied with little or no preparation, the motion to strike has educated him to all of the possibilities in the case, it has given him a good education in properly pleading his case, which he demonstrates by filing a legally sufficient and amended complaint, and has aroused him to a realization of the necessity of a thorough preparation for the trial of the case. He may then so thoroughly prepare himself for trial that it will result in *his* winning the case. This happens so frequently that it is a pretty good rule to usually decide against the impulse to make a motion to strike.

Motions to strike should only be made in those instances where the trial lawyer knows absolutely that his opponent cannot possibly plead a good cause of action or defense. Even then one should hesitate to make the motion to strike for fear it may suggest to opponent some grounds of defense or basis for claim that he has hitherto not realized.

The modern successful trial lawyer has found from bitter experience the many hidden traps and pitfalls surrounding the making of an apparently innocent and innocuous motion to strike and as a result he very seldom resorts to such procedure.

Before the advent of the changes in many Codes, it was possible to take advantage of the failure to set up a good cause of action in a pleading by a motion in arrest of judgment or for the first time on appeal, but according to the modern trend as evidenced by amendments to the Codes and by provision in the new Civil Practice Acts, no complaint can be raised as to the failure to plead a good cause of action for the first time on appeal. A motion to strike must be made in proper time or the defects will be considered as having been waived.

Even though this be true and though this knowledge is a temptation to the lawyer to make motions to strike, he must hesitate long enough to consider fully the harmful effects that may result from his making the motion. The obvious defect in the pleading may be a true indication of opponent's lack of knowledge of his case and of his subsequent inability to prove up a good cause of action. If he later fails to prove his case, it can be taken advantage of by a motion to direct a verdict when it will be too late for opponent to realize any advantage. It is easily apparent how much more valuable this procedure is in most cases. It eliminates all the harmful effects of an ill-advised motion to strike and is, therefore, recommended in most instances.

§ 124. — (2) Examination of adverse party.

In some states, provision is made in the various Codes for the physical examination before trial of the adverse party in all personal injury cases. Where this is possible it is always advisable for the defendant to take advantage of this additional help. In many States attempts on the part of those interested to secure legislation permitting defendants to examine physically those claiming damages for personal injuries have been unavailing. Though the modern trend is to provide for such examinations, many States still refuse to permit them.

From the view-point of the defendant, the right to examine physically an injured claimant is advantageous. It assists the defendant's attorney to acquire a full knowledge as to the extent of the injury. This will help him to prepare for the medical testimony. He will know the medical and anatomical facts with which he must become familiar. It will assist him also in arriving at a basis for possible settlement. If an examination is made shortly after the injury is sustained and another examination is made before trial, the possible extent of such injury is ascertainable. The attorney is then in a good position to advise his client in reference to the advisability of settling the case and on terms favorable to the defendant. At least most of the guess-work as to the extent of the injury is eliminated.

At this point it may be advisable to discuss the method to be followed in permitting an examination of the injured claimant in those states where the defendant has no right to demand such examination, but claimant's attorney being desirous of trying to effect a settlement of his case, accedes to the defendant's request for a medical examination of his client. In most instances this request should only be granted and the medical examination should only be permitted where defendant's attorney is willing to enter into a stipulation to the effect that the results of such examination will not be utilized for trial purposes; that is, the physician who makes the examination will not testify nor will any x-rays taken be permitted in evidence at the trial. It should further be agreed that no history or oral examination will be taken of the claimant. When this procedure is followed, particularly in those instances where the claimant has actually sustained severe and permanent injuries, the trial attorney will have protected the interests of his client as much as it was possible to do so under the circumstances.

One further and rather important suggestion is for the claimant to have a friendly physician present during this examination to see that no undue advantage is taken of the claimant and also to point out various phases of the injury likely to be overlooked either deliberately or unintentionally by opponent's physician.

Incidentally, it should also be stipulated or agreed that claimant's attorney be permitted to be present while his client is being examined. It will prove educational and will prevent opponent's physician from going beyond the scope of the intended examination. It will also prevent any unintended admission by the claimant.

§ 125. — (3) Discovery before trial.

While the subject of discovery before trial may properly include certain phases of the next two subject headings, namely, "Depositions" and "Admissions," they will be accorded separate attention and discussion. Under the heading of discovery before trial will be discussed the preliminary motions to be made to secure an examination of opponent's books, papers, and records before trial for the purpose of preparation for trial, and the taking of photographs of opponent's premises, or machinery involved in the law suit.

The modern practice act or Code usually provides for this method of discovery before trial. A motion duly made will be sufficient to authorize the Court to order the opponent to permit an inspection of his books and records so that the petitioner may properly prepare for trial.

Some Codes provide for this procedure in the following or somewhat similar provisions:

(1) Any party may, without filing an affidavit by motion seasonably made, either before or after issue joined and irrespective of the right to employ interrogatories in a complaint in equity, or to file a complaint for discovery, or to employ a subpoena duces tecum, apply for an order directing any other party to any cause or matter to file a sworn list of all the documents, including photographs, books, accounts, letters, and other papers, which are, or which have been, in his possession or power, material to the merits of the matter in question in said cause. If such order shall be made, as to any or all of said documents the documents embraced in such order shall be listed, with sufficient descriptions for identification, in two schedules, (1) all those which the party is will-

ing to produce, and the name and address of the party in whose possession or control such document now is; (2) all those which the party is unwilling to produce, with a statement of the reasons for his objection to production of the same and with the name and address of the party in whose possession or control such document now is. *Documents produced by the opposite party may be introduced in evidence by the party demanding them without further proof of genuineness.*

This rule shall not apply to memoranda, reports, or documents prepared by or for either party in preparation for trial, or to any communication between any party or his agent and the attorney for such party.

(2) As to documents listed in schedule 1, the other party may inspect and obtain copies of the same at any time not inconvenient for the party having possession thereof, and if leave so to do is unreasonably refused by the party listing it or by any other party at the instance of or by collusion with the party listing it, a motion may be made for an order that the party listing such document shall be nonsuited or have complaint dismissed, or that any pleading or part thereof filed by him shall be stricken out and judgment rendered accordingly, or that he may be debarred from any particular claim, defense, recoupment, set-off, counterclaim or replication respecting which discovery is sought, or an order of attachment as for contempt of court may be issued.

(3) As to documents listed on schedule 2, the party wishing discovery may apply to the Court by motion for an order that any or all of the documents so listed shall be produced for inspection and to be copied, at a time and place and in a manner to be fixed in the order, and if such order shall be made, and if such production shall be refused by the party listing said documents or by any other party at the instance of or by collusion with the party listing them, a motion may be made for, and the Court may enter an order that the party listing such document shall be nonsuited or his complaint dismissed, or that any pleading or part thereof filed by him shall be stricken out and judgment rendered accordingly, or that he may be debarred from maintaining any particular claim, defense, recoupment, set-off, or counterclaim or replication, respecting which discovery is sought.

(4) No document required by this rule to be listed and not listed shall be admissible in evidence at the instance of the party failing to list it, unless it shall be made to appear to the Court that the failure to list the same was due to the bona fide and reasonable belief of the party that such document was not material to the cause or matter in litigation.

(5) If any document listed in schedule 1 is not produced when reasonable demand is made for the same, such document shall not be admissible in evidence at the instance of the party listing it: (1) where it is in the possession or control of such party or (2) where it is in the possession or control of some other party unless the Court is satisfied that the refusal to produce was not due in any degree to the wilful connivance of the party listing it.

(6) No document listed in schedule 2 shall be admissible in evidence at the instance of the party so listing it, unless by leave of Court.

(7) Supplemental lists of documents may be filed as further documents are discovered by the party who has already filed a list, each supplemental list being supported by an affidavit stating facts showing in detail why the documents listed therein were not listed earlier, and if the Court shall be of opinion that the party has acted in good faith and that there was reasonable ground for the delay, the documents so listed may be introduced in evidence at the instance of the party so listing them on such terms as may be just. And such supplemental lists of documents shall be filed as additional documents come into the party's possession after the date of the order and before trial.

(8) Any party may at any time move for an order directing any other party or person to show cause why he should not produce specified documents, relating to the merits of the matter in question in said cause, for inspection and to be copied or photographed, where no list of documents has been demanded or where such documents have not been listed under section 1 of this rule, or produce for inspection or to be photographed articles or property relative to the merits of the said matter, such motion to be supported by affidavits showing that the other party. On the return or hearing of the order to show cause the Court may make such order as to discovery or such document or article is in the possession or control of

inspection as may be just, and, if the other party claims that the document or article is not in his possession or control he may be ordered to submit to examination in open court or by deposition regarding the locating of such document or article.

(9) The Court, on the application of any party to an action, also may enter an order requiring any other party to state by affidavit whether any one or more specific documents, to be specified in the application, is or are, or has or have at any time been in his possession or power, and if not then in his possession, when he parted with the same, and what has become thereof. Such application shall be made upon an affidavit stating that in the belief of the deponent the party against whom the application is made has, or has at some time had, in his possession or power the document or documents specified in the application, and that they relate to the matter in question in the case or matter, or to some of them.

(10) An order issued under section 1 or sections 8 or 9 of this rule shall operate to stay all other proceedings in the cause, until such order shall have been complied with or vacated; and the party obtaining such order, after the same shall have been complied with or vacated, shall have the like time to file and serve his complaint, answer, or replication, to which he was entitled at the time of making the order.

This particular form of discovery before trial is indicated in all instances where desired information is in the exclusive possession of the opponent. It should also be utilized in those instances where it is felt that the books, records, papers, or files of opponent will prove or show an admission of some fact of which the trial attorney is unable to produce corroboratory proof. For instance, the defendant may now deny that it ever purchased any merchandise of the plaintiff or that it has any knowledge of any such transaction. If the defendant is a large concern accustomed to keeping detailed records, it may be a comparatively simple matter to show from their records that the receiving clerk received the merchandise, that an invoice was sent and is in the files of the defendant, and that the ledger shows an entry evidencing an account payable to the plaintiff.

An examination of books and records is indicated in suits against stock brokers, in suits for accounting in claims for salesman's commissions, suits against banks, in fact in all cases where the details of the transaction are better known to the adverse party.

It is recommended that all trial attorneys become familiar with Ragland on "Discovery Before Trial." It contains many valuable suggestions as well as a worth-while collection of authorities and suggested forms.

The local statutes should always be examined to determine the extent of discovery rights permitted.

FORMS

§ 126. Motion for discovery of documents.

(Caption)

Now comes ——— by ———, his attorney, and moves the court to enter an order directing ———, ——— in the above entitled cause to file a sworn list of all the documents, including books, accounts, letters and other papers, which are, or which have been, in his possession or power, relating to the merits of the matter in question in said cause, pursuant to the statute and rules of court in such case made and provided.

§ 127. —Motion to produce listed document for inspection.

(Caption)

Now comes ———, ——— in the above-entitled cause, and shows to the court here that on ——— this court ordered ———, ——— herein, to file a list of all the documents in his possession relating to the merits of the matter in question in the above entitled cause; that pursuant to such order, ——— on ——— filed a list of said documents; that as one of said documents which ——— was unwilling to produce, said ——— listed in Schedule 2 (describe document). Wherefore, ——— moves that this court enter an order requiring said ——— to produce for inspection and to be copied at a time and place and in a manner to be fixed by the court, the said (describe document), pursuant to the statute and rules of court in such case made and provided.

§ 128. Motion for order requiring affidavit as to possession.

(Caption)

Now comes ———, ——— in the above entitled cause, and moves that the court enter an order requiring ———, ——— therein, to state by affidavit whether (describe document) is or has at any time been in his possession or power, and if not now in his possession, when he parted with same and what has become thereof. And in support of said motion ——— submits the affidavit attached.

(Attach affidavit.)

§ 129. Motion to show cause why document should not be produced.

(Caption)

Now comes ———, ——— in the above entitled cause, and moves that this court enter an order directing ——— to show cause why he should not produce (describe document) for inspection, and to be copied or photographed. And in support of such motion ——— submits attached affidavits showing that such document is in the possession of said ———.

(Attach affidavits.)

§ 130. Motion by defendant to dismiss for refusal to allow inspection of documents.

(Caption)

Now comes D. E. F., defendant in the above entitled cause, and shows to the court here that on ——— this court ordered P. L. F., plaintiff herein, to file a list of all the documents in his possession relating to the merits of the matter in question in the above entitled cause; that pursuant to such order plaintiff, on ———, filed a list of said documents; that as one of said documents which P. L. F. was willing to produce said P. L. F. listed in Schedule 1 (described document); that on ——— thereafter, defendant requested permission to inspect said (describe document) and obtain a copy thereof; that P. L. F. refused to allow defendant to inspect such (describe document) or obtain said copy; that said P. L. F. has unreasonably refused to allow defendant to inspect said (describe document) or obtain a copy thereof. Wherefore, defendant moves that this court enter an order dismissing the complaint of said P. L. F. and that judgment may be entered herein for defendant pursuant to the statute and rules of court in such case made and provided.

§ 131. Motion by defendant to dismiss for refusal to obey order to produce document.

(Caption)

Now comes D. E. F., defendant in the above entitled cause, and shows to the court that on the ——— day of ———, this court entered an order directing P. L. F., plaintiff herein, to produce (describe document) for inspection by D. E. F. at (name place) on (name date and hour) and to permit D. E. F. then and there to copy same by (describe manner); that P. L. F. did not produce said (describe document) at the time and place aforesaid but unreasonably refused so to do. Wherefore defendant moves that this court enter an order dismissing the complaint of said P. L. F., and that judgment may be entered herein for defendant, pursuant to the statute and rules of court in such case made and provided.

§ 132. Motion by plaintiff to strike answer for refusal to allow inspection of documents.

(Caption)

Now comes P. L. F., plaintiff in the above entitled cause, and shows to the court here that on ——— this court ordered D. E. F., defendant herein, to file a list of all the documents in his possession relating to the merits of the matter in question in the above entitled cause; that pursuant to such order defendant on ——— filed a list of said documents; that as one of said documents which D. E. F. was willing to produce, said D. E. F. listed in Schedule 1 (describe document); that on ——— thereafter, defendant requested permission to inspect said (describe document) and obtain a copy thereof; that D. E. F. has unreasonably refused to allow plaintiff to inspect said (describe document) or obtain a copy thereof. Wherefore, plaintiff moves that this court enter an order striking the answer of defendant from the files, and that plaintiff may have judgment in accordance with the prayer of his complaint, pursuant to the statute and rules of court in such case made and provided.

§ 133. Motion by plaintiff to strike answer for refusal of defendant to obey order to produce document.

(Caption)

Now comes P. L. F., plaintiff in the above entitled cause, and shows to the court that on the ——— day of ———, this court entered an order directing D. E. F., defendant herein, to produce (describe document) for inspection by P. L. F. at (name place) on (name date and hour) and to permit P. L. F. then and there to copy same by (describe manner); that D. E. F. did not produce said (describe document) at the time and place aforesaid but unreasonably refused so to do. Wherefore plaintiff moves that this court enter an order striking the answer of said D. E. F. from the files and that plaintiff may have judgment in accordance with the prayer of his complaint, pursuant to the statute and rules of court in such case made and provided.

§ 134. List of documents under discovery order.

(Caption)

Now comes ———, ——— in the above entitled cause, by ———, his attorney, and files herewith as "Exhibit A," hereto annexed a list of documents relating to the merits of the above entitled cause, pursuant to the order of this court entered ———.

EXHIBIT A.

Schedule 1.

——— lists under Schedule 1, as documents which he is willing to produce, the following:

Name of Document	Name and Address of Party Holding Same
___________	___________
___________	___________
___________	___________

Schedule 2.

——— lists herewith as documents which he is unwilling to produce, the following:

Name of Document	Name and Address of Party Holding Same
———	———
———	———
———	———

——— states that his objection to production of said documents is as follows: (state reasons).

State of ——— }
County of ——— } ss.

———, being first duly sworn, on oath deposes and says that he is the ——— in the above entitled cause; that pursuant to the order of this court entered ——— he files herewith a list of documents relating to the merits of said cause; that above "Exhibit A" is a true and accurate list of said documents and the names and addresses of the parties holding same; and that the matters and things therein stated are true.

Subscribed and sworn to, etc.

It is altogether probable that there will be times when the party filing the list is not in position to swear positively as to who is holding some document or documents. While the rule seems to make no specific allowance for this situation, it is hardly conceivable that a list which met it in the only possible way ——— by alleging upon information and belief ——— should be held insufficient, and in such event the form of verification would of course be altered accordingly.

§ 135. Supplemental list of documents under discovery order.

(Caption)

Now comes ———, ——— in the above entitled cause, by ———, his attorney, and files herewith as "Exhibit B" hereto annexed a supplemental list of documents relating to the merits of the above entitled cause, pursuant to the order of this court entered ———.

EXHIBIT B.

(Schedule documents as in "Exhibit A.")

State of ——— }
County of ——— } ss.

———, being first duly sworn, on oath deposes and says that he is the ——— in the above entitled cause; that pursuant to the order of this court entered ———, he files herewith a supplemental list of documents relating to the merits of said cause; that above "Exhibit B" is a true and accurate list of such documents discovered by affiant since he filed his previous list on ———, and that said documents were not listed earlier because (set out facts showing in detail the reason).

Subscribed and sworn to, etc.

§ 136. Motion for discovery.

(Caption)

To ———:

Please take notice, that on the ——— day of ———, 19—, at the hour of ——— o'clock ———M., or as soon thereafter as counsel can be heard, I shall appear before the Honorable ———, judge of the ——— court of ———, in the courthouse at ———, and move the court, pursuant to the statute and rules of court in such case made and provided, to enter an order directing ———, ——— in the above entitled cause, to file a sworn list of all the documents which are, or which have been, in his possession or power, relating to the merits of the matter in question in said cause, a copy of which motion is hereto attached.

Received a copy of the above notice and motion attached this ——— day of ———, A. D. 19—.

§ 137. Motion to produce listed document for inspection.

(Caption)

To ———:

Please take notice, that on the ——— day of ———, 19—, at the hour of ——— o'clock ———M., or as soon thereafter as counsel can be heard, I shall appear before the Honorable ———, judge of the ——— court of ———, in the room usually occupied by him as a court room in the courthouse at ———, Illinois, and move the court to enter an order requiring ——— to produce (describe document) for inspection and to be copied at a time and place to be fixed by the court, pursuant to the statute in such case made and provided.

Received a copy of the above notice with motion attached this ——— day of ———, A. D. 19—.

§ 138. Notice of motion by defendant to dismiss for refusal to allow inspection of documents.

(Caption)

To ———:

Please take notice, that on the ——— day ———, 19—, at the hour of ——— o'clock ——— M., I shall appear before the Honorable ———, judge of the ——— court of ———, in the room usually occupied by him as a court room in the courthouse at ———, Illinois, and move that plaintiff's complaint be dismissed and judgment entered for defendant because of the refusal of plaintiff to allow defendant to inspect (describe document) and make a copy thereof.

Received a copy of above notice with motion attached this ——— day of ———, A. D. 19 —.

§ 139. Notice of motion by plaintiff to strike answer for refusal to allow inspection of documents.

(Caption)

To ———:

Please take notice, that on the ——— day of ———, 19—, at the hour of ——— o'clock ——— M., or as soon thereafter as counsel can be heard, I shall appear before the Honorable ———, judge of the ——— court of ———, in the room usually occupied by him as a court room in the courthouse at ———, and move that the court enter an order striking the answer of defendant from the files for refusal to allow plaintiff the right to inspect (describe document) or obtain a copy thereof and that plaintiff may have judgment, in accordance with the statute and rules of court in such case made and provided.

Received a copy of the above notice with motion attached this ——— day of ———, A. D. 19—.

—————————.

§ 140. Notice of motion by defendant to dismiss complaint for refusal of plaintiff to obey order to produce.

(Caption)

To ———:

Please take notice, that on the ——— day of ———, 19—, at the hour of ——— o'clock ———M., or as soon thereafter as counsel can be heard, I shall appear before the Honorable ———, judge of the ——— court of ———, in the room usually occupied by him as a court room in the courthouse at ———, Illinois, and move that the complaint of plaintiff be dismissed and for judgment for defendant because of plaintiff's refusal to produce (describe document) pursuant to order of this court.

Received a copy of above notice with motion attached this ——— day of ———, A. D. 19—.

§ 141. Notice of motion by plaintiff to strike answer for refusal of defendant to obey order to produce.

(Caption)

To ———:

Please take notice, that on the ——— day of ———, 19—, at the hour of ——— o'clock ———M., or as soon thereafter as counsel can be heard, I shall appear before the Honorable ———, Judge of the ——— court of ———, in the room usually occupied by him as a court room in the courthouse at ———, Illinois, and move that an order be entered striking the answer of defendant from the files and that plaintiff have judgment because of defendant's refusal to produce, on order, a copy of (describe document).

Received a copy of the above notice with motion attached this ——— day of ———, A. D. 19—.

———————.

§ 142. Notice of motion to show cause why document should not be produced.

(Caption)

To ———:

Please take notice, that on the ——— day of ———, 19—, at the hour of ——— o'clock ———M., or as soon thereafter as counsel can be heard, I shall appear before the Honorable

———, judge of the ——— court of ———, in the room usually occupied by him as a court room in the courthouse at ———, and move that the court enter an order directing ——— to show cause why he should not produce (describe document).

Received a copy of above notice with motion attached this ——— day of ———, A. D. 19—. ————————.

§ 143. Notice of motion for order requiring affidavit as to possession of document.

(Caption)

To ———:

Please take notice that on the ——— day of ———, 19—, at ——— o'clock ———M., or as soon thereafter as counsel can be heard, I shall appear before the Honorable ———, Judge of the ——— court of ———, in the room usually occupied by him as a court room in the courthouse at ———, Illinois, and move that the court require ——— to state by affidavit whether (describe document) is or has been at any time in his possession or power, pursuant to the statute in such case made and provided.

Received a copy of the above notice this ——— day of ———, A. D. 19—.

————————.

§ 144. —Legal authorities.

The New York courts seem to be in conflict as to the right to discovery before trial. The following citations of authority are indicative of the situation there:

Section 288 New York Act was intended to prevent injustice resulting from the possible or probable inability of securing the evidence by the usual method and cannot be used simply for the convenience of an apparently friendly witness. Paparone v. Ader, 139 Misc. 281, 248 N. Y. S. 321.

Examinations in tort actions are to be cautiously and judiciously permitted. Schonhous v. Weiner, 138 Misc. 759, 246 N. Y. S. 73.

Defendant may be examined for the purpose of controverting defenses by avoidance but not for the purpose of disclosing defenses. Palmison v. First Nat. Bank of Tuckahoe, N. Y., 234 App. Div. 797, 253 N. Y. S. 896.

Generally, examination should be denied except when party has the affirmative, and the converse is true. Exceptional circumstances relax the rule. Frohman v. Samuel Stores, Inc., 142 Misc. 479, 255 N. Y. S. 606.

The Appellate Division, First Department, holds that there should be no general examination before trial in negligence cases, absent unusual circumstances; the Second Department is more liberal; Court of Appeals holds it discretionary and will not review the rulings. The courts of the Second Department should follow the Appellate Division there. Maher v. Orange & Rockland Elec. Co., 141 Misc. 573, 252 N. Y. S. 459.

There must be proof before the court, either by affidavits or the pleadings, that the testimony sought is material and necessary. Nedlin Realty Co., Inc. v. Bachner, 225 App. Div. 776, 232 N. Y. S. 126.,

General rule is that an examination is allowed only in support of applicant's own cause of action or affirmative defense. Schmitt v. Baptist Temple, Inc., 227 App. Div. 647, 234 N. Y. S. 888 (mem.).

Section provides only for the taking of necessary and material testimony of parties and witnesses and not production of documents. Citizens Trust Co. of Utica v. R. Prescott & Son, Inc., 221 App. Div. 420, 223 N. Y. S. 184.

"As to the Second Department, Oshinsky v. Gumberg, 188 App. Div. 23, 176 N. Y. S. 406, stated the rule to be that an applicant can have an examination only to prove his own case, although exceptions are recognized. The court has exercised its discretion in refusing to allow an examination by a party on an issue in which he did not have the affirmative, in Jannotta v. Bestmor Realty Corporation, 221 App. Div. 870, 224 N. Y. S. 337; Parkin v. Unity Protective Ins. Ass'n, 218 App. Div. 842, 219 N. Y. S. 27; Kimball v. John Budd Co., 215 App. Div. 724, 212 N. Y. S. 404, and O'Boyle v. Home Ins. Co., 226 App. Div. 767, 234 N. Y. S. 259.

"The Third Department, taking a more liberal view, has stated in Combes v. Maas, 209 App. Div. 330, 331, 204 N. Y. S. 440, 441, that the court, in its discretion, could, at the instance of a party litigant, order a general examination of his adversary before trial, and need not limit the examination to an issue on which the moving party has the affirmative. The

Court said: 'The limitations stated in cases under the Code of Civil Procedure upon the right to examine an adverse party were intended to assist the court in exercising its discretion and were not absolute rules which must be followed. And we hold that, under the Civil Practice Act, the examination need not be limited to those issues of which the moving party has the affirmative.'

"And the Fourth Department has taken much the same attitude in Marine Trust Co. of Buffalo v. Nuway Devices, Inc., 204 App. Div. 752, 198 N. Y. S. 715; Caskie v. International Ry. Co., 230 App. Div. 591.

§ 145. (4) Depositions.

This subject must be considered in two aspects, the first, as a means of discovery before trial, and the second, as a method of proof at the trial.

§ 146. — (a) As a means of discovery.

Some states make provisions for the use of depositions of not only the adverse party, but of any witness, as a means and basis of discovery to be used for preparation for trial. Some codes provide as follows:

(1) Any party to a civil action may cause to be taken, on oral or written interrogatories, by deposition before trial, in the manner provided by law for taking depositions in chancery cases, the testimony of any other party or of any other person, which is relevant to the prosecution or defense of the action, and, if hostile, such person may be examined as though under cross-examination.

(2) When the party or person to be examined is a corporation, joint stock company or unincorporated association, the testimony of one or more of its officers, directors, managing agents, or employees, which is relevant, may be so taken.

(3) When a party, without justification, takes or attempts to take a deposition for discovery, the court may assess the expense of taking such deposition, including a reasonable counsel fee for the time and attention devoted thereto, to be paid by the party taking such deposition.

(4) No disclosure as to any matter, whether obtained by complaint for discovery or by motion under rules, shall be conclusive, but may be contradicted by other testimony.

§ 147. — When use indicated.

The use of depositions for discovery purposes is indicated in those instances where it is desired to ascertain or to force the adverse party or some adverse witness to take a definite position in the case. It is, of course, always advisable to resort to depositions in those instances where the trial attorney is unable to otherwise ascertain the evidence which such adverse party or witness expects to give.

Since it is always preferable to know in advance all evidence harmful to the trial attorney's case, so that proper preparation can be made to refute such adverse testimony, it is better to secure a knowledge of such testimony as early as possible, and to have same recorded by a court reporter.

§ 148. — Early use advisable.

The use of depositions for discovery purposes should always be utilized as early in the proceedings as possible. In some cases, it is advisable to take the deposition of the adverse party before he has had an opportunity to adjust his story to the convenience of the occasion.

§ 149. — To ascertain proper parties to sue.

Another use of depositions in some states for discovery purposes is to ascertain the proper parties to be sued in the case, particularly in those instances where the claim is against some association, partnership or group where the names of the parties comprising such organizations are unknown to the plaintiff. A deposition examination of one or two of the known members will make it possible to quickly ascertain the names and addresses of all unknown members.

§ 150. — Commissioner.

In most states, it is possible to take depositions before any person competent to administer oaths. Some attorneys make it a practice to have these depositions taken before some Notary Public in their office, either on the theory that they are in a better position to control the Notary's actions or in an effort to eliminate expense. On the other hand, many attorneys would rather have the deposition taken before some court official, a Master in Chancery, a referee, or the like, because it is more impressive and more orderly.

§ 151. — Compelling attendance of witnesses.

In some instances, witnesses are somewhat reluctant and sometimes refuse to appear in answer to a Notary's subpoena to take depositions. The statutes in most cases provide the method by which such recalcitrant witness may be compelled to attend and to testify. It is usually provided that the Circuit or District Courts in the various jurisdictions upon petition duly made by the notary or commissioner designated to take the deposition will order such witness to appear and testify in answer to the subpoena, or subject himself to punishment for contempt of court.

§ 152. — Statutory provisions.

Statutory requirements for the taking of depositions may provide as follows:

Depositions of resident witnesses in chancery. When the testimony of any witness, residing or being within this state, shall be necessary in any suit in chancery in this state, the party wishing to use the same may cause the deposition of such witness to be taken before any judge, justice of the peace, clerk of a court, master in chancery or notary public, without a commission or filing interrogations for such purpose, on giving to the adverse party or his attorney ten days' notice of the time and place of taking the same, and one day in addition thereto (Sundays inclusive) for every fifty miles travel from the place of holding the court to the place of where such deposition is to be taken. If the party entitled to notice and his attorney reside in the county where the deposition is to be taken, five days' notice shall be sufficient.

§ 153. — (b) As method of proof.

The statutes of the various states usually provide for the method to be followed in taking depositions to be used in proof at trial of the cause of action. Some states provide two methods: one to govern the procedure in taking depositions in the trial of cases at law, and the other to govern the procedure of taking depositions of the trial of cases in equity or chancery.

However, some states have eliminated the distinction between law and equity under the various Codes.

§ 154. — Procedure.

The procedure usually followed in the taking of depositions is by service of a notice of the intention to cause a deposition or a commission to issue to a duly authorized person to take the deposition of a named witness. In most instances, the statute provides the length of notice that must be given to take a deposition of a witness outside of the jurisdiction of the court. In order that the deposition when taken may be properly utilized on the trial of the case, it becomes important that every requirement of the statute be strictly complied with.

§ 155. — Statutory provisions—Chancery cases.

Some Codes provide for depositions of non-residents as follows:

Deposition—When witness is non-resident, etc.—Notice (Chancery). When the testimony of any witness residing within this state more than one hundred miles from the place of holding the court, or not residing in this state, or who is engaged in the military or naval service of this state or of the United States, and is out of this state, shall be necessary in any civil cause pending in any court of law or equity in this state, it shall be lawful for the party wishing to use the same, on giving to the adverse party, or his attorney, ten days' previous notice, together with a copy of the interrogatories intended to be put to such witness, to sue out from the proper clerk's office a dedimus potestatem or commission, under the seal of the court, directed to any competent and disinterested person, as commissioner, or to any judge, master in chancery, notary public or justice of the peace of the county or city in which such witness may reside, or in case it is to take the testimony of a person engaged in such military service, "to any commissioned officer in the military or naval service of this state or the United States" authorizing and requiring him to cause such witness to come before him, at such time and place as he may designate and appoint, and faithfully to take his deposition upon all such interrogatories as may be inclosed with or attached to said commission, both on the part of the plaintiff and defendant, and none others; and to certify the same, when thus taken, together with the said commission and interrogatories, into the court in which such cause shall be pending with the least possible delay.

§ 156. — — Law cases.

Notice to non-resident party, etc. (Law). When the deposition of any witness is desired to be taken under the provisions of this act, and the adverse party is not a resident of the county in which the suit is pending, or is in default, and no attorney has appeared for him in such cause, upon filing an affidavit of such fact and stating the place of residence of such adverse party, if known, or that upon diligent inquiry, his place of residence cannot be ascertained, the notice required by this act may be given by sending a copy thereof by mail, postage paid, addressed to such party at his place of residence, if known, or if not known, by posting a copy of such notice at the door of the court house where the suit is pending, or publishing the same in the nearest newspaper, and when interrogatories are required, filing a copy thereof with the clerk of the court ten days before the time of suing out such commission.

§ 157. — — Oral examination.

When a party shall desire to take the evidence of a non-resident witness, to be used in any cause pending in this state the party desiring the same, or where notice shall have been given that a commission to take the testimony of a non-resident witness will be applied for, the opposite party, upon giving the other three days' notice in writing of his election so to do, may have a commission directed in the same manner as provided in Section 26 of this act, to take such evidence, upon interrogatories to be propounded to the witness orally; upon the taking of which each party may appear before the commission, in person or by attorney and interrogate the witness. The party desiring such testimony shall give to the other the following notice of the time and place of taking the same, to-wit: ten days, and one day in addition thereto (Sundays included) for every one hundred miles' travel from the place of holding the court to the place where such deposition is to be taken.

§ 158. Oral examination—costs.

When a party to a suit shall give the opposite party notice to take a deposition upon oral interrogatories and shall fail to take the same accordingly, unless such failure to be on account of the non-attendance of the witness, not occasioned by the fault of the party giving the notice, or some other unavoidable cause, the party notified, if he shall attend himself or by attorney, agreeably to the notice, shall be entitled to $2 per day for each day he may attend under such notice, and to six cents per mile for every mile that he shall necessarily travel in going to and returning from the place designated to take the deposition, to be allowed by the court where the suit is pending, and for which execution may issue.

§ 159. — Stipulations for issuance of dedimus.

However, in some instances opposing attorney may enter into a stipulation or an agreement waiving the strict requirements of the statute and agreeing that the deposition of the named witness may be taken before the designated commissioner at a certain time and place.

There are several different forms of stipulations usually used in this connection, depending upon whether the attorney is taking the deposition himself or whether he is merely acting in the capacity of an opponent. If the opposing side is taking the deposition, the trial attorney should see that the stipulation permits the making of objections to the questions and answers propounded and made before the commissioner at the time of trial, so as to be able to secure a ruling of the court on the propriety of such questions and answers. The following are some of the forms of stipulation used in taking depositions:

(Caption)

STIPULATION

IT IS HEREBY STIPULATED AND AGREED, by and between the parties hereto, by their respective attorneys, that the depositions of Dr. Philip L. Rock and Dr. Henry B. Leemon and other witnesses in behalf of the plaintiff and the defendant, of the City of Omaha, State of Nebraska, may be taken before Ida Walters, 418 Omaha National Bank Building, Omaha, Nebraska, a notary public, in and for the City of Omaha and

State of Nebraska, on the 17th day of August, 1932, at her office, 418 Omaha National Bank Building, Omaha, Nebraska, upon oral interrogatories, at two o'clock in the afternoon of said day.

It Is Further Agreed and Stipulated that a dedimus potestatum may be immediately issued by the Clerk of the said court to the said notary public to take the said depositions and that all prerequisite forms and notices required by the statutes are hereby waived by the respective parties, and the parties agree that the said depositions so taken shall have the same force and effect as if due notice of the suing out of the dedimus were given as required by statute or otherwise, the parties reserving unto themselves all right of objection that they would have if the depositions were taken upon the dedimus sued out upon the usual notice.

____
Attorney for Plaintiff

____
Attorney for Defendant

Dated at Chicago, Ill., July 29, 1932.

(Caption)

STIPULATION

It Is Hereby Stipulated and Agreed by and between the parties hereto, by their respective attorneys, that the depositions of Dr. Philip L. Rock, Dr. Henry B. Leemon, and of such other witnesses as may be present to testify in behalf of the plaintiff; and that the depositions of Dr. Harry Korn, Dr. William P. Mason, and such other witnesses as may be present to testify in behalf of the defendant, all of the City of Omaha, State of Nebraska, may be taken before Ida Walters, a notary public in and for the City of Omaha and State of Nebraska, at her office, 418 Omaha National Bank Building, Omaha, Nebraska, on August 17, 1932, at the hour of two o'clock in the afternoon, and the taking of said depositions may be by agreement of the parties from time to time adjourned until the same are completed, said depositions to be taken upon oral interrogatories and cross-interrogatories to be propounded to said witnesses and to be taken down in shorthand and transcribed.

IT IS FURTHER STIPULATED AND AGREED that all notices, statutory or otherwise, for the issuing of a dedimus potestatem or commission for the taking of said depositions are hereby waived, and that the Clerk of said Circuit Court of Cook County is hereby authorized and directed to issue a dedimus potestatem or commission directed to the said Ida Walters, 418 Omaha National Bank Building, Omaha, Nebraska, to take said depositions.

IT IS FURTHER STIPULATED AND AGREED that the depositions taken pursuant to this stipulation and such dedimus or commission may be read in evidence on the trial of said cause subject to the right of the parties to object to the materiality or competency of said oral interrogatories and cross-interrogatories, and to any of the same, and to any of the answers thereto, respectively, in like manner and upon the same grounds as if said witnesses were present and orally examined in open court upon the trial of said cause.

Dated at Chicago, Illinois, this 30th day of July, 1932.

____
Attorneys for Plaintiff

____
Attorneys for Defendant

§ 160. Attorney should take deposition personally if possible.

Many attorneys follow the practice of assigning the taking of depositions in their behalf to corresponding attorneys located in the jurisdiction where the witness' testimony is to be taken. While it is always advisable to have some local attorney associated in a case where foreign jurisdiction and questions of law may arise, yet the attorney should make every possible effort to be present and to take the deposition of such witness himself. No matter how competent the local attorney may be, it is impossible for him to be as completely familiar with the facts and the tactics which the lawyer intends to employ. No matter how detailed the statement to the correspondent may be, some unanticipated response by the witness may open up an entirely new field which the original attorney could appreciate in relation to all of the facts of his case, but which the local attorney can hardly be expected to follow and appreciate.

In some instances, the failure to take the deposition personally may require the retaking of additional testimony from the same witness to follow out the additional "leads." If the witness is not then available for the additional deposition, considerable harm may result to the client's cause.

§ 161. Oral interrogatories recommended.

In most jurisdictions provision is made for the taking of depositions by either written interrogatories or oral interrogatories. If the deposition is taken by the trial lawyer personally it is, of course, always advisable to have the deposition taken on oral interrogatories. If the deposition is to be taken by some correspondent in a foreign jurisdiction, it is also desirable that the deposition be taken on oral interrogatories, since the written interrogatories when prepared by the trial lawyer in his office may be so narrow and limited as not to cover all phases of the witness' story. When the additional precaution is taken of having the deposition on oral interrogatories, it will permit considerable leeway for the local attorney to take care of any details suggested on the spur of the moment by the responses of the witness.

§ 162. Care should be exercised in taking depositions.

Some attorneys believe that the taking of depositions should be done in a rather informal manner, and as a result some depositions are taken more in a slipshod, rather than an informal, manner. Depositions should be taken with as much seriousness and care as would be employed by the lawyer in the actual trial of a case. The deposition is one step in the proof he must present. That proof must be the best possible proof available under the circumstances. In some instances the proper care and attention to the details necessary to take a good deposition of the witness' testimony may make the difference between success and failure.

In some states the Codes provide that a hostile witness may be examined as though under cross-examination, for the purpose of taking depositions.

Where this provision appears in the local statute, the trial attorney should claim the benefit thereof on all occasions. It will materially broaden the scope of the examination and permit inquiry into subjects which might properly be subject to objection upon various grounds.

§ 163. Objections.

The attorney during the progress of taking depositions should always be on the alert to make proper objection to the question or answer of the witness wherever indicated. Objections are more important during the taking of depositions by far than objections during the trial of the case. In many instances during the trial, for fear of prejudicing the jury, objections may sometimes be waived or overlooked, but proper objections during the taking of depositions, particularly when such deposition is being taken by the opponent, may eliminate the use of such testimony in deposition form at the time of trial.

§ 164. Motions to suppress.

The law in various jurisdictions throughout the country should be investigated to determine the procedure in the various states provided to take advantage of proper objections made at the time the deposition was taken. In most jurisdictions matters of form must be taken advantage of by a "motion to suppress" the various objectionable features of the deposition a reasonable length of time before trial. Matters of competency of witnesses and of the competency of testimony in reference to the issues of the case may ordinarily be made for the first time at the trial of the case.

§ 165. Reading depositions.

As referred to under direct examination (page 272) the attorney offering the deposition in evidence should always employ an associate to assist him, the attorney to read the question and the associate to read the answer from the witness stand. This will serve to put "live" interest into deposition evidence, where ordinarily it would be lacking. This procedure has been held to be legally correct and permissible in the case of Vagaszki v. Consolidated Coal Co., 225 Fed. 913, 141 C. C. A. 37.

§ 166. (5) Interrogatories.

One of the most frequent methods of discovery resorted to by the trial attorney is the written interrogatory. The use of written interrogatories probably entails the least expense of all methods of discovery and may be the real reason why its use is so frequent and popular.

The proper and legal extent of the scope of written interrogatories in most jurisdictions is either a subject of much controversy or the scope has been limited and prescribed by the various statutes and codes.

In a few states hardly any limitation has been placed on the scope of the questions and information desired. In these states the main limitation seems to be placed on the number of questions that can be asked.

Other states have limited the scope of inquiry permissible under written interrogatories to facts necessary to prove the case of the proponent. Anything pertaining to the case of the adverse party has been prohibited, others prohibit the request for names and addresses of opponent's witnesses.

In view of the diversity of provisions, the local statutes, codes and authorities should always be referred to before presenting written interrogatories.

While the courts and legislatures of the various states should primarily be interested in dispensing justice and quickly arriving at the truth in the case, many statutory provisions merely serve to hinder rather than to aid justice. The restrictions placed upon the right to have full discovery aids the guilty person in most civil cases to evade liability and to delay the "day of reckoning."

The modern trend is toward full and free discovery and most states will soon follow the leadership of the few states which at present allow general discovery.

The following is form of one set of interrogatories used. Some judges, however, will not grant the request for interrogatories seeking the names and addresses of opponent's witnesses. The form of interrogatories should be changed to meet local requirements.

§ 166a. —Form of interrogatories.

(Caption)

Interrogatories to Be Propounded to Edgar Switzer, Defendant Herein, and to Be Answered in Writing Under Oath

(1) State your full name.

(2) State your residence address.

(3) What is your business or occupation?
(4) Give your business or office address.
(5) State what right, title, interest or equity you had on December 29th, 1933, either as owner, lessee or otherwise in the premises known as 517 Oakdale Avenue, Chicago, Illinois, generally called "Oaklane Apartments."
(5a) When did you acquire this building?
(6) Was McCluer & Company, a corporation, on December 29, 1933, in charge of these premises as agents to rent, manage, supervise and otherwise control the rental of the apartments and rooms therein and to employ janitors, elevator operators and other employees in the premises?
(7) When did McCluer & Company, a corporation, become employed or designated as agents of said premises, if at all?
(8) State the name of the manager of these premises in authority as manager on December 29th, 1933.
(9) Also, state his residence address and where he is now employed.
(10) Did you, or McCluer & Company, a corporation, as your agents, on December 29, 1933, have in your employ a mechanic, machinist, engineer or other person or persons whose duty it was to supervise, inspect and repair the elevators in this building?
(11) If yes, give the name or names and the respective duties of these persons.
(12) Also, give the residence address of each and where now employed.
(13) State the number of elevators in use on or about December 29, 1933, in these premises.
(14) State whether either or both of these elevators were used for special purposes, i. e., as freight or passenger, and just why and when they were used especially as freight or passenger elevators.
(15) Was either of these elevators inspected by an employee, agent or representative of yourself or of McCluer & Company on December 29th, 1933, or at any time within thirty (30) days prior thereto?

(16) If your answer is "yes," give the name or names of the person or persons making the inspection and what their official duties were with respect to their employment in or about these premises.

(17) State the dates on which these inspections were made.

(18) State how these inspections were made and what tests were used to discover whether these elevators were functioning and operating mechanically right.

(19) Was a report made or were there reports made to you or to McCluer & Company, your agents, or to anyone else in your employ or associated with you, stating the results of these inspections or tests?

(20) To whom were these reports made, if at all?

(21) If these reports were made in writing, attach a copy or copies to these Interrogatories.

(22) What, if anything, was done by your agents or employees in the way of adjusting or repairing these elevators, or either of them, on December 29, 1933, or within thirty (30) days prior thereto?

(23) Did you, or did McCluer & Company, defendant herein, or did any agent, servant or employee of yourself, or of your agents, receive a report or complaint from Mrs. Dorothy B. Frank, or her husband, or any tenant in the building, within thirty (30) days prior to December 29, 1933, to the effect that these elevators, or either of them, were in bad condition and needed repair?

(24) If such report was made to you, state the date this report was received, by whom it was received and by whom the report or complaint was made.

(25) What, if anything, was done towards adjusting or repairing these elevators, or either of them, after such complaint or report of their condition, or of either of them, was made?

(26) When were these elevators installed in this building?

(27) By whom were they installed?

(28) From whom were they purchased?

(29) Did you, or any agent, servant or employee of yours, know that on December 29th, 1933, one of these elevators, generally called the "freight elevator," was

out of repair or out of adjustment to the extent that it failed to stop on the level or even with the floors of the building?

(30) If you did know, how did you acquire this information?

(31) What was done about correcting this trouble or repairing this elevator, if at all?

(32) Did you, or did any servant, agent or employee, at any time prior to December 29, 1933, discover why or how this so-called "freight elevator" failed to stop on the level with the floors, particularly the first floor?

(33) Did you, or did any agent, servant or employee, discover on or after December 29, 1933, just why this "freight elevator" failed to come to a stop on the level with the floor of the premises and in particular the first floor?

(34) If the answer to either of the two foregoing questions is in affirmative, state just what the trouble was and what was done, if anything, toward correcting it.

(35) State by whom any alterations, repairs or inspections were made.

(36) Did any other tenant or person using this "freight elevator" notify you, or your agents, servants or employees, that that person using same had difficulty in operating this elevator?

(37) If such notice was received, state when and whether anything was done about making an adjustment of this elevator.

(38) Do you know who ordered a sign placed or posted in or near the elevators, directing tenants to use what was commonly called the "freight elevator," when the persons using same carried in and out of the building such property as parcels, bundles, etc.?

(39) If you do know, state the name of the person who ordered this card or sign placed, and give the date when this card or sign was displayed in these premises.

(40) Was there employed, on or about December 29, 1933, a person authorized to operate these elevators for

the benefit of tenants and others lawfully in the premises?

(41) If so, give his name and address.

(42) Was any operator employed at any time on or about December 29, 1933, to operate, manage or control the "freight elevator"?

(43) If so, what were his duties and what were his hours and what hours was he directed to be in actual service in this "freight elevator"?

§ 167. (6) Admissions.

The modern trend in most states is to adopt that procedure which will facilitate trials and at the same time assist the Court in speedily determining where the truth lies in a given cause of action. Code provisions which permit the parties to secure admissions from each other before trial have been found to be a worthwhile forward step in the administration of justice. These provisions have served the purpose in many instances of brushing aside the maze of legal technicalities often encountered in trials and as a result the real truth becomes exposed to the light of day with a considerable saving of the time of judges, juries, and court attachés.

Some states have adopted provisions for securing admissions in the following language:

(1) Either party may exhibit to the other or to his attorney at any time before the trial, any paper material to the action, and request an admission in writing of its genuineness. If the adverse party or his attorney fail to give the admission within 4 days after the request, and the delivery to him of a copy thereof, if such copy be required, and if the party exhibiting the paper be afterward required to prove its genuineness, and the same be finally proved or admitted on the trial, the expense of proving the same, including a reasonable counsel fee for the time and attention devoted thereto, to be ascertained and summarily taxed at the trial, shall be paid by the party refusing the admission, unless it shall appear to the satisfaction of the Court, that there were good reasons for the refusal, and an attachment or execution may be granted to enforce the payment of such expense.

(2) Any party, by notice in writing, given not later than 10 days before trial, may call on any other party to admit, for

the purposes of the cause, matter or issue only, any specific fact or facts mentioned in such notice, which can be fairly admitted without qualification or explanation as stated therein. In case of refusal or neglect to admit the same within 4 days after service of such notice, or within such further time as may be allowed by the Court or a Judge, the expenses incurred in proving such fact or facts, including a reasonable counsel fee for the time and attention devoted thereto, must be ascertained at the trial and paid by the party so neglecting or refusing, whatever the result of the cause, matter or issue may be, unless at the trial or hearing, the Court or a Judge certify that the refusal to admit was reasonable, or unless the Court or a Judge, at any time, shall order or direct otherwise. Any admission made in pursuance of such notice is to be deemed to be made only for the purposes of the particular cause, matter or issue, and not as an admission to be used against the party on any other occasion or in favor of any person other than the party giving the notice. The Court or a Judge, at any time, may allow any party to amend or withdraw any admission so made on such terms as may be just.

(3) When any public records are to be used as evidence, the party intending to so use them may prepare a copy of them in so far as they are to be used, and may seasonably present such copy to the adverse party by notice in writing, and such copy shall thereupon be admissible in evidence as admitted facts in the case if otherwise admissible, except in so far as its inaccuracy shall be pointed out under oath by the adverse party in an affidavit filed and served within 10 days after service of such notice and not less than 4 days before the case shall be called for trial.

§ 168. — Value of procedure.

From a reading of the foregoing paragraphs it becomes apparent that an admission of fact, an admission as to genuineness of records, and the like can lessen the trial attorney's burdens in many instances. It will eliminate the necessity of producing a number of witnesses. In some instances admissions can be readily obtained without which the trial lawyer might be unable to prove his case. Where there is an admission as to the genuineness of a document or an admission as to the contents of public records, it will save considerable expense.

These requirements of the Code as to admissions do not subject the opponent to any particular hardship, for it is only the fact that can be fairly admitted without qualification or explanation that comes within the Code. On the other hand, the penalties imposed may well force the adverse party to hesitate before he refuses to admit those facts which he is rightfully called upon to admit by his opponent.

The procedure to secure admissions may be based on the following forms:

§ 169. Admission in writing of genuineness of paper or writing.

(Caption)

To ———:

I hereby exhibit to you (describe paper) and request that within four days after this request you give your admission in writing of its genuineness, in accordance with the statute and rules of court in such case made and provided. A copy of said (describe paper) is hereto attached and delivered to you.

———————.

The above mentioned (describe paper) exhibited to me and a copy thereof received this ——— day of ———, A. D. 19—.

———————.

§ 170. Notice for admission of facts.

(Caption)

To ———:

Please take notice, in accordance with the statute and rules of court in such case made and provided that you are called upon to admit, within four days after service of this notice, for the purposes of the above entitled cause only, the following facts: (set out facts which can be fairly admitted without qualification or explanation as stated therein).

———————.

Received a copy of the above notice this ——— day of ———, A. D. 19—.

———————.

§ 171. —Limitations upon right.

In discussing provisions as to admissions, it is pointed out in Ragland's Discovery Before Trial (p. 200) that one of the most troublesome points in the actual use of the procedure concerns the type of fact which is the proper subject of a request to admit. "Is it intended," asks the author, "that a party may call upon his adversary to admit detailed items of evidence, about which there is room for argument and doubt, or is it intended that notices to admit shall include only items which are either true or false?" The conclusion reached is that different jurisdictions exhibit a variety of practice in this regard. This is a necessary conclusion, as is apparent from a glance at the manner in which various jurisdictions having similar provisions have interpreted them.

The Illinois provision closely follows section 323 of the New York Civil Practice Act. In a New York case, the court called attention to the fact that a notice served covered 115 folios, and contained 226 separately numbered paragraphs. "To allow all these demands," said the court, "would be calling upon the plaintiff to prove his adversary's case, to disprove his own, and at the same time, to pay all the expense. Some of the demands, if allowed, would call upon plaintiff to go to trouble and expense to acquire the knowledge to admit facts that are peculiarly within the knowledge of the defendant itself; some call for what, in so far as the papers before me show, is purely opinion evidence, or evidence that would be inadmissible at the trial. Others of the demands call for what, for want of a better term, we shall call half a fact, which standing alone, might have to the court or jury an entirely different meaning than if the whole face were presented." Koppel Industrial Car & Equipment Co. v. Portalis & Co., 118 Misc. 670, 195 N. Y. S. 24. The court further said, in this case: "This section may, and probably will, be abused in many instances, as is the case with rule 113. This rule 113, as I have had occasion to remark in a late decision, seems to have led to a practice of embarking on so-called 'fishing excursions'—attempting even to go into the merits of counterclaims, which are outside the provisions of that rule. So with section 323, which, unless carefully applied, will have the same tendency and will open a way for some to place upon an opponent the burden and expense necessary to prove their own case.

"Section 323, to my mind, provides only for an admission of facts to which one's adversary has no denial in any shape or form, and which are known to him, or the truth or falsity of which are easily ascertainable by him. The purpose of the section, as well as the general scope of the new Practice Act and rules, is to simplify the issues, shorten the trial, and save time and expense in matters that can be proven, but whose proof will necessarily impose labor and expense on the party seeking to prove them which in justice should not be imposed."

It is stated by Ragland (Ragland's Discovery Before Trial, p. 201) that some Wisconsin lawyers are using the device in exactly the same fashion which the New York court has thus condemned, and that the chief use of admission procedure in such form is a tactical weapon rather than as a means of eliminating undisputed items of proof. Quaere, as to the sound warrant for such a usage. The much maligned general issue had its use as a tactical weapon, par excellence.

A helpful suggestion comes from England. Order 32, rule 4, England, is as follows: "Any party may, by notice in writing, at any time not later than nine days before the day for which notice of trial has been given, call on any other party to admit, for the purposes of the cause, matter, or issue only, any specific fact or facts mentioned in such notice. And in case of refusal or neglect to admit the same within six days after service of such notice, or within such further time as may be allowed by the court or a judge, the costs of proving such fact or facts shall be paid by the party so neglecting or refusing, whatever the result of the cause, matter or issue may be, unless at the trial or hearing the court or a judge certify that the refusal to admit was reasonable, or unless the court or a judge shall at any time otherwise order or direct. Provided, that any admission made in pursuance of such notice is to be deemed to be made only for the purposes of the particular cause, matter or issue, and not as an admission to be used against the party on any other occasion or in favour of any person other than the party giving the notice: provided also, that the court or a judge may at any time allow any party to amend or withdraw any admission so made on such terms as may be just."

With reference to this provision it was said in Clarke v. Clarke, (1899) 34 W. N. (Eng.) 130: "As regards admission of fact, it is often urged, as it was here, that a litigant will hesitate to state on oath what he will without hesitation state in pleadings, and that there is difficulty in otherwise obtaining admission of facts, even though not really in dispute; and it is further urged that an admission by an affidavit in answer to interrogatories is useful in limiting the issues to be tried, and therefore in reducing the time occupied by the trial and the costs. I recognize the importance of this in the abstract; but practically I find that the interrogated party seldom makes such clean admissions as secure the advantages aimed at, and, failing that, little if anything is gained. As regards facts not really in dispute, I believe that the power of requiring admissions is not sufficiently used. If parties insist, as they generally do, on asking their opponents to admit facts, dates and events about which there is room for doubt or argument, of course the endeavor to obtain admissions breaks down; but if the demand is limited to facts not really in dispute, that is, which can be admitted cleanly, or subject to some simple qualifications, I find that it is generally acceded to, and the power which the court has of throwing the costs on any one who has increased them by declining reasonable admissions is not forgotten."

It has been held in both England and New York that a party served with what he deems to be an improper notice to admit cannot move to strike the notice. Crawford v. Chorley, 18 W. N. (Eng.) 198; Banca Nazionale di Credito v. Equitable Trust Co., 221 App. Div. 555, 224 N. Y. S. 617. As pointed out in the English case, the rule itself provides a remedy, which is that the notice can be left unanswered and if the refusal is reasonable nothing will be suffered. In Corr v. Hoffman, 128 Misc. 713, 220 N. Y. S. 65, the court said: "The plaintiff, prior to this motion called upon defendant, pursuant to section 323 of the Civil Practice Act, to admit, for the purposes of this action, 14 specific facts. Defendant has admitted these facts, with certain qualifications as to four of them. Plaintiff now moves to strike out from these admissions the qualifications recited, on the ground that they are irresponsive to the call. An admission of fact pursuant to such call is optional with the adverse party. If the refusal to admit is unreasonable, the statute provides an ample remedy in the shape of requiring the defaulting party to pay the expenses necessary in proving such facts, regardless of the outcome of the trial. A qualified admission of the fact may, under particular circumstances, be treated as a neglect or refusal to comply, in which event the plaintiff is furnished specific redress, as provided by the given section of the Civil Practice Act. In Colonial Knitting Mills, Inc. v. Hosiery Mfr's Corp., 120 Misc. 558, 199 N. Y. S. 854, Mr. Justice Mullan held that, upon an unsatisfactory compliance of the adverse party with a call to admit facts the court could not compel a fuller compliance.''

Under Civil Practice Act, Sec. 323, as amended by Laws 1926, ch. 679, authorizing party by notice to require the other party to admit for purposes of the cause any specific facts, if facts demanded are peculiarly within defendant's knowledge, demand should be complied with and answers given, that trial of issues may be shortened, and if defendant is not in position to answer, demand may be ignored, and defendant's rights protected by trial court holding that refusal to answer was reasonable. Banca Nazionale di Credito v. Equitable Trust Co. of N. Y., 221 App. Div. 555, 224 N. Y. S. 617.

In Colonial Knitting Mills v. Hosiery Mfr's Corp., 120 Misc. 558, 199 N. Y. S. 854, the court said: ''I am of the opinion that, speaking generally, no motion can be made at Special Term for motions under Section 323, except (1) for an extension of the time of the party receiving such notice to comply therewith; or (2) for permission to amend or withdraw an admission already made; or (3) for an order, in extreme and unusual cases, that the general rule of section 323 should not, because of peculiar circumstances, be applied. Except for slight variations, the section in question is an enactment of rule 4 of Order XXXII of the Rules of Practice of the Supreme Court of England. See White, K. & S. Am. Prac. 1922, p. 531. It seems to be the practice in England to require the party receiving the 'notice to admit,' as it is called there, to decide for himself whether he should make the admissions demanded or take the risk of being compelled, after the proofs are all in at the trial, to bear such expense as his adversary might be put to in procuring the evidence necessitated by the refusal to admit. Crawford v. Chorley, Wkly. Notes (1883) at page 198, cited by White, K. & S., supra, 532, and in 23 Halsbury Laws of England, 146. If that be the practice in England, where the admirable and businesslike system obtains of governing the preliminaries to a trial through trained and experienced masters who are really subordinate judges, how much more should it be the general rule here, where judges who sit in motion parts are already overburdened.

"As soon as the bar shall have become familiar with this important innovation and its tremendous possibilities, it is to be expected that notices to admit will be served in great numbers. Not only will the judges assigned to motion parts be unable to cope with the flood of disputes about notices to admit, but, even if they had the time to pass upon the numberless questions that would constantly be presented to them, I do not see how they could pass upon most of such questions with any degree of fairness or intelligence, isolated as such questions would necessarily be from the whole body of fact to be adduced thereafter upon the trial. Apparently, however, although, under both our statute and its English progenitor, the decision as to whether a refusal to admit was or was not reasonable is generally to be made after the proofs are in at the trial, a court or judge may nevertheless 'at any time' make an order certifying that a demanded admission need not be made. This presumably, is to take care of unusual situations, where it would obviously be unjust to place a party upon whom a notice to admit was served at the hazard of guessing correctly as to what the result would be to him if he did not make a demanded admission. Such a case would, I think, be very rare, as judges were once practicing lawyers, familiar with the difficulties that attorneys must labor under in making a determination as to what they should admit and what they should refuse to admit; and it is to be expected that the ultimate decision as to whether or not an admission should have been made will be governed by a desire upon the part of the judge who passed upon the matter to resolve every fairly doubtful question in favor of a refusal to admit that is ethically made.

"I see no occasion to fear that section 323 can be availed of unscrupulously, or in a spirit of terrorism, and it seems to me that the sound discretion of the justice who presides at the trial may be relied upon to settle with satisfaction any claims that the nonadmitting party acted improperly in causing his adversary to procure proofs to take the place of admissions that were refused. There is nothing in the present case that calls for action at the Special Term for Motions in respect of admissions under Section 323, except that I think that in view of the number and nature of the admissions demanded in the notice to admit the time of the defendant to admit or refuse to admit should be extended. Accordingly I direct that the defendant's time in that regard be, and it hereby is, extended to May 10, 1923. In other respects the motion is denied. No costs. Ordered accordingly."

Defendant, probably having no knowledge respecting certain facts it was called on by plaintiff's notice to admit before trial, was subjected to only half of expense of taking necessary depositions. (Civil Practice Act, Sections 322, 323.) Hart v. Automobile Ins. Co. of Hartford, Conn., 246 N. Y. S. 586.

As examples of the uses which have actually been made of such procedure elsewhere, Ragland mentioned (1) in a case involving a shipment by express, to prove that certain routine inspections were made at each stop between Milwaukee, Wisconsin, and Rochester, New York; (2) to prove a municipal ordinance; (3) to prove that a certain highway on which an accident had occurred was a public highway; (4) to prove the ownership of a certain automobile; (5) to prove an employer-employee relationship. Ragland, Discovery Before Trial, p. 205. See that work for further discussion. England and some twenty of the states have statutes or rules allowing a party to call upon his adversary for an admission of the execution or the genuineness of writings. This differs from the notice to admit facts only to the extent that documents, and not facts generally, are the subjects of the admission. Ragland, Discovery Before Trial, page 207.

§ 172. Public records.

(Caption)

To ———:

Please take notice that at the trial of the above entitled cause I intend to use as evidence a copy of (state nature of record) which same is attached to this notice and presented herewith, in accordance with the statute in such case made and provided.

——————.

Received a copy of the above notice and (state nature of record) this ——— day of ———, A. D. 19—.

——————.

§ 173. Admission of facts.

(Caption)

Plaintiff (defendant) in this cause only hereby admits the several facts hereinunder specified, saving all just exceptions as to their admissibility as evidence in this cause, and provided that this admission is made for the purposes of this action only, and is not an admission to be used against plaintiff (defendant) on any other occasion, or by any one other than defendant (plaintiff).

(Set out facts admitted.)

§ 174. Admission of genuineness of document.

(Caption)

Plaintiff (defendant) in this cause only hereby admits the genuineness of the document hereinunder described, saving all just exceptions to its admissibility as evidence in this cause, and provided that this admission is made for the purposes of this action only, and is not an admission to be used against plaintiff (defendant) on any other occasion, or by any one other than defendant (plaintiff).

(Describe document.)

§ 175. (7) Bills of particulars.

Almost all states have made provisions for Bills of Particulars. In most instances where the plaintiff has alleged his cause of action in a general and indefinite way, the defendant's attorney should make a motion for a bill of particulars. The advisability of making such a motion, however, should always be considered in the light of what has been discussed under the heading of "motions to strike." The motion and the argument before the court on such motion should never be so made as to awaken opponent to new possibilities in his case.

§ 176. — When indicated.

A motion for a bill of particulars is always indicated where the charges and allegations in the complaint are so broad that it is very difficult for the attorney for the defendant to know just what he will have to meet. A motion for a bill of particulars should always be made where the defendant's attorney desires to limit and narrow the issues and the plaintiff's evidence, as much as possible.

§ 177. — Value.

When it is considered that the plaintiff is limited in his evidence to the detailed facts alleged in his bill of particulars it is easily apparent why a bill of particulars should be frequently requested by the lawyer for the defendant. This limitation on the scope of the plaintiff's testimony is always desirable from the viewpoint of the defendant. The plaintiff's attorney should always file as broad and complete a bill of particulars as possible, so that he will be able to prove his entire case. If he attempts to present evidence beyond the scope of his bill of particulars, an objection by opposing counsel will be sustained. The failure to allege some important fact may prevent plaintiff's attorney from proving his case.

§ 178. — Code provisions.

In some states the Codes provide for bills of particulars and answers to be made under oath. The local Codes and Statutes should always be consulted as to the requirements. Some provisions are as follows:

(1) Where allegations are so wanting in details, that the opposite party should be entitled to a bill of particulars, the pleader shall file and serve a copy of such bill on being served with a notice demanding the same, which notice shall point out specifically the defects complained of or the details desired, and if such bill be demanded before the expiration of the time for filing a pleading, the opposite party shall have the same time to plead after receiving the bill of particulars to which he was entitled at the time of serving such notice.

(2) If the party shall unreasonably neglect to furnish a bill of particulars, or if the bill of particulars delivered be insufficient, the court may in its discretion strike the pleading, allow further time to furnish such bill of particulars or require a more particular bill to be delivered.

(3) Whenever a bill of particulars, in an action based on a contract, contains the statement of items of indebtedness and is verified by oath, the items thereof shall be deemed admitted except in so far as the opposite party shall file an affidavit specifically denying the same, and as to each item denied, stating the facts upon which such denial is based, unless such affidavit is excused by the court.

(4) When the party on whom a demand for a bill of particulars has been made believes that the party demanding the same is not entitled to the particulars asked for, he may move the court that the demand be denied or modified.

§ 179. Affidavit in opposition to demand for bill of particulars.

State of ——, }
County of —— } ss.

(Set out facts showing inability to furnish details demanded, or other good reason why demand should be denied or modified.)

Subscribed and sworn to, etc.

§ 180. Notice to furnish.

(Caption)

To ——, Attorney for Plaintiff:

I hereby demand that a bill of particulars of the plaintiff's claim in this action be served on me, within —— days, showing (*) (here state what items or particulars are demanded).

§ 181. Goods sold.

(Proceed as in Form 180 to asterisk, then as follows:) a statement of the dates, prices and quantities of the articles alleged to have been sold to defendant, and the amounts acknowledged to have been paid and credited therefor.

§ 182. Labor and materials.

(Proceed as in Form 180 to asterisk, then as follows:) a statement of the items of work done and materials furnished, with the times when same were done and furnished, and the reasonable value of each item thereof.

§ 183. Notice of motion to make pleading fuller and more particular.

(Caption)

To ———, Attorney for Plaintiff (or Defendant):

Please take notice that upon the complaint (or, answer) heretofore served (and filed) in this action the defendant(s) (or, plaintiff(s)) by his (or, their) counsel, will move the court at the courthouse in the city of ———, on the ——— day of ———, 19—, at the opening of court on that day or as soon thereafter as counsel can be heard, for an order requiring the said complaint (or, answer) in this action to be made fuller and more particular, by amendments, in the following respects, to wit:

1. In stating at what time the agreement therein mentioned was made.
2. In stating the nature and purport of the deed therein alleged to have been tendered.
3. In stating the dates and amounts of the several orders (or, certificates) mentioned therein.
4. In stating the facts claimed and pretended to constitute the usury alleged in said complaint so that the precise nature of the charge (or, defense) may be made apparent.
5. In setting forth the terms of the written contract and the plans and specifications of the same.
6. In separately stating the two causes of action therein mingled in one count or statement, to enable the defendant to plead separately thereto.
7. In stating the terms and conditions of the lease mentioned in said complaint (or, of the defeasance mentioned in said complaint).
8. In stating the facts on which the plaintiff relies to hold and charge the defendant as trustee of the property mentioned in the complaint.
9. In stating the nature and extent of the damages claimed to have been sustained by the plaintiff, by reason of the

breaches (or wrongs) mentioned in the complaint (or, whatever the case may be), (and for the costs of this motion).

Dated ———, 19—.

Received a copy of the above notice this ——— day of ———, A. D. 19—.

If any pleading is insufficient in substance or form the court may order a fuller or more particular statement; and if the pleadings do not sufficiently define the issues the court may order other pleadings, prepared.

§ 184. Notice of motion to strike pleading because no bill filed.

(Caption)

To ———:

Please take notice, that on the ——— day of ———, 19— at the courthouse in the city of ———, Illinois, at the opening of court, or as soon thereafter as counsel can be heard, we shall move the court to strike the (complaint), (answer), (counter-claim) heretofore filed in the above entitled cause, and for which a bill of particulars has heretofore been duly demanded, on the ground (of unreasonable neglect to furnish such bill of particulars), (that the bill of particulars delivered is insufficient).

———————————

Dated ———.

Received a copy of the above notice this ——— day of ———, A. D., 19—.

If the party shall unreasonably neglect to furnish a bill of particulars, or if the bill of particulars delivered be insufficient, the court may in its discretion strike the pleading, allow further time to furnish such bill of particulars or require a more particular bill to be delivered.

§ 185. Notice served with bill of particulars furnished on demand.

(Caption)

To ———, Attorney for (Defendant):

Please take notice that hereto annexed is a copy of the bill of particulars demanded by you, and that I have this date filed the original thereof.

(Date)

Received a copy of the above notice, with bill of particulars thereto annexed, the ——— day of ———, A. D., 19—.

§ 186. Motion that demand for bill of particulars be denied.

(Caption)

Now comes (defendant) in the above entitled cause, and moves the court that the demand of plaintiff herein for a bill of particulars be denied. In support of which said motion the affidavit of defendant is hereto annexed. (Attach affidavit.)

When the party on whom a demand for a bill of particulars has been made believes that the party demanding the same is not entitled to the particulars asked for, he may move the court that the demand be denied or modified.

§ 187. Form of bill of particulars.

(Caption)

On demand of (defendant) herein, plaintiff, P. L. F., by ———, his attorney, comes and files the following bill of particulars: (state items and dates with certainty, and if any cannot for good reason, be given, so state, together with the reason).

§ 188. Fraudulent sale of stock.

(Caption)

Now comes P. L. F., plaintiff by ———, her attorney, and files this her bill of particulars:

1. The names of the persons who it is claimed in plaintiff's complaint entered into the alleged conspiracy with defendant are as follows: (naming them), and other persons unknown by plaintiff or whose names cannot be recalled by her at this time.

2. The names of the persons who it is claimed by plaintiff dealt with her in connection with the purchase by plaintiff of the shares of stock in said X. Y. are as follows: The persons named above in preceding paragraph (1) and each of them, and other persons unknown by plaintiff or whose names cannot be recalled by her at this time.

3. The names of the persons who made the alleged false representations alleged in the complaint to have been made to the plaintiff are as follows: The persons named above in preceding paragraph 1 and each of them, and other persons unknown by plaintiff or whose names cannot be recalled by

her at this time. The dates of the alleged false representations made to plaintiff are as follows, to wit: (setting them out), and on various other dates between the ——— day of ———, 19—, and the ——— day of ———, 19—, the exact dates which cannot be recalled by plaintiff at this time.

4. The names of the officers, agents and servants who it is alleged in the complaint made the false representations are as follows: The persons named above in preceding paragraph 1 and each of them, and other persons unknown by plaintiff or whose names cannot be recalled by her at this time. The dates of said alleged representations are: The dates mentioned in paragraph 3 above, and at various times between the ——— day of ———, 19—, and ———, 19—, the exact dates which cannot be recalled by plaintiff at this time.

§ 189. (8) Notice to produce.

In every instance where it is desired to introduce secondary evidence of any document, instrument, or record, a notice to produce the original of such document, instrument or record should be served on opposing counsel a reasonable length of time prior to the trial or hearing of the cause. Upon the failure of opponent to produce the original document demanded, secondary evidence of the contents of such document is admissible.[1] In most instances a failure to serve such notice to produce will prevent the introduction of secondary evidence. However, in some jurisdictions it has been held that where the original document is in the possession of the opponent or his attorney and that either the adverse party or his attorney has the original document in court, no notice to produce is necessary.[2] Under such circumstances the

[1] Young v. Peo., 221 Ill. 51; Brownlee v. Reiner, 147 Cal. 641, 82 Pac. 324; British, etc., Co. v. Wilson, 77 Conn. 559, 60 Atl. 293; Singmaster v. Robinson, 181 Iowa 522, 164 N. W. 776; Muir v. Kalamazoo, etc., Co., 155 Mich. 624, 119 N. W. 1079; Peo. v. Gibson, 218 N. Y. 70, 112 N. E. 730; Hunter v. Lanius, 82 Tex. 677, 18 S. W. 201.

[2] Maxcy-Barton v. Glen Corp., 355 Ill. 228; Whelan v. Gorton, 15 Misc. 625, 37 N. Y. S. 344; Chadwick v. U. S., 3 Fed. 750; Overlock v. Hall, 81 Me. 348, 17 Atl. 169.

When in possession of opponent or attorney. Nicholson v. Tarpey, 70 Cal. 608, 12 Pac. 778; Truesdale v. Hoyle, 39 Ill. A. 532; Barker v. Barker, 14 Wis. 131; Gould v. Norfolk Lead Co., 9 Cush. 338 (Mass.); Howell v. Huyck, 2 Abb. Dec. 423.

Court may require the adverse party or his counsel to produce the document without any further notice. If counsel refuses to produce the said document the Court may then permit the introduction of secondary evidence.[3] This is also true in those instances where the adverse party denies all knowledge or receipt or possession of the original document or in all instances where the service of a notice to produce would have been unavailable or useless.[4] A notice to produce is not necessary where the original documents are in possession of the adverse party who must know that they are material to the opposing side's case and that he will necessarily have to rely upon such documents to prove his case.[5]

Even though the trial attorney may have the right to introduce secondary evidence without serving a notice to produce in some instances, it is suggested that he form the habit of always serving such notice in all cases where he expects to introduce secondary evidence. This is good policy because of the fear of a contrary ruling by some judges who seem to feel that the law requires the service of a notice to produce in every instance. Therefore, it is always better to take the precaution of serving notice.

In order to make a notice to produce effective it must definitely describe the document desired to be produced with such particular detail that the adverse party will know exactly what document is wanted. A general indefinite description of the document will invalidate the right to use such notice to produce as a basis for the introduction of secondary evidence. Care should, therefore, always be exercised in the preparation of the notice to produce.

If there are two or more documents of a similar nature dated the same day, it may even be advisable to set out in substance the contents of the instrument to be produced.

3 *Proof of secondary evidence.* By testimony of witnesses. Beecham v. Burns, 34 Cal. A. 754, 168 Pac. 1058; Fetherly v. Waggoner, 11 Wend. 599 (N. Y.); Ortiz v. De Benavides, 61 Tex. 60.

By copy: Bay, etc., Co. v. Susman, 91 Conn. 482, 100 Atl. 19; Braverman v. Bordacov, 202 Ill. A. 196; Pate v. Gallup, 195 S. W. 1151 (Tex.).

4 Taylor v. McIrvin, 94 Ill. 488.

5 Continental Life Ins. Co. v. Rogers, 119 Ill. 474.

The notice to produce may be in the following form:

State of Illinois }
County of Cook } ss.

In the Circuit Court of Cook County

Bernard Manning }
v. } No. 726446
Max Geltner }

Notice

To: Mr. H. K. Landie,
Attorney for defendant
160 No. La Salle St.,
Chicago, Illinois.

You are hereby notified to produce upon the hearing of the above entitled cause:

Letter dated September 10, 1925, addressed to Max Geltner, 221 East Hagler St., Miami, Florida, and signed Bernard Manning; and upon your failure to do so we shall offer secondary evidence of the contents thereof.

____

Attorneys for Plaintiff.

Received a copy of foregoing notice this first day of February, 1934 at ——— P. M.

____

Attorney for Defendant.

§ 190. (9) Subpoena duces tecum.

A subpoena duces tecum is used for the purpose of requiring a witness to bring with him certain books, papers, documents, or records which it is desired to introduce into evidence. A subpoena duces tecum is always used whenever the original document rather than secondary evidence will serve the trial attorney's purpose better. In most instances, it is more desirable to have the adverse party produce the original as it may seem to result in some sort of psychological admission. A subpoena duces tecum should always be used where the trial attorney is not in a position to produce satisfactory secondary evidence of a certain document. In the final analysis secondary evidence is never as fully satisfying as original or best evidence. Best evidence has always more psychological value and the trial attorney should, therefore, always endeavor to produce the best evidence possible under the circumstances.

In practically all instances, a subpoena duces tecum must be used to secure the production of original documents or records in the possession of witnesses or parties not involved in the particular law suit on trial.[6] A notice to produce served on someone not a party to the suit would be ineffective.

In many jurisdictions, a subpoena duces tecum will properly issue only upon a sworn petition to the court setting out definitely and particularly describing the document desired and with a showing of the materiality and necessity for its production during the trial of the case. An order of the court should be entered directing the clerk to issue the said subpoena duces tecum. Judges upon motion duly made are prone to vitiate the force of a subpoena duces tecum not based upon a sworn petition and an order of court that it issue.

A witness will not be required to bring into court a document called for by an improperly issued subpoena duces tecum not based upon an order of court or not describing in detail the particular document desired. However, the witness must respond to the subpoena portion requiring his presence in court.

As a matter of trial tactics, where the adverse party has been served with a defective subpoena duces tecum and the argument on the said subpoena is had in the presence of the jury, it is hardly worth while for the attorney to raise objections to the subpoena because of technicalities. As is generally known, juries abhor technicalities, and where the opponent may remedy the defects in the present subpoena by a motion made to the court for an additional order permitting the issuance of another subpoena, the objections to the defective one will be unavailing and may prove harmful. In

6 Banks v. Connecticut, etc., Co., 64 Atl. 14, 79 Conn. 116; Wuerth v. Frohlich, 232 N. W. 373, 251 Mich. 701; In re Makames, 265 N. Y. S. 515, 238 App. Div. 534; Stockwell v. Snyder, 51 S. W. (2d) 812.

Persons subject to process. Murray v. Elston, 23 N. J. Eq. 212.

Servants. U. S. v. Watson, 266 Fed. 736; Bank of Utica v. Hilliard, 5 Cow. (N. Y.) 153; Peo. v. Munday, 280 Ill. 32.

Adverse party. Peo. v. Dyckman, 24 How. Pr. (N. Y.) 222.

such instances it is always better to waive the defects and to produce the document called for.

The various forms that may be used in the issuance of a subpoena duces tecum including the petition, are as follows:

§ 190a. —Petition for subpoena duces tecum.

(Caption)

Your petitioner, ———, respectfully represents unto the Court that he is the duly authorized agent in this behalf of the plaintiff in the above entitled cause; that he has knowledge of the facts; that upon the trial of this cause to prove the issues therein on the part of the plaintiff and to prove the transactions on the purchase by the defendant of the merchandise herein sued for from the plaintiff and to prove that the defendant herein did purchase the same from the plaintiff, it will be necessary to produce in evidence the books of account, records, ledgers, memoranda, check books and check stubs and all other records and data on the books of account of said defendant corporation showing the purchases of merchandise from the plaintiff herein and payments therefor during the years 1926, 1927, 1928 and 1929, and that the said records, books of account, check books, check stubs, data and ledgers, etc., as aforesaid are in the possession of the defendant and its officers.

Wherefore your petitioner prays that the Clerk of this court be directed to issue a subpoena duces tecum commanding the said defendant and John Doe, its secretary, upon the hearing and trial of this cause to produce the said books of account, records, ledgers, memoranda, check books and check stubs and all other records and data on the books of account of said defendant corporation showing the purchases of merchandise from the plaintiff herein and payments therefor during the years 1926, 1927, 1928 and 1929.

———————————
Its duly authorized agent.

State of ——— }
County of ——— } ss.

——— being first duly sworn on oath says that he is the duly authorized agent of the plaintiff in this behalf; that he has read the foregoing petition by him subscribed, knows the contents thereof and that the same is true.

____

Subscribed and sworn to
before me this ——— day
of January, A. D. 1932.

____

Notary Public.

§ 191. (10) Change of venue.

The statutes and Codes of all States have made provision for changes of venue in the various courts throughout the country. In some instances client's interests require the filing of a petition for a change of venue. As a matter of good policy, the taking of a change of venue should be a rare occurrence. The trial attorney who makes a practice of filing petitions for change of venue will soon find that he has aroused the enmity and suspicion of every judge in his jurisdiction.

In some instances judges are prone to pass remarks during the arguments on preliminary motions which might be taken as indicative of their adverse attitude to the merits of the case at issue. For instance, the judge may say to the attorney that he does not see how he will be able to prove his case, or by some other remark indicate that his opinion on the merits of the case is adverse. The natural inclination of the lawyer is to ask for a change of venue because he feels that the handicap will be too great under which he will have to labor during the actual trial when the judge has already apparently expressed an adverse opinion. Some judges make this mistake, but do so in all fairness and honesty. They jump at a conclusion without knowing or fully considering all of the facts which will later be adduced upon the trial of the case. If the trial attorney feels that the judge is honorable and upright and if he feels there is merit in his case, he should not hesitate to go to trial before the same judge who has made the so-called derogatory remark, because in all probability that same judge, when all of the facts and testimony have been presented to him in a complete and orderly manner, will completely reverse his original opinion. However, every case and every judge must be separately considered. No hard and fast rule can be laid down to govern every instance.

§ 192. — Statutory provisions.

The statutes in reference to changes of venue provide somewhat as follows:

1. Causes. That a change of venue in any civil suit or proceeding in law or equity, including proceedings for the exercise of the right of eminent domain, may be had in any of the following cases:

First—Where the judge is a party or interested in the suit, or his testimony is material to either of the parties to the suit, or he is related to, or shall have been counsel for either party in regard to the matter in controversy. In any such case a change may be awarded by the court in term time, with or without the application of either party.

Second—Where either party shall fear that he will not receive a fair trial in the court in which the suit or proceeding is pending, because the inhabitants of the country are or the judge is prejudiced against him, or the adverse party has an undue influence over the minds of the inhabitants. In any such case the venue shall not be changed except upon application, as hereinafter provided, or by consent of the parties.

2. To what court. When a change of venue is granted it may be to some other court of record of competent jurisdiction in the same county, or in some other convenient county, to which there is no valid objection: Provided, that when the action is pending in either the Circuit or Superior Court of ——— County, and the only causes for a change of venue apply to one or more but not all of the judges of such court, the case may be tried before some one of the judges of such court to whom the causes do not apply.

3. Petition. Every application for a change of venue shall be by petition, setting forth the cause of the application and praying a change of venue, which petition shall be verified by the affidavit of the applicant.

4. Prejudice of inhabitants of county. If the cause for the change is the prejudice of the inhabitants of the county or the undue influence of the adverse party over their minds, the petition shall set forth the facts upon which the peti-

tioner founds his belief, and must be supported by the affidavits of at least two other reputable persons resident of the county. The adverse party may controvert the petition by counter affidavits, and the judge may grant or deny the petition as shall appear to be according to the right of the case.

5. When application may be made. The application may be made to the court in which the case is pending in term time, or to the judge thereof in vacation, reasonable notice thereof having been given to the adverse party or his attorney.

6. Not made after first term except, etc. No application for a change of venue after the first term shall be allowed, unless the party applying shall have given to the opposite party ten days' previous notice of his intention to make such application, except where the causes have arisen or come to the knowledge of the applicant within less than ten days before the making of the application.

7. Further exception. No change of venue shall be granted after the first term of the court at which the party applying might have been heard, unless he shall show that the causes for which the change is asked has arisen or come to his knowledge since the term at which the application might have been made.

8. Only one change. Neither party shall have more than one change of venue.

9. When there are several parties. When there are two or more plaintiffs or defendants, a change of venue shall not be granted unless the application is made by or with the consent of all the parties, plaintiff or defendant, as the case may be: Provided, that in proceedings for the condemnation of property, when the application is by or against all the owners of any parcel of property to be condemned, a change of venue may be made of so much of the case as affects them, if it can be done without prejudice to the other defendants or plaintiffs in such proceeding.

10. When granted in vacation. When a change of venue is granted in vacation, the judge granting it shall immediately transmit the petition and affidavits and his order directing the change of venue, to the clerk of the court in which the cause is pending, who shall file the same in his office, and make an entry of such order on the records of the court.

11. Conditions of change. The order for a change of venue may be made subject to such equitable terms and conditions as safety to the rights of the parties may seem to require, and the judge in his discretion may prescribe.

12. Expenses of change. The expenses attending a change of venue shall be taxed by the clerk of the court from which the case is certified, according to the rules established by law for like services, and shall be paid by the petitioner and not taken as part of the costs in the suit.

13. Order void if expenses not paid. The order shall be void unless the party obtaining a change of venue shall, within fifteen days, or such shorter time as the court or judge may prescribe, pay to the clerk the expenses attending the change.

14. When costs abide suit. Where the venue is changed without the application of either party, the costs of such change shall abide the event of the suit.

15. Transmitting papers, etc. In all cases of change of venue, the clerk of the court from which the change is granted shall immediately make out a full transcript of the record and proceedings in the case, and of the petition, affidavits and order for the change of venue, and transmit the same, together with all the papers filed in the case, to the proper court: Provided, that when the venue is changed, on behalf of a part of the defendants, to a condemnation proceeding, it shall not be necessary to transmit the original papers in the case, but it shall be sufficient to transmit certified copies of so much thereof as pertains to the case so changed. Such transcript and papers or copies may be transmitted by mail, or in such other way as the court or judge may direct.

16. Filing transcript, etc. — Docketing cause, etc. The clerk of the court to which the change of venue is granted shall file the transcript and papers transmitted to him and docket the cause, and such cause shall be proceeded in and determined in all things, as well before as after judgment, as if it had originated in such court.

17. Irregularity waived by trial and verdict. All questions concerning the regularity of the proceedings in a change of venue, and the right of the court to which the change is made to try the cause and execute the judgment, shall be considered as waived after trial and verdict.

The petition for change of venue must be served within a reasonable time after the petitioner has acquired knowledge of the prejudice or unfairness of the judge or of the citizens of the community in which he resides. What is a reasonable length of time depends entirely upon the circumstances of each case.[7] Most statutes provide that the notice should be served a certain length of time before the opening of the term of court. However, in some instances the notice of prejudice is not acquired until a day or two before trial. If such notice and petition is served immediately thereafter, the courts have held that it has been served within a reasonable length of time after acquisition of the notice of prejudice.

§ 193. Affidavit or verification.

State of ——— }
County of ——— } ss.

D. E. F., defendant in this cause, makes oath and says that the facts set forth in the foregoing petition by him subscribed are true in substance and in fact.

____

Subscribed and sworn to, etc.

§ 194. Affidavit opposing.

State of ——— }
County of ——— } ss.

———, being first duly sworn, says that he is the plaintiff (or defendant) in the above-entitled cause, and that the application of ——— for a change of venue in said cause on the ground of (whatever the ground is) ought not to be granted.

Affiant further says that the (traverse grounds set out for the change) and says that (here set out facts showing the absence of reason for prejudice).

(Add verification.)

7 Thompson v. Malmin, 204 Ill. A. 374; Hutson v. Wood, 105 N. E. 343, 263 Ill. 376; Goldfeder v. Greenberg, 178 N. Y. S. 581, 189 App. Div. 184; Township, etc. v. Empire, etc., Co., 253 Mich. 394, 235 N. W. 194; Ex parte Burch, 141 Pac. 813, 168 Cal. 18; Corpenny v. City of Sedalia, 57 Mo. 88; Wright v. Stevens, 3 Greene (Iowa) 63.

§ 195. Petition—Prejudice of judge.

(Caption)

The petitioner, D. E. F., respectfully shows to said court that he, the petitioner, is defendant in the above-entitled cause; that he fears that he will not receive a fair and impartial trial in said court if said cause will be tried before the Honorable ———, one of the judges of said court, because said judge is prejudiced against him, the petitioner, so that he cannot expect a fair trial by said judge. Petitioner further shows that said prejudice first came to the knowledge of this petitioner on ———.

Petitioner therefore prays a change of venue in this cause, or for an order that said cause be tried before some other judge than said ———, pursuant to the statute in such case made and provided.

(Add verification.)

§ 196. Petition—Undue influence—People prejudiced.

(Caption)

Your petitioner respectfully represents that he is the plaintiff (or defendant) in the above-entitled cause and that he fears that he will not receive a fair trial in this court because he believes ——— plaintiff or (Defendant), the adverse party in said cause, has an undue influence over the minds of the inhabitants of said county (or that the inhabitants of said county are prejudiced against your petitioner.)

Your petitioner further represents that this belief is predicated upon the following facts: (Set out facts).

Your petitioner further represents that he was unacquainted with the facts revealing such prejudice until ——— days ago.

Wherefore, your petitioner prays a change of venue in the cause, pursuant to the provisions of the statute in such case made and provided.

———————————

(Add verification.)

§ 197. (11) Continuances.

While most attorneys are in the habit of making motions for continuances as a mere matter of course, the provisions of the various statutes and Codes should be consulted in reference to the requirements concerning continuances. In most instances, the court will usually grant a continuance, particularly where the opponent agrees thereto, but considerable difficulty may be encountered where opposing counsel refuses to grant the request for a continuance and the motion is subsequently denied by the court. Unless proper preparation has been made, the trial attorney may be forced to trial without the benefit of certain opposing witness' testimony. On the other hand, it is important that the trial attorney appreciate the various steps that he may resort to in the event that opposing counsel makes the request for a continuance which for many reasons he cannot grant. In such case the trial attorney should require an affidavit from the opponent as to just what his witness will testify to. If the opponent happens to be in a hurry in the preparation of such affidavit and merely sets out a bare outline of what the witness will testify to, it will thereupon be good trial tactics for the trial lawyer to admit that such witness, if present, would so testify, with the added statement, of course, before the jury that he is not stipulating that the testimony of such witness is true, but just merely that if he did take the witness stand that he would so testify. This is particularly good policy in requiring such an affidavit and making such admission where the trial attorney's investigation and interview with such adverse witness has convinced him that the impression made by such adverse witness on the witness stand and the facts to which such adverse witness would testify to if in court would have by far a more harmful effect than just merely reading and admitting the facts set out in the affidavit. It is much easier to minimize the effect of the statements contained in an affidavit than it would be to persuade the jury to disbelieve the testimony given by such a witness from the witness stand.

The courts in most jurisdictions have held that where the attorney opposing the motion for continuance is willing to admit that a witness who is not present would testify to certain facts as alleged in an affidavit should in most cases deny the motion for a continuance. However, where equity and good conscience under the particular circumstances in each case show that the court should exercise his discretion in favor of granting the motion for continuance the exercising of the court's discretion in favor of granting the motion for continuance has been upheld.

The provisions of the Codes and Statutes in reference to continuances are usually in the following form:

§ 198. — Code provisions.

(1) When either party shall apply for a continuance of a cause on account of the absence of material evidence, the motion shall be supported by the affidavit of the party so applying or his authorized agent, showing that due diligence has been used to obtain such evidence, or the want of time to obtain it, and of what particular fact or facts the same consists, and if the evidence consists of the testimony of a witness, his place of residence, or if his place of residence is not known, showing that due diligence has been used to ascertain the same, and that if further time is given such evidence can be procured.

(2) Should the court be satisfied that such evidence would not be material, or if the other party will admit the affidavit in evidence as proof only of what the absent witness would testify to if present, the continuance shall be denied unless the court, for the furtherance of justice, shall deem a continuance necessary.

(3) It shall be sufficient cause for the continuance of any action that, in time of war or insurrection, a defendant, whose presence is necessary for the full and fair defense of the action, is in the military service of the United States or of this State; or that the party applying therefor or his attorney, solicitor or counsel, if his presence is necessary for the full and fair trial of the action, is a member of either house of the General Assembly and then in actual attendance on the sessions thereof, provided, in the case of such attorney, solicitor or counsel, that he was actually employed prior to the commencement of such session; and it shall be sufficient showing of diligence in seeking to obtain evidence that the absent witness is in the military service of the United States or of this State.

(4) No amendment shall be cause for continuance, unless the party affected thereby, or his agent or attorney, shall make affidavit that in consequence thereof, he is unprepared

to proceed to or with the trial of the cause. And if the cause thereof is the want of material evidence, such continuance shall be granted only on such further showing as may be required for continuance for that cause.

(5) The court may on its own motion, or with the consent of the adverse party, continue a cause for trial to a later day.

(6) No motion for the continuance of a cause made after the cause has been reached for trial shall be heard, unless a sufficient excuse is shown for the delay.

(7) When a continuance is granted upon payment of costs, such costs may be taxed summarily by the court, and on being taxed, shall be paid on demand of the party, his agent or attorney, and if not so paid, on affidavit of the fact, such continuance may be vacated, or the court may enforce such payment, with the accruing costs, by contempt proceedings.

§ 199. —Absent witness—Affidavit by defendant.

State of Illinois } ss.
County of ——— }

D. E. F., the above-named defendant, makes oath and says that he cannot safely proceed to the trial of said cause at the present term of this court on account of the absence of one W. I. T. (who resides at ———, or whose residence and whereabouts are to this affiant at present unknown), and who is a material witness in said cause on the part of this affiant; that this affiant expects to prove by the said W. I. T. the following matters, all of which are material to the issues involved in said cause, to wit: (here set forth fully and in detail the matters expected to be proved by the witness); that all the matters which affiant expects to prove by the said W. I. T. as above set forth are true (to the best of the knowledge, information and belief of this affiant).

And this affiant further says that (here set forth what efforts have been made to procure the attendance or testimony of the witness, and to ascertain his place of residence, if alleged to be unknown). And this affiant further says that he is informed and believes that upon the trial of said cause the material issues involved therein will be controverted and that the evidence relating thereto, introduced by the respective parties, will be exceedingly conflicting and contrary, and that he knows of no other person or persons than the said W. I. T. by whom he can so fully prove the matters above set forth. Affiant further says that if further time is given, the place of residence of the said W. I. T. can be ascertained, and such evidence can be procured. (Here set forth the reason for such expectation and belief.) And this affiant further says that the said W. I. T. is not absent by or with the procurement, connivance or consent of this affiant, either directly or indirectly given, and that this application is not made for delay, but that justice may be done.

(Add verification.)

§ 200. (12) Amendments.

The right to amend is an important one to the trial lawyer. All courts usually are in favor of permitting amendments to be made wherever it is felt the interests of justice will best be served. Not only juries, but courts, are not in favor of loss of rights by litigants solely and wholly as a result of technicalities.

§ 201. — Statutory provisions.

Most statutes are quite liberal in permitting amendments before trial, during trial and after verdict. Every lawyer should become familiar with his local Statutes and Codes in reference to amendments. Some states provide for amendments as follows:

(1) At any time before final judgment in a civil action, amendments may be allowed on such terms as are just and reasonable, introducing any party who ought to have been joined as plaintiff or defendant, discontinuing as to any plaintiff or defendant, changing the cause of action or defense or adding new causes of action or defenses, and in any matter, either of form or substance, in any process, pleading or proceedings, which may enable the plaintiff to sustain the claim for which it was intended to be brought or the defendant to make a defense or assert a cross demand.

(2) The cause of action, cross demand or defense set up in any amended pleading shall not be barred by lapse of time under any statute or contract prescribing or limiting the time within which an action may be brought or right asserted, if the time prescribed or limited had not expired when the orig-

inal pleading was filed, and if it shall appear from the original and amended pleadings that the cause of action asserted, or the defense or cross demand interposed in the amended pleading grew out of the same transaction or occurrence set up in the original pleading, even though the original pleading was defective in that it failed to allege the performance of some act or the existence of some fact or some other matter which is a necessary condition precedent to the right of recovery or defense asserted when such condition precedent has in fact been performed, and for the purpose of preserving as aforesaid such cause of action, cross demand or defense set up in such amended pleading, and for such purpose only, any such amendment to any pleading shall be held to relate back to the date of the filing of the original pleading so amended.

(3) A pleading may be amended at any time, before or after judgment, to conform the pleadings to the proofs, upon such terms as to costs and continuance may be just.

§ 202. —Motions should be accompanied by proposed amendment.

All motions for amendments should be accompanied by the proposed amendment. It should also be remembered that orders granting leave to amend are not in effect amendments. Amended pleadings must always be filed in addition to the order granting leave. Amendments have been permitted to conform to proof offered upon the trial after the verdict has been returned by the jury. In making motions for amendments to conform to proof the right of the judge to grant such motion in some instances may depend on the fact as to whether or not the opponent at the time the proof was offered during the trial of the case objected to the same on the grounds that such proffered proof was outside the scope of the pleadings on file. If such timely and specific objection was made by the opponent at the time the evidence was offered, it may legally prevent the court from granting leave to file the proposed amendment to conform to such proof.

§ 203. —Examine pleadings.

All pleadings and proposed proof should be carefully examined and considered in the light of the pleadings filed in the cause and if such proposed proof goes beyond the scope of the pleadings an amendment should usually be made. Some attorneys wait until the course of the trial develops the necessity for such amendment, before making their motions to amend. This is bad procedure in most instances because opponent may object to the granting of such motion to amend on the grounds that it changes the cause of action and that he is surprised and unable to continue with the trial if the amendment is permitted. In some instances, the court may properly sustain the objection and force counsel to proceed with the trial. He is then without the benefit of such additional proof and he may be forced to take a non-suit or continue the trial with the possibility of an unfavorable verdict. It is, therefore, suggested that motions for amendments should be made at the earliest moment, and usually a sufficient length of time before trial to obviate any possible objection by opponent.

§ 204. Affidavit of amendment.

(Caption)

D. E. F., the above-named defendant, being first duly sworn, on oath states that on the trial of said cause, the plaintiff, by leave of court, amended his complaint filed therein by filing an additional count thereto, in and by which it is alleged that (here state in substance the averments of additional count). Affiant further states that he is advised by his counsel and verily believes that said additional count states substantially a new and different cause of action from that made by said original complaint; that in consequence thereof this affiant is unprepared to and cannot safely proceed with the trial of said cause at the present term of court; that if the facts averred in the said additional count had been alleged in the original complaint, he would have been able to and would have successfully contradicted and disproved the same by the testimony of one W. I. T., who resides at, etc., and who would have, as affiant is informed and believes, testified to the following facts: (here insert the particular facts proposed to be proved by the witness), all of which said facts this affiant knows (or verily believes) to be true; that this affiant knows of no witness or witnesses other than the said W. I. T. by whom he can prove the facts above stated.

Affiant further states that until the filing of said additional count as aforesaid, he supposed that the plaintiff intended to prove and establish the averments of said original complaint only; that he had no reason to and did not anticipate the filing of said additional count, and that he was greatly surprised thereby. Affiant further states that he did not cause the said W. I. T. to be subpoenaed at the trial for the reason that he was unaware and did not anticipate that his testimony would be or become material to the issues made by the then pleadings. Affiant further states that the said W. I. T. is at present and has been for the past ——— weeks, in, etc., and that he verily believes that if this cause is continued he will be able to procure the attendance and testimony of the said W. I. T. to the facts above stated. Affiant further states that he believes that he has a complete and meritorious defense to the causes made by said amended count and said original complaint, and that this application is not made for delay, but that justice may be done.

(Add verification.)

§ 205. (13) Summary judgments.

Some modern codes governing practice and procedure in courts have made provision for summary judgments in the following language:

Subject to rules, if the plaintiff, in any action upon a contract, express or implied, or upon a judgment or decree for the payment of money, or in any action to recover possession of land, with or without rent or *mesne* profits, or in any action to recover possession of specific chattels, shall file an affidavit or affidavits, on the affiant's personal knowledge, of the truth of the facts upon which his complaint is based and the amount claimed (if any) over and above all just deductions, credits and set-offs (if any), the court shall, upon plaintiff's motion, enter a judgment in his favor for the relief so demanded, unless the defendant shall, by affidavit of merits filed prior to or at the time of the hearing on said motion, show that he has a sufficiently good defense on the merits to all or some part of the plaintiff's claim to entitle him to defend the action. If the defense is to a part only of the plaintiff's demand a judgment may be entered, and an execution or other suitable writ issued, for the balance of the demand, and the case shall thereafter proceed as to the portion of the plaintiff's demand in dispute as though the action had been originally brought therefor; and in such case the court may make such order as to the costs of the suit as may be equitable.

§ 206. Affidavits in proceedings for summary judgments.

(1) The affidavits in support of a motion for summary judgment shall be made on the personal knowledge of the affiants; shall set forth with particularity the facts upon which the plaintiff's cause of action is based; shall have attached thereto sworn or certified copies of all papers upon which plaintiff relies; shall not consist of conclusions but of such facts as would be admissible in evidence; and shall affirmatively show that the affiant if sworn as a witness, can testify competently thereto. If all the facts to be shown are not within the personal knowledge of one person, two or more affidavits shall be used.

(2) Affidavits of merits to prevent the entry of a summary judgment shall be drawn in the same manner as the affidavits mentioned in the foregoing paragraph of this rule.

(3) Should the affidavit of either party contain a statement that any of the material facts which ought to appear in such affidavit are known only to persons whose affidavits affiant is unable to procure, by reason of hostility or otherwise, naming such persons and showing why their affidavits cannot be procured, and what affiant believes they would testify to if sworn, with his reasons for such belief, the court may make such order as may be just, either granting or refusing the application for summary judgment, or making an order for a continuance to permit affidavits to be obtained, or for submitting interrogatories to or taking the depositions of any of the persons so named, or for producing papers or documents in the possession of such persons or furnishing sworn copies thereof. The interrogatories and sworn answers thereto, depositions so taken, and sworn copies of papers and documents so furnished, shall be considered as a part of the affidavit in support of plaintiff's claim or of the affidavit of merits as the case may be.

§ 207. —Summary judgments—Counterclaims.

Where, in a summary judgment proceeding, the defendant files a counterclaim against the plaintiff, the court, if it is of the opinion that there is merit in the defendant's counterclaim, may reserve action until all issues in the case have been determined, or may enter summary judgment for the plaintiff and stay execution upon such judgment until such time as the issues upon the counterclaim are decided.

If the amount of the counterclaim is less than the plaintiff's demand, judgment may be entered and execution or other suitable writ issued for the amount of the excess of plaintiff's demand over the defendant's counterclaim.

The summary judgment procedure may be employed by the defendant in filing a counterclaim. When so employed by the defendant, the provisions of this rule as to judgment and execution shall be applicable.

In many instances provisions for summary judgments have made possible the early disposition of cases with a saving not only of time, but of the expense entailed in the trial of a law suit.

§ 208. — Value.

While some lawyers may object to the advisability of Code provisions for summary judgments, yet the proper use of motions for summary judgments should go a long way toward "clearing" the congestion of most court dockets. It should make it possible to receive early trials in most cases by eliminating those in which unfounded defenses have been pleaded.

From the stand point of trial tactics, the motion for summary judgment may come to be used by the trial attorney for the purpose of ascertaining just what evidence he will have to contend with on the part of his opponent, especially in those instances when the defendant is fully aware of the plaintiff's case but the plaintiff is at a loss to know just what the actual defense is and what the adversary expects to produce in the way of evidence.

A motion for summary judgment properly supported by affidavits will force the defendant to disclose his case. In this way the plaintiff's attorney will know just what he must meet.

This provision was not passed for the purpose of using it as a "fishing expedition." However, it is quite obvious that many attorneys will use it just for that purpose.

§ 209. Affidavit for summary judgment—Recovery of money.

(Caption)

P. L. F., being first duly sworn, on oath deposes and says:

1. That he is the plaintiff in the above-entitled cause.

2. That said action is brought to recover the sum of ——— dollars which is alleged to be due upon (state basis or character of action).

3. That the facts and circumstances under which the causes of action alleged in the complaint arose are as follows: (set forth the evidentiary facts establishing existence of the cause of action alleged in the complaint, attaching sworn copies of any writing referred to, and making it affirmatively evident that plaintiff, if sworn as a witness, could testify competently to the facts alleged).

4. That by reason of the facts aforesaid, and after allowing to defendant all just deductions, credits and set-offs, the said sum of ——— dollars is now due and owing from the defendant to the plaintiff, P. L. F.

5. That affiant verily believes that there is no defense to this action. (This allegation is not affirmatively required by the Illinois statutory provisions set out above, but under corresponding procedure in other states is vital.)

Wherefore, affiant prays that judgment be ordered for the plaintiff and against the defendant for the sum of ——— dollars (with interest from ——— to ———).

§ 210. Affidavit for summary judgment—Recovery of land.

(Caption)

P. L. F., being first duly sworn, on oath deposes and says:

1. That he is the plaintiff in the above-entitled cause.

2. That said action is brought to recover possession of the following described real estate: (describe land).

3. That the facts and circumstances under which the cause of action alleged in the complaint arose are as follows: (set forth the evidentiary facts establishing existence of the cause of action alleged in the complaint, attaching sworn copies of any writing referred to, and making it affirmatively evident that plaintiff, if sworn as a witness, could testify competently to the facts alleged.)

4. That by reason of the facts aforesaid, plaintiff is entitled to possession of the land above described.

5. That affiant verily believes that there is no defense to this action. (This allegation is not affirmatively required by the Illinois statutory provisions set out above, but under corresponding procedure in other states is vital.)

Wherefore, affiant prays that judgment may be ordered for the plaintiff against the defendant; that plaintiff shall be restored to possession of the premises above described.

Subscribed and sworn to, etc.

Quaere as to whether this procedure is applicable to such proceedings as replevin and forcible entry and detainer.

§ 211. Affidavit of defense—To all of claim.

(Caption)

D. E. F., being first duly sworn, on oath deposes and says:

1. That he is the defendant in the above-entitled cause.

2. That he has a good defense on the merits to all of the plaintiff's claim.

3. That the nature of affiant's defense is as follows: (set out the evidentiary facts by way of denial or avoidance which establish the defense, attaching sworn copies of any writing referred to, and making it affirmatively evident that defendant, if sworn as a witness could competently testify to the facts alleged).

Wherefore, affiant says that he is entitled to defend the said action, and prays that the motion of plaintiff may be dismissed.

Subscribed and sworn to, etc.

§ 212. Affidavit of defense—To part of claim.

(Caption)

D. E. F., being first duly sworn, on oath deposes and says:

1. That he is the defendant in the above-entitled cause.

2. That he has a good defense on the merits to a part of plaintiff's claim.

3. That the nature of affiant's defense is as follows: (set out the evidentiary facts by way of denial or avoidance which establish the defense to the portion of the claim which is dis-

puted, attaching sworn copies of any writing referred to, and making it affirmatively evident that defendant, if sworn as a witness, could competently testify to the facts alleged).

Wherefore, defendant says that he is entitled to defend the said action over and above the amount of ——— dollars, which sum defendant admits to be due to plaintiff, and defendant says that he is entitled to defend said action as to any claim above said amount and prays that plaintiff's motion may be dismissed as to any amount in excess thereof.

Subscribed and sworn to, etc.

§ 213. Facts known only to hostile person.

(Insert paragraphs in affidavit, under appropriate circumstances, as follows:)

That certain facts material to affiant's (claim) (defense) are known only to H. W.

That affiant is unable to procure an affidavit from said H. W. because (here state reason why affidavit cannot be procured).

That affiant verily believes that if sworn, H. W. would testify as follows: (here state in detail to what H. W. would testify).

That the reasons for affiant's belief are as follows: (State reasons).

Wherefore, affiant prays that (ask appropriate relief).

Subscribed and sworn to, etc.

§ 214. Notice of motion for summary judgment.

(Caption)

To ———:

Please take notice that on the ——— day of ———, 19—, at the hour of ——— o'clock ———M., or as soon thereafter as counsel can be heard, I shall appear before his Honor, Judge ———, in the room usually occupied by him as a court room in the courthouse, ———, Illinois, and move that summary judgment be entered in accordance with the statute in such case made and provided and in support of said motion I shall present an affidavit, a copy of which is hereto attached.

Received a copy of the above notice, with affidavit attached, this ——— day of ———, A. D., 19—.

____

§ 215. Motion for summary judgment.

(Caption)

Now comes P. L. F., plaintiff, by ———, his attorney, and moves the court to enter judgment for the plaintiff for the relief demanded in his affidavit hereto attached, in accordance with the statute in such case made and provided.

(Attach affidavit.)

§ 216. New York authorities.

The antecedents of this rule are the English rules of the Supreme Court, order 14, rule 1. Commercial Credit Corp. v. Podhorzer, 221 App. Div. 644, 224 N. Y. S. 505.

The rule is based on a similar rule in the English rules of the Supreme Court (order 3, rule 6, and order 14, rule 1). Norwich Pharmacal Co. v. Barrett, 205 App. Div. 749, 200 N. Y. S. 298.

The purpose of the rule was to stamp out the practice of delaying judgment by the interposition of defenses which could not be substantiated by evidence. McAnsh v. Blauner, 222 App. Div. 381, 226 N. Y. S. 379.

Object of the rule is to require a defendant to make a showing that at least, he has an arguable defense. Commonwealth Fuel Co., Inc. v. Powpit Co., Inc., 212 App. Div. 553, 209 N. Y. S. 603.

It is not the purpose of this rule to authorize the trial of contested issues upon affidavits. L. R. Munoz & Co. v. Savannah Sugar Refining Corp., 118 Misc. 24, 193 N. Y. S. 422.

A summary judgment entered pursuant to this rule does not deny the defendant his constitutional right to a jury trial, notwithstanding section 261, Civil Practice Act, providing that an answer may contain either a general or specific denial of any material allegation of the complaint, or of any knowledge or information thereof sufficient to form a belief. Hanna v. Mitchell, 202 App. Div. 504, 196 N. Y. S. 43, aff'd 235 N. Y. 534, 139 N. E. 724.

Rule was not intended to deprive any one of jury trial of any issue of fact. Wrobel v. Call, 142 Misc. 610, 255 N. Y. S. 851.

Object of rule is to preclude interposition of frivolous defenses and defeat attempt to use a formal pleading as a means of delaying recovery of honest demands. Wrobel v. Call, 142 Misc. 610, 255 N. Y. S. 258.

This rule applies to counterclaims as well as to defenses. Salt Springs Nat. Bank of Syracuse v. Hitchcock, 144 Misc. 547, 259 N. Y. S. 24. (Quaere as to this being true under the Illinois statute, which refers to "plaintiff" and "complainant.")

Defendant must show real and substantial facts sufficient to entitle him to defend. Strasburger v. Rosenheim, 234 App. Div. 544, 255 N. Y. S. 316.

Rule requires defendant to show a bona fide issue, an arguable defense, and that he is not taking advantage of a technicality in pleading to prevent enforcement of an honest claim. Wrobel v. Call, 142 Misc. 610, 255 N. Y. S. 258.

A defendant must show real and substantial facts "sufficient to entitle him to defend" if he is to avert summary judgment under the rules which were carefully devised to eliminate unnecessary delay and further the prompt administration of justice. Strasburger v. Rosenheim, 234 App. Div. 544, 255 N. Y. S. 316.

Plaintiff's motion for judgment hereunder called upon defendant to assemble and reveal his proofs so as to show matters set up in answer were real and capable of being established at trial; having failed, denial of plaintiff's motion reversed. Dodwell & Co., Inc. v. Silverman, 234 App. Div. 362, 254 N. Y. S. 746.

The court does not become a trier of facts by listening to the affidavits of the respective parties on motion for summary judgment, but decides whether the case presents facts to be tried by a jury. Dibble Seedgrower v. Jones, 130 Misc. 359, 223 N. Y. S. 785.

Remedy under this rule is useful but drastic; it should be applied only where it is perfectly plain that there is no substantial issue to be tried. Moir v. Johnson, 211 App. Div. 427, 207 N. Y. S. 380.

If there is one good issue which must await trial, the purpose of the rule,—to save delay,—falls, and defendant is entitled to a trial in regular order. H. C. King Motor Sales Corp. v. Allen, 209 App. Div. 281, 204 N. Y. S. 555.

While several of the defenses set up were insufficient, summary judgment was denied, since facts in support of the remaining defenses might be made to appear. Stricks v. Siegel, 135 Misc. 608, 238 N. Y. S. 154.

The affidavit should set forth the evidential facts with such particularity that the court shall be satisfied of the plaintiff's actual right to recover. In re Littleton's Estate, 129 Misc. 845, 223 N. Y. S. 470.

In support of a judgment for plaintiff he must show evidentiary facts; statements of ultimate facts are insufficient. Kellogg v. Berkshire Bldg. Corp., 125 Misc. 818, 211 N. Y. S. 623.

CHAPTER IV

SELECTING THE JURY

§ 217. Importance.

It is frequently stated by all successful trial lawyers that the selection of the jury and the opening statement constitute the most important parts of the trial of the case. There may be some conflict of opinion as to whether or not this is literally true, yet no trial lawyer can successfully try cases without a full appreciation of the rules governing the selection and qualification of the jury. When the fact is taken into consideration that it is the jury that will decide the case either favorably or unfavorably, it can then be appreciated that the trial lawyer must sell both his client and himself into the good graces of the jury. Many lawyers haphazardly select the jury without any regard to their psychological "make-up." They then continue throughout the balance of the trial without apparently caring whether or not the testimony will have a favorable effect in influencing the jury to return the desired verdict. In many instances they fail to note the impression created by their witnesses by viewing the facial expressions of the various jurors. In other words, they totally disregard the jury when once they are sworn to try the issues. This is a serious mistake. In most cases it is found that the jury "tries" the lawyers rather than the clients. It is much easier for them to decide in favor of an attorney whom they like, and a friendly feeling occasioned throughout the trial on the part of the jury towards one of the lawyers trying the case before them usually assists in influencing a favorable decision. It, therefore, becomes important that the attorney should never lose sight of the fact that he is appealing *to the jury* to return a favorable verdict.

§ 218. When jury is to be demanded.

A jury should be demanded in every instance where the natural sympathies of the jury will favor the client. For instance the plaintiff will always seek a jury trial in those cases where the jury has a right to fix the amount of the damages, particularly in personal injuries where proper appeals to their sympathies may result in a larger verdict. A jury should always be demanded in cases where the defendant is a large corporation, a prominent or wealthy person, and also where the defendant is an insurance company, railroad corporation or banking concern. A jury should also be demanded in all instances where the client is a woman, child, an old man or an old woman, or an ignorant, illiterate or foreign-born person unable to read, write or speak English who would naturally excite the sympathies of the jury.

§ 219. New jury.

It is suggested as a matter of good trial tactics that where a lawyer represents the plaintiff in a personal injury case or in a case where the natural sympathies of the jury will run to his client, he make an endeavor to try the case before a *new jury*. It has been found that the juror trying his first personal injury case will pay more attention to the evidence, will be more responsive to a sympathetic appeal occasioned by the testimony of pain and suffering, and will always return a larger verdict. It has also been found that after a man has served as a juror on a number of such cases, he becomes somewhat hardened and calloused to testimony of pain and suffering and is more apt to return a smaller verdict. The same result is occasioned in the case of a charity worker who goes out to investigate her first appeal for charity. She will become almost unnerved by the striking evidence of poverty and want. Yet, after a number of such calls, each situation becomes merely another case worthy of the organization's attention.

This same suggestion in attempting to try the first case before a new jury always applies on behalf of defendant in criminal cases.

§ 220. Six-man jury or twelve-man jury.

In some jurisdictions the practice has arisen to try cases before either a six-man jury or a twelve-man jury. It is suggested that the plaintiff might be willing to try his case before a six-man jury because it is easier to get six men to agree on a proposition than it is to get twelve men to agree.

With the various types, races, creeds, and nationalities ordinarily selected to act as jurors in cases, it is much more difficult to get twelve men from twelve different walks of life to agree as to who is right or who is wrong in a case on trial. Therefore, it would seem to benefit the defendants to have trials in jury cases before a twelve-man jury. However, it should be kept in mind, from the viewpoint of the defendant, that it is only necessary to convince one man of the truth of the defendant's contentions so as to assure a disagreement which is always considered a victory for the defendant.

§ 221. Examining jurors in panels of four or twelve.

There seems to be considerable conflict of opinion between trial lawyers as to whether or not it is more advisable or beneficial to examine jurors in panels of four or twelve. It is possible in a poll of successful trial attorneys to receive as many opinions in favor of examining jurors in panels of four as one would receive in favor of examining in panels of twelve. Just as in all other features of trial work, there is no hard and fast rule governing the selection of jurors. Some attorneys feel that when representing the plaintiff, it is better to examine in panels of twelve on the ground that it affords a better opportunity to scrutinize the entire jury before exercising any of the challenges. On the other hand, many attorneys representing the defendants also feel that it is more advisable to examine jurors in panels of twelve because they have the last opportunity to examine and can definitely view all those remaining in the jury box after the plaintiff has exercised his right of challenge. Again, other attorneys feel that it is more advisable from the viewpoint of the defendant to examine in panels of four because it forces the plaintiff to take one or two unsatisfactory jurors in each panel of four by reason of his fear that if he should challenge one or two whom he deems to be unsatisfactory, that immediately thereafter the defendant's attorney will challenge the other one or two prospective jurors whom the plaintiff's attorney most desires to retain. Thus, the plaintiff's attorney when selecting jurors in panels of four will have accepted one or two in each panel of four who might be considered favorable from the viewpoint of the defendant. It is a generally recognized rule that one or two jurors favorable to the defendant may result in a disagreement. This is considered as a victory for the defendant, for successive trials usually tire out the plaintiff to the point where a settlement for a small sum may result. It is suggested that the trial lawyer experiment with both four and twelve panel examinations and arrive at a decision as to just which he prefers.

§ 222. Diagrams.

It is recommended that prior to the time the selection of the jury is commenced, a diagram be prepared and utilized for the purpose of recording all information in reference to the jurors. A sheet of paper, legal cap size, should be divided to represent the jury box as follows:

As each juror is examined all information in reference to that particular juror should be placed in the box in the diagram representing his position in the jury box. This is important, particularly during the final arguments where some point in issue comes within the particular experience of one or more of the jurors. This diagram will readily and quickly provide all information desired pertaining to the jurors, and the attorney then can direct his argument to that particular juror in reference to the point upon which his experience will best qualify him to influence the other jurors. This particular method compliments that juror, because he then feels that the attorney recalls him and has remembered his particular history. This will result in a favorable reaction.

The diagram is also of importance to the attorney for the defendant, because it enables him to ascertain quickly the name and business of a juror at a glance just prior to his examination of the said juror. In this way, it will appear to the jurors that the attorney for the defendant apparently remembers his name, or has taken the trouble to remember his name, and he will feel complimented. Some attorneys for the defendant have made it a practice to memorize the names and businesses of the twelve jurors by concentrated effort, and after considerable practice have been able to amaze the jurors with the fact of their remembering their names and their history. Yet a quick glance at the diagram just before passing on to the next juror to examine him will accomplish almost the same result.

§ 223. Types of jurors.

It is, of course, important that all trial lawyers become acquainted with the various suggestions in reference to types of jurors. Some leading exponents of the art of trial tactics ridicule the rules followed by many trial lawyers in reference to racial and other characteristics of prospective jurors, while the fact that some successful lawyers lose cases in court that they confidently feel they should have won, would tend to show that there are no hard and fast rules governing the selection of jurors, yet the trial lawyer must know what has been written and stated on the subject so that he can govern himself accordingly.

It has been suggested that where the trial lawyer represents the plaintiff in a case in which the sympathies of the jury will naturally be with his client, he should seek the type of juror that will most naturally respond to an emotional appeal. Most attorneys place the nationalities in the following category: The Irishman, the Jew, the Italian, the Frenchman, the Spaniard, and all Slavic races. These are the types that the defendant in a criminal case will ordinarily seek. The defendant in a civil case, where he seeks jurors that will not so readily respond to an emotional appeal, will try to get the Nordic type of juror, the Englishman, the Scandinavian, including the Swede and the Norwegian, the German, and such.

It follows that the prosecution in criminal cases will also seek the Nordic type of juror. They are considered to be more responsive to appeals for law and order and for the enforcement of the same. These suggestions are all subject to exceptions and are subject to modification dependent on the facts in each case. In one instance, a German banker was being prosecuted for embezzlement and larceny. The prosecutor in charge of the case, keeping in mind the instruction to secure as many English, German, and Scandinavian jurors as possible, lost sight of the fact that the defendant was a German. When the jury was selected there were six Germans on the jury. No one was surprised to learn that all of the Germans voted for acquittal.

It has been pointed out by many attorneys that the plaintiff in personal injury cases, and in all cases where the emotional appeal will be depended upon, should eliminate from the panel of prospective jurors all those who have had a great deal of contact with the general public, such as ex-policemen, ex-sheriffs and ex-justices, for as Donovan in "Modern Jury Trials" says, "such ex-officials have imbibed a deep seated prejudice for the plaintiffs whom they have served so long."

Under the same heading, it might, therefore, be proper from the viewpoint of the plaintiff to exclude those prospective jurors whose experience has been the adjustment of claims and complaints, as insurance adjusters, credit men, and the like.

For the plaintiff in personal injury cases and in all instances where the jury are to fix the amount of the verdict in their discretion, it is suggested that jurors be selected who are in the habit of thinking in large figures. It would seem that a laborer who has never earned more than ten or fifteen dollars a week will be more likely to think in terms of a smaller verdict, than would a person who is in the habit of handling large sums of money, or some man who thinks in terms of large figures. This type of jury would be more apt to compensate a plaintiff liberally for injuries sustained which result in cases of permanent deformities or cripple or incapacitate the victim for the rest of his life.

On the other hand, many plaintiff's lawyers favor the laborer type of juror on the ground that they have a reckless disregard for other people's money. However, the suggestion in the preceding paragraph is controlling in those instances where there is no question of liability, but where the main question is the amount of damages that shall be recovered. Where the important question to be decided by the jury is not so much the amount of damage, but the question of liability, then it should be the trial lawyer's desire to select men who are intelligent enough to be able to follow his theory of the case and to arrive at a favorable conclusion.

§ 224. Women jurors.

In those jurisdictions where women are accepted as jurors, most trial lawyers feel that they should be placed in the category of the emotional type of juror. That is, in all cases where the trial lawyer would seek the more emotional and sympathetic type of juror, he should also be willing to accept women jurors. Women jurors are considered as good jurors in that they usually pay more attention to the evidence, are serious, and strive to do their duty.

§ 225. Prior accidents.

It is always of the utmost importance in personal injury cases to examine the prospective jurors in reference to whether or not they or any members of their family or close friends have ever been involved in an accident, or whether or not they have ever sued or been sued as a result of an accident. From the viewpoint of the plaintiff, it would be harmful, of course, to have a man on the jury who had been previously sued as a result of some accident in which he had participated. On the other hand, it would be harmful from the viewpoint of the defendant to have a man sit on the jury who has sued for damages as a result of an accident, and who may not have recovered any damages as a result of that suit. It may be that some member of their family has been suing or has been sued as a result of an accident and that the results thereof may prejudice this prospective juror (either for or against you). It is, therefore, better policy to examine every juror in reference to prior accidents. It is always much better to have the defendant exhaust a challenge on some prospective juror who has sued as a result of some accident in which he had been involved rather than to neglect to ask a question in reference to prior accidents only to find that as a result of the defendant's examination the prospective juror had been sued in some prior accident and will probably be prejudiced. Ordinarily, it is too late to attempt to challenge a juror after he has been tendered to opponent for examination. Although it is within the discretion of the court to permit further examination and possibly to challenge such juror, it may prove to be very embarrassing if the court should refuse to grant such permission.

§ 226. One-man jury.

Care should be exercised in the selection of the jury to prevent the submission of the issues to a so-called "one-man jury." If a man is permitted to sit on the jury who is particularly experienced in that field of endeavor which is the basis of the law suit, all of the other jurors on the panel will naturally turn to this one man and will be governed mainly by his opinion as to who is right and who is wrong in the case. At first blush, it would seem preferable to have some man on the jury who would know all about the issues involved, but it is somewhat precarious when it is realized that there is the possibility of this one man disagreeing with the trial lawyer's theory of the case. His knowledge may be insufficient to permit him to grasp a contrary theory which is propounded by either the lawyer, the client, or his experts. The juror's experience or his reading may place him in a a position where he has arrived at a directly contrary conclusion and opinion to the one which the trial attorney is advancing. Having become friendly with the other jurors throughout the trial of the case and realizing his knowledge and experience in that particular field, the other jurors will naturally ask him for his opinion and his ideas and will accede to them in all probability. In this manner, it is possible for one man to decide the case. It would have been much better to have submitted the issues to a jury who had no knowledge of the particular subject and have them decide as between both the plaintiff and the defendant and their witnesses as to just who is right and who is wrong. Again it might seem preferable in a case involving the sale of office furniture to have another man on the jury in the same line of business. The lawyers would naturally ask him if he knew the parties involved, and he could probably truthfully answer that he did not. Yet being a competitor he may at some time have had a conversation with another competitor of the client who had reported to this prospective juror some derogatory report as to client's participation in some outside matter, and while this juror could truthfully say that he did not know client, yet his prejudice would be immediately aroused against the client by reason of what he had heard from the other competitor. This danger always exists and should be taken into consideration in the questioning of the prospective juror, and finally in determining whether or not it is wise to submit a case to a "*one-man jury.*" The tactics employed by some trial lawyers will sometimes place one in a position so embarrassing as to almost force him into a position where he is submitting the issues of the case to a one-man jury. For illustration, lawyers were engaged at one time in the trial of an occupational disease case involving carbon-tetrachloride poisoning, when one of the prospective jurors in answer to questions stated that he had made a study of carbon-tetrachloride. It became apparent immediately that the acceptance of this juror would probably result in a one-man jury, which was not desired by plaintiff. Counsel for the defendant thereupon openly and in a somewhat joking manner stated: "You're not afraid to leave him on the jury, are you? Let's leave him on so that he can follow this testimony." While counsel should not have made this remark, the making of it placed plaintiff in a position where if he excused the juror, it might have appeared to all the other jurors that plaintiff was afraid of his case and that he was trying to recover for something he was not entitled to. On the other hand, if left on the jury, his opinion on the subject might be different from plaintiff's and might have resulted in an unfavorable verdict. In a quandary plaintiff continued questioning and ascertained that he had at one time been employed in a certain large factory. One of plaintiff's experts who was to testify had also been employed at this large factory. Plaintiff knew that he was going to testify that this concern had employed all of the devices which plaintiff claimed the defendant in the present case had not employed, and that therefore the defendant was guilty of negligence in not having employed these so-called reasonable devices. With this additional fact in mind plaintiff's attorneys permitted themselves apparently to be placed in a position where they had to accept a one-man jury, since it was felt that this juror would accept as true testimony of plaintiff's experts as to what constituted reasonable devices which were utilized in a factory where both the juror and the expert had been employed.

§ 227. Study of law or medicine.

It is considered good policy to ask all jurors whether or not they have ever studied law. And in personal injury or medical and chemical cases all jurors should be asked whether or not they have ever studied medicine, or the particular subject involved in the case. It sometimes happens that a man who has studied law and is now in business is called as a juror, and with his *limited* knowledge of the law he is liable to come to a conclusion entirely different from *your* own, and the danger of the *"one-man jury"* will then become easily apparent. There are many disagreements as to what the law is between practicing attorneys, and the danger of such differences of opinion is enhanced many-fold in the case of the non-practicing attorney who has had limited connection with the law since his graduation from law school. This same thing, of course, is true on the part of the man who has studied medicine or the particular subject in discussion.

§ 228. Fairness.

It is, of course, good tactics to employ an attitude of fairness not only during the selection of the jury but throughout the entire trial. The greatest possible handicap under which any trial lawyer can labor would be the impression received on the part of the jury as to the unfairness of such trial lawyer. Any suggestion of unfairness will result in great harm to the cause of the client.

Should the occasion definitely show that a prospective juror can be successfully challenged for cause by opponent, it would be good policy to demonstrate one's fairness by stipulating that the juror may be excused by agreement of the parties. For instance, in larger communities where prospective jurors are usually excused because of their acquaintanceship with one of the parties to the law suit or to their attorneys in the case, it would be an evidence of fairness and good trial tactics to excuse such juror by agreement. These small gestures usually pay big dividends in the resulting good-will engendered in the trial lawyer's behalf on the part of the jury.

§ 229. Embarrassing prospective juror.

It is a common error and demonstrates bad trial tactics to embarrass any prospective juror or to ask him questions which would tend to make him appear ridiculous. Should the lawyer tactlessly commit this error, it would, of course, be foolhardy to permit such juror to remain to decide the case, for he would be definitely prejudiced against him. On the other hand, a great deal of harm may result even though he is excused from the panel, for some other juror on the panel may have become his friend and would naturally resent what has happened. It is bad policy to ask a question of a juror which would display to the world his ignorance. He will resent it, as would the others in the jury box.

§ 230. Testing juror's knowledge and education.

While one of the grounds of challenge for cause which will assist the trial lawyer in eliminating a prospective juror from the panel without resorting to a peremptory challenge is the lack or insufficiency of that juror's knowledge of the English language, and while some successful trial lawyers resort to this expediency on rare occasions and in emergencies, it should never become the practice of any trial attorney to utilize this privilege.

There is no more harmful method of embarrassing a prospective juror and of holding him up to apparent public ridicule than to demonstrate his lack of education and knowledge. Particularly is this true in those instances where the juror has already served as a juror in other cases with the members of the panel. They have probably all become very friendly during their past service together and, as a result, when one attorney or the other embarrasses or ridicules one of their number, he will succeed in arousing the resentment of the balance of the jury against the tactics of the lawyer who has apparently violated the proprieties of the occasion and has taken advantage of one of their new friends.

It can readily be appreciated that the attorney who starts his case in this manner will have erected an obstacle and a handicap that will require much effort to overcome.

Care should always be exercised in those communities where colored men are called for service as jurors. Some attorneys excuse colored jurors without regard to their qualifications. Some are intolerantly prejudiced and abruptly exercise their right of challenge. If it should happen that this prospective juror has already served on some case or other with the rest of the panel and they have come to respect his manner, or knowledge, a challenge openly made indicating that the colored man is being excused merely because of the attorney's prejudice will prove harmful even with those members of the panel who may be prejudiced themselves against others but whose prejudice against this one man has been allayed by reason of their mutual service.

§ 231. Technical terms.

The trial attorneys must ever be on the alert to see that the jurors understand all the terms and phrases used either by themselves or their witnesses during the selection of the jury as well as during the arguments and the testimony. No legal phrase or technical term should ever be used without restating the term or phrase or defining it immediately after its use. For instance, if during the selection of the jury the attorney uses a phrase like "preponderance of the evidence," he should immediately restate it to this effect: "Now, Mr. Jones, you understand, of course, that preponderance of the evidence merely means a greater weight of the evidence."

If it becomes necessary to use some medical term or to refer medically to some part of the anatomy, it should also be restated.

For illustration: Suppose it becomes necessary to inform the jury that the plaintiff sustained a fracture of the tibia. The attorney should immediately explain that the tibia is one of the bones in the leg and should also follow it up by indicating just where the bone is. Incidentally every medical expert in detailing to the jury the results of his examination should always be cautioned to restate the medical term in this way so that the jury at all times will know just what the witness is referring to.

§ 232. Manner.

All questions asked of any juror should be presented in the most friendly manner possible. It sometimes happens that the trial lawyer asks questions in a manner which irritates the prospective juror. For instance, in a case involving a railroad accident, the attorney may sometimes ask the juror—

"Q Do you ever ride in railroad trains?"

The attorney fails to appreciate the fact that almost everyone at some time or other has ridden in railroad trains, and, therefore, the better method would be to question him in this manner:

"Q Mr. Jones, of course you have ridden in railroad trains before, haven't you?"

In another instance a trial attorney asked a prospective juror this question:

"Q Do you know what a freight car looks like?"

The better method would have been:

"Q Mr. Johnson, you've seen a lot of freight cars in your day, haven't you, and you know just how they are made up generally, do you not?"

It is always better to phrase the question or statement to a juror as though he did know just what you wish him to know and is familiar with the object about which you are questioning him, even though he actually is not familiar with it. Questions and remarks which are prefaced with the statement "of course you understand, Mr. Jones," though he probably does not understand, compliments him to think that you believe that he does know and he is more apt to respond to your suggestions.

The phrases "as you know," "of course you understand" and "you realize" should be resorted to whenever possible in order to create good feeling.

It has been frequently stated that "to make friends we must be friendly ourselves." This is also true in the selection of the jury. If it is desired to create a friendly attitude on the part of the jury towards the lawyer, he must in the first instance show by his manner and questions a friendly feeling towards the juror. The more natural this friendly feeling on his part appears, the quicker and the greater the response will be on the part of the juror. It is, of course, unwise to carry this effort to such an extreme that the jury will feel that the lawyer is insincere.

One attorney who has had many years of success in the trial of personal injury cases, representing both the plaintiff and the defendant, recently made the suggestion that instead of asking the jury "By whom he is employed" to use the softer and more pleasing method of asking him, "With whom are you associated?" He found that this is an indirect soothing compliment to the prospective juror. However, on one occasion not long ago, a janitor was called as a prospective juror. The attorney asked the question of him as to whom he was associated with, and his only reply was "Huh?" Apparently this procedure is, as are all other suggestions contained herein, subject to exception and modification.

§ 233. Investigating jury.

In larger communities where the attorneys seldom know the members of the jury, and in large cities where there are many courts with many panels of jurors serving at the same time, first in one court room and then in another, it is always advisable to ascertain from the clerk of the court just what verdicts have been returned by the panel of jurors assigned to that court room, that is, whether they have been in favor of the plaintiff or the defendant, and just what types of cases were decided by them. With this information, the trial lawyer is in a better position to judge whether or not he desires the jurors who have been serving in that particular court room, and can exercise his judgment accordingly. If some of the jurors have come from another court room, it would be wise for the trial lawyer to have his associate step up to that court room and ascertain the information. If investigation discloses that they have decided cases of a similar nature, he will make inquiry as to whether or not anything occurred during the trial of the similar case which would tend to prejudice them one way or another in the present case. The natural response will be that nothing had occurred to prejudice them, but if the investigation has been made, he should then be in a position to determine whether or not they will make desirable jurors in the case on trial.

§ 234. Consult with client.

A good many writers on the subject of trial practice, as well as many successful trial lawyers, state that it is the duty and responsibility of the trial lawyer to determine whether or not a jury is satisfactory, and while this is true, yet good business tactics suggest that the trial lawyer consult with his client as to whether or not the jurors examined are satisfactory to him. It may be that during the course of the examination the client has noticed some facial expression on the part of the juror being examined which the attorney has failed to notice, or client may have noticed during the examination of a juror something which would tend to make him feel that the juror now being examined might be prejudiced against him, and, therefore, he does not feel quite satisfied to leave such prospective juror in the panel. In view of the fact that there are no set rules which can definitely point out to the trial attorney who is a good or a bad juror, and in view of the fact that there is always a desire for future business from the same client, it would seem to be good policy to accede to client's wishes in excusing certain jurors, particularly when there are still a number of challenges unexhausted. Should the lawyer fail to accede to his client's wishes in this respect, and if perchance there should happen to be an unfavorable verdict from the jury, the client will almost always feel that it was due to the one or two jurors to whom he took exception. It would seem to be the best plan to resolve all doubts in favor of the client.

A method sometimes employed by the trial lawyers in place of open consultation in front of the jury is to pre-arrange with client to signal in some manner that he does not desire a juror while the examination is being conducted. This can be done with a little pressure of the hand on the back of the attorney, a touch of the foot, or as is sometimes done by having client write down his objections or the reasons therefor on a pad of paper usually supplied for this purpose. Client should hand over the note at the time of the examination or immediately thereafter in such a way that the jury will not notice it. Incidentally, this pad should be provided for client's use throughout the entire trial so that he will not be whispering in the attorney's ear during the examination of the witnesses and thus divert his train of thought or prevent him from hearing just what is going on.

§ 235. Excusing jurors.

Challenging or excusing a juror should be accomplished in a quiet, dignified manner in the hope of not arousing the resentment of any other member of the jury or any friend that the excused juror may still have on the panel. The recommended procedure is not to excuse the juror at the time nor at the conclusion of the examination of him unless he is the last man to be examined. The better method is to go on to the next one or two jurors, and after having examined them, to quietly state to the court, "If the Court please, we will excuse Mr. Jones." By employing this method the rest of the jurors will probably have forgotten most of the questions which have been put to the juror to be excused, and with this casual method of challenging him, he will be on the way out of the jury box before they realize just what has happened, and with a minimum of ill feeling. When representing a corporation, many attorneys employ this method of excusing a juror: "If the court please, the defendant (or plaintiff) will excuse Mr. Jones." The request to excuse a juror or challenge should be made to the court and never to the juror himself. After all the court is the only one who has the power to excuse the juror, and the trial attorney must ever be alert not to encroach on the province of the court.

A nice way to excuse a juror whose answers are all 100% but who is not wanted is as follows:

"Q You live at 4758 Langley Ave.?

A Yes.

Q You have lived there quite a while, haven't you?

A Yes.

Q You know quite a lot of people in that neighborhood, don't you?

A Yes.

Q If the Court please, I believe we will excuse Mr. Jones." *

It sometimes happens that a juror in answering the question as to what his name is answers in an inaudible tone of voice some foreign sounding name which the attorney is unable to understand. The trial attorney sometimes then asks "What's the name?" or tells him he "didn't quite understand." The better and less irritating procedure would be to ask him just how he spells the last name.

§ 236. Recognizing prejudices and natural sympathies.

Many of our leading authors on the subject of trial practice call attention to the meaningless questions which the average trial lawyer asks the prospective juror. For instance, a question is usually put to the juror as to whether or not he would be prejudiced against the defendant because of the fact that the defendant is a corporation and the plaintiff is an individual. Invariably the answer from the juror is that he will not be prejudiced. Yet everyone knows that when that same juror goes to the jury room to deliberate upon the issues of the case that he will probably be the first one to vote in favor of a large-sized verdict for the plaintiff because of the fact

* Suggested by Abe R. Peterson.

that the defendant being a big corporation can well afford to pay five or ten thousand dollars, while the poor injured plaintiff requires a lot of help for the rest of his life, even though under the law there may be a serious question as to the liability of the defendant. It would seem to be better procedure to recognize the existence of these natural sympathies on the part of the juror for the adverse party and to put the question in this manner: "Mr. Jones, you'll try not to allow your natural sympathies for the plaintiff to influence your verdict against the defendant just because the defendant is a corporation, won't you?" If this method is utilized a number of times during the examination of the prospective jurors, it may result in one or more of the jurors championing the attorney's cause at least to the extent of trying to eliminate sympathy and prejudice. This, coupled with a proper instruction given by the court, as to sympathy and prejudice will be much more helpful than the old method of asking them whether or not they will be prejudiced.

§ 237. Accepting juror without questioning.

Some trial attorneys without fully appreciating the importance of examining each and every juror before accepting the jury, and feeling confident that they have an easy case to win, have gotten into the habit of stating to the court in the presence of the jury that "They will accept the first twelve jurors." To them this is an indication to the jury of confidence in their case and of confidence in the jury. They fail to realize that one unfriendly, unfavorable juror will be sufficient to prevent getting a favorable verdict. The lawyer has no means of knowing what nationalities, what creeds, what religions, what types of jurors, what businesses they are in, whether competitive with client or not, or any of the numerous things that may prejudice the jury against him. This practice, therefore, should never be followed. On the other hand, if these tactics are pursued by the trial lawyer's opponent and he represents the defendant, the announcement by the plaintiff's attorney that he will accept the first twelve jurors without questioning will tend to place him in an embarrassing position. If he does not follow suit and accept the twelve without questioning it may tend to show that he does not trust the jury or that he has something to be afraid of in the case.

A good method of relieving this situation is to state to the court, "there is no doubt but what the jury will be acceptable, but I would like to have the opportunity of getting their names and addresses just merely to get acquainted and also that my client may have some idea as to just who is on the jury." Then care, of course, should be used in excusing or challenging any of the members of this particular panel, but at least the lawyer will be in a position to know just who they are and as to whether or not he will want to excuse anyone.

When the fact is recalled that the qualification and selection of the jury is the attorney's only real chance to get acquainted and to get friendly with the jury, the opportunity to examine them should never be neglected. It is his duty to sell his client's cause to the jury as well as to sell himself, and the more he can talk with each juror in a friendly manner, the more friendly the juror will tend to be. This does not mean, however, that the examination of the juror should be unduly drawn out for both the judge and jury may become impatient and irritated and the extended examination may result in more harm than good.

§ 238. Brilliancy should not be overly displayed.

Some lawyers are so imbued with an exaggerated opinion of their ability as trial lawyers that they cannot seem to resist the temptation to display their brilliancy before the court, the jury and the spectators. Their main objective seems to be to "show-up" their opponent's lack of knowledge of the art of trying cases. While they may succeed in impressing the jury with their outstanding performance and ability, this procedure usually results in creating sympathy for the opponent's client. The jury begins to feel that they ought to help the adverse party because of his apparently poor selection of counsel. Their sympathies become aroused in favor of the supposed "under-dog" and result naturally in one of those verdicts for which outsiders seem unable to account. The egotistical lawyer of the supposed great ability is dumfounded and explains away the unfavorable verdict by blaming the ignorance of the jury. To him it merely proves the saying "that you never can tell what a jury will do." The real blame, in so far as the interests of the client are concerned, lies in the lawyer's failure to realize the psychological reactions of the jury to his "playing to the gallery."

The truth of this may be illustrated by the following article:

Beverly Smith in the American Magazine article entitled "Gentlemen of the Jury" tells of the question which was asked of the clerk of the court who had more than fifty years experience with juries.

"What is the mysterious and powerful influence," I asked him, "which makes juries bring in bad verdicts?"

He looked at me with his bland, wide-open blue eyes.

"Lawyers," he said.

"Years of experience in the courtroom have convinced me that he is right. The greatest single mistake of jurors is to take sides for or against the *lawyers* rather than for or against the *evidence* which the lawyers adduce. The juror seated in the box is like a spectator at a play. And the lawyers are the leading actors on the stage. They open the performance with their speeches. They dominate the witnesses. They provide the comedy and the heroics. They are men of strong personality, overshadowing the dry details of confused testimony.

"It takes a juror of extraordinary mental strength and detachment to see through the lawyers to the evidence. The natural human tendency is to like one lawyer better than the other. As the trial progresses, all that he says seems right and all that his opponent says seems wrong. Even veteran judges have admitted to me that they are caught in the same thrall.

" 'But a sensible man,' you say, 'can see through these smooth lawyers.'

"I have a very sensible friend. College graduate, business manager of a large publishing house, widely traveled, widely read, a man of the world. Two months ago he was one of a jury which tried an important damage suit. I happened to know a good deal about the case and was astounded when the jury brought in a verdict for the plaintiff. When I saw my friend, I asked him how come?

" 'Well,' he explained, 'this lawyer the plaintiff had was an awfully stupid little chap. Amiable, likable, and all that, you understand, but always blundering at the crucial moment.

The lawyer for the defense was a whiz. A big, handsome fellow, eloquent, suave, brilliant. But we saw through him. It was a pretty intelligent jury, if I do say so myself. We got together and decided we ought to help the dumb little chap out. We gave him the verdict.'

"A great light dawned on me.

"'I see,' I said. 'And do you happen to know that the dumb little chap's fees average $200,000 a year? And that the handsome, brilliant chap is lucky if he makes a tenth that much?'

"My friend was amazed.

"'Why? How can that be?' he asked.

"'I've never heard a better explanation than the one you've just given,' I said.

"They have a right to challenge you 'for cause'—that is, because of legal ineligibility."

§ 239. Use of the word "please."

After many years of observation, one must come to the conclusion that it is only the truly successful trial lawyer who really appreciates the importance of acting the part of a gentleman before juries during the trial of cases. To many young attorneys, the art of being a gentleman seems entirely unknown. At least they give every appearance of this being true. Some men, who take pains to appear at their best socially seem to relax their every effort in this regard when they step into the court room to try a case. If being a gentleman is important socially, it is of equal or greater importance in the court room.

Both the court and the jury always react favorably to the pleasing gentlemanly lawyer, especially when the opponent is a loud, boorish, snarling, nasty type, apparently lacking in breeding and honorableness.

The word "please" should be frequently used. This does not mean that the trial attorney should resort to insincere fawning, but a dignified (not too stiff) gentlemanly and friendly attitude should be maintained.

In the selection and qualification of the jury, a courteous request of the prospective juror as to his name, coupled with the word "please" is a great deal better than a gruff, curt demand that the juror state his name.

The trial attorney should always couple this request with an indication by a nod or pointing with a finger to the juror he wishes to interrogate. This will save some embarrassment as it frequently happens that the jurors are unable to determine just who the attorney desires to question first. This is particularly true where the trial attorney wears glasses and due to the reflection of the glasses the jurors are unable to see clearly at whom the attorney is looking.

Sometimes when the juror does not speak clearly or loudly enough to be heard, the attorney may explain that because of the position of the jurors seated against a wall, it is much easier for the jury to hear the lawyer since the sound of his voice has only a short distance to carry and is stopped by the wall while the juror's voice just carries right out into the court room and, therefore, makes it harder for the lawyer to hear. In other words, this is just another illustration of the trial lawyer's assuming the blame in a gentlemanly way rather than taking the risk of arousing a juror's resentment.

The lawyer should never hesitate to use the words "thank you" wherever called for. If the trial attorney in court will adopt the same manners he uses to impress a new acquaintance or prospective friend he will have gone a long way toward winning his client's case.

Some lawyers ask questions of a prospective juror in a tone of voice and manner which indicate that they do not believe what the juror is telling them. Any indication of a lack of confidence in the statements of a prospective juror will harm the trial attorney immeasurably. Resorting to sarcasm or trying to be funny by making a pun out of some juror's name will also re-act unfavorably. Courtesy should be the watchword and guide throughout the trial of all cases.

§ 240. Stress the law.

Where one represents a defendant or a plaintiff where the defense or basis of claim is a legally technical one, it is always good policy to get the prospective juror to commit himself to the proposition that he will follow the law as given to him by the Court in the instructions. In most instances where the defense relied upon is purely legal and technical and devoid of emotional appeal, the jurors should be interrogated and committed to the proposition that they will follow the law and enforce it as given in the instructions even though that law is contrary to their own ideas on the subject, and contrary to their conception of what the law is or should be.

Their duty as citizens should be indirectly emphasized to accept the law as made for them by their representatives in the legislature and to abide by the laws until changed.

Some lawyers in qualifying a juror frequently ask the juror "if he will take the law from the Court or follow his own conception of the law if his idea is different from that given by the court." Some jurors answer that they will follow their own conception of the law and are considerably embarrassed when the attorney then tells them they must follow the law given by the court or be challenged for cause. This procedure, whether consciously or unconsciously, will arouse the juror's resentment as he will feel that the lawyer has deliberately led him into a trap in order to "make a fool out of him." On the other hand this reply might indicate unruly and radical tendencies on the part of the juror.

The better procedure would be to explain to the prospective juror, "It is the duty of all citizens to abide by the law. We do not make the laws, but the laws are made for us by our representatives in the legislature. It is, therefore, our duty to follow the law even though we feel that the law should be to the contrary. If accepted as a juror, you will not hesitate to follow the law as given to you by His Honor in the instructions will you? Even though your idea of the law is entirely different from that given you in the instructions"?

When this method is followed, any fair-minded juror will appreciate his duty and be more willing to abide by it.

If the statute of limitations or some such defense is relied upon, a short statement as to the reasonableness of such a statute should be made known to the jury—perhaps something to the effect that law and justice abhor stale claims; that the statute of limitations merely means that a claim is so old that it has become outlawed. These few words, plus a statement that old claims are barred, because witnesses sometimes die or disappear or records are destroyed after a reasonable length of time, and therefore the law says that if one wants to sue in this class of case he must do so before five years, will give the juror the proper understanding of the statute.

When stating the law, the trial lawyer should always have an exact copy of the instruction in his hand so as to state the law completely and correctly. Objections by opponent on the ground of an improper statement of the law which are sustained several times during the selection of the jury will result in a loss of "caste" before the jury. It is but a simple precaution for the attorney to provide himself with an instruction which properly and fully states the law applicable.

§ 241. Preventing statements on the law.

Some trial lawyers in an effort to prevent their opponents from continually stating their conception of the law call the Court's attention directly or indirectly to the fact that opponent is seeking to invade the province of the Court. Since some judges are "jealous" of the fact that it is their sole prerogative to instruct the jury as to the law in the case, it seems to require but a word or two to call the Court's attention to the so-called "indiscretion" of opponent, in this manner: "If the Court please: It seems to me that your Honor is the one to instruct the jury as to the law in this case and not Counsel." The Court usually replies, "Yes, counsel, the Court will instruct the jury as to the law at the proper time."

§ 242. Plaintiff's attorney should talk of damages.

During the selection of the jury, the plaintiff's attorney should not hesitate to inform the prospective jurors that his client is seeking damages. The plaintiff's right to damages, as well as an indication that he is suing for a substantial amount based upon permanent injuries (in a personal injury case) should be stated. Direct and indirect reference may be made to the type of injury sustained.

Illustration

Q Now, Mr. Jones, you do not have any prejudice against a man who is suing for damages for another's negligence which results in the loss of a leg, do you? or

Q Have you any quarrel with the law which permits a person to sue for legitimate compensation for the loss of a limb occasioned by the negligence of another? or

Q Mr. Jones, if we prove our case as required by law and under the instructions of the court, you will not hesitate to do your duty as a juror by bringing in a verdict in our favor for whatever compensation we prove this man is entitled to for the loss of his leg, will you?

No hesitancy should ever be shown on the part of the plaintiff's attorney in letting the jury know that he and his client expect the jury to return a substantial verdict in their favor.

§ 243. Watch number of challenges.

A most important and worth-while precaution on the part of an attorney qualifying a jury is to remember and to be able always to tell just how many peremptory challenges he has exhausted. Every trial lawyer should adopt some method of keeping count of his challenges. Some have a slip of paper numbered one to five or six or ten, whatever the number of challenges permitted by the local statute. As each challenge is utilized, they run a line through the next number. For example, as the first challenge is used they strike off number two with a diagonal line (/). They also keep a list to account for the number of challenges used by the opponent.

Another method which may be followed where the trial lawyer has adopted the policy of making a diagram for the jury, as heretofore suggested, is to indicate on the diagram the number of challenges in this way:

	P # 3			P # 2	
	P # 1		D #1		D # 2

This clearly indicates which juror was challenged and by whom. Writing down the number will constantly remind the attorney as to how many challenges have been exhausted both by himself and by his opponent.

The importance of keeping count of the challenges used may be illustrated in the experience of one lawyer who was selecting a jury in a large mid-western city. It also illustrates what not to do as to manner of interrogating a prospective juror.

This attorney was endeavoring to get the prospective juror to understand a certain question which he was propounding. The young man did not seem to clearly know himself the propositions of law which he was trying to explain. Finally he seemed to lose his temper and he almost shouted at the juror the following question:

Q Do you get what I'm driving at?

A (The juror) No, I don't.

Counsel: All right, I'll excuse you.

Opponent: I'm sorry, but you have exhausted all of your challenges.

One can well imagine the predicament of this young lawyer with the prospect of having on the jury a juror whom he had quite obviously offended, embarrassed, and ridiculed. Luckily for the lawyer, his opponent was a veteran at the bar who took this opportunity of showing his fairness by stating that he would permit the lawyer to excuse the juror if he so desired, even though his challenges were exhausted. However, the young lawyer had irretrievably harmed himself before the rest of the jurors by his irritating, ungentlemanly questioning.

It has been suggested that it is always advisable for the plaintiff's attorney to hold two challenges in reserve while the defendant's attorney should hold one challenge in reserve.

§ 244. Prepare questions in advance.

It is recommended that the trial lawyer block out or prepare the questions he expects to ask the jurors during their selection and qualification before the trial commences.

The experienced trial lawyer will require no more than a word to remind him of the question he wishes to ask.

The young trial lawyer, however, should write out the questions almost verbatim until he has them practically memorized. It is sometimes pitiful to watch a young lawyer flounder around in an effort to put questions in a proper form to the prospective juror. As he realizes that the question is not in proper form, his natural nervousness increases until he can hardly ask any question.

The questions should be written out where the law involved is to be included in such question. If the question is not actually written out a copy of the instruction intended to be given should be in the hands of the trial attorney while he is framing the question as heretofore suggested.

§ 245. Watch jurors as they take seats.

It is always good policy for the trial attorney to closely observe each prospective juror as he walks to his seat in the jury box. The manner and gait of each one should be noted. The aggressive and positive walk of some, the slouched, sliding movement of others, their apparently interested or disinterested manner should all be looked for and considered in trying to determine those desired. The walk and posture of most men indicate their character.

It is suggested that all prospective jurors be viewed in this way to determine those who are crippled or deformed.

One defense lawyer in a personal injury case who failed to note the prospective jurors as they took their seats was shocked to learn at the first recess period that he had accepted as a juror a man who had an artificial limb in a case where another man was suing for $50,000.00 damages as a result of being forced to have a leg amputated which had been hurt in an automobile collision.

Some attorneys hesitate to accept crippled or deformed men on their juries as they claim that this type of juror is ''soured'' on the world.

§ 246. Street-car motormen as jurors.

Some attorneys for the plaintiff in automobile accident cases in the larger cities have accepted street car motormen to serve as jurors in their cases. Others fully and completely examine such prospective jurors and then challenge them because they seem to come to the conclusion finally that they do not care to accept them.

A certain judge who had been a successful trial lawyer prior to his elevation to the bench once decried the practice of accepting motormen as jurors. He claimed that this procedure should not be followed. He had found from years of experience that street car motormen make poor jurors for the plaintiffs in automobile cases. In most instances of automobile collision cases he even felt that street car motormen are mostly undesirable even for the defendants. His thought was that motormen have had such unsatisfactory experience with motorists that they will and do condemn all motorists. As a rule, motormen feel that all motorists "hog the road," violate all the rules of traffic, and that they are responsible for all accidents.

There is a great deal of common sense in this observation and all trial lawyers would do well to consider it seriously.

He further suggests that street car motormen should be excused without any detailed examination for fear of indicating to the balance of the jury that this class of juror is not desired.

§ 247. Where judge questions jury.

In some jurisdictions, it is now the practice for the trial judge to ask the jury all the general qualifying questions. This practice has arisen in the interests of facilitating the trial of cases. It saves time from the view-point of the court. However, from the view-point of the trial attorney, it takes away the one real opportunity he has of getting acquainted with the juror and more particularly the juror's opportunity of getting acquainted with the lawyers in the case.

In some instances where this practice prevails, the judge may ask all of the preliminary and general questions and then permit the attorneys to ask some additional questions. The trial lawyer should always avail himself of this opportunity. He should have noted all questions he desires to ask on a slip of paper. The court will not permit the attorneys to ask any question which has already been answered by the jurors.

In those jurisdictions where the judge asks all of the questions, but, at the conclusion, permits the attorneys to suggest further questions to be asked, the suggestions are made in the following form: "Will your Honor please ask Mr. Jones how long he has been employed by Blank & Co. and also what his business was prior to his association with Blank & Co.?"

When this procedure is followed most judges will permit all the additional questions the trial lawyers wish to have answered.

In some jurisdictions where the judge asks all the questions, as many as fifteen to twenty-five jurors are examined, then a recess is declared to permit the attorneys to determine just which jurors they desire to challenge. All this occurs outside of the presence of the jury. The jurors have no idea which lawyer has challenged them and the trial proceeds with the twelve acceptable jurors remaining.

This procedure is much to be desired, especially in the smaller communities. It is also worth-while in the larger cities from the view-point of the trial lawyer. It eliminates to a great extent the possibility of antagonizing some member or members of the jury remaining on the panel. It could always be used in those instances where the jury is selected in panels of twelve.

§ 248. **Challenges after tender or acceptance.**

In most jurisdictions it is permissible in the discretion of the court to challenge a juror after he has been tendered to the opponent for examination. This is also true in the discretion of the court even after the juror has been accepted, but not yet sworn to try the issues. However, most judges frown upon the practice. It is always bad policy to rely on the hope that the judge will exercise his discretion in favor of the "challenger." All challenges should be made before the juror is tendered if possible.

In some instances, upon good cause shown, the court may permit a challenge even after the jury is sworn to try the issues. These occasions are rare. It must be upon a showing that considerable harm may result unless the right to exercise the challenge is allowed. Incidentally this attempted challenge should be made outside the presence of the jury. Precaution should be taken that no member of the jury receives the least intimation of the intention to make the motion to challenge so that ill-feeling may not be aroused in the event that the judge denies the motion.

§ 249. **Do not question all jurors in detail.**

The fear of tiring and boring all jurors should be sufficient to deter the desire of the trial lawyer to examine each juror by asking each one every possible question he can recollect. It is always poor policy to subject each and every juror to the same detailed questioning which is usually reserved only for the first or second prospective jurors. It is through the questioning of the first, second, or third jurors that the trial lawyer is able to make his "points" and impressions. After he has conveyed to the juror his idea of the case and the duty of the jurors, only the most important questions should be submitted to the rest of the jurors. Sometimes it is advisable to plan to ask a number of general questions of one juror and use others on the next juror. In this way all questions may be utilized.

Some lawyers follow the method of asking the remaining jurors some question which will require the jurors to recall all of the other questions, but permits them to be disposed of by answering one question to this effect:

"Q Mr. Jones, you heard all of the questions which I asked the other jurors and you heard the answers that they gave. Now if I should ask you the same questions would your answers be substantially the same?"

However, it is probably better policy to restate some of the general questions in other language and use several for each juror until the entire list has been utilized.

§ 250. Objections.

In those instances where the trial lawyer feels that in order to maintain his defense, it will be necessary for him to interpose numerous objections throughout the trial, he should take some steps during the examination of the jury to eliminate the natural prejudice of the jury against "objecting lawyers," if possible. It is generally known that most jurors view the "objecting lawyer" with suspicion. They feel that he is attempting to keep the true facts from them and that he is relying mainly upon technicalities to keep all of the evidence away from the jury. To their mind the objections are resorted to mainly for the purpose of withholding information. In order to overcome this condition the following questions and explanations have been evolved:

Q Now, Mr. Jones, you understand, of course, that cases are tried and governed by rules just as is everything else in life, do you not?

A Yes.

Q You also understand do you not, that just as all sports have their rules as to what is fair, that is also true as far as the trials of cases are concerned?

A Yes.

Q Now, if it should become necessary for either the attorney for the plaintiff or myself to make objections to certain evidence offered, you will understand, will you not, that we, by objecting, feel that the evidence that is being offered is not proper according to the rules, and that it is our duty to our client to object. The judge will either sustain or overrule the objection. If he sustains the objection he agrees that the evidence is not being offered according to the rules. If he overrules the objection it means that he feels that the evidence is proper and is being offered according to the rules. If either one of us should make such objections during the trial of this case, you will understand, will you not, that we are just trying to keep what we consider improper evidence out of the case, and you won't hold that against either one of us, will you?

With an explanation similar to this it is quite apparent that a good deal of the suspicion of the jurors will be eliminated in so far as objections are concerned.

§ 251. Opening remarks and conclusion.

It is always advisable for the trial lawyer representing the plaintiff to adopt some particular method of informing the jury in a few words as to the type of law-suit they may be called upon to decide and to let them know the names of the parties involved, as well as the names of the attorneys. The statement as to the issues involved must be very general and very brief. No detail should be given as to what the proof will be as that should be reserved for the opening statement.

The opening remarks are usually made by the attorney for the plaintiff. He gives a friendly salutation to the court upon rising and then stands before the prospective jury. The opening remarks usually take but a moment or two. Many attorneys fail to adopt a method that will result in a *graceful conclusion* and which will permit them to return to their seats without an awkward pause.

In those jurisdictions where the attorneys are permitted to question the jury the opening remarks and the conclusion may be as follows:

"If the Court please (wait for the judge to acknowledge greeting) and gentlemen of the jury: At this time I would like to briefly tell you in a general way just what this case is about. This is a suit instituted by Henry Thompson, the plaintiff, who sits at the table to my left. He is suing Edward

Simmons, the defendant, who sits on the right-hand side of the table in the second chair. The defendant is represented by the firm of Rand, Walker and Hurley, attorneys. Mr. John Hurley of that firm is here representing the defendant. He is the gentleman sitting in the chair in front of the defendant. My name is Edward Smith and I represent the plaintiff, Henry Thompson. Mr. Thompson is suing the defendant for personal injuries he sustained in an automobile collision which took place at the intersection of Jones and 7th Streets. We are charging that Henry Thompson sustained permanent injuries in this collision which resulted from the negligence of the defendant.

(Here the attorney would start backing into his chair, while he continues to say the following:) At this time both the attorney for the defendant and I will ask you a few questions in reference to your acquaintanceship with either of the parties to this law suit or with their attorneys. (By this time the attorney should have returned to his seat and taken up his trial book or memorandum pad, prepared to question the first juror.) He will indicate with his index finger the juror whom he wishes to question and continue as follows:

Counsel: Q. The first gentleman, (indicating) may I have your name please?

§ 252. List of questions to jury—For the plaintiff.

1. The first gentleman (indicating) may I have your name, please?
2. Will you spell it, please? (Where the name is a difficult one.)
3. And what is your address?
4. What is your business or profession, Mr. Jones?
5. Are you in business for yourself?
6. How long has that been your business?
7. (If employed) With whom are you associated? (or by whom are you employed?)

7a. In what line of business is the White Co.?

8. In what capacity are you employed by them?
9. How long have you been employed by the White Co.?
10. What was your business before you went with the White Co.?

11. With what firm were you connected?
12. In what line of business are they?
13. In what capacity were you connected with them?
14. Are you a married man, Mr. Jones? (Where it is felt that this is worth knowing).
15. Any family?
16. About how old a man are you, Mr. Jones?
17. Have you ever been in the real estate business (or whatever line the adverse party is engaged in)?
18. Mr. Jones, do you know any of the parties involved in this case?
19. Either, the plaintiff, Mr. Henry Smith, the defendant, Edward Thompson, Mr. James Simpson, the attorney for Mr. Thompson or any member of his firm, which is Banks, Ryan & Thompson, or do you know me or any member of my firm? As you know, my name is Robert Barnes and the name of my firm is Hawks, Barnes and Simons.
20. Have you ever heard of this case before?
21. Has anyone attempted to discuss it in your presence?
22. Have you ever been involved in a similar law-suit either as a party or as a witness?
23. Is there anything about the nature of this case or about the parties involved that would make you hesitate to sit on this jury?
24. Mr. Jones, have you any prejudice against this particular type of case?
25. This is your first week of service as a juror is it not?
26. Have you ever served as a juror before this term of court?
27. Have you acted as juror before in a similar case?
28. Did anything occur during the trial of that case which would tend to prejudice you in this matter?
29. You understand, of course, Mr. Jones, that each case must be decided on its own facts and according to the law, do you not?
30. Have you any quarrel with any of the rules of law that were given to you in that previous case?

Q I take it then, Mr. Jones, that you are familiar with most of the rules that govern the trial of cases and that they were all explained to you?

If juror has not served before:

Q Mr. Jones, you will probably hear something said about the burden of proof and the preponderance of evidence. As you no doubt know the plaintiff must prove his case by a preponderance of the evidence which *merely* means that we must prove our case by the greater weight of the evidence and that it is our duty to prove the defendant guilty as we charge in our complaint. Now, if we do so prove the defendant guilty as required by law, you won't hesitate to return a verdict in our favor, will you?

(Note: This is practically the only time that the plaintiff's attorney mentions preponderance of the evidence and burden of proof. Any repetition must come from the defendant's counsel. If defendant's counsel alludes to it as he should, plaintiff's attorney proceeds to reply during his questioning of a subsequent juror to the effect that he understands, of course, that preponderance *merely* means the greater weight of the evidence.)

If juror has only served in Criminal Court:

Q You understand, of course, Mr. Jones, the difference in the requirements as to proof. In a civil case such as we have here, the plaintiff must prove his case by a preponderance of the evidence, which merely means a greater weight of the evidence. In a criminal case, the State must prove its case beyond a reasonable doubt which is a far greater degree of proof. However, you will only require us to prove our case by a preponderance of the evidence, will you not, Mr. Jones?

In automobile accident case.

Q Do you own an automobile?

Q Do you drive or have you ever driven an automobile?

Q Have you ever been involved in an accident?

Q Has anyone ever made a claim against you as a result of an accident?

Q Were you ever sued as a result of an accident?

Q Has any member of your family or close friend been involved in an automobile accident case?

Q Or any accident case?

If juror states he was in an accident ask this further question:

Q Were you a claimant or was the claim made against you?

(If he answers that he was the claimant the plaintiff's attorney should not question him any further. If he states that the claim was made against him, he should be further interrogated about the accident.)

Q Will you just tell us briefly, Mr. Jones, what the circumstances of your accident were?

(If he states the type of accident was something entirely different from that involved in this case, make light of it and say "That is an entirely different situation. Of course, that would have nothing to do with this case.")

Q Mr. Jones, was that case tried or was it disposed of in some other way?

To find out if a juror is prejudiced against women auto drivers:

Q Do you have an automobile?

A Yes.

Q Does your wife drive it?

A Yes.

Q Then I suppose you have no prejudice against women driving do you?

But if a man is married, has an auto, and his wife doesn't drive you want to know why:

Q Is it because of any prejudice on your part that your wife doesn't drive?

Counsel:

Q Now, Mr. Jones, you do not have any prejudice against a man who is suing for damages for negligence which results in the loss of a leg, do you? or

Q Have you any quarrel with the law which permits a person to sue for legitimate compensation for the loss of a limb occasioned by the negligence of another? or

Q Mr. Jones, if we prove our case as required by law as given in the instructions of the Court, you will not hesitate to do your duty as a juror by bringing in a verdict in our favor for whatever compensation the evidence shows this man is entitled to for the loss of his leg, will you?

Q Mr. Jones, do you know of any reason that I have not asked you about why you could not be a fair and impartial juror for both sides in this case?

Q You understand, do you not, that that is what *both* counsel for the defendant and myself are seeking—twelve fair and impartial jurors to decide this case.

Q And you feel, Mr. Jones, that you can give both sides in this case a square deal, do you not?

A Yes.

Q I believe you can also. We will tender the jury.

§ 253. — For the defendant.

Q Mr. Jones, I believe you said that you were in the retail grocery business on Fourth Avenue for the past ten years, did you not?

(Note: This will show that you took sufficient pains to remember the juror's name and history.)

Q Do you know either the plaintiff or his attorneys?

Q Mr. Jones, do you have any feeling against my client just because he has been sued in this case?

Q As you sit there now, do you have any feeling that this defendant is the sole and only cause of this accident or he would not have this suit filed against him, Mr. Jones?

Q You realize, of course, Mr. Jones, that all anyone has to do to file a suit is to hand the papers to the clerk, pay the necessary filing fees and then the other man has to come into court and defend the case whether he is guilty or not. You do not have any prejudice against a man who is forced to come into court and defend himself, do you?

Q You do not feel, Mr. Jones, as you sit there that just because we have been sued in this case that we are liable, do you?

Q In other words, Mr. Jones, unless the plaintiff offers sufficient evidence under the law to show that he is entitled to recover in this case by a preponderance of the evidence, you will not return a verdict in his favor, will you?

Q You understand, Mr. Jones, do you not, that the provision of the law requiring the plaintiff to prove his case by a preponderance of the evidence is a substantial one and is not merely a matter of words or formality.

Q Mr. Jones, will you make the plaintiff prove his case by a preponderance of the evidence?

Q If the plaintiff fails to prove his case by a preponderance of the evidence you won't hesitate to do your duty by returning a verdict in our favor, will you?

Q In other words, Mr. Jones, you will make the plaintiff prove everything that the law requires him to prove, will you not?

Q I take it, Mr. Jones, that you understand that it is not our duty to prove that we are not guilty (or not liable) in this case, but that it is the plaintiff's *duty* to prove *us guilty.*

Q Mr. Jones, will you make the plaintiff prove us guilty as required by law?

Q In other words, Mr. Jones, the burden of proof in this case is on the plaintiff and you will make him assume that burden, will you not?

Q Now, Mr. Jones, our position in this case is that this accident happened through the plaintiff's own fault and negligence; that the plaintiff himself is to blame for what happened and not the defendant. In law that is known as the defense of contributory negligence, that is, that a person cannot recover because he himself was negligent and contributed to the accident. Now, Mr. Jones, if the Court should instruct you that contributory negligence where shown by the evidence is a good defense, will you follow and apply that law?

Q I take it, Mr. Jones, that as a good citizen you will follow the law as given you by the court in its instructions, will you not?

Q Of course you realize that it is our duty as citizens to follow the law even though our conception of what it ought to be differs from what it actually is, do you not?

Q And you will follow that law in spite of any sympathy you might feel for either of the parties here, won't you?

Q Of course, you know, Mr. Jones, that sympathy has no place in the trial of a case, do you not?

Q And neither has prejudice?

Q Now Mr. Jones, will you try to prevent any sympathy you might feel for the plaintiff from interfering with your returning a just verdict based solely and wholly on the law and the evidence in the case?

Q Of course, we realize, Mr. Jones, that it is natural for all of us to sympathize with any man who has been injured, but you would not deliberately take money from us and turn it over to the plaintiff just because you might have a feeling of sympathy for him, would you?

Q Mr. Jones, will you try to keep your feelings of sympathy from preventing you from doing your duty as a citizen and as a juror, and will you only return a verdict based on the law and the evidence that will meet with the approval of your conscience.

Q In this case, Mr. Jones, the plaintiff has the privilege of putting on his witness first; after he gets through, if we desire to do so, we have the right to put on our witnesses. Naturally while the plaintiff is putting on his witnesses we will not be able to put on ours. Will you try to keep in mind that we expect to put on witnesses to refute all that the plaintiff attempts to prove during his case. In other words, will you try to keep a clear open mind until you have heard all of our witnesses also, before you make up your mind as to who is right and who is wrong.

Q I take it, Mr. Jones, that you realize that there are always two sides to every question?

Q Mr. Jones, will you give due consideration to any defense which the court permits us to offer?

Q Mr. Jones, have you ever been involved in an accident case before, either as a party or as a witness?

Q Have you ever been hurt in any accident?

Q Has any member of your family or close friend ever been injured?

Q Have you ever sued anyone for damages arising out of an accident?

Q Have you ever made a claim against anyone for damages arising out of an accident?

Q Did anyone make a claim for personal injuries against any firm that you were connected with that you had anything to do with?

Q Mr. Jones, do you own an automobile?

Q Have you ever driven an automobile?

Q Are you familiar with the operation of a Buick automobile?

Q Mr. Jones, will you try not to allow any feelings you may have against corporations to interfere with your returning a just verdict in this case?

Q Will you try to give both sides here a fair, square and impartial trial, Mr. Jones, even though the plaintiff is an individual and my client is a corporation?

Q You feel, do you not, Mr. Jones, that my client is entitled to a fair hearing in this case?

Q And you will give us a fair trial, will you not?

Q Mr. Jones, you understand do you not that you do not have to believe a thing is so just merely because someone says it is so, especially if what that witness says does not seem to be correct when viewed in the light of your past experience in life?

Q In other words, Mr. Jones, just because you may take an oath to act as a juror in this case, it doesn't mean that you are going to leave all of your experiences in life outside the jury box, does it?

Q You will view all the evidence in this case in the light of your past experiences and under the instructions of the court and then make up your mind as to who is telling the truth, will you not?

Q Now, Mr. Jones, you understand, of course, that cases are tried and governed by rules just as everything else in life, do you not?

A Yes.

Q You also understand, do you not, that just as all sports have their rules as to what is fair that that is also true as far as the trials of cases are concerned?

A Yes.

Q Now, if it should become necessary for either the attorney for the plaintiff or myself to make objections to certain evidence offered, you will understand, will you not, that we by objecting feel that the evidence that is being offered is not proper according to the rules and that it is our duty to our client to object. The judge will either sustain or overrule the objection. If he sustains the objection he agrees that the evidence is not being offered according to the rules. If he overrules the objection, it means that he feels that the evidence is proper and is being offered according to the rules. If either one of us should make such objections during the trial of this case you will understand, will you not, that we are just trying to keep what we consider improper evidence out of the case, and you won't hold that against either one of us, will you?

Q Mr. Jones, suppose some witness should take the stand whom you happen to know or of whom you know, will you subject his testimony to the same tests that you will any other witness?

Q You understand, Mr. Jones, that even people we know may be mistaken sometimes, do you not?

Q And so you will view their testimony in the light of all the facts and circumstances in this case, will you not?

Q Mr. Jones, just because my client happens to be a corporation, you will not require any greater degree of care or proof on our part, will you, other than what the law requires of any individual?

Q In other words, Mr. Jones, you will not visit this man's misfortunes upon my client until the plaintiff has proved his case according to every requirement of the law, will you?

Q If under the instructions of the court, one of the requirements of the law is that plaintiff shall prove that he was exercising due care and caution for his own safety at the time this accident occurred, you will make the plaintiff prove that he *was* exercising due care and caution for his own safety before you will return a verdict of guilty in this case, will you not, Mr. Jones?

Q You realize, of course, Mr. Jones, that there may be an injury sustained by one person due to his own fault for which no one else may be liable, do you not?

Q If the evidence should show that the plaintiff was injured through his own negligence, will you give such evidence due consideration under the instructions of the court as to the law governing such situations.

Q And you will apply that law in arriving at your verdict, will you not, Mr. Jones?

Q Mr. Jones, do you know of any reason about which I have not asked you any questions, which you feel would tend to make you prejudiced in this case? I do not want to pry into your personal affairs, therefore, I am putting this squarely up to you to decide.

Q Then you feel that you can give both sides a fair and square deal, do you?

Q All right, I believe you will also. We will tender the panel (or we will accept the panel).

§ 254. Kinds of challenges.*

Generally, challenges are classified as:

(1) Challenges for cause.

(2) Peremptory challenges.

A challenge for cause is a challenge to a juror for which some cause or reason is alleged. At common law such challenges were divided into challenges for *principal cause* and *to the favor,* the former being based upon grounds from which, if shown to exist, the disqualification of the juror followed as a legal conclusion, and the latter upon grounds which merely raised a suspicion of bias to be determined as a question of fact.

Peremptory challenges are challenges which may be made or omitted according to the judgment, will, or caprice of the party entitled thereto, without assigning any reason therefor, or being required to assign a reason therefor.

§ 254a. Statutory provisions.

Statutory provisions governing the qualification and selection of jurors vary in the different states. *Local codes and statutes should be consulted.* Some states provide as follows:

Jurors in all counties must have the legal qualifications herein prescribed, and shall be chosen a proportionate number from the residents of each town, or precinct, and such persons only as are:

First—Inhabitants of the town, or precinct, not exempt from serving on juries.

Second—Of the age of twenty-one (21) years, or upwards, and under sixty-five (65) years old.

Third—In the possession of their natural faculties, and not infirm or decrepit.

Fourth—Free from all legal exceptions, of fair character, of approved integrity, of sound judgment, well informed, and who understand the English language.

Exceptions. The following persons shall be exempt from serving as jurors, to-wit: The Governor, Lieutenant Gov-

* 35 C. J. 381 and 405.

ernor, Secretary of State, Auditor of Public Accounts, Treasurer, Superintendent of Public Instruction, Attorney General, members of the General Assembly during their term of office, all judges of courts, all clerks of courts, sheriffs, coroners, postmasters, mail carriers, practicing attorneys, all officers of the United States, officiating ministers of the Gospel, school teachers during the term of school, practicing physicians, dentists registered and assistant pharmacists, constant ferrymen, mayors of cities, policemen, active members of the fire department, embalmers, undertakers and funeral directors actively engaged in their business, and all persons actively employed upon the editorial or mechanical staffs and departments of any newspaper of general circulation printed and published in this state, all legally qualified veterinarians actively engaged in the practice of their profession: Provided, That every fireman who shall have faithfully and actively served as such in any volunteer fire department in any city of this state, for the term of seven years, may thereafter be exempt from serving on juries in all courts.

When regular panel exhausted—Seeking to be juror or to get person on a jury. When by reason of challenge in the selection of a jury for the trial of any cause, or by reason of the sudden sickness or absence of any juror for any cause, the regular panel shall be exhausted, the court may direct the sheriff to summon a sufficient number of persons having the qualifications of jurors to fill the panel for the pending trial; but, upon objection by either party to the cause to the sheriff summoning a sufficient number of persons to fill the panel, the court shall appoint a special bailiff to summon such person: Provided, the same person shall not be appointed special bailiff more than once at any term of court. Any person who shall seek the position of a juror, or who shall ask any attorney or other officer of the court or other person to secure his selection as a juryman, shall be deemed guilty of a contempt of court, and be fined not exceeding $20, and shall thereby be disqualified from serving as a juror for that term, and such fact shall be sufficient ground for challenge. Any attorney or party to a suit pending for trial at that term who shall request or solicit the placing of any person upon a jury, shall be deemed guilty of a contempt of the court and be fined not exceeding $100, and the person so sought to be put upon the jury shall be disqualified to serve as a juror at that term of court.

Causes for challenge. It shall be sufficient cause of challenge of a petit juror that he lacks any one of the qualifications mentioned in section two of this act; or if he is not one of the regular panel, that he has served as a juror on the trial of a cause in any court of record in the county within one year previous to the time of his being offered as a juror; or that he is a party to a suit pending for trial in that court, at that term. It shall be the duty of the court to discharge from the panel all jurors who do not possess the qualifications provided in this act, as soon as the fact is discovered: Provided, if a person has served on a jury in a court of record within one year he shall be exempt from again serving during such year, unless he waives such exemption: Provided further, that it shall not be a cause of challenge that a juror has read in the newspapers an account of the commission of the crime with which the prisoner is charged, if such juror shall state, on oath, that he believes he can render an impartial verdict, according to the law and the evidence: And, provided, further, that in the trial of any criminal cause, the fact that a person called as a juror has formed an opinion or impression, based upon rumor or upon newspaper statements (about the truth of which he has expressed no opinion), shall not disqualify him to serve as a juror in such case, if he shall, upon oath, state that he believes he can fairly and impartially render a verdict therein, in accordance with the law and the evidence, and the court shall be satisfied of the truth of such statement.

Impaneling Petit Jurors

Drawing by lot. It shall be the duty of the clerk of the court, at the commencement of each week of the term, to write the name of each petit juror summoned and retained for that week on a separate ticket, and put the whole into a box or other place for safe keeping; and as often as it shall be necessary to impanel a jury, the clerk, sheriff or coroner shall, in the presence of the court, draw by chance twelve names out of such box or other place, which shall designate the twelve to be sworn on the jury, and in the same manner for the second jury, in their turn, as the court may order and direct.

Passing upon jurors. Upon the impaneling of any jury in any civil cause now pending, or to be hereafter commenced in any court in this state, it shall be the duty of the court, upon request of either party to the suit, or upon its own motion, to order its full number of twelve jurors into the jury box, before either party shall be required to examine any of the said jurors touching their qualifications to try any such causes: Provided, that the jury shall be passed upon and accepted in panels of four by the parties, commencing with the plaintiff.

§ 255. Competency and qualifications.[1]

Public officials are generally exempt from jury duty by statute.

It is well settled that a person is incompetent to serve as a juror in any case where he has a direct financial interest in the result of the action.[2]

A person is incompetent to serve as a juror upon the trial of a case where he is bail for defendant's appearance,[3] and, if he has once been such surety, it is immaterial that he has been discharged.[4]

A stockholder in a corporation is incompetent to act as a juror in a case in which the corporation is a party,[5] or has any pecuniary interest.[6]

1 35 C. J. 313–337.

2 Ill.—Essex v. McPherson, 64 Ill. 349.

Ind.—Zimmerman v. State, 115 Ind. 129, 17 N. E. 258.

Mich.—Michigan Air Line R. Co. v. Barnes, 40 Mich. 383.

Mo.—Vessels v. Kansas City Light, etc., Co., 219 S. W. 80.

N. H.—Page v. Contoocook Valley R. Co., 21 N. H. 438.

N. J.—Peck v. Essex County, 21 N. J. L. 656.

S. C.—Lynch v. Horry, 1 S. C. L. 229.

S. D.—Rogers v. Gladiator Min., etc., Co., 21 S. D. 412, 113 N. W. 86.

Vt.—Citizens' Sav. Bank, etc., Co. v. Fitchburg Mut. F. Ins Co., 86 Vt. 267, 84 A. 970; Phelps v. Hall, 2 Tyler 401.

3 Brazleton v. State, 66 Ala. 96; Anderson v. State, 63 Ga. 675; Peo. v. McCollister, 1 Wheel. Cr. (N. Y.) 391; State v. Prater, 26 S. C. 198, 613, 2 S. E. 108.

4 Phelps v. Hall, 2 Tyler (Vt.) 401.

5 Mich.—Peninsular Ry. Co. v. Howard, 20 Mich. 18.

Nev.—Fleeson v. Savage Silver Min. Co., 3 Nev. 157.

N. C.—Murchison Nat. Bank v. Dunn Oil Mills Co., 150 N. C. 683, 64 S. E. 883.

N. H.—Page v. Contoocook Valley R. Co., 21 N. H. 438.

Pa.—Silvis v. Ely, 3 Watts & S. 420; Respublica v. Richards, 1 Yeates 480.

6 Ala.—Citizens' Light, etc., Co., v. Lee, 182 Ala. 561, 62 S. 199.

N. C.—Featherstone v. Lowell Cotton Mills, 159 N. C. 429, 74 S. E. 918.

Members of a mutual insurance company liable to be assessed to pay losses incurred by the company are disqualified from serving as jurors in an action to which it is a party,[7] or in which it is interested.[8]

It has been held, however, that a person is not competent as a juror on a trial for a particular offense, if he is a member of, and under obligation to contribute to, a society organized for the prosecution of such offenses.[9]

A juror is incompetent and subject to challenge if he is related within the prohibited degree to either party,[10] which is reckoned according to the rules of the civil law.[11]

N. H.—Page v. Contoocook Valley R. Co., 21 N. H. 438.

Ore.—Putnam v. Pacific Monthly Co., 68 Ore. 36, 130 P. 986, 136 P. 835, 45 L. R. A. (N. S.) 338, Ann. Cas. 1915 C 256, L. R. A. 1915 F 782.

Pa.—Secherman v. Wilkes-Barre Co., 255 Pa. 11, 99 A. 174; Silvis v. Ely, 3 Watts & S. 420; Respublica v. Richards, 1 Yeates 480.

Vt.—Spinney v. Hooker, 92 Vt. 146, 102 A. 53.

7 Church v. Stoldt, 215 Mich. 469, 184 N. W. 469; Martin v. Farmers' Mut. F. Ins. Co., 139 Mich. 148, 102 N. W. 656.

8 Church v. Stoldt, 215 Mich. 469, 184 N. W. 469.

9 Fla.—Blackwell v. State, 76 Fla. 124, 79 S. 731, 1 A. L. R. 502.

La.—State v. Moore, 48 La. Ann. 380, 19 S. 285.

Mass.—Comm. v. Moore, 143 Mass. 136, 9 N. E. 25, 58 Am. R. 128; Com. v. Eagan, 4 Gray 18. But see Com. v. O'Neil, 6 Gray 343 (where it was held that mere membership in such a league, and having contributed to its funds, did not disqualify a juror; but it was intimated that if he had promised, but not yet paid, a contribution, it might be otherwise).

Mo.—State v. Fullerton, 90 Mo. App. 411.

N. Y.—Jackson v. Sandman, 18 N. Y. S. 894.

Tex.—Counts v. State, 78 Tex. Cr. 410, 181 S. W. 723.

10 Ala.—Thomas v. State, 133 Ala. 139, 32 So. 250.

Cal.—Mono County v. Flanigan, 130 Cal. 105, 62 Pac. 293.

Ga.—Ledford v. State, 75 Ga. 856.

Ind.—Hudspeth v. Herston, 64 Ind. 133.

Kan.—Bailey v. Turner, 108 Kan. 856, 197 Pac. 214, 216 (cit. Cyc.).

Mich.—Hasceig v. Tripp, 20 Mich. 216.

Mo.—State v. Walton, 74 Mo. 270; Price v. Patrons', etc., Home Protection Co., 77 Mo. A. 236.

N. C.—State v. Potts, 100 N. C. 457, 6 S. E. 657; State v. Perry, 44 N. C. 330.

N. J.—Hinchman v. Clark, 1 N. J. L. 446.

N. Y.—Peo. v. Clark, 62 Hun 84, 16 N. Y. S. 473, 695, 10 N. Y. Cr. 57; Paddock v. Wells, 2 Barb. Ch. 331.

Pa.—Balsbaugh v. Frazer, 19 Pa. 95.

Tenn.—Parrish v. State, 12 Lea. 655.

Tex.—Veramendi v. Hutchins, 56 Tex. 414; Texas, etc., R. Co. v. Elliott, 22 Tex. Civ. App. 31, 54 S. W. 410; Davidson v. Wallingford (Civ. App.), 30 S. W. 286; Stringfellow v. State, 42 Tex. Cr. 588, 61 S. W. 719.

11 Ala.—Danzey v. State, 126 Ala. 15, 28 So. 697.

Ga.—Davis v. State, 153 Ga. 669, 113 S. E. 11; O'Berry v. State, 153

A person is not competent to serve as a juror in an action where there exists any business relation between him and one of the parties calculated to influence his verdict.[12]

A juror who has rendered a verdict in a case is incompetent to serve as a juror upon a subsequent trial of the same case.[13]

One who served as a grand juror on the finding of an indictment is incompetent to serve as a petit juror on the trial of the offense.[14]

A juror is clearly incompetent who admits that he has such a feeling with regard to one of the parties or the nature of the case as would influence his verdict,[15] or that he would be so influenced in case a certain state of facts should be developed

Ga. 644, 113 S. E. 2; Merritt v. State, 152 Ga. 405, 110 S. E. 160.

Ind.—Tegarden v. Phillips, 14 Ind. App. 27, 42 N. E. 549.

Kan.—Bailey v. Turner, 108 Kan. 856, 197 Pac. 214, 216 (cit. Cyc.).

Me.—Hardy v. Sprowle, 32 Me. 310.

N. Y.—Peo. v. Clark, 62 Hun 84, 16 N. Y. S. 473, 695, 10 N. Y. Cr. 57.

Ohio—Kahn v. Reedy, 8 Ohio Cir. Ct. 345, 4 Ohio Cir. Dec. 284.

Vt.—Churchill v. Churchill, 12 Vt. 661.

(1) By the canon law persons were considered as near related to each other as they were to their common ancestor, and therefore the number of degrees most distant from their common ancestor was their degree of relationship; but by the civil law persons are related only in that number of degrees which exist between them to be counted by reckoning from one up to their common ancestor and down to the other. Churchill v. Churchill, 12 Vt. 661. (2) In this computation the person from whom the count begins is excluded and he in whom it ends is counted. Peo. v. Clark, 62 Hun 84, 16 N. Y. S. 473, 695, 10 N. Y. Cr. 57.

12 Iowa—Stumm v. Hummell, 39 Iowa 478.

13 Mich.—Hester v. Chambers, 84 Mich. 562, 48 N. W. 152.

N. Y.—Barclay v. Peo., 8 Alb. L. J. 104.

Tex.—Holmes v. State, 52 Tex. Cr. 352, 106 S. W. 1160. Statutory provision to this effect, see Willis v. State, 9 Tex. App. 297; Jacobs v. State, 9 Tex. App. 278; Dunn v. State, 7 Tex. App. 600.

14 Ill.—Peo. v. Mooney, 303 Ill. 469, 135 N. E. 776.

Mass.—Com. v. Hussey, 13 Mass. 221.

Tex.—Greenwood v. State, 34 Tex 334; Franklin v. State, 2 Tex. App. 8.

Wis.—Bennet v. State, 24 Wis. 57.

15 Cal.—Fitts v. Southern Pac. Co., 149 Cal. 310, 86 Pac. 710, 117 Am. S. R. 130.

N. Y.—Peo. v. Decker, 157 N. Y. 186, 51 N. E. 1018; Haas v. Newberry, 181 App. Div. 772, 169 N. Y. S. 175.

Ohio—Lingafelter v. Moore, 95 Ohio St. 384, 117 N. E. 16.

Tex.—Gulf, etc., R. Co. v. Gilvin (Civ. App.), 55 S. W. 985; Muse v. State, 94 Tex. Cr. 71, 249 S. W. 861; St. Louis, etc., R. Co. v. Hooser, 44 Tex. Civ. App. 229, 97 S. W. 708; Withers v. State, 30 Tex. App. 383, 17 S. W. 936.

on the trial,[16] or if he is doubtful of his ability to render an impartial verdict.[17]

A juror is incompetent if he is so prejudiced against defendant's race or nationality,[18] or that of his attorney,[19] that he could not on this account give him a fair and impartial trial, but not where he merely has a general unfavorable opinion of persons of that race or nationality which he testifies will in no way influence his verdict.[20]

A juror is incompetent if he has such a prejudice against corporations as would influence him in his consideration of the particular case.[21]

A juror who entertains a prejudice against a class of which defendant is a member cannot act with entire impartiality, and is therefore incompetent.[22]

A juror is not disqualified by reason of general bias entertained against a class of actions, where it appears from his testimony that he can lay aside that prejudice, and, uninflu-

16 Marande v. Texas, etc., R. Co., 124 Fed. 42, 59 CCA 562 (writ of error dismissed 197 U. S. 626 mem., 25 Sup. Ct. 800 mem., 49 L. ed. 912 mem.); Peo. v. Decker, 157 N. Y. 186, 51 N. E. 1018.

17 Cal.—Quill v. Southern Pac. Co., 140 Cal. 268, 73 Pac. 991.

18 Pinder v. State, 27 Fla. 370, 8 So. 837, 26 Am. S. Rep. 75; State v. McAfee, 64 N. C. 339; Potter v. State, 86 Tex. Cr. 380, 216 S. W. 886.

Illustration.—That a juror was prejudiced against the colored race to such an extent that he would not believe what a negro said when opposed to the statement of any white person renders him incompetent. Makey v. Dryden (Tex. Civ. App.), 128 S. W. 633.

19 State v. Sanders, 103 S. C. 216, 88 S. E. 10.

20 Iowa—State v. Giudice, 170 Iowa 731, 153 N. W. 336, Ann. Cas. 1917 C 1160; State v. Buford, 158 Iowa 173, 139 N. W. 464, 465 (cit. Cyc.).

N. Y.—Balbo v. Peo., 80 N. Y. 484 (aff. 19 Hun 424).

Tex.—Bass v. State, 59 Tex. Cr. 186, 127 S. W. 1020; Moore v. State, 52 Tex. Cr. 336, 107 S. W. 540.

21 Ill.—Winnesheik Ins. Co. v. Schueller, 60 Ill. 465.

Tex.—St. Louis, etc., R. Co. v. Hooser, 44 Tex. Civ. App. 229, 97 S. W. 708.

22 Naylor v. Metropolitan St. R. Co., 66 Kan. 407, 71 Pac. 835; State v. Brooks, 57 Mont. 480, 188 Pac. 942; Beach v. Seattle, 85 Wash. 379, 148 Pac. 39.

Member of Ku Klux Klan.—A juror cannot be said to be fair or impartial toward a defendant nor qualified to weigh evidence touching guilt or innocence on a criminal charge, when he admits that in weighing the evidence he will be prejudiced against defendant solely because defendant was a member of the Ku Klux Klan, an organization to which the juror was opposed. Peo. v. Vitelle (Cal. App.), 215 Pac. 693.

enced by it, try the cause at issue solely upon the evidence and the instructions of the court as to the law.[23] But the rule is otherwise where his bias or prejudice is such as to affect his verdict,[24] or where he would on account of his prejudice, require stronger proof than if it was an action of another kind.[25]

A juror is incompetent if there exists any hostility between him and one of the parties,[26] although it has no connection with the action to be tried.[27] But the fact that a juror has had business difficulties,[28] or a dispute,[29] or trivial misunderstanding,[30] with one of the parties is not sufficient to render him incompetent where he swears that he is without prejudice and entirely impartial between the parties. A juror is also incompetent if he admits a friendship for one of the parties,[31] or members of his family,[32] which, other things being equal, would influence his verdict, or would cause him to believe such party unless contradicted by witnesses with whom the juror was personally acquainted,[33] or where he admits a feeling of

23 Fitts v. Southern Pac. Co., 149 Cal. 310, 86 Pac. 710, 117 Am. S. R. 130; Young v. Bridges, 34 La. Ann. 333; Ruschenberg v. Southern Electric R. Co., 161 Mo. 70, 61 S. W. 626; Denham v. Washington Water Power Co., 38 Wash. 354, 80 Pac. 546.

24 Fitts v. Southern Pac. Co., 149 Cal. 310, 86 Pac. 710, 117 Am. S. R. 130. See Galveston, etc., R. Co. v. Manns, 37 Tex. Civ. App. 356, 360, 84 S. W. 254 (dictum).

"Prejudice against a class of litigation under which the plaintiff's cause of action comes, is tantamount to a prejudice against the law which gives him the right to recover in his suit. And its existence in the mind of a juror, in the trial of the case, might work a greater injury than actual prejudice against him personally by the juror would cause him." Galveston, etc., R. Co. v. Manns, supra.

(a) Rule applied to damage suits against corporations. Quill v. Southern Pac. R. Co., 140 Cal. 268, 73 Pac. 991.

25 Fitts v. Southern Pac. Co., 149 Cal. 310, 86 Pac. 710, 117 Am. S. R. 130; Quill v. Southern Pac. R. Co., 140 Cal. 268, 73 Pac. 991.

26 McLaten v. Birdsong, 24 Ga. 265; Billmeyer v. St. Louis Transit Co., 108 Mo. A. 6, 82 S. W. 536; Brittain v. Allen, 13 N. C. 120.

27 Brittain v. Allen, 13 N. C. 120.

28 Heucke v. Milwaukee City R. Co., 69 Wis. 401, 34 N. W. 243.

29 Pietzuk v. Kansas City R. Co., 289 Mo. 135, 232 S. W. 987.

30 Memmler v. State, 75 Ga. 576.

31 Cal.—Lombardi v. California St. R. Co., 124 Cal. 311, 57 Pac. 66.

N. Y.—Rosenberg v. Rubin, 164 N. Y. S. 201.

One who has entertained defendant at a hotel is incompetent. Rosenberg v. Rubin, 164 N. Y. S. 201.

32 State v. Faulkner, 185 Mo. 673, 84 S. W. 967; Collins v. State, 15 Okl. Cr. 96, 175 Pac. 124.

33 Stinson v. Sachs, 8 Wash. 391, 36 Pac. 287.

gratitude and obligation for services rendered him by one of the parties;[34] and where it appears that the relations between a juror and one of the parties are of such an intimate character as would be reasonably calculated to influence his verdict it is proper to exclude him.[35]

A juror who has formed an unqualified, fixed, or decided opinion as to the merits of the case, or the guilt or innocence of accused,[36] or who has formed such an opinion as to any material issue involved in the case,[37] is incompetent, regardless of the source of the information upon which it is based.[38]

While it has been held that hypothetical questions having correct reference to the law of the case, and which do not call for a prejudgment of the case or of any supposed case on the facts, may, in the sound and reasonable discretion of the trial court, be propounded,[39] it is not proper to propound hypothetical questions purporting to embody testimony that is intended to be submitted,[40] regardless of whether or not they

34 Texas Cent. R. Co. v. Blanton, 36 Tex. Civ. App. 307, 81 S. W. 537.

35 Rooker v. Deering Southwestern R. Co. (Mo. App.), 247 S. W. 1016; Omaha St. R. Co. v. Craig, 39 Neb. 601, 58 N. W. 209; Com. v. Mosier, 135 Pa. 221, 19 Atl. 943.

36 Cal.—Peo. v. Brotherton, 43 Cal. 530.

Ill.—Coughlin v. Peo., 144 Ill. 140, 33 N. E. 1, 19 L. R. A. 57.

Iowa—State v. Shelledy, 8 Iowa 477.

N. Y.—Greenfield v. Peo., 74 N. Y. 277, 6 Abb. N. Cas. 1, 2 Cow. Cr. 479; Peo. v. Allen, 43 N. Y. 28, 1 Cow. Cr. 263 (rev. 57 Barb. 338).

Ohio—Mangano v. State, 17 Ohio Cir. Ct. (N. S.) 595.

Tex.—Gulf, etc., R. Co. v. Dickens, 54 Tex. Civ. App. 637, 118 S. W. 612; Choctaw, etc., R. Co. v. True (Civ. App.), 80 S. W. 120; Muse v. State, 94 Tex. Cr. 71, 249 S. W. 861; Harris v. State, 72 Tex. Cr. 117, 161 S. W. 125; Slack v. State, 67 Tex. Cr. 460, 149 S. W. 107; Ross v. State, 53 Tex. Cr. 162, 109 S. W. 153; Ward v. State, 19 Tex. App. 664.

37 Pine v. Callahan, 8 Idaho 684, 71 Pac. 473; State v. Otto, 61 Kan. 58, 58 Pac. 995; State v. Tomblin, 57 Kan. 841, 48 Pac. 144; Johnson v. Park City, 27 Utah 420, 76 Pac. 216.

38 Leigh v. Terr., 10 Ariz. 129, 85 Pac. 948; McGough v. State, 113 Ark. 301, 304, 167 S. W. 857; Peo. v. Gehr, 8 Cal. 359; Wright v. Com., 32 Gratt (73 Va.) 941; Armistead v. Com., 11 Leigh (38 Va.) 657, 37 Am. D. 633.

39 Pope v. State (Fla.), 94 So. 865. See Henwood v. Peo., 57 Colo. 544, 143 Pac. 373, Ann. Cas. 1916 A 1111 (where it was said: "Perhaps to a limited extent hypothetical questions are proper").

40 Cal.—Peo. v. Copsey, 71 Cal. 548, 12 Pac. 721.

Ill.—Peo. v. Robinson, 299 Ill. 617, 132 N. E. 803; Chicago, etc., R. Co. v. Fisher, 141 Ill. 614, 31 N. E. 406 (aff. 38 Ill. App. 33).

Ohio—State v. Huffman, 86 Ohio

correctly epitomize the testimony.[41] Thus it is not competent to examine jurors as to how they would act or decide in certain contingencies,[42] or in case the court should give certain instructions,[43] or in case certain evidence or a certain state of evidence should be developed on the trial,[44] or as to his attitude toward a particular witness who is expected to testify in the case.[45]

St. 229, 99 N. E. 295, Ann. Cas. 1913 D 677.

Tex.—Houston v. State, 83 Tex. Cr. 190, 202 S. W. 84; Merkel v. State, 75 Tex. Cr. 551, 171 S. W. 738.

(a) If one party has been allowed to ask hypothetical questions based upon his theory of the case, the other party may, on cross-examination, also ask hypothetical questions based upon his theory of the case. Peo. v. Copsey, 71 Cal. 548, 12 Pac. 721.

41 Dicks v. State, 83 Fla. 717, 93 So. 137.

42 Cal.—Peo. v. Hinshaw, 40 Cal. A. 672, 182 Pac. 59.

Ill.—Peo. v. Robinson, 299 Ill. 617, 132 N. E. 803; Ventriss v. Pana Coal Co., 155 Ill. A. 152.

Ohio—State v. Huffman, 86 Ohio St. 229, 99 N. E. 295, Ann. Cas. 1913 D 677.

Tex.—Campbell v. Campbell (Civ. App.), 215 S. W. 134.

Wis.—Hughes v. State, 109 Wis. 397, 85 N. W. 333.

Illustrations.—It is not competent to ask a juror: (1) Whether upon certain stated facts he will find for plaintiff. Ventriss v. Pana Coal Co., 155 Ill. A. 152. (2) What his verdict would be in case the indictment was read but no evidence put in. State v. Turley, 87 Vt. 163, 88 A. 562. (3) Whether he would stand on his opinion of not guilty, formed after due deliberation in the jury room, or would yield his opinion merely to reach a verdict. State v. Huffman, 86 Ohio St. 229, 99 N. E. 295, Ann. Cas. 1913 D 677.

43 Fish v. Glass, 54 Ill. A. 655; State v. Foster, 150 La. 971, 91 S. 411; State v. Perioux, 107 La. 601, 31 So. 1016; Moffett v. State, 32 O. C. A. 337; Collins v. State, 77 Tex. Cr. 156, 178 S. W. 345.

44 Ill.—Peo. v. Robinson, 299 Ill. 617, 132 N. E. 803; Chicago, etc., R. Co. v. Fisher, 141 Ill. 614, 31 N. E. 406 (aff. 38 Ill. A. 33, and overruling Galena, etc., R. Co. v. Haslam, 73 Ill. 494; Chicago, etc., R. Co. v. Buttolf, 66 Ill. 347; Chicago, etc., R. Co. v. Adler, 56 Ill. 344); Fish v. Glass, 54 Ill. A. 655.

Iowa—State v. Dillman, 183 Iowa 1147, 168 N. W. 204.

N. Y.—Peo. v. Hughson, 154 N. Y. 153, 47 N. E. 1092.

Ohio—State v. Huffman, 86 Ohio St. 229, 99 N. E. 296, Ann. Cas. 1913 D 677.

Tex.—Parker v. Schrimsher (Civ. App.), 172 S. W. 165.

45 Ellis v. State, 69 Tex. Cr. 468, 154 S. W. 1010; Mainville v. State, 173 Wis. 12, 179 N. W. 764; Chybowski v. Bucyrus Co., 127 Wis. 332, 106 N. W. 833, 7 L. R. A. (N. S.) 357.

CHAPTER V

OPENING STATEMENTS

§ 256. In general.

The next step in the trial of cases as well as the next in importance to properly selecting the jury is the *opening statement.* Successful trial lawyers claim that a carefully selected jury and a good opening statement will do more than anything else to help the trial lawyer win cases. Yet a visit to any court room will soon convince one that many lawyers, young and old, fail to appreciate the important part that an opening statement plays in the trial of cases. Judges are almost unanimous in their criticism when trial lawyers fail to inform the jury properly of just what the case is about in their opening statements.

§ 257. Purpose.

The *purpose* of an opening statement is to give to the jury a "bird's eye-view" of the evidence that is to be presented to them during the course of the trial so that it will enable them to understand each bit of evidence and testimony properly in its relation to the whole case *at the time it is presented to them in "piece-meal" fashion.* If an improper or incomplete opening statement is made, the jury may be kept in ignorance of the theory of the case until the completion of the testimony. As a consequence the jury fails to appreciate the importance of each detail of the evidence and thus the convincing effect of the testimony is materially weakened. It must forever be kept in mind that the jury are convinced only in proportion to the amount of understanding and appreciation they have of the effect of the evidence at the moment that evidence is presented.

§ 258. Failure to make a good opening statement.

Many attorneys fail to make a good opening statement for the reason that they do not keep upper-most in mind the fact that the jury is composed of "laymen" and that they know absolutely nothing about the case to be tried nor about the evidence which will be presented. The trial lawyer usually thinks in legal terms and of the legal effect of the evidence which he expects to produce. This may be the real reason why so many poor opening statements are made.

To the uninitiated, the telling of just what the case is about seems to be a comparatively simple matter and yet the inability of many lawyers to make a good opening statement seems to be responsible, in a measure, for their failure to win cases.

§ 259. Testing opening statement.

The best test and the best method of determining whether or not the trial lawyer has prepared a proper opening statement is for him *to stand up before one of his other clients or before some non-professional friend* and to tell him about the case just as he would before a jury. When he has finished he should ask his friend whether he understands the case clearly. Have the friend tell what impression he got from the opening statement. It will be amazing to learn in most instances how little he understood. Usually the friend will have to ask about a dozen or more questions. If this is true, in a friendly discussion with an intelligent friend, it can well be imagined what impression the statement will make on a mixed jury.

The result of this experiment will serve notice that more care and preparation must be utilized in making opening statements. It will usually suggest a thorough revision.

It is strongly recommended that this method of trying out opening statements on "laymen" friends and clients be followed in every case. This habit, once established, will repay the trial attorney a hundredfold for this additional effort. It will help him to win many more cases.

§ 260. Detailed or short opening statement.

One perplexing problem facing the trial lawyer in the preparation of an opening statement is whether to make a short statement or *a long detailed one.* The decision must be determined by the facts in each particular case. No set rule can be followed nor given that will control every situation. In most instances the opening statement should not be too long nor too detailed. The length and detail of the opening statement should be governed by the thought that opening statements should serve the same purpose that a good introduction serves in a really worthwhile lecture. The function of a good introduction is to create good will towards the speaker and to create interest in the subject matter as well as to arouse curiosity and interest as to the method and manner of proving the speaker's contentions. It must make easily understandable the maze of evidence which is to follow.

Just as an introduction cannot and should not contain the entire speech or lecture, so the opening statement should not be so detailed that every bit of evidence later to be adduced will lose its interest and appeal.

Thus, it will be seen that an *overly detailed opening* statement is subject to the *objection* that the jury will lose interest in the evidence to be given by the witnesses for the reason that the jury already knows every word of the testimony that will be presented. The evidence thus becomes "stale" for them and of no interest. The overly detailed statement is also legally objectionable and prohibited.[1]

In all instances, where the shorter and more general opening statement is indicated, few of the names of the witnesses, if any, should be given nor should the testimony of each witness expected to be called be recited to the jury in the opening statement. Something new should be left for the jury to discover during the presentation of the evidence.

While the shorter opening statement in most instances is to be desired, understanding, clarity, and interest should never be sacrificed for the sake of brevity. It must be remembered that no rule can govern every case.

The short opening statement is *not* indicated and should *not* be used in *very complicated* cases. The main function of the opening statement is to clarify the testimony which is to follow and to set out the issues involved. In a complicated case, it will be necessary to give a more detailed word-picture of the case and theory. The more involved the case, the more detailed the statement, unless some medium can be arrived at which when used for illustration purposes makes a seemingly complicated situation a simple one to understand. (See Argument to Jury, page 611, for illustration.)

Detailed opening statements are also indicated in all cases where the main witnesses relied upon are *ignorant* or *illiterate*

1 Pietsch v. Pietsch, 92 N. E. 325, 245 Ill. 454, 29 L. R. A. (N. S.) 218; Scripps v. Reilly, 35 Mich. 371, 24 Am. R. 575.

or foreigners who do not speak English or where it is expected the witnesses will have difficulty in interestingly telling their stories. In these instances, the appeal by the witnesses to the jury cannot be depended upon entirely. The trial lawyer must, therefore, rely more on his own efforts to sell his theory of the case to the jury in the opening statements and in the arguments. He dare not leave much for the jury to gather from the evidence as the evidence will probably be "choppy" and hard to understand.

§ 261. Directed verdict on opening statement.

In some states, judges have the right to direct a verdict on motion duly made by opposing counsel on the ground that the opening statement made shows insufficient basis for a favorable legal verdict. The importance of making a good and legally sufficient opening statement can readily be appreciated when the right of the court to direct a verdict is realized.

While most courts are properly hesitant in directing verdicts on the basis of an insufficient opening statement, and while appeal courts frown upon this practice, yet in instances where the suit is brought upon a document illegal as against public policy, the court may direct a verdict on an opening statement on its own motion.

The failure of counsel in his opening statement to recite all of the material facts necessary to a recovery will not warrant the court in taking the case from the jury.[2] However although the practice is not universally recognized [3] under certain circumstances, the trial court may direct a verdict against a party on his opening statement.[4] Thus when plaintiff, in his open-

[2] 64 C. J. 239–241; Martin Emerich Outfitting Co. v. Siegel, 108 Ill. App. 364; Goodman v. Brooklyn Hebrew Orphan Asylum, 165 N. Y. S. 949, 178 App. Div. 682; Fini v. Perry, 146 N. E. 358, 119 Ohio St. 367; Redding v. Puget Sound Iron, etc., Works, 79 Pac. 308, 36 Wash. 642.

[3] In Wisconsin, the practice of granting a nonsuit, on the opening statement of the case by counsel for plaintiff, does not prevail, and never has prevailed. Haley v. Western Transit Co., 45 N. W. 16, 76 Wis. 344.

[4] Illinois Power & Light Corporation v. Hurley, 49 F. (2d) 681 (cert. den. 52 S. Ct. 19, 284 U. S. 637, 76 L. Ed. 541); Bowe v. Wright, 281 F. 946; Houk Mfg. Co. v. Cowen Co., 267 F. 787 (cert. den. 41 S. Ct. 9, 254 U. S. 637, 65 L. Ed. 450); Bias v. Reed, 145 Pac. 516, 169 Cal. 33; Moffitt v. Ford Motor Co., 292 Pac. 698 (superseded 297 Pac. 553, 212 Cal. 73); Sun Oil Co. v. Garren, 261 Ill. App. 513; Gray v. City of Boston, 178 N. E. 286; Compton-Price Piano Co. v. Stewart, 25 Ohio Cir. Ct. (N. S.)

ing statement, distinctly sets out facts the existence of which preclude his recovery the court may dismiss the complaint.

It is generally declared that the practice of disposing of a case upon the mere opening of counsel is ordinarily a very unsafe method of deciding controversies, where there is or ever was anything to decide,[5] and counsel should be allowed to qualify, explain or supplement it so far as the truth will permit,[6] and before directing a verdict the court should inform counsel as to the particulars in which he has failed to make a case.[7]

Self-preservation and the client's interests demand a good and sufficiently legal opening statement so as to prevent the direction of a verdict in the case.

§ 262. Administrators, executors, trustees, and next friends.

When representing a plaintiff who is suing in the capacity of an administrator, executor, trustee, or as the "next friend" that fact and the reason for it should be explained to the jury as early as possible in the opening statement or during the selection of the jury so that the jury may understand the purpose and reason for it. The legal terms involved and their meaning is thus made plain to them.

270; Carter v. King County, 208 Pac. 5, 120 Wash. 536; Gross v. Bennington, 100 Pac. 846, 52 Wash. 417.

5 Bias v. Reed, 145 Pac. 516, 169 Cal. 33; Mahutga v. Minneapolis, St. P. & S. S. M. Ry. Co., 234 N. W. 474, 182 Minn. 362; Hoffman House v. Foote, 65 N. E. 169, 172 N. Y. 348; Malcolm v. Thomas, 201 N. Y. S. 849, 207 App. Div. 230 (aff. 144 N. E. 899, 238 N. Y. 577); Gross v. Bennington, 100 Pac. 846, 52 Wash. 417.

Except where it unmistakably appears that action is based on contract prohibited by morality or public policy it is not a safe practice to decide a case upon the opening statement of counsel to the jury. Lane v. Portland Ry., Light & Power Co., 114 Pac. 940, 58 Ore. 364.

6 Oscanyan v. Winchester Repeating Arms Co., 103 U. S. 261, 26 L. Ed. 539; Spicer v. Bonker, 8 N. W. 518, 45 Mich. 630. And see Barto v. Detroit Iron, etc., Steel Co., 118 N. W. 738, 155 Mich. 94; Mahutga v. Minneapolis, St. P. & S. S. M. Ry. Co., 234 N. W. 474, 182 Minn. 362 (cert. den. 51 S. Ct. 494, 283 U. S. 847, 75 L. Ed. 1456); Donnelly v. Paramount Organization, 160 A. 569, 109 N. J. Law 57 (rev'g 155 A. 377, 9 N. J. Misc. 57); Cornell v. Morrison, 87 Ohio St. 215, 100 N. E. 817.

7 Haynes v. Maybury, 131 N. W. 1110, 166 Mich. 498. See also Rodeff v. Lake Shore & M. S. Ry. Co., 7 Ohio App. 73.

Illustration

"Gentlemen: This suit is brought by Albert Johnson. He was appointed by the Probate Court as administrator of the Estate of John Franklin who died January 14th, 1932."

This procedure not only explains who Albert Johnson is, but gives him the added prestige of having been appointed as a sort of representative of one of the courts.

If the suit is brought by Albert Johnson, a minor, by Edward Johnson, his father and next friend, this statement might be made: "Gentlemen, this suit is brought by Albert Johnson, a minor. He is the little boy who was hurt in this case. Our law permits a minor to bring suit in his own name but it must also be started in the name of some adult. This is for the protection of the minor's interests. That adult is usually called the child's 'next friend.' In this case the father, Edward Johnson, brings this suit as the 'next friend' of his child, Albert Johnson."

§ 263. Waiving or reserving opening statement.

When representing a defendant in the case it frequently becomes necessary to decide whether it will be better to make an opening statement or to waive it entirely. Sometimes in Criminal cases it is advisable to waive the opening statement on the part of the defendant where there is every indication that the defendant may be guilty. This is also true in personal injury cases where there is no question but that client is liable and also where the only hope is to keep the verdict as small as possible.

Waiving the opening statement may be indicated in those instances where the attorney relies upon a *secret defense,* that is, where he has information, witnesses, and evidence unknown to the plaintiff which will completely refute and destroy plaintiff's case. Let us take a personal injury case where the plaintiff claims to have been confined to bed during all the time from the date of the accident to the date of trial and where he also claims he is permanently injured and unable to leave his bed. The attorney has caused moving pictures to be taken of the plaintiff a month prior to trial which shows him leaving his home and working around the house fixing and repairing things—normal in all respects. In such a situation some attorneys feel it is better to waive the opening statement so as not to warn the plaintiff of impending danger. However, in some jurisdictions the defense is permitted by motion duly made to the court to *reserve the defendant's opening statement* until after the plaintiff has proved his direct case. It is usually discretionary with the court to permit the defense to reserve its opening statement, but in some states the rules of court in civil cases provide that the defendant's opening statement must follow that of the plaintiff's.[8]

Where permitted, the request to *reserve* the opening statement may be made in the following form: "If the Court please, the defense would like to have permission to reserve its opening statement until the close of plaintiff's case."

It is always good policy for the plaintiff to object to this request and to attempt to force the defendant to "disclose his hand."

§ 264. Forcing defendant to make opening statement.

In those instances where it is thought that the defendant does not intend to make an opening statement there are several methods usually utilized by plaintiff's attorneys in an effort to arouse the jury's suspicions in case the defendant's attorney fails or refuses to make an opening statement. This is usually accomplished in the few introductory remarks by the plaintiff's attorney.

Illustration

"If the Court please, and Gentlemen of the Jury: As you know, *it is customary* at this stage of the trial, *for both the attorney for the plaintiff and the attorney for the defendant,* to tell you just what we each expect to prove. First I will tell you what our case is about on behalf of the plaintiff, Henry Johnson, and then, Mr. Jones, for the defendant, will tell what he expects to show———."

Another Illustration

"———After I get through telling you what we expect to show on the part of the plaintiff, Mr. Jones, the attorney for the defendant will tell you his theory of the case and also what evidence and proof he expects to produce to meet our case."

8 Rule 50, Circuit and Superior Courts of Cook County, Illinois.

When this method is used, the jury will look with surprise at the defendant's failure to state openly what his case is about.

Another method used by some attorneys to cast suspicion on the motives of the defendant's lawyer *in seeking* permission to reserve his opening statement until the close of the plaintiff's evidence is illustrated by the following incident: The attorney for the defendant requested permission to reserve his opening statement until the close of the plaintiff's case, whereupon the attorney for the plaintiff made the following statement:

"Mr. David: It seems to me, your Honor, in a case where a suit is in assumpsit, and an Affidavit of Claim is filed to which an Affidavit of Defense is filed where the defendant is supposed to state his complete defense, that it is unfair both to the plaintiff and the jury to permit defendant to reserve a statement so that the jury does not know until we are through what the defense is. The issues should be defined now. Counsel is making objections on the ground that it has nothing to do with the issue. He objects to my stating from the affidavit what the issues are and objects to stating to the jury himself what the issues are. What is his defense?

Court: He is reserving that. I will permit him to reserve it.

Mr. David: Exception—I have never known a defense to reserve a statement in a contract case. I have heard it in an action of tort where they file a general issue.

Mr. Finn: I object to arguing before the jury.

Court: Objection sustained.

§ 265. Where secret defense.

It is suggested that in most instances it is *not* necessary to waive the defendant's opening statement even where the defense is a secret one. Sufficient can be stated in a few words and much more can be suggested by innuendo so as to arouse the curiosity of the jury and to intimate that there is a great deal more to the case than appears on the surface. A very brief short statement may be made which will serve to make the jury listen to the plaintiff's witnesses with the thought in their minds that they must not accept the plaintiff's testimony unreservedly in the light of defendant's statement that everything will be proved to the contrary.

Illustration

"Gentlemen of the Jury: The attorney for the plaintiff has told you what he expects to prove. If he proves it by a preponderance of the evidence as required by law, you return a verdict in his favor. But we are sure that he will not be able to prove his case because the evidence will show that this accident did not happen as he claims it did. The evidence will also show that the plaintiff was not injured as he states, nor is he permanently injured as claimed. All we ask is that you keep an open mind until all of the evidence is presented to you."

In very few instances in Civil cases is it advisable to waive the defendant's opening statement entirely. First impressions are sometimes difficult to eradicate from the minds of the jurors. If the plaintiff's outline of his case should be favorably received it will require more evidence to change the opinion of the jury. However, if doubt and suspicion are cast on the story of the plaintiff by a short opening statement by the defendant it will have a beneficial psychological effect.

Most successful trial lawyers suggest that the defendant should nearly always make an opening statement.

§ 266. Motion to exclude witnesses.

Before the opening statements are made it is usually advisable to make a motion to exclude all witnesses. This is a motion addressed to the presiding judge who in his discretion may order all witnesses excluded from the court room during the trial so that each witness will not hear to what the other witnesses testify. By making this motion before the opening statements are made, it will prevent opponent's witnesses from knowing what the evidence will show and will not forewarn them as to what to expect on cross-examination. If the witnesses are excluded as early as possible, it will eliminate the possibility of changing their stories. Having the exclusion of witnesses is of considerable value in those instances where it is felt that opponent's witnesses are not telling the truth. A motion to exclude should always be made where opponent has the greater number of witnesses. In such a case, there is a greater possibility of showing differences between the testimony of the various witnesses. Sometimes these differences will be great enough to discredit opponent's contentions entirely. In some instances, excluding the witnesses serves to emphasize the lack of truth and credence to be given to a number of witnesses who take the witness stand and testify to the same thing in identical language, showing a carefully rehearsed and memorized story.

The order to exclude all witnesses will not apply to either the parties plaintiff or defendant. The parties have a right to be present in open court during the entire trial and to face all witnesses presented.

The order to exclude witnesses will not apply to one representative of the party plaintiff or defendant where they are corporations or where the plaintiff or defendant is absent. Where this situation arises, a motion should be addressed to the court for permission to have one representative remain in court to act in an advisory capacity.

It is sometimes advisable in those instances where opponent places an expert witness on the stand to request the court's permission to have a friendly expert sit behind the trial lawyer while opponent's expert testifies so as to have the benefit of such expert's knowledge for cross-examination purposes. The court will usually grant such request.

Should any witness violate the order of exclusion by the court and remain in the court room during the testimony, an objection should be made to his testifying. If the violation of the exclusion order has been intentional, the court may refuse to permit the witness to testify, particularly if his testimony goes directly to the matter in controversy. If the violation has been unintentional and the witness is to testify as an expert or as to some phase of the case not decisive of the point in issue or where the witness is to testify in rebuttal only, the court may in its discretion permit the witness to testify.

The request to the court to exclude the witnesses may be made in this form:

"If the Court please, we wish to make a motion at this time to exclude all witnesses."

The Court: "All witnesses, except the parties will retire to the witness room or will retire to the corridor until called to testify."

§ 267. Over-statement and exaggeration.

It is always a great mistake for the trial attorney to tell the jury that he expects to prove a great many things which he knows he will be unable to prove. It will materially weaken his case in the eyes of the jury. The jury, depending on the lawyer's exaggerated opening statement, listens to all the evidence waiting for testimony which will prove such over-statements, and when such proof is not presented an unfavorable verdict may result. Some attorneys tell the jury that they will overwhelmingly prove their case not only by a preponderance of the evidence but will prove it beyond all reasonable doubt and to a mathematical certainty. Some say they will prove their case beyond a shadow of a doubt.

A great advantage can be taken of this error by opposing counsel in the final arguments when he points out to the jury that the rash statements made in the opening statement have not been proved. The effectiveness of this can well be imagined on the minds of the jury when the following illustration is considered:

Illustration (in the final arguments)

"Gentlemen of the Jury: Counsel in his opening statement told you that he would prove so and so———. Did he prove it? No.

He also told you that he would prove———. Did he prove that? No.

And then he stated that he would prove———. Did he prove that? No.

And then he stated that he would prove———. Did he? No. (and so on).

§ 268. "We expect to prove.".

Many lawyers have fallen into the error of commencing almost every sentence in their opening statement with the words "we expect to prove," or "the evidence will show," or "we expect to show you" etc. This procedure weakens the psychological effect of the statement. The introductory remarks may contain a statement to the effect that the purpose of the opening statement is to inform the jury as to what each side expects to prove, but that should be about the only time that the statement "we expect to prove" should be made.

The purpose in making an opening statement is to present to the jury a graphic picture of the case. The interpolation after every few words of the statement "we expect to prove" breaks up the picture and takes the mind of the jury away from that picture.

§ 269. Pictures.

The opening statement should stress "pictures" rather than witnesses. The completion of the statement to the jury should leave with them a vivid mental picture of just how the accident happened (in a personal injury case) who the parties are, their positions and all the factors upon which is based the right of recovery.

§ 270. Logical sequence.

This picture must be presented in logical sequence or failure will result. Unless all events are related in the order of their happening, the jury will be unable to appreciate their full significance in the scheme of things. Some young lawyers commence with the time of starting suit, and then work back to the beginning of the relationship between the parties. This is a mistake. It only serves to confuse the jury. They should start from the beginning and then relate everything in order just as it happened.

In a suit by a beneficiary of a life insurance policy, it is more logical to start by telling of the assured, his name, with some history as to date of application, payment of premium, medical examination, then a statement as to the type of insurance, who the defendant is, then showing that the plaintiff is the beneficiary of policy, that assured died, proofs made, and claim of amount of policy.

In every instance where the plaintiff sues in some representative capacity, as assignee, trustee, or in the name of a third party for use of the real plaintiff, the opening statement should commence with the original parties and their claims and then trace the relationship between the parties as well as the events in logical sequence and order.

§ 271. "As you know."

It is, of course, the height of folly to ever intimate that either the court or the jury is lacking in understanding. Yet lawyers are guilty of this breach of good trial procedure every day. One method of preventing this violation of good trial tactics is through the use of the words "as you know."

§ 272. — The jury.

The jury may not know nor realize just what is happening nor understand the significance or legal effect of certain evidence, but no successful trial lawyer will so indicate by his words or manner. Every person is susceptible to subtle flattery and everyone likes to feel that others consider that he possesses knowledge greater than that which he actually has. This psychological fact must be ever kept uppermost in the trial lawyer's mind. At the same time, it must also be kept in mind that actually the jurors may not and probably do not understand the theory, position, or procedure that is being followed.

The compliment to their supposed intelligence may be given through the use of the words "as you know." In most instances they do not actually know, but it makes them feel better to think that the attorney seems to believe that they do know. "As you know," however, must always be followed up with a complete explanation of the point to be made just as though the jury actually knew nothing about the point to be conveyed.

§ 273. — — The court.

This may be a good place to consider the psychological method of addressing the judge on a somewhat similar though different basis. In arguing with the court some proposition of law or method of proof which the trial attorney knows is correct, but which the judge does not seem to be able to follow, it is always advisable to assume the blame for the Court's lack of understanding rather than to irritate him by intimating either by words or manner that it is all due to his lack of intelligence. The trial lawyer, in such an instance, must have the proverbial "patience of a saint" and exercise the greatest mental control. Instead of saying as some do that "the Court does not seem to understand" or "you do not seem to get my idea," it is far better to adopt a somewhat apologetic tone and say something to this effect: "If the Court please, I am sorry I have not made myself clear. Perhaps I should have stated it this way———etc."

When this method is followed a further hearing will be obtained with a striving on the part of the Court to understand the advocated theory. The trial lawyer should always assume the blame in this situation. It will repay him many times over.

§ 274. Demeanor.

The manner in which the opening statement should be made is in a conversational tone of voice. The statement should not be delivered in a monotone, nor in a dull, lifeless way, but should be lively, with a change of "pace" as to expression and tone. Only simple words and short sentences should be used. Any legal or technical terms should be restated and defined so that the jury will not be at a loss to understand all that is being stated. No particular vehemence should be indulged in by the plaintiff; this should properly be left for the final arguments to the jury. While no loud nor boisterous voice should be used, yet sincerity and earnestness should be shown, as well as confidence in the merits of the case.

When representing the defendant, a little more spirit may be shown in an effort to impress the jury with the theory of the defense as being directly contrary to the facts stated by the plaintiff. This will serve to have the jury keep in mind the fact that all evidence presented on the part of the plaintiff should be considered by them only in the light of the evidence which the defendant has stated he expects to prove. It will help to eliminate a whole-hearted acceptance of the stories of plaintiff's witnesses in view of the possible doubt engendered by the thought of the contrary evidence which the defendant has stated he will produce.

§ 275. Argument.

The opening statement being merely a statement of what each side expects to prove, the law prohibits the attempt to couple such statement with an argument seeking to convince the jury of the truth of each side's case.[9] Objections should

9 Posell v. Herscovitz, 130 N. E. 69, 237 Mass. 513; Wells v. Ann Arbor R. Co., 150 N. W. 340, 184 Mich. 1, Ann. Cas. 1917 A 1093; Zucker v. Karpeles, 50 N. W. 373, 88 Mich. 413; F. L. Dittmeier Real Estate Co. v. Southern Surety Co. (Mo.), 289 S. W. 877; McQuary v. Quincy, O. & K. C. Ry. Co., 269 S. W. 605, 306 Mo. 697; Baker Matthews Lumber Co. v. Lincoln Furniture Mfg. Co., 139 S. E. 254, 148 Va. 413; Cincinnati St. Ry. Co. v. Adams, 169 N. E. 480, 33 Ohio App. 311.

be made to any obvious attempt on the part of an attorney to argue his case in the opening statement. An illustration of an objectionable argument in an opening statement is contained in the following excerpt:

"Now it appears that as the truck backed out somebody came out from the sidewalk toward the car track, but he never got to the back end of the truck. Who he was, we don't know, unless he was somebody who was connected with that truck, but this man coming out as he did before the truck started, visible under the back end of the truck, *was one of the reasons that Mr. Mowat had his automobile under control so that he would be able to handle it for anybody who so came out to get on the street car.*

Mr. Hinshaw: If the Court please, it is pure argument.

The Court: I think the last part is argumentative. Objection sustained."

§ 276. Anticipating defense.

While ordinarily it is not proper [10] for the plaintiff's attorney in his opening statement to take up the case of the defendant and to inform the jury thereof, and while the attorney for the defendant may object to the plaintiff's stating his side of the case on the theory that that is his province and right, however, in some jurisdictions the attorney may state an anticipated defense of his opponent in so far as it appears of record. In those instances where the jury may become prejudiced against the plaintiff upon hearing from the defendant facts which would constitute a perfect defense to the case, but which if the opportunity to reply were given, plaintiff might be able to show that the defense is untenable, then and in that event plaintiff should indirectly anticipate such defense. For illustration, in a contract action where suit is brought for a sum due for goods, wares and merchandise sold and delivered the defense is that the merchandise was not as per sample. The plaintiff replies that the defendant had ac-

10 Mulligan v. Smith, 76 Pac. 1063, 32 Colo. 404; Maxfield v. Jones, 76 Me. 135; Ayrault v. Chamberlain, 33 Barb. (N. Y.) 229. See also Kansas City Southern R. Co. v. Murphy, 85 S. W. 428, 74 Ark. 256 (where counsel said the defense would be "the same old stereotyped one," the court on appeal declared that this was not within the proper confines of an opening it being neither a statement of counsel's claims nor of the evidence, supporting it and that the court should have dealt with the statement emphatically).

cepted and sold all of said merchandise and, therefore, is precluded from raising any such defense. Ordinarily, the plaintiff in his opening statement might be limited to the statement concerning the original purchase, sale, and delivery and the terms in reference thereto. However, in order to give the jury a complete picture of the cause of action the attorney might not only state all of the facts in reference to the sale and delivery, but would then go on to say that his client thereafter made a claim for the money and that at that time the defendant first raised the question that the merchandise was not as per sample. He would then go on to say, "but we will show you that the defendant instead of relying on his claim that the merchandise was not as per sample proceeded to sell all of said merchandise at regular prices and made a profit thereon, thus, as I believe the Court will later instruct you, waiving any claim, if he had one, in reference to the merchandise not being as per sample."

By this procedure the possible effect of defendant's opening statement will have been completely nullified. This method does not violate any rule prohibiting plaintiff from going into the defense or anticipating the defense in his opening statement, and yet completely refutes any such possible defense.

§ 277. Objections.

Objections should almost always be made to opponent's opening statement which contain improper statements as to the law. An improper statement as to the law applicable to the case, unless objected to, may leave an uneradicable impression on the minds of some of the jurors.

A statement by opposing counsel to the effect that he expects to prove certain facts and to produce certain evidence or documents which are inadmissible under the limited issues created by the pleadings should also be objected to in most instances. The possible effect that the knowledge of these extraneous facts may have on the minds of the jury should always be considered.

The only time when such objection should not be made is where there is a hesitancy in calling the attention of the opposing lawyer to the defects and narrowness of his pleadings because of the possibility of amendment. Yet if on this account no objection is made there may be a waiver of the defect.

§ 278. Citing the law.

Many trial judges will not permit attorneys to read or to cite the law applicable to the case, though there are authorities which hold that it is permissible.[11] While the court may be jealously watchful and on guard to prevent any encroachment of his judicial province in instructing the jury on the law, a general statement that the case is based upon a certain statute is permissible and is recommended.

For example, should the cause of action be based on a statute giving the driver of an automobile approaching from the right the right of way, the attorney for the plaintiff would state to the jury that "the plaintiff's claim is based on the statute which gives the driver of an automobile approaching from the right the right of way—the details of the statute and the law applicable thereto will be given to you later by the Court."

Thus a statement of the law has been made and yet the province of the court has not been invaded.

§ 279. Harmful evidence.

Wherever the opponent is in possession of information which is harmful to the proponent's case, it is always advisable for the trial lawyer to mention that fact so as to mitigate the bad effect of it as much as possible. If one of his witnesses has a bad reputation which is well known to the other side, it is always better to make that fact known in such a way that the jury will appreciate that circumstances make it necessary to produce such witness. An attempt to hide this fact, allowing it to become known through cross-examination by the opponent or in his opening statement, will result in a great deal more harm.

§ 280. Plaintiff and defendant.

Some attorneys in the early stages of the trial continually refer to their client as either the plaintiff or the defendant

11 Paige v. Illinois Steel Co., 84 N. E. 239, 233 Ill. 313 (aff'g 136 Ill. App. 410); Jones v. Detroit Taxicab & Transfer Co., 188 N. W. 394, 218 Mich. 673; Steel Furniture Co. v. Pearce, 170 N. W. 80, 203 Mich. 652; Baughman v. Metropolitan St. Ry. Co. (Mo. App.), 177 S. W. 800.

(a) Misstatement of nature of action by counsel where it does not mislead adverse party is not error. Lee v. Campbell, 46 N. W. 497, 77 Wis. 340.

(b) Discretionary with the court. San Miguel Consol. Gold Min. Co. v. Bonner, 79 Pac. 1025, 33 Colo. 207.

without realizing that in some instances the jurors have no idea as to whom the attorney is referring. This method makes it difficult for the jury to understand "at first blush" just who the parties are. It is preferable and more easily understandable to say Edward Johnson, the plaintiff, or the plaintiff, Edward Johnson. When this method is followed there can be no question in the minds of anyone as to whom the attorney is referring. Psychologically, it is better to couple the name of the client with the identification of him as either the plaintiff or the defendant, for the sooner the jury associates the name of the person with the party to the law suit the better will be the results. It is, therefore, recommended and suggested that both the name of the individual and the identification of him as either a party plaintiff or defendant be coupled and associated together. However, the opposing party need not be so identified. He may be referred to as the "defendant."

§ 281. Admissions.

The trial attorney is cautioned in reference to the making of admissions in his opening statement to the jury because of the legally binding effect such admissions will have on his client throughout the remainder of the trial. In most states an outright admission of a fact in the opening statement may eliminate the necessity for legal proof of such fact by the opposite side.[12] Admissions on the part of an attorney are

[12] U. S.—Lehigh Valley R. Co. v. McGranahan, 6 F. (2d) 431.

Kan.—Security State Bank of Eskridge v. Mossman, 292 P. 935, 131 Kan. 508.

Mich.—Zabowski v. Loerch, 237 N. W. 386, 255 Mich. 125.

Mo.—Eaton v. Curtis, 4 S. W. (2d) 819, 319 Mo. 660; Frisby v. St. Louis Transit Co., 113 S. W. 1059, 214 Mo. 567; Wasmer v. Missouri Pac. Ry. Co., 148 S. W. 155, 166 Mo. App. 215.

N. Y.—Bowman v. Seaman, 137 N. Y. S. 568, 1112, 152 App. Div. 690, 937, 28 N. Y. Cr. 279.

Okla.—Hunt v. W. T. Rawleigh Medical Co., 176 P. 410, 71 Okl. 193.

(a) Admission of consideration by execution.—Answer and opening statement admitting note sued on was executed in place of notes on which defendant was liable, admitted consideration for note sued on. Security State Bank of Eskridge v. Mossman, 292 P. 935, 131 Kan. 508.

(b) Effect of admission on right to instruction. — Defendant, having in opening statement admitted primary liability leaving only the amount of recovery to be determined to plaintiff, could not except to court's refusal to give instruction not pertaining to amount of damages. Rorvick v. As-

binding on his client when made during any portion of the trial. However, in some circumstances the binding effect of such admission is limited to that particular trial, though in some states such admission may be shown in a retrial of the same case.

§ 282. "We."

It is a well recognized fact that in most cases the jury "tries" the lawyers rather than the clients. Without realizing it the jurors gradually allow their opinions on the evidence to be swayed in favor of the side represented by the lawyer they like. This is common knowledge among successful trial lawyers.

toria Box & Paper Co., 299 P. 333, 136 Ore. 381.

(c) Concession by counsel for defendant in his opening that the loan sued upon had in fact been made will oblige the court to deny defendants' motion for judgment at the close of plaintiff's case. United States Trust Co. v. Tuchowska, 227 N. W. 539, 249 Mich. 16.

Steel Furniture Co. v. Pearce, 170 N. W. 80, 203 Mich. 652; Simmons v. Harris, 235 P. 508, 108 Okl. 189; McMurrough v. Alberty, 215 P. 193, 90 Okl. 4; Hunt v. W. T. Rawleigh Medical Co., 176 P. 410, 71 Okl. 193; Patterson v. Morgan, 155 P. 694, 53 Okl. 95.

(a) Mere preliminary outline is not such a solemn admission of facts as will dispense with proof thereof. Fillingham v. St. Louis Transit Co., 77 S. W. 314, 102 Mo. App. 573.

(b) Alleged admission of doubtful meaning is not conclusive, especially where nullified by other statements. Patterson v. Morgan, 155 P. 694, 53 Okla. 95.

(c) Where causes are tried on formal written pleadings, it is only where the so-called statement of counsel is distinct and formal and made for the purpose of dispensing with formal proof of some fact at the trial that it may be looked to to supply proof of a fact material to the plaintiff's cause of action. McMurrough v. Alberty, 215 P. 193, 90 Okl. 4.

(d) Where parties failed to have opening statement taken down by court reporter, and where attorneys in the lower court stipulated that case-made, which omitted opening statements, contained all evidence of proceedings, and trial judge certified that it contained all evidence and proceedings, such opening statements were not solemn admissions to be relied on as part of evidence. Simmons v. Harris, 235 P. 508, 108 Okl. 189.

(e) Lack of right to sue.—In an action by an assignee of claims for services, a statement by plaintiff's counsel in his opening statement to the jury that plaintiff was a nominal plaintiff in the case did not constitute an admission that plaintiff was not the real party in interest as required by statute. Dyer v. Title Guaranty & Surety Co., 179 P. 834, 106 Wash. 186.

(f) Admission not established. — Paepke v. Stadelman, 300 S. W. 845, 222 Mo. App. 346.

One method frequently resorted to by attorneys in an effort to take advantage of this knowledge is to put themselves right into the case with their clients by use of the pronoun "we." Instead of John Jones, the plaintiff did so and so—the attorney says "we" did so and so. If the attorney has made himself agreeable and likeable to the jury and thus projects himself into the cause by "we" the jury will more readily be inclined to accept his statements as true. For, after all, the attorney has had the center of the stage throughout the trial. He has played the leading part. His client is virtually a stranger to the jury. The client has taken the witness stand, testified for a short while and then has figuratively faded into oblivion. The personality of the lawyer is constantly before the jury and he gradually absorbs the client's cause to such an extent that unconsciously in the minds of the jury it becomes the lawyer's cause. The jurors take sides for or against him in proportion to their liking for him. The use of "we" will, therefore, bring about a more ready acceptance of his theories and is recommended. It should be used in the opening statements when indicated, but may be used a great deal more effectively in the closing arguments after a good impression has been made throughout the trial as a result of maintaining a friendly, gentlemanly, and honorable attitude.

§ 283. Calling attention to adverse witness' idiosyncrasies. It is sometimes possible to obviate the damaging effect of an adverse witness where proper preparation has been made by interviewing such witness. If the interview has shown the witness to possess certain peculiar traits they may be called to the attention of the jury during the opening statement which may lead them to question the witness' mental stability. This procedure is not recommended as it may tend to excite the sympathy of the jury. Yet, not long ago, a young attorney in a criminal case in Iowa utilized this method to secure a disagreement of the jury. The case was never re-tried and his client was freed.

In the preparation for the trial, he had learned by questioning the complaining witness of certain peculiarities of manner of the said witness, which might be taken as symptoms of insanity. This young lawyer proceeded to discredit this witness before the jury. In his opening statement to the jury, he told them to watch the complaining witness when he testified for these particular mannerisms, describing them, and subtly conveyed to them the idea that this witness was either insane or completely irresponsible. When the witness took the stand, the jury watched for these details and some of the jurors evidently came to the conclusion that he was insane or not to be believed. This constituted almost his entire defense. It secured him a disagreement of the jury.

§ 284. Framing the opening statement for plaintiff.

The opening statement should include for plaintiff:

(1) Introduction.
(2) Parties.
(3) Theory of case.
(4) Description of scene of accident (In personal injury case.)
(5) Word-picture of accident.
(6) Injuries sustained.
(7) Medical, surgical, and other care.
(8) Extent of injuries.
(9) Monetary loss.
(10) Conclusion.

§ 285. (1) Introduction—personal injury case.

The introduction should be commenced in a friendly, genial manner, the salutation to the court and to the jury being more than merely the statement of a few words. When the statement is made "If the Court please" or "May it please the Court" the attorney should face the judge and speak the words to the judge in a friendly manner of greeting. He should pause in the salutation to the court long enough to receive in turn a friendly nod or reply from the court acknowledging such salutation. Should the court in acknowledging the greeting reply by stating the attorney's name in acknowledgment of such friendly salutation it will create a much better psychological atmosphere. The same is true in reference to the salutation to the jury. When the attorney turns from the judge and then faces the jury and states directly to them the words "Gentlemen of the Jury" it must be done in a manner and with an attitude that will secure their friendly attention. While the actual words used are "gentlemen of the jury" the attorney's manner and attitude must be denoting a salutation in effect using the words "friends" or "fellows."

The introduction may consist of a few words or it may consist of a number of paragraphs. It should take sufficient time to permit the jury to become accustomed to the manner of the attorney and to his voice, diction, and method of speaking. The attorney should not go into the main facts which he expects to cover in the opening statement until the jurors have had an opportunity to focus their attention upon him and his statement.

The preliminary remarks of introduction may be in the following form:

Illustration

Counsel: "If the Court please and gentlemen of the jury, as you know, it is customary at this stage of the trial for both the attorney for the plaintiff and the attorney for the defendant to tell you in more detail just what this case is about and what we each expect to prove. First, I, as the attorney for Henry Simpson, the plaintiff in this case, will tell you our theory of the case; then Mr. Jones, the attorney for the defendant, will tell you his theory of the case and just what he expects to prove, and also just what evidence he expects to produce to meet our case. Of course, as you know, any statement that either Mr. Jones might make or that I may make in telling you what we each expect to prove is not to be considered by you as evidence. So that if either one of us should tell you that we expect to prove certain facts and you find at the close of all the evidence that either he or I have failed to prove such fact, just disregard it."

§ 286. (2) Parties.

In order that the jury may properly follow the outline of the case which is to be given by the attorneys in their opening statements, it is always advisable as early as possible to acquaint the jury with the names and the general history of the parties involved in the law suit. This may properly include the naming and the giving of the history, including a statement of the relationship of parties besides those who are included as parties plaintiff or parties defendant. This would be true in all cases where the suit is brought in a representative capacity, such as administrator of an estate, executor, trustee, or the next friend, as well as instances where suit is commenced by the beneficiaries under life insurance policies or where the action is brought for the use of a third person.

It is sometimes good policy under this heading to immediately name all of the parties and to identify them through their relationship with each other and then continue with the statement showing the cause of action relied upon.

Illustration

"* * * Mary Lind, the plaintiff in this case, is a housewife, the wife of John Lind. The defendant, Arthur Simons, is a hauling contractor in the business of hauling ashes in this city. Mary Lind and her husband were riding in an automobile with Joseph Rand and his wife and their son Henry."

§ 287. (3) Theory of the case.

Under this heading a statement would be made in a general way as to the basis of liability. It may be no more than a general statement of the nature of the case which was made in the preliminary remarks just prior to the qualification of the jury. In a personal injury case it might be stated as follows:

"The plaintiff's claim in this case is for damages by reason of the violation of the right of way statute by the defendant in failing to give the right of way to the plaintiff who was approaching from the right of the defendant."

§ 288. (4) Scene of the accident.

It is, of course, important that the jury understand as soon as possible the location of the scene of the accident. This may be done by giving a word picture description of the streets, designating their location and the directions in which each run. If one of the streets happens to be a "through" street or a boulevard, or if there are street car tracks on either of the streets, that fact should be made known to the jury.

In many instances it is advisable to secure an agreement from opposing counsel to utilize in the opening statements specially prepared diagrams or photographs showing the scene of the accident, which diagrams and photographs will in all probability be introduced in evidence during the trial. A statement in the presence of the jury addressed to opposing counsel just before the commencement of the opening statement as to whether or not the diagram or photograph correctly portrays the scene of the accident will usually be followed by a request from opposing counsel to examine the diagram or the photograph. If such diagram or photograph has been fairly and honestly prepared he will undoubtedly agree as to its correctness. This should be followed by a request that he stipulate (in the presence of the jury) that the diagram and photographs may be considered as exhibits received in evidence and may be used by either attorney during the opening statements so that the jury may get a better idea as to the scene of the accident. When this procedure is followed, it will be found that in almost all instances the opposing attorney will agree to the use of such diagrams and photographs. With these aids it is then a comparatively simple matter to present to the jury clearly a description of the place where the accident happened.

In the event diagrams and photographs are *not* used, then the scene of the accident should be described somewhat as follows:

"* * * Gentlemen, this accident took place at Raven Street and Newark Avenue in Norwood Park. Newark Avenue is about 6700 West and Raven Street is about 6200 North. Raven Street runs East and West. Newark Avenue runs North and South. The neighborhood at Raven Street and Newark Avenue is a residential neighborhood with buildings on the Northwest corner of Newark and Raven set back some distance from the sidewalk line. At this Northwest corner of Newark and Raven are some shrubs. Both Raven Street and Newark Avenue at this point where they come together are each approximately 30 feet wide."

Another illustration

If a diagram is used by agreement of the parties it can be utilized in this way:

"* * * Now, gentlemen, this accident took place at the intersection of Raven Street and Newark Avenue in Norwood Park. Newark Avenue is about 6700 West and Raven Street is about 6200 North. Raven Street runs East and

West and Newark Avenue runs North and South. Now I will just refer to this diagram which has been marked Plaintiff's Exhibit 1 and received in evidence by agreement between counsel for the defendant and myself. You will notice that Raven Street runs East and West and that Newark Avenue runs North and South. On the Northwest corner of Newark and Raven, which I now indicate, there is a building set back some distance from the sidewalk line. Just beyond the sidewalk line is a hedge of shrubs. From the diagram you will notice that a very short distance to the south of Raven Street on Newark is Navarre Avenue * * *."

§ 289. (5) Word picture of accident.

In detailing how the accident occurred, it is important that a clear graphic picture be given to the jury as to all of the incidents concerned in the accident. The facts should be told in an interesting manner, each incident following the other in logical sequence so that the jury will have no difficulty in understanding just what happened and just how it happened. The position of the parties should be set out.

Illustration

"On August 2, 1931, Joseph Rand and his wife invited Mary Lind and her husband, John Lind, to take a trip with them in their automobile. They were to go to Bangs Lake, a distance of about fifty miles. This was on a Sunday, a sort of holiday trip. Joseph Rand's car was a five passenger Ford. Henry Rand, the son, was also to go with them. They spent the day at Bangs Lake and started their return at about 4:00 P. M. As they approached the City, Joseph Rand and his son Henry were in the front seat. Joseph Rand was driving. In the rear seat Mary Lind, the plaintiff in this case, was sitting on the outer left-hand side right next to the window on the left-hand side. Next to her in the center was Mrs. Rand and on the outer right hand John Lind was seated. Joseph Rand was driving his Ford about 20 to 25 miles per hour on Raven Street. Raven Street, as you have heard, runs East and West. The Rands and the Linds in the Ford were driving in an Easterly direction on Raven Street. As they approached Newark Avenue, which runs North and South, they noticed a "slow" sign near the corner, so Joseph Rand slowed down the speed of the Ford to 10 to 15 miles per hour. I might add that Raven Street as it reaches Newark Avenue is on a downward incline.

As Joseph Rand approached the intersection of Raven Street and Newark Avenue he looked to his left and noticed a car approaching from the left on Newark Avenue. This car was proceeding in a southerly direction from the North. The car from the left was a large Viking Sedan driven by the defendant. The Viking Sedan was coming along at a very rapid rate of speed. There is also a "slow" sign on Newark Avenue just before you reach the intersection at Raven Street.

As I said, Joseph Rand in the Ford looked to the left and noticed this big sedan coming up Newark Avenue but figured that the Viking would stop as it arrived at the intersection. Rand's car, the Ford, had already arrived at the corner first, so he glanced to the right again to see if there were any cars approaching from the right and started slowly across the street at about 10 to 15 miles per hour. Then he glanced to the left again and noticed the big Viking Sedan almost on top of him. He gave his steering wheel a jerk to the right in an effort to avoid the crash. He managed to swerve the car around so that he was almost facing South on Newark Avenue.

The Viking apparently had not slackened speed nor seemed to make any attempt to avoid the impact. It was still traveling at a high rate of speed and crashed into the rear left side of the Ford car. The defendant, Arthur Simons, had failed to give the Ford car the right of way.

Mrs. Mary Lind and Mrs. Rand just before the impact screamed. Mrs. Lind was thrown from her seat very violently. The rear left side of the Ford was crushed in, crushing Mrs. Lind against the back of the front seat."

§ 290 (6) Injuries sustained.

In stating the injuries sustained it is not necessary to give every minute detail. However sufficient should be told so that the jury will appreciate the seriousness of the case. Care should be exercised in stating a description of the injuries. It should never be done in technical medical terms only. If possible, the injuries should be designated in terms familiar to the layman. If the injury sustained is a fracture of the arm, this should be said. The lawyer should not say the plaintiff sustained a fracture of the humerus. If it is desired to familiarize the jury with the medical terms so that they will appreciate the later medical testimony, it may be advisable to say "the plaintiff, John Jones, suffered a fractured arm. The medical term is humerus."

Illustration:

(Continuing with our illustrative case)

"As Mrs. Lind was crushed against the back of the front seat of the Ford, she felt a terrific pain all around her hips and waist, which the doctors call the pelvis or pelvic girdle. She felt pain in her back, legs and chest."

§ 291. (7) Medical, surgical, and other care.

Here again most of the detail should be left for the testimony of the plaintiff and her attending physician.

Illustration

"Mrs. Lind was taken out of the car and then taken home. A doctor was called. Mrs. Lind was ordered taken to the hospital and put to bed."

§ 292. (8) Extent of injuries.

Under this heading would be included the various types of examinations by the attending physicians, such as physical and x-ray examinations. The same admonition as to too much detail must also be observed in this connection.

Illustration

"The Doctor examined Mrs. Lind and ordered x-rays to be taken. The examination disclosed bruises on legs, back, and chest. The x-rays showed four fractures of the pelvis. Mrs. Lind was immobilized, that is kept in one position by sand bags holding her down to the bed. Later she was put in a complete body cast."

§ 293. (9) Monetary loss.

Here would be stated the basis for recovery, the pain and suffering, the medical and hospital bills, the cost of hiring nurses, maids and others to do all the housework, as well as the permanency of the injury.

Illustration

"Mrs. Lind remained in the hospital for nine weeks. Throughout most of this period she suffered extreme and excruciating pain day and night. After the nine weeks in the hospital she was taken home. She was unable to take care of her household duties for more than nine months. She had to have a nurse for about four weeks after she left the hospital. During all the nine months at home she had to have a woman come in and do all the housework. She had a large hospital and doctor's bill to pay. I believe around $700.00 or $800.00.

She is now able to do her housework, but must rest after short periods of time. She still suffers pain and is extremely nervous. This condition is permanent and she will continue to suffer throughout the rest of her days."

§ 294. (10) Conclusion.

Any few words that will bring the opening statement to a graceful conclusion is permitted. Some attorneys, where they feel that the evidence as to damages will more than support the claimed ad damnum refer to the amount sued for. Others just merely state that the statements made in the opening represent what the case is about.

Illustration

"That in brief, gentlemen, is what the plaintiff expects to prove in this case. Thank you."

Another illustration

"Gentlemen: That is the evidence upon which the plaintiff expects to ask you to return a verdict in this case for the $10,000.00 that we are suing for. Thank you."

Another illustration

"Gentlemen: That is the theory of the plaintiff in this case. This is the evidence that we expect to produce in proof of the defendant's negligence and upon which we expect to ask you to return a verdict in favor of Mrs. Mary Lind, the plaintiff here. Thank you."

§ 295. The opening statement for defendant should include:

(1) Introduction.
(2) Establishing the issue.
(3) Party defendant and his agents.

(4) A picture of how accident happened from view point of the defendant.
(5) The theory of the defendant.
(6) Conclusion.

§ 295a. (1) Introduction.

What has been stated under the heading of the introduction to the opening statement for the plaintiff will also apply to the introduction of the defendant's opening statement. The manner must be friendly. The salutation to the court and jury must be genial and likeable. In many instances, some remark or statement by the plaintiff's attorney will give the basis for the defendant's introductory remarks. Sometimes the defendant's attorney adopts the suggestion made by the plaintiff's attorney that the statements of counsel are not to be considered as evidence. Sometimes the defendant's attorney will call attention to the proverbial saying that there are two sides to every question and that the defendant's evidence will prove that there are two sides to this case.

Illustration

"If the Court please, and Gentlemen of the Jury, as counsel explained to you these statements made at this time are, of course, not evidence, and are not to be received by you as evidence. The theory is that after we have made these opening statements, you, gentlemen, will know what we each expect to prove. You will then be able to sift the chaff from the wheat and be able to tell what really did happen.

Naturally the stories of the two sides as usual are not alike. The evidence for the defendant will show that there are two sides to this case also."

§ 296. (2) Establishing the issue.

It is almost always advisable to inform the jury as early as possible as to the real issue as seen from the view-point of the defendant. In a personal injury case the defendant may frequently take issue with the plaintiff on the basis of the failure of the plaintiff to exercise ordinary care and caution for his own safety. In other words, it would be the intention of the defendant to establish the issue of contributory negligence.

In the case used for illustration purposes in the discussion of the various steps in the plaintiff's opening statement, the defendant could properly establish the issue on the basis that the plaintiff did not have the right of way.

Illustration

"* * * Counsel for the plaintiff has told you that he expects to prove that the plaintiff had the right of way in this case. We will show you by the witnesses that the plaintiff did not have the right of way."

It will be recalled that the defendant in his opening statement should adopt a confident, somewhat positive manner, in detailing his side of the case. Some successful trial attorneys recommend a rather spirited (but not too much so) opening statement for the defendant.

§ 297. (3) Party defendant and his agents.

The attorney for the defendant should always inform the jury at this point a little of the history of the defendant so that they may know just who the defendant is. This is especially true where the attorney for the plaintiff has failed to tell the jury about the defendant or where plaintiff's counsel has attempted to prejudice the jury against the defendant by misdescribing him (or it, where defendant is a corporation).

For instance, suppose in the illustrative case the plaintiff's attorney had attempted to picture the defendant unfairly as a rich hauling contractor and to give the impression that the defendant would not miss a mere $10,000.00 that the plaintiff was seeking. In such a case it would be necessary to show to the jury quickly that while the defendant may be designated as a hauling contractor, he barely makes a living hauling ashes for a number of people.

Illustration

"* * * Counsel for the plaintiff has told you that the defendant is a hauling contractor. He neglected to tell you that Arthur Simons operates a one-man business of hauling ashes on the South Side. He has been hauling ashes for the past ten years. At the time of this accident he owned a Viking automobile which was then about three years old."

§ 298. (4) A picture of how accident happened from viewpoint of defendant.

A plain and vivid word-picture description should be stated of how the accident happened as to be shown by the defendant's witnesses. All facts should be detailed which refute the plaintiff's contentions. This does not include secret defenses.

In the illustrative case, it will be shown that the defendant, naming him, was out visiting; that he was proceeding in a southerly direction on Newark Avenue; that he arrived first at the intersection, honked his horn, and started across the street; that plaintiff's car did not slow up, but proceeded at an excessive rate of speed across the intersection and refused to permit the defendant to pass and that the accident happened through the fault of the driver of the Ford.

Illustration

"Now, gentlemen, let us see how this accident actually occurred as will be shown by the evidence. On August 2nd, 1931, Arthur Simons was out driving with his wife and another couple. They were returning from a visit to a mutual friend. At about 6:30 P. M. they were proceeding South on Newark Avenue. Arthur Simons was driving his Viking Automobile about 15 miles per hour. As he approached Raven Street he slowed up in accordance with the "slow" sign near the corner. He looked to his right and noticed another car coming from the West on Raven Street. Raven Street coming from the West at Newark Avenue is on a steep incline. Mr. Simons reached the corner first. He started across the street at a leisurely rate of speed. Having already started across the street he looked to the left. There were no cars approaching from that direction so he continued on. As he looked again to the right he was surprised to see the Ford car coming down the incline on Raven Street at a faster rate of speed. The driver of the Ford car seemed to be making no effort to turn off so Mr. Simons tried to swerve to the left. By this time the Ford started to swerve to the right. The two cars came together."

§ 299. (5) Theory of the defendant.

Under this heading would come a general statement as to why the defendant feels that he is not liable. The jury should in most cases know the basis of the defendant's claim of non-liability.

In the illustrative case it might be done in this way:

"Now, gentlemen, it is the theory of the defendant, and the witnesses will tell you, that the plaintiff or the driver of the Ford did not have the right of way; that Arthur Simons got to the corner first and, therefore, as I believe, the Court will instruct you the Ford even though approaching from the right had lost any claim to the right of way. In fact, Arthur Simons had the right of way and not the Ford. It is also the claim of the defendant, Mr. Simons, that this accident happened through the fault of Mr. Rand, the driver of the Ford car.

§ 300. (6) Conclusion.

After a discussion of the theory of the defendant, the conclusion that follows shows that the defendant is not liable and that the defendant is entitled to a verdict of not guilty.

Illustration

"We are sorry for Mrs. Lind. We regret very much that she was hurt, but her claim is not against Mr. Simons. Her claim is against Mr. Rand. It was he who is to blame for causing this accident. The evidence will show and the witnesses will tell you that it was Mr. Rand's stubborn refusal to stop and let Mr. Simons pass or else it was his negligent inability to stop his car on the incline after traveling at an excessive rate of speed that caused this accident. Based on this evidence, the defendant at the close of all the testimony will ask you to return a verdict of 'Not Guilty.' Thank you."

§ 301. Contract case.

The outline to be followed in making an opening statement for the plaintiff in a general contract or assumpsit case is slightly different from that used in personal injury or tort cases. In a contract or assumpsit case the outline for the plaintiff will consist of the following:

(1.) Introduction.
(2.) The Parties.
(3.) Theory of the Case.

(4.) Picture of the cause of action, including relationship of the parties and the duties of each.
(5.) Damages.
(6.) Conclusion.

§ 302. (1) The introduction.

In a contract case the introduction is about the same as in a tort case. The various suggestions set out under the heading of the introduction in the outline for a personal injury case hold good as well in most instances in contract cases.

§ 303. (2) The parties.

The same thing is true under this heading with the possible additional suggestion that in a contract case it is frequently advisable to give a little more history of both the plaintiff and the defendant.

§ 304. (3) Theory of the case.

As has been advocated under this heading in a personal injury case, a general statement should be made as to the nature of the case.

Illustration

"Gentlemen: The plaintiff, Henry Simpson, is suing the defendant for damages for breach of contract."

§ 305. (4) Picture of cause of action.

This portion of the opening statement would include a clear, plain word picture of the relationship of the parties, how they came together, what the basis of their dealings was, the duties and obligations imposed upon each, and the breach of such duties by the defendant.

Illustration

"* * * John Hampton the plaintiff in this case as you have heard was employed in the radio business for a number of years. He had successfully marketed a number of different types of radios.

The defendant, Harry Hunt, had been in the wholesale grocery business. He had retired some years ago. In 1932 he decided to enter the radio business with a man by the name of Johnson. They manufactured a type of radio called the Exeter. After a year they gave it up as a bad job. That left the defendant Harry Hunt with a radio factory and a great number of Exeter Radios on his hands. He was unable to move them.

Someone told him about John Hampton. So Harry Hunt decided to hire John Hampton to market the Exeter Radios. After several conferences they arrived at certain terms.

John Hampton was to get a contract. He was to draw $100.00 per week as salary and 5% commission on every radio sold. He was to devote his entire time and attention to the business.

He did devote his entire time and attention to selling Exeter radios. At first and for a while the sales were small and business was very slow. Gradually Hampton began to show results. This took about three or four months. During this time John Hampton drew his $100.00 per week, but did not receive a written contract covering the commission of 5%. He asked the defendant for the contract, but was told not to worry about it. Hunt told Hampton to go right ahead selling the radios and that he would take care of him on the commission.

A year went by. John Hampton succeeded in disposing of all the Exeter radios on hand and had successfully put the Exeter on the market.

The defendant, Harry Hunt, profited from all of the efforts put forth by John Hampton, but failed to give Hampton a written contract to cover the 5% commission on all radio sales. The sales on radios amounted to about $100,000.00."

§ 306. (5) Damages.

In telling of the damages sustained by the plaintiff, the attorney for the plaintiff would detail the amount sued for and how that amount is arrived at.

Illustration

"* * * The sales having amounted to $100,000.00 John Hampton is entitled to 5% of the amount or $5,000.00. This is the sum that we are suing for."

§ 307. (6) Conclusion.

The same form of conclusion may be used as suggested under the same heading for tort or personal injury cases.

§ 308. Opening statement for defendant in contract case.

The opening statement for the defendant in a contract case is based upon the same outline and the same suggestions contained in opening statement for the defendant in personal injury or tort cases. The same general plan should be followed.

§ 309. Opening statement for plaintiff in suit for real estate commission.

May it please the Court and gentlemen of the jury: As you know, it is customary at this stage of the proceedings for both the attorneys for the plaintiff and the attorneys for the defendant to tell you just what we each expect to prove. Perhaps it may be advisable to review the names of the various parties who are concerned in this matter.

As you have been told, Henry Glass and John Rice are the plaintiffs. They are members of the firm of Glass & Rice, Real Estate brokers doing business at West Street and North Avenue. John McCarthy, whose name has already been mentioned, is employed as a real estate broker by the plaintiffs, Mr. Glass and Mr. Rice. Mr. McCarthy has been employed with the plaintiffs, Glass and Rice, for a number of years.

The defendant, Hugo Anderson, is in the manufacturing business in this city. In 1925 Anderson erected a large building at 70th & Oglesby. This building is located on the Southeast corner. The plaintiffs, Mr. Glass and Mr. Rice were employed by the defendant Anderson as renting agents for his building at 70th and Oglesby.

Miss Mary Maroney, another of the parties whose name has been mentioned, is a principal of one of the public schools in this City. I believe it is called the Graham School. She later became a purchaser of the building owned by the defendant, Hugo Anderson.

These are the main parties whom I shall refer to in this statement. Mr. Glass, Mr. Rice, the plaintiffs; Mr. John McCarthy, their real estate broker, and one of their agents; the defendant, Hugo Anderson, who owned the building; and Miss Mary Maroney, who later purchased the building.

In the summer of 1925, the defendant Hugo Anderson listed his building for sale with the plaintiffs, Glass and Rice, that is the plaintiffs, Glass and Rice were employed by the defendant Mr. Anderson to sell his large apartment building at 70th and Oglesby Avenue. At the time that the defendant Anderson listed the building with the plaintiffs Glass and Rice for sale, he, Anderson, agreed that he would pay 3% commission on the purchase price if Glass and Rice sold the building for him. The purchase price at which the defendant Anderson listed his building was at that time $160,000.00.

This suit, as you have heard and know, has been started by the plaintiffs, Glass and Rice, against the defendant, Hugo Anderson, for a commission of 3% on the selling price of $149,500.00, at which the building was later sold.

Mr. John McCarthy, who was employed as an agent and salesman by Glass and Rice, was given the job of selling Mr. Anderson's building. He made various efforts to sell it shortly after it was listed with the plaintiffs for sale in the summer of 1925. He worked on a certain deal which fell through. Then Mr. McCarthy had a further talk with Mr. Anderson, the defendant, and told him that in his opinion $160,000.00 was too high a price for this particular building. Thereupon Mr. Anderson told John McCarthy, who was Glass and Rice's agent, as I have stated, to sell it for $150,000.00.

About the end of February, 1928, John McCarthy became acquainted with Miss Mary Maroney. As you have heard, she was a principal of one of the public schools, the Graham School. He brought the property to her attention. Mr. McCarthy called on Miss Maroney several times at her residence, which was the Lexington Hotel. This was during the month of March, 1928. Finally Mr. McCarthy made an appointment to take Miss Maroney out to show her that building when she expressed some interest in it, and on the 28th of March, 1926, Mr. McCarthy took Miss Maroney out and showed her throughout the building.

That day is fixed, because on the following day Mr. McCarthy on behalf of Glass and Rice sent a notice in writing to Mr. Anderson to the effect that he had a prospective purchaser, naming her, Miss Maroney, and that she was interested in those premises. A few days later, which would be around the first or second or third of April, Mr. McCarthy went to see Mr. Anderson in his home, and told him that

Miss Maroney was interested in this building at 70th and Oglesby, that she liked the building and might buy it, but she stated that the price was too high.

Mr. Anderson then said, "Well, keep on trying." Mr. McCarthy later in the day went back to his office. Mr. Anderson also came to the office and had a talk with Mr. Glass. In McCarthy's presence, Glass remarked to Mr. Anderson, "McCarthy has a deal on for your building." Anderson said, "I know that, but I came here on other matters."

Then on the following Sunday, which was about April 4th, 1926, Mr. McCarthy again took Miss Maroney out to that building at 70th and Oglesby. At that time they were accompanied by Miss Maroney's brother. Miss Maroney wanted him to look at the boiler of the apartment building to see whether it was in good condition. Again she expressed a liking for the building.

She remarked about the leases and general appearance of the building and on the way home, she said to her brother, "I like that building and I expect to buy it."

At various times after this visit to the building, the second visit, Mr. McCarthy saw Miss Maroney. In fact, he kept on seeing her throughout the month of April, 1926. Her only complaint at that time was that she thought the purchase price was high.

At the end of April, or possibly the beginning of May, the exact date is not fixed, Mr. McCarthy received information that Anderson had been in a deal, and that the building had been sold. Thereupon McCarthy naturally ceased his efforts to sell the building. Mr. Emme, the renting agent of the plaintiffs, Glass and Rice, who had taken care of collecting rents and paying expenses on the building, which was a large apartment building, had a conversation with Mr. Anderson, the defendant, when he came in, to this effect. This conversation was late in April, or early in May, as I have said. Mr. Anderson came in and told Mr. Emme not to pay out any more expenses on that building. Mr. Emme knew they had been working on the sale of it, and he naturally asked Anderson "Why, have you got a deal?" and Mr. Anderson concealed the fact that he had then already sold that building, and sold it to Miss Maroney, and said, "Well, maybe yes, and maybe no, but don't pay any more expenses, and you pay the June rent to West Englewood National Bank." Glass and Rice had been paying the rent over to Anderson, who had been the owner.

Gentlemen, on April 27th, or around that date, Mr. Anderson, without saying anything to Messrs. Glass and Rice who had done the work, made a contract with Miss Mary Maroney to sell her that very property.

The property was deeded not directly to Miss Maroney, but it was deeded to the West Englewood Trust & Savings Bank as trustee, and that bank held the title for Miss Maroney until late in November. Glass and Rice knew nothing about the sale having been made to Miss Maroney, until late in the summer, or in the fall, and after they had discovered it, or about that time, then the West Englewood Trust & Savings Bank deeded the property directly to Miss Maroney.

We will show you that the purchase price that Miss Maroney paid for this property was $149,500.00, $500 less than the amount that Mr. McCarthy had been authorized by Mr. Anderson to sell it.

After Mr. Glass had made inquiries, both at the West Englewood Trust & Savings Bank and from Miss Maroney, and had been refused information, Miss Maroney had told him that she did not have any interest in it. This was in October, 1926, while that bank was holding the title for her, but after the title was deeded over to Miss Maroney by the bank, and the fact that she was the purchaser, was no longer hidden, then Glass and Rice made a demand for commissions and were refused, and that is what this suit is brought for. Thank you.

§ 309a. Opening statement for defendant in suit for real estate commission.

Mr. Scott: If the Court please.

The Court: Mr. Scott.

Mr. Scott: And gentlemen of the jury:

From counsel's opening statement one might get the impression that there is considerable mystery about this case. There is none. You will concede that it is plain, simple, and aboveboard when you have heard all of the testimony.

Hugo Anderson, the defendant, whom you have seen sitting behind me at the table has been in the manufacturing business for some time. As you have been told, he owned a certain piece of property on the south side. This property was heavily mortgaged and as was told to the plaintiffs, the burden was just a little too heavy to carry. So Mr. Anderson wanted to dispose of it as soon as possible, and for as large a price so as to lose as little as possible.

Mr. Anderson listed his property for sale with a number of real estate men all over the city. The plaintiffs were only one of many with whom he listed this building for sale. However, none of these various real estate brokers had the exclusive right to sell this property. The first one that produced a buyer at a reasonable price would receive the commission. The commission was to be 3% of the selling price. All of these real estate men had this building for sale on the same basis.

It is our contention that we do not owe the plaintiffs anything in this case. They did not sell the building. Another agent sold the building and collected the commission.

Now this is how the whole thing happened.

Mr. McCarthy the agent of the plaintiffs, Glass and Rice, was given a price of $149,500 to sell this property for. It is true that he got in touch with Miss Maroney, and he offered the property to Miss Maroney and Miss Maroney told him that she would not pay that much.

Now, the best offer that Mr. McCarthy was ever able to submit to Mr. Anderson in this case was several thousand dollars, in fact $145,000, $4,500 less than the price that was actually received for it. After he had been to Mr. Anderson, Mr. McCarthy, I mean, he went back again to Miss Maroney and again he came back to Mr. Anderson and said the best offer I can get is $145,000, and Mr. Anderson then told him he would not take $145,000.

Thereupon Anderson went further with him, and he said, "See if your client will pay $149,500," and Mr. McCarthy then told him that $145,000 was the best he could get, and unless Anderson would come down in price, to $145,000, he was through with this deal.

Mr. Anderson told him he would not take $145,000, and Mr. McCarthy told him he had done everything he could do, and left. That was the last Mr. Anderson ever heard of Mr. McCarthy in this deal.

Subsequently, the evidence will show, another agent came to Mr. Anderson and asked them if they could have the listing of this property and he told him, "Yes" and gave them a price. That agent was able to get $149,500 for the property, for which it was sold, and he got Miss Maroney to pay it, something you will find from the evidence that McCarthy was unable to do. A commission was paid to the other agent, McCarthy had nothing to do with the sale and, therefore, the plaintiffs have nothing coming. That is our defense, gentlemen, and based upon that at the close of all the evidence we shall ask you to return a verdict in our favor.

§ 310. Opening statement for plaintiff in suit for damages to real estate.

May it please the Court and gentlemen of the jury: As you know, it is customary at this time for both the attorney for the plaintiff and the attorney for the defendant to tell you what we expect to prove. The plaintiff, Frank E. Scholl, leased the premises involved in this case for a period of ten years from the owners. The property is located at 437–439 West Van Buren Street. It is a six-story brick building. In 1924 Frank Scholl entered into a sub-lease with the Ackerman Printing Company, the defendants in this case. The sub-lease was for a period of three years, which was in 1927 extended to expire in 1931. There is a building on the premises at 437–439 West Van Buren Street, six stories high and constructed of brick. Under the terms of the sub-lease between my client, Frank E. Scholl, the plaintiff, and the Ackerman Printing Company, the defendant, it became the duty of the defendant, the Ackerman Printing Company to return the premises at the expiration of the lease in good order and repair. This suit is brought to recover the amount of damages which we claim the Ackerman Printing Company caused during the time that they occupied the premises under the sub-lease.

Under the terms of the lease, the defendant agreed that they received the premises from Frank Scholl in good order and repair. They further agreed that they would maintain the premises in a clean, healthful condition; that they would repair and replace all broken glass at their own expense and would repair the premises throughout during the period of the lease. By the terms of this lease it was the duty of the defendant to return the premises in as good a condition as they received it, loss by fire and ordinary wear and tear excepted.

The evidence will show that when the defendant, the Ackerman Printing Company, vacated the premises in 1931 that they did not return the premises to Frank E. Scholl in good order and repair, as provided in the lease, but that on the contrary the building was greatly damaged and that this damage was not due to ordinary wear and tear.

When the premises were turned over to Frank Scholl by the defendant, certain beams and posts were damaged by acid throughout the building, the plaster in various parts of the building was broken, damaged, and torn out, floors and windows throughout the building were badly damaged, window sills were eaten away by acid, the freight elevator was broken and damaged and not fit to be used, the electric wiring and light fixtures were damaged and torn out, toilet facilities all through the building were in bad shape and unable to be used.

The witnesses will tell you that in its present condition due to the damage by the defendant that this building is not fit to be rented to any other tenant and that repairs costing in excess of seven or eight thousand dollars must be made, all of which we contend the defendant is liable for, and based upon this evidence we will ask you to return a verdict in our favor. Thank you.

§ 311. — Opening statement for defendant in suit for damages to real estate.

May it please the Court and Gentlemen of the Jury: As you know there are usually two sides to every case. At this time I would like to have you know our position in this matter.

My client, the Ackerman Printing Company, has been engaged in the printing business for a great many years. We admit that the lease under which we occupied this building provided that the building was to be turned over at the end of the lease in a condition of good order and repair, except for ordinary wear and tear. It is our contention gentlemen, and the evidence will show, that the damage complained of, if any, was due to ordinary wear and tear and that under the circumstances, of which Mr. Scholl was fully aware at the time he entered into this lease, my client does not owe Mr. Scholl one single solitary dollar.

In the first place, as we will prove, Mr. Scholl himself, has been in the printing business for more than 35 years and at the present time is connected with a large printing company in a responsible position, so that he knew exactly how and for what his building was going to be used by my client who is also in the printing business. Mr. Scholl knew at the time he entered into this lease that we could not carry on our business unless we had printing presses in his building, he knew that these printing presses are necessarily heavy pieces of machinery and that in order to be installed in the first place and removed when the lease was up they had to be moved back and forth across the floors. Also, gentlemen, the evidence will show that in the ordinary course of business, it was necessary for us to move large, heavy rolls of paper back and forth across the floors, that we even put additional braces and supports in the building to hold up our machinery properly; also that in the ordinary course of our business it was sometimes necessary to use certain acids in various ways.

The evidence will show that we leased the premises for seven years. During all of that time the plaintiff did no painting, decorating or repairing.

The parties when they entered into this lease knew the nature of the business we were to conduct there. The so-called damage to beams was not any damage at all. The plaintiff knew that the beams had to be altered at the time to permit the installation of our machines. He did not object to it at the time. The same thing is true as to the floors. The plaster is broken in some spots, but it was due to the age of the plaster and not to our fault. We took care of this property as though it were our own. We believe the evidence will show that we do not owe the plaintiff anything at all. Thank you.

§ 312. Opening statement in wrongful death case for plaintiff.

If the Court please and gentlemen of the jury: As you know, it is customary at this stage of the trial for both counsel for the plaintiff and counsel for the defendant to tell you what each side expects to prove. Of course, anything that either one of us, either Mr. Jones for the defendant, or I for the plaintiff, may say is not to be considered as evidence. If either one of us should tell you that we expect to prove certain facts and we should later be unable to prove those facts, just try to forget our statements—just disregard them.

Karl Fugiel during his lifetime was a heater employed at the Republic Steel Mills. He was killed when the automobile in which he was riding was struck by a street car. Lloyd Hill, the plaintiff in this case, was appointed by our Probate Court as the administrator of the estate of Karl Fugiel to prosecute this case. Lloyd Hill, the administrator, is suing the Chicago Surface Lines and Charles Warren who was driving the automobile in which Karl Fugiel was riding. This suit is brought by Lloyd Hill in behalf of Karl Fugiel's widow and his children for damages resulting from wrongful death.

You, gentlemen, are probably familiar with the territory where this accident occurred, between South Chicago and Hegewisch. Avenue O, is a state highway running North and South. It crosses 118th Street which runs east and west. There is a street car line on 118th Street. The ground in that locality is low and swampy and both 118 Street and Avenue O are raised 3 or 4 feet above the ground level. There is a heavy growth of bullrushes or weeds in this swamp along both sides of Avenue O, and on the night of the accident those weeds were high enough to keep people traveling along Avenue O in an automobile from seeing a street car coming up to the crossing of Avenue and 118th Street.

The night of October 31, 1932, was a dark night. About 11 o'clock Karl Fugiel and five other men were coming home from a meeting in an automobile owned and driven by one of them, Charles Warren. The car was a five passenger Locomobile sedan, in good condition. Its brakes and tires were in good condition. The car was going south on Avenue O at about twenty or twenty-five miles an hour, with headlights burning brightly. The men in the car were silent, there was nothing to distract the attention of anyone; in other words, Karl Fugiel was in the exercise of due care and caution for his own safety.

Karl Fugiel and the driver of the car had traveled this road frequently and had ridden on the street car line crossing this road at Avenue O. The evidence will show that street cars were accustomed to sound their gongs as they approached this crossing and to stop on the near side of the highway before crossing it.

There you have the picture—An automobile with good brakes and tires carrying five silent men through the dark night between the high weeds on either side of the road, moving at a moderate rate of speed toward the street car crossing. As the automobile reached the crossing, when it was within a few feet of the crossing, a street car going at high speed, suddenly, and with no warning gong burst into view from behind the tall weeds on the east side of the highway and bore down on the automobile.

Because the road was raised here the automobile could not swerve, and it was too late to stop. The street car struck the automobile on the side near the back and carried it a way and turned it completely around. All those in the car were seriously injured. Karl Fugiel died of a fractured skull and internal injuries within a few hours.

On the night of the accident the weeds were so high that it was impossible for the occupants of an automobile coming along here to see a street car approaching. A day or two after the accident those weeds were cut down. Just who cut them down we do not know, but they were cut down low enough so that those driving in automobiles are now able to see street cars approaching.

Karl Fugiel was 43 years old, and in good health. He had a life expectancy of about 25 years. The witnesses will tell you that Karl Fugiel was a good steady worker, a good provider for his family. He was a heater at the Republic Steel Mill and for the year before his death his average earnings were between $250 and $300 a month. He was the sole support of his wife and four children. He provided a home for his family; clothed and fed them, and educated his children. We claim that Karl Fugiel wrongfully came to his death due to the negligence of the defendant. This suit is brought by his administrator under the laws of this state which provide for the recovery of damages by the dependents and family of one killed through the negligence and fault of another, in an amount not exceeding $10,000.00.

It is our contention that Karl Fugiel was wrongfully killed and that it was due to the negligence of the defendants. As you will later be instructed by the court, this suit is brought by Lloyd Hill as the administrator to recover damages not exceeding Ten Thousand Dollars under the statutes of this state for the use and benefit of Karl Fugiel's dependents, his widow and his fatherless children.

§ 313. Opening statement in wrongful death case for defendant.

May it please the Court and gentlemen of the jury: The evidence for the defendant will show you that counsel is mistaken as to his impression of how this accident occurred. The evidence will demonstrate that my client, the Surface Lines, were not negligent and are not liable in this case.

Counsel for plaintiff has told you that Karl Fugiel was exercising due care and caution for his own safety at the time of and just before the accident. We will show, gentlemen, that he was not exercising due care and caution for his own safety and neither was the driver of the car, Charles Warren.

The evidence will show that the night of October 31, 1932, was dark, but clear. The street car in this accident was moving east on 118th Street at about 18 miles an hour. The highest speed that this type of car could make under the most favorable conditions was only 28 miles an hour. The brakes and controls on the car were in good working order. The lights in the car and the headlight were burning brightly. The motorman was an old timer in the service, who had an excellent record of many years of prudent, careful operation of street cars.

Now, gentlemen, you will recall that this was a clear, dark night. Lights in the street car were plainly visible for some distance. This street car as it approached this intersection was a number of feet higher and above any weeds that were there. Anyone looking ahead could see the lights of the approaching street car. Witnesses will tell you that anyone looking could easily see the lights and know that a car was coming around the bend. The evidence will show that other drivers of automobiles coming along Avenue O right behind Charles Warren's car were able to see and did see the lights of this approaching street car and stopped to avoid danger, but that Charles Warren and the five men in his car made no effort to stop or to avoid the collision.

Since the lights of the street car were so plainly seen it is our contention that we are not liable in this case because of the fact that this accident happened through the fault of the driver of the automobile and the occupants of the car. They were negligent themselves in not seeing the street car and were, therefore, guilty of contributory negligence. I believe his Honor will later instruct you as to the law applicable under these circumstances.

Now let us see just what happened.

As the street car came to the crossing the motorman slowed it down to eight or ten miles an hour. As the street car started across the highway the automobile darted up the road at a high rate of speed, not pausing or slowing down for the crossing, struck the street car on the side of the front vestibule, opposite the entrance, shattering the glass in that part of the car. Then the automobile swerved in front of the car, was struck by it, carried along and turned around.

When the automobile struck the street car, the motorman shut off the current and put on the air brakes, but the shock of the impact threw him back into the car on the floor and in falling, he released the air brakes. He scrambled to his feet and put on the brakes again.

The evidence will show that Karl Fugiel was accustomed to pass along this road, to pass the street car tracks at this location. On the night of the accident the weeds were not high enough to shut out the view of a street car moving along those tracks from the occupants of automobiles on the highway.

Karl Fugiel did not warn the driver of the approach of the street car. He probably did not look either. As a consequence neither Karl Fugiel nor Charles Warren were exercising that due care and caution for their own safety which the law requires.

We are terribly sorry for what happened to Karl Fugiel, but it was not our fault. We are blameless. We did everything we could under the circumstances. If anyone is to blame it is Charles Warren. This claim should be made against him alone and not against us. Thank you.

CHAPTER VI

DIRECT EXAMINATION

§ 314. What is included.

That portion of the examination of a witness by the lawyer who calls such witness to the stand to maintain his case, is usually designated as direct examination or examination-in-chief. The exceptions to this definition are such cases where under statutes in various states the adverse party may be called as for cross-examination.

While the discussion in this chapter will deal with plaintiff's direct examination the principles enunciated herein apply with equal force to all direct examinations for and in behalf of the defendant as well as for the plaintiff. Successful trial attorneys deprecate the lack of instruction and published material on this important subject of direct examination. Volumes have been written on the subject of cross-examination with illustrations demonstrating the particular skill used, yet it must be admitted that in cases thoroughly and properly prepared, where both sides are ably represented, that the winning of a case solely through skillful cross-examination is a rare occurrence. The primary object in the trial of a case should be *proving the attorney's case* rather than disproving his opponent's case. The most important part of the trial is the direct examination. The direct examination should be sufficiently comprehensive,

(1) To prove all elements necessary to merit a favorable verdict.

(2) To present a picture of the cause of action with clarity, understanding and interest.

(3) To present the witnesses to the greatest advantage so as to secure acceptance of their stories as true by court and jury.

(4) To present this story and picture by proper questioning according to the rules of evidence.

(5) To present all documentary evidence to prove and to corroborate the contentions of the trial lawyer.

§ 315. (1) To prove all the elements necessary to merit a favorable verdict.

If proper preparation of the facts, and the law have been made in accordance with the suggestions outlined in the chapters under those headings, it should be a comparatively simple matter to prove all the elements necessary to merit a favorable verdict. A complete investigation of the law involved should furnish the elements necessary to prove the cause of the action. The proper use of the diagram suggested to be made in the preparation of the facts and the use of detailed statements secured from the witnesses outlined in accordance with the suggestions herein should be of considerable assistance.

Some trial attorneys fail to take into consideration the importance of direct examination. They are satisfied to prove up a rather "skimpy" prima facie case barely sufficient to prevent the direction of a verdict against them, then if the opposition presents a strong defense which completely overshadows the plaintiff's direct case, they attempt to supply the deficiencies by presenting witnesses in rebuttal to make the proof complete. An objection by the opposing counsel that such witness or witnesses should have been presented by the plaintiff in his direct case may in many instances be sustained and properly so, and plaintiff's attorney thereupon finds himself with a weak and unconvincing case before the jury. It must, therefore, be kept uppermost in mind that the first purpose of direct examination is to prove fully and completely all of the elements necessary to establish a right to a favorable verdict. While nothing should be done to prolong the trial of a case unduly there must be no fear of overproving by competent evidence the major and material issues involved.

The trial lawyer must not be afraid of "overproving" his case as to the important and material issues which are definitely in conflict. All credible evidence possible should be produced when it goes to prove the main contentions between the parties. When the major point in controversy is considered, the tendency should be towards "over-proving" rather than to take a chance on "under-proving" the case.

§ 316. (2) To present a picture of the cause of action with clarity, understanding and interest.

It has been said that "true art is to achieve the natural in all things." This is also true in the proper presentation of the facts to the jury. To be natural in the presentation of facts in the trial of cases is difficult to achieve. It must always be remembered that the story to be told to the jury is new and unknown to them. Ordinarily the story is presented to them as though they knew the entire history and background of the case. Great care should be observed that the story is presented to them plainly and simply so as to be easily followed and understood. The presentation of facts should be so planned as to present them in a natural sequence so that the jury may arrive at a natural and logical conclusion. The presentation of the facts must run smoothly and plausibly and not require unusual effort to be followed and understood. It must not be "jumpy," "haphazard" or "choppy." If the facts and testimony of various witnesses are not at once understandable to the jury then the case has not been properly presented. The well prepared, intelligently planned and properly presented case is a joy to behold. It identifies the able trial lawyer.

The presentation of the facts and witnesses should be so planned as to reach an interesting climax. When the direct examination has been thus planned, the plan should be adhered to strictly, if possible. Some trial attorneys put a witness on the stand, then without completing his testimony, withdraw that witness for the purpose of putting on another witness to prove other facts. This should not be done unless some emergency arises, as it breaks up the logical sequence of the case and produces a bad psychological effect.

The proof of facts must be presented only after a serious consideration of their psychological value. Planned procedure, as well as the thought of securing the best possible setting for the reception of such evidence in point of order and sequence, must always be sought and desired. This procedure will prove to be of great value in securing a favorable response on the part of the jury.

Elliott in the Work of the Advocate has this to say:

> "Groups of facts must be arranged in natural order, and the rules of logical relation determine their respective positions with relation to each other. A ragged, straggling, disorderly body of facts creates confusion; one treads upon another, one hides another, and one pushes another, like urchins scrambling in a rush for the

playground. Many are dimly seen, none clearly perceived. No pains should be spared to secure an orderly grouping of facts, nor should any labor be omitted to keep each group in its place and filled with its full complement of facts. Until one group has been completed, it should be the sole object of attention; but, when completed, it should be allowed to stand in its place until another compact and finished group arises at its side.

"Facts cannot be effectively grouped together unless a natural method is adopted. What in natural order is entitled to the first place must be awarded it. The thing which a reasonable mind would naturally expect to first appear must lead off, followed in natural order by attendant facts. Obedience to this fundamental principle will sometimes prevent the advocate from putting forward his brightest witness at the outset, but it is safer to adhere to the principle, even though the witness who is chosen to lead the way is not the best. This fundamental principle of arrangement should be steadfastly adhered to, but the best witness of the group which stands first in natural order should always speak the opening words. In filling out the groups the strongest witness should be called first, and after him should come, in orderly succession, those whose testimony is most nearly allied to his, for by this means the jurors start with quickened attention and an intelligent view of the subject. With such a start they readily follow, without perplexity or confusion, the testimony as it falls from the witnesses. If, however, the connection between the testimony of the witnesses is not clearly maintained, the minds of the jurors will be distracted by the introduction of new subjects, and the force of the testimony will be much weakened. Where the groups are not filled in an orderly way confusion and obscurity result, burdening the memory and wearying the understanding. One who has never followed an intricate case throughout its development cannot form an adequate conception of the strength given the case by a careful assemblage of the facts in clusters, with each cluster filled out in logical order."

It has been urged that all trials be opened with the making of only formal proof. Leading trial lawyers, however, disagree with this method of procedure, because it violates one of the primary purposes of direct examination. The making of but formal proof without taking into consideration the logical sequence of all facts to be presented makes it impossible for the jury to appreciate the full import of such evidence. The trial lawyer is, therefore, urged to present all evidentiary facts in a natural sequence. The jury must grasp the significance of each fact at the time it is presented and understand it in its relationship with all other facts in the case.

§ 317. (3) To present the witnesses to the greatest advantage so as to secure acceptance of their stories as true by court and jury.

Since it is the purpose of the trial lawyer to convince the jury of the justice of his side of the case he must depend upon the manner and demeanor of his witnesses in telling their stories to secure belief. It must be remembered that the trial lawyer is in fact a salesman attempting to sell the theory of his cause to the jury. His evidence is his stock in trade, and his witnesses are his means of presenting and offering the evidence. Care should, therefore, be taken to present the best witnesses possible under the circumstances and to present them in such a manner that their stories may be more readily acceptable.

If the occupation or office of the witness is such as will lend dignity and credence to his testimony, the witness should be permitted by proper introduction to state his occupation, position or duty. Where, of course, an expert witness is put upon the stand it is then not only permissible but necessary to qualify the witness by showing the various connections he may have with public or private institutions, his experience and any distinction he may have earned in his particular field of endeavor.

To present the witnesses to the greatest advantage, it becomes of the utmost importance that the trial attorney remain in the background as much as possible and permit the witnesses to "sell" themselves to the jury, rather than attempt to convince the jury of the attorney's great ability as a trial lawyer by putting himself in the foreground. Practically all successful trial lawyers agree that the more prominence given to a lawyer by his method of questioning, the greater the harm to the cause of the client.

§ 318. (4) To present the story and picture by proper questioning according to the rules of evidence.

In order to present all the facts legally and properly in direct examination, it is necessary that all trial attorneys become familiar with the technique to be employed in laying the foundation for the reception of all types of evidence. Familiarity with the many illustrations contained in this book should sufficiently provide the groundwork for the proper introduction into evidence of all facts necessary to be proved in direct examination. If detailed question and answer statements have been taken from all witnesses, as previously suggested, they should be used as the basis for the proper presentation of their testimony.

Some authors have cautioned trial attorneys against the preparation of all questions in advance and suggest that only a few preliminary questions be prepared for each witness. Experience with lawyers who are trying their first few cases establishes the fact that the more questions prepared in advance, the better it has been for all parties concerned. There is a natural nervousness which every lawyer feels and experiences when he is about to try his first case. That nervousness, in many instances, increases as the trial progresses and is such that he may forget all the plans he has made in reference to the procedure to be followed. This tends to contribute to a lack of self-confidence and results in utter confusion. Where, however, the attorney has prepared practically all important questions in advance, both on direct and cross-examination, he gains confidence as he finds the trial progressing smoothly. Even if he should still continue to be nervous, with everything having been prepared, he is in a position to continue and will probably succeed in spite of his nervousness. He will find that he has made a complete legal proof of his side of the case. The preparation of questions in advance is, therefore, strongly recommended to all lawyers until the trial technique and plan of procedure have become almost second nature. This should be done until confidence and experience warrant its discontinuance. It is reported that one of the ablest trial lawyers of today, after many years of success, still prepares his cases by writing out almost every question.

Trial technique should be studied and practiced intensely until such time as the technique becomes familiar and habitual. All questions as they are prepared should be subjected to a rigorous self-examination by the trial attorney to see whether or not they are subject to any of the many objections under the rules of evidence, viz., leading, immaterial, irrelevant, calling for conclusions, etc. If questions are prepared without subjecting them to this close scrutiny, they will be of little assistance.

§ 319. — Have witnesses visit court room.

Whenever possible, witnesses should be requested to make visits to various court rooms while trials are in progress, so as to familiarize themselves with the procedure of the court room. Not only is this good advice for witnesses, but young trial lawyers should at every opportunity observe recognized and competent trial lawyers in "action," so as to familiarize themselves with the proper demeanor, practice and procedure of the attorney in the court room.

§ 320. — Interviewing witnesses.

After the questions are prepared, and just prior to the trial, each witness should be called in and examined in the same form and manner as he will be on the trial so as to familiarize him with the form of questions to which answers will later be required. Each witness should be warned against testifying to conclusions such as "he agreed," "it was understood," hearsay evidence, etc., with illustrations as to each of these objectionable features and with suggestions as to how the same answer may be given without violating the rules of evidence. They should also be directed merely to answer the questions and not to volunteer any information. The witnesses should all be warned against losing their tempers. A good method to follow is to tell them that the opposing lawyer will endeavor to get them angry in an effort to discredit them before the jury.

§ 321. — Connectives.

One of the greatest boons of the trial attorney in properly presenting testimony upon direct examination is through the use of *connectives*. Connectives are those few words generally utilized to inconspicuously prompt and guide the witness in telling his story. It assists the witness and enables the trial attorney to make his proof much more simply. It helps to lead the witness over troublesome situations without being subject to objection [1] and at the same time helps put the witness at ease. It also eliminates "jerky spots" as well as embarrassing pauses and gaps in the continuity of the witness' story. It helps to keep the interest alive in a more natural telling of the story. These connectives should be used whenever possible and necessary. The following are some of the connectives most commonly utilized:

1. "What happened then, if anything?"
2. "What did you then do, if anything?"
3. "What did he then do, if anything?"
4. "What occurred then, if anything?"
5. "What followed then, if anything?"

The use of the words "if anything" in conjunction with these connectives, eliminates the possible objection that the examining lawyer is assuming that something further happened or that something further was done. The words "if anything" should therefore always be added. It is not an uncommon occurrence to have the witness on the stand forget certain facts. In order to have the witness testify to these forgotten facts it becomes necessary to refresh his memory. In anticipation of this possibility and in preparation for such a contingency, all witnesses prior to taking the witness stand should, in response to such connectives as have been discussed in the preceding paragraph, be warned to answer *"That is all that I can recall"* or *"That is all that I can recollect just now."* This answer serves the purpose of showing that the witness' recollection has been exhausted and will permit the examining attorney to suggest the subject of further inquiry by a direct question.[2] The witness should be admonished never to say "That is all that happened" or "That is all that was said." Such an answer forecloses further inquiry into

[1] Peo. v. Hodge, 141 Mich. 312, 113 A. S. R. 525, 104 N. W. 599. Schlesinger v. Rogers, 80 Ill. A. 420, at p. 422.

[2] Schlesinger v. Rogers, 80 Ill. A. 420; Graves v. Merchant etc., 82 Ia. 637.

the subject except by express permission of the court. Direct or leading questions are permissible in direct examination under the circumstances above explained or in cases where the witness does not speak or understand English with adequate sufficiency, is ignorant and illiterate. They are permissible in examining children and proved hostile witnesses and in all cases where the subject of inquiry is *merely preliminary* and not involving the material issues of the case. In fact in the last mentioned instance, leading questions are favored as they tend to expedite the trial of the case without harm to either side.[3]

§ 322. "Tell the Court and jury, please."

As previously pointed out in selecting the jury, the trial lawyer must always show that he is cognizant of the presence as well as the power of the jury. His appeal, as well as that of his witnesses, must be to the jury who are to return the verdict in the case.

While the attorney must heed and recognize the necessity of the appeal to the jury he must be careful not to slight the authority and power of the judge. Therefore some of the questions should be propounded in this form:

Illustration

"Q. Mr. Jones, *will you tell the Court and jury, please,* what kind of a day it was?"

§ 323. Right to correct testimony.[4]

Every witness who has given incorrect testimony, has a legal right to take the witness stand later and to admit that his former testimony was not correct. He may then testify as to the true state of affairs.

The trial lawyer should not hesitate to have a witness do this, particularly where he has mistakenly testified on some *material* point.

A request addressed to the court for permission to recall the witness for this purpose will usually be granted.

3 See Leading Questions, p. 258.

4 Moreau v. Grandmaison, 189 N. W. 860, 220 Mich. 238; Teutonia Ins. Co. v. Tobias (Tex.), 145 S. W. 251.

§ 324. Refreshing memory.[5]

It often occurs that the recollection of a witness testifying with respect to the happening or non-happening of a certain event fails him. When this occurs resort must be had to outside sources. It may be that at the time of the happening or non-happening of the event the witness made a memorandum or record. If the memorandum or record was true and correct and was made at the time of the occurrence in the usual and ordinary course of business, it may be utilized for

[5] See Re-Direct Examination, p. 597, for additional suggestions.

Any memorandum that will refresh the memory of a witness may be used for that purpose. Peo. v. Cassidy, 283 Ill. 398; T. Barbour Brown & Co. v. Canty, 161 Atl. 91, 115 Conn. 226; Com. v. McDermott, 152 N. E. 704, 255 Mass. 575.

It must first be shown that a witness cannot recall the facts before he will be permitted to examine the memorandum. Precourt v. Driscoll, 157 Atl. 525, 85 N. H. 280; Haack v. Fearing, 28 N. Y. Super. 528; Diamond Glue Co. v. Wietzychowski, 227 Ill. 339.

A witness may refresh his recollection from a memorandum prepared by another person where he can testify as to its correctness. Walsh v. Chicago Rys. Co., 303 Ill. 339; Stillman v. Chicago R. I. & P. Ry. Co., 192 N. W. 860, 196 Ia. 612.

As for example, where the memorandum had been prepared under the supervision of the witness. Com. v. Levine, 181 N. E. 851, 280 Mass. 83; Laub v. DeVault, 139 Ill. App. 398.

Or in the presence of the witness. Crystal Ice Mfg. Co. v. San Antonio etc., 27 S. W. 210, 8 Tex. Civ. App. 1.

The memorandum must have been made at or near the time when the facts were fresh in the mind of the witness. Peo. v. Majors, 190 Pac. 636, 47 Cal. App. 374; Peo. v. Cassidy, 119 N. E. 279, 283 Ill. 398; State v. Hassan, 128 N. W. 960, 149 Ia. 518; Texas Employers Ins. Ass'n. v. Birdwell, 39 S. W. (2nd) 159 (Texas); McCourt v. Peppard, 105 N. W. 809, 126 Wis. 326.

The witness must be able to testify from an independent recollection without the aid of the memorandum. Peo. v. Maddox, 162 Ill. App. 95; Johnson v. Culver, 19 N. E. 129, 116 Ind. 278; Tabor State Bank v. Brewer, 69 N. W. 1011, 100 Ia. 576.

However, it has been held that when the witness testifies that the memorandum is true and was made contemporaneously with the transaction, he may testify although he has no independent recollection. Graham v. Dillon, 121 N. W. 47, 144 Ia. 82; Prudential Trust Co. v. Coghlin, 144 N. E. 283, 249 Mass. 184; Sorell v. State, 167 S. W. 356, 74 Tex. Cr. 100; Linch v. Nebraska etc. Co., 235 N. W. 456, 120 Neb. 819; Martin v. Good, 14 Md. 398; Wait v. Wenks, 186 Ill. App. 296, at 299.

Opposing counsel has the right to examine the memorandum. Peo. v. Cassidy, 119 N. E. 229, 283 Ill. 398; Peo. v. Schaepps, 186 N. W. 508, 217 Mich. 406; Richardson v. Nassau El. R. Co., 180 N. Y. S. 109, 190 App. Div. 529.

Cross-examination as to refreshing memory, see p. 491.

the purpose of refreshing the recollection of the witness. The technique to be employed in that event is as follows:

Witness: A. I just cannot recall right now the individual items that I packed.

Q. Do you know of anything that will help refresh your recollection?

A. Yes, there is a shipping ticket.

Q. Who prepared the shipping ticket?

A. I did.

Q. Was that shipping ticket written out by you?

A. Yes, it was.

Q. Was it true and correct at the time you wrote it?

A. Yes.

Q. Was it made by you in the ordinary course of business?

A. Yes, it was.

Q. And at the time you shipped these items?

A. Yes.

Q. Would a reference to that shipping ticket help you to refresh your recollection?

A. It would.

Q. I show you Plaintiff's Exhibit 4 for identification and ask you whether or not that is the shipping ticket you have referred to?

A. It is.

Q. Will you examine it, please?

A. I have.

Q. Please return it to me. (Witness does so.) Now after having examined Plaintiff's Exhibit 4 for identification have you an *independent recollection* as to what individual items you shipped?

A. I have.

Q. What are they?

A. Two maple chairs, one breakfast table, etc.

If the witness can then remember only a few items and there are many more, the same technique may be employed over again until the witness has recollected and testified to all of the items.

If, after examining the exhibit, the witness still has no independent recollection of the items, but testifies as to all of the preliminary steps showing that it was true and correct at the time it was made and that it was made in the ordinary course of business at the time of the transaction, then the memorandum or exhibit may be introduced in evidence.[6]

§ 325. Leading questions.[7]

A leading question is one that is so formed as to suggest to the witness the answer that is desired. Not only are lead-

6 Peo. v. Krauser, 315 Ill. 478 at 508; Marron v. Great Northern Ry. Co., 129 Pac. 1055, 46 Mont. 593; Pickering v. Peskind, 183 N. E. 301, 43 Oh. App. 401; Howard v. McDonough, 77 N. Y. 592.

7 *A leading question is one which suggests to the witness the answer expected or desired:* Harvey v. Osborn, 55 Ind. 535; Collins v. Gleason Coal Co., 140 Iowa 114, 18 L. R. A. (N. S.) 736, 115 N. W. 497, 118 N. W. 36; Stoudt v. Shepard, 73 Mich. 588, 44 N. W. 696; Roth v. Travelers etc., Co., 102 Tex. 241, 132 A. S. R. 871, 20 Ann. Cas. 97, 115 S. W. 31; Proper v. State, 85 Wis. 626, 55 N. W. 1035; People v. Schladweiler, 315 Ill. 553, 146 N. E. 525.

Or which assumes a fact to be proved which is not proved: People v. Mather, 4 Wend. (N. Y.) 229, 21 Am. Dec. 122; Brannan v. Henry, 142 Ala. 698, 110 A. S. R. 55, 39 So. 92; Damas v. People, 62 Colo. 418, L. R. A. 1918 D 591, 163 Pac. 289; Carpenter v. Ambrason, 20 Ill. 170; Hill v. State, 141 N. E. 639 (Ind.); State v. Christy, 198 Iowa 1302, 210 N. W. 42; Williams v. Craig, (Texas) 252 S. W. 876.

The allowance of leading questions is a matter within the discretion of the Court: People v. Fong Ah Sing, 70 Cal. 8, 11 Pac. 323; Crean v. Houmigan, 158 Ill. 301, 4 N. E. 880; Kyle v. Miller, 108 Ind. 90; State v. Pugsly, 75 Iowa 742, 38 N. W. 498; Webb v. Feather, 119 Mich. 473, 78 N. W. 550; McDermott v. Jackson, 97 Wis. 64, 72 N. W. 375; Stratford v. Sanford, 9 Conn. 279; Downs v. N. Y. C. R. R. Co., 47 N. Y. 83; Devereaux v. Clemons, 17 Oh. Cir. Ct. 33, 9 Oh. C. D. 647; International & G. N. R. Co. v. Dalwigh, 92 Tex. 655, 51 S. W. 500; Kohler v. West Side R. Co., 99 Wis. 33, 74 N. W. 568.

A question is not objectionable as leading because it can be answered by "Yes" or "No": Gully v. Nystel, 233 S. W. 122 (Tex.); Ingwerson v. Carr & Brannon, 180 Iowa 988; Schlesinger v. Rogers, 80 Ill. A. 420; McKeon v. Harvey, 40 Mich. 226; but see: International G. N. R. Co. v. Dalwigh (Tex.) supra, and Daly v. Melendy, 32 Neb. 852, 49 N. W. 926.

While leading questions are generally objectionable to one's own witness, the Court may, in its discretion, permit it under the following circumstances: *Where the witness has taken the party by surprise:* St. Clair v. United States, 154 U. S. 134, 14 Sup. Ct. Rep. 1002; Babcock v. People, 13 Colo. 515, 22 Pac. 817.

Where the witness is hostile or evasive: Rosenthal v. Bilger, 86 Iowa 246, 53 N. W. 255; Moody v. Rowell, 17 Pick. (Mass.) 490, 28 Am. Dec. 317; McBride v. Wallace, 62 Mich. 451, 29 N. W. 75; People v. Sexton, 187 N. Y. 495, 116 A. S. R. 621, 80 N. E. 396; Shaw v. State, (Tex. Cr. Repts.) 229 S. W. 609; Peo. v. Curran, 286 Ill. 302, 121 N. E. 637.

Where the witness is reluctant: Cassen v. Galvin, 158 Ill. 30, 41 N. E.

ing questions usually objectionable according to the rules of evidence, but they are bad psychologically. In an effort to secure a favorable verdict the attorney, who is in effect *testifying* by means of leading questions and the securing of "yes" or "no" answers by the witness, places the witness in a very poor light and minimizes the chances of securing acceptance of the story as true by both court and jury.

§ 325a. Handling of witnesses.

Handling of witnesses properly is an important factor in trial technique. The attorney should serve merely as a friendly guide, interrupting as little as possible and permitting the witness to tell his story in his own way. The simplest and plainest language should be used in forming questions, keeping in mind that both the witness and the jury are laymen and must understand every question. All witnesses should be warned against exaggeration and acting "smart alecky" but should be instructed to adopt a natural, friendly, honest attitude, showing a willingness to answer all questions. They should be warned that the same attitude must be maintained *on cross-examination* as well as during the direct examination. They should also be told to say that

1087; Robinson v. State, (Tex. Cr. Repts.) 49 S. W. 386; Schuster v. State, 80 Wis. 107, 49 N. W. 30.

Where the witness is very young: Peo. v. Schlodweiler, 315 Ill. 553, 146 N. E. 525; Moody v. Rowell, (Mass.) supra; State v. Megorden, 49 Ore. 259, 14 Ann. Cas. 130, 88 Pac. 306.

Where the witness is ignorant: Cheeney v. Arnold, 18 Barb. (N. Y.) 434; Doran v. Mullen, 78 Ill. 342; Rodriguez v. State, 23 Tex. App 503, 5 S. W. 255.

Where the witness is infirm: Belknap v. Stewart, 38 Neb. 304, 56 N. W. 881; Cheeney v. Arnold, (N. Y.), supra.

Where the memory of the witness is exhausted: Graves v. Merchants' & B. Ins. Co., 82 Iowa 637, 31 A. S. R. 507; Hatsfield v. State, (Tex. Cr. Repts.) 29 S. W. 777; Turney v. State, 8 Smedes & M. (Miss.) 104, 47 Am. Dec. 74; People v. Limeberry, 298 Ill. 355, 131 N. E. 65; Schlesinger v. Rogers, 80 Ill. App. 420 at 422.

Where the question is merely preliminary: State v. Castelli, 92 Conn. 58, 101 Atl. 476; Seymour Water Co. v. Lebline, (Ind.) 144 N. E. 30; State v. Golden, (Iowa) 190 N. W. 509; Greenup v. Stoker, 8 Ill. 202; Cronan v. Cotting, 99 Mass. 334; People v. Hodge, 141 Mich. 312, 113 A. S. R. 525, 104 N. W. 599; People v. Mather, N. Y., supra.

Leading questions are generally permissible on cross-examination: People v. Considine, 105 Mich. 149, 63 N. W. 196; Legg v. Drake, 1 Oh. St. 286; Hempton v. State, 111 Wis. 127, 86 N. W. 596; Phares v. Barber, 61 Ill. 271.

they "do not remember" or "do not know" whenever that is the fact. They should not testify too positively about minor details or dates.

At the risk of repetition, but because of the prominent part that direct examination plays in the trial of a law suit, we quote from Harris "Hints on Advocacy:"

> "One of the most important branches of advocacy is the examination of a witness-in-chief. * * *
>
> "One fact should be remembered (by the attorney) to start with, and it is this: the witness whom he has to examine has probably a plain straight-forward story to tell, and that upon the telling it depends the belief or disbelief of the jury, and their consequent verdict. If it were to be told amid a social circle of friends it would be narrated with more or less circumlocution and considerable exactness. But all the facts would come out; and that is the first thing to ensure if the case be, as I must all along assume it to be, an honest one. I have often known half a story told, and that the worse half too, the rest having to be got out by the leader in re-examination, if he have the opportunity. If the story were being told as I have suggested, in private, all the company would understand it, and if the narrator were known as a man of truth, all would believe him. It would require no advocate to elicit the facts or to confuse the dates; the events would flow pretty much in their natural order. Now change the audience; let the same man attempt to tell the same story in a Court of Justice. His first feeling is that he must not tell it in his own way. He is going to be examined upon it; he is to have it dragged out of him piecemeal, disjointedly, by a series of questions—in fact, he is to be interrupted at every point in a worse manner than if everybody in the room, one after another, had questioned him about what he was going to tell, instead of waiting till he had told it. It is not unlike a post mortem; only the witness is alive, and keenly sensitive to the painful operation. He knows that every word will be disputed, if not flatly contradicted. He has never had his veracity questioned perhaps, but now it is very likely to be suggested that he is committing rank perjury.
>
> "This is pretty nearly the state of mind of many a witness, when for the first time he enters the box to be examined. In the first place then he is agitated, confused, and bewildered. Now put to examine him an agitated,

confused and bewildered young advocate, and you have got the worst of all elements together for the production of what is wanted, namely, evidence. First of all the man is asked his name, as if he were going to say his catechism, and much confusion there often is about that, the witness feeling that the judge is surprised, if not angry, at his not having a more agreeable one, or for having a name at all. He blushes, feels humiliated, but escaping a reprimand thinks he has got off remarkably well so far. Then he faces the young counsel and wonders what he will be asked next.

"Now the best thing the advocate can do under these circumstances is to remember that the witness has something to tell, and that but for him, the advocate, would probably tell it very well, 'in his own way.' The fewer interruptions therefore the better; and the fewer questions the less questions will be needed. Watching should be the chief work; especially to see that the story be not confused with extraneous and irrelevant matter. The chief error the witness will be likely to fall into will be hearsay evidence, either he says to somebody, or somebody says to him something which is inadmissible and delays the progress of events. But the witness being very nervous, you must be careful how you check the progress of his 'he says says he's,' or you may turn off the stream altogether. Pass him over those parts as though you were franking him through a turnstile, and then show him where he is; or as if you were putting a blind man with his face in the direction he wishes to go, and then left him to feel his way alone. * * *

"Judges frequently rebuke juniors for putting a question in this form: 'Do you remember the 29th of February last?' In the first place, it is not the day that has to be remembered at all, and whether the witness recollects it or not is immaterial. It is generally the facts that took place about that time you want deposed to, and if the date is at all material, you are putting the question in the worst possible form to get it. A witness so interrogated begins to wonder whether he remembers the day, or whether he does not, and becomes puzzled. We don't remember days. You might just as well ask if he remembers the 1st of May, 1886 (the day on which he was born), instead of asking him the date of his birth. This is one of the commonest and at the same time one of the stupidest blunders that can be made. I will, therefore, at the risk of repetition, give one more illustration. Suppose you ask a witness if he remembers the 10th of June, 1913; he probably does not, and both he and you are bewildered, and think you are at cross purposes; but ask him if he was at Niagara in that year; and you will get the answer without hesitation; inquire when it was, and he will tell you the 10th of June. In this way you avoid taxing a witness's memory, always a dangerous proceeding, and much more within the province of cross-examination than examination-in-chief. Many a good case has been lost—and many more will be—by clumsy questions of this kind at the commencement of a witness's examination. If you leave his mind in a state of bewilderment and confusion, your work will only need to be followed up by a well-delivered question or two in cross-examination to demolish the whole of his evidence; and then, in all probability, you will think the case would certainly have been won if you had not had so stupid a witness. * * *

"The rule is this, that in examining a witness the order of time ought always to be observed.

"Stated in writing it looks simple enough, and everybody says 'of course.' Plain as one of the ten commandments, and as often violated by young advocates. Just step into court, and you will see events running over one another like ants on an ant-hill. Not only is the rule not acted upon, it is never even recognized. True, the principal events in a story are generally placed in something like order, because the judge requires that his notes should be correct. But with what difficulty this is accomplished when an inexperienced junior gets out a detail here and a detail there and mixes them up with wrong events and dates, leaving the judge to match them as if he were playing a game of 'Patience.'

"While a witness is telling his story in a natural manner (which he will generally do if left to himself and with due attention to the order of time), counsel suddenly breaks in with some such observation as this: 'One moment. What was said when you spoke to the defendant?'

"The thread of the story is immediately broken; the witness's mind is carried back like a wounded soldier to the rear, and it is some time before he can be brought to the front again. Nor is this all. The judge is angry (if a judge can be), and the mind of the jury is prevented from following the course of the narrative. If the question be of importance the judge's notes must be altered, and probably will be confused. Had the order of time been observed the notes would have required no correction, and it is possible that the subsequent events will take a different colour from the answer. Besides this, the breach of this rule tends to multiply itself. The question having been interposed at the wrong time, the judge asks: 'When was that said?' The witness becomes confused, tries to recollect, and very likely puts it in the wrong place after all, is reminded that that cannot be, is ordered to recollect himself and be careful, and so on, to the confusion of everybody except the opposing counsel, into whose hands the inexperienced junior is playing. It shows the necessity of every event being placed in its natural order, and of every material circumstance and conversion accompanying that event being given in connection with it, so that everything is exhausted as the story proceeds. If this be not done the client had better have been without your services.

"Let therefore the events be told in the order in which they occurred, with the accompanying conversations, if important and admissible, and their minor incidents if material.

"Another fault of too frequent occurrence is the repetition of the phrases: 'You must not tell us what was said, but what was done.' 'Did he say anything to you? Don't tell us what it was.' The jury, who know very little of the rules of evidence, must sometimes think from the tone as well as the language that the counsel is afraid of something being told that would be adverse to his case, and must wonder at an advocate who asks if somebody said something, but anxiously cautions the witness not to tell what it was. It may be said the caution was necessary, so it might be; but it need not be made the prominent feature in the examination. There need not be a fuss about it, as though you wanted to impress the world with your vast knowledge of the rules of evidence. In ninety-nine cases out of a hundred, it is obvious that something was said; the fact will not be disputed, and a leading question will pass the witness over the difficulty, and not confuse his mind by sending it upon an inquiry as to why he must not give the conversation.

"Another rule to observe is this:

"Never cross-examine your own witness. This, again, seems remarkably obvious. But it requires an effort to obey it nevertheless. You will hear an advocate cross-examine his witness over and over again without knowing it, if he have not the restraining hand of his leader to check him.

"Before Mr. Justice Hawkins, some years ago, a junior was conducting a case, which seemed pretty clear upon the bare statement of the prosecutor. But he was asked: 'Are you sure of so and so?' 'Yes,' said the witness. 'Quite?' inquired the counsel. 'Quite,' said the witness. 'You have no doubt?' persisted the counsel. 'Well,' answered the witness, 'I haven't much doubt, because I asked my wife.'

"Mr. Justice Hawkins: 'You asked your wife in order to be sure in your own mind?' 'Quite so, my lord.' 'Then you had some doubt before?' 'Well, I may have had a little, my lord.'

"This ended the case, because the whole question turned upon the absolute certainty of this witness' mind. Of course, it is not suggested that a fact should be suppressed that is necessary for the ascertainment of truth, and in this particular instance the learned counsel was quite right in pressing the witness upon a material point upon which the prosecution rested; but it is no part of an advocate's duty to shake his witness' testimony to pieces if he believes it to have been honestly given. Nay, more. A cross-examination of one's own witness may most unjustly bring about a disastrous result. A witness may get confused, and although at first might feel absolutely positive and be justly positive, yet, by perpetually harassing him, he may begin to doubt whether he is positive or not, and leave an impression that he is doubtful. Such questions as: 'Are you quite sure, now? Are you certain?' are cross-examination, and do not fall properly within the scope of an examination-in-chief. 'Are you quite sure you have the money in your hand?' would be certain to raise a doubt in the mind of a conjurer asked the question.

"But although it is by far the best to let a witness tell his story in his own way as much as possible, it is absolutely necessary to prevent him from rambling into irrelevant matter. Most uneducated witnesses begin a story with some utterly irrelevant observation, such as, if they are going to tell what took place at a fire, they will say, 'I was just fastening up my back door, when I heard a shout.' Get him as soon as you can at the fire and the evidençe will come with little trouble. * * *

"Another common error is worth noting, and that is the not permitting a witness to finish his answer, or tell all he knows on a material matter. In the very midst of an important answer a witness is very often interrupted by a frivolous question upon something utterly immaterial. This seems so absurd on paper that it needs an example. A witness is giving an answer when some such question as this is interposed: 'What time was this?' or, 'Had you seen Mr. Smith before this?' A question is often left half answered by such interruptions, the better half perhaps being untold. 'He never asked me about that,' says the witness after the case is over; or, 'I could have explained that if he had let me.' If the question be material, by all means let the answer be taken down; if immaterial it ought not to have been asked. All unnecessary interruptions produce confusion in the mind of the witness and jury and tend to damage your case."

§ 325b. General suggestions.

Complex and verbose questions should be avoided. The question should be clear and simple. It is much more advantageous to put two or more short questions than to propound one lengthy and complex one. The question has to be understood not only by the witness but also by the jury (if the case is being tried before a jury). Each witness should be instructed to listen carefully to every question as it is propounded and not to answer any question unless he understands it. The witness should be advised not to hesitate to indicate that he does not understand the question if he actually fails to understand it. All witnesses should be warned against chewing gum or having anything in their mouths while testifying as this is not only undignified but sometimes makes it difficult for the judge and counsel on both sides as well as the jury, in jury cases, to understand the witness. The witness should answer all questions distinctly and in a naturally modulated tone of voice. Witnesses should come to the court room dressed in clean conservative street clothes in order to make the best possible impression.

§ 326. Interview all witnesses.

Every witness should be personally interviewed and prepared wherever possible, for two reasons. One, that the witness himself, by the retelling of his story, may, on the witness stand, testify in an easy, natural and favorable manner; and two, that the interview or examination prior to the trial will give the attorney an opportunity to acquire additional information which may not have been given to him by his client. It will avoid the possibility of the witness either giving surprise testimony or testifying with respect to an important phase of the case of which the lawyer has no knowledge or information. This will eliminate an embarrassing court situation. There is nothing so humiliating as to have a witness who is expected to testify along certain lines, state, in response to such questions as are propounded that the witness was not there or did not see the happening or event, but that he got his information indirectly, so that his testimony is incompetent.

It is therefore recommended that all witnesses be personally interviewed by the trial attorney at least once before they are permitted to take the witness stand. This precaution should be taken as to each witness without regard to the relative importance of his testimony.

No witness should be permitted to memorize his story as this procedure is fraught with danger, and when recognized by either the court or jury as being a memorized story, tends to indicate that the story is untrue. This is only a natural impression, for if the story is true, there should be no reason to memorize it.

In the event that the witness should testify contrary to expectations, the attorney should not show any irritation or surprise, but should unobtrusively gloss the incident over as quickly as possible by interrogating the witness on some other phase of the testimony. It is, of course, clearly inadvisable to stop the examination upon receiving a harmful answer. The effect thereof will be greatly minimized by proceeding as has been above outlined, a showing of unconcern and passing on to another subject of inquiry.

Professor Wigmore's "Principles of Judicial Proof" contains worthwhile suggestions for the handling of various types of witnesses. A thorough study of this work will prove invaluable to the trial attorney.

§ 327. Exhibits.

In most states exhibits may be offered in evidence only during the direct examination of a witness. The subject of "exhibits," however, is treated separately under the chapter on "Exhibits."

§ 328. Offer of harmful evidence.

Wherever an investigation of the facts conclusively shows certain harmful features of a case, and it is certain they are known to the opposition and will be introduced in evidence by them, it is best to offer such evidence directly rather than to have the opposition introduce it. By careful preparation the harmful evidence can be introduced in a much less damaging manner than it would be if presented by the adverse party. Then when it is offered and introduced by the other side it will be found to have lost much of its effectiveness. It will be like using the opponent's thunder. Not only does it have the advantage of weakening the effectiveness of this testimony, but it also creates a good psychological effect upon the jury tending to show the attorney's fairness and honesty.

§ 329. Fairness.

As has been previously observed, it is of the utmost importance that throughout the entire trial of the case the lawyer maintain an attitude of fairness. Any suggestion communicated to the jury which indicates that the attorney is trying to take undue advantage of any situation that may arise during the trial will harm him immeasurably. No suggestion of "taking advantage of technicalities" must appear. Any evidence of unfairness will create antagonism in the minds of the jury. For instance, suppose a case where the opposing attorney has failed to serve notice to produce a certain letter. The letter happens to be in court and in the possession of the trial lawyer. It would be foolhardy for him to raise any serious objection to producing the letter particularly in view of the fact that in most jurisdictions the law does not require any notice to produce, when the document called for is in court and in the possession of the attorney. The better procedure would be for the trial lawyer to announce before the court and the jury that counsel has not served notice to produce but that he will not take any technical advantage of the situation. It is much better to produce the letter in this way.

§ 330. Affectation.

Care should be taken not to adopt an affected manner, voice, or attire. The jury is quick to sense and resent any affectation. It must be remembered that the aim is to secure the good will of the jury. This can be best attained by a natural unstilted demeanor.

§ 331. Never attack a woman's character.

All successful trial attorneys are unanimous in stating that a woman's character should never be attacked in court by the proffer of evidence, unless the proof of such bad character is overwhelming. Even in that event this procedure should only be utilized *in an emergency.* An attempt to attack a woman's character even by innuendo or insinuation will definitely result in harm to the case. This is particularly true in *defending* a law suit against a woman. An attack upon her character is very likely to create sympathy in her favor. In such instances the jury, with a sense of "courtroom chivalry" with the defendant's money are prone to add an additional sum to the verdict to assuage the tender feelings of the plaintiff whose character has been attacked.

§ 331a. General illustrations.

The following illustrations, in addition to those listed in the chapter on "Exhibits," "Expert Witnesses" and "Hypothetical Questions," will enable the trial attorney to prove up all the facts in the ordinary and average case. The reference to the text material and illustrations set out in the chapter on "Objections" will suggest what to avoid in framing questions to be used in direct examination.

§ 332. Conversations.

A proper foundation must be laid for admission of all conversations had with parties to the suit or their agents. Such foundation includes:

(1) Identification of the parties.

(2) Testimony as to the time when the conversation took place.

(3) Testimony as to the place where the conversation was had.

(4) Testimony as to who was present at that time and place.

(5) Testimony as to the conversation.

Illustration

Q. Do you know Paul Simpson, the defendant in this case?

A. Yes, I do.

Q. Did you ever have any conversations with him?

A. Yes.

Q. When was the first time you had a conversation with him?

A. The first part of June, 1934.

Q. Where did the conversation take place?

A. At his home, 922 Clark Street.

Q. Who else was present, if anyone?

A. Just he and I.

Q. Will you tell the Court and Jury please, what he said to you and what you said to him, if anything?

A. He said ———. I said ———.

§ 333. Telephone conversations.

Testimony in reference to telephone conversations is admissible.[8] The foundation usually required to make such testimony admissible is the identification of the parties, the time and the means, the proof as to what steps were taken to insure connection with the telephone of the party being called, identification of the voice, if possible, and then stating the con-

[8] Thede v. Matthews, 203 Ill. App. 507; Lord El. Co. v. Morrill, 178 Mass. 305, 59 N. E. 807; Harrison Granite Co. v. Penn. Co., 145 Mich. 712, 108 N. W. 1081; Peo. v. Strollo, 191 N. Y. 42; Stein v. Jascula, 165 Wis. 317, 162 N. W. 182; Old Motor Works v. Churchill, 175 S. W. 785 (Tex.).

versation. In cases where the witness is testifying to a telephone conversation where the witness was called, rather than the witness calling the other party, it is necessary that the witness be able to identify the voice of the party to whom he was talking over the telephone.[9]

Illustration

Q. Did you have a conversation with Paul Simpson after that?

A. Yes, I did.

Q. When?

A. About July 2, 1934.

Q. How was the conversation carried on?

A. Over the telephone.

Q. Did you call him or did he call you?

A. I called him.

Q. Just what did you do?

A. I looked up the telephone number of his office in the telephone book.

Q. Do you remember that number?

A. Yes, I do. It was State 1234.

Q. What did you then do, if anything?

A. I dialed the number, State 1234.

Q. What happened then, if anything?

A. Someone answered the phone and said, "Good morning, State 1234." I asked for Mr. Paul Simpson and then Paul Simpson answered the telephone.

Q. Did you ever talk to him over the telephone before?

A. Yes, I have, many times.

Q. Did you recognize the person's voice who answered the telephone?

A. Yes, I did.

Q. Whose voice was it?

A. Paul Simpson's.

Q. What did you say to him and what did he say to you, if anything?

A. I told him ———. He said ———.

Note: If telephone used was not a dial phone, witness, in answering as to what he did, would say he lifted up the

[9] Mankes v. Fishman, 163 App. Div. 789, 149 N. Y. S. 228; Tabor Coal Co. v. Cohen, 189 Ill. App. 190; Cox v. Cline, 147 Iowa 353, 126 N. W. 330.

receiver, and, when the operator answered, he asked to be connected with State 1234. Sometimes the witness will testify that he did not recognize the voice of the person answering the telephone. Opposing counsel will probably make an objection to the admission of any testimony with reference to a conversation with a person whose voice the witness did not recognize. The weight of authority is to the effect that telephone calls to *business houses,* who have placed their number in the telephone book, invite the transaction of business over the telephone, and that under such circumstances it is *not* necessary for the witness to be able to recognize the voice of the person with whom he is talking over the telephone in order to make such conversation admissible.[10]

§ 334. Fixing time.

It is the general rule that the time of any conversation or happening of any event does not have to be fixed with any degree of certainty unless the question of time is material to the issues involved. The witness will be permitted to fix the time of any conversation or happening of any event as closely as he can.

§ 335. Stipulations.[11]

It is, of course, important that the trial attorney see that all stipulations and agreements between counsel are set out in the record of the case on trial. This may be done by either reading the stipulation into the record to the court reporter or by filing a written stipulation signed by the attorneys for

10 Gen. Hospital Soc. v. New Haven, etc., Co., 79 Conn. 581, 65 Atl. 1065; Godair v. Ham Nat. Bank, 225 Ill. 572, 80 N. E. 447; Collins v. Wells, 140 Iowa 304, 118 N. W. 401; Theisen v. Detroit Taxicab Co., 200 Mich. 136, 166 N. W. 901; Missouri Pac. R. Co. v. Heidenheimer, 82 Tex. 195, 117 S. W. 608; Wolfe v. Missouri Pac. Ry. Co., 97 Mo. 473, 11 S. W. 49, 3 L. R. A. 539; Mankes v. Fishman, 163 App. Div. 789, 149 N. Y. S. 228; R. I. & P. R. R. v. Potter, 36 Ill. App. 590.

11 Stipulations do away with the necessity of introducing evidence: Vickery v. Valdez, 113 Cal. App. 135, 295 Pac. 151; Rowe v. Brooklyn Heights R. Co., 71 A. D. 474, 75 N. Y. S. 893; Sovereign Camp, etc., v. Downer, (Texas), 241 S. W. 228; Central Shoe Co. v. Rashid, 203 Iowa 1103, 212 N. W. 559; General Const. Co. v. Industrial Com., 314 Ill. 59.

the respective parties. Where it is read into the record it is usually done in this manner: "Let the record show that it has been stipulated and agreed by and between counsel for the defendant and myself, as attorney for the plaintiff, that the defendant waives the filing of an answer by the plaintiff to the intervening petition of this defendant."

§ 336. Admissions by attorneys.[12]

When we consider the fact that admissions by the attorneys during the trial of the case are binding upon their client, it becomes important that the record show each and every such admission by the opposing counsel. An admission by counsel of any fact necessary to be proved will obviate the necessity of offering proof of such fact. It must be kept in mind therefore that care must be exercised not to make admissions of facts which the opponents are unable to prove.

§ 337. Depositions.

The method of securing the benefit of depositions previously taken as part of the evidence on direct examination is as follows: The dedimus or commission is usually read before the jury for the purpose of the record and to show the authority and the manner of having taken such depositions. (This particular formality may be waived by agreement of counsel and the agreement shown in the record.) Then the direct examination of each witness is read to the jury by the attorney for the plaintiff, while the cross-examination of each witness is read to the jury by the attorney for the defendant. This procedure, however, results in loss of much of the psychological good usually accomplished by the personal attendance of the witness while giving testimony in court. To eliminate this objection, it has been suggested that the trial attorney

12 Abbott v. Lee, 86 Conn. 392, 85 Atl. 526; Bechat v. Knisley, 144 Ill. App. 551; Mercier v. Union St. R. Co., 230 Mass. 397, 119 N. E. 764; Peo. v. Mole, 85 App. Div. 33, 82 N. Y. S. 747.

Admission in Opening Statements—see Opening Statements, p. 218.

Admissions are limited to the case on trial: Weisbrod v. Chicago, etc., R. Co., 20 Wis. 419; Hardin v. Forsythe, 99 Ill. 312; Cadigan v. Crabtree, 192 Mass. 233, 78 N. E. 412; State v. Buchanan, Wright (Ohio), 233; unless made without limitation: Kircheimer v. Barrett, 125 Ill. A. 56; Stemmler v. New York, 179 N. Y. 473, 72 N. E. 581.

presenting evidence by depositions ask the questions, while his associate sitting in the witness chair reads the answers. With a little practice between the trial attorney and his associate, a proper reading of the deposition in this manner will make it seem as though the witness was present in court and personally testifying, and add greatly to the effectiveness of the testimony. In cases where a large portion of the direct examination is based upon depositions, this method of procedure is invaluable. This procedure has been held to be legally correct.[13]

§ 338. Identifying persons.[14]

Whenever it becomes necessary for a witness to identify another person in the court room, the record should be completed so as to show the name of the person being identified and the method of such identification.

Illustration

Witness: I don't know the name of the man, but I saw him in the court room this morning.

Q. Describe the man.

A. He is short, rather stout, dark man with glasses with a scar on his right cheek.

Counsel: If the Court please may we have the man described by the witness step into the court room so that we may have him identified for the record.

The Court: Mr. Bailiff you will ask the gentleman to step into the court room.

Counsel: (To the witness) Is this the man you have referred to?

A. Yes, he is.

Counsel: (To the man described) Will you state your name and address please?

Man: Henry Davis, 1202 Ford Street.

In the event the witness fails to identify the person this should also be noted in the record.

13 Vagaszki v. Consolidation Coal Co., Inc., 225 Fed. 913, 141 C. C. A. 37.

14 For purposes of identifying persons in court, witnesses may be asked leading questions. Com. v. Whitman, 121 Mass. 361; Rice v. Rice, 47 N. J. Eq. 559, 19 Atl. 736; Sadler v. Murrah, 5 Miss. 195; Peo. v. Mather, 4 Wend. (N. Y.) 229, 21 Am. Dec. 122; Peo. v. Curran, 286 Ill. 302.

Illustration

My name is Mae F. Quinlivan.

Q. Did you see the defendant, John Brown in the Court Room?

A. Yes, I did.

Q. Point him out.

A. That is he over there.

Counsel: Will you kindly rise, sir.

Q. Is this the man?

A. Yes.

Counsel: Let the record show that the witness has identified Mr. George Russell, an attorney, as the defendant, John Brown.

§ 339. Amendments.

Whenever it becomes apparent during the course of the trial that the evidence which it is sought to be introduced does not come within the purview of the issues of the case as made by the pleadings, or where some error has apparently been made in drafting the pleading, a motion should be immediately made to the court for leave to amend the pleadings.[15] It must be remembered, however, that the procuring of leave to amend the pleadings is of itself insufficient, but must be supplemented by the actual filing of the amended pleadings.[16] It is a practice with some attorneys to ask leave to amend a pleading on its face. In cases where a pleading is sworn to, this, of

15 Weinberg v. John A. Vaughan Corp., 29 Pac. (2nd) 862; Botsford v. Wallace, 69 Conn. 263, 37 Atl. 902; Bell v. Toluca Coal Co., 272 Ill. 576, 112 N. E. 311; Henri Pelandeau, etc. v. Fred Gillespie Lumber Co., (Mass.) 188 N. E. 380; Mastrobuono v. Lange, 270 N. Y. S. 564; Missouri Pac. R. Co. v. South Texas Candy Co., 65 S. W. (2nd) 325; Gates v. Paul, 117 Wis. 170, 94 N. W. 55; Gilliland v. Wallace, Tapp. 168 (Ohio); In re Farmers, etc., Bank, 194 Mich. 200, 160 N. W. 601.

16 Peo. v. Cleveland, etc., R. Co., 314 Ill. 455, 145 N. E. 647; Chicago, etc., R. Co. v. Reyman, 73 N. E. 587 (Ind.); Carroll v. Palmer Mfg. Co., 181 Mich. 280, 148 N. W. 390; Dexter v. Ivins, 133 N. Y. 551, 30 N. E. 594; Central, etc., Assoc. v. Seeley, 267 Pac. 138 (Cal.).

However, it has been held that when the parties treat the proposed amendment as made, a failure to file the pleading is not fatal. Sobieski v. Chicago, 241 Ill. App. 180, 325 Ill. 259, 156 N. E. 279; Parmenter v. McDougall, 172 Cal. 306, 156 Pac. 460; Farnam v. Doyle, 128 Mich. 696, 87 N. W. 1026.

course, should not be allowed, unless the affiant who swore to the pleading is present in court and is resworn thereto.[17] This at best is a slovenly practice. The court will usually grant sufficient time to file either an amendment or an amended pleading. In the event that proof is offered and received beyond the scope of the pleadings that are on file, a motion should be made for leave to file an amended pleading so as to conform to the proof offered and received.[18] Wherever possible the proposed amendment should be presented at the time the motion is made. If this is impossible, sufficient time should be requested within which to file it and then the lawyer must be sure to file the amendment or amended pleading within the time allowed. The court in its discretion may allow a motion for leave to file an amendment or an amended pleading at any time during the trial or within a very short time thereafter.

Illustration

Counsel: I ask leave to file an amended affidavit of merits alleging and setting forth as an additional defense that the work was done in an unskillful, unworkmanlike, careless and negligent manner.

The Court: Leave granted.

§ 340. Where witness indicates.[19]

Whenever it becomes necessary during the course of the trial for the witness to indicate a person, a part of the court

17 Amendment by interlineation is permissible subject to the discretion of the court. Ward v. Steel Co., 17 Ohio N. P. (N. S.) 331; Chamberlain v. Lowenthal, 138 Cal. 4, 70 Pac. 932.

But this practice has been severely criticized. Moorhead v. Briggs, 15 Ill. App. 361.

18 Sharp v. Pitman, 166 Cal. 501, 137 Pac. 234; Frank v. Hanly, 215 Ill. 216, 74 N. E. 130; New Castle Bridge Co. v. Doty, 160 Ind. 259, 79 N. E. 485; Young v. Mandis, 191 Ia. 1328, 184 N. W. 302; Pizer v. Hunt, 250 Mass. 498, 146 N. E. 7; Troutman v. Gates, 176 N. W. 187; Smith v. Wetmore, 167 N. Y. 234, 60 N. E. 419; Supreme, etc. v. Everding, 20 Oh. Cr. Ct. 689, 11 Oh. Cir. Dec. 419; Durbin v. Knox, 132 Wis. 608.

19 The extent of physical demonstration by witnesses is a matter within the discretion of the court. Com. v. Borilli, 113 Atl. 663, 270 Pa. 388; Stale v. McGann, 66 Pac. 823, Idaho, Where witness was permitted to show where person was shot by placing hand on his own body. Hukox v. State, 285 S. W. 621, 104 Tex. Cr. 649; Rachmel v. Clark, 54 Atl. 1027, 205 Pa. 314, 62 L. R. A. 959.

room or some place about his body, the record should be made to show such act. It is usually done in the following manner:

Attorney examining the witness, or opposite attorney will state:

"The witness indicates the defendant, John Jones," or
"The witness indicates about three feet," or
"The witness indicates the left side of her face."

§ 341. Interpreters.[20]

Whenever a foreign witness is put on the witness stand to give testimony and he is unable to speak the English language, the proper method of securing such testimony is by means of an interpreter. In selecting an interpreter care should be exercised to find one who is sufficiently versed in the foreign language and intelligent enough to translate the same in understandable English. He should be a person who is impartial and not have any interest in the case nor be connected with either of the parties to the suit. The clerk of the court usually swears in the interpreter to translate the questions from the English language to the foreign language and to correctly translate the answers from the foreign language into the English language. The interpreter should be sworn to translate the questions and answers literally. The questions should be submitted through the interpreter just as though the questions were submitted directly to the witness. For instance, the question would be asked "What is your name?"

§ 342. Witness resuming stand.

Wherever witness has been withdrawn before his testimony is completed to permit another witness to testify, or where there is an adjournment during the course of the witness' testimony and upon the convening of court the witness again

20 The qualifications of a person to act as an interpreter is in the court's discretion. Peo. v. Rardin, 255 Ill. 9, 99 N. E. 59, L. R. A. 1916 F 1207. And also the necessity for the use of an interpreter is a matter within the discretion of the court. Peo. v. Lacang, 1 P. (2nd) 7, 213 Cal. 65; Menella v. Metropolitan St. R. Co., 86 N. Y. S. 930.

resumes the stand, the record should indicate this fact. It is usually done in this manner:

Q. You are the same John Jones who was previously sworn and testified, are you not?

A. I am.

§ 343. Withdrawing witness.

Whenever it becomes necessary to withdraw a witness to permit another to testify that fact should be shown by the record in this manner:

If the Court please, counsel for the defendant has agreed that we may withdraw this witness to permit Dr. John MacDougall to testify. He has to leave town in the morning.

The Court: Very well.

§ 344. Offering incompetent witnesses.

Wherever by the statute a wife is declared incompetent to testify for or against her husband or where any other witness is disqualified from testifying, the record should show that the attorney has these witnesses ready to testify. The witness should be placed upon the stand and sworn. The opposing counsel may then be permitted to object. This has a better psychological effect on the jury as most jurors do not know of the statutory restrictions and they may wonder why the witnesses were not produced. An instruction should also be given stating the statutory restrictions.

§ 345. Absent witnesses.

On those occasions where it is found that one or more of the witnesses are unable to appear for various reasons, this fact should be made known to the jury, and put into the record so as to account for their absence otherwise the jury may feel you have deliberately failed to present the testimony of an eye witness because such testimony would be unfavorable. It may be done in various ways, one of which is as follows:

Mr. Guthrie: I want it to appear in the record that Mr. Thomas J. Hall, who was to appear here and testify for and in behalf of the plaintiff, was subpoenaed on January 27th. I have the return of the subpoena here. Mr. Hall, I was informed late on the day he was subpoenaed, was sick in bed in his home with a high fever and was not permitted to leave the house.

It is, of course, always advisable to subpoena witnesses who are strangers to the case so as to show that the attorney has taken every reasonable step in order to assure their attendance at the trial.

§ 346. Proof of distance.[21]

Sometimes it becomes important to establish proof of certain distances. This may be done in the following manner:

Illustration

Q. State your name, please?
A. Joseph A. Marshall.
Q. Where do you live, Mr. Marshall?
A. 4942 St. Anthony Court.
Q. Mr. Marshall, did you at my request go to the corner of Crawford and Addison Street, Chicago, and measure the distance from the North side of Addison Street on the East side of Crawford Avenue up to a garage that is located at 3617 Crawford Avenue?
A. Yes, sir.
Q. And did you take the measurements up to the office door, that is the north door of that garage?
A. Yes, sir.
Q. What equipment did you use in making your measurements?
A. I used a steel tape.
Q. Where did you measure from?
A. I measured from the sidewalk right in front.
Q. Was that the inside or outside sidewalk line?
A. Well, it is along the building there.
Q. By the building?
A. Yes, sir.
Q. What was the distance?
A. Forty feet.

21 Proof of distance may be made although no measurement was taken. McComb v. Atchison T. & S. F. Ry. Co., 294 Pac. 81; Hermes v. Chicago, etc., R. Co., 80 Wis. 590, 50 N. W. 584.

The distance a moving body has gone may be shown. St. Louis, etc., R. Co. v. Brown, 62 Ark. 68, 39 S. W. 72 (train); I. C. C. R. R. Co. v. Swisher, 53 Atl. 413, at 417.

Or how far a person could see. Pasachone Water Co. v. Slandart, 97 Cal. 476, 32 Pac. 532; Chicago City R. Co. v. Hagenback, 228 Ill. 290, 81 N. E. 1014.

§ 347. Proving interest.[22]

In cases where the plaintiff is entitled to interest on his claim it is necessary that the amount of interest be proved, the same as every other fact in the case. Testimony must be offered to prove the amount of interest that the plaintiff is entitled to. This may be done in the following manner:

Illustration

Q. You are an attorney associated with Tenney, Harding, Sherman & Rogers?

A. I am.

Q. Have you made a computation of the amount of interest at the statutory rate of 5% on the sum of $7,500.00 from February 19, 1930, to date?

A. I have.

Q. What does it amount to?

A. $731.50.

§ 348. Forgotten questions.

Sometimes counsel announces that he has finished his examination and then remembers something that he has forgotten to ask about. In most instances he can readily secure permission to ask the question by requesting such permission from the court. When this request is made the court will, almost as a matter of course, permit counsel to continue his examination. Ordinarily, opposing counsel will not object, knowing that to do so would only put him in a bad light.

§ 349. Custom.[23]

Proof of custom as well as denial of existence of such a custom may be made in accordance with the following illustration:

Q. What is your name, please?

A. John Langley.

22 The court may permit a witness on the stand to compute and state the amount of interest due. West Chicago Alcohol Works v. Sheer, 8 Ill. A. 367.

23 Proof of customs and usages in any calling may be made by the testimony of witnesses who have knowledge of them. Wilson v. Bauman, 80 Ill. 493; Wilmarth v. Cal. Pac. Mut. L. Ins. Co., 168 Cal. 536, 143 Pac. 780; Thayer v. Smoky Hollow Coal Co., 121 Iowa 121, 96 N. W. 718; Noah v. Bowery Savings Bank, 225 N. Y. 284, 122 N. E. 235; State v. Ampt, 6 Oh. Dec. (Reprint) 699, 7 Am. L. Rev. 469; Sullivan v. Owens (Texas) 90 S. W. 690; Chandler v. Prince, 214 Mass. 180, 100 N. E. 1029; Lamb v. Kraus, 30 Wis. 94; see Conestoga Cigar Co. v. Finka, 13 L. R. A. 438.

Q. What is your business?

A. I am engaged as a salesman in the bond and investment business.

Q. How long have you been in that business?

A. For the past twenty-two years.

Q. Where have you engaged in that business during that period of time?

A. I have been acting as a salesman in the bond and investment business during that period of time in practically all of the big cities from the Pacific coast to the Atlantic seaboard.

Q. With what kind of firms have you been associated with during that period of time?

A. I have been associated with the largest investment houses in the Country.

Q. Have you been engaged exclusively in the bond and investment business during that period of time?

A. Yes, I have.

Q. Were you familiar with the customs and trade practices in the investment and bond business in and about the City of Chicago in the year 1932?

A. I was.

Q. Was there a custom in the investment and bond business in and about Chicago in the year 1932 with reference to the compensation of a broker who has performed the services that you have testified you performed in this case?

A. Yes, sir.

Q. What is the custom in investment and bond houses with reference to a broker who has performed the services that you have testified were performed by you in this case?

A. It was a common practice and custom among real estate bond houses or other bond houses dealing in real estate mortgage bond issue loans to recognize a broker who was a duly licensed broker under the State laws and such a broker is entitled to a commission commonly known on the street between brokers as a "finder's commission" in connection with the financing of a real estate project, and that commission has by such practice and custom been fixed at one percent of the par value of the bond issue.

Mr. Morrow: I move to strike out the answer of the witness because both the question and answer are incompetent, irrelevant, and immaterial and cannot and do not establish any contract or obligation on the part of the defendant in this case to pay Langley any commission, and in the second place because it is at variance with the allegations in his declaration.

The Court: Objection overruled.

Q. When does the commission become payable?

A. At the time of the consummation of the deal.

Q. Assume that a person or corporation having an interest in real estate wishes to borrow Five Million Dollars evidenced by its bonds and secured by a mortgage on its interest in the realty, and suppose that a duly licensed broker gets the details of the bond issue from the president and treasurer of the mortgagor and then goes to a bond house and tells the bond house about this and the bond house gets in touch with the mortgagor and thereafter the bond house purchases from the mortgagor this proposed five million dollar bond issue at 96% of par, which is $100.00, is there among investment houses, banking houses, and bond houses a custom as to the compensation of such brokers?

A. Yes, sir, there is. Territorily the area covers, of my own personal knowledge, the Central part of the United States and the Eastern part, I would say as far west as Minneapolis, St. Paul and St. Louis and all the way to New York.

Q. Will you state what that custom is?

Mr. Morrow: I object.

The Court: Objection overruled.

A. The custom is that the broker receives one per cent of the face value of the securities so placed, unless there is a definite understanding as to some other amount. The broker always looks to the financing house for his protection and for his commission. From my personal knowledge the custom was in general use when I started to practice real estate.

§ 350. Denial of existence of a custom.

Q. Will you state your full name, please?

A. Cuthbert C. Adams.

Q. Where do you live Mr. Adams?

A. I live in Winnetka.

Q. Will you state your business, please?

A. I am in the investment bond business.

Q. With whom are you associated?
A. With T. E. Joiner & Company, Incorporated.
Q. And what is their business?
A. They are an investment bond house.
Q. How long have you been associated with them?
A. I have been with them and their predecessor for about eleven years.
Q. How long have you been in the bond business?
A. In the City of Chicago about twenty-five years.
Q. Are you familiar with the customs and practices in the investment bond business?
A. I am.
Q. Was there in existence in the City of Chicago on November 3, 1924, and for some time prior thereto a general and uniform custom and usage among investment brokers, investment bankers and bond houses, in the absence of an express agreement to the contrary, to pay a commission or a so-called finder's commission to a person or broker who voluntarily and without solicitation, and without any promise of reward as a condition thereof, furnishes information to an investment banker who, acting upon the same, secures a bond deal?
A. No, there was not.

§ 351. Demonstrations and experiments.[24]

It is common practice justified by judicial decisions to display before the jury and to formally introduce in evidence

[24] Woodruff Coal, etc., Co. v. Commercial Coal Co., 221 Mich. 175, 190 N. W. 686; Painter v. People, 147 Ill. 444; Boerner Fry Co. v. Mucci, 158 Iowa 315, 138 N. W. 866; Thornhill v. Carpenter-Morton Co., 220 Mass. 593, 108 N. E. 474; Ballard v. Breigh, 262 S. W. 886 (Texas); Hiller v. Johnson, 162 Wis. 19, 154 N. W. 845; Schroeder v. Hotel Commercial Co., 147 Pac. 417, 84 Wash. 685; B. & O. R. Co. v. Fouts, 88 Oh. St. 305, 104 N. E. 544, Ann. Cas. 1915 A 1256.

Models—Texas Mach. etc., Co. v. Ayers Ice Cream Co., (Texas) 150 S. W. 750; Lush v. Parkersburg, 127 Iowa 701, 104 N. W. 336; Andrews v. State, 33 Oh. Cir. Ct. 564; Everson v. Casualty Co. of America, 208 Mass. 214, 94 N. E. 459; McKeon v. Proctor, etc., Mfg. Co., 162 App. Div. 784, 147 N. Y. S. 1012; Harris v. Seattle, etc., R. Co., 65 Wash. 27, 34, 117 Pac. 601; I. C. C. R. R. Co. v. Berens, 208 Ill. 20.

Maps and Diagrams—Foley v. Cal. Power Co., 165 Cal. 103, 130 Pac. 1183; Lee v. Farmers Mutual Rail, etc., Co., 241 N. W. 403 (Iowa); Lavene v. Freidrichs, 186 Ind. 333, 115 N. E. 324,

physical objects which form a part of or serve to illustrate the transactions or occurrence which is the subject of investigation. Evidence of this character is frequently resorted to, both in civil and criminal cases and the propriety of its use cannot be successfully called into question. It is well settled that plats, drawings, casts, maps, photographs and real objects or things which are material to a controversy are admissible in evidence although testimony may be required to enable the jury to understand and apply such evidence to the issues in the case. If the manner in which the plaintiff was injured or the nature or character of the injury can better be explained by the production of physical objects, such evidence may be admitted. In criminal cases, however, exhibits are not admissible, unless they are the instruments with which it is alleged the crime was committed or have a tendency to prove controverted facts.[25] The admission or rejection of exhibits for inspection of the jury is within the discretion of the trial judge, since it depends on the circumstances of each individual case whether the exhibition of physical objects will explain better than anything else the occurrence under investigation or whether they will only tend to mislead and confuse.[26]

View by jury[27] or by the judge when case is tried without a jury, of the locus in quo is permissible in actions involv-

116 N. E. 421; Hews v. Troiani, 179 N. E. 622 (Mass.); Cincinnati Traction Co. v. Harrison, 24 Oh. Cir. Ct. N. S. 1; Close v. Ann Arbor R. Co., 169 Mich. 592, 134 N. W. 346; Govier v. Brechler, 159 Wis. 157, 149 N. W. 740; Wightman v. Campbell, 217 N. Y. 479, 112 N. E. 184, Ann. Cas. 1917 E 673; Criswell v. Robbins, (Texas) 152 S. W. 210; Hageman v. Freeburg, 162 Atl. 21, 115 Conn. 469; Reinke v. Sanitary District, 260 Ill. 380.

Casts—People v. Smith, 121 Cal. 355, 53 Pac. 802, 41 L. R. A. 157 (foot prints); Earl v. Lefler, 46 Hun. 9 (N. Y.).

25 People v. Arnold, 248 Ill. 169; Zipkie v. City of Chicago, 117 App. 418.

26 It is within the discretion of the court to permit a view by the jury of locus in quo.

27 Gibson v. Miller, 246 N. W. 606 (Iowa); Carlson v. Assoc. Realty Corp., 114 Conn. 699, 159 Atl. 885; City of Indianapolis v. Barthal, 194 Ind. 273, 141 N. E. 339, 142 N. E. 409; Nordman v. Mechem, 198 N. W. 586, 226 Mich. 86; Manuta v. Lazarus, 117 N. Y. S. 1076, 104 Misc. 135; (but see Buffalo Structural Steel v. Dickson, 90 N. Y. S. 268, 98 App. Div. 355, where the court held that it had no power to send the jury out to view premises except where authorized by statute).

Hovey v. Sandres, (Texas) 174 S. W. 1025, but see Bailey v. Woodrum Trunk Lines, (Texas) 36 S. W. (2nd) 1090;

ing real estate if the court in the exercise of sound discretion considers such view necessary or proper to enable jury to better understand and apply the evidence, but the jury must be instructed that their view is not evidence.[28]

§ 352. Use of demonstrative evidence.

It has been held that models of machinery may be introduced in evidence for demonstrative purposes to assist a witness in explaining the operation of such machinery to the jury.[29] So, a model of a locomotive or a coal hoist [30] is admissible.

Instruments of crime, or articles having a tendency to prove controverted facts are admissible in a criminal case.[31] So, a revolver and bullet are competent evidence in prosecution for homicide in murder prosecution,[32] the bed in room where person was murdered, and mattresses, sheets and other bed clothing pertaining thereto may be introduced.[33] A buggy in which deceased was sitting when he was shot is competent evidence and may be used to enable a witness to explain position of deceased, position of accused, range of shot which passed through deceased and lodged in back cushion.[34]

In a civil action if the manner in which plaintiff was injured, or the nature or character of the injury can better be explained by the production of physical objects, such evidence may be admitted.[35] So, in a civil action for negligently killing a person, torn clothing worn by party at time of injury may be shown.[36]

Max L. Bloom Co. v. U. S. Casualty Co., 210 N. W. 689, 191 Wis. 524; Springer v. Chicago, 26 N. E. 514, 135 Ill. 552, 12 L. R. A. 609; McPherson v. West Coast T. Co., 94 Cal. App. 463, 271 Pac. 509; People v. Thorn, 42 L. R. A. 370.

28 Geohegan v. Union El. R. R. Co., 258 Ill. 352.

29 I. C. R. R. v. Berens, 208 Ill. 20; (see also note 24).

30 Penn v. Kelly, 156 Ill. 9.

31 Peo. v. Arnold, 218 Ill. 169; Painter v. People, 147 Ill. 444; Peo. v. Kinney, 124 Mich. 486, 83 N. W. 147; Com. v. Brelsford, 161 Mass. 61, 36 N. E. 677; State v. Gorman, 168 Iowa 216, 150 N. W. 9; Peo. v. Byrne, 160 Cal. 217, 116 Pac. 521; State v. Laudano, 74 Conn. 638, 51 Atl. 860; Siberry v. State, 133 Ind. 677, 33 N. E. 681; Collins v. State, (Texas) 178 S. W. 345; Peo. v. Morse, 196 N. Y. 306; Roszczyniala v. State, 125 Wis. 414, 104 N. W. 113.

32 McCoy v. People, 175 Ill. 224.

33 Painter v. People, 147 Ill. 444.

34 Henry v. People, 198 Ill. 162.

35 Tudor Iron Works v. Weber, 129 Ill. 535.

36 Quincy G. & E. Co. v. Baumann, 203 Ill. 295.

In an action against a common carrier for breaking or puncturing cans of yeast, a can of yeast similar to that shipped is properly shown to the jury.[37]

§ 353. Experiments.[38]

The same rules generally apply to experiments as to the use of demonstrative evidence. That is, the burden of proof is upon the party desiring to show the results of an experiment, to establish that the experiments were conducted under circumstances very similar to those connected with the act to be illustrated.[39] When the similarity of conditions has been established, the results of the experiment are admissible as direct evidence. But if it is not shown that the circumstances under which the experiments were conducted were identical or at least very similar to those under which the fact in question occurred, the result of the experiment is not admissible. So, in an action against a carrier for damages to a shipment of cantaloupes, evidence of refrigeration tests with other shipments of cantaloupes is not admissible without first showing similarity of the shipments.[40] In an action for negligence, where the questions to the witness did not tend to show that experiments made shortly after the accident were made under substantially *similar conditions* to those that prevailed when the accident occurred,[41] they are not admissible.

37 Amer. Express Co. v. Spillman, 90 Ill. 455.

38 Com. v. Scott, 123 Mass. 222, 25 Am. R. 81 (voice); Peo. v. Levine, 85 Cal. 39, 22 Pac. 969, 24 Pac. 631; Chicago Tel. Supply Co. v. Marne, etc., Tel. Co., 134 Iowa 252; (telephone test permitted in presence of jury); Nat. Cash Register Co. v. Blumenthal, 85 Mich. 464, 48 N. W. 622 (operating cash register in presence of jury); Clark v. Brooklyn Heights R. Co., 78 App. Div. 478, 79 N. Y. S. 811; Schweinfurth v. Cleveland, etc., R. Co., 60 Oh. St. 215, 54 N. E. 89 (running train over crossing); St. Louis, etc., R. Co. v. Ewing (Texas) 126 S. W. 625; Benson v. Superior Mfg. Co., 147 Wis. 20, 132 N. W. 633 (showing that hook, when locked, could not be removed from staple); Pennsylvania Coal Co. v. Kelley, 156 Ill. 9. (Some states contra.)

39 Upthegrove v. Chicago Great Western R. Co., 154 Ill. App. 460; Peo. v. Saloni, 6 Col. App. 103, 91 Pac. 654; Interboro Brewing Co. v. Independent, etc., Co., 95 Misc. 24, 156 N. Y. S. 574; Chicago, etc., R. Co. v. Champion, 32 N. E. 874 (Ind.); Dow v. Bulfinch, 192 Mass. 281, 78 N. E. 416; Texas, etc., R. Co. v. Graham, 174 S. W. 297 (Texas).

40 Arakelian v. San Pacific Co., 220 Ill. App. 160.

41 Johnson v. Gustafson, 233 Ill. App. 216.

§ 354. — Preliminary proof.

When it is sought to use an article or other physical object as an exhibit in a lawsuit, it must be properly identified before it is admissible.[42] It must be *shown that articles* that are produced for use as an exhibit are in substantially the same condition that they were when such condition was material to the issue, or if they have been broken, marred, worn or altered since such time it should be shown in which particular they have been changed, the use to which they were put, and if material, the test or circumstances under which they were broken or marred, the rule in this respect is the same whether the article is produced to prove a fact or for the purposes of illustration.[43] If the articles produced as exhibits have been in the custody of the sheriff or other officer of the court, they are not admissible unless it is first shown how they came into his possession, that they were kept by him in the same condition as when delivered to him up to the time that they were offered in evidence and that they are the same articles.[44] Where it is not proved that the articles used as exhibits are in the same condition as they were when such condition was material to the issues in the case, it is error to admit such exhibit.[45] So, in an action for the price of beans sold defendant where it was alleged that 17% of the beans sold were wormy or rotten, it was error to admit in evidence a number of paper bags containing supposed samples of the beans where the proof was not satisfactory that the samples were in the same condition as at the time of the delivery, especially where a witness testified that there might be a greater percentage of worms in them at the time of trial.[46]

It is no objection to the use of articles as exhibits or for demonstrative purposes that they have been illegally taken from the possession of the defendant or otherwise unlawfully obtained, so long as they were not obtained in violation of some constitutional right.[47] Ordinarily the court will rule

[42] Quincy G. & E. Co. v. Baumann, 203 Ill. 295.

[43] Stover Carriage Co. v. American & British Mfg. Co., 188 Ill. App. 635.

[44] People v. Mankus, 215 Ill. App. 518.

[45] Yohalem v. Matalone, 225 Ill. App. 221.

[46] Ibid.

[47] People v. Castree, 311 Ill. 392. (Some states contra.)

upon the admissibility of evidence without inquiring into the method by which it was procured. Articles which have been obtained by artifice or deceit or unlawfully or by stealth or force by an individual not acting under the authority of the state are admissible, but articles which have been obtained by violation of the defendant's constitutional rights, such as by unlawful search and seizure by an officer having no warrant are not admissible.[48] So, intoxicating liquors illegally seized under a search warrant issued upon information and belief, and not on an affidavit of facts, as required by statute, are not admissible in evidence in a prosecution for violation of the prohibition act where the question of their admissibility is properly presented by a motion to exclude alleging unlawful search and seizure and demanding the return of such articles.[49] However, it has been held in a criminal case that where certain books and records of an institution with which defendant had been connected had been taken from his possession unlawfully, but not in violation of his constitutional rights that they were admissible.[50] The rules governing the use of illegally obtained evidence are the same in civil cases and criminal cases in Illinois, although in some states the rule is different in civil cases, allowing greater latitude in the use of such evidence.[51] Demonstrations and experiments should be utilized whenever necessary to clarify proof in the record.

§ 355. Speed.[52]

In proving opinions of witnesses as to speed, a proper foundation must first be laid to show familiarity with the speed or familiarity in estimating speeds of the vehicles in question. For instance, in proving speed of an automobile witness must show that he has had occasion to ride in auto-

48 People v. Castree, 311 Ill. 392; Peo. v. Brocamp, 307 Ill. 448.

49 People v. Elias, 316 Ill. 376.

50 People v. Munday, 204 Ill. App. 24.

51 Massman v. Thorson, 118 Ill. App. 574.

52 An observer may testify as to the speed of an automobile. Faulkner v. Payne, 191 Mich. 263, 157 N. W. 565; Dilger v. Whitteen, 33 Cal. App. 15, 164 Pac. 49; Becvar v. Batesole, 265 N. W. 297 (Iowa); Book v. Aschenbrenner, 165 Ill. App. 23, 70 A. L. R. 541 n; American Motor Car Co. v. Robbin, 181 Ind. 417, 103 N. E. 641; Creedon v. Galvin, 226 Mass. 140, 115 N. E. 307; or of a street car, 34 L. R. A. (N. S.) 784; or of a train, 34 L. R. A. (N. S.) 790.

mobiles, that there were speedometers on each of these automobiles and that he had occasion to check the speed of each of these automobiles by watching the gauge of the speedometer and from this experience is able to form an opinion as to the speed at which the automobile is operated.

Illustration

Q. Mr. Hahn have you ever driven an automobile?
A. Yes, I have.
Q. For how long?
A. Off and on for ten years.
Q. What make of machine?
A. All kinds.
Q. Did those automobiles have speedometers?
A. Yes they did.
Q. Did you have occasion to watch the gauge on your speedometer while you were driving?
A. Yes, I have many times.
Q. During those ten years you were driving?
A. Yes, sir.
Q. From that experience are you able to estimate the speed at which an automobile is being driven?
A. I am.
Q. Have you an opinion as to what rate of speed the defendant's car was being driven just prior to the impact?
A. I have.
Q. What is that opinion?
A. He was going about 35 miles an hour.

§ 356. Reading testimony given at previous trial.[53]

Upon a retrial of a cause of action where witness who has previously testified is dead at the time of the retrial, his

[53] Reading former testimony is permissible when it is shown that the parties to the subsequent trial are the same. McInturff v. Ins. Co. of America, 248 Ill. 92, 97, 93 N. E. 369; Pratt v. Tailer, 135 App. Div. 1, 119 N. Y. S. 803; Pfeiffer v. Chicago, etc., R. Co., 163 Wis. 317, 156 N. W. 952; Austin v. Dungan, 46 (Texas) 236.

. . . or in privity, as administrator, agent or assignee. Fredericks v. Judah, 73 Cal. 604, 15 Pac. 305; In re Durant, 80 Conn. 140, 67 Atl. 497; Stephens v. Hoffman, 263 Ill. 197, 104 N. E. 1090.

The issues must be substantially the same as in the previous trial. Frick v. Kabaker, 116 Ia. 494, 90 N. W. 498; Cohen v. Long Island R. Co., 154 App. Div. 603, 139 N. Y. S. 887.

It must be shown that the opposing party had an opportunity to cross-examine the witness whose testimony is

testimony, both direct and cross-examination, may be read upon the retrial of the case. This is also true where the witness is outside the jurisdiction of the court, and by affidavit it is shown that his residence is unknown, the testimony would then be presented in the following manner (after competent proof of death, absence of witness, etc.):

Illustration

"Mr. Molthrop: Now, if your Honor please, I desire to read the testimony given by Mr. Godfrey Langhenry at the last trial, he having died since.

Mr. Molthrop reading:

Q. What is your name, please?

A. Godfrey Langhenry.

Q. Where do you live?

A. 5823 Wayne Ave., Boston, Mass.

Q. What is your profession?

A. I am a lawyer.

Q. Where is your office, please?

A. At 82 Washington St.

Q. How long have you been an attorney?

A. About twenty years.

Q. Were you acquainted with Elizabeth Brownlee, the deceased in her lifetime?

A. I was.

Q. Look at the instrument now shown you purporting to be the last will and testament of Elizabeth Brownlee, deceased

being read. London, etc., Co. v. American Cereal Co., 251 Ill. 123, 95 N. E. 1064; Ephraims v. Murdock, 7 Blackf. 10 (Ind.); Taft v. Little, 178 N. Y. 127, 70 N. E. 211; Trinity, etc., R. Co. v. Geary, 194 S. W. 458 (Texas); Laine v. Brainerd, 30 Conn. 565, 579; Kemble v. Lyons, 169 N. W. 117 (Iowa).

It must also be shown that it is impossible to procure the attendance of such witness because of *death.* Marshall v. Hancock, 80 Cal. 82, 22 Pac. 61; Shaw v. N. Y. El. R. Co., 18 N. Y. 186, 79 N. E. 984.

. . . *or absence.* Cameron v. Ah Quong, 175 Cal. 377, 165 Pac. 961; Heminway, etc., Silk Co. v. Porter, 94 Ill. App. 609; Karwick v. Pickards, 181 Mich. 169, 147 N. W. 605; Schomer v. State ex rel. Bettman, 190 N. E. 638, 47 Oh. App. 84; Mutual L. Ins. Co. v. Anthony, 50 Hun 101, 4 N. Y. S. 501.

. . . *or disqualification.* Hutchins v. Corgan, 59 Ill. 70; Morehouse v. Morehouse, 41 Hun 146 (N. Y.).

. . . *or mental incapacity.* Stout v. Cook, 47 Ill. 530; Ibanez v. Winston, 222 Mass. 129, 109 N. E. 814.

. . . *or illness.* Chicago, etc., R. Co. v. Mayer, 91 Ill. App. 372; Collins v. State, 5 S. W. 848 (Texas).

and state whether that instrument bears your name and signature?

A. It does.

Q. At whose request did you sign your name to the instrument?

A. At Elizabeth Brownlee's request.

Q. For what purpose did you sign your name to the instrument?

A. As a witness to the will.

Q. Did you see her sign her name to the instrument?

A. Yes.

Q. Did she see you sign your name to the instrument?

A. Yes.

Q. Who was present when the testatrix signed?

A. Simon Sutton, Henry Jones and myself.

Q. Were the same parties present when you signed?

A. Yes.

Q. On what date was the instrument signed by the testatrix and the witnesses; was it signed on March 26, 1922, the date it bears?

A. Yes.

Q. About how old was she at that time?

A. 52 years.

Q. Do you believe she was of sound mind and disposing memory at the time she signed her name to the instrument?

A. Yes she was.

Q. Did you so believe her to be of sound mind and disposing memory when you signed your name to the instrument as witness?

A. Yes, I did.

Q. Did she get married after signing the instrument?

A. No, she did not.

Q. Was there any child or children born to her or adopted by her after signing the instrument?

A. No.

Q. Look at the instrument, and state if it is in the same condition as it was when you signed it?

A. Yes, it is.

§ 357. Market price and value.

Evidence as to market price or value must always be presented by means of expert witnesses.[54] (See Expert Witnesses), except in so far as the subject concerns household furnishings.[55] In that event any householder is competent to testify as to value. In the absence of contrary evidence, testimony as to the price paid in the open market at fair sale in ordinary course of business will be received as evidence of value.

Illustration

Q. What is your name please?
A. Don Yaeger.
Q. And your address?
A. 6720 South Wabash Avenue.
Q. What is your business?
A. I am in the automobile repair and painting business. We also buy and sell parts for all makes of automobiles.
Q. How long have you been in that business?
A. Eighteen years.
Q. Are you familiar with the fair reasonable value and market price of Ford automobile fenders in Chicago in January 1934?
A. I am.
Q. What was the fair reasonable value and market price of one Ford automobile fender for a 1932 Model Sedan car in Chicago in the month of January, 1934.
A. $———.

§ 358. Pain and suffering.

In personal injury cases and in other instances where pain and suffering are involved as an element of damage of the case, it is permissible for plaintiff to testify to the usually objectionable subjective symptoms of pain and suffering in response to the question, "How did you feel after the im-

54 J. J. Jackson & Sons v. N. Y. C. R. R., 167 Ill. App. 461; Hudson v. No. Pac. R. Co., 92 Ia. 231, 60 N. W. 608; Rodee v. Detroit, etc., Ins. Co., 74 Hun 146, 26 N. Y. S. 242; Western Union Tel. Co. v. Gorman, 174 S. W. 925 (Texas); Maguire v. Pan American Amusement Co., 211 Mass. 22, 97 N. E. 142. (Some states contra.)

55 International, etc., R. Co. v. Davis, 175 S. W. 509 (Texas); Hood v. Bekans, etc., Co., 172 Pac. 594 (Cal.); Chicago City R. Co. v. T. W. Jones, etc., Co., 92 Ill. App. 507; Names v. Union Ins. Co., 104 Ia. 612, 74 N. W. 14; Berry v. Ingalls, 199 Mass. 77, 85 N. E. 191; Rademacher v. Greenwich Ins. Co., 75 Hun 83, 27 N. Y. S. 155.

pact?" or "What was your condition after the impact?"[56] An attending physician is also permitted to testify to the history of present pain and suffering given to him by the plaintiff.[57]

§ 359. Qualifying child witness.

More latitude should be allowed in the examination of a child of tender years and who has difficulty in understanding questions. In such a case leading questions are permissible providing a proper foundation has been laid. Such foundation should establish the age, education and ability to distinguish between right and wrong. In order not to frighten the child, which would ruin the chances of getting correct answers from him, a very familiar friendly attitude should be assumed.

Illustration*

Q. Now Johnnie, can you give us your full name please?
A. John Arthur Jackson.
Q. Where do you live, Johnnie?
A. 814 Wilson Ave.
Q. Johnnie, what grade are you in school?
A. I am in 3B.
Q. What school do you go to?
A. Wells School.
Q. Can you read from books?
A. Yes, sir.
Q. Can you write Johnnie?
A. Yes, sir.
Q. Johnnie, when you raised your hand a moment ago before that man over there, did you know what that was for?
A. Yes, sir.
Q. Just tell us what that was for Johnnie?
A. That I must tell the truth.
Q. Are you going to tell the truth, Johnnie?
A. Yes, sir.

---

* Suggested by Stanley A. Tweedle.

56 North Chicago St. R. Co. v. Cook, 145 Ill. 551, 33 N. E. 958; Martin v. Sherwood, 74 Conn. 475, 51 Atl. 526; O'Brien v. Chicago, etc., R. Co., 89 Ia. 644, 57 N. W. 425; Pierpont v. Fifth Avenue Coach Co., 151 App. Div. 40, 135 N. Y. S. 322; Wright v. Ft. Howard, 60 Wis. 119, 18 N. W. 750; El Paso El. Co. v. Cannon, 69 S. W. (2nd) 532 (Texas).

57 See Expert Witnesses, p. 385.

CHAPTER VII

EXHIBITS

§ 360. In general.

The young trial lawyer begins to appreciate the important part that "exhibits" play in the trial of cases when he first hears the judge sustain his opponent's objection to an important document (upon which his right to recovery is based) on the ground that no sufficient foundation has been shown for its admission into evidence. The subsequent loss of that case usually awakens him to the need for knowledge of the technique to be employed in the introduction of all classes of exhibits.

Successful trial lawyers emphasize the corroboratory and convincing value of all forms of written evidence. A good exhibit will continue to argue the merits of the attorney's cause long after his voice has been stilled. The jury may forget some of the oral testimony, but they cannot very well overlook or forget the exhibit which serves as an ever-present reminder of the truth of his contentions.

It is usually an exhibit introduced into evidence that turns the scales of justice, one way or another. All exhibits offered by an opponent, seemingly disproving a client's contentions, should be closely examined and tested to determine whether or not they are genuine or spurious.

As in all other phases of trial procedure, exhibits should only be offered in evidence at that stage of the case where they may be most logically understood and where, psychologically, they may tend most convincingly to prove the truth of the attorney's case. This is also the point at which the exhibit should be read to the jury so as to acquaint them with the contents thereof.

§ 361. Exhibits must be material.[1]

All exhibits must be material to some issue in the case—that is:

1. The action must be based upon the instrument, as in an action on a contract, note, lease, guaranty, etc.; or

[1] McGarrity v. Byington, 12 Cal. 426; Dunham v. Boyd, 64 Conn. 397, 30 Atl. 62; Grover, etc., Co. v. Newby, 58 Ind. 570; Crate v. Decorah, 15 N. Y. S. 607;

2. It must tend to prove some phase of the case or corroborate some witness' testimony as by letter, statements, books of account, receipts, etc.; or

3. It must tend to impeach or contradict some witness' statement either written or oral.

§ 362. Preliminary foundation.[2]

The following procedure should be utilized in offering exhibits in evidence:

First: The instrument should be identified and marked[3] for identification.

Second: A foundation must be legally laid for its admission.

Third: It should be shown to opposing counsel for examination and possible objection.[4]

Fourth: It must be offered in evidence.

Fifth: A ruling must be obtained from the court as to its admissibility.

Sixth: The record should show that it is received in evidence.

Seventh: It is good practice to request the court reporter with permission of the court to strike off the identification mark so that no question can be raised later from the notations on the instrument that it has not been received in evidence. This is particularly important in long drawn-out cases where there are frequent changes of court reporters. Whenever questions are raised by counsel as to whether or not certain exhibits have been received in evidence it is very seldom that the same reporter is available to check the record. If the identification mark has been stricken at the time the exhibit

Perry State Bank v. Elledge, 99 Ill. App. 307.

2 Where documentary evidence is offered, each piece should be presented by itself to the court, exhibited to opposing counsel, identified by the court stenographer with marks, and the genuineness established. Vergie v. Stetson, 73 Me. 452.

3 The marking of the exhibit does not make it evidence. Casteel v. Millison, 41 Ill. App. 61; Shelton v. Holzwasser, 91 N. Y. S. 328, 46 Misc. 76; Byerley v. Sun Co., 181 Fed. 138.

4 It is error to admit documentary evidence without permitting opposing counsel to examine it. Tonseth v. Portland Ry. Light & Power Co., 141 Pac. 868, 70 Ore. 341.

is received in evidence there can be no question about it. (See illustration on page 297.)

Eighth: Upon the admission of an exhibit in evidence it should be read to the jury.[5] In some states the failure to read the exhibits to the jury will prevent their use in the case. The record should show that the exhibits have been read to the jury unless by permission of the court and with the stipulation and agreement of the adversary it is agreed that the reading of the exhibits may be dispensed with and that it be considered that the exhibits have been read. The record should also show this stipulation with the further agreement of counsel that the exhibits may be referred to during the final arguments to the jury as though the formality of reading them to the jury had been complied with.

If the lawyer is opposing the admission of the exhibit and objects to it (after stating the grounds of his objection), and if the court rules adversely to him and admits the exhibit in evidence it is sometimes necessary, in order to properly preserve the question for review, to save an exception to the ruling of the court.

§ 363. Objections to exhibits.

All objections to offered exhibits should be specifically stated.[6]

Illustration

Plaintiff's Exhibits K and L marked for identification.

Mr. Brown: I now offer these two documents in evidence.

Mr. Stanton: I object to the exhibit known as Document K for the reason that there is no proof in the record as to who J. H. Bacon, the person mentioned in Plaintiff's Exhibit K was. Because there is no proof in the record that the plain-

5 It is ordinarily within the discretion of the court, whether document should be read. O'Reilly v. Duffy, 105 Mass. 243; Brill v. Flagler, 23 Wend. (N. Y.) 354.

A party has a right to insist that it be read. Billings Appeal, 49 Conn. 456; Novelty Showcase Co. v. Samuel I. Davis & Co., 155 N. Y. S. 345, 92 Misc. 210; Palmer v. Parker, 158 Pac. 1017, 91 Wash. 683.

6 Milliken v. Barr, 7 Pa. 23; Wilson v. Steers, 18 Misc. 364; Gage v. Eddy, 186 Ill. 432, 57 N. E. 1030; Page v. Grant, 127 Iowa 249; Shippers, etc., Co. v. Davidson, 80 S. W. 1032 (Texas); Ohio R. Co. v. Walker, 113 Ind. 196, 15 N. E. 234.

tiff was the procuring cause for the execution of the document known as Exhibit K; and therefore that Plaintiff's Exhibit K is incompetent, irrelevant and immaterial upon any theory of the case.

I object to the introduction in evidence of Plaintiff's Exhibit L for the reason that there is no testimony in the record showing who J. H. Bacon was, what his connection with the Yeoman of America was, or the Brotherhood of American Yeoman was, and that there is no proof in the record that the plaintiff was the procuring cause for the execution of the document known as Plaintiff's Exhibit L, and that therefore Plaintiff's Exhibit L is incompetent, irrelevant and immaterial to any of the issues in this case.

I might say further, there is no foundation laid for the introductions of either of these documents; they are not the best evidence as to what occurred if anything did occur at any time between Mr. Bacon and the defendant Dr. Heuser. The deeds themselves are the best evidence, may it please your Honor. That is another ground of objection.

A further ground of objection: There is no proof as to who J. H. Bacon was, the person who signed that signature, no proof of the authenticity of the signature upon the original deed and that it is secondary evidence of the fact, if there is any fact, adduced by either of those exhibits and therefore they are incompetent.

§ 364. Identifying exhibits.

It should become the practice of the trial lawyer to have each exhibit marked for identification before any evidence in reference thereto is offered. Unless this is done it is impossible to determine from the record which exhibit the testimony refers to, by reason of the fact that counsel failed to mark the exhibit for identification before commencing his examination in reference thereto.

It is improper and poor technique to ask such questions as, "Have you ever seen this before?"—"Did you sign this?" or "When did you sign this?" Such a record does not disclose what exhibits were referred to by the questions.

The proper procedure would be something like this:

Q. Mr. Reporter, will you please mark this instrument Plaintiff's Exhibit 1 for identification? (Paper is marked.)

To witness: Mr. Jones, I show you Plaintiff's Exhibit 1 for identification and ask you if your name and signature appears thereon?

A. Yes, it does.

Q. Was it signed by you on or about the date it bears?

A. It was.

Counsel: I offer Plaintiff's Exhibit 1 for identification, being the letter dated October 2nd, 1933, in evidence as Plaintiff's Exhibit 1.

The Court: It may be received.

Counsel: And I will ask that the identification mark be stricken and the instrument marked as Plaintiff's Exhibit 1 in evidence.

Note: (Court reporters usually designate exhibits when marked for identification in this way: "Pl. Ex. 1 for id." When the identification mark is stricken it appears as "Pl. Ex. 1 ~~for id.~~").

The Court: The identification mark may be stricken.

§ 365. "What is it?"

Many trial attorneys in identifying exhibits do so by asking the witness "if he knows what the instrument is?" This question is usually followed by the objection of counsel "that the instrument speaks for itself."

Illustration

Q. Do you know what this is?

A. Yes, I do.

Q. What is it?

A. A guarantee.

Mr. Opponent: I object to that. The document speaks for itself. I move that the last answer be stricken.

The Court: Your motion allowed.

Longenecker in his "Hints on the Trial of a Law Suit" makes this comment on the propriety of the foregoing questions and answers:

"Many lawyers object to this question, confusing it with questions that call for the contents of a paper, or again, they claim such a question calls for a conclusion and that the paper speaks for itself. This disconcerts the young trial lawyer.

but he should remember and reason that no paper speaks for itself, that is, determines what it is, that the question is not a vital one and is only *preliminary* to naming the papers by identifying it for the record, so that anyone reading the record afterward may understand what was being spoken of.

"The answer that 'It is a letter,' 'It is a contract,' or 'It is a deed,' binds no one, because it is the contents that bind and affect the parties, and the materiality will be passed upon when it is offered in evidence."

It is suggested that this objection may be obviated in part by adopting the following method of identifying exhibits:

Illustration

(After paper is marked Plaintiff's Exhibit 1 for identification.)

Q. I show you Plaintiff's Exhibit 1 for identification, *purporting to be a letter* and ask you whether or not you have ever seen that before?

A. Yes, I have.

§ 366. When exhibits offered.

Exhibits should always be offered in evidence during the direct or re-direct examination of a witness or during the direct case of the party. Offering exhibits in evidence during the cross-examination is subject to objection in some States.[7] Exhibits will not be received in evidence, in some states, during cross-examination of a witness without the express and stipulated consent of opposing counsel as well as the Court. Of course if no objection is raised by an oppo-

7 It has been held that the writing may be introduced on cross-examination of a witness who has testified concerning it; Spitler v. Kaeding, 65 Pac. 1040, 133 Cal. 500; Graham v. Plotner, 151 N. E. 735, 87 Ind. App. 462; Laserowitch v. Reiman, 6 N. Y. St. 246, 116 N. Y. 659; Chicago, etc., R. Co. v. Holland, 13 N. E. 145, 122 Ill. 461, where the witness stated the contents of a letter on direct examination.

Where the witness used the writing on direct examination to refresh his memory, it was permitted to introduce it on cross-examination. Smith v. Jackson, 71 N. W. 843, 113 Mich. 511; Remson v. Metro. El. R. Co., 41 N. Y. S. 593, 9 App. Div. 533; Chang Sim v. White, 277 Fed. 765; Haas v. Commerce Trust Co., 69 So. 894, 194 Ala. 672; Schworm v. Fraternal Banker's Res. Soc. 150 N. W. 714, 168 Iowa 579; MacBard Coal v. Wyatt Coal Co., 17 Oh. App. 38.

nent, the objection will be deemed to be waived. It has been held, however, *not* to be reversible error to admit exhibits on cross-examination.

Exhibits may usually be taken by the jury into the jury-room during their deliberations. (Some states contra.)

§ 366a. Offering exhibits identified by opponent.

Whenever the attorney desires to offer in evidence exhibits which have been marked for identification by his opponent but which are not offered in evidence by such opponent, he may have opponent's exhibit marked as one of his own exhibits and offer it in evidence as such.

§ 367. Photostatic and certified copies.

In some instances it becomes advisable to substitute photostatic or certified copies in place of original documents. This can be done by agreement of counsel and permission of the court. However, it is always necessary to have the record show this stipulation and agreement so that no question can later be raised to the effect that there are differences between the originals and the substituted copies.

Illustration

Mr. Sullivan: If the Court please, I would like to request the indulgence of the Court and counsel to the extent of being privileged to substitute photostatic copies of the original exhibits which have been introduced in evidence.

The Court: No objection, Mr. O'Shaughnessy?

Mr. O'Shaughnessy: No objection.

The Court: All right.

Mr. Sullivan (for the record): It is hereby stipulated and agreed by and between the parties hereto, by their respective counsel, that any of the exhibits offered here in evidence today by the defendant, may be supplanted, for the purpose of the record, after the hearing in Court by photostatic copies thereof.

Mr. Sullivan (continuing): You agree to that stipulation, Mr. O'Shaughnessy?

Mr. O'Shaughnessy: Yes.

In each instance where original exhibits are withdrawn and photostatic copies are substituted, the photostatic copies should also be marked as exhibits.

Illustration

Counsel: Now, if the Court please I would like to withdraw Plaintiff's Exhibits 1, 2, and 3 and to substitute photostatic copies of them. The checks do not belong to us. I will also ask that the photostatic copies be marked Plaintiff's Exhibits 1a, 2a, and 3a.

Mr. King: That is all right. *Subject to the same objection* as to the original exhibits.

The Court: Motion allowed.

§ 368. Offering both sides of exhibits.

Where it is important that *both* sides of an exhibit be considered by the court and jury, it is advisable to offer in evidence *both* sides of the instrument.

Illustration

Counsel: If the Court, please, at this time I wish to offer Plaintiff's Exhibit 11 for identification, being the check dated Jan. 3, 1934, *both the face and reverse sides thereof,* in evidence as Plaintiff's Exhibit 11.

§ 369. Re-offering exhibits.

Some trial attorneys have made it a practice to *re-offer* and to *re-introduce* all of their exhibits just before they rest their case at the close of all the evidence as an added precautionary measure against the possible error of having forgotten to offer some one or more exhibits in evidence. This procedure is recommended.

Illustration

Counsel: At this time, if the Court, please, in order to make sure that the record shows all of the exhibits as received in evidence, I wish to *re-offer* all of Plaintiff's Exhibits, Nos. 1 to 16 inclusive and ask that they may be received in evidence as Plaintiff's Exhibits 1 to 16 inclusive.

The Court: They may be received and so marked.

However, it is generally held by all courts, that where both sides, by their conduct, treat a certain instrument as though it had been received in evidence and argue it before the Court and jury, it will be considered as though it had been offered and received in evidence.[8]

The better practice, it would seem, is to re-offer all exhibits before the attorney rests his case.

§ 370. Changes, alterations and interlineations.

All changes, alterations, and interlineations on all written instruments should be explained by witnesses before the exhibit is offered in evidence so as to avoid any suspicion as to its genuineness.[9] The trial attorney should not wait for opposing counsel to call attention to this by cross-examination. He should always account for the continuous possession of the exhibit prior to date of trial.

§ 370a. Motion to reserve decision on admissibility.

Sometimes the trial attorney's investigation and knowledge of the case convinces him that certain exhibits offered by his opponent should not be received in evidence. Sufficient foundation has *apparently* been laid to warrant the Court in receiving the exhibit in evidence but knowing that a little cross-examination will disclose the fact of its inadmissibility, he should request the Court to withhold his ruling until after he has had an opportunity to cross-examine in reference to the instrument.[10] In most instances the Court will usually grant this request.

Illustration

Opponent: I offer Plaintiff's Exhibit 10 for identification in evidence as Plaintiff's Exhibit 10.

Counsel: If the Court please, we would like to have your Honor reserve his decision on the admissibility of this exhibit until after we have had an opportunity to cross-examine as to it.

The Court: Very well.

8 McChesney v. Chicago, 152 Ill. 543, 38 N. E. 767; Zeiverink v. Kemper, 50 Oh. St. 208, 34 N. E. 250; Wright v. Roseberry, 81 Cal. 87, 22 Pac. 336.

9 Herrick v. Malin, 22 Wend. (N. Y.) 388; Hutchison v. Kelly, 276 Ill. 438; Morgan v. Tutt, 52 Tex. C. A. 301, 113 S. W. 958.

10 Trussell v. Scarlett, 18 Fed. 214.

§ 371. Examine each offered exhibit.

It is of the utmost importance that the trial lawyer examine every exhibit offered by his opponent before stating his grounds of objection. Some attorneys make the general objection of "incompetent, irrelevant, and immaterial" without closely examining the instrument. After the general objection is overruled and the exhibit is read to the jury, it then becomes apparent that he should have made a specific objection, which might have been sustained, but it is usually too late. The harm is done when the jury hears the statement as to the contents of the exhibit.

§ 372. Limiting purpose of exhibit.

It frequently happens that an exhibit is generally inadmissible, but may become admissible for only one purpose. Where the exhibit is admitted into evidence by the court, the record should show that it is only being received for that purpose, and only such portions of the exhibit that tend to prove the one phase for which it is received should be read to the jury.

All other parts of the exhibit should be covered in some way, or else the material portion (if a written document) should be copied on another piece of paper and by stipulation received into evidence.

§ 373. Simple foundation.

In most instances a perfectly natural and simple method of laying a foundation for the admission of an exhibit arises when the witness is led on by asking him "what did you do then, if anything?" and he answers that "I gave him a check" or "I sent him a letter." The next step, obviously, is to have the check or letter marked for identification and to ask the witness: Q. "I show you Plaintiff's Exhibit 1 for identification and ask you whether or not that is the letter you have referred to." A. "Yes, it is." Then offer it in evidence, and it is received without any further formality.

§ 374. Carbon copies of letters, etc.

A little more difficulty is experienced when it becomes necessary to introduce in evidence carbon copies of letters, etc. The first step usually required is to serve notice a reasonable length of time in advance of the trial on the opposite party to produce the original letter and, that upon his failure to do so, secondary evidence will be offered of its contents.[11]

§ 375. —The notice to produce—Form.

State of ——— }
County of ——— } ss.

In the Circuit Court of ———

John Brown }
v. } No. 726446
George Smith }

Notice

To: MR. H. K. WILSON
Attorney for Defendant
160 No. Western Rd.

You are hereby notified to produce upon the hearing of the above entitled cause:

Letter dated September 10, 1925, addressed to George Smith, 100 W. Main St., Miami, Florida, and signed John Brown; upon your failure to do so we shall offer secondary evidence of the contents thereof.

____

Attorneys for Plaintiff.

Received a copy of foregoing notice this first day of February, 1934, at 2:00 P. M.

____

Attorneys for Defendant.

11 Young v. People, 221 Ill. 51; Singmaster & Son v. Robinson, 181 Iowa 522, 164 N. W. 776; McDowell v. Aetna Ins. Co., 164 Mass. 444, 41 N. E. 665; Martlock v. Williams, 76 Mich. 568, 43 N. W. 592; Foster v. Newbrough, 58 N. Y. 481; Walsh v. Methodist, etc., Church, (Tex.) 173 S. W. 241.

But, where the document is in Court, notice is not necessary; McGregor v. Wait, 10 Gray (Mass.) 72, 69 Am. Dec. 305; Hanselman v. Doyle, 90 Mich. 142, 51 N. W. 195; Whelan v. Gorton, 37 N. Y. S. 344; Chotean v. Raitt, 20 Oh. 132; Maxcy-Barton v. Glen Bldg. Corp., 355 Ill. 228; Truesdale Mfg. Co. v. Hoyle, 39 Ill. A. 532; where document was in attorney's possession.

Notice must be given a reasonable time before trial. Jack v. Rowland, 98 Ill. App. 352; Welch v. N. Y., etc., R. Co., 176 Mass. 393, 57 N. E. 668; Continental Fire Ass'n v. Bearden, 69 S. W. 982 (Texas); Muir v. Kalamazoo Corset Co., 155 Mich. 624, 119 N. W. 1079.

Form and substance of notice. Walden v. Davidson, 11 Wend. (N. Y.) 65, 25 Am. Dec. 602; Arnstine v. Treat, 71 Mich. 561, 39 N. W. 749; McDowell v. Aetna Ins. Co., (Mass.) supra; Nussbaum v. U. S. Brewing Co., 63 Ill. App. 35.

§ 376. — Original letter produced.

If, after notice to produce is served, opposing counsel brings the exhibit into court, and upon request produces it, the trial attorney may then introduce it into evidence.

Illustration

Counsel: If the Court please, we served notice on Mr. Wilson, the attorney for the defendant, to produce the original letter dated September 10th, 1925, addressed to George Smith, 100 W. Main St., Miami, Florida, and signed John Brown. I now call on Mr. Wilson to produce that letter.

Mr. Wilson: Yes, I have it. (Produces letter.)

Counsel (to the reporter): Please, mark that Defendant's Exhibit 1, for identification.

Q. Calling your attention to Defendant's Exhibit 1 for identification, I ask you if you received that? (Handing paper to witness.)

A. Yes, I received it.

Counsel: I offer Defendant's Exhibit 1 for identification being the letter dated September 10, 1925, in evidence as Defendant's Exhibit 1.

The Court: It may be received.

§ 377. — Proof of carbon copy.

If, however, when called upon in open court and during the trial, to produce the original letter in pursuance of the notice served upon the opponent, opponent fails to produce it, then a proper foundation must be laid for the admission of the carbon copy. It must be shown that the letter was dictated, correctly transcribed and typed, properly addressed to the party intended, that full, sufficient and uncancelled postage stamps were properly affixed to the envelope, and that it was duly deposited in a regular United States Post Office mail chute or post-office. If any reply is received or response made by the party to whom the letter was addressed, it should also be shown as it tends to prove that the letter was duly received. With this foundation shown by proper witnesses the carbon copy of the letter will be received in evidence.

The notice to produce should be registered and filed for record in the case so as to show that all preliminaries were complied with.

Illustration

(To the Court): If the Court please, we served notice upon counsel to produce the letter dated September 10, 1925, addressed to George Smith and signed John Brown. In accordance with this notice, I now ask counsel to produce said letter.

Opponent: We have no such document.

(Note: Then proceed to lay the foundation for the admission of the carbon copy.)

§ 378. — Proof of preparation of original and carbon copy.

Illustration

Q. Will you state your full name, please?

A. John Brown.

Q. What is your profession, Mr. Brown?

A. I am a lawyer.

Q. Where do you live, please?

A. 4919 Madison St., Chicago.

Counsel: I will ask that this document be marked Plaintiff's Exhibit 2 for identification. (The said document is so marked.)

Q. I show you document marked Plaintiff's Exhibit 2 for identification (handing exhibit to witness). Did you have anything to do with the preparation of that document?

A. I dictated the original of that document.

Q. What did you do with the original, if anything?

A. I read it and then signed it.

Q. At the time you received the original letter did you receive anything else?

A. Yes, a carbon copy of the original.

Q. Is Plaintiff's Exhibit 2 the carbon copy you have referred to?

A. Yes, it is.

Q. What did you do then, if anything?

A. The envelope, the original letter and carbon copy were delivered by me to my secretary, Helen Jones.

Q. Is Plaintiff's Exhibit 2 for identification, a true and correct copy of the original?
A. Yes, it is.

§ 379. —Proof of mailing.[12]

Illustration

Q. What is your name, please?
A. Helen Jones.
Q. Where do you live?
A. 6964 North Ave., Chicago.
Q. What is your business?
A. I am a stenographer.
Q. What was your business in the month of September, 1925?
A. I worked for the firm of Brown and Henry as Mr. Brown's secretary.
Q. How long did you work for them?
A. Three years.
Q. I show you Plaintiff's Exhibit 2 for identification and ask you whether or not you have ever seen it before?
A. Yes, I have.
Q. Was that prepared by you?
A. Yes, I typed it.
Q. At the time you typed Plaintiff's Exhibit 2 for identification, did you type anything else?
A. Yes, the original.
Q. When?
A. 1925, when it was dated, September 10th.
Q. By whom was it dictated, if anyone?
A. By Mr. Brown.

12 *When a letter is properly addressed and mailed and postage prepaid, there is a presumption that it was received by the addressee.* Grade v. Mariposa County, 132 Cal. 75, 64 Pac. 117; Huntley v. Whether, 105 Mass. 391; De Bolt v. German American Ins. Co., 18 Iowa 671, 165 N. W. 55; Foote v. Greilick, 166 Mich. 636, 132 N. W. 473; Mishkind-Feinberg Realty Co. v. Sidorsky, 189 N. Y. 402, 98 N. Y. S. 496, 82 N. E. 448; Western Union Tel. Co. v. McDavid, 103 Texas 601, 132 S. W. 115; Clark v. People, 224 Ill. 554, 79 N. E. 941.

Q. That paper you have, Plaintiff's Exhibit 2 for identification, is that a carbon copy of something?
A. Yes, this is a carbon copy of the original letter.
Q. Is that a true and correct copy of the original?
A. It is.
Q. In whose possession has Plaintiff's Exhibit 2 for identification been?
A. In mine.
Q. After you typed and prepared the original and carbon copy, what did you do with them?
A. I took them to Mr. Brown.
Q. What did Mr. Brown do, if anything?
A. He read the original letter and signed it.
Q. And after it was signed what did Mr. Brown do with it?
A. He returned it to me with the copy, and I put the original in an envelope and mailed it down the chute.
Q. How did you address it?
A. To Mr. George Smith, 100 W. Main St., Miami, Fla.
Q. And after addressing the envelope what did you do with the original of that letter?
A. I enclosed the original in the envelope.
Q. What else did you do then, if anything?
A. I sealed the envelope after enclosing the letter, and put a stamp on it.
Q. What kind?
A. A three cent stamp.
Q. Cancelled or uncancelled?
A. Uncancelled.
Q. A United States postal three cent stamp?
A. Yes.
Q. Where did you deposit it?
A. The mail chute in the building.
Q. Which building?
A. At Clark and Madison Street.
Q. The same building in which your office was?
A. Yes.
Q. And was that a United States mail chute?
A. Yes, it was.
Q. Do you remember the character of the envelope that you enclosed the original in?

A. It had the name of our firm and the address on the upper left-hand corner for return address purposes.

Q. Let me have that please. (Asking for letter.) How do you identify all letters that were dictated to you and by you transcribed from your notes and written on the typewriting machine?

A. I put the initials of the person who dictated the letter and my initials at the lower left-hand corner of the letter.

Q. Did you do that on Plaintiff's Exhibit 2 for identification?

A. Yes, I did.

Q. Who receives all mail in your office?

A. I do.

Q. Was the original of Plaintiff's Exhibit 2 which you mailed ever returned to your office?

A. No sir.

Counsel: I now offer Plaintiff's Exhibit 2 for identification being the carbon copy of letter dated September 10th, 1925, in evidence as Plaintiff's Exhibit 2.

The Court: It may be received.

§ 380. Books of account.

Some statutes and codes provide for the admission of books of account into evidence as follows:

Where, in any civil action, suit or proceeding, the claim or defense is founded on a book account, any party or interested person may testify to his account book and the items therein contained; that the same is a book of original entries; and that the entries therein were made by himself,[12a] and are true and just; or that the same were made by a deceased person, or by a disinterested person, a non-resident of the state at the time of the trial, and were made by such deceased or non-resident person in the usual course of trade, and of his duty or employment to the party so testifying; and thereupon the said account book and entries shall be admitted as evidence in the cause.

§ 381. — In general.

A book to be admissible in evidence as an account book,

12a See § 383.

must contain entries or transactions as they occurred in the regular course of business.[13]

It must be a book of original entry,[14] and made at time of transaction.[15]

§ 382. —Ledger.

The book of original entry must be produced, the ledger alone is not sufficient.[16]

Where no foundation is laid for the introduction of an account book in evidence, it is error to permit a witness to read into the record items contained in such book.[17]

Ledger leaves offered in evidence, not shown to be from a book of original entries or that the entries made thereon were made by the witness or were true and correct, or were made by a deceased person or non-resident or in the usual course of business, are not admissible under the statute to prove books of account.[18]

A witness is competent to identify a book of original entries kept by himself, notwithstanding that he has a pecuniary

13 Yick Wo v. Underhill, 5 Cal. App. 519, 90 Pac. 967; Nouman Printer's Supply v. Ford, 77 Conn. 461, 59 Atl. 499; Pittsburgh, etc., R. Co. v. Fawsett, 56 Ill. 513; Kossuth County St. Bank v. Richardson, 132 Iowa 370, 106 N. W. 923, 109 N. W. 809; Riley v. Boehm, 167 Mass. 183, 45 N. E. 84; Evans v. Rogers, 159 N. Y. S. 898; Fruit Dispatch Co. v. Sturgis, 28 Oh. Cir. Ct. 65, 78 N. E. 1125; Bouldin v. Atlantic Ricemills Co., 86 S. W. 795 (Tex.); Kibbe v. Bancroft, 77 Ill. 18.

14 Kerns v. McKean, 76 Cal. 87, 18 Pac. 122; McDavid v. Ellis, 78 Ill. App. 381; Cogswell v. Dolliver, 2 Mass. 217, 3 Am. Dec. 45; Baldridge v. Penland, 68 Tex. 441, 4 S. W. 565; Skipworth v. Deyell, 83 Hun 307, 31 N. Y. S. 918.

Entries may be original although transferred from some other memorandum. Faxon v. Hollis, 13 Mass. 427; McGoldrick v. Wilson, 18 Hun 443 (N. Y.); Chisholm v. Beaman Mach. Co., 160 Ill. 101, 43 N. E. 796.

However, the transfer must be made within a reasonable time. Landis v. Turner, 14 Cal. 573; Redlich v. Bauerlee, 98 Ill. 134.

15 Kearns v. McKean, 76 Cal. 87, 18 Pac. 122; Bouldin v. Atlantic Ricemills Co., (Tex.) 86 S. W. 795; Mahoney v. Hartford Inv. Co., 82 Conn. 280, 73 Atl. 766; Chisholm v. Beaman Mach. Co., 160 Ill. 101, 43 N. E. 796; Trainor v. Robyn, 164 Iowa 508, 146 N. W. 450; Davis v. Sanford, 91 Mass. 216; Greisheimer v. Tannesbaum, 124 N. Y. S. 650, 26 N. E. 957; Fruit Dispatch Co. v. Sturgis, 28 Oh. Cir. Ct. 65, 78 N. E. 1125; Hill Co. v. Sommer, 55 Ill. App. 345.

16 McCormick v. Elston, 16 Ill. 204; Harper v. Ely, 70 Ill. 581.

17 Osgood v. Poole, 165 Ill. App. 63.

18 Baretti v. Theurer, 206 Ill. App. 164.

interest in result of litigation and adverse party is defending in representative capacity.[19]

§ 383. —Records made by others.

In order to entitle a book of account made up of entries transcribed from temporary memoranda to be read in evidence, such book must be supported not only by the suppletory oath of the party who made the entries in the book but by the person who made the temporary memoranda in the first instance,[20] unless the witness testifies that all records were kept under his direction and supervision. In some jurisdictions, rules of court permit the introduction of records proved to be kept in the ordinary course of business by anyone, whether the records were made by the witness or not. However, this is the exception rather than the rule.[21]

Books of Account

Illustration

Q. What is your name, please?
A. David L. Jones.
Q. Where do you live?
A. 4400 Wilcox Street.
Q. What is your business?
A. I am a bookkeeper.
Q. Employed by whom?
A. The Electric Corporation.
Q. Were you so employed in that capacity by the Electric Corporation in April, 1930?
A. I was.
Q. And were your duties the same at that time?
A. They were.
Q. Who is in charge of the bookkeeping department there?
A. I am.
Q. Were all the entries in the books and records of the Electric Corporation made under your supervision and direction?
A. They were.

19 McGlassen v. Housel, 127 Ill. App. 360.

20 Trainor v. B. A. Building Ass'n, 204 Ill. 616.

21 Rule 166 Mun. Ct. of Chgo.

Q. What books of account do you use?

A. A ledger, cash-book, journal, and invoice or sales book.

Q. Will you describe the method you follow in keeping your books?

A. Sales tickets are made for all sales and from there posted to the general ledger. The sales tickets are bound together in what we call a sales book. All cash received is entered in the cash book and then posted to the ledger. The journal is used for general entries.

Q. I show you Plaintiff's Exhibit 1 for identification, purporting to be a ledger sheet account of the Brass Tool and Manufacturing Company and ask you in whose handwriting it is, if you know?

A. In mine.

Q. Was Plaintiff's Exhibit 1 for identification made in the usual and ordinary course of business?

A. It was.

Q. Is it true and correct?

A. It is.

To Court reporter: Mark these Plaintiff's Exhibits 2, 3, and 4 for identification.

Q. I show you Plaintiff's Exhibit 2 for identification and ask you whether or not this is the sales book you have referred to?

A. It is.

Q. Who posted those items shown in Plaintiff's Exhibit 2 for identification to Plaintiff's Exhibit 1 for identification?

A. I did.

Q. I show you Plaintiff's Exhibit 3 for identification and ask you whether or not that is the cash book that you have referred to?

A. It is.

Q. Were Plaintiff's Exhibits 2, 3, and 4 for identification kept and prepared under your supervision and direction?

A. They were.

Q. Are they true and correct?

A. They are.

Q. Were they kept in the usual and ordinary course of business?

A. They were.

Q. In whose handwriting are Plaintiff's Exhibits 2, 3, and 4 for identification?
A. In my assistant's, Tom Herman.
Q. Is Tom Herman here?
A. He is not.
Q. Where is he?
A. I do not know. I have not been able to find him.
Q. What did you have to do with these records?
A. I posted all items from the sales tickets and cash book to the ledger.
Q. And by cash book you refer to Plaintiff's Exhibit 3 for identification, and by sales tickets you refer to Plaintiff's Exhibit 2 for identification?
A. Yes.
Q. I now offer Plaintiff's Exhibits 1, 2, 3, and 4 for identification in evidence as Plaintiff's Exhibits 1, 2, 3, and 4.
Court: They may be admitted.

Where certain pages of these records are to be admitted instead of the entire book, the following method is suggested:

Illustration

Q. Mr. Jones, I show you Plaintiff's Exhibit 1 for identification (the ledger sheet) and ask you to tell the Court and jury what the figures on both sides of that sheet represent?
A. The figures on the left-hand side represent the debits or charges while the figures on the right-hand side represent the credits or payments on account.
Q. Directing your attention to the first item on the left-hand side, the debits, where did you get that information?
A. From page 27 of the sales book.
Q. Will you refer to Plaintiff's Exhibit 2 for identification, the sales book, and indicate on page 27, the item posted to Plaintiff's Exhibit 1 for identification?
A. Here it is (indicating).
(Note: The same procedure would be followed as to all debits.)
Q. Now, Mr. Jones, directing your attention to the first item on the right-hand side of Plaintiff's Exhibit 1 for identification (the credits) where did you get that information?
A. From page 7 of the cashbook.

Q. Will you refer to Plaintiff's Exhibit 3 for identification, the cashbook, and indicate on page 7, the item posted to the credit side of Plaintiff's Exhibit 1 for identification which is the ledger sheet?

A. Here it is (indicating).

(Note: The same procedure would be followed as to all credits.)

Q. I now offer Plaintiff's Exhibit 1 for identification in evidence as Plaintiff's Exhibit 1.

Court: It may be admitted.

Counsel: I now offer pages 27, 39, 58, and 69 of Plaintiff's Exhibit 2 for identification in evidence and ask that pages 27, 39, 58, and 69 be marked Plaintiff's Exhibits 2a, 2b, 2c, and 2d respectively.

Court: They may be admitted and so marked.

Counsel: I now offer pages 7, 11, and 12 of the Plaintiff's Exhibit 3 for identification in evidence and ask that the said pages 7, 11, and 12 be marked Plaintiff's Exhibits 3a, 3b, and 3c respectively.

Court: They may be admitted and so marked.

Q. Referring to Plaintiff's Exhibit 1, the ledger sheet, will you tell the Court and jury please, what the total debits are?

A. $927.50.

Q. Now, please tell us what the total credits are, as shown by Plaintiff's Exhibit 1.

A. $527.50.

Q. What is the balance after deducting all credits from the debits as shown by Plaintiff's Exhibit 1?

A. $400.00.

> Note: Some attorneys object to a witness telling the state of an account by reading from a ledger sheet after it has been received in evidence on the ground that the document "speaks for itself." However, it must be remembered that a document prepared by an expert in a specialized field does not always speak for itself. Anything that requires explanation by an expert in a field outside the general knowledge of a "layman" jury does not speak for itself.[21a] In the case of Estate of Smythe v. Evans, 209 Ill. 376, on page 388, the court held:

21a Where the entries in books of account are not stated in a form which is self-explanatory, it is essential that they be explained by proper evidence. Walker v. Skliris, 34 Utah 353, 98 Pac. 114.

"It is also proper, for the convenience of the jury, to take the evidence of a bookkeeper, accountant or other person skilled in work of that character, to show the footing of a column of figures or to show the result of any calculation from a complicated set of figures which cannot be readily carried in mind by the jury, where the calculation is purely mathematical."

In some states one further step is required in laying the foundation for the introduction of books of account. In New York, California and Texas, in addition to the proof required as hereinbefore illustrated, the testimony of one of plaintiff's customers who has found client's books to be correct must be introduced in evidence.[22]

Illustration

Testimony of one of plaintiff's customers:

Q. Do you know the John Jones, the plaintiff in this case?

A. Yes, I do.

Q. Have you had occasion to do business with him?

A. Yes, I have.

Q. For how long a period of time?

A. For the past five years.

Q. On a cash or credit basis?

A. On a credit basis.

Q. In what manner have you settled your accounts with the plaintiff during that time?

A. According to his books.

Q. Did you keep books and records as to your transactions with John Jones?

A. Yes, I did.

Q. From time to time, did you receive invoices and statements of your account with John Jones?

A. Yes, I did.

Q. Have you always found plaintiff's books to be correct?

A. Yes.

22 *In some states correctness is proved by customers who testify that they had dealt with the party and settled by his books and that they had always found his accounts correct.* Smith v. Smith, 163 N. Y. 168, 53 L. R. A. 545, 57 N. E. 300; Colburn v. Parrett, 27 Cal. 541, 150 Pac. 786; American Fire Ins. Co. v. First Nat. Bank, (Tex.) 30 S. W. 384. (See New York statute for changes.)

Q. How do you know the accounts were correct?
A. His records always corresponded with mine.
Q. Have you your books of account with you?
A. Yes, I have.
Q. Will you produce them please?
Counsel: Will you please mark these Plaintiff's Exhibits 2, 3 and 4 for identification.

(Proceed to prove as suggested above and offer in evidence.)

§ 384. Promissory note.[23]

Illustration

Q. I show Plaintiff's Exhibit 3 for identification and ask you whether or not you have seen that before?
A. Yes, I have.
Q. From whom did you receive it, if anybody?
A. From James Simpson.
Q. The defendant in this case?
A. Yes, sir.
Q. Whose signature appears on Plaintiff's Exhibit 3 for identification, if you know?
A. James Simpson.
Q. Was it signed by him in your presence?[24]
A. It was.

23 Sufficiency of foundation: Patton v. Bank of Lafayette, 124 Ga. 965, 5 L. R. A. (N. S.) 592, 4 Ann. Cas. 639, 53 S. E. 664; Bevan v. Atlanta, 142 Ill. 302.

24 Execution of documents may be proved by the testimony of a person who was present and saw it executed: Dundee v. Chambers, 23 Ill. 369; In re Chismore, 166 Iowa 217, 147 N. W. 97; Cohen v. Elias, 176 App. Div. 763, 163 N. Y. S. 1051; Graham v. Burggraf, 10 Oh. Cir. Ct. (N. S.) 594.

The most satisfactory evidence of execution is the testimony of one who saw the signatory sign his name: Lefkowitz v. First Nat. Bank, 152 Ala. 521, 44 So. 613; State v. Matlack, (Del.) 64 Atl. 259; Menley v. Zeigler, 23 Tex. 88.

Also where the witness has seen the party write his name on other occasions, he may testify that the signature is that of the party: Haynes v. Thomas, 7 Ind. 38; Rutherford v. Dyer, 146 Ala. 665, 40 So. 974; Pate v. Peo., 8 Ill. 644.

If the instrument purports to be executed by an agent, the authority of the agent must be proved: Pallidine v. Imperial V. F. L. Ass'n, 65 Cal. App. 727, 225 Pac. 291; Darst v. Doom, 38 Ill. App. 397.

Q. On or about the date it bears?
A. It was.
Q. What did he do with it after he signed it, if anything?
A. He gave it to me.

Counsel: I offer this note dated June 1, 1927, and marked Plaintiff's Exhibit 3 for identification in evidence as Plaintiff's Exhibit 3.

Court: It may be admitted and received in evidence.

§ 385. Contracts.

Illustration

(To Court reporter): Please mark this Plaintiff's Exhibit 4 for identification.

Q. Mr. Jones, I show you Plaintiff's Exhibit 4 for identification, and ask you whether your signature appears thereon?
A. Yes, it does.
Q. Was it signed by you on or about the date it bears?
A. It was.
Q. Who else's signature appears on that instrument, if you know?
A. George Smith.
Q. The defendant in this case?
A. Yes.
Q. Where was it signed by him, if you know?
A. In my presence at his office.
Q. When did he sign it?
A. At the same time I did.
Q. After he signed Plaintiff's Exhibit 4 for identification, what did he do with it, if anything?
A. He gave it to me.

Counsel: I offer Plaintiff's Exhibit 4 for identification in evidence as Plaintiff's Exhibit 4.

Court: It may be admitted.

§ 386. Check.

Illustration

(To the Court reporter): Please, mark this Plaintiff's Exhibit 2 for identification.

Q. I show you Plaintiff's Exhibit 2 for identification, purporting to be a check and ask you whether or not your signature appears thereon?

A. Yes, it does.

Q. Was it signed by you on or about the date it bears?

A. It was.

Q. *Referring to the reverse side,*[25] whose signature appears thereon, if you know?

A. John Walsh's.

Q. What did you do with Plaintiff's Exhibit 2 for identification, then, if anything?

A. I gave it to John Walsh.

Q. The defendant in this case?

A. Yes.

Q. When did you next see it?

A. When I got it back from my bank marked cancelled and paid.

Counsel: I offer this check marked Plaintiff's Exhibit 2 for identification in evidence as Plaintiff's Exhibit 2.

Court: It may be admitted.

Counsel: And I will ask that the identification mark be stricken to show it is received as Plaintiff's Exhibit 2.

Court: That may be done.

§ 387. Lease.

The technique to be employed is the same as suggested for a contract.

Another method would be to call the *adverse party* as a witness and ask him whether or not he signed and delivered the lease.

Illustration

Counsel: If the Court, please, I would like to call the defendant, Henry Michaels, as the next witness. (To witness): Mr. Michaels, I show you Plaintiff's Exhibit 2 for identifica-

25 Though a check may be identified and execution shown so as to be admissible, indorsements and marks on the check are not admissible as part thereof over objection unless also authenticated. Martin v. N. Y. Life Ins. Co. (N. M.) 234 Pac. 673.

tion (the lease) and ask you whether or not it bears your signature?

A. It does.

Q. Was it signed and delivered by you on or about the date it bears?

A. It was.

Q. Who else signed it, if anyone?

A. Axel Johnson.

Q. The plaintiff?

A. Yes.

Counsel: I offer Plaintiff's Exhibit 2 for identification in evidence as Plaintiff's Exhibit 2.

The Court: It may be received.

§ 388. Weather reports.

From the standpoint of the psychological value of a witness' testimony it is more advisable to have someone from the government's weather bureau to testify as to weather conditions, but where that is somewhat difficult to arrange, a *certified* copy of the weather report for the month in question should be obtained and introduced into evidence,[26] in those states where permissible under the code or statute.

Illustration

Counsel (to Court Reporter): Please, mark this Plaintiff's Exhibit 4 for identification. (To Court): If the Court, please, at this time I want to offer Plaintiff's Exhibit 4 for identification, which is a certified copy of the weather report for the month of June, 1934, in evidence as Plaintiff's Exhibit 4.

The Court: It may be received.

Note: The form of the certification appearing as part of the weather report is as follows:

26 Chicago, etc., R. Co. v. Trayes, 17 Ill. App. 136; Hart v. Walker, 100 Mich. 406, 59 N. W. 174; Commonwealth v. King, 150 Mass. 221, 5 L. R. A. 536, 22 N. E. 905; Miller v. Indianapolis, 123 Ind. 196, 24 N. E. 228.

UNITED STATES OF AMERICA
DEPARTMENT OF AGRICULTURE, WEATHER BUREAU

Chicago, Ill., August 24, 1934.

As custodian of the records of the U. S. Weather Bureau, at Chicago, Ill., I hereby certify that the data hereon, front and reverse sides, are accurate and authentic, and that they have been compiled from the original official records made at the U. S. Weather Observatory, located at Rosenwald Hall, University of Chicago, near 58th Street and University Avenue, Chicago, Ill. (All data are in Central Standard Time.)

(Signed) C. A. Donnel
Principal Meteorologist, in Charge.

§ 389. Delivery receipts.[27]

Illustration

Q. Will you state your full name, please?
A. Henry Faxon.
Q. What is your address?
A. 928 4th Avenue.
Q. What is your business?
A. Deliveryman for the Busy Bee.
Q. Do you know Edward Johnson, the defendant in this case?
A. Yes, I do.
Q. How long have you known him?
A. About three years.
Q. Have you ever delivered any merchandise to him?
A. Yes, I have.

Counsel (to Court Reporter): Please mark this Plaintiff's Exhibit 8 for identification. (To witness): I show you Plaintiff's Exhibit 8 for identification and ask you whether or not you have ever seen that before?

A. Yes, I have.
Q. When?
A. When I delivered the merchandise listed on it.

27 Possession of tickets issued as token for delivery is presumptive evidence of delivery. Bumsted v. Hoadley, 11 Hun 487 (N. Y.).

Q. Did you see Edward Johnson on that occasion?
A. Yes, I did.
Q. Just tell the court and jury what happened, if anything?
A. I delivered the suit to Mr. Johnson personally and asked him to sign the receipt.
Q. Did he sign it in your presence?
A. Yes, he did.
Q. Is this his signature on Plaintiff's Exhibit 8 for identification?
A. Yes, it is.
Counsel: I now offer Plaintiff's Exhibit 8 for identification in evidence as Plaintiff's Exhibit 8.
The Court: It may be received.

§ 390. Mortgage.

Illustration

Q. Mr. Carlson, I show you Defendant's Exhibit 17 for identification and ask you if that bears your signature (showing document to witness)?
A. Yes.
Q. Was the document executed by you on or about the date it bears?
A. Yes.
Q. Was it acknowledged by you as indicated before John Williams, a notary public?
A. Yes.
Counsel: I offer the instrument in evidence as Defendant's Exhibit 17 together with the recording data.
The Court: It may be admitted.

§ 391. Lost instruments.

A lost instrument is one which cannot be found after that thorough, careful and diligent search which the law requires to be shown before secondary evidence can be introduced of its contents.

The loss or unintentional destruction of a written instrument in no way affects the liabilities of the parties to it.[28]

[28] Conlin v. Ryan, 47 Cal. 71; Prussing v. Jackson, 208 Ill. 85; McCarin v. Randall, 17 N. E. 75; Paw Paw Bk. v. Free, 205 Mich. 52; Homberg v. Kekhaffer, 43 Minn. 205; Streever v. Ft. Edward Bk., 34 N. Y. 413.

The burden of proof is on the person seeking to establish a lost instrument to show its former existence, execution, delivery, loss and the making of a proper search therefor, and that he is the owner at time of trial.[29]

§ 392. Lost instrument—proof of copy.

Illustration

Q. Was there more than one agreement signed?
A. No. I had the only signed agreement.
Q. Have you that original agreement that was signed by you and John Jones?
A. No. I have not.
Q. Where is it now, if you know?
A. I do not know where it is.
Q. When did you see it last?
A. The day it was signed.
Q. Where was the last place you saw it?
A. In my office.
Q. What did you do with it?
A. I put it in my desk.
Q. How long ago was that?
A. About three months ago.
Q. Have you seen the agreement since?
A. No, I have not.
Q. When did you first look for it after that?
A. About two weeks ago.
Q. Did you find it?
A. No.
Q. Where did you look?
A. All through my desk, on top of the desk and every place where I ordinarily keep my papers.
Q. What else have you done in an effort to find it?
A. I have searched every place I could think of where it might be.
Q. Did you find it?
A. No, I did not.

29 Mullens v. McCort, 170 Ky. 547, 186 S. W. 137; Borstelman v. Brohan, 81 N. J. Eq. 401, 87 Atl. 145; Shepley v. Shepley, 274 Ill. 506; Nofftz v. Nofftz, 290 Ill. 36, 124 N. E. 838; Rice v. Taliaferro, 156 S. W. 242 (Tex.).

Q. Have you tried to find it since?

A. Yes, a number of times.

Q. Do you believe the original agreement is lost or destroyed?

A. Yes.

Q. Did you intentionally misplace or destroy it?

A. No, sir.

Q. (To court reporter): Please mark this Plaintiff's Exhibit 1 for identification. (To witness): I show you Plaintiff's Exhibit 1 for identification and ask you if you have ever seen that before?

A. Yes, sir.

Q. When and where?

A. At my office at the same time I saw the original agreement which John Jones and I signed. This is a carbon copy of the original agreement.

Q. Is it a true and correct copy of the original?

A. Yes, sir. It was made at the same time.

Counsel: If the Court, please, I offer Plaintiff's Exhibit 1 for identification being a carbon copy of the original agreement in evidence as Plaintiff's Exhibit 1.

The Court: It may be received.

§ 393. Proof of lost instrument where there is no copy.

Illustration

Q. When you returned the bond, what happened, if anything?

A. Mr. Jones gave me a receipt for it.

Q. What did you do with the receipt?

A. I placed it among my personal papers in my office.

Q. When did you see it last?

A. The day it was signed.

Q. Where was the last place you saw it?

A. In my office.

Q. How long ago was that?

A. About three months ago.

Q. Have you seen the receipt since?

A. No, I have not.

Q. When did you first look for it after that?

A. About two weeks ago.

Q. Did you find it?
A. No.
Q. Where did you look?
A. All through my desk, on top of the desk and every place where I ordinarily keep my papers.
Q. What else have you done in an effort to find it?
A. I have searched every place I could think of where it might be.
Q. Did you find it?
A. No, I did not.
Q. Have you tried to find it since?
A. Yes, a number of times.
Q. Do you believe the original receipt is lost or destroyed?
A. Yes.
Q. Did you intentionally misplace or destroy it?
A. No, sir.
Q. Was the receipt made out in duplicate?
A. No, sir.
Q. Was there any copy made of it at any time?
A. No, sir.
Q. Do you recall the contents of that receipt?
A. Yes, sir.
Q. Will you tell the Court and jury, please, as nearly as you can the words or the substance of that receipt?
A. It was dated February 3, 1934, and stated as follows: "Received of Harry Doe One $500.00 Real Estate Bond on the Palace Apartments and was signed John Jones."

§ 394. X-rays—skiagraphs.

Photographs taken by the x-ray process are admissible in evidence after proper preliminary proof of their correctness and accuracy has been made.[30] It is sufficient proof to admit

[30] Bruce v. Western Pipe, etc., Co., 177 Cal. 25, 169 Pac. 660; Chicago City R. Co. v. Smith, 226 Ill. 178, 80 N. E. 716; Ingebretsen v. Minneapolis, etc., R. Co., 176 Iowa 74, 155 N. W. 327; Doyle v. Singer Sewing Mach. Co., 220 Mass. 327, 107 N. E. 949; Lake Shore El. Co. v. Hobart, 32 Oh. Cir. Ct. 154, 13 Oh. Cir. Ct. (N. S.) 592; Chicago, etc., R. Co. v. Smith, (Tex.) 197 S. W. 614; Mauch v. Hartford, 112 Wis. 40, 87 N. W. 816; Bruce v. Beall, 99 Tenn. 303, 307, 41 S. W. 445; Kimball v. Northern El. Co., 159 Cal. 225, 113 Pac. 796; Chicago & J. El. R. Co. v. Spence, 213 Ill. 220, 72 N. E. 796; Rickel v. Stockman, 168 Atl. 467, 111 N. J. Law, 294; Wosoba v. Kenyon, 243 N. W. 569; Stephens v. Ill. Cent. R. R., 306 Ill. 370.

an x-ray where a physician testifies that he was present when they were taken, that he waited while the plate was taken into the dark room and developed, and that he examined the plate and is positive that it is the skiagraph of the injured member.[31] When a person who is an expert in taking x-rays has established his status as an expert on the basis of experience, training or other qualifications, a sufficient foundation is laid when such expert testifies that he made the exposure, developed the negative and printed the picture therefrom and that it was an accurate and correct representation. The person making the photograph need not identify further the x-ray pictures if the plaintiff identifies it in his testimony as the one taken and the doctor identifies it as a true representation of the leg and the leg itself was also presented to the jury so that even if the skiagraph was incorrect, the jury would not be misled by it.[32]

The witness need not be a physician in order to qualify as an expert on x-rays, so where a witness testifies that he was an x-ray expert and regularly engaged in taking such photographs for physicians, that he took the negative from which the photograph was developed and it was an accurate and correct representation it was held that he had qualified as an expert and that the x-ray pictures were admissible.

X-rays

Illustration

Q. What is your name, please?
A. John Simpson.
Q. What is your profession?
A. Roentgenologist, an X-ray expert.
Q. Are you connected with any Hospital, doctor?
A. Yes, sir, with the Burnside Hospital as Roentgenologist.
Q. What does Roentgenologist mean, doctor?
A. It means one who is qualified to make and interpret skiagraphs or X-rays.

31 Wicks v. Cuneo-Henneberry Co., 319 Ill. 344.

32 Clay v. Aluminum Ore Co., 186 Ill. App. 506.

Q. How long have you been connected with the Burnside Hospital in that capacity?

A. I have been doing that work for six years.

Q. On August 30, 1925, did you see the plaintiff, Edward Johnson, at the Hospital?

A. I did.

Q. Did you take care of him professionally that day?

A. Yes, sir, I fluoroscoped him.

Q. What is a fluoroscope?

A. With a fluoroscope you lay your patient on the table, and your tube is under the table and the light is thrown up through. You have a fluoroscent chemically treated screen that you look down through, and see the bones, and whatever you may be looking for. You see shadows of them on the screen. The bones cause a shadow.

Q. When did you next see plaintiff, if at all?

A. September 6, 1925.

Q. What did you do then, if anything?

A. I took an X-ray of him.

Q. How many pictures did you take on that occasion?

A. Several.

Q. Will you please produce them?

Counsel: (To Court reporter) I would like to have this X-Ray film marked Plaintiff's Exhibit 1 for identification. (To witness) Will you please examine Plaintiff's Exhibit 1 for identification and tell us if you can idenitfy it?

A. Yes, I can. This is the first one I took.

Q. When did you take this X-ray?

A. September 6th, 1925.

Q. How do you identify this picture as the picture of the plaintiff, Edward Johnson, in this case?

A. I have his name, address and date on it, which I placed on there myself. The same exposure that took the X-ray also recorded the identification data.

Q. At the time and place just named, were you familiar with the operation of the machine?

A. Yes, sir.

Q. What was its operative condition?

A. Good condition, first class condition.

Q. How many X-ray pictures had you taken prior to this date with that same machine, doctor?

A. About a thousand.

Q. How frequently have you taken pictures on this machine?

A. Daily for about three years previous to this date.

Q. Who developed these pictures, if you know?

A. I did.

Q. Does this picture correctly portray what it is intended to show, doctor?

A. It does.

Q. Is it in the same condition now as when it was taken?

A. It is.

Q. Does it correctly show the conditions of that part of the body which it purports to show?

A. It does.

Counsel: I offer Plaintiff's Exhibit 1 for identification, the X-ray film in evidence as Plaintiff's Exhibit 1.

Court: It may be received.

(Note: For another and more complete illustration, see page 391, Expert Witnesses.)

§ 395. Photographs.

Photographs are admissible:[33]

1. To assist jury in understanding case.
2. To show scene of accident and the physical situation at time of accident.
3. To show the proper proportions of a document that is already in evidence.
4. To reproduce documents which are out of the jurisdiction of the court and cannot be obtained.

[33] People v. Loper, 159 Cal. 6, 112 Pac. 720, Ann. Cas. 1912 B 1193; N. Y., etc., R. Co. v. Robbins, 38 Ind. App. 172, 76 N. E. 804; Wooley v. Fall River, 220 Mass. 584, 108 N. E. 367; Harrison v. Green, 157 Mich. 690, 122 N. W. 205; Archer v. N. Y., etc., R. Co., 106 N. Y. 589, 13 N. E. 318; Mahar v. Montello Granite Co., 146 Wis. 46, 130 N. W. 949; Cincinnati, etc., R. Co. v. De Onzo, 87 Oh. St. 109, 100 N. E. 320; McKarren v. Boston, etc., R. Co., 194 Mass. 179, 80 N. E. 477; Alberti v. N. Y., etc., R. Co., 118 N. Y. 77, 23 N. E. 35, 6 L. R. A. 76; Peo. v. Elmore, 167 Cal. 205, 138 Pac. 989; State v. Cook, 75 Conn. 267, 53 Atl. 589; So. Pac. Co. v. Eckenfels, (Tex.) 197 S. W. 1003.

5. To prove forgery of a document.
6. To supplement scale drawings.
7. To show condition of real estate prior to, at time of, and subsequent to injury by floods, trespassers, etc.
8. To show machinery.
9. To establish identity of persons.
10. To show appearance of injured party as he appeared at time of accident.

§ 396. — Admissibility.

To make a photograph admissible in evidence it must be shown that it is a correct and substantial representation of the thing it purports to show, who made the photograph, his skill, the kind of instrument used, how it was used, that it was a picture of the locus in quo and when it was taken.[34]

A photograph taken by an amateur,[35] who is *not* qualified, is not admissible, unless proof is shown that it is a true and correct representation of what it purports to show. Nor will it be received in evidence if the conditions have changed. If the scene or objects have been posed or arranged by one party, for the purpose of taking the photograph, in the way or manner sought to be shown, the photograph will not be admissible.[36]

It seems that even when there has been a slight change in the physical condition of the scene of an accident, photographs which are shown to be correct representations of the premises where the accident happened are admissible.[37] It has been held that where a photograph is a correct repre-

[34] People v. Rogers, 163 Cal. 476, 126 Pac. 143; State v. Hasty, 121 Iowa 507, 96 N. W. 115; Conn v. Morgan, 159 Mass. 375, 34 N. E. 458; Davis v. Adrian, 147 Mich. 300, 110 N. W. 1084; People v. Smith, 121 N. Y. 578, 24 N. E. 852; Houston, etc., R. Co. v. Chick, (Tex.) 84 S. W. 852; People v. Webster, 139 N. Y. 73, 34 N. E. 730; In re Jessup, 81 Cal. 408, 21 Pac. 976, 22 Pac. 742, 6 L. R. A. 594.

[35] C. C. C. & St. Louis Ry. Co. v. Monaghan, 140 Ill. 474 (taken by amateur).

[36] Grant v. C. & N. W. Ry. Co., 176 Ill. App. 292. (Some states contra.)

[37] Smith v. Hausendorf, 92 Conn. 573, 103 Atl. 939; Chicago, etc., R. Co. v. Corson, 198 Ill. 98, 64 N. E. 739; Indiana, etc., Co. v. Scribner, 47 Ind. App. 621, 93 N. E. 1014; Ingebretsen v. Minneapolis, etc., R. Co., 176 Iowa 74, 155 N. E. 327; Lynch v. C. J. Larivee Lumber Co., 223 Mass. 335, 111 N. E. 861; Cohen v. Elias, 176 App. Div. 763, 163 N. Y. S. 1051; Lake Shore El. R. Co. v. Lathrop, 32 Oh. Cir. Ct. 154; Missouri, etc., R. Co. v. Heacker (Tex.) 168 S. W. 26.

sentation of the locus in quo except that snow was on the ground when the photograph was taken some three weeks after the accident, that it was properly admitted.[38]

However, if the difference between the conditions at the time of the accident and the time when the photograph was taken is of such a nature that the result of the trial would probably be different if the conditions as they formerly existed were shown, the photograph is not admissible. Where the view at a railroad passing was obstructed by vegetation at the time of the injury and the vegetation had all been removed at the time of the photograph, it was held that the photograph was not a correct representation and was not admissible.[39] Where the changes in conditions are not primarily involved in the case, photographs may be received in evidence. A photographic likeness may be admitted in evidence without proof of taking and developing of picture where shown to be a true and correct representation of person in question.[39a]

§ 396a. — Documents.[40]

Photographic copies of documents have been held to be admissible when it is shown that the original instrument is out of the jurisdiction of the court and cannot be obtained, and preliminary proof as to accuracy has been made.[41] An enlarged photograph of such a document would be admissible because it makes the proportions of the handwriting, etc. plainer.[42]

§ 396b. — Injured persons.

Photographs of injured person taken soon after injury and shown by the testimony to be correct representations of such party as he appeared at the time, are competent.[43]

38 Fitzgerald v. Hedstrom, 98 Ill. App. 109; see also Grim v. E. St. L. Ry. Co., 180 Ill. App. 92.

39 Althoff v. I. C. R. Co., 227 Ill. 417.

39a Brownlie v. Brownlie, 357 Ill. 117; People v. Herbert, 361 Ill. 64.

40 People v. Mooney, 132 Cal. 13, 63 Pac. 1070; Corbet v. Union Dime Sav. Inst., 67 Misc. 175, 122 N. Y. S. 268; Ayers v. Harris, 77 Tex. 108, 13 S. W. 768; Baxter v. Chicago, etc., R. Co., 104 Wis. 30, 80 N. W. 644.

41 Stitzel v. Miller, 250 Ill. 73.

42 Diller v. No. Cal. Power Co., 162 Cal. 531, 123 Pac. 359; Howard v. Illinois Trust, etc., 189 Ill. 568, 59 N. E. 1106; Hoffman v. Prussian Nat. Ins. Co., 181 App. Div. 412, 168 N. Y. S. 841; Potvin v. West Bay, etc., Co., 156 Mich. 201, 120 N. W. 613.

43 Peoples Gas Light Co. v. Amphett, 93 Ill. App. 194.

§ 397. **— Photographs, proof of.**

Illustration

Q. What is your full name, please?
A. Jack Connors.
Q. Where do you live?
A. 171 Long Ave.
Q. What is your business or profession?
A. I am a photographer.
Q. How long have you been a photographer?
A. Twenty-five years.
Q. On the 17th of September, 1930, did you go up to a garage that is located about 3600 North Crawford Ave.?
A. Yes, sir, I did.
Q. What did you do there, if anything?
A. I took a picture of an automobile that was standing in front of the door of that garage.

(To Court Reporter) Mark this Defendant's Exhibit 12 for identification. (To witness) I show you Defendant's Exhibit 12 for identification and ask you whether or not that is a true and correct picture and representation of the auto as you saw it there in the garage on the left side of the street?

A. Yes, sir.
Q. Is it a clear and true picture of the auto as you saw it?
A. It is.
Q. Who developed the picture?
A. I did.

Counsel: The picture that I have called attention to, if the Court please, was marked Defendant's Exhibit 12 for identification, and I now wish to offer it in evidence as Defendant's Exhibit 12.

The Court: It may go in.

Counsel: Did you, at the same time, Mr. Connors, make a photograph of Crawford Street looking south as your camera was directed toward the south from a position a little bit north of that garage?

A. Yes, I did.
Q. Is Defendant's Exhibit 13 for identification, the picture you took?

A. Yes, sir, it is.

Q. Does that picture fairly and accurately represent what it purports to show in the street there as it existed on the morning of the 17th of September, 1930 when you took the picture?

A. Yes, sir.

Q. Who developed the picture?

A. I did personally.

Counsel: I wish to offer Defendant's Exhibit 13 for identification in evidence as Defendant's Exhibit 13. I wish to offer that in evidence, and I will offer proof showing that there was no change in the street between midnight of the night before the taking of the picture and the time the picture was taken.

Opponent: Subject to further evidence I want to object to the offer.

The Court: It may be received, subject to further proof.

§ 398. Notice to city before suit.[44]

In all suits against the City for personal injuries, where required, the statutory notice should be marked as an exhibit and introduced into evidence to complete proof as to compliance with the Statute.

Illustration

Counsel: (To Court Reporter) Mark this Plaintiff's Exhibit 1 for identification. (To the Court) At this time, I offer in evidence Plaintiff's Exhibit 1 for identification being the statutory notice served on the City as required by statute and ask that it be received in evidence as Plaintiff's Exhibit 1.

Opponent: No objection.

The Court: It may be received.

§ 399. Foreign statutes and laws.

Many statutes and codes of the different states provide for

44 Statutes usually require the notice to set forth the time, place, cause and nature of the injury. Ouimette v. Chicago, 242 Ill. 301, 90 N. E. 300 (time); Shaw v. Waterbury, 46 Conn. 263 (place); Rushville v. Morrow, 54 Ind. App. 538, 101 N. E. 659 (cause); Tattan v. Detroit, 128 Mich 650, 87 N. W. 894 (nature of injury); Ryan v. Schenectady, 91 Misc. 296, 154 N. Y. S. 890 (service).

the introduction of all foreign statutes and laws into evidence as follows:

Printed Statutes. The printed statute books of the United States, and of this state, and of the several states, of the territories and late territories of the United States, purporting to be printed under the authority of said United States, any state or territory, shall be evidence in all courts and places in this state, of the acts therein contained.[45]

Exemplified Statutes. An exemplification by the Secretary of the State, of the laws of the other states and territories, which have been or shall hereafter be transmitted, by order of the executive or legislatures of such other states or territories, to the Governor of this state, and by him deposited in the office of said Secretary, shall be admissible as evidence in any court of this state.[46]

Reports of Courts. The books of reports of decisions of the supreme court, and other courts of the United States, of this state, and of the several states and the territories thereof, purporting to be published by authority, may be read as evidence of the decisions of such courts.[47]

Court records—How certified. The papers, entries and records of courts may be proved by a copy thereof certified under the hand of the clerk having the custody thereof, and the seal of the court, or by the judge of the court if there be no clerk.[48]

Records, etc., of cities, etc.—How certified. The papers, entries, records and ordinances, or parts thereof, of any city,

45 Cochran v. Ward, 5 Ind. App. 89, 29 N. E. 795, 31 N. E. 581; Hecla Powder Co. v. Signa Iron Co., 157 N. Y. 437, 52 N. E. 650; Manhattan L. Ins. Co. v. Fields, (Tex.) 26 S. W. 280; Rudolph Hdwe. Co. v. Price, 164 Iowa 353, 145 N. W. 910; Ann. Cas. 1916 D 850, and note 853. Bride v. Clark, 161 Mass. 130, 36 N. E. 745; Dawson v. Peterson, 110 Mich. 431, 68 N. W. 246; McGraney v. Glos, 222 Ill. 628.

46 See U. S. Constitution, Art. 4, Sec. 1; U. S. Revised St. Sec. 905. (U. S. Comp. St. 1901, p. 677); State v. Twitty, 9 N. C. 441, 11 Am. Dec. 779; Ashley v. Root, 4 Allen (Mass.) 504.

47 Brush v. Scribner, 11 Conn. 388, 29 Am. Dec. 303; Chicago, etc., R. Co. v. Tuite, 44 Ill. App. 535; McRae v. Mattoon, 13 Pick. (Mass.) 53.

48 *Court Records* (certified copies). Dixon v. Smith-Wallace Shoe Co., 204 Ill. App. 336; McGlasson v. Scott, 112 Iowa 289, 83 N. W. 974; Clark v. Dasso, 34 Mich. 86; Arndt v. Burghardt, 165 Wis. 312, 162 N. W. 317; Royal Ins. Co. v. Texas, etc., R. Co., 115 S. W. 117, 123; Woolsey v. Saunders, 3 Barb. 301 (N. Y.).

village, town or country, may be proved by a copy thereof, certified under the hand of the clerk or the keeper thereof, and the corporate seal, if there be any; if not, under his hand and private seal.[49]

Thus a book purporting on its title page to be the statutes or laws of a foreign state, published by the authority of its legislature and to be in force is admissible in evidence.[50]

Wherever such laws are the basis of a law suit the attorney should introduce the statute in evidence and read the law applicable to the jury.[51]

§ 400. Ordinances—Judicial notice.

In some jurisdictions, proof of ordinances is provided for in the following language:

Courts of Original Jurisdiction. Every court of original jurisdiction in addition to the matters of which courts of original jurisdiction have heretofore been required to take judicial notice, shall take *judicial notice* of the following:

First. All general ordinances of every municipal corporation within the city, county, judicial circuit, or other territory for which such court has been established, or within the city, county judicial circuit or other territory for which such court has been established, or within the city, county or judicial circuit from which a case has been brought to such court by change of venue or otherwise.

Second. All laws of a public nature enacted by any state or territory of the United States.

Third. All rules of practice in force in the court from which a case has been transferred by change of venue or otherwise.

49 *Record of Cities, etc. (certified copies).* Gage v. Chicago, 225 Ill. 218, 80 N. E. 127; Green v. Indianapolis, 25 Ind. 490; Bayard v. Baker, 76 Iowa 220, 40 N. W. 818; Peo. v. Wilson, 16 N. Y. S. 583.

50 Eagan v. Conley, 107 Ill. 458.

51 Mode of proving: Grafton v. St. Paul, etc., R. Co., 16 N. D. 313, 22 L. R. A. (N. S.) 1, 113 N. W. 598, 15 Ann. Cas. 10; Green v. Ashland Water Co., 101 Wis. 258, 43 L. R. A. 117, 70 A. S. R. 911, 77 N. W. 722; Bugg v. Houlka, 122 Miss. 400, 9 A. L. R. 480, 84 So. 387.

Books or pamphlets purporting to contain the ordinances of a city and to be published by municipal authority are frequently made prima facie evidence of such ordinances. St. Louis, etc., R. Co. v. Garber (Tex.) 108 S. W. 742; I. C. C. R. Co. v. Warriner, 229 Ill. 91.

§ 401. Ordinances, proof of.

In other jurisdictions, proof of ordinances may be made as follows:

Illustration

Q. What is your name?
A. Henry Jones.
Q. What is your business?
A. Clerk in the City Clerk's Office.
Q. Where do you live?
A. 1328 Rosedale Avenue.
Q. Have you with you the ordinances of the City of Chicago, which relate to the use of the streets by the Chicago Surface Lines?
A. Yes, I have.
Q. Will you read them please?

The witness: Under the heading:

"Street Paving, Section 15:

"The company shall at its own expense, fill, grade, pave and keep in repair that portion of the streets occupied by it, as more specifically provided for in Exhibit B."

In Exhibit B, the paragraph entitled: "Maintenance of Streets."

"The company as respects filling, grading, paving and keeping in repair, sweeping, sprinkling, keeping clean or otherwise improving the streets or parts of streets occupied by its railway shall fill, grade, pave, keep in repair, sweep, sprinkle and keep clean and free from snow, eight feet wide of all streets and public ways or portions thereof occupied by it with single track rail and sixteen feet in width of all streets and public ways or portions thereof occupied by it with a double track railway."

In Exhibit B of the ordinance, under the heading: "Pavement."

"The company, upon order of the commissioner of public works and approval of the board of supervising engineers shall pave, repave, or repair portions of the streets and public ways which by this grant it is required to keep paved and in repair whenever and as often as the same shall reasonably require paving, repaving or repairing, and shall at all times keep the surface of all of its paving at least up to the top of the rail."

§ 402. Records.

A copy of the record required by law to be kept by a City, duly certified as required by statute, is original evidence and its introduction in evidence does not depend upon the fact that the record itself is lost or destroyed.[52]

§ 403. Certificates.[53]

Birth certificates are no proof of the identity of the persons named in them with the parties to this controversy. The fact of their identity must be established by other evidence.[54]

A death certificate duly certified may be introduced to prove prima facie cause of death.[55]

§ 404. — Clerks of County and Circuit Court.

Certificate of magistracy by county clerk must be attached to certificate of justice where proceedings are in another county.[56]

§ 405. — Notary.[57]

A certificate under seal, by a foreign notary, is not prima facie evidence of his authority to administer oaths unless it contains a recital of the fact of his authority.[58]

52 City of E. St. Louis v. Freeds, 17 Ill. App. 339.

53 Admissibility: Grand Pass Shooting Club v. Crosby, 181 Ill. 266, 54 N. E. 913; York v. Sheldon, 18 Iowa 569; Weitzel v. Brown, 224 Mass. 190, 112 N. E. 945; Richards v. Robin, 178 Ap. Div. 535, 165 N. Y. S. 780; Typer v. Tonn, (Tex.) 132 S. W. 850; Peters v. Reichenbach, 114 Wis. 209, 90 N. W. 184.

54 Lewandowski v. Zuzak, 305 Ill. 612; Hyde v. Kloos, 134 Minn. 165, 158 N. W. 920.

55 Henninger v. Interocean Cas. Co., 217 Ill. App. 542; Shamhan v. Equitable Acc. Co., 226 Mass. 67, 115 N. E. 46. (Some states contra.)

Marriage Certificate: State v. Schweitzer, 57 Conn. 532, 6 L. R. A. 125, 18 Atl. 787; State v. Behrman, 114 N. C 797, 25 L. R. A. 449, 19 S. E. 220.

56 Crossett v. Owens, 110 Ill. 378.

57 Usually the certificate of a foreign notary must be authenticated by some other official showing the appointment and power to act. Hill Clutch Co. v. Independent Steel Co., etc., 74 W. Va. 353, 82 S. E. 223; Harding v. Curtis, 45 Ill. 252; Stephens v. Williams, 150 N. Y. S. 667; Johnson v. Brown, 154 Mass. 105, 27 N. E. 994.

The courts take judicial notice of the official character of a notary. Hertig v. People, 159 Ill. 237, 42 N. E. 879; Sloan v. Anderson, 57 Wis. 123, 13 N. W. 684, 15 N. W. 21; Butts v. Purdy, 63 Ore. 150, 125 Pac. 313, 127 Pac. 25.

58 Des Noyers Shoe Co. v. Bank, 183 Ill. 312.

Statutes of the United States provide that copies of any books, records, papers or documents in any of the executive departments, under the seals of such departments, respectively shall be admitted in evidence equally with the originals thereof.[59]

§ 406. Certified copies.[60]

All certified copies should be marked for identification and then offered in evidence as exhibits.

Illustration

Counsel: (To Court Reporter) Please mark this Plaintiff's Exhibit 8 for identification. (To the Court) If the Court please, at this time I wish to offer Plaintiff's Exhibit 8 for identification which is a certified copy of the corporate charter of the Blank Optical Co. in evidence as Plaintiff's Exhibit 8.

The Court: It may be received.

Another Illustration

Counsel: (To Court reporter:) Please mark this Plaintiff's Exhibit 2 for identification.

I offer in evidence, if the Court please, Plaintiff's Exhibit 2 for identification which is a certified copy of the record of the Industrial Board, purporting to be a record of rejection of the

59 Am. Surety Co. v. N. S., 77 Ill. App. 106.

60 Admissibility: Gage v. Chicago, 225 Ill. 218, 80 N. E. 127; Mitcheltree School Township v. Hall, 68 N. E. 919; Hoffman v. Metropolitan L. Ins. Co., 135 App. Div. 739, 119 N. Y. S. 978; Fox Lake v. Fox Lake, 62 Wis. 486, 22 N. W. 584; Stone Land, etc., Co. v. Boon, 73 Tex. 548, 11 S. W. 544; Emmett v. Lee, 50 Oh. St. 662, 35 N. E. 794; In re Baker, 176 Cal. 430, 168 Pac. 881; Commonwealth v. Hayden, 163 Mass. 453, 40 N. E. 846.

Public Records: Rich v. Lancaster R. Co., 114 Mass. 514.

Judicial Records: McGlasson v. Scott, 112 Iowa 289, 83 N. W. 974; Clark v. Dasso, 34 Mich. 86; Royal Ins. Co. v. Texas, etc., R. Co. (Tex.), 115 S. W. 123; McCloud v. Hogle, 200 Ill. App. 483.

Official Records kept by public officers, who are required to record particular transactions occurring in the course of their public duties, are admissible in evidence. D. I. Mofziger Lumber Co. v. Solomon, 13 Cal. App. 621, 110 Pac. 474; Hay v. Springfield, etc., 181 Ill. App. 23; Robinson v. State, 182 Ind. 329, 106 N. E. 533; Richard v. Robins, 178 App. Div. 535, 165 N. Y. S. 780; Denton v. English (Tex.), 171 S. W. 248.

provisions of the Workmen's Compensation Act by the Victor Chemical Works as Plaintiff's Exhibit 2.

(Handing paper to opposing counsel.)

Opposing Counsel: No objection.

The Court: Let it be admitted.

§ 407. Mortality tables.

In most jurisdictions courts take judicial notice of standard recognized mortality tables [61] such as those prepared by Wigglesworth, Northampton, Carlisle and Farnsworth. Tables can usually be obtained from any insurance company or general legal encyclopedia.

Illustration

Counsel: Now, if the Court please, I want to offer as Plaintiff's Exhibit in evidence the mortality tables showing the expectancy of life at the age of 33 years. I offer those as contained in the 20th volume of the American and English Encyclopedia of Law, page 85.

The Court: Any objection to that?

Opponent: No, I have no objection.

Counsel: Showing that the expectancy of life at the age of thirty-three is 33.21 years.

§ 408. Corporate minutes.

In order to render the books and corporate record of a corporation admissible in evidence they must be duly authenticated and identified as such, and it must be made to appear that they are the books of the corporation, kept as such by the proper officer.[62]

61 Mortality Tables . . . are admissible in evidence, where shown to be of standard authority, without any further proof of authenticity and correctness. The court will take judicial notice of the correctness and authenticity. Marshall v. Marshall, 252 Ill. 568, 96 N. E. 907 (Carlisle); Pearl v. Omaha, etc., R. Co., 115 Ia. 535, 88 N. W. 1078 (American); Scagel v. Chicago, etc., R. Co., 83 Ia. 380, 49 N. W. 990 (Northampton); Winn v. Cleveland, etc., R. Co., 239 Ill. 132, 87 N. E. 954 (Wigglesworth); Missouri, etc., R. Co. v. Ransom, 41 S. W. 826 (Tex.) (Flatchcraft Ins. Manual).

62 Hurwitz v. Gross, 5 Cal. App. 614, 91 Pac. 109; Bartholomew v. Farwell, 41 Conn. 107; Monger v. New Era Assoc., 171 Mich. 614, 626, 137 N. W. 631; St. Stanislaus Church v. Verien, 31 App. Div. 133, 52 N. Y. S. 922; Trainor v. German-American, etc., 204 Ill. 616, 68 N. E. 650; Ney v. Eastern Iowa Tel. Co., 162 Iowa 525, 144 N. W. 383.

Illustration

Q. Have you the book in which the minutes are kept of meetings of the 201 East Delaware Building Corporation.

A. Yes.

Q. Will you produce it, please?

A. Yes.

Q. (To Court reporter) Please mark this Plaintiff's Exhibit 4 for identification. (To witness): I call your attention to notice of a special meeting of the Board of Directors to be held March 1, 1927, and the minutes of the meeting held on that day pursuant to said notice, and ask you to state if those are the original minutes?

A. Yes.

Q. I call your attention to the signatures on Plaintiff's Exhibit 4 for identification. Whose signatures are they, if you know?

A. All of the directors.

Q. What are their names?

A. Charles Smith, that is mine, Albert B. Henry and George Case.

Q. Those were the three directors at that time?

A. Yes.

Q. And the only directors?

A. Yes.

Q. The minutes show on the second page, signed George Case, Secretary, is that his signature?

A. Yes.

Q. And to the left are the signatures of three directors, Albert B. Henry, Charles Smith and George Case; those are the signatures of those directors?

A. Yes.

Mr. Young: I offer in evidence Plaintiff's Exhibit 4 for identification being the minutes of a special meeting of the board of directors of the 201 East Delaware Building Corporation held on March 1, 1927 pursuant to waiver of notice signed by the three directors, as appears on the original record book of the corporation, as Plaintiff's Exhibit 4.

The Court: It may be received.

§ 409. Repair bills.

In some jurisdictions a *paid* repair bill is prima facie evidence that charges made are fair and reasonable unless rebutted by expert testimony.[63]

Illustration

Q. What was the condition of your car just prior to the accident?
A. It was in good condition. It had just been overhauled.
Q. What was the condition of the car after the impact?
A. The left fender and left running board were crushed and bent and the left side of the body was bent in badly.
Q. What was the condition of the left fender just prior to the impact?
A. It was in good condition.
Q. What was the condition of the left running board prior to the impact?
A. It was in good condition.
Q. What was the condition of the body prior to the impact?
A. It was in good condition.
Q. What did you do with the car after the impact, if anything?
A. I had it repaired.
Q. Where?
A. At the Palmer Park garage.
Q. And where is that located?
A. I do not know the exact address. It is in the vicinity of 113th, and just off of South Park Avenue.
Q. Is it a regularly established repair shop and garage?
A. Yes, it is.
Q. In business out there?
A. Yes.
Q. When your car was taken in there, was it in the same condition that it was immediately after the impact?
A. Yes, sir.

63 Receipted bills for repairs are admissible to prove that plaintiff paid for repairs. Galveston H. El. R. Co. v. English (Tex.), 178 S. W. 666.

They are admissible to prove that plaintiff paid so much money. Roth v. Fleck, 242 Ill. App. 396; Byalos v. Matheson, 328 Ill. 269, 159 N. E. 242; Singer v. Cross, 257 Ill. App. 41; Finch v. Carlton, 249 Ill. App. 60.

Q. What did they do to the car, if anything?

A. They repaired it.

Q. Just what did they do, if you know?

A. They straightened out the body and put on a new fender and running board.

Q. In the regular course of business?

A. Yes, sir.

Q. Did they render you a bill?

A. Yes, sir.

Counsel: Will you mark this Plaintiff's Exhibit 1 for identification. Now, Mr. Gordon, I show you Plaintiff's Exhibit 1 for identification and ask you if that is the bill that was rendered to you by the Palmer Park Garage?

A. Yes.

Q. Was that bill paid?

A. Yes, sir.

Q. Did you pay it?

A. Yes, sir.

Counsel: I offer Plaintiff's Exhibit 1 for identification, being the paid bill, in evidence as Plaintiff's Exhibt 1. (Showing same to counsel).

The Court: It may be received.

§ 410. —Where repair bill is not paid.

Where the repair bill has not been paid or where the repairs have not actually been made, proof of the cost of the repairs must be made by a duly qualified automobile mechanic.

Illustration

Q. Will you state your full name, please?

A. John Jones.

Q. Where do you live, Mr. Jones?

A. 1902 Harris St.

Q. What is your business, please?

A. Automobile mechanic.

Q. Under what name do you do business?

A. The Halsted Garage & Repair Shop.

Q. How long have you been in that business?

A. Ten years.

Q. How long have you been an automobile mechanic?

A. About fifteen years.
Q. What makes of automobiles have you repaired?
A. All makes.
Q. Do you deal in new parts for all kinds of automobiles?
A. Yes, sir.
Q. Does that include buying and selling parts?
A. Yes, sir.
Q. And installing them?
A. Yes, sir.
Q. When did you first see Henry Thompson's car?
A. June 4th, 1934.
Q. What make of automobile was it?
A. Buick 1933, Sedan Model.
Q. Where did you see it?
A. At Fourth and Main St.
Q. Did you examine it at that time?
A. Yes, sir.
Q. What did your examination disclose?
A. Left side of the body was damaged, the left fender was badly smashed and the left rear wheel was broken.
Q. What did you do then, if anything?
A. I had the car towed to my garage.
Q. What did you do then, if anything?
A. I repaired and straightened out the body and painted it, put on a new left rear fender and a new left rear wheel.
Q. Could the fender and wheel have been repaired?
A. No, sir.
Q. Are you acquainted with the *fair, reasonable,* and *customary charge* for work and labor in straightening out a dent in the left side of the body and installing a new left rear fender and a new left rear wheel on a 1933 Buick Sedan in the city of Detroit and State of Michigan on June 4th, 1934?
A. Yes, sir.
Q. What was it?
A. $17.50.
Q. Are you acquainted with and do you know the fair, reasonable *market price* of one new left rear fender and one new left rear wheel for a 1933 Buick Sedan in the City of Detroit and State of Michigan on June 4th, 1934?

A. Yes, sir.
Q. What was it?
A. $———.

§ 411. Foreign judgment.[64]

Illustration

Proof of foreign judgments may be made as follows:
Q. Will you state your full name, please?
A. John Jones.
Q. Are you the plaintiff in this case?
A. Yes, I am.
Q. Do you know John White, the defendant in this case?
A. I do.
Q. How long do you know him?
A. Ten years.
Q. Have you had any business dealings with him?
A. Yes, sir.
Q. For how long?
A. During the past ten years.
Q. Where was the place of business of John White the defendant during that time?
A. Blankstown, Ohio.
Q. Directing your attention to March 15th, 1932 did you have an occasion to bring suit against John White, the defendant in this case?
A. I did.
Q. In what state was that suit started?
A. In Ohio.
Q. And in what county?
A. Blankstown.
Q. What kind of a case was it?
A. I sued him on a note which he gave me for a debt.
Q. I show you this paper marked Plaintiff's Exhibit 1 for identification (showing exemplified copy of a judgment wherein John Jones appears as the plaintiff and John White as the defendant) and ask you whether you are the plaintiff

64 Admissibility of exemplified copy. Griswold v. Pitcairn, 2 Conn. 85; Lincoln v. Battelle, 6 Wend. (N. Y.) 475; Wolf v. King (Tex.), 41, 107 S. W. 617; Calhoun v. Ross, 60 Ill. App. 309.

mentioned in this action and whether John White the defendant in this case is the defendant in that action?

A. Yes.

I offer in evidence as Plaintiff's Exhibit 1, an exemplified copy of the judgment of the Superior Court, State of Ohio, County of Blankstown. (This copy shows the judgment to be duly entered in the office of the Clerk of the County of Blankstown on March 15, 1932.)

The Court: It may be received.

Counsel: Has any part of this judgment been paid?

A. No.

Q. Have you computed the interest at the statutory rate of 5%?

A. Yes.

Q. How much is it?

A. $200.00.

§ 412. Stipulations of facts.

Stipulations of fact when reduced to writing should be read to the jury and filed in the case. They bind the parties as a judicial admission.[65]

Form of Stipulation

(Caption)

It is Hereby Stipulated and Agreed by and between the plaintiff and the defendant, by their respective attorneys, and the following stipulated facts may be admitted in evidence, in lieu of other testimony or documentary evidence, subject, however to the general objection on the part of either party as to competency, materiality and relevancy.

1. It is agreed that on October 29, 1930, the plaintiff had a margin account with the defendants, Roll Bros., which had been running for a considerable length of time and that the

[65] Nathan v. Diersson, 146 Cal. 63, 79 Pac. 739; Catlin v. Traders Ins. Co., 83 Ill. App. 40; Jones v. Clark, 37 Iowa 586. When made for a specific purpose they possess no force after the purpose has been accomplished. Perry v. Simpson Waterproof Mfg. Co., 40 Conn. 313; Dennie v. Williams, 135 Mass. 28. If unqualified on its face, no limitation to the pending trial is implied, and it may be received in subsequent trial between the parties. Nathan v. Diersson, supra; Stemmler v. N. Y., 179 N. Y. 473, 72 N. E. 581.

total value of all securities on deposit with the defendants on that date was $31,348.00. There was due from the plaintiff, Sol Keller, to Roll Bros. on said account the sum of $3,743.39.

2. It is agreed that the securities purchased and sold in the account of Sol Keller were purchased and sold by the defendants, Roll Bros., on or about the respective dates as shown in the respective accounts appearing on the books of Roll Bros., and that the prices shown on said account of Sol Keller, and at which said securities were purchased or sold, represented the fair cash market value of said securities at the time and place of sale.

3. It is further Stipulated that on November 6, 1930, and November 7, 1930, the defendants, Roll Bros., sold the following stocks belonging to the plaintiff, Sol Keller, at the respective market prices:

40 shares Elec. Bond & Share @ 48¾....	$1,942.40
199/200 share Elec. Bond & Share @ 46½..	46.08
100 shares Union Carbide @ 59¾.........	5,953.60
150 shares Chgo. Yellow Cab @ 23¼......	3,465.75
100 shares Chgo. Yellow Cab @ 23½......	2,333.50
100 shares Chgo. Yellow Cab @ 23½......	2,333.50
100 shares Chgo. Yellow Cab @ 23¼......	2,310.50
200 shares Chgo. Yellow Cab @ 23¼......	4,621.00
200 shares Chgo. Yellow Cab @ 23½......	4,667.00
	$27,673.33

and that said total of $27,673.33 represents the fair cash market price at the time of the said sales and that said sales aggregate the sum of $27,673.33.

That after October 29, 1930, the Plaintiff, Sol Keller, became indebted on his said account in the following items: Interest $63.29; Grain account—$762.50; Interest $28.24; Total—$854.03; and was entitled to the following credits: Interest—$1.47; Dividend on 50 shares Chgo. Yellow Cab—$12.50; Total $13.97, or a balance of additional indebtedness of $840.06.

It is further Stipulated and Agreed that between the 29th day of October, 1930, and the 6th day of November and 7th day of November, 1930, there were no stocks of any kind, nature or description bought by the defendants, Roll Bros., for Sol Keller, and that the total value of securities on deposit belonging to Sol Keller remained of comparatively the same value as of October 29, 1930, there being a total depreciation of about One Hundred Forty-eight Dollars ($148.00) between said October 29th, 1930 and said November 7th, 1930.

Jones and Smith,
Attorneys for Plaintiff.
Williams and Hale,
Attorneys for Defendants.

CHAPTER VIII

OBJECTIONS

§ 413. In general.

A knowledge of the law governing "objections" as well as a knowledge of the mode of making objections is almost indispensable to the trial lawyer. It is also necessary to know the propriety or impropriety of objecting to certain testimony. A *timely* and *proper objection* may serve to keep out of the record evidence which might prejudice a cause before a jury, as well as before some appeal tribunal. On the other hand, an objection, *improper in form,* may *fail* to keep incompetent and prejudicial evidence out of the case and may result in an unfavorable verdict.

When it is realized that every case tried may be appealed, it becomes important to keep that fact in mind throughout every trial. Unless the record is preserved by *proper* objections the trial lawyer may not prevail on appeal and thus all of his efforts may be for naught.

§ 414. Ruling must be obtained.

It has been repeatedly held by appellate courts that they will not review rulings of trial courts unless the injured or complaining party has objected to the evidence sought to be introduced and has obtained a ruling on such objection by the trial court and, in some jurisdictions, has preserved an exception to the ruling of the trial court.[1] The rule is the same whether the case is tried before a jury or by the court without a jury.[2]

§ 415. How objections should be made.

Objections should be made clearly and openly so that all the parties, opposing counsel and the court may hear them.

1 Shaw v. Shaw, 160 Cal. 733, 117 Pac. 1048; Feld v. Loftis, 240 Ill. 105, 88 N. E. 281; Bremer v. Hoag, 151 Iowa 449, 131 N. W. 667; Miller v. Williams, 210 Mass. 516, 96 N. E. 1103; Bertolami v. United Eng., etc., Co., 181 N. Y. 71, 91 N. E. 267; Smith v. Olson, 92 Tex. 181, 46 S. W. 631.

2 Ross-Lewin v. Gould, 211 Ill. 384.

It has been held that the court may properly disregard objections that are made in an undertone or in such a low voice that they are not audible to the court and the opponent.[3]

§ 416. Types of objections.

There are two types of objections, *General* and *Specific*. *General objections* are those which in effect state to the court that the offered proof has no probative value whatever. They are usually stated "I object" or "Objection." It has also been held that an objection to the evidence on the grounds "that it is incompetent, irrelevant and immaterial" is no more than a general objection and will not be considered as proper in those instances where a specific objection should have been interposed.

§ 417. — General objections.[4]

General objections are sufficient to preserve errors for the consideration of a reviewing court only where the nature of the evidence is such that it will clearly appear "at first blush" to be improper.[5] The materiality of the offered proof may be reached by a general objection.[6]

Generally, courts look with disfavor upon general objections inasmuch as it is the purpose of an objection to advise the court and opposing counsel of the improper nature of the evidence so as to enable counsel to correct the error, if possible, by re-framing the question or by laying the proper foundation for its admissibility. Only the party who is affected by the introduction of evidence may object.[7]

3 Quincy Gas & Elec. Co. v. Baumann, 203 Ill. 295.

4 General objections . . . as a general rule are insufficient, except where the ground therefor is so manifest that the trial court could not fail to understand it, as when evidence is clearly irrelevant or incompetent or inadmissible for any purpose. Quaker Oats Co. v. Kidman, 179 N. W. 128, 189 Iowa 906; Tozer v. N. Y., etc., R. Co., 11 N. E. 846, 105 N. Y. 659; Taylor v. Adams, 115 Ill. 570; McKinsey v. McKee, 9 N. E. 771, 109 Ind. 209 (incompetent); Fraher v. Eisenman, 270 Pac. 704, 94 Cal. 48 (irrelevant); Brown v. Wakeman, 18 N. Y. S. 363 (immaterial); Glens Falls Ins. Co. v. Bendy (Tex.), 39 S. W. (2d) 628 (prejudicial); Crouch v. Nat., etc., Co., 217 N. W. 557, 205 Iowa 51.

5 McCabe v. Swift, 143 Ill. App. 404, 407.

6 Scott v. Caldwell, 152 Ill. App. 172.

7 Rice v. Rice, 108 Ill. 199.

§ 417a. Legal requirements.

Objections should be made *at the time* question is propounded.[8] If cause for objection to testimony is apparent at the time it is given, a motion to exclude comes too late after the witness is excused from the stand. It is not sufficient objection for counsel to advise the court that he *will object* to a given line of testimony, but objection must be made after question is stated.[9] Counsel's statement "I will preserve my objection" upon introduction of photographs is not a sufficient objection to their admission.[10]

§ 418. —Specific objections.

Specific objections are those which state or point out in detail the grounds or reasons why the offered evidence is legally insufficient to be admitted. Specific objections must be made in all instances where the objection, if specifically pointed out, might be obviated or remedied; that is, in all cases where the error complained of can be obviated by further evidence so as to lay a proper foundation for its reception, or where an objectionable question might be re-framed to correct the error.[11]

The form in which a specific objection should be stated varies with the individual case, depending largely on the nature of the evidence offered. The words used should clearly and completely inform the court of the specific grounds of objection.

In some jurisdictions, the grounds of the specific objection must be stated and then coupled with the general statement

8 McFeeley v. Industrial, etc., 223 Pac. 413, 65 Cal. App. 45; Kreigh v. Sherman, 105 Ill. 49; Wood v. State, 30 N. E. 309, 130 Ind. 364; Culbertson v. Salinger, 117 N. W. 6 (Iowa); Colrick v. Swinburne, 12 N. E. 427, 105 N. Y. 503; Bohanan v. Hans, 26 Tex. 445. . . . Or as soon as the objectionable nature of the evidence becomes apparent: Toledo, etc., R. Co. v. Stevenson, 122 Ill. App. 654; Holland v. Riggs, 116 S. W. 167 (Texas). Objections to improper questions must be made at the time the question is asked: Ruddy v. McDonald, 91 N. E. 651, 244 Ill. 494; In re Merrill's Est., 211 N. W. 361, 202 Iowa 837; Link v. Sheldon, 32 N. E. 696, 136 N. Y. 1.

9 City of Charleston v. Newman, 130 Ill. App. 6.

10 Sorenson v. Chi. Rys. Co., 217 Ill. App. 174.

11 Everdson v. Mayhew, 21 Pac. 431, 85 Cal. 1; Curtis v. Marrs, 29 Ill. 508; Wightman v. Campbell, 112 N. E. 184, 217 N. Y. 479; McCarty v. Johnson, 151 S. W. 774 (Tex).

that "therefore it is incompetent" or "therefore it is irrelevant" or "therefore it is immaterial." Any two or all of these general conclusions may also be coupled with the specific objection.

§ 419. — **When necessary.**

Specific objections must be made in all of the following instances (*a general objection will be overruled*): when leading questions are asked on direct examination;[12] when the answer of a witness is not responsive to the question asked;[13] where the evidence offered is not the best evidence;[14] when evidence is offered of a transaction with a deceased person in violation of provisions of a statute;[15] when the proof offered is variant from the pleadings;[16] that documentary evidence offered is incompetent for any reason;[17] that photographs of the locus in quo of an accident are inadmissible;[18] questions as to the validity, existence or legal passage of statutes or municipal ordinances;[19] that a proper foundation has not been laid for the admission of documents, photographs, X-rays and all exhibits;[20] giving wrong instructions or refusing to give proper instructions;[21] when expert testimony

12 Edmandson v. Andrews, 35 Ill. App. 223; Gill v. McNamee, 42 N. Y. 44; Waller v. Leonard, 35 S. W. 1045, 89 Tex. 507; Teegarden v. Caledonia, 6 N. W. 875, 50 Wis. 292.

13 . . . Motion to strike answer must be made: Yaeger v. So. Cal. R. Co., 51 Pac. 190 (Cal.); Latman v. Douglas & Co., 127 N. W. 661, 149 Iowa 699; Burns v. Brier, 90 N. E. 399, 204 Mass. 195; Shaw v. N. Y. El. R. Co., 79 N. E. 984, 187 N. Y. 186; Math v. Chicago City Ry. Co., 90 N. E. 235, 243 Ill. 114; Western Union Tel. Co. v. Johnsey, 109 S. W. 251 (Tex.).

14 Rich v. Township, etc., 41 N. E. 924, 158 Ill. 242; Porter v. Tenant, 197 N. W. 79, 197 Iowa 200; Folts v. Ferguson, 24 S. W. 657 (Tex.).

15 Foxton v. Moore, 87 N. W. 492 (Iowa); Christianson v. Dunham, etc., Co., 75 Ill. App. 267; Levin v. Russell, 42 N. Y. 251; Mousseau v. Mousseau, 42 Minn. 212, 44 N. W. 193.

16 Davey v. So. P. Co., 45 Pac. 170 (Cal.); Levinson v. Home Bank & Trust Co., 169 N. E. 193, 337 Ill. 241; McDonald v. Smith, 102 N. W. 668, 139 Mich. 211; Kent v. Thelin, 195 Ill. App. 440.

17 When sufficient foundation has not been laid for the admission of documentary evidence: Wyman v. City of Chicago, 98 N. E. 266, 254 Ill. 202; McDaneld v. McDaneld, 36 N. E. 286, 136 Ind. 603; Krolik v. Graham, 31 N. W. 307, 64 Mich. 226; Morris v. Murray, 49 N. Y. S. 1093, 22 Misc. 697.

18 Sorenson v. Chi. Rys. Co., 217 Ill. App. 174.

19 When the validity of an ordinance is questioned: Wabash R. Co. v. Kamradt, 109 Ill. App. 203; George v. St. Joseph, 97 Mo. App. 56, 71 S. W. 110.

20 Gage v. Eddy, 186 Ill. 432.

21 When the objection is to an instruction, or a part thereof, where the

is improperly excluded; if a question asked on cross-examination improperly goes beyond the scope of the testimony brought out on the direct examination;[22] where a question is asked which has been previously asked and answered; propounding an improper question on re-cross examination;[23] where hypothetical questions are defective;[24] where the identity, form or contents of a deposition are questioned;[25] when the question calls for a privileged communication;[26] where the form of the question is objectionable;[27] when the evidence is admissible in part;[28] where the evidence is admissible for any particular purpose;[29] when the method of proving a fact is objectionable;[30] when the question calls for a conclusion of the witness;[31] when the evidence is hearsay;[32] when question impeaches own witness;[33] when document offered is

instruction or the part objected to contains separate and distinct propositions: Love v. Anchor, etc., Co., 45 Pac. 1044 (Cal.); Razor v. Razor, 142 Ill. 375; Roselli v. Riseman, 182 N. E. 567 (Mass.); Jones v. Gould, 103 N. E. 720, 209 N. Y. 419; Stedman Fruit Co. v. Smith, 45 S. W. (2d) 804 (Tex.).

22 I. C. C. R. R. Co. v. Puckett, 210 Ill. 140.

23 When improper cross-examination: Allen B. Wrisley Co. v. Burke, 67 N. E. 818, 203 Ill. 250; Knapp v. Schneider, 24 Wis. 70.

24 Reynolds & Heitsman v. Henry, 185 N. W. 67, 193 Iowa 164; Dameron v. Ansbro, 178 Pac. 874, 39 Cal. App. 289; Griswold v. Chicago Rys. Co., 253 Ill. App. 498, 170 N. E. 845.

25 Smith v. Smith, 149 Ill. App. 21.

26 Tooley v. Bacon, 70 N. Y. 34; Satterlee v. Bliss, 36 Cal. 489.

27 Tracy v. People, 97 Ill. 101; Westfield Cigar Co. v. Teutonic Ins. Co., 169 Mass. 382, 47 N. E. 1026; Waller v. Leonard, 89 Tex. 507, 35 S. W. 1045.

28 People v. McFarlane, 71 Pac. 568, 72 Pac. 48, 138 Cal. 481, 61 L. R. A. 245; Martin v. Sherwood, 51 Atl. 526, 74 Conn. 475; McGuffey v. McLain, 30 N. E. 296, 130 Ind. 327; Simpson v. Foundation Co., 95 N. E. 10, 201 N. Y. 479; Tuttle v. Robert Moody & Son, 97 S. W. 1037, 100 Tex. 240.

29 Sneed v. Osborn, 25 Cal. 619; Gage v. Eddy, 53 N. E. 1008, 179 Ill. 492; Boston Food Co. v. Wilson & Co., 139 N. E. 637, 245 Mass. 550; Dalton v. Smith, 86 N. Y. 176; Youngblood v. Youngblood (Tex.), 46 S. W. (2d) 390.

30 Gelpecke-Winslow & Co. v. Lovell, 18 Iowa 17; Murphy v. People, 4 Hun (N. Y.) 102.

31 Crouch v. Nat. Live Stock, etc., Co., 217 N. W. 557, 205 Iowa 51; Mortimer v. Manhattan R. Co., 29 N. E. 5, 129 N. Y. 81.

32 C. C. Snyder Cigar, etc., Co. v. Stutts, 107 So. 73, 214 Ala. 132; Gagnon v. Sperry, etc., Co., 92 N. E. 761, 208 Mass. 547.

33 H. F. Cady Lumber Co. v. Wilson, etc., Co., 114 N. W. 774, 80 Neb. 607; Wise v. Wakefield, 50 Pac. 310, 118 Cal. 107; Cincinnati First Nat. Bank v. Kelly, 57 N. Y. 34.

self-serving;[34] where the evidence violates the parol evidence rule;[35] and where witness is incompetent.[36]

§ 420. — Waiver of objections.

An objection may be waived either expressly or by implication.[36a] An objection is expressly waived by withdrawal of the objection, even after it has been sustained.[37] Waiver may be implied from the conduct of the objector which induces the court and opposing counsel to believe that the objection has been withdrawn.[38] An objection to improper evidence is not waived by a cross-examination of the *same* witness in respect thereto,[39] but error in admission of evidence is waived by the objecting party subsequently examining *other* witnesses on the *same point.*[40]

A specific objection waives objection to all other points not specified or relied upon, especially if these points might have been cured had they been raised during the trial.[41] However, a general objection may be made which reserves the right to make specific objections at a later time, and under such circumstances, specific objections can be made to certain parts of the evidence without waiving objections to the admissibility of other parts of the evidence.[42]

34 Pleason Realty, etc., Co. v. Kleinman, 206 N. W. 645, 165 Minn. 342.

35 Piretti v. Firestone Tire & Rubber Co., 120 N. Y. S. 782; Hock v. Allendale Tp., 126 N. W. 987, 161 Mich. 571; Anderson v. Crane, 183 Ill. App. 21.

36 Burdick v. Raymond, 77 N. W. 833, 107 Iowa 228; Rosengren v. Manufacturers Nat. Bank, 220 Ill. App. 608; Boyce v. Manhattan R. Co., 54 N. Y. Super. 286, 118 N. Y. 314; In re Menzner's Est., 207 N. W. 703, 189 Wis. 340.

36a Craney v. Schlowman, 145 Ill. App. 313; Hinkle v. Jas. Smith & Son, 65 S. E. 247, 133 Ga. 255; In re Riggs, 210 Pac. 217, 105 Oregon 531; Wallerich v. Smith, 66 N. W. 184, 97 Iowa 308; Hopes' Appeal, 12 N. W. 682, 48 Mich. 518; N. Y. Mut. L. Ins. Co. v. Baker, 31 S. W. 1072 (Tex.); Com. v. Nefus, 135 Mass. 533.

37 Crawford v. Burke, 201 Ill. 581.

38 Thomasson v. Wilson, 146 Ill. 384.

39 Laver v. Hotaling, 46 Pac. 1070 (Cal.); Aetna Ins. Co. v. Paul, 23 Ill. App. 611; Metropolitan Nat. Bank v. Commercial State Bank, 104 Iowa 682, 74 N. W. 26.

40 Huling v. Century Pub. Co., 108 Ill. App. 549.

41 Village, etc. v. Schoening, etc., 248 Ill. 57; In re Huston's Est., 124 Pac. 852, 163 Cal. 166; Plumb v. Curtis, 33 App. 998, 66 Conn. 154; Kleiner v. Third Ave. R. Co., 56 N. E. 497, 162 N. Y. 193.

42 People v. Looney, 314 Ill. 150.

Failure to make timely objections waives any objections to the competency, relevancy, admissibility, etc., of the evidence introduced without protest.[43] But objections as to the sufficiency of the evidence to make out a case are not waived.[44] Incompetent evidence not objected to may be received and given such probative value as it naturally carries.

Objections may be waived by the objector introducing evidence of a like nature that is also objectionable.[45]

§ 420a. Subject to objection and reserving ruling.

Where objections are made and the court allows evidence to go in subject to objection or when the court reserves a ruling on a certain objection, the objection is waived unless a further and a final ruling is requested before the end of the trial.[46]

§ 420b. Legally preserving record.[47]

To preserve the record properly for appeal an objection must be made, a ruling of the court obtained and this is usually followed by a motion to strike the answer and an exception taken (where necessary).

Some attorneys who are examining witnesses, when objections are made, continue with their examination without giv-

43 Robinson v. Halley, 100 N. W. 378, 124 Iowa 443; Walters v. Geo. A. Fuller Co., 77 N. Y. S. 681, 74 App. Div. 388; Webb v. Sweeney, 69 N. E. 200, 32 Ind. App. 54.

44 Roberts v. Chan Tin Pen, 23 Cal. 259; Lowe v. Bliss, 24 Ill. 168; Gillaspie v. Murray, 66 S. W. 252 (Tex.).

45 Mayer v. Swygart, 17 N. E. 450, 125 Ill. 262; McCarty v. Waterman, 96 Ind. 594; Miller v. Montgomery, 78 N. Y. 282; San Antonio, etc., R. Co. v. Cockrill, 10 S. W. 702, 72 Tex. 613; Kreuziger v. C. & N. W. R. Co., 73 Wis. 158, 40 N. W. 657; Budd v. Meridian El. R. Co., 69 Conn. 272, 37 Atl. 683; Pickrel v. Doubet, 239 Ill. 555.

46 Ashdown v. Ely, 140 Iowa 739, 117 N. W. 976; Putnam v. Harris, 193 Mass. 58, 78 N. E. 747; Indiana Union Tract. Co. v. Jacobs, 167 Ind. 85, 75 N. E. 325.

When evidence is permitted to go in subject to objection upon a promise to connect, failure to renew objection operates as waiver. Napa v. Howland, 87 Cal. 84, 25 Pac. 247; Gaar Scott & Co. v. Nichols, 115 Iowa 223, 88 N. W. 382; Chicago City Ry. Co. v. Hyndshaw, 116 Ill. App. 367; Williams v. Grand Rapids, 53 Mich. 271, 18 N. W. 811; Hoxie v. Home Ins. Co., 32 Conn. 21.

47 Party who objects is entitled to ruling. Faulkner v. I. L. Elwood Mfg. Co., 79 Ill. App. 544.

Ruling should be made as soon as possible. Clopton v. Clopton, 121 Pac. 720, 162 Cal. 27.

Construction of ruling. Reiche v. Gleicher, 172 N. Y. S. 200.

ing the court an opportunity to rule on such objection. This should never be permitted. An objection to all subsequent questions and answers should be made until the court has ruled upon the previous objection.

In some instances judges are prone to ignore proper objections, evidently unable to make up their minds as to their decisions. If the objection is important, a ruling should be respectfully and quietly insisted upon, so as to preserve the question for review.

In some jurisdictions an exception must also be taken to the court's ruling.[48] In most states Practice Act provisions make exceptions unnecessary.

§ 421. Improper remarks of counsel.

Objections should be made to improper remarks of counsel, if any, with a request that the court instruct the jury to disregard them, and if important enough it should be requested that a juror be withdrawn and the case declared a mistrial.

Improper Remarks of Counsel [49]

Illustration

Q. Did he lie there where he had landed and only moved two inches, or did he get up and go to the end of the ladder?

Mr. Opponent: Now isn't that just rotten; I think that is so utterly unfair. I never heard anything like this going on in a court-room at all.

Counsel: I object to the improper remarks of counsel and wish to preserve an exception to them.

The Court: Sustained.

Counsel: I now move that they be stricken from the record and the jury ordered to disregard them.

The Court: They will be stricken and the jury will disregard the statements made.

48 Raymond v. Glover, 55 Pac. 398, 122 Cal. 471; Mortimer v. Bristol, 180 N. Y. S. 55, 190 App. Div. 452.

49 What should be done to correct misconduct is within court's discretion. Smith v. Hendrix, 128 N. W. 360, 149 Iowa 255; Reehil v. Fraas, 90 N. E. 340, 197 N. Y. 64; Perkins v. Norris (Tex.), 25 S. W. (2d) 979; Deel v. Heiligenstein, 91 N. E. 429, 244 Ill. 239; Herman v. Teplitz, 148 N. E. 641, 113 Oh. St. 164.

§ 421a. Exceptions to court's remarks and conduct.[50]

Exceptions to remarks or conduct of the court as a matter of policy should not be taken unless such conduct or remarks seem to be seriously damaging. To the jurors, the judge is considered impartial. In most instances they have been acting as jurors in a number of other cases, and have discussed those cases with the court after each decision, frankly and openly and in a friendly manner. They will be quick to resent any apparent antagonism against the judge. Some lawyers take exception to the remarks or participation of the judge in the trial in a loud tone of voice. Better results can be obtained by calling the court reporter out of the hearing of the jury and in the presence of the judge ask that the record show an objection and exception to the remarks or attitude of the court, specifying the grounds thereof. In many instances, this has served to bring to the attention of the court unintentional but prejudicial misconduct on his part. Most judges being fair-minded and not desiring to commit reversible error will tell the jury to disregard their own remarks and actions. This method eliminates antagonism on the part of the court. In many instances it creates a friendly feeling towards the trial attorney.

Exceptions to Court's Remarks

Illustration

The Court: You file pleas of the General Issue in a suit and special information by this plea on file. Counsel could not have filed it without receiving information from some source.

Mr. Opponent: Mr. Reporter just step over here a moment, please. (Outside of presence of jury). If the Court please, I wish the record to show an exception to the Court's remark. I am sure it was unintentional, but I believe it will be viewed by the jury in the wrong light. I feel that your Honor should instruct the jury to disregard the remark.

50 Williams v. Perrotta, 111 Atl. 843, 95 Conn. 529; Marsh v. Burnham, 179 N. W. 300, 211 Mich. 675; Roseberry v. Nixon, 11 N. Y. S. 523, 58 Hun (N. Y.) 121; Hines v. Messer (Tex.), 218 S. W. 611; Chicago City R. Co. v. Enroth, 113 Ill. App. 285.

§ 422. Few objections should be made.

Very few objections should be made in court. Only in those instances where evident harm may result should the trial lawyer object. A mere matter of form or preliminary foundation should never be objected to especially if the opposing attorney is competent and is actually familiar with the proper technique. For example, in actual practice, if the opposing lawyer fails to lay a proper foundation for some immaterial conversation, a little side remark to him to fix the time, place and who was present is all that is necessary.

Incessant objections on immaterial matters are, of course, bad trial tactics. Both the court and jury will resent such procedure. If the matter is deemed to be important, however, no hesitancy should be shown in interposing objections.

Elliott in "The Work of the Advocate" makes some very helpful suggestions on the subject of "Objections" as follows:

> "A constant and determined guard must be maintained to prevent the introduction of incompetent evidence that may do harm. Such evidence should never reach the ears of the jurors if "skill of fence" can prevent it. If possible it should not be heard at all, although it is promised that on future consideration it may be struck out. Evidence once heard, if important, leaves an impression. An impression once made requires evidence to remove it, and thus makes the task more difficult than it would be if minds free from all impressions were to be convinced. Quick and strong should be the interposition to prevent the introduction of harmful and incompetent evidence, but if it gets to the jury let the subsequent effort to reject it be quiet and mild, rather than earnest and determined; for the stronger the effort to get rid of it, the more importance jurors will attach to it, and the deeper it will sink into their minds. The better plan is to put the motion to reject in writing specifying the grounds of objections, and hand the paper to the court without argument. If, however, the advocate deems it expedient to fasten the minds of the jurors upon the matter, as sometimes happens, then the more earnest the argument the better.
>
> "It is only evidence that is likely to do harm to which an objection should be made, except, perhaps where the purpose is to prevent a useless waste of time, or the con-

cealment of important facts by a mass of immaterial matter. It is folly to make objections where there is no reason to believe that the testimony will do harm. If the testimony is not harmful it is far better to let it go in than to be thought a technical, carping critic. Those who fritter away time in unimportant objections bring upon themselves a reproach which much impairs their power with the jury. A man who abounds in objections finds no favor with court or jury. 'Never object to a question from your adversary,' says David Paul Brown, 'without being able and disposed to enforce your objection.' The reason for this rule is not far to seek. If objections are fruitlessly made an air of weakness is given to the case, for jurors are apt to infer that an advocate against whom the court often rules has a feeble case, which he is attempting to prop by technical objections. So, too, they are apt to regard it as an effort to keep the truth from them or to give them only a partial view of it. They, be sure, know of the charge so persistently, and most often so unjustly laid against lawyers, of attempting by tricks and artifices to bewilder courts and juries, and so defeat justice. It is but reasonable, therefore, to expect them to look with great disfavor on anything that looks like a professional trick or a lawyer's technicality. What they want is full information, and they resent any effort to keep it from them.[a]

"If an objection is worth the stating, it is worth supporting. If an objection is stated, let the best and strongest reasons that can be commanded be brought to its support. Once it is made the true policy is to stand to it, earnestly, but courteously, and not let it pass without a struggle. Of course, no struggle will be openly made after the court has announced its opinion, for that would be not only discourteous, but mischievous. Unless the judge is clearly in the wrong, or is unfit for his position, the jury will sympathize with him, since they will regard him as just and impartial, and look upon the advocate as a prejudiced man, working only for a reward.[b] If a fight

(a) "The habit of making constant objections to the introduction of evidence, without being able to assign any reason for such objections indicates a desire to suppress the truth, and a jury are not slow in discovering that fact."—Quoted from Law Notes for December, 1910.

(b) "In their zeal to serve their clients counsel sometimes indulge a habit of objecting when it must be apparent that no valid ground of obis to be made, let it be made as vigorously as you will before the ruling is announced. A hearing courteously requested will seldom be denied. There are cases where it may not be improper to ask leave to again argue an objection, and when this is necessary the wise advocate will ask it courteously and respectfully, but openly and frankly, and will not seek to accomplish his object by indirection. It is seldom that an objection should be withdrawn but it may happen that it is better to withdraw it, and when this does happen, let it be withdrawn openly and candidly. A frank acknowledgment of error is better than a covert attempt at an evasive retreat.

"There are cases in which, from rulings on the pleadings or rulings on the evidence, the advocate will have reason to expect that the court will rule adversely to him upon objections to evidence, and where there is reason to expect this it is well to write objections in advance, and with a little comment, deliver them to the court. Repeated statements of objections serve to fasten the obnoxious evidence in the minds of the jurors, and prudence dictates that, in general, there be as few repetitions as possible. There are, as we have hinted, cases where it is desirable to state and argue objections, even though they are certain to be overruled; but these are exceptional cases, seldom arising in actual practice. When the advocate is quite sure that the evidence he assails can be overcome, it is well enough to persistently object, since that will make it seem the more important, and when it falls the greater will be the impression produced by its downfall.

"Where a willing witness is being led by questions plainly objectionable, because they are leading, it is good policy to do no more than say enough to attract attention to the fact that counsel is suggesting answers. This may be done without formal objection, as by a playful remark, or a suggestion to the examiner; but enough must be

jection exists. Objections of the character indicated do not tend to preserve a record, but rather tend, as is suggested by counsel, to cause the jury to infer that the trial court, by repeated rulings against the objections, is adverse to the position of the objecting party upon the merits of the case. The injury resulting from such an inference by the jury would be very appreciably obviated if counsel would limit their objections." — Quoted from opinion in Walker v. Chicago & C. R. Co., 149 Ill. App. 406, 411.

done to bring the matter to the attention of the jury. If once they can be made to believe that the witness is testifying as counsel dictates, little weight will the testimony of that witness be accorded. In argument, the manner of counsel and witness will be fair matter of comment, and the man who can not profit by it has mistaken his vocation. Nor is this the only reason why such a course is sometimes expedient. Another reason is, that a witness who has been uttering the answers suggested by leading questions leans entirely on his mentor, and when, on cross-examination, that prop is pulled from under him, he goes down. But it is not safe to assume in every case that the jury will see that leading questions suggest the desired answers, for they are often so adroitly framed that even the witness is unconscious that the counsel is suggesting his answers. A skillful examiner will often so frame his questions as to suggest the answers and yet conceal from the jurors his purpose; and when this is the case, the only course is to expose the artifice and press the objection with determination and vigor. If the judge declines to interfere, as he may do (for the matter is much one of discrimination), the jury, if the advocate has done his duty and fully exposed the unfairness of such an examination, will not be prejudiced by the decision of the judge against the objecting party; on the contrary, they will be very apt to take sides with him. If, however, the matter is not important, or the witness is an unwilling one, it is not expedient to object, for the probability is that the objection will be unavailing; and even if it is sustained, the jury are not unlikely to infer that a fair opportunity was not allowed opposing counsel to get all the facts from the witness."

A lecture delivered by Judge Samuel H. Silbert of Cleveland, Ohio, gives a good idea as to how the average judge feels on the subject of "Objections":

"Objections are the bane of our official lives. I have seen lawyers object to one stating one's age, on the ground that such evidence was hearsay! Some of these objections are wholly absurd and immaterial. Some are so trivial that the court ignores them entirely, letting the objection go by default. Leading questions! They do not seem to realize that generally they are discretionary with the court; that there are occasions where they are even desirable. It is only where the leading questions suggest the answer on *material matters* that the court should exclude them entirely. And the joke of it all is that in many instances after the court has ruled against them, the lawyers fail to note their exceptions. And when the court does order it out, they forget it's still in—the jury has it. Consider a negligence suit, for instance. You know, of course, that the object of the plaintiff's lawyer is to recover a verdict, and to make that verdict stick; yet by his insistent objections, he may succeed in getting the court into error, and in having that verdict reversed. I would point out to these unconscientious or unconscious objectors that some of our best lawyers when in doubt under such circumstances have the court rule against them deliberately. The real lawyer today has stopped objecting unless it is something vital. These objectors merely take up the court's time, clog up the records with inconsequential objections and achieve no perceptible results."

§ 423. Subject to objection.

Some judges, whether from lack of knowledge or in an attempt to take the easiest way out, have erroneously adopted the practice in *law* cases of allowing questions to be asked and answered "subject to objection." This may allow harmful evidence to be heard by the jury. A far greater harm, however, results in those instances where the trial lawyer later fails to renew his objections to such testimony. Such failure to secure a final ruling by the court on the previous objections to questions or answers which were allowed in evidence "subject to objection" waives such previous objection. In this way an appellate court could sustain the judgment of the lower court, when perhaps the main evidence to support such judgment is the evidence erroneously admitted because of the trial lawyer's failure to renew his objections and motions to strike.

§ 424. Promise to connect.

It is, however, proper for the judge to allow certain testimony to be received on the promise of counsel to "connect it up" legally with other evidence to be adduced later. If counsel fails to produce such evidence a motion to strike the previously objectionable evidence should be made.

Illustration

Counsel: Q. What conversation did you have with Mr. Cherry, if any?

Opponent: I object. There is undoubtedly sufficient foundation laid to show that Mr. Cherry was employed by the plaintiff here, but as to a discussion of this particular matter that is in controversy there is no evidence as yet that will throw any light on that question.

The Court: *I will allow the conversation at this time subject to your objection to strike out later on if they don't show that he had authority.*

§ 425. "Withdraw the question."

Some trial attorneys unfairly ask questions that they know are improper and frequently prejudicial. Upon objection they request permission or state that they will "withdraw the question" in an effort to eliminate reversible error. In many instances the harm has been done, for the jury has heard the question which is usually put in statement form. If the opposing attorney persists in this conduct, an exception should be taken and the court's attention called to the practice with the request that counsel be admonished to desist from employing such unfair tactics.

§ 426. Offers of proof.

In all instances where the court refuses to permit the lawyer to present testimony which he feels is competent and material and necessary to prove his case, the method of properly preserving the record and thus saving the question for review is through the making of an *offer of proof*. This may be done in the presence of the jury in the discretion of the court. The offer should be made in reference to what the witness would testify to if permitted, in detail, and not merely to offer to prove conclusions of fact. (Some states contra.)

Illustration

Mr. Oppenheim: What did you do then, if anything?

Witness: I picked up a telephone book, looked up the number of the Blank Life Insurance Co., called for that number and someone answered stating that it was the Blank Life

Insurance Co. I told the person answering that I was ill and wanted to be examined by one of their doctors.

Opponent: I object unless he can state to whom he was talking or that he recognized the voice of the person.

The Court: Sustained.

Counsel: If the Court please, I wish to make an offer of proof at this time. The plaintiff offers to prove by John Terry, this witness, and he will testify, if permitted, that about the middle of May, 1930, he examined a telephone book in Omaha, Nebraska, to see if the Blank Life Insurance Company, defendant herein, had an office in Omaha, called the number listed in the telephone book and requested the operator of the telephone company to connect him with said number; that someone answered the telephone and that he asked that person whether or not he was connected with the Blank Life Insurance Company. The person at the other end of the line replied that he was connected with the Blank Life Insurance Company; that he thereupon told the party answering the telephone for and in behalf of the Blank Life Insurance that he was a policyholder in their company; that he was sick and would probably have to file a claim under his policy with their company, and asked that they furnish him with the name of one of their examining physicians so that he could go to see him; that thereupon the party answering the telephone for and in behalf of the Blank Life Insurance Company gave him the name of Dr. Thomas Green and two others who were examining physicians for the Blank Life Insurance Company, and the party answering the telephone thereupon told this witness to go to any one of the three.

John Terry will further testify, if permitted, that he later met Dr. Thomas Green at the Country Club in Omaha, Nebraska, at which time he was introduced to Dr. Green by one, Harry Meyers; that on the occasion of this meeting at the Country Club this witness told Dr. Green that it was quite a coincidence that he had been given his name by the Blank Life Insurance Company and that the girl in the office of the Blank Life Insurance Company had told him to see Dr. Green for examination in reference to a possible claim that he might file under the health policy which he held with the Blank Life Insurance Company.

We further offer to prove by John Terry, and he will testify, that thereafter when he went to Dr. Thomas Green for examination that Dr. Green told him that he was the examining physician for the Blank Life Insurance Company.

We further offer to prove by John Terry, and he will testify, if permitted, that the later insurance policy taken out from the Blank Life Insurance Company and the one from the Central Life Insurance Company were without provisions for disability benefits, and further that Dr. Green and the examining physician for the Central Life Insurance Company did not make a full and complete physical examination of John Terry, the plaintiff in this case prior to the issuance of said policies and that the later policy issued by the Blank Life Insurance Company marked Plaintiff's Exhibit 14 for identification was taken out after a conversation with said Dr. Thomas Green in which Dr. Green stated in reply to John Terry's question as to whether or not he had tuberculosis that he would procure for him further and new insurance to prove to him that he did not have tuberculosis and that John Terry, the plaintiff, thereupon requested the further issuance of said policy and that the same was issued without any other or further examination by said Dr. Green or any other doctor for the Blank Life Insurance Company.

Mr. Opponent: To all of which offer the defendant objects.

The Court: Sustained.

§ 427. — Requisites and sufficiency of offer of proof.

What constitutes

To constitute an offer of proof, counsel must make a statement of what he expects to prove by the witness. Mere conversation between court and counsel does not constitute an offer of proof.[51]

The right to make offer

Examining counsel has the right to make offer of proof, and, if properly made, it is error to refuse this right. The purpose and necessity for this rule is twofold: (1) to inform

[51] Kilbourn v. Muller, 22 Iowa 498; Goyette v. Keenan, 82 N. E. 427, 196 Mass. 416; Crew v. Penn. R. Co., 153 N. E. 95, 21 Oh. App. 143; Chicago Rys., etc. v. Carrol, 206 Ill. 318.

court what is expected to be proved, and (2) procuring exceptions to the exclusion of the offered evidence so that the upper court may determine from the record whether the proposed evidence is competent.[52]

Time for making

An offer of proof is made at the proper time when (1) objection is made to the question put to the witness, and (2) the court has sustained the objection.[53]

Conclusions

An offer to prove a conclusion of law, as for example, insolvency, delivery of a deed, consideration, or acceptance, is improper. The offer must contain specific facts and circumstances which constitute the transaction.[54]

The offer must be specific

The offer must contain specific evidence, competent upon the subject, which tends to prove the desired fact.[55] Nothing that is offered should be left to inference. When counsel desires to prove particular meanings of words in a trade, he must offer to show the word has a special meaning in the trade. An offer to prove the making of an agreement by a corporation must show by whom the agreement was made, and by whom the agents were authorized.

Part competent

Where the offer contains both competent and incompetent matter, it is bad and may be properly rejected.[56]

Limiting proposal

When an offer is competent for one purpose, but incom-

52 Maxwell v. Haber, 92 Ill. App. 510.

53 Harmon v. Indian Grave Drainage Dist., 217 Ill. App. 502; Hoover v. Patton, 64 N. E. 10, 158 Ind. 524.

54 Manning v. Den, 24 Pac. 1092, 90 Cal. 610; Somers v. Loose, 86 N. W. 386, 127 Mich. 77; Martin v. Hertz, 224 Ill. 84.

55 Smith v. East Branch Min. Co., 54 Cal. 164; Lessing v. Davis, 125 N. E. 579, 72 Ind. App. 111; Cook v. Farnum, 154 N. E. 577, 258 Mass. 145; Hellreigel v. Manning, 97 N. Y. 56; Goodrich v. Chicago, 218 Ill. 18; Nat. Bank of Decatur v. Board of Education, 205 Ill. 57.

56 Harman v. Indian, etc., supra; Newell v. Baird, supra; Boyle v. Boston El. R. Co., 94 N. E. 247, 208 Mass. 41; Gardner v. Barden, 34 N. Y. 433; Donan v. Donan, 256 Ill. 244.

petent otherwise, it must be stated that the offer is made for the competent purpose.[57]

Documentary evidence

Where documentary evidence is offered, the contents should be disclosed in order to determine its competency.[58] Reading it in substance, at the time the offer is made, is sufficient disclosure. An offer of part of a document is bad. But, a portion of the document may be offered only when offered in corroboration or contradiction of various contentions, and when so done, the opposition may offer and read the remainder.

Offer en masse

An offer of documentary evidence en masse is improper and may be properly rejected.[59]

Ruling on offer

The ruling on the offer may be orally, and the court has the right to state grounds which form the basis of the ruling. The ruling is not within the statute requiring instructions to be in writing.[60]

Re-offer

Where the court already has ruled that a certain line of proof is incompetent and counsel has taken exception, it is not necessary to re-offer the same to preserve the error.[61]

However, where the testimony is ruled out on the grounds that it is improper cross-examination, incompetent, it must be

57 Stotts v. Fairfield, 145 N. W. 61, 163 Iowa 726; Hubbard v. Allyn, 86 N. E. 356, 200 Mass. 166; Quincy v. White, 63 N. Y. 370; Adams v. Foley, 173 N. E. 197, 36 Oh. App. 295; Bank of Commerce v. Elkins, 214 Ill. App. 417.

58 Dwyer v. Rippetoe, 10 S. W. 668, 72 Tex. 520; Smith v. Young, 179 Ill. App. 364; Chicago Rys. v. Cepak, 68 Ill. App. 500.

59 Newell v. Baird, 192 N. W. 817 (Iowa); Board of Ed. v. Keenan, 55 Cal. 642; Dowie v. Priddle, 116 Ill. App. 184.

60 T. Barbour Brown & Co. v. Canty, 161 Atl. 91, 115 Conn. 226; Campion v. Downey, 245 Pac. 1098, 77 Cal. App. 125; O'Mara v. Jesma, 121 N. W. 518, 143 Iowa 297; People v. Horn, 309 Ill. 23.

61 Cadwaller v. Martin, 257 Pac. 538, 83 Cal. App. 666; International Text Book Co. v. Mackhorn, 158 Ill. App. 543; Smith v. Plant, 103 N. E. 58, 216 Mass. 91; Campbell v. Germania Fire Ins. Co. of N. Y., 158 N. W. 63, 163 Wis. 329. . . . Unless court indicates that it would be useless. Mebius, etc., Co. v. Mills, 88 Pac. 917, 150 Cal. 229; Lichtenstein Millinery v. Peck, 110 N. Y. S. 410, 59 Misc. 93

re-offered. The rule, that where an adverse ruling has once been obtained and exception taken, other offers governed by such ruling need not be made has no application where the question is excluded as improper cross-examination.

Where documentary evidence is excluded, as, for example, a letter, because no notice to produce is shown, and later it is established that the letter was never received, a re-offer is necessary on the ground that the letter was not held incompetent, but was excluded simply because no foundation was laid for its admission.

Where an offer is excluded on the grounds of immateriality and the court indicates that no evidence of that character will be received, it is not necessary to call all other witnesses and interrogate each one of them in order to preserve the error.[62]

Presence of jury

If the court believes that the offer is not made in good faith or is made simply to improperly influence the jury, the jury may be ordered to retire, or it may be so made that the jury cannot hear.[63] When the offer is equivalent to a statement of what the answer would have been, the court may properly exclude it completely.[64]

§ 428. General illustrations—Leading questions.

The following are illustrations of different types of objections:

Improper Leading Questions

Illustration

Q. Well, did he tell you to sell the farm for him?

Mr. Opponent: Just a minute. That is objected to as leading and suggestive.

The Court: The objection is sustained.

62 Bartholomew v. Davis, 276 Ill. 505.

63 Litsinger v. Panhandle & S. F. R. Co., 286 S. W. 1107 (Tex.); Curtis v. McAuliffe, 288 Pac. 675, 106 Cal. App. 1; Starks v. O'Hara, 165 N. E. 127, 266 Mass. 310; Schabel v. Onseyga Realty Co., 251 N. Y. S. 280, 233 App. Div. 208; Carroll County v. O'Connor, 35 N. E. 1006, 37 N. E. 16, 137 Ind. 622; Maxwell v. Habel, 92 Ill. App. 510.

64 People v. Rosenbaum, 299 Ill. 93.

Another Illustration

Q. Was there anything ever said by Ralph Christian to you about the weight of this cast being from 1,100 to 1,300 pounds?

Mr. Opponent: I object to the form of the question. It is leading and suggestive.

The Court: Sustained.

§ 429. — Exhausting recollection.

Questions which direct the witness' attention to certain subjects are permissible when recollection of the witness has been exhausted. The request for permission to use direct or leading questions should be addressed to the court and the purpose announced, namely, to refresh the recollection of the witness.[64a]

§ 430. — Proper direct or leading question.

Illustration

Witness: He told me I did not have to worry about the account, that his claim would be paid in full; that he had a note with the bank and he was going to offset his claim against the bank against their claim to the note. Otherwise our company did not have to worry for payment thereof. We had a general conversation, but that, I would say, would be the meat of the conversation, that he wanted to see his lawyer before we could go ahead with such a proposition. *That is all that I recall of that conversation.*

Counsel: What did he say, if anything, in reference to losing on the transaction?

Opponent: I object to that as leading.

Counsel: I have exhausted his recollection.

The Court: He has exhausted his recollection. He has a right to ask him that. It may stand.

Witness: He told me that I would not lose anything.

§ 431. Counsel assuming facts in question.

Illustration

Q. And he wanted you to give him the combination of the safe, didn't he?

64a See Leading Questions, pp. 258–259n (where the memory of the witness is exhausted).

Mr. Opponent: I object to the form of the question. It assumes facts and is leading and suggestive.

The Court: Sustained.

§ 432. Not responsive to question.

Illustration

When I saw Fugate working on the wedge it was down.

Q. Down where?

A. Well, the bolt was screwed out, I imagine. (Motion to strike out answer as not responsive, sustained.)

Another Illustration

Q. What would happen if you double that dose to a patient?

A. Well, that is a larger dose than ordinarily is administered.

Counsel: I move that the answer be stricken, as not responsive.

The Court: It may be stricken.

Objection to non-responsive answer can be made only by the party examining the witness;[65] if the answer is proper, the examining party has the right to let it stand if he chooses,[66] and it cannot be stricken on the objection of the adverse party.[67] Where a party asks to have a part of an answer stricken, which is done, he is bound by the part which remains.[68]

§ 433. No foundation for conversation.

Illustration

Counsel: Did you see your prescription there?

A. I did.

Q. What was said about the drug that went into it?

65 In re Hoyt's Estate, 163 N. W. 430, 180 Iowa 1250; In re Dunahugh's Will, 107 N. W. 925, 130 Iowa 692; Merkle v. Bennington Tp., 24 N. W. 776, 58 Mich. 156, 55 Am. R. 666; Hamilton v. People, 29 Mich. 173; Jones v. New York Cent., etc., R. Co., 61 N. Y. S. 721, 46 App. Div. 470.

66 Holzer v. Read, 13 P. (2d) 697, 216 Cal. 119; In re Dunahugh's Will, 107 N. W. 925, 130 Iowa 692; Merkle v. Bennington Tp., 24 N. W. 776, 58 Mich. 156, 55 Am. R. 666.

67 Barnett v. Chicago City Ry. Co., 167 Ill. App. 87; In re Hoyt's Estate, 163 N. W. 430, 180 Iowa 1250; Reagan v. Manchester St. R. Co., 56 A. 314, 72 N. H. 298.

68 People v. Wilkinson, 14 N. Y. S. 827.

Mr. Crowe: I object. He is asking about a conversation this witness had with somebody, I don't know who it was. I object unless we fix who it was and where, when and who was present.

The Court: Objection sustained.

Another Illustration

The Witness: I remember meeting Mr. McQueeny there.

Q. Well, what did you talk about?

Opponent: I object to that, your honor, no foundation laid for its admission.

The Court: Objection sustained.

§ 434. Double questions.

Illustration

Q. Did you have anything with you at that time? What did you do or say to Mr. Farmer?

Opponent: I object to that. That is a double question.

The Court: Sustained.

§ 435. Hearsay.

Illustration

Witness: I heard that Mr. Simons had gone away.

Counsel: I object to the hearsay.

The Court: Sustained.

Another Illustration

Witness: Mr. Simons told me that Mrs. Simons was on her way there.

Counsel: I object to what somebody else told her outside of the presence of the defendant. It is hearsay.

The Court: Sustained.

§ 436. Indefinite term.

Illustration

Witness: There was an *unusual* condition there.

Opponent: I object. The word unusual is an indefinite term.

The Court: Yes, sustained.

§ 437. Characterizing conclusion.

Illustration

Q. What was the next thing that you noticed after that?
A. I couldn't see, I couldn't hear, it was a terrible pressure in my head, and I was sick, *terribly sick* all over.
Q. How do you mean? That doesn't mean anything. How did you feel?
A. Well, I was, oh, *deathly sick*.
Q. I can't hear you; what?
A. I was just *deathly sick*.
Opponent: I move to strike out the characterization of it.
The Court: Yes, that may go out.

§ 438. Conclusions.

Illustration

The Witness (continuing): I went over there to his place —he evidently didn't know I was coming.

(Motion by defendants to strike "he didn't know I was coming" as a conclusion, sustained.)

Another Illustration

Witness: Concerning the next occurrence with reference to this transaction, well, she came down to the store one day and made a *terrible rumpus* down there.

("Terrible rumpus" stricken out on motion of defendants.)

Other Illustrations

He agreed.
He admitted.
It was understood.

§ 439. Document speaks for itself.

Illustration

Counsel: I want to ask you, Mr. Bright, whether under this agreement it was necessary for you to obtain any and all escrow receipts which you had issued or which you held?

Opponent: I object. If it was, it was in the document itself.

The Court: I will sustain the objection.

Counsel: Mr. Bright, this escrow receipt of January 11, 1927, had to be returned?

A. Yes.

Q. It had to be returned under this agreement to the Montreal Trust Co.?

Opponent: I object to that. The agreement speaks for itself.

The Court: Yes, the form of the question is objectionable.

Another Illustration

Q. When were you to pay the note?

Counsel: I object—the note speaks for itself.

The Court: Sustained.

§ 440. Best and secondary evidence.

Illustration

Q. Do you know whether the books and records of the John Fox Co. show any sales of sugar owned by them in the month of August to Simmons & Co.?

Mr. Opponent: I object—the books are the best evidence.

The Court: Sustained.

§ 441. Parol evidence rule—Exceptions thereto.

A written contract cannot be varied, contradicted, or modified by parol evidence of anything that occurred at or prior to the time when such contract was executed.[69]

Date

Parol evidence is admissible to show date of a contract.[70]

69 Pierce v. Avakian, 167 Cal. 330, 139 Pac. 799; Goodno v. Hotchkiss, 88 Conn. 655, 92 Atl. 419; Roberts v. Dazey, 284 Ill. 241, 119 N. E. 910; Schlosser v. Nicholson, 184 Ind. 283, 111 N. E. 13; Farrell v. Wallace, 161 Iowa 528, 143 N. W. 488; Com. Trust Co. v. Coveney, 200 Mass. 379, 86 N. E. 895; Boston, etc., Co. v. Pontiac Clothing Co., 199 Mich. 141, 165 N. W. 856; Lese v. Lamprecht, 196 N. Y. 32, 89 N. E. 365; Furnace, etc., Co. v. Heller Bros., 84 Oh. St. 201, 95 N. E. 771; Cauble v. Worsham, 96 Tex. 86, 70 S. W. 737; State v. Steber, 161 Wis. 576, 155 N. W. 146; Robbs v. Herkel, 200 Ill. App. 471.

70 Gately v. Irvine, 51 Cal. 172; Lambe v. Manning, 171 Ill. 612, 49 N. E. 509; Hindenlang v. Mahon, 225

Part in writing

Where only part of a contract is reduced to writing and the part so reduced is merely a partial execution of a part of an entire agreement, the whole agreement may be proven.[71]

Subsequent agreements

Parol evidence is admissible to show contracts under seal have been released, abrogated, cancelled and surrendered by an executed parol agreement, and the question whether a sealed contract is so abrogated is a question for the jury.[72]

Waiver

A waiver need not be shown by an express agreement between the parties; it may be established by their acts and conduct with respect thereto. It may be inferred from facts and circumstances sufficiently indicating an intention to waive, and a new consideration is not essential.[73]

Contract not intended binding

Parol evidence is competent to show that an instrument was never intended to become operative.

The rule that parol evidence of contemporaneous agreement is not admissible to contradict or vary terms of a valid written agreement is not infringed by the introduction of parol evidence which shows that the instrument never had a legal existence or binding force.[74]

Mass. 445, 114 N. E. 684; Germania Bank v. Distler, 64 N. Y. 642; Perry v. Smith, 34 Tex. 277; Schaeppi v. Slade, 195 Ill. 62.

71 Whittier v. Los Angeles, etc., Bank, 161 Cal. 311, 119 Pac. 92; Caulfield v. Hermann, 64 Conn. 325, 30 Atl. 52; Mason v. Griffith, 281 Ill. 246, 118 N. E. 18; Matson v. Mitchell, 156 N. W. 838 (Iowa); Studwell v. Bush Co., 206 N. Y. 416, 100 N. E. 129; Magnolia, etc., Co. v. Davis, 108 Tex. 422, 195 S. W. 184.

72 Arpo v. Ferguson, 175 Cal. 646, 166 Pac. 803; Snow v. Greisheimer, 220 Ill. 106, 77 N. E. 110; Amer. Food Co. v. Halstead, 165 Ind. 633, 76 N. E. 251; O'Brien v. Peck, 198 Mass. 50, 84 N. E. 325; Grand Traverse, etc., Exch. v. Thomas Canning Co., 200 Mich. 95, 166 N. W. 878; Tyson v. Post, 108 N. Y. 217, 15 N. E. 316; Self v. King, 28 Tex. 552.

73 Union Trust Co. v. Best, 160 Cal. 263, 116 Pac. 737; Mallow v. Estes, 179 Ind. 267, 278, 100 N. E. 836; Duplanty v. Stokes, 103 Mich. 630, 61 N. W. 1015; Gilson v. Boston Realty Co., 82 Conn. 383, 73 Atl. 765; Brady v. Cassidy, 145 N. Y. 171, 39 N. E. 814; Mars v. Morris, 48 Tex. C. A. 216, 106 S. W. 430; Globe Brewing Co. v. Amer. Malt Co., 152 Ill. App. 194.

74 Wiltse v. Fifield, 143 Iowa 332, 121 N. W. 1086; Woodard v. Walker, 192 Mich. 188, 158 N. W. 846; Pech-

Fraud and deceit

Misrepresentations made to induce execution of contract may be proved by parol evidence, notwithstanding the terms of contract may be reduced to writing. In such a case, the action is not upon the contract, but upon the representations and deceit. Fraud is not extinguished by the covenants.[75]

Proof of fraud may be made by facts and circumstances which raise the inference that fraud was perpetrated.[76]

Consideration

Where suit is brought upon a simple contract, resort may be had to parol evidence for purpose of impeaching consideration.[77]

The statements as to amount and receipt of consideration in a deed are formal recitals, the legal operation is to prevent a resulting trust and may be explained, varied or contradicted by parol evidence.

Construction of parties

Where a contract is silent, doubtful or ambiguous, it is proper to show the interpretation put upon it by the parties themselves.[78]

Receipt

Parol evidence is admissible to explain, vary or contradict

ner v. Phoenix Ins. Co., 65 N. Y. 195; Rush v. Amarillo First Nat. Bk. (Tex.), 160 S. W. 609; Van Norman v. Young, 129 Ill. App. 542.

75 Venture, etc., Co. v. Warfield, 174 Pac. 382 (Cal.); Grubb v. Milan, 249 Ill. 456; Franke v. Kelsheimer, 180 Iowa 251, 163 N. W. 259; McLaughlin v. Thomas, 86 Conn. 252, 85 Atl. 370; Solomon v. Stewart, 184 Mich. 506, 151 N. W. 716; Callanan v. Keeseville, etc., R. Co., 199 N. Y. 268, 92 N. E. 747; U. S. Gypsum Co. v. Shields, (Tex.), 106 S. W. 724.

76 Swift v. Yanoway, 153 Ill. 197.

77 Roger v. Kelly, 174 Cal. 70, 161 Pac. 1148; Reddington v. Blue, 168 Iowa 34, 149 N. W. 933; Way v. Greer, 196 Mass. 237, 81 N. E. 1002; Stotts v. Stotts, 198 Mich. 605, 165 N. W. 761; Keuka College v. Ray, 167 N. Y. 96, 60 N. E. 325; Groves v. Groves, 65 Oh. St. 442, 62 N. E. 1044; Taylor v. Merrill, 64 Tex. 494; Robinson v. Yetter, 238 Ill. 320; Lloyd v. Sandusky, 203 Ill. 621.

78 Balfour v. Fresno, etc., Co., 109 Cal. 22, 41 Pac. 876; Cravens v. Eagle Cotton Mills Co., 120 Ind. 6, 21 N. E. 981; Whidden v. Jordan, 215 Mass. 189, 102 N. E. 436; Barney v. Forbes, 118 N. Y. 580, 23 N. E. 890; Converse v. Langshaw, 81 Tex. 275; Con. Coal Co. v. Schneider, 163 Ill. 393.

a receipt and this though plaintiff is suing for balance after giving receipt in full.[79]

§ 442. Vary a written instrument by parol.

Illustration

Q. Now, after you had been up in the property of the Gold Mining Syndicate and you had these various conversations which you just explained to the jury, did you ever come to any agreement with Mr. Ross contrary or different than the agreement which is shown by the contract of May 10, 1926?

Opponent: I object to that as attempting to vary the terms of a written instrument by parol.

The Court: Sustain the objection.

§ 443. Merged in contract.

Illustration

Witness: I had previously signed contracts with the Blank Piano Co. Mr. Lawton called me on the last day of December, 1927, and said in order to make his quota he would like me to sign a contract for that piano.

Counsel: I object to that conversation prior to the signing of the contract.

The Court: Sustained. I rather think that a detailed history of what went on before is not competent because it is merged in the contract.

§ 444. Offers of compromise—In general.

A proposition made by one party to the other simply for the purpose of effecting a compromise is not binding unless

79 Carpenter v. Markham, 172 Cal. 112, 155 Pac. 644; Butler v. Hamburg, etc., Bank, 173 Iowa 659, 155 N. W. 999; Seeley v. Osborne, 220 N. Y. 416, 116 N. E. 97; Pool v. Chase, 46 Tex. 207; Atherton v. Shelly, 217 Ill. App. 419; McKinnie v. Lane, 230 Ill. 544. (Some states contra.)

accepted and cannot be shown on trial as evidence of an admission of facts.[80]

Letters containing offer of compromise are inadmissible.[81]

Illustration

Witness: We met again the following week at Thompson's office and tried to settle the matter.

Counsel: I object to any conversation in reference to any settlement or attempt to compromise.

The Court: Sustained.

Another Illustration

Witness: Mr. Livingston called me up and wanted to know if we would pay anything to compromise the case, and I wrote the company and got $100 and submitted the offer to them, and after that, I had another conversation with him in which he said he would take $120 which was $120 and costs.

Opponent: I object on the grounds that an offer of compromise is not admissible.

The Court: Sustained.

Counsel: And I move that the answer be stricken and the jury directed to disregard it.

The Court: It will be stricken and the jury will disregard the answer.

§ 445. —Voluntary admissions.

Admissions of independent facts, though made in negotiating compromise, are competent.[82]

80 Dennis v. Bolt, 30 Cal. 247; Fowles v. Allen, 64 Conn. 350, 30 Atl. 144; Schultz v. Starr, 180 Iowa 1319, 164 N. W. 163; Barker v. Bushnell, 75 Ill. 220; Strauss v. Skurnik, 227 Mass. 173, 116 N. E. 404; Crane v. Ross, 168 Mich. 623, 135 N. W. 83; Bradley v. McDonald, 218 N. Y. 351, 113 N. E. 340; International, etc., R. Co. v. Ragsdale, 67 Tex. 24, 2 S. W. 515.

81 Sanford v. John Finnegan Co. (Tex.), 169 S. W. 624; Harrison v. Trickett, 57 Ill. App. 515; Knowles v. Crampton, 55 Conn. 336, 11 Atl. 593; Pelton v. Schmidt, 104 Mich. 345, 62 N. W. 552.

82 Rose v. Rose, 112 Cal. 341, 44 Pac. 658; Sipes v. Barlow, 197 Ill. App. 239; Louisville, etc., R. Co. v. Wright, 115 Ind. 378, 16 N. E. 145; Ewing v. Hatcher, 175 Iowa 443, 154 N. W. 869; Durgin v. Somers, 117 Mass. 55; Wallace v. Noble, 168 N. W. 984 (Mich.); Manhattan, etc., Co. v. White Co., 78 Misc. 401, 138 N. Y. S. 314; International, etc., R. v. Ragsdale, supra.

Independent admissions, made during negotiations to compromise, are competent unless expressly stated made in confidence or without prejudice.[83]

In an action for breach of contract, a declaration by defendant before the controversy arose that "he claimed that I owed him two hundred fifty dollars; I claimed that I owed him two hundred dollars" held to be an admission of an independent fact and not a statement made in an effort to compromise.

§ 446. Customary method.

Illustration

Witness: I mopped the floor and put down cardboard to prevent people from slipping.

Q. And is that the usual customary method that you had pursued in the care of premises of a similar character?

Mr. Opponent: I object, your Honor.

A. Yes, sir.

Counsel: Under similar conditions?

Mr. Opponent: I object and move to strike the answers.

The Court: Sustained. The answers will be stricken.

§ 447. Making of one specific objection as waiver of all other objections.

Illustration

Counsel: I ask this be marked Defendant's Exhibit 8 for identification and I offer this carbon copy in evidence as Defendant's Exhibit 8.

Mr. Opponent: I object. This document is not competent under the issues here.

The Court: May I see the document, please? It may be objectionable on the ground that no foundation has been shown for the admission of secondary evidence but I will overrule the objection on the grounds you have stated. The document will be received in evidence.

83 Alminowicz v. People, 117 Ill. App. 415; Bowers v. Hanna, 101 Iowa 660, 70 N. W. 745; White v. Old Dominion S. S. Co., 102 N. Y. 660, 6 N. E. 289; Sanford v. Finnegan (Tex.), 169 S. W. 624.

§ 448. Conjectural.

Illustration

Q. If there is a scar in the cornea at the place where you removed the pterygium—if there is a scar at that point today, it could be found by a specialist looking at that eye?

(Objection by defendant as to the form of the question as to what a specialist could find in the opinion of the witness, as being conjectural.)

§ 449. Incompetent witness.

(Wife as Witness—In Some States)

Illustration

Q. What is your name?
A. Mary Jones.
Q. Where do you live?
A. I live at 4080 Lunt Avenue.
Q. You are related in some way to the defendant, John Jones?
A. I am his wife.
Opponent: Your Honor, please, I object to any testimony by this witness. She is incompetent to testify.
The Court: She is his wife, is she?
Counsel: Yes, we are tendering her as a witness—
The Court: Call another witness.
Counsel: All right, step down.

(Note: An incompetent witness should always be offered as a witness even though you know your opponent will object to his testifying, for the psychological effect on the jury.)

§ 450. —Statutory provisions.

In some states, the husband or wife of a party to a suit is declared incompetent to testify with some exceptions as follows:

Husband and wife. No husband or wife shall, by virtue of Section 1 of this act, be rendered competent to testify for or against each other as to any transaction or conversation occurring during the marriage, whether called as a witness during the existence of the marriage, or after its dissolution, except in cases where the wife would, if unmarried, be plaintiff or defendant, or where the cause of action grows out of a personal wrong or injury done by one to the other or grows out of the neglect of the husband to furnish the wife with a suitable support; and except in cases where the litigation shall be concerning the separate property of the wife, and suits for divorce; and except also in actions upon policies of insurance of property, so far as relates to the amount and value of the property alleged to be injured or destroyed, or in actions against carriers, so far as relates to the loss of property and the amount and value thereof, or in all matters of business transactions where the transaction was had and conducted by such married woman as the agent of her husband, in all of which cases the husband and wife may testify for or against each other, in the same manner as other parties may, under the provisions of this act: Provided, that nothing in this section contained shall be construed to authorize or permit any such husband or wife to testify to any admissions or conversations of the other, whether made by him to her or by her to him or by either to third persons, except in suits or causes between such husband and wife.

However, in some states, amendments have been passed to modify the above restrictions as follows:

"In all civil actions, husband and wife may testify for or against each other, provided that neither may testify as to any communication or admission made by either of them to the other or as to any conversation between them during coverture, except in actions between such husband and wife, and in actions where the custody or support of their children is directly in issue, and as to matters in which either has acted as agent for the other."

§ 451. Objections must be made in time.

Illustration

Q. Had you ever had any experience in gold mines?
A. None whatsoever.
Q. Did you ever see one before?
A. No, sir.
Q. Did you know anything about them?
A. Not a thing.

Opponent: I object, if your Honor please, to the last three questions and the answers thereto because they have absolutely no bearing upon this contract or this case.

The Court: I will let it stand.

Q. Have you ever had any opportunity to dispose of those units or any stock at any price?

A. No, sir.

Opponent: May it please the Court, I, at this time want the record to show that I want to object to the last three questions and the answers thereto because they are purely conclusions of the witness and do not say what he did in order to sell them or anything leading to that opportunity to sell.

The Court: The objection is overruled, you should have objected in time.

§ 452. General objections.

Illustration

Q. Is this a true and correct carbon copy?

A. Yes, sir.

Counsel: I offer this carbon copy in evidence as Plaintiff's Exhibit 4.

Opponent: I object to the question, I object to the answer, if your Honor please, on the ground that they are absolutely *immaterial, unnecessary and irrelevant* in this case.

The Court: Overruled.

(Note: There should have been a specific objection as to failure to lay proper foundation.)

§ 453. Variance.

An answer in garnishment was "no funds." The garnishee offered proof that it (a bank) had charged off the deposit against the indebtedness. To this proof counsel made an objection that it was "incompetent, irrelevant, immaterial, vague and indefinite."

The Court held in Levinson v. Home Bank & Trust Company, 337 Ill. 241 on page 245 that "This objection did not go to the question of variance but was general in its nature." (Note: There should have been a specific objection of variance.)

§ 454. Not bearing on issues.

Illustration

Q. What was this check issued for?

A. It was issued to assist in carrying on or to raise some funds to pay some of the obligations that Acadia had acquired and had remained unpaid at that time. We appealed to meet the payroll and such things as that, a lumber bill.

Opponent: May it please the Court, just a moment. I object to the question, I object to the answer, on the ground that it has absolutely no bearing on the suit whatsoever.

The Court: Sustained.

§ 455. Immaterial.

Illustration

Counsel (to witness on direct examination): What was the reason, Mr. Christnelly that you were pushing out the steel erection work towards the piers before the piers were completed?

Opponent: I object. The reason is immaterial.

Court: Sustained.

§ 456. Alternative questions.

Illustration

Q. And what happened to the Ford after it was pushed over on the car tracks?

A. What happened to the Ford?

Q. Yes. Did it remain standing up or stay there, or what happened to it?

A. It stayed there for a short while. The street car came up after the truck had pulled over to the side.

Q. Just describe how this truck came out, Mr. Witness. What I mean is this: When it was in the runway, was it pointing straight at the building or was it slanting?

Opponent: If the Court please, I object to counsel giving an alternative in each question. Almost every question he has put to this witness has been in the alternative, was it one way or the other, giving him a choice, instead of letting him tell.

The Court: Objection sustained.

§ 457. Privileged communications.

(Cross-Examination)

Illustration

Opponent: Now what did you tell your lawyer about that?

Counsel: I object, your Honor, what he told his former lawyer is privileged and counsel knows it.

Court: Sustained.

§ 458. Self-serving documents.

Self-serving documents should be objected to and as a rule are not admissible in evidence.

Illustration

Opponent: I offer this letter, Plaintiff's Exhibit 4 for identification in evidence as Plaintiff's Exhibit 4. (The letter was taken from Koban v. Gordon Supply Co., 253 Ill. App. 569.)

Mr. Adolph Koban,
440 S. Dearborn St.
Chicago, Illinois.
Gentlemen:

This letter is to confirm a personal conversation our Mr. Ben Gordon had with your Mr. Adolph Koban and Mr. M. A. Getz when you were at our yard a few days ago, which was that your Mr. Adolph Koban said to our Mr. Ben Gordon that any money or account the Great Lakes Iron & Metal Co. owes the Gordon Supply Co. is to be charged to Adolph Koban and he will pay for same. Any scrap iron now on hand belonging to the Great Lakes Iron & Metal Co. is to be invoiced to Adolph Koban in the usual way and as was told and instructed by Mr. Adolph Koban that our future transactions should continue on the same ledger account of the Great Lakes Iron & Metal Co. with the exception that we should change the name to Adolph Koban and continue the same as before. We shall also immediately mail you a statement of the account (of the Great Lakes Iron & Metal Co.) as of July 1, 1926. If the above is not in accordance with our conversation we shall expect an answer by return mail, otherwise we shall consider this above confirmed.

Yours very truly,
GORDON SUPPLY CO.
BENJ. GORDON

Counsel: I object, your Honor, the letter is self-serving.
The Court: Sustained.

§ 459. Where insurance company defends.

It is improper in personal injury cases and in all cases where an insurance company is defending, to inform the jury of that fact. It will immediately warrant the court, on proper motion, to declare a mistrial, withdraw a juror and continue the case. However, as appears in the following illustration, where an indefinite, general, inadvertent reference is made, the courts are loath to allow such a motion.

Illustration
(Cross-Examination)

Q. Now, besides Dr. Ingraham, did any other doctor call on you? Was Doctor Ingraham the only doctor that called on you from November until April?
A. There was. It was the insurance doctor.
Q. He came out?
A. He came out to see me.
Q. What was it? What is his name?
A. I don't know his name.
Q. Now, how long were you home?
A. I was home all the time.
Opponent: I move, at this time, if the Court please, as this was not responsive to my question—
Counsel: He said he was home all the time.
The Court: Temporarily we will deny it.
Opponent: I move to withdraw a juror and continue the case.
The Court: Yes, I know.

Later

Opponent: Let the record show that at the close of plaintiff's evidence, I wish to renew my motion to withdraw a juror and continue the case, on the ground of this insurance being mentioned by the plaintiff himself.

The Court: No, that is not grounds enough. It did not get far enough so that the court can do that.

(Discussion.)

The Court: It was so slight and apparently unnoticed by the jury that I do not think that in any way they got the point at all, when he said it was the insurance company's doctor—certainly not—unless they know all about these cases, and they do not. They don't know about any of them, about these cases.

The Court: Well, the motion, which is renewed, of course, is denied. I do not think it amounts to anything in this case. Are you going ahead?

Opponent: Yes.

§ 460. Cross-examination of or impeaching own witness.

Illustration

Witness (on direct examination): I did not see the accident.

Counsel: Didn't you tell me that you did see the accident?

Opponent: I object, your Honor, he is trying to impeach his own witness.

The Court: Yes—sustained.

§ 461. Arguing with witness.

Illustration

Q. That does not mean anything to me. Can't you describe what you mean by alignment?

A. Yes, sir.

Q. What is it?

A. That is the expression we use, the alignment of the box.

Q. I don't care what you use.

Opponent: We object to counsel arguing with this witness, if the Court please.

Q. Can you tell this jury what you mean by alignment of the box so that we will know what you are talking about?

Opponent: I object to that highly improper form of question.

The Court: Sustained.

Another Illustration

Q. You never told counsel about this jerk or you never talked to anybody about your testimony?

A. No.

Q. Don't you know you aren't telling the truth?

Opponent: I object to that.

Court: Sustained.

§ 462. "What is the fact"?

A frequently objectionable question sometimes put to a witness by defense counsel after plaintiff's witnesses have testified to a certain fact and the attorney for the defendant assumes in his question that his witnesses know the facts and are the only ones testifying to the truth is usually in the following form:

Q. *What is the fact* as to whether or not the stairway at the time that you got there was passable, that is, could a person have gone up and down it?

Mr. Opponent: I object, if the Court please, to the form of the question. It assumes that this witness is the only one who knows the fact; it calls for a conclusion and invades the province of the jury. That is one of the questions the jury is called to pass upon.

The Court: Sustained.

§ 463. In some states it is objectionable to introduce exhibits on cross-examination.

Illustration

Witness (cross-examination): I do not remember seeing the instrument which you now show me. The signature to that document is mine. (Document marked Defendant's Exhibit 3 for identification.)

Counsel: I want to introduce this into evidence as Defendant's Exhibit 3. You can look at it now.

Opponent: Before looking at it, I object to it; I object to the introduction at this time because this is not the time for the defendant to introduce documentary evidence. Cannot introduce exhibits on cross-examination.

The Court: Sustained.

CHAPTER IX

THE EXPERT WITNESS

§ 464. Opinion evidence.

The complexities of modern civilization in recent years have made necessary an exception to the general rule that witnesses should testify as to facts and not to opinions. As we know, the opinions of witnesses are, in general, irrelevant.[1] To this general rule, there are, however, important exceptions. One of these is opinion evidence. Evidence of this character is usually held admissible upon subjects that are not within the knowledge of all men of common education and experience. Opinion evidence is said to be admissible from necessity, as the best evidence, under certain circumstances, possible to be obtained. In many cases, where the subjects under investigation are wholly unfamiliar to the jury, if expert testimony were rejected, there could be no adequate way of arriving at a satisfactory conclusion. Because of this, courts have adopted the rule of admitting the opinions of witnesses whenever the subject matter of inquiry is such that inexperienced persons are unlikely to prove capable of forming a correct judgment upon it without such assistance. While it is often difficult to draw the line between legitimate inference and bare conjecture, only such inferences may be drawn as are rational and natural. Mere surmise or conjecture is never regarded as proof of a fact and the jury will not be allowed to base a verdict thereon. No one is permitted to testify what he has never learned, whether it be ordinary or scientific facts. If a witness has not sufficient and adequate means of knowledge, his evidence should not be considered.

1 Cameron v. Ayers, 175 Cal. 662, 166 Pac. 801; Inter-State Finance Corp. v. Com. Jewelry Co., 280 Ill. 116, 117 N. E. 440; Gardner v. Kiburz, 168 N. W. 814 (Iowa); Pool v. Montague Tp., 194 Mich. 476, 160 N. W. 549; Goodman v. Caledonian Ins. Co., 222 N. Y. 121, 118 N. E. 523; Swing v. Rose, 75 Oh. St. 355, 79 N. E. 757; Romania v. Boston El. R. Co., 226 Mass. 532, 116 N. E. 218; Tweed v. Western Union Tel. Co., 107 Tex. 247, 166 S. W. 697; 177 S. W. 957.

§ 465. In general.

Expert evidence is not confined to classed and specified professions, but is applicable wherever peculiar skill and judgment applied to a particular subject are required to explain results or trace them to their causes. Expert evidence is admissible when the witnesses offered as experts have peculiar knowledge or experience not common to the world, which renders their opinions, founded on such knowledge or experience, an aid to the court or jury in determining the questions at issue.

§ 466. Sciences and trades.

Experts or persons instructed by experience; or "men of science" may give opinions on questions of science and skill or trade, as to the genuineness of handwriting, the cause of disease and death, the consequences of wounds, the sanity and insanity of persons, or others of like kind.

§ 467. Questions for court.

The question of the qualification of an expert rests largely on the discretion of the trial court. There can be no arbitrary or fixed test but necessarily only a relative one, dependent somewhat upon the subject and the particular witness.[2]

While the question of the competency of witnesses is left largely to the discretion of the trial judge, there is no presumption that a witness is competent to give an opinion, and his competency must be shown.

§ 468. Study.

A witness is not incompetent to testify as an expert by reason of the fact that his special knowledge of that particular subject of inquiry has not been derived from experience or actual observation, but from reading and the study of standard authorities.[3]

2 Vallejo, etc., R. Co. v. Reed Orchard Co., 169 Cal. 545, 147 Pac. 238; Ferguson v. Rochford, 84 Conn. 202, 79 Atl. 177; Graham v. Deuterman, 244 Ill. 124, 91 N. E. 61; Pierce v. Coffee, 160 Iowa 30, 139 N. W. 1092; Barrie v. Quimby, 206 Mass. 259, 92 N. E. 451; Dolan v. Herring, etc., Co., 105 App. Div. 366, 94 N. Y. S. 241; Blackwell v. St. Louis, etc., R. Co., 168 S. W. 52 (Tex.).

3 Thayer v. Tyler, 169 Cal. 671, 147 Pac. 979; Citizens, etc., Co. v. O'Brien, 19 Ill. App. 231; Romona Oolitic Stone

A medical expert, in giving his opinion as an expert, is not confined to opinions derived from his own observation and experience, but may give an opinion based upon information derived from medical books.[4]

§ 469. Subjective symptoms—Pain and suffering.

Plaintiff, in a personal injury case, may testify to subjective symptoms.[5] Attending physician may also testify as to subjective symptoms,[6] but a doctor who is not the attending physician cannot do so.[7]

The attending physician may testify only as to history of *present* pain and suffering *at time of examinations.*[8]

§ 470. Examination solely for purpose of testifying.

A physician may testify even though the examination he made was solely for the purpose of testifying.[9] Such testimony, however, is limited to the examination only, and not to statements made by the patient to him during the examina-

Co. v. Shields, 173 Ind. 68, 88 N. E. 595; Beverley v. Boston El. R. Co., 194 Mass. 450, 80 N. E. 507; Hall v. Murdock, 114 Mich. 233, 72 N. W. 150; Callen v. Collins, 154 S. W. 673 (Tex.); Kath v. Wisconsin Cent. R. Co., 121 Wis. 503, 99 N. W. 217.

4 Siebert v. Peo., 143 Ill. 571.

5 Martin v. Sherwood, 74 Conn. 475, 51 Atl. 526; No. Chi. St. R. Co. v. Cook, 145 Ill. 551, 33 N. E. 958; O'Brien v. Chicago, etc., R. Co., 89 Ia. 644, 57 N. W. 425; Pierpont v. Fifth Ave. Coach Co., 151 App. Div. 40, 135 N. Y. S. 322; Wright v. Ft. Howard, 60 Wis. 119, 18 N. W. 750.

6 Peo. v. Lowen, (Cal.) 42 Pac. 32; Gilmore v. American Tube, etc., Co., 79 Conn. 498, 66 Atl. 4; Peoria Cordage Co. v. State Ind. Board, 284 Ill. 90, 119 N. E. 996; Indiana, etc., Co. v. Jacobs, 167 Ind. 85, 78 N. E. 325; State v. Blydenburg, 135 Iowa 264, 112 N. W. 634; Fleming v. Springfield, 154 Mass. 520, 28 N. E. 910; Leedy v. Hoover, 160 Mich. 449, 125 N. W. 394; Kennedy v. Rochester, etc., R. Co., 130 N. Y. 654, 29 N. E. 141; Wheeler v. Tyler S. E. R. Co., 91 Tex. 356, 43 S. W. 876; Curran v. A. H. Stanger Co., 98 Wis. 598, 74 N. W. 377.

7 Shaughnessy v. Holt, 236 Ill. 485.

8 Atlanta, etc., R. Co. v. Gardner, 122 Ga. 82, 49 S. E. 818; Omberg v. U. S. Mut. Acc. Assoc., 101 Ky. 303, 40 S. W. 909; Barber v. Merriam, 11 Allen (Mass.) 322; West Chicago St. Ry. Co v. Carr, 170 Ill. 478; Declarations as to past pain by the patient to the physician are not admissible. Gulf, etc., R. Co. v. McKinnell, 173 S. W. 937 (Tex.).

9 Eckels v. Bryant, 137 Ill. App. 234; Cronin v. Fitchburg, etc., R. Co., 181 Mass. 202, 63 N. E. 335; International etc., R. Co. v. Williams, 160 S. W. 639 (Tex.)

tion.[10] However, such medical witness has been permitted to testify as to exclamations of pain during the course of the examination, as wincing, for example.[11]

§ 471. Reasons.

Experts are permitted to give reasons for their opinions.[12]

§ 472. Health and physical condition.

Witnesses who are *not* experts, that is, "laymen," may express their opinions as to the physical condition of persons whom they have observed [13]—that is, they may state whether, in their opinion, such persons appear to be in good health, have the ability to perform work, whether they appear to be suffering pain, *are conscious or unconscious*, and in possession of their mental faculties. Nor will the party whose condition is subject of inquiry, be presumed to feign disease, pain or distress, under the condition in which he is ordinarily observed by strangers or his friends and neighbors.[14]

Non-experts may state that plaintiff was sick or in a nervous condition. Note: They may also testify as to sanity, insanity,[15] the value of household furnishings,[16] etc.

10 O'Dea v. Mich. C. R. Co., 142 Mich. 265, 105 N. W. 746; Davidson v. Cornell, 132 N. Y. 228, 30 N. E. 573; Coburn v. Moline, etc., R. Co., 243 Ill. 448.

11 Jones v. Niagara Junction R. Co., 63 App. Div. 607, 71 N. Y. S. 647; St. Louis S. W. R. Co. v. Pruit, 157 S. W. 236 (Tex.); Krakowski v. Aurora, etc., R. Co., 167 Ill. App. 469.

12 Loban v. Boston El. R. Co., 188 Mass. 414, 74 N. E. 633; Boehm v. Detroit, 141 Mich. 277, 104 N. W. 626; Venuto v. Lizzo, 148 App. Div. 164, 132 N. Y. S. 1066; Cincinnati v. Scarborough, 6 Oh. Dec. (Reprint) 874; International, etc., R. Co. v. Williams, 160 S. W. 639 (Tex.); Nielson v. Chicago, etc., R. Co., 58 Wis. 516, 17 N. W. 310; Reclamation, etc., v. Inglin, 31 Cal. App. 495, 160 Pac. 1098; O'Neill v. Beland, 133 Ill. App. 594 (handwriting expert); McCabe v. Swift, 143 Ill. App. 404 (Physician).

13 In re Loveland, 162 Cal. 595, 123 Pac. 801; Atwood v. Atwood, 84 Conn. 169, 79 Atl. 59; Craig v. Trotter, 252 Ill. 228, 96 N. E. 1003; Langdon v. Ahrends, 166 Iowa 636, 147 N.W. 940; O'Neil v. Hanscom, 175 Mass. 313, 56 N. E. 587; Smalley v. Appleton, 70 Wis. 340, 35 N. W. 729; Pullman Co. v. Hoyle, 52 Tex. C. A. 534, 115 S. W. 315; Cannon v. Brooklyn City R. Co., 9 Misc. 282, 29 N. Y. S. 722.

14 Lauth v. Chi. Union Trac. Co., 244 Ill. 244.

15 Mayville v. French, 246 Ill. 435; Jamison v. People, 145 Ill. 357; State v. Wright, 112 Iowa 436, 84 N. W. 541 ("absent-minded"); LaPlante v. Warren Cotton Mills, 165 Mass. 487, 43 N. E. 294 ("bright and quick"); Vivian's Appeal, 74 Conn. 257, 50 Atl. 797 ("easily impressed"); In re Sparks, 198 Mich. 421, 164 N. W. 267; Rankin v. Rankin, 134 S. W. 392 (Tex.); but, contra: In re Snowball, 157 Cal. 301, 107 Pac. 598.

16 Testimony of layman as to value of household furnishings, see page 291.

Witnesses may testify as to whether a person appeared sick or well, and may compare appearances at different times,[17] and state whether assistance was necessary under certain conditions.[18]

§ 473. Facts.

The facts [19] upon which the opinion of the expert is sought must be proved, but they need not be proved by other witnesses if the expert himself has personal knowledge of them, and can, therefore, testify as to those facts from his own personal knowledge. The expert in such case occupies a dual role of fact and expert witness. Where he has personal knowledge of all the facts upon which his opinion is predicated, the hypothetical question may be dispensed with, provided he has previously testified as to those facts.

§ 474. Selection of expert.

With these general principles of law in mind governing opinions of experts, the first important step in the preparation of a case for trial involving expert opinion is the *proper selection* of the expert who is to testify. Failure to use proper discretion in the selection of an expert may result in an unfavorable verdict. Ordinarily it might be supposed that an expert who is a leading authority in his field should be the one to select. While knowledge of the subject is one of the most important considerations, yet, it is but one of many. The expert must be one who has the ability to explain his

17 St. Louis & S. W. R. Co. v. Lowe, 97 S. W. 1087 (Tex.).

18 Salem v. Webster, 192 Ill. 369; West Chicago St. R. Co. v. Kennedy-Cahill, 165 Ill. 496, 46 N. E. 368; Bailey v. Centerville, 108 Iowa 20, 78 N. W. 831. Witness may testify as to intoxication. Bidwell v. Los Angeles, etc., R. Co., 169 Cal. 780, 148 Pac. 197; Ward v. Chicago City R. Co., 237 Ill. 633, 86 N. E. 1111; Ewing v. Hatcher, 175 Iowa 443, 154 N. W. 869; Felska v. N. Y. C. R. Co., 152 N. Y. 339, 46 N. E. 613. When acquainted with handwriting of a person witness may state opinion. Richmond Dredging Co. v. Atchison, etc., R. Co., 31 Cal. App. 399, 160 Pac. 862; McDonald v. McDonald, 142 Ind. 55, 41 N. E. 336; Stone v. Hubbard, 7 Cush. 595 (Mass.); Stretch v. Stretch, 191 Mich. 418, 158 N. W. 185; Sheldon v. Benham, 4 Hill 129 (N. Y.); Dolan v. Meehan, 80 S. W. 99 (Tex.); Putnam v. Wadley, 40 Ill. 346.

19 Witness must state facts on which his opinion is based as far as is possible. Grant v. Thompson, 4 Conn. 203; Teter v. Spooner, 279 Ill. 39, 116 N. E. 673; In re Martin, 166 Iowa 233, 142 N. W. 74; In re Curtis, 190 Mich. 377; In re Campbell, 136 N. Y. S. 1086; Daly v. Whitacre, 207 S.W. 350 (Tex.).

technical subject in language easily understandable to a "layman" jury. He must also be the type of individual who is a student in his field. He should be one who is accustomed to testifying in court, but not one who spends his entire time in court. He should also be the type who believes in proper and thorough preparation before trial, that is, one who looks up his authorities in advance and has them available for the trial attorney for perusal and study, and one who will prepare counsel for the cross-examination of experts presented by the adversary.

Stryker in his book "Courts and Doctors" presents these as the necessary qualifications of a good expert witness:

"First, honesty; second, good character and reputation; third, quick intelligence and attentive ears; fourth, courage—the determination not to be brow-beaten from what he knows to be the truth; fifth, good personality and a presentable appearance; sixth, good manners and tact; and seventh, terseness, the quality of answering briefly and of not volunteering."

§ 475. Qualifying expert.

Since the expert is not permitted to express an opinion unless the trial court is satisfied as to his qualifications, it is necessary to lay the foundation for his testimony by showing that he is competent to express an opinion.[20] This foundation is properly laid by showing that the witness has had the necessary education, training and experience in the particular field which is involved in the law suit. Obviously, if his training and experience does not involve the particular subject in question no weight will be given to his testimony. Any teaching position or university connection, any special research work the witness has done, any books or articles he has written on the subject should be brought out. If he has held any official position with any of the governmental agencies, such as city, county, state or national governments, it should also be made

[20] Peo. v. Lamperle, 94 Cal. 45, 29 Pac. 709; Currelli v. Jackson, 77 Conn. 115, 58 Atl. 762; Peo. v. Jennings, 252 Ill. 534; Isenhour v. State, 157 Ind. 517, 62 N. E. 40; Piehl v. Albany R. Co., 162 N. Y. 617, 57 N. E. 1122; Koons v. State, 36 Oh. St. 195; Wehner v. Lagerfelt, 27 Tex. C. A. 520, 106 S. W. 221; Schantes v. State, 127 Wis. 160, 106 N. W. 237.

known. If he is connected with any particular institutions, hospitals, societies, etc., this should also be shown.

The illustrations in this chapter showing the technique of qualifying various kinds of experts, with some slight variations, should enable the trial lawyer to qualify all classes of witnesses.

§ 476. Admitting qualifications of expert.

Sometimes, when a particularly well-qualified expert is presented as a witness, opposing counsel will make it a practice of immediately, but very quietly, admitting the qualifications of the witness. This serves the purpose of keeping from the jury a full knowledge of just who the witness is and what his standing is in his particular field or profession. If the jury are thus prevented from knowing all about the witness they naturally cannot give his testimony the full consideration it should deserve. Some trial lawyers overcome this admission by their opponents by stating to the court, "I just desire to show the witness' standing to the jury very briefly."

Illustration

Mr. Jones: We will admit the witness' qualifications.

Mr. Simpson: If the Court, please, it may be that some of the jurors are not familiar with Dr. Blank's standing and I would like to have him briefly tell us about his study and experience.

One can easily appreciate the psychological effect on the jury of these few remarks.

§ 477. Qualifying expert by cross-examination of opponent's expert.

Where the lawyer represents the defendant, another method of qualifying his expert is to ask the opponent's expert during cross-examination of him, if he knows his expert, and secure an admission from him that the attorney's expert is recognized as an authority in his field. This has a good psychological effect on the jury, secures approval of his testimony before he testifies, and assures a favorable reception on the part of the court and jury of his expert's testimony as well as proving that he is qualified. This method has also been followed by plaintiff's attorneys in cross-examination of defendant's experts, where plaintiff's experts are outstanding in their field and generally recognized as authorities by their contemporaries.

Illustration

Q. By the way, Doctor, do you know Dr. Jones of Johns Hopkins University Medical School?
A. I certainly do.
Q. Do you consider him an expert on toxicology?
A. I do.

§ 478. The paid expert.

If the expert is being compensated, the lawyer should not wait for opposing counsel to bring out that fact on cross-examination, but should minimize whatever bad effect there might be by bringing it out himself on direct examination. This "steals the other fellow's thunder," and if the expert's testimony is well-founded medically, it helps to eliminate damaging cross-examination as to bias and interest on the part of the opponent. It then appears to be perfectly natural to the jury that the expert is being paid.

Illustration

After name and address and general qualifications:
Q. By the way, doctor, you have been in Chicago since last Monday?
A. Yes, sir.
Q. And I have promised you that you are going to be paid for your time and expenses?
A. Yes, sir, you have.

§ 479. Withdrawing witnesses.

In many instances in large cities where expert witnesses are so busy and compensation for their time runs so high it has become a usual custom for the trial attorney to withdraw "lay" witnesses in the midst of their examination and to put the expert on the stand in his stead to conserve time and expense. There is no absolute right in law on the part of counsel to do this, as generally it is required that each witness complete his testimony, both direct and cross-examination, before another witness is proffered. However, in some jurisdictions, the right to withdraw witnesses is discretionary with the trial court.

Usually, a request in open court, addressed to opposing counsel and the judge, will result in an agreement and stipulation to withdraw a witness to permit an expert to testify. However, this method of "chopping" up testimony is not recommended and should not be utilized unless absolutely necessary. (For illustration as to technique to be employed in withdrawing witness see Direct Examination, page 277.)

§ 480. Methods of qualifying expert witnesses in various fields.

The Doctor—X-Rays, Foundation for Admission—Objective and Subjective Symptoms, Opinions as to Permanency, etc.

Q. Doctor, will you please state your full name to the Court and jury?

A. Arthur C. Jones.

Q. Where do you reside?

A. 1605 Meadow Lane.

Q. What is your profession?

A. Physician and surgeon.

Q. Are you duly licensed to practice as a physician and surgeon in the State of Illinois?

A. I am.

Q. How long have you practiced medicine, Dr. Jones?

A. Thirty-seven years this coming June, next month.

Q. Of what medical school are you a graduate, doctor?

A. I graduated from the Hahnemann Medical College in 1895.

Q. What other study or training did you have?

A. I served one year as interne in the Hahnemann Hospital. Then, after a few years of practice, I took post graduate work in the University of Chicago, Department of Pathology and Bacteriology and in the Chicago Clinical School of Electro-therapeutics; also the graduate department, Harvard University, Boston, some post graduate work in the New York Post Graduate, New York City; I visited the clinics of the Johns Hopkins University, and visited the clinics at Mayo Brothers and various other important centers.

Q. Have you held a teaching position in any medical institution?

A. Yes, I have.

Q. Tell us, briefly, about that.

A. I was instructor in bacteriology and pathology in Hahnemann Medical College.

Q. What do you mean by pathology?

A. Pathology is that portion of medical science which has to do with diseased conditions, especially applying itself to a study of the changes in the tissues; bacteriology has to do with the study of the bacteria, especially in medicine the forms of bacteria that produce disease in the human.

Q. Now, have you taught at any other institutions other than the one you have mentioned?

A. Yes, sir. The Illinois Post Graduate Medical School, where I was a professor of physical diagnosis up until the time of the World War.

Q. As a part of your work, Dr. Jones, have you had experience in the taking and reading of X-ray pictures?

A. I have.

Q. Tell us briefly what your experience along that line has been.

A. I had my first X-ray machine in 1897. It was one of the kind that you handled with a crank, 16 plates of glass, and it took about 2½ to 3 minutes to take a picture of the hand and wrist. I have used the X-ray in my practice from that time until today and at the present time I have a large, modern equipment of X-ray in my office, the Snook type of transformer, and the Victor table, large control stand, and can take pictures with 100,000 volts current.

Q. Have you had occasion in the course of your practice to take and examine X-ray pictures?

A. I have, thousands of them.

Q. What specialty, if any, have you made in your medical practice?

A. Diagnosis.

Q. By diagnosis, you mean what, in the laymen's language?

A. Diagnosis is that department of medical effort which concerns itself particularly with the evaluation of a man's physical condition. It has to do with not only the naming of a disease or ailment from which he may be suffering, but to ascertain the cause of it, the amount of damage which has been done by an ailment, a disease or injury, its course, and in my work, its ultimate recovery.

Q. As a part of your training and in actual practice, have you made a thorough study of the anatomy of the human body?

A. Yes, sir.

Q. Doctor, do you know Mr. Walter B. Casey, the plaintiff in this case?

A. Yes, I do.

Q. Now, Doctor, did you attend and take care of, as *attending* physician, Mr. Walter B. Casey, the plaintiff in this case?

A. Yes, sir, I did.

Q. When did he first become a regular patient of yours, to the best of your recollection?

A. On or about September 23 or 24 of last year, 1931.

Q. What did you do on that occasion, if anything?

A. I made a thorough physical examination of him.

Q. Now, will you just describe the method of examination and technique that you used in examining him?

A. The method of examination consisted, first, a physical examination in which I used my eyes and hands. Second, a chemical and microscopic examination in which I used chemicals and the microscope. Lastly, X-ray examination in which I used my X-ray machine.

Q. Now, doctor, please tell the court and jury what objective findings your examination disclosed?

A. I had him strip naked so that I could observe the movements of all muscles, etc., etc. . . . I found . . .

Q. Now, doctor, tell us what your subjective findings were?

A. I found . . . having him relax and move every joint, the wrist joint, the elbow joint, the shoulder joint, and then after doing that with the upper extremities, I directed my attention to his lower extremities and took his legs and flexed them on his body so that the knee came up almost to the chest.

On the right side, when I did this, *I produced pain as evidenced by a sudden pallor* of the region of the testicles, the scrotum and the contraction of the cremasteric muscle into a firm contractual effort which produces a reaction of all of the muscles, all of the tissues overlying this muscle. When I did the same thing on the left side, I got the same reaction, *a pallor of the surface of the scrotum* and contraction of the cremasteric, *an objective, unmistakable symptom of pain,* and when I brought the knees up toward the chest, there was complaint on his part of extreme pain. This was most marked on the left side, but also present on the right.

Then, because of the complaint of pain in the region of the left hip bone next to the sacrum and shooting down the leg, and also because of the . . .

Q. What did you then do, doctor?

A. I took an X-ray.

Q. Just tell us, what you did.

A. I placed the patient in the standard position upon my X-ray table and proceeded to take stereoscopic films of the pelvis on 14 by 17 films, and after these films were developed in my presence and dried under my control, I examined them in my stereoscope and examined each one of them separately.

Q. Doctor, as I understand, you examined it through the stereoscope?

A. Yes, sir.

Q. What is the stereoscope?

A. The stereoscope is an instrument that we use in observing X-ray films, to reproduce the conditions under which objects are seen with the eye.

The normal man has two eyes placed at a relatively common distance apart, and when he views an object, he sees two images of that object, one with the right eye and one with the left; these two images are coordinated in the brain centers, in the optical centers and visual centers, so he gets the impression of contour and depth as well as breadth and shading, the shading of an object, and in order to reproduce that information regarding the interior of the body, we take two X-ray films with the patient in one position, in a fixed position, the tube on one side being moved from the absolute center the distance which exists from the middle of the nose to the center of the pupil and then make our flash and get our picture. Then we move the tube back to a point which would be similar to our visual center, to the visual center of the left eye, and take another picture. So, that we get a cross-fire, a true perspective, by having these films in a stereoscope.

Now, the stereoscope is an instrument made of two such view boxes as we have here, one set to your left and one set to your right, a mirror in the middle so that the rays of light coming through these illuminated films are reflected to the eye and you get the exact reproduction of the conditions under which the film was made. So that you get depth as well as a flat shadow. This simply shows the film in a flat shadow, what we call in Roentgenological parlance, a flat film.

Q. Doctor did you examine Mr. Casey under the fluoroscope?

A. I did.

Q. What is a fluoroscope?

A. A chemically treated screen used in conjunction with the X-ray machine to show the condition of parts of the body in a darkened room.

Q. Now, Doctor, before you tell us anything about the film perhaps we better have them marked for identification.

(To Court reporter) Please mark these Plaintiff's Exhibits 4 and 5 for identification. (To witness) Now, I hand you Plaintiff's Exhibits 4 and 5 for identification and ask you to state whether or not those are the films you took of Mr. Casey?

A. Yes, these are my films, the ones I took.

Q. By what means do you identify them other than by recognition of the structures?

A. My own private marker, the patient's name and my name, the serial number, the date and my address and a lead letter "R" are all imprinted in the film, being taken at the same time that the shadow of the bones themselves were made.

Q. Now, what type of X-ray machine or apparatus did you use in taking those films?

A. The Snook type transformer with the Victor No. 8 X-ray table and a stabilizer, all standard equipment, manufactured by the General Electric Company.

Q. What was the operative condition of the machine and all of the apparatus at the time those pictures were taken?

A. They were in good working order.

Q. Will you describe the method of technique to the jury that you used in the taking of those films, Plaintiff's Exhibits 4 and 5 for identification?

A. I placed the casette or carrier, which holds the film, and protects them from the daylight, it has an aluminum front window under the patient and in the slide drawer, or a Bucky diaphragm, and the subject, Mr. Casey, was then placed on his back in the hollow of this Bucky diaphragm. He was so placed that he lay absolutely flat on the surface and he was padded around with cushions and pillows so that there would be no strain on his muscular structures and no effort to readjust himself for comfort while the films were being taken.

Then the carrier for the X-ray tube was brought over his body, a distance of 26½ inches from the film, and first centered over the center of the films. Then, locked in that position, except that the little shift for the tube was left free and that tube was shifted first to the left for the first picture and then to the right for the second picture, just the distance which exists between the two pupils of the eyes and in each case when everything was set, the exposure was made by turning on the current and turning it off after the proper number of seconds.

Q. Who developed the films, doctor?

A. They were developed in my presence by my technician in my dark room, and I examined them while they were still wet.

Q. In your opinion, do these films correctly portray that portion of the body or anatomy which they purport to show and which you took?

A. Yes.

Q. Were those films designed to portray tissue itself, or merely the bony structure of the body?

A. Chiefly the bony structure; certain soft tissues are shown, however, in the films.

Q. Is there a different method of technique used in the taking of pictures, for example, of the kidney itself, so as to get the complete outline and position of the kidney?

A. Yes, sir.

Q. Now, are they, in your opinion, clear, workmanlike films?

A. Yes.

Counsel: If the Court please at this time I want to offer these X-ray films being Plaintiff's Exhibits 4 and 5 for identification in evidence as Plaintiff's Exhibits 4 and 5.

The Court: They may be received and so marked.

Q. Doctor, will you take the X-rays, Plaintiff's Exhibits 4 and 5 and interpret them for the Court and jury. Just tell us what they show.[21]

A. Plaintiff's Exhibit 4 shows . . . . Plaintiff's Exhibit 5 shows . . . .

Q. Now, Doctor, from your study of the X-ray films, which you took, from your study of the X-ray pictures Plaintiff's Exhibits 4 and 5 which you have just read, and from your own physical examination, consisting of examination by both palpation, as you have described it, by examination with your eyes and hands and by microscopic examination, did you form an opinion, based upon a reasonable medical certainty, as to what the diagnosis in this case was?

A. I did.

Q. Will you tell us briefly what your complete diagnosis was, based upon your own objective physical examination and your own reading of the X-ray films in question?

A. Laceration of the ligaments and attachments of the left sacro-iliac joint with relaxation of that joint and movement in that joint. And movement, abnormal movement. At the beginning of the treatment, both right and left kidneys were floating and displaced, detached, and this displacement of the kidneys, associated with a tear, or laceration, extending into the pelvis, of the left kidney, with the production of scar tissue in the left kidney, and traumatic nephritis, associated with the appearance in the urine of blood, both as individual corpuscles and blood casts.

21 X-rays may be interpreted and explained to the jury: Dooley v. Chicago City R. Co., 166 Ill. App. 312; State v. Matheson, 142 Iowa 414, 120 N. W. 1036; Marion v. B. G. Coon Const. Co., 157 App. Div. 95, 141 N. Y. S. 647; Missouri, etc., R. Co. v. Coker, 143 S. W. 218 (Tex.).

X-ray is sufficiently identified where a physician testifies that he was present when the exposure was made, that he waited while the plate was taken into the dark room and developed, and that he examined the plate and is positive it is a skiograph of the injured member. Wicks v. Cuneo-Henneberry Co., 319 Ill. 344.

Q. When did you last examine Mr. Casey?

A. The last time was about the 5th of April, this year.

Q. Was there any change in the condition as you have described it, at the time of your last examination?

A. There was some improvement in the condition of the hip. There was . . . the kidneys, with the belt on, and for the time that he would lie on the table, were in normal position, but the changes in the left kidney, as evidenced by the condition of the urine, persistence of tenderness, persistence of spastic contraction of the left lower abdominal quadrant, had not improved.

Q. Have you an opinion, based upon a reasonable medical certainty, from your examination and study of the case, as to whether or not the condition of the hip joint of the left hip as you have described it is temporary or permanent in nature?

A. Yes, sir.

Q. What is your opinion?

A. Permanent.

Q. Doctor, are you acquainted with what the fair, reasonable and customary charge in Chicago, Cook County, Illinois, is for the treatment of patients such as you have described during the year 1931 and 1932? [21a]

A. Yes.

Q. All right, now, tell the Court and jury what the fair, reasonable and customary value of such medical services as you rendered the plaintiff in this case over the entire period of time from last September, when you undertook the treatment, down to the present day, is?

A. About $500.

Q. Is that a fair and reasonable charge?

A. Yes.

Q. Have you an opinion, based on a reasonable medical certainty, as to whether it will be necessary for the plaintiff to continue under medical treatment?

A. Yes, I have an opinion.

Q. What is your opinion?

A. That he will require future medical treatment.

[21a] See Wicks v. Cuneo-Henneberry Co., 319 Ill. 344, where paid physician's bill is involved. Considered prima facie evidence of reasonable charge.

§ 481. Alienist and psychiatrist.

Q. Will you state your full name, please?
A. H. Douglas Singer.
Q. Where do you live?
A. At 6856 Oglesby Avenue.
Q. What is your profession?
A. Physician.
Q. Duly licensed to practice in this state?
A. Yes, sir.
Q. Of what school are you a graduate, doctor?
A. Graduate of the Institute of London, in England.
Q. And what year?
A. 1898.
Q. When were you admitted to practice as a physician and surgeon?
A. In the same year, 1898.
Q. And had you taken any post graduate study of any kind?
A. Yes. I had six years post graduate work in London.
Q. In any particular line, or specialty, doctor?
A. Four years I was in general medicine, and two years in nervous and mental diseases.
Q. How long were you in London?
A. I was born there. I left there in 1904.
Q. And where did you go to?
A. I went to Omaha, Nebraska.
Q. Did you practice as a physician and surgeon there?
A. I practiced as a physician, not as a surgeon.
Q. Have you specialized in any particular branch of medicine?
A. I have.
Q. What is that?
A. Nervous and mental diseases.
Q. And how long have you specialized in nervous and mental diseases?
A. Since 1904, continuously and two years before that in a special hospital in London.
Q. At the special hospital in London, was that for the treatment of nervous and mental diseases?
A. Yes, more nervous than mental.

Q. Now, doctor, have you held any official position with the State of Illinois?
A. I have.
Q. Tell us what, please?
A. I came to Illinois in 1907 as director of the State Psychopathic Hospital.
Q. Located where?
A. At Kankakee, Illinois, on the grounds of the Kankakee State Hospital.
Q. How long were you there, doctor?
A. I was at Kankakee until 1919.
Q. What did you do after that?
A. Then they moved the institute from Kankakee to the Chicago State Hospital at Dunning.
Q. In Chicago, Illinois?
A. Yes, sir.
Q. And what position did you hold there, doctor?
A. I was still director of that same institute.
Q. In charge?
A. Yes, sir.
Q. And how long were you at that place?
A. Until 1921.
Q. And then what did you do, if anything?
A. I entered private practice in the City of Chicago.
Q. Have you written any books on the subject of mental diseases, doctor?
A. I have written one book in conjunction with Dr. William O. Krohn, who is since deceased.
Q. On what subject, doctor?
A. On "Insanity and Law."
Q. Any other books?
A. I have written another one which is not yet published, but is in the press now.
Q. Have you written any papers, or articles for any societies on that subject?
A. Yes, a number of them.
Q. Tell us something about your practice, doctor?
A. Well, I am in practice in the city, in consultation in cases of mental and nervous diseases, see patients in my office; I am an attending psychiatrist at the sanitarium located

in Milwaukee, and also called in consultation in other hospitals, and in patients' homes.

Q. Now, during all your experience with the Kankakee Hospital and the Chicago State Hospital, in these various cases, have you been in active practice and attendance, doctor?

A. Not only those hospitals, but at all of the state hospitals, I had the duty of visiting all of the state hospitals in Illinois and giving instructions to the members of the staff of those hospitals, and I used to have new members and some of the old members of the staff of those hospitals sent to me for a course of instruction.

Q. Have you served in the capacity of instructor anywhere, doctor?

A. I am Professor of Mental Diseases in the University of Illinois Medical School.

Q. At the present time?

A. Yes, sir.

Q. How long have you been there, doctor?

A. I was an associate professor the first time, I think it was 1914, or 1915, until 1920, when I was made full professor and head of the department.

§ 482. Toxicologist.

Q. Doctor, state your name, please?

A. William J. Maxwell.

Q. Where do you live?

A. 3734 North Avenue.

Q. What is your profession?

A. I am a toxicologist and a physician.

Q. Of what medical school are you a graduate, Doctor?

A. I graduated from the University of Michigan and the Rush Medical College.

Q. When did you graduate?

A. I graduated from the University of Michigan in 1905, and 1920 from the Rush Medical College.

Q. And what did you graduate as from the University of Michigan?

A. As a scientist and chemist.

Q. Now, in between—after 1905, what did you do?

A. I was a chemist at the Union Stockyards, Illinois, a chemist.

Q. What company?

A. Armour and Company, and chemist in charge of the laboratories of the National Stockyards, in the stockyards for Armour and Company.

Q. For how long?

A. Until 1908, and in 1908 I came to Chicago as superintendent for a drug company, manufacturers of drug sundries, then became chief chemist at the Health Department until 1913, and in 1913 in June I began as chief coroner and toxicologist for the coroner's office in Cook County.

Q. How long were you connected with the Coroner's office?

A. I was connected with the Coroner's office until March, 1929.

Q. And what were your duties in that connection?

A. My duties were the examination of organs for the presence of poisons and conducted research work regarding poisons, and from 1925 to 1929 I was conducting post mortems as chief coroner's physician.

Q. While you were connected with the Coroner's office, how many organs and bodies have you examined in conducting post mortems there?

A. Well, I have examined the organs of many people that I did not hold post mortems on, in number over ten thousand people that I have examined the organs of as toxicologist for the Coroner's office.

Q. Deceased persons?

A. Deceased persons.

Q. Now, you graduated from Rush Medical College in what year?

A. 1920.

Q. After you graduated from there, what did you do?

A. I still continued in the same line of work, general medicine and internal medicine and toxicology, research work at the Rush Medical College.

Q. Do you hold any teaching position at the present time?

A. I am associate professor of toxicology at the Rush Medical College.

Q. How long have you been so teaching?
A. Since 1913.
Q. Have you written anything on the subject?
A. I have written a number of articles on poisons and their detection; have articles in text books; one with Peterson & Haines on Gaseous Poisons.
Q. What is toxicology?
A. Toxicology is the science that treats of poisons, their origin, and their detection by chemical or other means.
Q. What do you mean by poison?
A. A poison is a substance which when taken into the system is capable of seriously affecting health or causing death, and that is its chief action.

§ 483. Chiropractor.

Q. What is your name, Doctor?
A. Norman Baxter.
Q. Where do you live?
A. 10727 Calumet Avenue.
Q. What is your profession?
A. I am a chiropractic doctor.
Q. Where is your office?
A. 1112 Michigan St.
Q. Are you duly licensed to engage in and practice in the State of Michigan?
A. I am.
Q. Have you attended any professional schools?
A. I have attended the National College of Chiropractics.
Q. Is that school recognized by the State?
A. Yes, it is.
Q. How long did you attend that school, Doctor?
A. Four years of eight months each.
Q. And how long have you been engaged in the practice of chiropractic?
A. Since June, 1926.
Q. By the way, Doctor, may I ask you at this time, just what is the nature of your work?
A. I specialize principally in spine work, occasionally using some adjuncts, such as heat, hydrotherapy, or electrotherapy.

Q. What courses do you have to study, in this school that you attended?

A. We studied anatomy, all branches, chemistry, physical diagnosis, pathology, hygiene, jurisprudence and various other subjects.

Q. Do you get a diploma from this school?

A. Yes, we do.

Q. Did you have to take any competitive examination in order to receive a diploma?

A. Yes, we did.

Q. Did you successfully pass those examinations?

A. Yes, I did.

Q. Did you ever at any time examine the plaintiff, Harry Gordon?

A. Yes, I did.

§ 484. Handwriting expert.[22]

Q. What is your full name, please?

A. Vernon Faxon.

Q. Where do you reside, Mr. Faxon?

A. Wilmette, Ill.

Q. What is your business or profession?

A. I am an examiner of disputed documents.

Q. Just what does your work consist of?

A. I examine and report matters submitted to me concerning the genuineness of a document and matters of disputed typewriting, interlineations, erasures, matters of paper, pens and inks.

Q. How long has that been your profession?

A. I have followed it as a profession since 1920 in Portland, Oregon and Chicago, Illinois.

Q. Do you devote your entire time to this work?

A. Yes. Since I have been in Chicago and for some time before I have devoted my entire time to this work.

Q. Have you had occasion to testify in courts relative to disputed documents?

22 Qualifications generally: Pate v. Peo., 8 Ill. 644; Eisfield v. Dill, 71 Iowa 442, 32 N. W. 420; Dubois v. Baker, 30 N. Y. 355; Dolan v. Meehan, 80 S. W. 99 (Tex.).

A. I have testified in thirty different states and in Cuba and Canada.

Q. What study have you made to prepare yourself as an examiner of disputed documents?

A. I have read all the books in English on the subject of disputed documents and allied subjects, microscopy, paper and paper making, inks, ink manufacture and photography. I have also provided myself with all necessary apparatus, have examined novel and disputed questions of disputed documents for years, interchanged ideas and criticisms with other experts. I maintain an office and laboratory exclusively for this work.

Q. Where is your office?

A. 134 N. LaSalle St., Chicago, Illinois.

Q. Are you able to compare handwriting of known origin with handwriting the origin of which is not known and form an opinion as to whether or not they were written by the same person?

A. Yes, I am.

Q. Have you seen Proponent's Exhibit A?

A. I have.

Q. Did you examine it at any time?

A. Yes, I did. On or about June 22, 1934.

Q. Have you seen Proponent's Exhibit B?

A. I have.

Q. Did you examine it at any time?

A. Yes, I did, at the same time I examined Proponent's Exhibit A.

Q. Have you made an examination and comparison of Proponent's Exhibits A and B for identification for the purpose of determining whether or not in your opinion they were written by the same party?

A. Yes, I have.

Q. From the examination you have made, and based upon your study and experience as an examiner of disputed documents, have you an opinion as to whether or not the signature of James Simpson, appearing on both Exhibits A and B were written by one and the same person?

A. I have an opinion.

Q. What is that opinion?

A. My opinion is that they were written by one and the same person.

Q. Upon what do you base that opinion?

A. On the fact . . .[23]

§ 485. Engineer.

Q. What is your name, please?

A. William Daniels.

Q. Where do you live, Mr. Daniels?

A. 8024 Lafayette Ave.

Q. What is your profession?

A. I am professor of experimental engineering at the Armour Institute.

Q. How long have you been connected with Armour Institute in that capacity?

A. I have been instructor and professor there for eight years.

Q. What is the Armour Institute?

A. Armour Institute is a technical school teaching engineering exclusively.

Q. What kinds of engineering?

A. Mechanical, electrical, civil, fire protection engineering and architecture.

Q. Is it recognized as a school of standing?

A. It is recognized as being second to none.

Q. What professions does it give degrees to?

A. It issues Bachelor degrees and Master degrees in the various engineering branches that I have mentioned; for example, Bachelor of Science in mechanical engineering.

Q. Have you had any experience, professor, with problems of ventilation and exhaust devices?

A. That has been the work which I have specialized in at the Institute. I have charge of the laboratory which does that work.

Q. How long have you specialized in that line of work?

A. Ever since I have been there, eight years.

23 Handwriting expert may testifiy as to: alterations, Vinton v. Peck, 14 Mich. 287; erasures, Dubois v. Baker, 30 N. Y. 355; forgery, Hess v. State, 5 Oh. 5, Dolan v. Meehan, 80 S. W. 99 (Tex.); age of writing, Eisfield v. Dill, 71 Ia. 442, 32 N. W. 420.

Q. What is the general aim and object of that work, professor?

A. In ventilation, one object is to provide sufficient supply of air, oxygen, to maintain health, but, in the industries it is used in addition to remove impurities that may be created by the work.

Q. Have you ever had occasion to examine plants or make studies and reports and observations as to problems for various manufacturers in different parts of the country?

A. Under the direction of Prof. Gebhardt, who has charge of all that work, we do that frequently.

Q. About how many such reports have you made, professor, and examinations in the course of the last eight years?

A. Well, I would say possibly fifty or so.

Q. That brought you in contact with different varieties of plants?

A. Yes.

Q. Now, generally speaking, professor, are you familiar with ventilation and exhaust problems connected with the use of emery paper or emery cloth?

A. Yes.

Q. What is the problem presented wherever emery is used in connection with metal?

A. Whenever emery or any other abrasive substance is used in connection with metal, there is dust created which is generally considered a hazard to the health, and the problem consists of installing some system to remove that dust or use precautions to prevent it or settle it by means of a liquid or keeping it moist.

Q. Now, can you state, professor, whether or not there has been for the last ten years any approved and accepted device for dealing with dust wherever emery and metal come in contact with a revolving surface?

A. Why, in such a case, as in most cases where dust is produced by a machine, by the operation on a machine, where it is reasonably well concentrated, it has been the common practice for many years to use an exhaust fan or commonly called a blower to carry a stream of air over the work in such a way that it will carry with it the dust.

Q. Now, in a room where there are, say, fifteen or twenty machines of metal spinning variety, together with a number of other mechanisms, but where the metal spinning machines are used part of the time only, for the purpose of polishing by means of emery various metals such as brass, aluminum and steel with an emery cloth. Have you an opinion as to what would be the proper, accepted and approved device for the general ventilating of that room?

A. I would say that in such case there should be two distinct systems installed. In the first place, an exhaust system, one consisting of one fan and connected by a series of ducts to each machine liable to produce this dust in the proper way. If the machines are not in continuous service, in order to prevent the excessive expenditure of energy keeping them in operation all the time, each individual hood can be provided with a damper that can be shut off and, as soon as you cut down the air flow, the amount of power required by the fan is cut down and in that way it is not wasted. Then in addition to that there should be a general ventilating system for maintaining a steady flow of fresh air through the room.

§ 486. Real estate appraiser and broker.[24]

Q. Will you state your full name and address, please?

A. Hugh McLane, 300 North Michigan Avenue.

Q. Will you state your business?

A. Building contractor.

Q. How long have you been in that business?

A. Over twenty-five years.

Q. Have you built any office buildings or other large structures in Chicago?

A. Yes, sir.

Q. Will you name a few of them?

A. The Evening Post Building; the Bell Building; the 300 West Adams Building; the Jackson-Franklin Building; the Finchley Building—

Q. I think that is enough. Have you had occasion to appraise or value fireproof buildings in the City of Chicago?

A. Yes.

[24] De Freitas v. Suisan City, 170 Cal. 263, 149 Pac. 553; Geoghegan v. Union El. R. Co., 266 Ill. 482, 107 N. E. 786; N. Y., etc., R. Co. v. Hammond, 170 Ind. 493, 83 N. E. 244; Yore v. Meshow, 146 Mich. 80; Clark v. Baird, 9 N. Y. 183; J. P. Watkins, etc., Co. v. Campbell, 98 Tex. 372, 84 S. W. 424; Jefferey v. Osborne, 145 Wis. 351, 129 N. W. 931.

Q. During your experience as a contractor?

A. Yes.

Q. Have you ever appraised or valued buildings in the central business district of Chicago, commonly known as the loop district?

A. Yes, sir.

Q. Are you familiar with the cost of construction of fireproof buildings in November, 1929, in the City of Chicago?

A. Yes, sir.

Q. And in the loop district of Chicago?

A. Yes.

Q. Are you familiar with the building at the southwest corner of State and Washington Streets, commonly known as the Reliance Building?

A. Yes.

Q. How long have you known that building?

A. Ever since it was erected. I think about 36 years ago.

Q. That would make it about 1895?

A. Yes.

Q. Have you estimated the cubic content of that building, Mr. McLane.

A. Yes, sir.

Q. Have you made an inspection of the building?

A. Yes, sir.

Q. For what purpose?

A. For the purpose of determining the kind of construction, the design, and other incidental features.

Q. What is the cubic content of that building?

A. 1,031,693 cubic feet.

Q. Have you an opinion as to the useful life of a building of that type?

A. Yes.

Q. What is it?

A. Fifty years.

Q. Have you an opinion as to the cost of reproducing that building in November, 1929?

A. Yes.

Q. With material of like kind and quality?

A. Yes.

Q. What was the fair, reasonable, market cost of the reproduction of that building in Chicago, Illinois, in November, 1929?

A. $514,930.

Q. You say that you have appraised buildings in the loop district of Chicago?

A. Yes, sir.

Q. A number of times?

A. Yes, sir.

Q. At whose request?

A. At the request of mortgage bankers and investment houses.

Q. And have they accepted your appraisals?

A. Yes.

Q. Have you an opinion as to the fair market value in November, 1929, of the Reliance Building, the building in question?

A. Yes.

Q. What is your opinion, was the fair market value of that improvement as of November, 1929?

A. $175,077.

§ 487. Chemist.

Q. State your name, please?

A. Edward Jackson.

Q. Where do you live?

A. 805 W. Main.

Q. What is your business?

A. I am a professional chemist and technical engineer.

Q. Tell the court and jury your preliminary college education along those lines?

A. I am a graduate of the public schools of New York, the universities of Berlin and Goettingeo, Germany.

Q. What degrees, if any, do you hold?

A. The degree of Doctor of Philosophy.

Q. What study of chemistry have you made?

A. Well, I studied chemistry for five years at Columbia University, for two and a half years abroad, as my collegiate education; I have had practical experience for about 26 years.

Q. What has been your practical experience?

A. I have been in charge of manufacturing institutions; for the last 15 years as consulting chemical expert and technical engineer in business for myself.

Q. With what concerns were you chemist in charge?

A. I have been engaged as chemist in charge of superintendent in charge in the glucose starch sugar business; since in private practice, with a tremendous large number; I could not really enumerate all of them, in the general line.

Q. Doctor, are you familiar with vats and tanks used in chemical factories in mixing chemicals, treating shops, machinery, vats, blow pipes, suction devices and appliances in general use in chemical plants?

A. Yes, sir.

§ 488. Jeweler.

Q. Will you state your name in full, please?

A. William Brown.

Q. And your address?

A. 55 E. Washington St.

Q. What is your business, Mr. Brown?

A. Jeweler.

Q. How long have you been in the jewelry business?

A. Since 1907.

Q. What has your work consisted of during the time that you said you were in the jewelry business?

A. During that time I have been occupied chiefly in diamonds and pearls and other precious stones, and in that connection I have had a fairly broad experience.

Q. With whom have you been associated during that time?

A. I was with Shaw & Co.

Q. How long were you with them?

A. I started in 1909. My occupation there was in the diamond section; also assistant manager.

Q. And your work in the diamond section, what did that consist of, generally speaking?

A. In that particular business, well, we were occupied chiefly in purchasing, also passing on the various qualities of diamonds and pearls or other precious stones that were presented for either an appraisal or for resale.

Q. What did you do after you left Shaw & Co.?

A. I started in business with another gentleman named Holland in 1929.

Q. The present name of your company is what?

A. Holland and Brown.

Q. On or about the 2nd day of May, 1931, were you engaged in that same business with Holland?

A. Yes, sir.

Q. Did you have occasion at that time to buy and sell various kinds of jewelry and diamonds?

A. Yes, that is our business from day to day to constantly keep in touch with what is available; also as to prices.

Q. Now, have you an opinion, Mr. Brown, as to the fair reasonable market value in the City of Oakland and State of California, on or about May 2, 1931, of a diamond platinum bracelet which is set with the following stones: One marquis diamond weighing 1 carat, 95 hundredths, a perfect stone of white, a fairly good color, two marquis diamonds about 81 one-hundredths carat each, total 1 carat 62 hundredths for both, of about the same quality as the last stone; 229 diamonds having a total weight of 12 carats, 95 hundredths, which may be described as stones of a fairly good quality; 56 diamonds having a total weight of 1 carat, 23 hundredths, of the same general quality; 44 emeralds of the kind usually matched in a bracelet of that kind?

A. Yes, I have an opinion.

Q. What is that opinion?

A. The fair reasonable market value would be $5600.00.

§ 489. Limit expert to scope of question.

Some expert witnesses are so clever at testifying that they attempt to answer beyond the scope of the question. If proper and timely objections are made, it serves the purpose of breaking up the expert's story and prevents the witness from resorting to these unfair tactics.

The following testimony, with objections, illustrate the point:

Q. Doctor, in the course of your medical experience have you had occasions to observe the disease known as syphilis?

A. I have.

Q. Will you explain to the Court and Jury the effects of syphilis on the human anatomy, in its various stages based upon your experience?

A. Well, there is a great change of symptoms in persons suffering with syphilis, depending upon the stage in which it is taken. A person may come into the office without any outward manifestation of an eruption or any serious illness and can have a loss of appetite or some stomach disturbance, and we take a blood test and do quite a routine examination, and we may find—

Mr. Corey: I object to this narrative testimony of routine procedure as to what they do and find in other cases.

Mr. Reese: Well, I will put it this way: Will you state some of the effects upon living persons of the presence of a syphilitic infection?

A. In an acute case *we usually find a lesion* known as a chancre, it may be on the private parts and it may be on the tongue or lips and even the nose. This is an erosion sometimes like a punch-out ulcer which the patient says he is unable to heal by all medications that he has applied. In other cases, you will see them with rash, with a blood tint red to a pink tint over the whole body. Other cases will come in with a lesion that I have already mentioned and will have an eruption all over their whole bodies, and it may be on the face or the hair or the arms. Others in later periods of this disease may not have any of these eruptions and we may be able to trace the scar in the former chancre, but when we get from them a history of having had a chancre or loss of hair and start throughout—

Mr. Corey: I still object to this form of testimony, your Honor.

The Court: Sustained.

Mr. Corey: I move it be stricken out.

Mr. Reese: What part do you want stricken out?

Mr. Corey: The latter part, everything that he finds in some patients or others.

The Court: Sustained.

Mr. Reese: After the stages of lesion and the rash, will you state what are the other symptoms?

The witness: Another stage may be where the individual comes in with great distress in the stomach—

Mr. Corey: Wait. I object to that. He can state what the symptoms are without adding a story.

The Court: Sustained.

Mr. Reese: All right.

Q. What are the symptoms referable to gastrointestinal tract in syphilis?

A. A person may have a gastric crisis, and at this state he may think—

Mr. Corey: I object to that.

Mr. Reese: What is a gastric crisis?

A. Where there is a great pain in the stomach that causes a person to double up with pain, he may be operated on for appendicitis and he may be operated for—

Mr. Corey: I object to that and move that it be stricken out.

The Court: That may go out, the latter part.

§ 490. Cross-examination.

A clever expert witness, under cross-examination, can by proper response to opposing counsel's questions, signal a necessity for questions to be asked on re-direct examination. This is usually done in those instances where the witness is apparently compelled to admit some damaging factor under cross-examination. In those instances, he usually admits the fact as true, but adds "that's true under certain conditions." This is a signal to ask, on re-direct examination: "Doctor, you said that so and so was true under certain conditions—just tell the Court and jury under what conditions that would be true."

The law in almost all jurisdictions permits great latitude in the cross-examination of expert witnesses[25] but that fact in itself should not make the ambitious trial lawyer forget the oft-repeated admonition, "never to cross-examine an expert in his own field." This is good advice if the witness is actually an expert in that particular field and if it is found, after

[25] Matter of Higgins, 156 Cal. 257, 104 Pac. 6; Ewing v. Hatcher, 175 Iowa 443, 154 N. W. 869; McMahon v. Chicago City R. Co., 239 Ill. 334, 88 N. E. 223; O'Hare v. Gloag, 221 Mass. 24, 108 N. E. 566; Michigan, etc., Co. v. Wilcox, 78 Mich. 431, 44 N. W. 281; Palestine, etc., Co. v. Terminal Warehouse Co., 67 Misc. 456, 123 N. Y. S. 346; Missouri, etc., R. Co. v. Hart, 196 S. W. 960 (Tex.); Brey v. Forrestal, 151 Wis. 245, 138 N. W. 645.

an exhaustive study of the subject under discussion, that the expert has testified truthfully and honestly and fully on the subject. If after a full consideration of the medical authorities, and after consultation with his own expert, the lawyer is convinced that the expert witness is *not* fully qualified or has *overstepped the bounds,* then he should be cross-examined, all depending, of course, upon the amount and completeness of the preparation he has made before trial.

If it is decided that the expert is qualified and is competent and that he has testified truthfully, the cross-examination should be limited to showing his relationship with the parties and the lawyers, the amount of his fee for treatment and for time spent in court testifying. If it is known that he spends a great deal of time in court testifying, that fact should be brought out. If he always testifies for the plaintiff or for the defendant, either one side or the other exclusively, that should be the point of attack. Anything that will show he is interested in the outcome of the case should be shown. Sometimes expert witnesses are employed on a contingent basis.[26] If the amount of their fee is dependent on the winning of the case, that fact, when made known to the jury, will cast suspicion on the expert's testimony.

A complete and exhaustive examination of an expert in his own field usually serves the purpose only of giving the expert an opportunity to expand on his own views and to convince the jury of his great fund of knowledge. The better practice is to try to secure an admission on several points which the lawyer has learned from a perusal of text-books that the expert must, if honest, admit. This will corroborate the lawyer's position and also gain credence for the testimony of his experts.

The lawyer should never allow an expert too much opportunity to explain, by putting a question so broad as to permit the witness to explain away his case. He should be careful also not to ask a question on cross-examination which will permit the expert to supply everything that he might have left out on direct examination.

26 Contingent fee contracts are held to be against public policy. Burnett v. Freeman, 115 S. W. 488, 134 Mo. App. 709.

The lawyer must forever keep in mind his theory of the case. His main purpose is to prove his case rather than to seek to destroy his opponent's witnesses. (See Cross-Examination for rules and principles.) The following is an illustration:

In the taking of depositions in the case of Harry Simon v. Natural Life Insurance Company (suit based on health insurance policy), it became necessary to prove all symptoms and ailments upon which to base a hypothetical question that would sufficiently permit doctors to state that the plaintiff was suffering from tuberculosis of the larynx prior to June 26, 1930. When the defendant's doctors were presented for cross-examination, it was planned to gain admissions that plaintiff had the following symptoms: that he was hoarse, had a dryness in the throat, disorders in the abdomen, suffered loss of weight, lack of appetite, that he had a tubercular growth in the vocal chords and larynx, and that the growth was not a papilloma or singer's node, but was in fact a tuberculoma. The object was to prove that under the medical authorities, the growth which was found in the larynx of the plaintiff was a tuberculoma, one of the distinctive features of which is that it is rigid and not freely movable. On the other hand, a papilloma is supposed to be soft, pliable and freely movable according to Turner.

It had to be proved that no conclusive diagnosis of tuberculosis could be made without full and complete X-rays of the chest and repeated examination of the sputum by laboratory tests to determine the presence of tubercle bacilli. It, therefore, became necessary to secure an admission that no X-ray had been taken of the plaintiff's chest and that no laboratory examination had been made of the sputum. In view of the subsequent history of plaintiff's being confined to a sanitarium with an advanced case of pulmonary tuberculosis of the larynx, the lawyers knew that admissions by opposing doctors to the effect that they had not taken X-rays of the chest and laboratory tests of the sputum would prevent the defendant from absolutely ruling out the possibility of plaintiff's having had tuberculosis since June, 1930. It was also necessary to prove that the plaintiff's confinement in the sanitarium almost a year after original examinations made by opposing doctors was due to the continuous disability of the same ailment from which he was suffering in June, 1930, so that the cross-examination was thereupon conducted with a view to showing that the plaintiff was under the continuous care and treatment of opponent's doctors until the time that he left town. To show that he was disabled during this period of time it was also necessary to corroborate the attorney's position by admissions from opponent's doctors that they had advised him against working, the main portion of his work being the use of the voice, and that they had ordered him not to use it. It was also necessary to prove that a diagnosis made by another doctor in Kansas City that the plaintiff was suffering from tuberculosis of the larynx, was communicated to opponent's doctors for the purpose of corroborating that physician and to give the plaintiff's testimony greater weight and credence in an effort to show that the claim was not recently "trumped up." The doctors were, therefore, cross-examined as follows:

Dr. Sampson's cross-examination (in part)

Q. You stated that you had a talk with Dr. Jones, who had previously examined Mr. Simon?

A. Yes, sir.

Q. —and you said he mentioned the possibilities of cancer and syphilis?

A. Yes.

Q. By that do you mean that he didn't mention to you the possibility of tuberculosis?

A. Yes.

Q. What do you mean?

A. He made no definite diagnosis, he said there is a possibility—

Q. (Interrupting) Did he say there was a possibility of tuberculosis?

A. I remember he mentioned cancer and syphilis.

Q. Would you say, then, that he didn't tell you there was any possibility of tuberculosis?

A. I would not say so.

Q. Counsel asked you whether you saw an open ulcer there?

A. Yes.

Q. Did you or did you not?

A. No, sir.

Q. Ulcers and ulcerations are a matter of difference in growth or degree, is that right?

A. Yes, sir.

Q. Some lesser and some greater?

A. Yes.

Q. And some ulcers in the larynx are not easily seen, is that right?

A. Yes, sir.

Q. So that there might have been an ulceration there without your having seen it?

A. Yes.

Q. Did you see any growth on any portion of the larynx at the time you saw Dr. Graydon examine him?

A. There was a large swelling, protrusion or enlargement on which it might have had a growth underneath the inflamed area.

Q. As a matter of fact, you know there was some growth there?

A. A swelling or a growth there, yes.

Q. But whether it was a papilloma or tuberculoma, you don't know?

A. I couldn't tell.

Q. When Mr. Simon returned from the examination by Dr. Jones, what was Mr. Simon's condition? (To show that Dr. Jones had communicated his findings to client.)

A. Very much upset, nervous and excited, and very, very, upwrought.

Q. Did you have a conversation with him at that time in reference to that examination?

A. Yes, sir.

Q. In fact, at one time there he became so excited you threatened to send him to the hospital, is that right?

A. Yes.

Q. As a doctor, of course you are familiar with all nose and throat symptoms of ailments in the larynx, either tuberculosis, cancer or syphilis?

A. Yes.

Q. —and those are the three things that are usually suspected, is that right?

A. Those are the most common.

Dr. Graydon—concluding portion of direct examination

Q. At the conclusion of your treatment, what shape was the laryngeal mucosa in?

A. It still was thickened, the chronic laryngitis was still present, the acute factor had seemingly disappeared.

Q. At the end of your treatment, you say that he appeared to be in good shape?

A. The acute factor had cleared up but the chronic process was still present.

Q. During any time during this period that you treated him, did the symptoms you found present the typical appearance of a tuberculous condition or of malignancy or syphilis?

A. We were uncertain at first as to whether it might not be one or all.

Q. But at no time was it typical in appearance?

A. No.

Cross-examination

Q. Now, doctor, while you say that it didn't present a typical appearance, still it was not of such an appearance that you ruled out tuberculosis, was it?

A. No, the tuberculosis can be implanted upon any of these problems that you may have in a throat such as he had. The inflammatory problem, tuberculosis can be implanted upon that at any time.

Q. Why did you rule out tuberculosis of the larynx at that time after your examination?

A. He was sent to Dr. Sampson for that very purpose, and Dr. Sampson reported to me that there was no lesion present in the lungs, nor was he able to find anything that would lead him to think there was any tuberculosis any place else.

Q. Doctor, what chest examinations would be necessary upon which you would rule out tuberculosis of the larynx?

A. Well, to rule out tuberculosis of the larynx, it is essential that there be a careful physical examination of the X-rays taken of the chest, and that a careful check be made for tubercle bacilli in the sputum by making a number of examinations.

Q. In your first examination, did you take a history of his case?

A. We did.

Q. Will you tell us what was included in that history?

A. It shows increased hoarseness for several months and considerable difficulty in prolonged use of his voice.

Q. Any other history that you took at that time?

A. No.

Q. Anything about loss of weight?

A. No.

Q. Did you ask him about that?

A. If I did I have forgotten it. I probably did, but I have forgotten it.

Q. Were you depending upon Dr. Sampson for a general physical examination?

A. Where we refer a patient that way we always rely upon his findings.

Q. You say you gave him rest treatment, doctor?

A. Yes.

Q. That is also the treatment for tuberculosis of the larynx, is it not?

A. Yes.

Q. Now, doctor, Mr. Simon was under your treatment off and on from June 28, 1930, until February 13, 1931, is that right?

A. Yes, sir.

Q. During all that period of time was this chronic laryngitis condition present?

A. To a marked degree it had cleared up very decidedly before he went away. We must not forget that when an acute inflammation is implanted upon a chronic condition, it always aggravates the latter condition.

Q. But that condition prevailed throughout that time?

A. There was a chronic laryngitis present.

Q. The thickening of the mucosa was also present at that time, throughout that time?

A. Yes.

Q. Was this growth present during all of that time?

A. It had largely subsided.

Q. But it was still present during all of that time?

A. There was still a small part of it, but it had very largely disappeared. I remember sometime in September or August, it was practically all gone.

Q. Tell us what the condition of his ventricular bands were in June, 1930.

A. All of his membranes were thickened and this was noted on the anterior of the left cord.

Q. Did you have a consultation with Dr. Sampson about it?

A. Yes, we had several.

Q. What was your finding after those consultations and examinations?

A. That he had a chronic laryngitis with papilloma.

Q. Would you say absolutely that there was not tuberculosis present in June, July, August, 1930?

A. No, I would not say that.

Q. Now, this papilloma that you saw, doctor, will you describe that, please?

A. A small elevation probably a little over an eighth of an inch where it is attached to the cord at an elevation of a little less than an eighth of an inch.

Q. Was that an eighth of an inch out from the cord?

A. Yes.

Q. What diameter?

A. Its location out on the cord, and its attachment to the cord was more or less round, and a little more than an eighth of an inch in diameter.

Q. Did you attempt to get at this growth in any way?

A. Dr. Sampson was advised that treatment would be of no avail, that it would be necessary to remove it. In fact, I am rather of the opinion that if I remember correctly at the end of the first week or ten days, we had about decided that it would be advisable to operate.

Q. *I take it was movable?*

A. No, it was firmly fixed and rigid.

Q. Would you say that it was unusually rigid?

A. No, it was firmly fixed and rigid.

Q. Doctor, it is an easy thing, is it not, to mistake a papilloma for tuberculoma?

A. Oh, yes.

Q. Now, Doctor, if an examination of the sputum had disclosed tubercle bacilli at that time, would that have changed your diagnosis?

A. Very decidedly.

Q. Doctor, if one is suffering from tuberculosis of the larynx, it is of a secondary nature and not primary, as far as you are concerned?

A. We always expect it to be secondary.

Q. The fact that it is secondary or even primary, would that affect the ulceration process? The ulceration merely designates whether it is more advanced or in the early stages, does it not?

A. Ulceration shows that is active.

Q. So that you could have tuberculosis of the larynx without ulceration appearing; is that right?

A. Yes.

Q. Ulceration would be red around where it breaks down?

A. Yes, we may have tuberculoma without that.

Q. That would not mean that there was not tuberculosis present?

A. No.

Q. Tell us something about the color of the larynx, on June 28, 1930.

A. These membranes, as I told you, were very much thickened; I don't know what you mean by color. There is a certain normal color that is a pinkish red; the condition we found these in was more of a deeper red, thickened, the circulation had been blocked back and the membranes were more of a deeper, going over into a darker red.

Q. The condition that you have described that you found there was a deep red, wasn't it?

A. Yes.

Q. That condition is present in all tuberculosis cases of the larynx, is that right?

A. No, they usually have a paling down. One of our early signs is a paling of the membranes, and if we have deeper red, we tend towards a malignant thing. If it is paler than usual, we lean toward the tubercular diagnosis until we have proven it.

Q. Does the color change during the various stages of tuberculosis?

A. That depends upon the ulcerations. If there is an ulceration present, it is a deeper red around the ulceration and pales down into a pale stage in a membrane that does not have ulceration.

Q. So that if ulceration were present, there would be a deeper red rather than the ashen pallor?

A. Yes, sir.

Q. At that time, did he tell you anything about having pain in swallowing?

A. He had considerable difficulty in swallowing at that time.

Q. —and the hoarseness continued practically all of the time he was under your care, is that right?

A. Yes.

Q. Did you tell him to keep on using his voice or to stop using his voice?

A. I told him to give as much rest to his voice as he could, told him to use it as little as he could.

Q. Did he also tell you that he was coughing?

A. I have forgotten that.

Q. Do you know whether or not he was actually coughing at that time?

A. Well, there is always a certain cough attending a condition of that kind. I don't remember whether it was an unusual cough or not.

Q. .You do know, don't you, that he was coughing during that time?

A. There is always a cough with trouble such as his.

Q. Did he tell you anything about losing weight?

A. I have forgotten it if he did.

Q. Do you know whether or not he lost any weight?

A. I do not know.

Q. Do you know whether or not he stated anything to you about fever or hot flushes or complained of excessive perspiration?

A. No, if we asked him that as we went along, we made no mention of it.

Q. Did he complain of weakness or of being unusually fatigued?

A. He complained of considerable fatigue early in our experience.

Q. Did he say anything about bringing up mucus?

A. There is always a certain amount of mucus.

Q. Did he say anything to you about it?

A. Nothing, unusual, it has slipped my mind if he did.

Q. Do you know or did you know, whether or not Dr. Sampson had had an X-ray examination made of his chest?

A. He reported to me over the telephone that he had gone over Mr. Simon and that there was nothing about him that would lead him to suspect tuberculosis of anything.

Q. Please answer the question as to whether or not you knew that Dr. Sampson had or had not had an X-ray taken of Mr. Simon's chest.

A. I have forgotten if I asked that question over the telephone.

Q. Was your diagnosis based upon the assumption that an X-ray had been taken of Mr. Simon's chest?

A. It is always, and when we ask for an opinion upon a chest, and especially as to the tubercular problem, we expect an X-ray of that chest, and we expect a careful sputum examination.

Q. In taking into consideration your findings, you assumed that a sputum examination had been made either by Dr. Sampson, and that a negative finding had been returned, is that right?

A. We always assume that an examination has been properly conducted; we don't stop to ask how it was done; we know that the man is competent; and when he tells us that his findings are negative, we don't ask him what he did; that would be questioning his ability.

Q. I must insist that we get a direct answer to the question. When you made your diagnosis, based upon the report of Dr. Sampson that physically Mr. Simon was O. K., did you, assume that there had been an X-ray examination made and a laboratory test of the sputum, both of which had been returned negative?

Mr. Opponent: Object to any assumptions.

Q. Is that right, Doctor?

The Court: Overruled.

A. The question, as I understand it, is that when Dr. Sampson reported to me that he had given this man a negative finding that then I assumed that he had put him through these different tests, which means an X-ray of his chest and a careful physical examination; *I did.*

Counsel: That is all.

§ 491. Cross-examination as to qualifications.[27]

If the lawyer has doubts as to the witness' qualifications, or if his examination of the Medical Blue Book or other medical directories, has shown that the witness specializes in a field other than the one in question, that fact should be shown. The cross-examination should be conducted in a seemingly casual and quiet manner, without permitting the witness to feel that he is suspected or that the attorney has any particular object in mind.

Where the subject under discussion is one which is outside of the field of the expert, this method may be employed: (A question of internal medicine was involved.)

Q. Doctor, what is your listing in the medical blue book?

A. I beg your pardon.

27 Cross-examination may be directed to the qualifications of the witness. Princeton, etc., Co. v. Howell, 46 Ind. App. 572, 92 N. E. 122; Johnson v. Bay State, etc., R. Co., 222 Mass. 583, 111 N. E. 391; Andre v. Hardin, 32 Mich. 324; Walter v. Hangen, 71 App. Div. 40, 75 N. Y. S. 683; Levant, etc., Co. v. Wells, 186 App. Div. 497, 174 N. Y. S. 303; S. W. Portland Cement Co. v. Kezer, 174 S. W. 661 (Tex.); Coman v. Wunderlich, 122 Wis. 138, 99 N. W. 612. Such as his skill, knowledge and experience: Reclamation Dist. No. 730 v. Inglin, 31 Cal. App. 495, 160 Pac. 1098; Ewing v. Hatcher, 175 Iowa 443, 154 N. W. 869; Peo. v. Cochran, 313 Ill. 509. Although it is permissible to show lack of qualification, the evidence offered to prove it must be relevant. Chicago, etc., R. Co. v. Schmitz, 211 Ill. 446, 71 N. E. 1050; Galveston, etc., R. Co. v. Young, 148 S. W. 1113 (Tex.); Buckman v. Missouri, etc., R. Co., 100 Mo. App. 30, 73 S. W. 720, where the expert witness had been a railroad employe, and had been discharged and could not get employment with any other railroad. This fact could not be shown to impair his opinion unless it was shown that his discharge was due to incompetency. Southern R. Co. v. Parham, 10 Ga. App. 531, 73 S. E. 763, where a medical expert could not be impeached by showing he previously made a mistake in diagnosing a case. Adams v. Sullivan, 100 Ind. 8; Carley v. N.Y., etc., R. Co., 1 N. Y. S. 63, where the court held it was improper to ask the expert witness if the opponent's expert knew anything about the particular subject-matter.

Q. What is your listing in the medical blue book?

A. What is my listing?

Q. Yes.

A. Well, there is a paragraph in there, I do not know just how it reads, I have not looked at it lately.

Q. Just give us an idea now how you are listed there, will you?

A. I think at the present moment—

Mr. Opponent: Well, now, just a moment. I object.

Q. I am asking how he is listed whether as a surgeon or otherwise.

The Court: He may answer.

Q. You are listed as a surgeon, aren't you?

A. Yes, sir.

The following method has been employed to very good advantage in some instances:

During the course of a personal injury suit, a certain doctor was qualified as an expert witness, and he was asked, among other things, whether he was affiliated with any hospital at the present time. He replied that he was, and proceeded to enumerate five or six well-known hospitals. He mentioned his connection with each of them by saying that he was a staff surgeon at one hospital, consulting surgeon on the staff of another, etc.

On cross-examination, counsel proceeded as follows:

Q. Doctor, you say that you are on the staff of Blank Hospital as a surgeon?

A. Yes, that's right.

Q. Doctor, can you tell us how many cases you have taken to this hospital in the past week?

A. I don't believe I had any there in the past week.

Q. Well, Doctor, have you had any cases there in the past two weeks?

A. Well, I don't think so.

Q. Don't you know, Doctor?

A. I don't believe I did have any cases at that hospital in the past two weeks.

Q. Doctor, have you had any cases there in the past month?

A. (Very slowly) No, I don't think so.

Q. Have you had any cases there in the past two months?

A. No, I haven't.

Q. Well, Doctor, have you had any cases there in the past six months?

A. No, I cannot recall.

Q. Have you had any cases there in the past year?

A. No, I don't believe I have.

Q. Doctor, you say you are affiliated with the State Hospital?

A. Yes.

Q. Your position there is that of consulting surgeon. How many cases have you been consulted in at the State Hospital in this past week?

A. Well, I don't believe I was consulted in any cases this past week.

(Note: This method should not be attempted unless you feel the so-called expert is a charlatan.)

The same tactics were pursued in examining the doctor as to his affiliations with the other hospitals he had mentioned in qualifying as an expert; and it developed that this particular doctor was a member of the staff of the various hospitals in name only and had practically no experience either as an operating surgeon, consulting surgeon, or in any other capacity on the staff of any of these hospitals.

§ 492. Cross-examination as to subjective symptoms.

Where a doctor's opinion is based almost solely upon subjective symptoms, and it is suspected that the plaintiff's claim is not a just one, a cross-examination, in part, such as follows, may be used:

Q. In making a diagnosis of this patient's supposed ailment you had to take his word for the question of whether or not he was suffering pain, didn't you?

A. Why, no. It was by my giving him the examination and by flexation and mobility of the leg it elicited pain.

Q. And the way you determined whether or not he had pain was what he said about it?

A. And—

Q. And his voluntary wincing, is that right?

A. I don't know whether it was voluntary or involuntary.

Q. I see. You don't know whether it was voluntary or involuntary?

A. I could only take the patient's word for it.

Q. So that you had to take the patient's word for it. Now then you could not see the pain, of course, could you?

A. No.

Q. And you could not see the sciatic nerve, could you?

A. No.

Q. And you determined whether or not the sciatic nerve was injured by what the man said when you manipulated his leg?

A. I formed—I ran my finger along the course.

Q. And by the demonstration he gave you at the time you ran your finger along the course of the nerve?

A. I wanted to see what pain was elicited.

Q. There were no objective symptoms from which you could come to the conclusion that the sciatic nerve was injured, were there?

A. Only by my observation of the limb, that when I moved it or anything of course it elicited pain.

Q. Pain is not an objective symptom, is it, Doctor?

A. Subjective.

Q. We will go back to the original question then. From objective symptoms you could not determine that he had an injury to the sciatic nerve, could you?

A. Not any more than what I told you.

Q. In other words the answer to the question is, Yes, you could not, is that right, Doctor?

A. No, you can't say it could not, but I don't know what way—

Q. All right, Doctor. When you made your diagnosis of the alleged injury to this man, what if any objective symptoms did you take into consideration?

A. Well, from the patient.

Q. From the patient?

A. Yes. Of course you can't see the sciatic nerve.

Q. But I say that is not an objective symptom, is it Doctor? That is a subjective symptom, isn't it?

A. It might be objective, for I have taken that man and turned him on his abdomen, and when he was not looking I would follow the sciatic nerve, and as soon as I touched it he would wince.

Q. You call that objective, do you?

A. Objective.

Q. Was there anything else you call objective besides that from which you—

A. Well, it showed by that that he moved involuntarily, so it must have hurt him.

Q. The man was not paralyzed, was he?

A. He was not paralyzed.

Q. He could feel your finger at any place you touched him, couldn't he?

A. Yes. Anybody else can.

Q. He could do that whether he had his face up or down, couldn't he, Doctor?

A. Yes.

Counsel: That is all, Doctor.

§ 493. Cross-examination to test recollection.

Where a doctor or other expert witness professes to remember all details of many years ago, the following form of cross-examination is suggested:

Part of direct examination

Q. Will you tell the Court and jury, what Mr. Herman was complaining of when he came into the hospital, and what your treatment consisted of and what your diagnosis was?

A. He complained of a burning sensation in the stomach and some nausea and some indefinite pains in the abdomen.

Q. All right, then what did you do?

A. I took his history and made a physical examination, and made a gastro-intestinal X-ray study.

Q. Have you got it with you?

A. The X-ray?

Q. Yes.

A. No.

Q. Do you know what happened to it?

A. Why they were destroyed. They are all destroyed after a period, when they get four years old.

Q. Have you got the history with you?
A. The history?
Q. Have you got the history that he gave you?
A. I haven't the history he gave me—no.
Q. Do you know what it is?
A. Yes, essentially I gave it to you.
Q. What kind of treatment did you give him in the hospital?
A. I gave him three quart feedings, three hour feedings of food, intending not to excite the secretions of hyperchloridia acids any more than possible. I gave him powders, called citric powders, and kept him in bed at the time he was in the hospital.
Q. Well did you make a diagnosis at that time?
A. Yes, sir.
Q. What was your diagnosis?
A. Hyperchloridia with a probable diagnosis of gastric ulcers.

Cross-examination

Q. Now, you have no history sheets there, doctor?
A. I have no sheets with the history on, no, sir.
Q. How many people have you had there at that hospital since 1925, how many patients?
A. Well, we have a daily average of about twenty.
Q. And that keeps on throughout all of the year, does it?
A. The daily average?
Q. Yes.
A. Yes, that will run about like that over the period.
Q. What is the most you have there at any one time?
A. Oh, a capacity of forty beds there.
Q. Have you ever had those beds filled during any time between 1925 and today?
A. I don't know for sure. We had them filled just a few days before—a few weeks before that date there, April 20th, because that was during the cyclone they had down there, and we had it filled at that time, but I don't remember since then.
Q. Well, are all history sheets disposed of within four years?
A. No.

Q. How long do you keep history sheets?

A. Always.

Q. You keep those all the time?

A. We have all that we made since we have owned the hospital.

Q. Now, you didn't make out any history sheet for Herman, is that right?

A. No, I didn't.

Q. All this that you are testifying to is from your memory so far as his history is concerned?

A. Yes, sir.

Q. Doctor, he was only there a few days, for a few days, eight or nine days altogether, is that right?

A. Nine days, yes, sir.

Q. Now, tell us the name and symptoms of the history of another patient that you had there at the same time that he was there.

A. Well, I couldn't now.

Q. Give us the name and history of a patient that came the day before or the day after he was there. Can you do that, Doctor?

A. No, sir.

Q. Can you name anybody within one month prior to Mr. Herman's time there, from your memory, as to just what he suffered from and how long he was in the hospital, and all about it?

A. No, I cannot.

Q. Now, the X-ray didn't show any ulcers, did it?

A. No, sir, the X-ray didn't show any ulcers, no.

Q. Did your X-rays show he had hyperchloridia?

A. Indirectly, yes.

Q. And you are making that statement from your memory, as to what the X-ray showed five or—let us see, eight years ago?

A. Well, that is from memory and treatment on the chart.

Q. That means you are not sure it was there, you meant that that might be, is that right, the gastric ulcers?

A. Yes, sir.

Q. It might be there?

A. Yes.

Q. Now, did you make a gastric analysis at all, Doctor, of Mr. Herman?

A. No, sir, I didn't.

Q. Is it necessary to make some analysis in order to determine that, doctor?

A. Well, not always.

Q. Why not, please?

A. Whenever the symptoms of the patient together with the other findings, it isn't necessary always to make a gastric analysis.

Mr. Reeve: I wish the record to show that Dr. Harris is assisting plaintiff.

Mr. Gould: Yes, please, have the record show that.

Mr. Reeve: In framing the questions.

Mr. Gould: Because I don't claim to be a doctor.

Mr. Reeve: I limited my cross-examination on the theory that the doctor wanted to get away from here.

Mr. Gould: I will put him back on again. We wouldn't limit you for the world.

(Note: Mr. Reeve, throughout the trial, undermined the effect of this expert's testimony, by showing the expert's inordinate interest in the outcome of the case. On cross-examination, he showed that the doctor's fees, up to that time, amounted to three thousand dollars, and at every opportunity called the jury's attention to the unusually great interest shown by expert.)

Q. Now, the record shows that the patient had a fever when he came in there, is that correct?

A. Yes, it shows the temperature of 99 in one or two instances.

Q. That case that I called your attention to, is there a fever register there of 99 44/100, doctor?

Q. Is that in your handwriting?

A. No, sir.

Q. Whose handwriting is that?

A. I don't know, a nurse's—

Q. Was that fever at that time?

A. That is a slight fever.

Q. Now is that usual finding in gastric ulcers?

A. Well, I wouldn't say it was usual, it could be there.

Q. On the other hand, it indicates some infection present, doesn't it?

A. Yes.

Q. Does an infection make one feel sick to his stomach, doctor, with fever?

A. Quite often, yes.

Q. And if you have that feeling in the stomach, don't you always have symptoms of after-taste and belching, accompanying a fever and infection?

A. Not always.

Q. But you do have it, doctor?

A. Yes, sure, you could.

Q. And that lets up after the infection is over, isn't that right?

A. Yes, a sick stomach from an infection clears up usually when the infection is over.

Mr. Gould: That is all, doctor.

§ 494. Cross-examination where expert relies on some authority.

In some instances, it is possible to trap the expert where he does testify honestly as far as he goes, but deliberately leaves out some facts, so as to mislead the jury. One such incident took place in a recent occupational disease case, involving carbon tetrachloride poisoning. An expert was placed on the stand by the defendant, and was duly qualified. Among a great many things he testified as follows (on direct examination):

Q. Will you state the symptoms of carbon tetrachloride poisoning?

A. Among the symptoms that a patient experiences, that is supposed to have been poisoned by these substances, are nausea, vomiting, a sense of fullness in the abdomen, diarrhea, sometimes faulty stools, dizziness, stupor, cough, bronchial irritation; under very severe acute attacks, we have pulmonary hemorrhage and pneumonia, also irritation of the eyes.

Q. Have you known of such cases to result fatally?

A. I have never seen any.

Q. Do such cases make partial or complete recoveries?

A. All that I have ever seen made a complete recovery.

Q. Within how short a time?

A. Within a period of thirty to sixty days.

(Note: It was the theory of the plaintiff that his liver had become affected permanently and the functions of the liver had become impaired by reason of inhalations of carbon tetrachloride.)

In detailing the above, the expert deliberately left out of his enumerations of the symptoms, all reference to the liver and stated that there was no such thing as delayed poisoning. Counsel for the plaintiff had read the latest article by Dr. Carey McCord, an authority, in which he listed the liver as sometimes being affected by carbon tetrachloride, and also that delayed poisoning was possible. He therefore, cross-examined as follows:

Cross-examination

Q. Now, doctor, I listened to you giving the various symptoms of carbon tetrachloride poisoning, let's see if I got them all, will you? You said nausea, vomiting, fullness in the abdomen, diarrhea, bloody stools, dizziness, stupor, coughing, pulmonary hemorrhage, irritation of eyes?

A. Pneumonia, I said.

Q. That's right?

A. Yes, sir.

Q. That's all that you said?

A. I said bloody stools occasionally.

Q. Why did you leave out the liver, doctor?

A. Why did I leave out the liver?

Q. Yes, why did you leave out the liver?

A. I was giving symptoms mainly. I was giving symptoms.

Q. Is pneumonia a symptom or a disease?

A. It is a disease.

Q. Is pulmonary hemorrhage and all of the rest of the things, those are all symptoms?

A. Yes, they are all symptoms.

Q. Did you leave out the liver on purpose, doctor?

A. No, sir.

Q. You are an expert in carbon tetrachloride poisoning?

A. Occupational diseases.

Q. Occupational diseases, and don't you know that the liver is one of the things affected in the human body by carbon tetrachloride poisoning?

A. No, sir, I would not say so.

Q. Is it ever affected?

A. Oh, yes.

Q. But you left that out?

A. It might be affected.

Q. You left that out in your listing.

A. Because it is not characteristic.

Q. It is not characteristic?

A. No, sir.

Q. Citing whom, doctor?

Mr. Reeve: What do you mean "citing whom?"

Mr. Gould: Do you understand me, doctor?

A. Yes, I understand you.

Q. Citing whom?

Mr. Reeve: I object to that. He did not cite anybody.

Mr. Gould: I am asking him.

The Court: He has made a statement, and he is asking him[28] for his authority.

Mr. Gould: That's right. That's just what I want.

A. I am citing my own experience.

Q. Citing anybody else, somebody else that has done any work with carbon tetrachloride and published any article?

A. Yes, I think McCord does not include the liver.

Q. McCord does not include the liver?

A. Yes, sir.

Q. Who is McCord?

Mr. Reeve: He said he thinks.

Mr. Gould: Will you wait a moment. I will ask that counsel be admonished.

The Court: Yes.

28 The witness may be asked as to the basis of his opinion. Oakland v. Adams, 174 Pac. 947 (Cal.); Wilcox v. International, etc., Co., 278 Ill. 465, 116 N. E. 151; Tracy v. Mt. Pleasant, 165 Iowa 435, 146 N. W. 78; Matter of East 161st St., etc., 159 App. Div. 662, 144 N. Y. S. 717; Pecos, etc., R. Co. v. Holmes, 177 S. W. 505 (Tex.). Whether authorities lay down a contrary opinion. Chicago Union Tract. Co. v. Ertrachter, 228 Ill. 114, 81 N. E. 816; Matter of Hock, 74 Misc. 15, 129 N. Y. S. 196. Use of text books in cross-examination of experts, see Hypothetical questions, page 475.

Mr. Gould: Who is McCord?

A. He is a specialist on occupational diseases.

Q. As a matter of fact, he is the outstanding authority in this country on carbon tetrachloride today, isn't he?

A. No, I would not say that.

Q. Well, he is big enough for you to cite, is that right?

A. He is one of the specialists.

Q. Tell me, what is the article by Gary McCord, that is his name?

A. No, Carey McCord.

Q. Pardon me, Carey McCord is right; tell me which article he wrote where he says that carbon tetrachloride does not affect the liver?

A. I did not say that.

(Note: Counsel, in his anxiety allowed the witness to know that he was familiar with the McCord article. He should not have done so. He should have led the witness on more and more until he had fallen into the trap. As it was the witness was on his guard against committing any further indiscretions.)

Mr. Gould: Will you please tell us, doctor, which one of Carey McCord's articles said that the liver is not involved?

A. In an article on carbon tetrachloride.

Q. In what?

A. December 1932, "Industrial Medicine."

Q. Did he say anything about its effect upon the liver?

A. I think he does, yes.

Q. What does he say about it?

A. I cannot tell you exactly.

Mr. Reeve: I object to that. I object to the contents of any medical authority.

The Court: Objection overruled.

Q. When was the last time that you read that article?

A. I don't know, but it was about a month ago, I believe.

Q. All right; now tell us what he says about the effect of carbon tetrachloride on the liver?

A. I don't remember that he mentions that carbon tetrachloride has any specific effect on the liver.

Q. Well, then, you would say that he did not say that it affects the liver at all, would you, is that right?

A. No, I could not say that, because I don't remember what he says.

Counsel: That is all.

§ 495. Cross-examination as to relationship with parties and lawyers.

One suggested method of casting suspicion on a plaintiff's case with a possibility of affecting the credibility of an expert's testimony is as follows:[29]

Q. Doctor, you were hired by Mr. Gordon, the attorney for the plaintiff in this case, were you not?

A. For this service, yes.

Q. He sent his client there to you, didn't he?

A. That is not my understanding.

Q. How did she come over to you, have you got any idea? She doesn't live in Chicago. She lives in Buffalo, doesn't she?

A. She was sent to me by some friend of hers, according to her statement.

Q. It was suggested by Mr. Gordon, wasn't it?

A. I don't know.

Q. Well, Mr. Gordon sends cases to you, doesn't he?

A. Not for treatment.

Q. No, not for treatment. Merely to be examined and come in and testify?

A. Yes.

Q. You do a lot of that, don't you?

A. A certain amount.

Q. How much do you get for it, Doctor?

A. It depends on the amount of time given.

Q. Well, now, how much do you expect to charge Mr. Gordon for your services to him today?

Mr. Gordon: I object to that, as assuming a charge to me, your honor.

The Court: He may answer.

29 Cross-examination may be directed to the expert's interest in the litigation, if any. Oakland v. Adams, 174 Pac. 947 (Cal.); Dempsey v. Goldstein, etc., Co., 231 Mass. 461, 121 N. E. 429; McMahon v. Chicago, etc., R. Co., 239 Ill. 334, 88 N. E. 223 or matters tending to show bias. Di Tommaso v. Syracuse Univ., 172 App. Div. 34, 158 N. Y. S. 175; St. Louis, etc., R. Co. v. McMichael, 115 Ark. 101, 171 S. W. 15, where it was held permissible to ask the witness if he testified frequently for the defendant.

Q. You look to Mr. Gordon, the attorney for plaintiff, for pay, don't you?

A. Yes.

Q. How much do you expect to get?

A. Approximately one hundred dollars for each appearance in court.

§ 496. Cross-examination of non-expert as to mental condition.

A doctor was called to testify as to the mental condition of one of his patients. He had operated on the patient and based upon his observation of before and after the operation, he gave the following opinion:

A. My opinion is that the man had a form of senile dementia before he was operated on, and apart from the operation, the conditions present at the operation. The operation neither made the mental condition better nor worse, except insofar as when I saw him in coma, that condition was produced by the obstruction. The obstruction removed, the coma was removed, but he went back into the status that existed before and apart from the operation. That is exactly the situation. He was of poor mental status without respect to the physical condition. The physical condition made it worse. The physical condition, relieved by an operation, improved it, insofar as that condition made the mental condition worse. He lapsed back into what was the normal mental status, that is to say, of unsound, defective mental condition which existed prior to and apart from the operative condition.

Cross-examination

Q. How long did you know Giles McClendon prior to 1923, Doctor?

A. I didn't know him at all.

Q. Did you ever see him before that?

A. Not to my knowledge.

Q. How long after 1923 did you know him, that is, have personal contact with him?

A. One year.

Q. And how frequently did you see him during that year?

A. Oh, I would see him, during the time of the operation and following the operation. For six weeks following the operation, I saw him every day.

Q. Now, you treated him during those six weeks, did you?

A. As a consultant, I treated him.

Q. When?

A. Well, in the latter part of 1923 and during 1924.

Q. Have you your records here?

A. I haven't the records here, no.

Q. Has the other gentleman that you conferred with about the dates, has he the record here?

A. No.

Q. Just when did you perform this operation, Doctor?

A. Well, I was not able to get the date. I tried to get in touch with Dr. Turner this morning. They are not a part of my personal record, because I saw him with Dr. Turner.

Q. How many times did you talk with McClendon prior to the operation?

A. Well, I didn't have any very successful conversations with him at all.

Q. Well, as a matter of fact, did you have *any* conversation with him, Doctor?

A. I talked to him.

Q. He was in a state of coma—

A. Absolutely.

Q. —when you were called to operate on him?

A. Yes.

Q. Did you talk to him then?

A. We did not operate on him while he was in coma.

Q. When did you operate on him?

A. After a few days treatment. It will be necessary for me to explain that we did the operation in two stages.

Q. All right.

A. We first did a super-pubic cystotomy, that is, the bladder was opened and drained.

Q. With a drain for about how long?

A. For about two weeks.

Q. And then after that, did you remove the gland?

A. We did.

Q. During those two weeks with the drain, was he in the hospital?

A. He was.

Q. And it was after he was in this state of coma?

A. Yes.

Q. Now, the toxemic condition there, Doctor, how long had it been since you observed it? Could you tell from his condition at that time how long he had been in that state?

A. He was brought to the hospital. I saw him after he arrived in the hospital with a history of urinary obstruction.

Q. I didn't ask you anything about the history, Doctor.

A. Well, I don't know.

Q. Well, your testimony has been based upon a history that somebody gave you, is that right?

A. No.

Q. Well, now, prior to this operation in 1923, just tell us what portion of your opinion with reference to his mental condition is based upon your examinations and personal contact?

A. I never saw him before he came into the hospital.

Q. So that you have no direct knowledge of his mental condition prior to his appearance at the hospital, is that right?

A. I have an opinion.

Q. I asked you whether you had any personal knowledge of his condition mentally, his mental condition, prior to the time he appeared at the hospital?

A. I had no personal knowledge, no.

Q. Now, how long was he in the state of coma?

A. Oh, a few days.

Q. What portions of the day did you come to visit him at the hospital?

A. In the morning, and sometimes afterwards, in the day.

Q. For how long a period of time?

A. I saw him throughout the period of six weeks every day.

Q. For how long?

A. It would vary from fifteen minutes to an hour and a quarter.

Q. Just tell us what you did the first day you saw him?

A. The first day that I saw him, I subjected him to a rather thorough physical examination.

Q. He was in a state of coma?
A. Yes.
Q. What else did you do?
A. We made an attempt to pass catheters.
Q. Did you succeed?
A. We did finally succeed.
Q. And that passing was through what?
A. Through the urethra into the bladder.
Q. When was the next time that you saw him?
A. I saw him that same night.
Q. What did you do?
A. I looked at the chart, took note of his pulse and temperature, of his general condition, and took particular note of the laboratory findings, and gave orders.
Q. What did you do the next day?
A. Took note of changes, present condition and changes that have occurred in the interim, between when I saw him the night before.
Q. Well the second day.
A. We did the super-pubic cystotomy.
Q. Anything else?
A. Put him back to bed.
Q. Was he under an anesthetic at that time?
A. That was done under local anesthetic.
Q. Then what else did you do?
A. Then he was put back to bed with a bladder drain, and he was given fluids.
Q. What did you do the next day?
A. Well, from then on it was just a question of allowing his bladder to drain, under our observation, until such time as we felt his condition warranted the removal of the prostate gland.
Q. When did you have your first conversation?
A. I made attempts to converse with him from day to day. Now I don't remember just which particular hour or moment he came out of the coma.
Q. Was he out of the coma when you performed the systotomy?
A. Yes, he was partly out of it. He was clouded still, he remained clouded.

Q. Tell us when you had your first conversation with him, that you can recall.

A. Well, I conversed with him from the time he came in, and when he became semi-conscious I spoke with him. His answers were not coherent, if you can call that a conversation.

Q. That was while he was semi-conscious, is that right?

A. Semi-comatose.

Q. Now, have you ever talked to anybody else in that semi-comatose state, Doctor?

A. I have talked with persons.

Q. How many?

A. Well, I couldn't tell you that.

Q. Approximately?

A. Well, I wouldn't attempt to say.

Q. Well, you have performed 2,143 operations. How many of those did you converse with in a semi-comatose state?

A. Well, every patient who takes inhalement of anesthesia, there is a stage where they are—

Q. Semi?

A. (Continuing) —semi, and if you want to split it up to one-half and one-quarter, until they are finally completely unconscious, they are all stages.

Q. Out of those numbers that were in a semi-comatose state, how many of them gave you coherent answers to questions that you asked them?

A. None of them could be called perfectly coherent, and yet some particular thing that they might say would be coherent.

Q. Yes, but on the whole you would not say that they were in good mental condition at that particular time, would you, Doctor?

A. No, I wouldn't.

Q. You wouldn't say they were normal in all respects.

A. Absolutely not.

Q. As far as their mental condition, would you?

A. No.

Q. Therefore, at the time you talked to Giles McClendon when he was in a semi-conscious state of mind, you did not expect him to be normal mentally, did you, Doctor?

A. I did not. I did not base my opinion on that.

Q. Pardon me, I will get around to that.

A. I beg your pardon.

Q. Now, when was the next time you talked to him, Doctor?

A. Well, I talked with him every day, or made attempts to talk with him every day.

Q. Take the first day and tell us what you talked to him about, the first attempt that you made.

A. I would not be able to answer that specifically. The probabilities are that I asked him how he felt, and "What is your name," and "if anything hurts you," in an effort to get at something about the case.

Q. That's it exactly. Your position was surgeon in that particular case, wasn't it, Doctor?

A. Absolutely.

Q. You were called in for that particular purpose?

A. Yes.

Q. All you were interested in at that time was to see that he came along properly and successfully after you operated on him?

A. (Witness nods head.)

Q. And also for the purpose of determining the proper time to complete the prostate gland operation, is that right?

A. (Witness nods head.)

Q. Nobody had called you in there, Doctor, to test this man's mental powers, did they?

A. No.

Q. And you have never studied psychiatry, nor any of its branches, have you?

A. Not as a specialty.

Q. By the way, have you ever testified as a psychiatrist in any case?

A. I never have.

Q. Have you ever testified in any case, called in as an expert, to give your opinion on the mental condition of any patient?

A. Not as an expert.

Q. Just merely as a layman, just as any other layman, is that right?

A. No, no. As a physician, but not as a psychiatrist.

Q. Tell us what you said to the gentleman the next day that you talked to him, Doctor?

A. Oh, I couldn't tell you that.

Q. What's that?

A. I couldn't tell you that. I don't remember.

Q. Well, tell us any other day thereafter of any conversation you had with Giles McClendon, give us the details of it?

Mr. Smith: Now, if the Court please, I have tried to be as patient as possible, but I do make an objection to counsel unnecessarily encumbering the record, and asking unnecessary questions. He has been over it two or three times.

The Court: Overruled.

Counsel: Please give us the details of any conversation you can remember that you had with Giles McClendon during any of that period he was in the hospital?

A. I can't give you any details of conversations.

Q. Can you give us the substance of any conversation you had with him during any of that time?

A. My conversations were purely related to his physical condition. I had no personal conversations with him about anything, about any matter.

Q. That was during your entire connection with him in the hospital, is that right?

A. Absolutely. I had no personal contact with him at all.

Q. Tell us, after he left the hospital, Doctor, of any conversation you had with him, any particular conversation?

A. I have had no particular conversations with him at any time, except with reference to his physical condition.

Q. You were looking for physical symptoms, is that right, Doctor?

A. Absolutely, but I could not overlook the mental.

Q. When was the last time that you saw Giles McClendon?

A. I wouldn't be able to tell you that date. It has been some years ago. It has not been since 1926.

Q. Can you specify any particular date, or give us the details of any conversation you had with him since 1924?

A. I cannot.

Q. Now, I believe you did state that the removal of the prostate gland did not accentuate any mental infirmities he might have had, is that right?

A. No, I didn't say that the removal— It did not accentuate any, that is correct, yes.

Q. I thought I understood you correctly. In fact, it would improve his condition, because it would have relieved it from physical pain and discomfort, and the obstruction in his bowels, and so forth, so that it would improve his mental condition, is that right?

A. Yes.

Counsel: That is all.

§ 497. Cross-examination in handwriting cases.

A number of methods of cross-examination, where handwriting is in question, are suggested by Albert S. Osborn, in his book "The Problem of Proof." They are excellent illustrations of cross-examination of both lay and self-styled, but not qualified, expert witnesses. The comments and illustrations are as follows:

"The most common error in document expert testimony is made by the bank clerk or ordinary business man, who testifies that he can look at a signature and at once decide that it is genuine from its general appearance alone. Witnesses of this class can often be effectively cross-examined by a series of questions like those here given. If the questions, however, are not given with accuracy and the witness is not held strictly to a definite line of inquiry, the whole effect is often lost.

"It is entirely proper for the examiner to have in hand a series of questions fully written out.

First Series

"The following examination will sometimes decidedly weaken, if not entirely destroy, the testimony of a witness who is mistaken and depends only on general appearance as the basis for an opinion:

"Point: Writing can be skillfully imitated, especially by the tracing method, and when so imitated, may resemble genuine writing that the witness who judges by general appearance alone is easily deceived.

Illustration:

"Q. You have said that this signature is in your opinion genuine?

Q. Is there such a thing as forgery of signatures?

Q. Is it possible for one person to imitate with some degree of success the form and general appearance of the handwriting of another?

Q. In your opinion some imitators would be more successful in this than others, would they not?

Q. And if this was done well enough it would be difficult to detect, would it not?

Q. It might be done well enough, could it not, so that from the general appearance alone it would be dangerous to say positively that the writing is genuine?

Q. You know, do you not, that, because only this general appearance test was applied, that hundreds of thousands of dollars are paid on forgeries every year by banks and business men?

Q. You have said that this signature is genuine because its design and general appearance are the same as your memory of the genuine signatures of this writer?

Q. Are we to understand that your point is that when you look at this signature it looks to you like a genuine signature and your opinion is based upon this view of the signature as a whole?

Q. Have you ever seen what is described as a forgery by tracing?

Q. Do you understand what a traced forgery is?

Q. What is it?

Q. If a tracing was well made, would it not show the same form as the model?

Q. If then the design was correct would it not have the same general appearance as a genuine signature, and, according to the method you have applied in this case, would you not be obliged to say that it is a genuine signature?

Q. Then is it not true that this very signature itself may be such an imitation?

Q. As a matter of fact (to a bank clerk), and you would not pay out money on handwriting alone, would you?

Q. With a check payable to bearer, endorsed and presented by a total stranger, with this signature on it, would you pay it if the check was for $5?

Q. Would you pay such a check payable to bearer to a total stranger if it called for $500 of your money or your bank's money?

Q. How about paying a $5000 check under those circumstances?

Q. Would you pay it without requiring identification?

Q. Why would you require identification?

Q. If this disputed signature, as it appears, was attached to a letter ordering you to send $5000 of a depositor's money by express, would you send it without investigation?

Q. You would not, of course. Now, why would you not send it?

Q. It is because, is it not, that you would not depend upon your opinion regarding the handwriting alone?

Q. This being true, would you think it safe to depend upon your opinion here in this case?

Q. Have you ever paid a forgery?

Q. Has a forgery ever been paid by your bank?

Q. Do you know of a forgery ever having been paid by any bank?

Q. If a forgery was so paid it was because the paying teller thought the signature was genuine, is not that true?

Q. And now finally, do you think it would be safe here to depend upon your opinion?

"If the questions of this first series are asked of an uninformed witness and it is shown that he is not qualified to testify, other incompetent witnesses may thus be kept off from the witness stand. In some cases a whole troop of similar witnesses have been assembled to give similar testimony. It is very important that the questions be asked, accurately and in the proper order. As they can all, or nearly all, be answered by yes or no, a yes or no answer should be firmly insisted upon. The witness should be kept strictly within the line of the questions and not allowed to wander."

Second Series

"This series of questions are intended to show that the ordinary untrained witness is not qualified to give an opinion as to the identity of a handwriting, and is not qualified to give technical testimony as to the genuineness or forgery of a disputed signature. The problem is a scientific one and uninformed and inexperienced witnesses cannot furnish reliable assistance. With one who is not a bank clerk the examination should begin with the eighth question.

"Point: To show that the witness has made no study of the subject, is posing as an expert, and is not qualified.

"Q. As a paying teller (if the witness is a bank clerk) or as a business man passing on handwriting, did you, or do you not, make a careful study of every check presented to you for payment?

Q. There would not be time for this at a teller's window, would there?

Q. What you do is to look at the check, look at the one that presents it, and if the circumstances are regular and the check is not too large, you pay it, do you not?

Q. You, in fact, pay if all the surrounding circumstances are regular, do you not?

Q. Have you ever paid a forgery?

Q. How many forgeries has your bank paid?

Q. Was the general appearance of the forged signature good?

Q. Have you made a study of the subject of handwriting identification?

Q. Do you know anything about the various systems of handwriting?

Q. Would not two writers of the same system be more likely to write in a similar way than two writers of different systems?

Q. Two writers of the same system might write much alike, is not this true?

Q. Would you say that a signature is genuine or not genuine from one characteristic in it or one thing about it?

Q. Is there anything about this signature that causes you to hesitate at all in reaching the conclusion that it is genuine?

Q. Did you compare it with any signatures or give any opinion from recollection?

Q. What signatures did you have?

Q. How many were there?

Q. Were there some particular qualities in this disputed signature that led you to think that it was genuine?

Q. What were they?

Q. Would the characteristics you have described as indicating that this signature is genuine be likely to be imitated in a careful imitation?

Q. Would they be likely to be reproduced in an accurate tracing?

Q. If so reproduced, you would then think the signature genuine even though it is not?

Q. It is true, is it not, that you may be mistaken in your opinion regarding this signature?

Q. You would advise other means of determining whether or not it is genuine than merely your opinion alone?

Q. If the question involved $10,000 of your own money would you still depend upon your own judgment?

Q. You, of course, do not hesitate to say that you may be mistaken in your opinion?

Q. What special instruments for use in this work do you possess?

Q. Have you at any time made any serious study of the subject?

Q. Do you know there are special books on the subject?

Q. What books on the subject have you read?

Q. Have you ever read or seen (showing book) Osborn on 'Questioned Documents'?

Q. Have you ever read or seen (not showing book but having some book in hand) Ames on 'Forgery'?

Q. Did you ever hear of it?

Q. Have you ever read or seen (not showing book but having some book in hand) Hagan on 'Disputed Handwriting'? (There is such a book.)

Q. Have you ever seen or read (have some book in hand) Farnsworth on 'Forged Documents'? (There is no such book.)

Q. Have you ever even heard of any of these books on this subject before today?

(As a rule these men will admit not having read any books on the subject and it will thus appear they have made no real study of the question. If the witness says he has heard of, or read, 'Farnsworth,' this point should at once be followed up by mentioning other fictitious books and authors, and then finally telling him which are real and which fictitious.)"

Third Series

"If the corrupt witness who has testified against obvious facts has not himself exposed the unreliable character of his testimony he may be asked the questions given below.

"Point: To show that the witness has misinterpreted or ignored significant evidence, has exaggerated certain details by which he has attempted to befog the question and mislead the jury. In some cases it is advisable to make a witness still further emphasize the incredible testimony he has given.

"As already suggested, it may be bad policy to cross-examine a witness of this kind on the technical question involved, except under the conditions already outlined in this chapter. If, however, a witness of this class has defended a crude and obvious forgery, saying that it is genuine, some of the following questions should be asked:

"Q. Is there anything of any kind about this disputed signature that requires excuse, apology, or explanation?

Q. Did you find about it anything of any kind that was suspicious in any degree?

Q. Do you consider it an average, normal, genuine signature of this writer of this date?

(If the witness says the signature is not suspicious in any way the question can be followed up as follows):

Q. Comparing the disputed signature with the signatures nearest in date to it, do you find any differences that even remotely suggest that the signature may not be genuine?

Q. You see none?

Q. You do see differences though, do you not?

Q. If there were twice as many as you find would you still say the signature is genuine?

Q. If there were four times as many differences of this same character, would you still say the signature is genuine?

Q. Have you simply ignored the differences you have found or excused them?

(If the witness says there are no differences whatever and that the disputed signature is an average, normal signature, he then should be asked):

Q. If this disputed signature, apart from the document on which it appears, was submitted to you with three or four of the standard signatures nearest in date, would you be able to tell which signature was under suspicion if you were not told?

Q. You would, of course, know at once which was disputed, wouldn't you?

Q. Do you think your judgment on the subjects is based on such reasons as to make it reliable and trustworthy?

(If the signature is a palpably divergent one and this divergence can be seen by the jury, and has been minimized or ignored by the witness, the following questions should be asked. During this inquiry and the preceding one the photographs should be in the hands of the jury):

Q. How long did it take you to reach the conclusion that this is a genuine signature?

Q. Who submitted the matter to you?

Q. What standards did you have?

Q. Did you make a memorandum of what standards you examined?

Q. Have you that memorandum?

Q. Did you make a report in the case?

Q. To whom was the report made?

Q. Was it oral or written?

Q. Did you ask for any additional standard signatures?

Q. Was your first report the same as your latest?

Q. Do you have a copy of your report with you, and if so, are you willing to submit it or are you willing to submit the original that you submitted in the case?

Q. Did you not say at the beginning that there were some suspicious qualities in this signature that needed explanation?

Q. Have you your notes of the examination with you?"

CHAPTER X

HYPOTHETICAL QUESTIONS

§ 498. In general.

A recognized method of obtaining opinions of experts in trials is through the medium of hypothetical questions. Its use is indicated in all cases where the facts upon which an opinion is desired are not within the personal knowledge of the expert. Where the witnesses' knowledge of the facts is gained from someone else and would, therefore, be hearsay, his opinion must be obtained by means of a hypothetical question. Since he has no personal knowledge of the truth of the facts, his opinion cannot be given directly upon them.

§ 499. Value.

A hypothetical question, when properly prepared, has a favorable psychological effect as it serves to sum up for the jury all of the important material facts and evidence which the propounder of the question feels should entitle his client to a verdict.

§ 500. Preparation of hypothetical question.

The hypothetical question to be most effective should almost always be prepared in advance. It should be prepared in conjunction with, or submitted to the expert before the trial. All phases of the question should be discussed with the medical or other adviser to be certain that all of the material facts of the case are properly included. The witness will then have all necessary factors in logical sequence, which will give him a true basis upon which to render his opinion. In some instances where hypothetical questions are not prepared in advance, experts have been compelled to admit that they were unable to give an opinion based upon the floundering, incomplete hypothetical question the trial attorney was trying to submit to them during the stress and excitement of the trial.

§ 501. —Method of preparation.

With a little practice and a knowledge of the general rules of law governing hypothetical questions, it should be a comparatively simple matter for the trial attorney to prepare a legally sufficient hypothetical question in his office. Some attorneys claim this cannot be done. However, if the case has been fully and properly prepared and all witnesses have been interviewed in accordance with the suggestions heretofore made, it should be a comparatively simple matter to prepare a hypothetical question long before trial. The attorney then knows the theory upon which he intends to proceed, and also knows just what the testimony of each witness will be. If on the trial, one or two or more material facts are brought out which were not considered in preparing the question, it is a very simple matter to include such facts in the proper place while propounding the question to the expert. As a result of preparing the question in advance, it is then only necessary to keep in mind the one or two additional material facts brought out on the trial; and what ordinarily might have been a hesitant, floundering, incomplete and disconnected question, becomes instead a smooth and legally correct one. A better impression is made on both the court and jury with the correspondent feeling of confidence always brought about by complete preparation. Some lawyers object to the preparation of a hypothetical question in advance by writing it out, on the grounds that it loses some of its psychological value in reading it before the jury. They contend that it does not sound like a natural question. While this may be true in some instances, still when properly prepared and properly read by the trial lawyer in a clear, well modulated voice, not too rapidly, nor in a tiresome monotone (after some practice in reading the question aloud prior to trial) it will be found that very little psychological value is lost due to the reading of the question, while a great deal of good results from such early preparation.

§ 502. Elements.

Usually, the more troublesome features, in the preparation of a hypothetical question, are the *commencement* and the *conclusion* of the question. A full and complete itemization of all the important material facts of the proponent's case usually insures the inclusion of all necessary factors in the *body* of the hypothetical question.

§ 503. Commencement.

Most jurisdictions require that the question to be presented to the expert shall be in *hypothetical form,* which directs the witness to *assume* as true all the factors included in the *body* of the question.

In many states, the commencement of the question is usually in the following form:

"Doctor, *assume* a young man twenty-six years of age . . ."

Sometimes, instead of the word "assume," the words "supposing" or "consider" have been used by trial attorneys.

§ 504. Body.

The body of the question contains all of the *material* (not each and every detail) facts upon which the opinion of the witness is desired. It must also be in hypothetical form. Each material factor, or series of factors, is sometimes preceded by a direction to witness to further assumptions, such as:

"Assume further, doctor, that the young man was employed as an electric arc-welder, for a period of two years, and that he—etc."

§ 505. —Limit use of word "assume."

While the question must be hypothetical in form, it is not advisable from a psychological point of view to over emphasize that fact as a great deal of value may be lost so far as the jury is concerned. Therefore, the use of the word "assume" should be limited as much as possible in the body of the hypothetical question. Some trial attorneys use the words "assume further" after each thought or sentence. Too much prominence is thus given to the fact that it *is* a hypothetical situation.

On the other hand, where the word "assume" is used just sufficiently to comply with the legal requirements, and all the facts are graphically and interestingly detailed in the *body* of the question, the hypothetical question then becomes, psychologically, a much greater moving force in favorably influencing the jury.

It is suggested that by only including *material* facts in the question that the lawyer will not be guilty of unduly drawing out the question and possibly tiring the jury.

§ 506. Conclusion.

The *conclusion* is usually the most troublesome part of the hypothetical question. To keep from "invading the province of the jury" and to determine just how far a conclusion may go frequently causes great concern. An improper conclusion invalidates the entire question.

§ 507. — Forms of conclusions.

Ordinarily, in cases where the facts are in dispute, the *conclusion* must confine the opinion to be given to the probable result of the combination of facts or circumstances assumed. It may be in one of the following forms:

(1) Doctor, have you an opinion, based upon reasonable medical certainty as to whether or not there might or could be a causal connection between the accident described and the condition of ill-being found as set forth in this question?

(2) Have you an opinion, based upon a reasonable medical certainty as to whether there is or may be a direct causal connection between the particular traumatism or fall described and the resulting pathology as described to you in this hypothetical question?

(3) Have you an opinion, based upon reasonable medical certainty whether or not the given condition or malady of the hypothetical person may or could result from and be caused by the facts stated in the hypothetical question?

(4) Doctor, assuming those facts to be true, have you an opinion, based upon a reasonable certainty and from a medical and surgical point of view as to whether the facts assumed in the question and the injury assumed, namely, the dislocation of the vertebrae and the fracture of the lamina of the sixth cervical vertebra, are sufficient to cause the symptoms and the conditions assumed in the question?

(5) Doctor, have you an opinion, based upon reasonable certainty and from a medical and surgical viewpoint, if the facts assumed could cause the condition assumed and existing up to the present time?

(6) Doctor, have you an opinion, based upon a reasonable medical certainty, as to what might or could have caused the death of the hypothetical man?

(7) (In an occupational disease case) Have you an opinion, doctor, as to whether there might or could, with reasonable medical certainty, be a causal relationship between this employment which I have described in this question and the condition of this young man in June 1931 and down to the present time?

(8) (Aggravation of a pre-existing ailment) Have you an opinion, based upon reasonable medical certainty as to whether or not there is or may be a direct causal connection between the accident described, the pre-existing ailment related herein, and the condition of ill-being found as set forth in this question?

(9) (In malpractice case—Doctor) Doctor, assuming the facts stated in this question to be true, have you an opinion, based upon reasonable certainty and from a medical and surgical point of view, as to whether or not the course pursued by the operating surgeon was such a course as could be pursued by a skillful and careful physician and surgeon engaged in the same line of work in the City of —— and State of —— in January, 1932?

(10) (In malpractice case—Lawyer) Mr. Jones, assuming the facts to be as stated in this hypothetical question, have you an opinion as to whether or not Mr. Blank in the defense and trial of the case of Henry Thompson, used and exercised the same degree of care and diligence and ability that is usually, ordinarily and reasonably used by lawyers in good standing in the City of —— and State of —— in June, 1933?

§ 508. Several opinions on same hypothesis.

Several conclusions or opinions may be requested of the witness, based upon the same hypothesis, for example, as to whether the condition is *temporary* or *permanent.*

Illustrations

(1) Now, doctor, assuming the facts set forth in the same hypothetical question, have you an opinion, based upon reasonable medical certainty, as to whether or not the conditions described are temporary or permanent?

(2) Doctor, assuming the same hypothesis, have you an opinion, based upon reasonable certainty and from a medical and surgical viewpoint, as to whether or not the conditions set forth in the hypothetical question are temporary or permanent?

Some lawyers also follow up with a question in reference to *future medical care and attention.*

Illustration

Doctor, assuming the facts set forth in the same hypothetical question, have you an opinion, based upon reasonable medical certainty, as to whether or not it will be necessary for the hypothetical person *to continue under medical treatment?*

§ 509. Some requirements.

The hypothetical question should be so framed as to reflect the theory of the party propounding it, as shown by the facts admitted or proved.[1] With the permission of the court, facts assumed in a hypothetical question may be predicated upon testimony which the court is assured that counsel will adduce later.[2] Whether the facts stated in a hypothetical question

1 22 C. J. 708–712 (excerpts). Roche v. Baldwin, 143 Cal. 186, 76 Pac. 956; C. & E. I. R. Co. v. Wallace, 202 Ill. 129; Saintman v. Maxwell, 154 Ind. 114, 54 N. E. 397; Stutsman v. Des Moines, etc., R. Co., 180 Iowa 524, 163 N. W. 580; Peo. v. Bowen, 165 Mich. 231, 130 N. W. 706; Middleton v. Whitridge, 213 N. Y. 499, 108 N. E. 192; Presbyterian Church, etc. v. Bevan, 34 Ohio Cir. Ct. 318; Brewster v. Forney, 196 S. W. 635 (Tex.); Sullivan v. Minneapolis, etc., R. Co., 167 Wis. 518, 167 N. W. 311; Barber's App., 63 Conn. 393, 27 Atl. 973, 22 L. R. A. 90; Poole v. Dean, 152 Mass. 589, 26 N. E. 406.

The facts upon which the question is based need not be proved to a certainty. Sprengel v. Schroeder, 203 Ill. App. 213; Frankfort v. Manhattan R. Co., 12 Misc. 13, 33 N. Y. S. 36; Gulf, etc., R. Co. v. Abbott, 146 S. W. 1078 (Tex.); Tebo v. Augusta, 90 Wis. 405, 63 N. W. 1045; Graves v. Union Oil Co., 36 Cal. App. 766, 173 Pac. 618; In Quin v. Higgins, 63 Wis. 664, 24 N. W. 482, it was held that the question could not be excluded on the ground that in the opinion of the judge the facts were not established by a preponderance of the evidence.

2 Conrad v. St. Louis, etc., R. Co., 201 Ill. App. 276; Eckels v. Halsten, 136 Ill. App. 111; Delaney v. Framingham, etc., R. Co., 202 Mass. 359, 88 N. E. 773; Darling v. Grand Rapids, etc., Co., 184 Mich. 607, 151 N. W. 701; Jarvis v. Metropolitan St. R. Co., 65 App. Div. 490, 72 N. Y. S. 829; Gulf, etc., R. Co. v. Abbott, 146 S. W. 1078 (Tex.).

are sufficiently established by the proof, is a question for the jury.[3] The length of the question is a matter almost wholly within the discretion of the court.[4] While no truly material fact should be left out, the question should not be unduly drawn out for fear of tiring the jury; though it is generally necessary to include all material facts in disputed cases, it is permissible to use only part of the facts, if they are sufficient upon which to base an opinion consistent with the propounders' theory of the case.[5] *Slight* exaggeration, coloring, or evidencing partisanship in relating the assumed facts to the witness will not make the question objectionable in the discretion of the court,[6] but when indulged in to the extent of being misleading, is fatal.[6a] The exact language of the witness who gave evidence of a fact need not be used if meaning is the same.[7] There may be more than one question based upon the same hypothesis without repeating the entire hypothetical question. In order to take advantage of defects in hypothetical questions in most instances, it is necessary that the *objections be specific.* The objection, to be availing, must specifically point out the deficiencies so that counsel propounding the question may have an opportunity to remedy the defects;[8] otherwise the defect is waived. A general objection to a hypothetical question only goes to its materiality. A specific objection raised for the first time on appeal will not be permitted. In New York, it seems that where the wit-

3 Public Utilities Co. v. Handorf, 185 Ind. 254, 112 N. E. 775; C. & E. I. R. Co. v. Wallace, 202 Ill. 129.

4 Barber's App., 63 Conn. 393, 27 Atl. 937, 22 L. R. A. 90; Jones v. Portland, 88 Mich. 598, 50 N. W. 584, 34 N. Y. S. 572.

5 Barker v. Louis Storage & Transfer Co., 79 Conn. 342, 65 Atl. 143; Botwinnes v. Allgood, 113 Ill. App. 188; In re Henry, 167 Iowa 557, 149 N. W. 605; Stowell v. Standard Oil Co., 139 Mich. 18, 102 N. W. 227; Van Wycklen v. Brooklyn, 118 N. Y. 424, 24 N. E. 179; Hite v. Keen, 149 Wis. 207, 134 N. W. 383, 135 N. W. 354.

. . . All material facts should be stated. Fuchs v. Tone, 218 Ill. 445, 75 N. E. 1014; Peo. v. Lake, 12 N. Y. 358; Sargeant v. Barnes, 159 S. W. 366 (Tex.); Blume v. State, 154 Ind. 343, 56 N. E. 771.

6 Woodworth v. Brooklyn El. R. Co., 22 App. Div. 501, 48 N. Y. S. 80; Murphy v. Marston Coal Co., 183 Mass. 385, 67 N. E. 342.

6a . . . Williams v. Brown, 28 Ohio St. 547; Beck v. Hanline, 122 Md. 68, 89 Atl. 377; Swanson v. Hood, 99 Wash. 506, 170 Pac. 135.

7 Presbyterian, etc. v. Bevan, 34 Ohio Cir. Ct. 318; Trinity, etc., R. Co. v. McCune, 154 S. W. 237 (Tex.); Grill v. O'Dell, 113 Md. 625, 77 Atl. 984.

8 See Specific Objections, page 347.

ness has observed part of the phenomena on which his opinion is desired, a hypothetical question may be propounded which sets forth the unobserved facts and assumes the facts observed without enumerating them.[9]

§ 510. Objections.[10]

A hypothetical question may be objectionable because it is a purely theoretical question, too indefinite to permit the witness to form a judgment of any value, misleading, ambiguous, unintelligible, where it shows misconception of the evidence, when it is complicated, vague, involved or obscure, argumentative, when it calls for mere conjecture, where it does not present sufficient facts upon which to base a reasonable conclusion, where it calls for a categorical answer and the witness says he cannot answer it, or where it is based on an assumption which is false or assumes facts which are not in evidence. It is objectionable if question includes with other facts the opinion of another expert and when it generally includes examination of witness without fully setting out the evidence of such examination.

9 Blake v. Bedford, 170 Iowa 128, 151 N. W. 74; Sellack v. Janesville, 100 Wis. 157, 75 N. W. 975; In re Flint, 100 Cal. 391, 34 Pac. 863; Peo. v. Johnson, 70 Ill. App. 634; Bonner v. Mayfield, 82 Tex. 234, 188 S. W. 305; Matteson v. N. Y. C. R. Co., 35 N. Y. 487; The Clipper v. Logan, 18 Ohio 375.

10 Question is objectionable when it is argumentative: Houston, etc., R. Co. v. Johnson, 118 S. W. 1150 (Tex.); . . . when it is conjectural: Hamilton v. Michigan Cent. R. Co., 135 Mich. 95, 97 N. W. 392; . . . when the question does not present sufficient facts to afford reasonable grounds for a conclusion: In re Henry, 167 Iowa 557, 149 N. W. 605; when it does not contain all the essential facts: Catlin v. Trader's Ins. Co., 83 Ill. App. 40; Knight v. Overman Wheel Co., 174 Mass. 455, 54 N. E. 890; . . . when it is too indefinite to form a judgment of value: Barber's App., 63 Conn. 393, 27 Atl. 973, 22 L. R. A. 90; Kuhns v. Wisconsin, etc., R. Co., 70 Iowa 561, 31 N. W. 868; Turner v. Ridgeway Tp., 105 Mich. 409, 63 N. W. 406; McGinnis v. 3rd Ave. R. Co., 104 App. Div. 342, 93 N. Y. S. 787; . . . when it is misleading: Carpenter v. Bainley, 94 Cal. 406, 29 Pac. 1101; Barber's App., supra; McCormick, etc., Co. v. Gray, 100 Ind. 285; Farrell v. Haze, 157 Mich. 374, 122 N. W. 197; Middleton v. Whitridge, supra; . . . when it is ambiguous: Currie v. Consolidated R. Co., 81 Conn. 383, 71 Atl. 356; . . . when it is unintelligible: Thayer v. Smoky Hollow Coal Co., 121 Iowa 121, 96 N. W. 718; . . . when it is complicated, involved or obscure: Chicago Union Tract. Co. v. Sugar, 117 Ill. App. 583; Howes v. Colburn, 165 Mass. 385, 388, 43 N. E. 125, 22 C. J. 709–712.

§ 511. Previous good health.

Previous good health should be shown.

§ 512. Improper commencement.

In some states, in a case where the facts are in dispute, a hypothetical question which commences, "Doctor, assuming that a man whose present condition is as you disclose the condition of the plaintiff to be" has been held to be improper.[11]

§ 513. Modifying question.

Where an objection is made to a hypothetical question which the court indicates is well founded, it is always advisable for the attorney to state that he will modify or adopt as part of his question the facts stated by opponent as having been left out. The expert should then be asked to assume such additional facts, and the conclusion should be repeated, asking the expert if he has an opinion based upon the entire question as *modified.*

This is a simple method of securing an answer to an objectionable hypothetical question. An attempt to repeat the entire question and to add the additional or modifying facts will give opposing counsel an opportunity to think of a number of other objections, one or two of which may be of sufficient importance to prevent the using of the prepared question at all. Opponent by making one or two specific objections waives all other possible objections.

§ 514. Note all objections.

Objections to hypothetical questions must be specific under the authorities cited herein. One method of preparing for possible objections to be made to opponent's hypothetical question is to note on a piece of paper each ground of objection as the question is read, particularly as to the form of the commencement, all material facts which have been left out in the body of the question and as to the form of the conclusion. During the early days of the trial attorney's experience he should not depend upon his memory alone. If the question is a long one and there are more objections to be

11 Hammond v. Bloomington Canning Co., 190 Ill. App. 511.

raised as the question progresses he will find that he has forgotten the first few objections he was going to make. They may have been the really important ones while the later objections may not be so material and may be properly overruled. It can readily be seen, therefore, how much better it is to note down a word or two to indicate all of the objections the attorney expects to interpose.

§ 515. Copies of hypothetical questions.

In some jurisdictions the practice requires the proposed hypothetical question to be prepared in duplicate, with one copy to be furnished to the opposing counsel. Generally, however, there is no legal requirement to supply one's opponent with a copy of the hypothetical question. Still, some attorneys make it a practice to request opposing counsel (in the presence of the jury) for permission to see the prepared hypothetical question so that they may intelligently make their objections. If possession of the question is secured in this manner the making of objections is considerably facilitated.

§ 516. Having question re-read.

If counsel refuses such request then the attorney should ask that the court-reporter be permitted to re-read the question to him *out of the presence of the jury*. There is considerable harm possible in the re-reading of a well-planned hypothetical question before a jury.

The court will rarely object to the re-reading of the question if the lawyer did not hear all of it. While the court reporter is re-reading the question he can make notes as to the possible objections. The objections should then be stated to the court in the presence of the jury and a ruling secured thereon.

§ 517. Anticipating cross-examination.

In all instances where the hypothetical question is submitted to the expert before he has taken the witness stand, (which should be done in every possible case), it should become the practice, during the early portion of the direct examination of the expert, to make known the fact that the expert has seen the hypothetical question before the trial and that the lawyer has discussed it with him as he would with any other witness. This will tend to eliminate possible prejudicial cross-examination by the opponent in reference to this point. It will then appear to the jury as a perfectly natural and honorable thing to do. If this procedure is not followed and counsel brings this fact out for the first time on cross-examination, he will usually do it in a manner and in a tone of voice that will tend to cast suspicion upon the testimony of the expert.

Illustration

Q. Doctor, I have discussed this hypothetical question and your testimony with you before just as I would with any other witness, have I not?

A. Yes, sir.

Q. All right, doctor. Will you assume . . . (Here read the hypothetical question.)

§ 518. Answers to hypothetical question.

The answer to a hypothetical question must be based on the hypothesis stated and should not be argumentative, conjectural, or indefinite, and must be responsive.[12] Where the question asks the expert if he has an opinion, the proper answer is that he has an opinion. This is followed by the question as to what his opinion is. In most instances, the answer must correspond with the question part of the conclusion. If the conclusion is as to the "causal connection," the witness must state, that, in his opinion, there was a causal connection between the accident and the condition described. Then, if desired, it is permissible to ask the witness to state his reasons for the opinions expressed by him or to explain how his conclusion was reached.[13] In New York it has been held that an answer to the effect that an ulcer was "apt," "liable," and "likely" to re-open instead of "probable" was competent.[14]

[12] 22 C. J. 720–721; Cobb v. United, etc., Co., 191 N. Y. 475, 84 N. E. 395; Taylor v. McClintock, 87 Ark. 243, 112 S. W. 405; . . . nor conjectural: Swenson v. Brooklyn Heights R. Co., 15 Misc. 69, 36 N. Y. S. 445.

[13] The expert may give reasons for his opinion: See Expert Witnesses, page 386; Reclamation Dist., etc., v. Inglin, 31 Cal. App. 49, 160 Pac. 1098; Quincy Gas Co. v. Schmitt, 123 Ill. App. 647.

[14] Moran v. Duke Drug Co., 134 N. Y. S. 995.

Illustration

Q. Have you an opinion (as to accident and condition)?
A. Yes, I have an opinion.
Q. What is your opinion?
A. My opinion is that there is a causal connection between the present condition of the hypothetical person and the accident.

§ 519. As to temporary or permanent.

Illustration

Q. Have you an opinion based upon the same hypothesis, as to whether or not the condition is temporary or permanent?
A. Yes, I have an opinion.
Q. What is that opinion?
A. That the condition is permanent.

§ 520. If basis of opinion is desired.

Illustration

Q. What is the basis of your opinion?
A. . . .

§ 521. Motion to strike.

If the answer is objectionable, and the proper basis of objection is stated to the court, it should always be coupled with a motion to strike the answer on the grounds stated, so as to preserve the record properly for review.

§ 522. Using opponent's hypothetical question.

In some instances it is possible to use opponent's hypothetical question against him with damaging effect. Let us take the case where a lawyer represents the defendant and the medical or other expert advises him that the opposing expert has given an opinion based on the hypothetical question which is not well-founded or true. A copy of the hypothetical question which is not well-founded or true, should be secured from the court reporter during the recess period and then the same hypothetical question should be propounded to the defendant's expert with the preliminary remark before the court and jury that it is the same question that was propounded by the opponent to his expert. If defendant's expert has been duly qualified and then gives a directly contrary opinion on the same facts, the opponent's testimony will be greatly minimized if not destroyed by one or two more of defendant's experts also concurring in the same contrary opinion.

This procedure has proven unusually effective in a number of cases.

§ 523. Hypothetical question in personal injury case.

Illustration

Q. Doctor, assume that a man forty-six years old, in good health, who on the 10th day of August, 1929, had been riding in a motor bus seated on the back seat of the bus which was being driven along a country road, and which suddenly ran into some ruts or depressions in the highway causing a jolting or jarring of the bus sufficient to throw him from or dislodge him from his seat, causing him to fall backward in such a manner that he sustained an injury, a compressed fracture of the first lumbar vertebrae; immediately following the fall against the seat, he experienced severe and excruciating pain in his back; he was placed lying down on the seat, and the bus was then driven slowly for five or six or eight miles; and, when it arrived at a small town it was met by a doctor who took him to the hospital, strapped his back or immobilized it and put him in bed in the hospital for a period of five or six days.

During this time the patient was experiencing great pain and was given morphine and other narcotics to alleviate his pain and suffering; he was then removed to another city where he was examined and X-ray pictures were taken of him; the X-ray pictures disclosed that this fracture of the first lumbar vertebrae was interfering with his ability to walk, and was causing him excruciating pain; his bowels up to that time had not moved or functioned from the time of the accident; an ambulance was then called, and he was taken to a train and sent to Chicago. He was taken to another hospital, and other X-ray pictures were taken which disclosed the same condition in the back, namely a compressed fracture of the first lumbar vertebrae; and it showed the abnormal condition of the lumbo-sacral joint with the sacrum itself out of alignment to the extent of forty-five degrees; the conditions shown in the first X-ray films taken in the hospital in Chicago, August 20th, are substantially the same conditions that are shown in all X-ray films, with the exception that there is now a bone splint appearing in the back from the dorsal down to the lumbar vertebrae and over the junction of the first lumbar; he was placed in bed in the hospital and in an extension, or with weights on his legs with a view to straightening out the spine or causing some relief; during all this time he suffered greatly, and was given narcotics or morphia to relieve his suffering; during this period of time and in the interim he suffered spasms of the legs and muscles throughout his body and limbs; on the 10th of September, the same year, 1929, he was operated on by a competent physician and surgeon, who, after cutting away the muscles and removing the ligaments from the spinus processes, cut a bone out of his tibia seven inches long, three-quarters of an inch wide, and approximately one-half an inch in thickness, and was grafted or welded into his back, which resulted in a stiffening of that part of the back where the bone graft was made; following the operation he was unconscious for a period of practically five days, and for an additional period of five days he had a very vague recollection of the events, and was not fully conscious; thereafter he was conscious, and remained in bed for six or eight weeks; during all this time he was in a weakened condition, but after a period of about three months he was able to be up and about the hospital wearing a Taylor brace; when he is on his feet for ten or fifteen minutes he suffers excruciating pain in the lower part of his back which is relieved when he lies down or becomes at rest; when he sits down after standing he gets some relief for five or ten minutes, but after he is seated for a time he again suffers pain, and must lie down in order to get relief; that condition is present up to this time; Doctor, assuming these facts to be true, have you an opinion based upon reasonable certainty, and from a medical and surgical standpoint as to whether there might or could be a causal connection between the accident described and the condition of ill-being found as set forth in this question?

A. I have an opinion.

Q. What is your opinion, Doctor?

A. My opinion is that there is a causal connection between the present condition of the hypothetical person and the accident.

Q. Doctor, assuming the same hypothetical person and the same hypothesis, have you an opinion based upon a reasonable certainty and from a medical and surgical standpoint, as to whether that condition as described at the present is permanent or temporary?

A. I have an opinion.

Q. What is your opinion, Doctor?

A. The condition is permanent.

Q. Doctor, what is your opinion as to whether another operation performed upon this man would correct the deformity in the lower part of his spine?

A. In my opinion it could not be done.

Q. Why, Doctor?

A. The deformity in the lower part of the spine is of such a nature it would require separation of these vertebrae in order to put them in a natural and normal position. The separation of those vertebrae entails a degree of surgical shock and damage to the tissues and to the spinal nerves that come down through that region that would make it impossible to do it and have the man survive the operation.

Q. Well, assume, Doctor, that the operation you have in mind were successful, what kind of a back would he have then?

A. He would be as rigid as a poker from his hips up to the shoulders.

Q. Have you an opinion as to whether such an operation would restore the function of his legs and the muscle spasms that he has from time to time?

A. It would not if he survived the operation.

Q. Then you would not advise it, Doctor?

A. I would not.

§ 524. Defendant's hypothetical question.

Illustration

Q. Now, doctor, assuming that a person has a pterygium in his right eye extending into the pupillary area until the area of the pterygium is about a millimeter from the center of the pupillary area, and that that pterygium has been developing for eleven or twelve years past, and on October 31, 1929, that pterygium is dissected and buried under the conjunctiva; on May 16, 1930, a small particle of cinder or rust is found on the area of the pterygium scar in the right eye, superimposed upon the scar, and that following the removal of that small piece of cinder or rust an ulcer develops, which is treated with medicines for a period from May 16, 1930, to August, 1930; and that in August, 1930, the ulcer is healed tight, and on October 1, 1930, the hypothetical person's right eye is refracted that the vision is shown to be 20/70ths, corrected to 20/50ths; that on January 6, 1932, or between January 6 and January 11, 1932, an opaque condition of the right eye is found upon examination and that separating that opaque condition from the scar of the pterygium and ulcer is a clear space of 1/12th of an inch or 2 millimeters of clear tissue, have you an opinion as to whether that opaque mass discovered on January 6 to January 11, 1932, could with reasonable certainty, reasonable medical and surgical certainty, have resulted from the ulcer on the pterygium scar?

A. I have an opinion.

Q. What is the opinion, doctor?

A. That it could *not* be related.

Q. Why?

A. For several reasons. The first, that if the vision was 20/70ths corrected to 20/50ths in October of 1930, then there could not be a mass so spoken about being present; secondly, if there is an intervening portion of clear tissue two millimeters or 1/12th of an inch between the ulcer that you state existed on the side of the pterygium and this other mass, that would preclude the same being related to the ulcer.

If a person has an opaque mass on his right eye, encompassing approximately 5/6ths of the pupillary area of his right eye, it would be impossible to refract the eye to show a 20/70ths vision. If a person's right eye is refracted on October 1, 1930, and the vision found to be 20/50ths, he absolutely could not at that time have had an opaque mass on the pupillary area of his right eye encompassing about 5/6ths of the pupillary area.

§ 525. Death case.

The following is an example of a hypothetical question which was put to a physician of standing and experience, for his opinion as to the cause of a sickness, the outcome of which was the death of a little girl:

Illustration

[15] Q. Suppose a girl between seven and eight years of age who has always been in good health, on the 9th day of January, 1887, to have been run over by a runaway horse, with sleigh attached, to have been knocked insensible to the ground, the horse and sleigh passing over her, inflicting three cuts, one upon the top, one upon the side, and one upon the back of her head from the hoofs of the horse or otherwise: that she thereafter was attacked with vomiting, and was confined to the house for two months, suffering great pain in the back and front of the head; at intervals, thereafter, increasing in frequency and intensity till the date of her death, on May 18, 1892, she was attacked with violent pains in the head accompanied with vomiting; that in the last few months of her life her sight gradually failed, and she became totally blind; that her legs became unsteady, and her control over them uncertain; that she suffered almost continually great pain in the front and back of her head; that after her death, on examination, it was found that she had one or more tumors on the cerebellum, or at the base of the brain—what, *in your opinion, was the exciting cause of the illness from which she suffered from January 9, 1887, the date of the accident, till the date of her death, May 18, 1892?* (Hardiman v. Brown, 162 Mass. 585.)

§ 526. Mind and memory.

Illustration

[16] Q. Assume a man makes what is claimed to be a will on the 31st day of August, 1921, and died on the 25th day of March, 1923, and at the time of his death was of the age of eighty-five years, three months and six days, that this man had never been married; he had lived on the same farm for over forty-five years; that the writing claimed to be a will, except the signatures thereon, was in the handwriting of the

[15] Mitchell, The Doctor in Court.

[16] Pendarvis v. Gibbs, 328 Ill. 282.

person who was named as executor in such instrument; that such person obtained the two persons who acted as witnesses to go to the house of such man to act as such witnesses; the man in the presence of the person named as executor, and the two witnesses, signed his name to the instrument, and the person named as executor told him to tell the witnesses that it was his will and he wanted them to sign it; the man did then tell them it was his will and that he wanted them to sign it; the writing consisted of three sheets of paper fastened together at one corner with a pin; when the person named as executor and the two witnesses were departing from the house of such person, within not more than five minutes after the signing of such instrument, that such man said: "We have lots of company. See those fellows up in the tree out there?" and that such persons looked and saw nothing; that the person named as executor and the two witnesses arrived at such man's house about three-quarters of an hour before sundown of August 31, 1921, and departed about one-half hour later; the two other men stayed with the man at this home that evening and night of August 31, 1921, and that about dusk he told one of the men to get an axe on a mattock, that these people were going to kill him, and that the man then entered through a door to a room in which there was only one window; the window was fastened down, and the man fastened the door from the inside and remained in the room the remainder of the night.

The man in his early years was about six feet tall and weighed about 175 pounds, and was very strong, and in the year of 1915 had broken one of his legs and had later injured his hip; he suffered pain from these injuries and it was difficult for him to walk; he used intoxicating liquors and at times became intoxicated; that the man talked about going to California in the days of 1849; that he had talked of the events that had occurred a number of years before; that he was the owner of about 350 acres of land on which there was no indebtedness and the fair cash market value of which on August 31, 1921, was not less than $42,000 and not more than $47,000, and that he also had on deposit in a bank about $900 and owned 5 shares of bank stock worth about $1,100 and also owned about $1,400 of Liberty Bonds and $75 of War Savings Stamps and had between three or four thousand bushels of corn; that he had a bank account in the two banks during the years of 1920 and 1921 and that during such years he drew 150 checks against such accounts and that in none of such checks was there anything written by him on the checks except his signature; and that seven of such checks were signed by his mark and his name written by some other person; that in June, 1921, this man while in his home and in conversation with another man, pointed up in the trees and spoke about seeing people up there. In December, 1922, this man sometimes sat in a chair in his home and struck out with a cane, and stated there were men in the house and asked another person to drive them out; that this condition existed from the last of February, 1923, until a short period before his death and that for a period of three or four days before his death he spent some time in his bed and did not eat but very little food; that this man did not know persons who called to see him, although he had been acquainted with them for some time; that in 1921 this man asked another person to take a barrel of kerosene and burn up the trees in his yard, saying that the people in the trees bothered him. That on September 6, 1921, this man stated that he had $10,000 worth of bank stock in a certain bank when in fact he did not have and never had any stock in this bank; that in the year 1921 this man stated that he could not raise any more corn as the Indians tramped it down; that during the year 1921 and 1922 this man was feeble and on September 6, 1921, was affected with arterio-sclerosis and that on that date his eyes were glassy and his hands shook.

Now, doctor, assume the facts stated above to be true, have you an opinion as to whether or not the man above mentioned was of sound mind and memory upon August 31, 1921?

Mr. Gordon: If the Court please, we wish to object to the question, and we would like to have the use of the question for the purpose of stating our objection.

The Court: All right.

Mr. Gordon: It may take some time to do it. In the first place, we object to the question as incompetent, immaterial and irrelevant; as not being a fair or proper or correct summary of the evidence in this case, or of the facts which have been proved, as omitting matters testified to by witnesses on the part of the complainants in this case, the contestants of the will, witnesses produced by themselves, which have a necessary and material bearing on the question; as containing statements which are not borne out by the evidence, and as containing statements of matters which are not of such character as would under any circumstances tend to show mental incompetency. And now, then, we wish to object to this hypothetical question as to each and every paragraph and statement contained in it, that it is not based upon the evidence in this case, and that there is no evidence justifying the insertion of it in a hypothetical question of this nature. I state it this way because to go through and take these statements, one by one, would be interminable and that is the reason I state it in that way, that each and every of these paragraphs and each and every statement in the paragraph of facts is not supported by the evidence, or is not justified as being inserted in here under the evidence in the case or upon any correct or proper theory of the evidence, and the whole question itself is unfair and misleading as being summary of certain alleged statements of testimony of witnesses, and omitting many other things that were testified to by the same witnesses and in the same connection, which have a necessary material bearing upon the question involved, and upon the question propounded.

That the dates are not correctly fixed in the opinion, and in some instances the pronouns used are uncertain as to what person or persons they apply to. (Note: These objections were not specific.)

The Court: Objection overruled.

Answer: Yes, sir, I have.

Q. Was such a man of sound mind and memory, or not?

A. He was not of sound mind and memory.

§ 527. Specific objections—Amending and correcting hypothetical question.

Illustration

Q. Doctor, assume that on the 22nd day of October, 1930, a young woman 34 years of age in good health, was struck by an automobile and thrown to the pavement; that she was momentarily dazed, but was able to arise with some slight assistance, and walk a few yards to an automobile and with assistance get into the automobile; that she got out of the automobile with assistance, and walked to an elevator, and went into a doctor's office, where she remained for some time; that while in the doctor's office she suffered some pain in her leg and some in her back and head, but not a very severe pain; that she then left the doctor's office, and after she got off the elevator she was unable to walk and had to be carried to a nearby automobile, where she was then taken to the hospital; that upon arriving at the hospital X-ray pictures were taken, and they showed the same condition that appears in Plaintiff's Exhibits 18 and 23, which you have just interpreted for the jury; she remained in bed at the hospital from October 22nd to November 9th of the same year, and during this time was treated by a competent physician, and ice packs were put on her head and on her leg; her ankle was immobilized and placed in a splint, and she remained in that condition for the greater part of the time while in the hospital; that during the latter few days of her stay there she was able to be up and about; she felt some better, but still experienced severe pain in her back, and headaches more or less continuously; she went to her home on November 9th and remained at home for a period of nine days, and again returned to the hospital and remained there until December first; while she was in the hospital the second time she was treated by the same doctor and given physio-therapy treatments for her back; after she left the hospital, December 1st, she remained at home, up and about, in bed part of the time and up and about the house part of the time, until December 17th, at which time she resumed her former employment, that of an interior decorator; that her condition was such, however, on account of her head condition, having occasional headaches, she could not work steadily, but worked only part time; that X-ray pictures were taken of her within the last few days, or to be exact, on July 10th, and the X-ray pictures disclosed the condition that you have found in your interpretation of Exhibits 18 and 23, and that her condition, and these X-ray pictures which were taken July 10th show substantially the same condition that existed on October 22, 1930, when she was admitted to the hospital; doctor, this hypothetical person has improved greatly, but her right ankle becomes swollen and has been swollen continuously up to the present time more or less; that she has pain in the back very frequently, and she suffers from headaches; now assuming these facts to be true, Doctor, have you an opinion, based upon a reasonable certainty and from a medical and surgical standpoint, as to whether the facts assumed in the question and the injury ensuing therefrom, are sufficient to cause the condition which now exists?

Mr. Truitt: I object.

The Court: Overruled.

Mr. Truitt: Just a moment, please. I want to state my objection, if the Court please.

The Court: State your objection if you like.

Mr. Truitt: My objection is that the question is not consistent with the evidence. In one instance, that when she got to the hospital X-ray pictures were taken, showing that position shown in Exhibits 18 and 23. That is inconsistent because 23 wasn't taken until July the—

Mr. Hulbert: I will correct that.

Mr. Truitt (continuing): twenty-second.

Mr. Hulbert: I will correct that question, Mr. Counsel.

The Court: Very well. Point out any further objection.

Mr. Hulbert: I correct that, your Honor. I noticed that myself, but I thought I would correct that in another question.

Mr. Truitt: Now, he asked him to testify from conditions which he has found in the X-ray plates, and that invades the province of the jury and doesn't tell us just what he is basing his opinion upon; we are entitled to know exactly what he is basing his opinion on; he would have to confine it to exactly what he testified to and nothing else. He is assuming that the conditions that were shown in the X-rays taken July 10th showed the same condition as those taken on October 22nd and 23rd, and the evidence doesn't so show. And it assumed that the ankle had been swollen continuously, and at this time the evidence doesn't so show, because this doctor says he just measured them and they were both alike; and this is inconsistent with the evidence. Also it assumed that the lady worked part time at her office, due to headache from the injury, which has not been shown; and you asked the doctor to testify in broad terms as to whether these assumptions are sufficient to cause the condition which he now finds, without telling us what particular conditions he expects to testify to. Nobody can show that a thing is final on any specific thing that has been proved or hasn't been proved.

Mr. Hulbert: Your Honor, I desire to correct one or two statements there in the question. I desire to modify or change that question to read: doctor, that when this hypothetical person reached the hospital and when she was X-rayed, the X-rays disclosed the condition appearing in Exhibits Nos. 1 and 10 which you have just interpreted, and of course confining your answer strictly and exclusively to that alone; and I wish to further modify or amend the question to read that her ankle has been swollen the greater part of the time since the accident occurred up to the present time, but was not swollen on the 14th day of July, when she was examined by a doctor. Now, then, I wish also to impress upon you, doctor, that in answering that hypothetical question you must confine your answer solely and exclusively to the facts mentioned in the picture, and to the interpretation of these pictures as you have just given it to the jury. Do you understand me now?

A. I understand.

Q. Now, then limiting or modifying the question, or amending it to that extent, have you an opinion, based upon a reasonable certainty, as to whether the facts assumed in the question, are sufficient to cause the present condition of the hypothetical person as assumed in the question?

Mr. Truitt: I object for the reason the question is too broad, and that as it is amended you can't follow it; besides it invades the province of the jury.

The Court: Overruled.

Mr. Hulbert: Have you an opinion, first, doctor?

A. I have.

Q. What is your opinion?

A. My opinion is that there is a causal connection between the present condition and the accident.

Mr. Truitt: Move the answer be stricken.

The Court: Overruled.

(Note: Counsel in the body of the above hypothetical question asks the doctor to assume that the X-rays showed the same condition that appears in certain exhibits which he had just interpreted for the jury. While in some states this might be technically objectionable, opposing counsel did not object to the question on this ground and therefore waived such objection. Both attorneys being expert personal injury trial lawyers, opposing counsel knew it would be a waste of effort to object. It would only serve to emphasize that part of the testimony as the attorney would have easily re-framed that portion of the question.)

§ 528. Cross-examination as to hypothetical questions.

Ordinarily great latitude is permitted in cross-examinations of expert witnesses, particularly in reference to answers given to hypothetical questions. The witness' qualifications, skill and knowledge and experience may be questioned. His interest in the litigation and any matter showing excessive bias may be shown. It is pertinent to find out what authorities he bases his opinion on and to contradict him with the authorities if possible. This is true though the witness does not state on direct examination that he bases his opinion on certain authorities.[17]

§ 529. Medical books.[18]

It is not competent for counsel to read from medical works, and much less is it competent to attempt to prove the contents of such books by witnesses testifying solely from memory; such evidence is mere hearsay and incompetent.

Scientific books are not admissible in evidence as proof of the facts they set forth, but if a witness assumes to base his opinion on such books, extracts may be read from them to

17 Wilcox v. International Harvester Co., 278 Ill. 465, 116 N. E. 151.

18 Questions may be framed by the use of quotations from or reading from standard treatises. Allen v. Boston El. R. Co., 212 Mass. 191, 98 N. E. 618; Gulf, etc., R. Co. v. Dooley, 62 Tex. C. A. 345, 131 S. W. 831. . . . this is permissible only to show what authors have declared on the subject when the expert bases his opinion wholly or in part on medical books, to contradict him. Griffith v. Los Angeles, etc., Co., 14 Cal. App. 145, 111 Pac. 107. But if the witness bases his opiniin upon his own experience this cannot be done. Ullrich v. Chicago City R. Co., 265 Ill. 338, 106 N. E. 828.

contradict him.[18a] Having expressed an opinion upon a matter material to the issue, a medical expert witness may be cross-examined as to whether that opinion is based upon personal experience or upon books which he has read, and this whether he has stated in his direct examination the basis of his opinion. Should he testify for the first time upon cross-examination that his opinion is based upon what he has read, counsel has the same right to interrogate him as to the authorities upon which he relies, and then contradict him with those authorities if he can, the same as if he had testified in direct examination that his opinion was based upon such authorities.[19] The mere fact that the witness on direct examination has expressed his opinion generally will not foreclose counsel, upon cross-examination, from eliciting from the witness the basis of his opinion.[19a]

§ 530. Breaking up question into parts.

The attention of the witness may be called to any fact omitted from the hypothetical question asked him on direct

[18a] Bloomington v. Schrock, 110 Ill. 219; Com. v. Sturtivant, 117 Mass. 122; Marshall v. Brown, 50 Mich. 148, 15 N. W. 55; Peo. v. Schuyler, 106 N. Y. 298, 12 N. E. 783; Galveston, etc., R. Co., v. Hanway, 57 S. W. 695 (Tex.); Knoll v. State, 55 Wis. 249, 12 N. W. 369. It is hearsay. Chicago City Ry. v. Douglas, 104 Ill. App. 41.

[19] The witness may be asked to name the authors upon whom he relies. Peo. v. Goldenson, 76 Cal. 328, 19 Pac. 161; Wilcox v. International, etc., Co., 278 Ill. 465, 116 N. E. 151; Hall v. Murdock, 114 Mich. 233, 72 N. W. 150, but see Peo. v. Vanderhoof, 71 Mich. 158, 39 N. W. 28; Pierson v. Hoag, 47 Barb. 243 (N. Y.); Ripon v. Bettel, 30 Wis. 614.

The witness may be asked what the authorities hold on a particular question. Broadhead v. Wiltse, 35 Iowa 429, 430.

The witness may be asked whether the authorities have an opinion different from his. Wittenberg v. Onsgard, 78 Minn. 342, 81 N. W. 14, 47 L. R. A. 141; Matter of Hock, 74 Misc. 15, 129 N. Y. S. 196.

But where the witness has *not relied* upon any authorities, the position of the authorities cannot be elicited. Ullrich v. Chicago City R. Co., 265 Ill. 338, 106 N. E. 824; Hanway v. Galveston, etc., R. Co., 94 Tex. 76, 58 S. W. 724; . . . nor can he be asked whether or not a certain author has an opinion different from his own. Mann v. Blair, 195 Ill. App. 254.

Some courts refuse to permit the reading of extracts from a book to the witness. In re Du Bois, 164 Mich. 8, 128 N. W. 1092.

It is also improper to ask the witness to read on cross-examination an extract from the book and state what it says. Byers v. Nashville, etc., R., 94 Tenn. 345, 29 S. W. 128.

[19a] Wilcox v. International Harvester Co., 278 Ill. 465, 116 N. E. 151.

examination.[20] The facts stated in the hypothesis which are considered unimportant may be sifted out.[20a] The question may be broken up into small parts and thus show that the conclusion arrived at by the witness is not reasonable.

§ 531. Show witness prepared question—Testing recollection.

One method of casting suspicion upon an expert's testimony is to show that the witness helped to prepare the hypothetical question. It may be shown that he has read the question before taking the stand, and had already stated what his opinion would be. If the witness has not had question read to him before or helped to prepare it, and it is a long, complicated and involved one, a good procedure is to ask the witness to repeat all of the material factors he took into consideration in arriving at his conclusion. He may be asked to point out all factors in the question which he considers unnecessary to base his opinion upon. This serves the purpose of occasionally forcing the expert to point out that his opinion is really based upon one or two factors only. Frequently, the trial lawyer is then in a position to show by proper authorities that these few factors are not controlling and are not sufficient upon which to arrive at such a conclusion.

20 C. & E. I. R. Co. v. Wallace, 202 Ill. 129; State v. Wood, 112 Iowa 411, 84 N. W. 520; Green v. Boston El. R. Co., 207 Mass. 467, 93 N. E. 837; Lake Shore, etc., R. Co. v. Whidden, 23 Ohio Cir. Ct. 85; Schoff v. Shephard, 196 S. W. 232 (Tex.); Zoldoske v. State, 82 Wis. 580, 52 N. W. 778.

20a Prentis v. Gates, 93 Mich. 234, 53 N. W. 153, 17 L. R. A. 494.

The court will generally permit imaginary questions assuming facts or theories not in evidence in order to elicit the reason for the opinion or ascertain the extent of the knowledge of the witness. Kenna v. Calumet, etc., R. Co., 284 Ill. 301, 120 N. E. 295; Bever v. Spangler, 93 Iowa 576, 61 N. W. 1072; Dilleber v. Home L. Ins. Co., 87 N. Y. 79; Uniacke v. Chicago, etc., R. Co., 67 Wis. 108, 29 N. W. 899.

But the court will not permit it if the question is conjectural. Root v. Boston El. R. Co., 183 Mass. 418, 67 N. E. 365; . . . or assuming facts not pertinent. Chicago San. Dist. v. Corneau, 257 Ill. 93, 100 N. E. 517; McCann v. California, etc., 176 Cal. 359, 168 Pac. 355; Commonwealth Bank v. Goodman, 128 Md. 452, 97 Atl. 1005.

The witness may be asked what his opinion would be assuming the facts to be as cross-examining counsel claims the evidence shows them to be. Taylor v. Taylor, 174 Ind. 670, 93 N. E. 9; Peo. v. Thurston, 2 Park Cr (N. Y.) 49.

§ 532. Emphasizing hypothetical nature of question.

It is good policy for the attorney against whom a hypothetical question has been propounded to try to keep before the jury the fact that the opinion submitted by the expert was based only upon assumed and hypothetical facts. It naturally follows that the attorney propounding the hypothetical question is interested in disguising the hypothetical nature of the question as much as possible.

§ 533. Requesting opponent's hypothetical question.

Where opponent has prepared a written hypothetical question in advance it is always good policy to ask to see it in the presence of the jury and then use it as a basis of cross-examination.

§ 534. Admissions.

If there are certain facts stated in the hypothetical question which the expert must admit have no material bearing on his opinion, he should be questioned about them. Every admission under cross-examination that a fact included in the question would have no bearing in arriving at his opinion will serve to narrow and limit the facts upon which he bases his opinion.

Illustration

Q. Doctor, counsel in his hypothetical question included the fact of so and so. . . . What importance did you place on that fact in arriving at your opinion?

A. None.

(Note: The same form of question can be put as to all other factors deemed immaterial.)

§ 535. Additional facts.

If the attorney's preparation has been thorough and under the advice of his expert he knows that his opponent's expert, if truthful, must admit that his opinion will be different if certain additional facts are added to the hypothetical question which are or will be introduced in evidence by the trial attorney, then opponent's expert should be asked to assume such additional fact or facts, and then asked whether or not that would change his opinion.

Illustration

Q. Now, doctor, if you were told to assume these additional facts, namely . . ., and . . ., would your opinion still be the same?

A. No, it would not.

§ 536. Using opponent's question.

It is very seldom that one will be able to get a paid partisan expert to change his opinion. The better practice might be to secure a copy of opponent's hypothetical question and propound the same to one's own expert adding the additional facts which he propounded to opponent's expert. Then the trial lawyer's expert will be able to give a contrary opinion and also a full explanation as to the reasons why he claims that the few additional facts would indicate a contrary opinion. This procedure, including the method in the above illustration, should tend to clarify the entire situation before the jury with the attendant psychological value of a verbal dissection of a usually complicated and not easily followed hypothetical question. There is always a great deal of value in using the identical hypothetical question propounded by an opponent and thus pointing out that opponent has unfairly tried to gain an advantage without taking into consideration *all* of the facts in the case. This can also be used to good effect in the final arguments.

§ 537. Disproved facts.

Another method of cross-examination which can be used to good advantage arises where counsel includes in his hypothetical question facts which are material as a basis for his possible recovery but which facts are either disproved by friendly witnesses or by facts and circumstances in the case of which the attorney is sure that other witnesses or evidence which he intends to produce later will completely refute. In such a situation it is good policy to ask the expert if his opinion would still be the same if *such* facts were eliminated from the hypothetical question.

Illustration

Q. Doctor, would your answer to the hypothetical question have been the same if counsel in putting the question to you had left out of consideration the statement that the doctor was unable to flex the leg when he made the examination?

(Note: Assuming that this fact was controlling in the hypothetical question and that the doctor must have given prominent consideration to it in arriving at his opinion, if the doctor still persists in his opinion the attorney would then ask him to leave out of consideration all additional disproved facts.)

§ 538. Unnecessary elements in question.

One method of attacking an opinion given in response to a hypothetical question frequently resorted to by some trial lawyers is to limit the facts upon which such opinion is based by means of the following question:

Illustration

Q. Doctor, were there any elements in that hypothetical question which counsel propounded to you which were not necessary to your affirmative answer?

A. Yes, so and so—.

Q. Were there any other elements in the hypothetical question which were not necessary to your affirmative answer?

A. Yes, these further facts. . . .

§ 539. Where expert has not examined injured person.

Where the witness is an expert, but has not examined the injured person, he may be cross-examined as follows:

Illustration

Q. Doctor, you did not examine this injury, did you?

A. No, sir, I have never seen the individual involved in this case.

Q. Your answers in this matters are, so far as your conclusions about the individual are concerned, entirely theoretical?

A. My answers were based on the hypothetical question.

Q. Now doctor, you do not know whether the facts stated in the hypothetical question are true or not, do you, that is, of your own knowledge?

A. No, I do not.

Q. Your opinion is limited to just those facts set out in the hypothetical question?

A. Yes.

Q. If additional facts were given you they might cause you to change your opinion, of course?

A. Yes, of course.

Q. Doctor, did you help prepare the hypothetical question that counsel put to you?

A. I did not.

Q. Did you go over it with counsel before you took the stand?

A. I did.

Q. So you knew just what you were going to be asked?

A. Yes, sir.

Q. And you had your answer already prepared?

A. Yes.

Q. Please tell the court and jury just which facts in the hypothetical question you based your opinion on.

A. On all of the factors.

Q. Were there any factors in the question which you could leave out and still give the same opinion?

A. Yes, sir.

Q. Which ones are they?

A. Why, so— and so—.

Q. Any other factors that you could eliminate?

A. Why, yes, one other . . . etc., etc.

Q. So that you would leave these facts in the question upon which you base your opinion, . . . is that so?

A. Yes.

(Note: If the expert is not truthful or if he is not competent, this method will give the attorney's experts a chance to entirely discredit opponent's expert.)

§ 540. Testing recollection.

If the expert, under the above cross-examination answers that he did not help prepare the hypothetical question, that the question was never submitted to him before the trial and where the hypothetical question is a long and involved one, the following additional questions may be used:

Illustration

Q. Now, doctor, you say that counsel never submitted that hypothetical question to you before you took the witness stand?

A. No, he did not.

Q. Will you please repeat all of the factors in the question upon which you base your opinion?

A. Why, I took into consideration the fact that the hypothetical person was . . .

(Note: If not properly prepared the witness will not be able to remember more than a few of the factors.)

Q. Well, doctor, are those the only factors in the hypothetical question upon which you base your opinion?

A. No, there were some others, but I have forgotten just what they were.

(Note: This will tend to discredit the expert who has a definite opinion on the facts related to him in a hypothetical question, but is now unable to remember all of the facts upon which he bases his opinion.)

Q. Doctor, your opinion remains the same although you cannot remember all of the factors upon which you base your opinions, is that right?

A. Yes.

§ 541. Testing each detailed fact—Sanity and testamentary capacity.

A particularly effective method of cross-examination of experts who have given untruthful opinions in response to detailed hypothetical questions is to examine in reference to each detailed fact included in the question and to ask him whether that fact alone is an indication of sanity or testamentary capacity or the lack of either. The expert will usually admit that this fact standing alone is not sufficient on which to base an opinion. The same procedure can be followed as to each individual detail with the result that he will be discredited before the jury.

§ 542. Mind and memory.

Two effective illustrations of proper cross-examination of experts in reference to opinions given in answer to hypothetical questions are contained in Cornelius on "Cross-examination of Witnesses" together with the following comments:

"Experts, for example in will contests, usually base their conclusions upon hypothetical questions. These hypothetical questions must be grounded on the testimony already given in the case, and must not contain any evidence of assumed facts or circumstances not already in evidence. The cross-examiner first of all then should be on the alert to see that the hypothetical question submitted contains nothing but facts already in evidence in the case. It may be assumed from the outset that the hypothetical question put to the expert for the contestants in a will case, will present no testimony tending to show the sanity or normality of the testator. Here it is sound for the cross-examiner to interrogate the expert concerning those qualities possessed by the testator which tend to indicate his sanity. In this connection, it must be kept in mind that even a person who is actually insane may often display the qualities of normalcy; that even as to such a person many witnesses might be called who had talked with him and discussed various subjects with him and who noticed no insanity or eccentricities. It is, therefore, good practice for the cross-examiner to proceed to prepare the jury for the testimony which is to follow by interrogating the expert as to whether or not he knew the testator possessed these various characteristics; if the testator attended to his business or any part of it, or executed legal documents, or if no one had ever accused him of being insane during his lifetime. The expert should be quizzed about each one of these facts and whether or not he knew that such was the case and had taken these facts into consideration in giving his opinion. The following is an example of how this may be accomplished:

"A lady fifty-five years old, on May 15, 1923, began muttering and talking to herself a great deal, expressing the fear that certain organizations were intending to harm her. She gradually grew violent until on or about the first day of July of the same year, she was adjudged insane and placed in a hospital. During the interim, when the first signs of depravity began to appear, she exhibited certain mental derangements, such as ordering some of her friends who had called to see her, from her home; expressing dread that the Catholic church had a particular grudge against her and was seeking to destroy her, and other abnormal mental traits.

"After her death and the probate of her will, executed some two weeks after she had begun to show said signs of mental derangements, the attorney for the contestants, unquestion ably, if he knew his business, should have compiled all of these abnormal mental actions of the deceased into a single statement of fact and asked the expert witness whether or not in his opinion from such assumed statement of facts, the testatrix was sane or insane, and had the mental capacity to make the will in question. This, of course, would be answered in the negative. An effective cross-examination under the circumstances would develop all of the conduct of this woman tending to indicate sanity and normalcy. The following cross-examination of Dr. C. may serve as an example:

Q. Now, doctor, you say that upon the assumed statement of facts just read to you, that this woman on the date the will was made lacked testamentary capacity?

A. Yes, sir.

Q. Did you know that she was working every day in her home?

A. The question does not state whether she had or not.

Q. And that she cooked the meals for her husband, and waited upon him in her usual and customary manner and that she prepared her children for school each and every day, and that most of her friends and acquaintances did not notice anything abnormal about her mental condition?

A. The question does not cover such facts.

Q. Now, doctor, if she got her children ready each morning and sent them to school, she would on that date, know who her children were, would she not?

A. Yes, sir.

Q. And if she cooked the meals for her husband, she would know who he was?

A. Yes, sir.

Q. As to the husband and children, she would know what she wanted to give them for their meals?

A. I think she would.

Q. And when she made the will, she would know who her husband and her children were and what she wanted to give them—they were beneficiaries under the will of her, proper?

A. I think she would.

"The answer to this last question was, of course, practically an admission of testamentary capacity by the expert and rendered his opinion almost valueless to the contestants."

§ 543. — Another illustration.

"Another method of cross-examining the expert is to show that the alleged eccentricities of the testator relied upon are possessed by many other persons, admittedly not insane and sometimes to separate the hypothetical question into its component parts, selecting therefrom the essential elements which the contestants rely upon, wring from the expert the admission that not one of these elements in itself is sufficient to establish insanity. For example, we will assume in a certain given case that the contestants of the will have produced testimony to show (a) that the testator talked to herself in a rambling manner, (b) that she cursed and swore violently at her children almost habitually, (c) that she would fall asleep while receiving callers, and (d) that she wanted to sell her farm for about half of its actual value. All these facts were embodied in a hypothetical question and submitted to an expert witness who testified that the testatrix was of unsound mind. The cross-examination follows:

"Q. Now, doctor, one of the factors set forth in the hypothetical question and upon which you base your opinion that this woman was insane at the time she executed the will, is that she talked to herself in a rambling manner?

A. Yes, sir.

Q. Now, doctor, you have known during your lifetime a number of people who were perfectly sane and yet who frequently talked to themselves?

A. Yes, sir.

Q. And, when an individual talks to himself he usually lets his thoughts run at will and is therefore liable to talk in a rambling manner?

A. Yes, sir.

Q. So that having known many persons who have been perfectly sane and talked to themselves in a rambling manner, you would not be prepared to say that the fact that this testatrix talked to herself in a rambling manner, was standing alone, any proof of insanity?

A. No, sir.

Q. Now, doctor, the next thing we come to in this case is that she cursed and swore violently at her children. Is that one of the factors in the case upon which you base your opinion that this woman was insane?

A. Yes, sir.

Q. You are, however, acquainted with very many people both women and men, who occasionally curse and swear at their children?

A. Yes, sir.

Q. And often, they get angry at their children and curse and swear at them in a loud tone of voice in what we would ordinarily term a violent and angry manner?

A. Yes, sir.

Q. And these people of whom I am now speaking are perfectly sane?

A. Yes, sir.

Q. You would not say, therefore, that the fact standing alone that this testatrix cursed and swore at her children was any proof of insanity?

A. No, sir.

"This method was continued as to all of the factors in the case and, in the end, the doctor admitted that the testatrix had testamentary capacity."

CHAPTER XI

CROSS-EXAMINATION

§ 544. In general.

Cross-examination is one of the greatest instrumentalities for good known to the trial lawyer, yet it may be one of the most dangerous. Effective cross-examination will win many doubtful cases, but with improper use it can *destroy* the lawyer. It is truly "a two-edged sword." The injudicious use of cross-examination always helps to strengthen an opponent's case.

To the lawyer just out of law school, with a lack of knowledge of the art of cross-examination, announcement by opposing counsel that "you may cross-examine," leaves him almost spellbound and speechless. He does not have the least idea of where to start, what to do, or how to do it. Unless some-one directs him to a special work on cross-examination, he does not seem to realize that there are certain fundamental rules of procedure to be followed in the cross-examination of witnesses. Very frequently, facts come to his attention, which in the hands of a skillful cross-examiner, would absolutely ruin the opponent's case, but in the hands of one who is unfamiliar with the tools to be used in cross-examining witnesses, the telling effect of such facts is almost entirely lost. We have all seen lawyers, who in their anxiety to make their point, have either overplayed their hand entirely or have played it so poorly that the witness is able to evade the "trap" and to explain away the apparently "ruining" fact upon which counsel had depended.

§ 545. Objects of cross-examination.

Proper cross-examination in the trial of cases has two objects. The *first and primary object* is its use as a vehicle for securing admissions of facts that tend to prove the lawyer's contentions or to corroborate proof of his claims already in the record. *The secondary object* of cross-examination is to discredit opponent's witnesses or their stories. The technique employed in effecting this secondary object is generally known as "impeachment."

Many trial lawyers never seem to appreciate nor to realize the primary purpose of cross-examination. They direct their sole attention to the attempt to discredit the witness or his story.

In actual practice and in cases where there are able counsel on both sides, who investigate their clients and have prepared their witnesses, a cross-examination directed solely with the one object in view of discrediting the witness or his story will frequently fail. Destructive impeachment of witnesses is the rare event rather than the usual thing in well prepared, ably represented cases.

The technique to be employed in discrediting witnesses and their stories is treated in the next chapter under the heading of "Impeachment."

§ 546. Primary purpose of cross-examination.

The attorney's attention is first directed to the primary purpose of cross-examination, namely, the securing of admissions that will tend to prove his case. (For illustration, see Expert Witnesses, pages 416 to 425.)

The "building up" of a case by securing admissions of facts in corroboration of counsel's testimony is far more important than the negative effect of discrediting his opponent's witnesses. One cannot "paint his client white by painting his opponent black."

Admissions secured from the lips of opponent's client and his witnesses ordinarily have greater weight with the jury than does the testimony of one's own witnesses. These admissions, especially where they are secured in a number of instances tending to prove the attorney's contentions, will be the basis for a successful argument to persuade the jury to accept his theory in its entirety, because so many elements of the case have been admitted as true by the opponent. Therefore counsel can argue that it is more reasonable to believe that the truth is on his side.

§ 547. — Right to cross-examine.

The right to cross-examine a witness is absolute.[1]

1 In re Cullberg's Estate, 146 Pac. 888, 169 Cal. 365; Peo. v. Andrews, 158 N. E. 462, 327 Ill. 162; Com. v. Gallo, 175 N. E. 718, 275 Mass. 320; Warrick v. Moore County, 291 S. W. 950 (Tex.).

§ 548. — Scope of cross-examination.

A witness may be cross-examined as to his direct testimony in all its bearings and as to whatever goes to explain, modify or to discredit what he has stated in his first examination.[2]

The cross-examination of a witness is limited to an inquiry as to the facts and circumstances connected with the matters stated in his direct examination.[3] In the application of this rule much is left to the discretion of the court. However, in some jurisdictions a party in interest may be cross-examined beyond the scope of the direct examination.[4]

It is always permissible to inquire into the details of the events testified to in chief by a witness and to develop and unfold the whole transaction about which he has only been partially interrogated.[5]

[2] Bancroft-Whitney Co. v. McHugh, 134 Pac. 1157, 166 Cal. 140; Kendall v. Luther, 74 Atl. 879, 82 Conn. 523; Warth v. Lowenstein, 219 Ill. 222; Sax v. Zanger, 111 N. E. 1, 184 Ind. 262; State v. La Barre, 210 N. W. 918; Clark-Rice Corp. v. Waltham, etc., 166 N. E. 867, 267 Mass. 402; Peo. v. Swanson, 185 N. W. 844, 217 Mich. 103; Peo. v. Sexton, 80 N. E. 396, 187 N. Y. 495; Alsabrook v. Bishop, 295 S. W. 646 (Tex.); Gibson v. Milwaukee, etc., Co., 128 N. W. 877, 144 Wis. 140.

[3] Ellsworth v. Palmtag, 143 Pac. 602, 168 Cal. 360; Finch v. Weiner, 145 Atl. 31, 109 Conn. 616; Peo. v. Geidras, 170 N. E. 219, 338 Ill. 340; Schaffer v. State, 173 N. E. 229, 202 Ind. 318; Hall v. Allemania F. Ins. Co., 161 N. Y. S. 1091, 175 App. Div. 289; Graves v. Rib Lake Lumber Co., 138 N. W. 86, 151 Wis. 99; International, etc., R. Co. v. Biles & Ruby, 120 S. W. 952, 56 Tex. C. A. 193.

[4] In Civil Actions. Generally, a wider range of cross-examination is permitted. In re Strong's Est., 156 Pac. 1026, 172 Cal. 441; Chicago Union T. Co. v. Miller, 72 N. E. 25, 212 Ill. 49; Albaugh v. Shrope, 196 N. W. 743, 197 Iowa 844; Freeman v. Freeman, 130 N. E. 220, 238 Mass. 150; In re Klink's Est., 178 N. W. 14, 210 Mich. 614; Page v. Thomas, 47 S. W. (2nd) 894 (Tex. C. A.); Ward v. Thompson, 131 N. W. 1006, 146 Wis. 376; Hoberg v. Sofrancy, 217 N. Y. S. 97, 217 App. Div. 546.

May cross-examine party beyond scope of direct examination. Felsenthal v. Northern Assurance Co., 284 Ill. 343 (but see Brownlie v. Brownlie, 357 Ill. 117).

[5] Chapman v. Strong, 127 N. W. 741, 162 Mich. 623, where the driver of a car testified as to how an accident happened, could be asked whether or not he had been drinking prior to the accident.

Bell v. State, 54 So. 116, 170 Ala. 16, where it was held that an alibi witness could be asked how long it takes to walk from his store to a certain street car line. Thomas v. Winthrop, etc., 111 N. E. 173, 222 Mass. 456, where the witness testified that the sidewalk was rough, could be asked as to the condition at the point in issue. Peo. v. Bolton, 171 N. E. 152, 339 Ill. 225, where the witness testified as to the identification of the defendant, it was held that it was error to refuse to permit defend-

§ 549. — Court may ask questions.

The general rule is that the trial judge has a right to ask questions of witnesses.[6]

§ 550. — Counsel assuming facts in questions.

In examination of witnesses counsel are prohibited, even upon cross-examination, of assuming any material facts in issues and which is to be found by the jury, or from assuming that particular answers have been given contrary to the facts.[7] A question asked of a witness on cross-examination, "What was the name of the car repairers' association to which you belonged, if you know," held improper as assuming that the person referred to was a member of a car repairers' association.[7a]

§ 551. Contradiction on immaterial fact.

A witness cannot be cross-examined as to any fact which is collateral and irrelevant to the issue, merely for the purpose of contradicting him by other evidence.[8]

§ 552. — Insulting, etc., questions.

Insulting, disparaging[9] or argumentative[9a] questions are not permitted.

ant's counsel to ask as to the circumstances surrounding the identification.

Witness may be asked as to the reason for his actions: Del Visco v. Gen. El. Co., 126 N. E. 799, 235 Mass. 415, where it was permissible to ask the witness why he had discharged a certain workman, to bring out the fact the workman was negligent and caused the injury to the plaintiff and was discharged for that reason.

6 Peo. v. Perrin, 231 N. Y. S. 557, 224 App. Div. 546; Ingle v. Ingle, 131 S. W. 241, 62 Tex. C. A. 205; Peo. v. Lurie, 276 Ill. 630; Peo. v. Keys, 255 Pac. 897, 82 Cal. App. 602.

7 Hand v. Soodeletti, 61 Pac. 373, 128 Cal. 674; Parker v. Crane Co., 185 Ill. App. 377; C. & O. R. Co. v. Fultz, 161 N. E. 835, 91 Ind. App. 639; State v. Curran, 49 N. W. 1006, 51 Iowa 112; Commonwealth v. Sacco, 151 N. E. 839, 255 Mass. 369; Davis v. Willis, 22 N. Y. S. 339.

7a Davis v. E. St. Louis Lodge, 197 Ill. App. 25.

8 Selby v. Detroit R. Co., 81 N. W. 106, 122 Mich. 311; Benedict v. Dakin, 243 Ill. 384.

9 Peo. v. Durrant, 48 Pac. 75, 116 Cal. 179; Peo. v. Malkin, 164 N. E. 900, 250 N. Y. 185; Libby, etc. v. Cook, 123 Ill. App. 574; Redick v. State, 202 S. W. 743, 83 Tex. Cr. 225.

9a Houston v. Maunula, 255 Pac. 477, 121 Or. 552.

§ 553. Repetition.

Questions asked on cross-examination, the purpose of which is merely to require the witness to repeat what he has already stated, may be disallowed.[10] This is discretionary with the court, however. (See § 563.)

§ 554. Refreshing memory.

Witness may be cross-examined as to writing he has used to refresh his memory.[11] He may also be cross-examined to test his recollection before he uses the writing to refresh his memory[12] and opposing party may examine such writings for that purpose.[13]

§ 555. Planning cross-examination in advance.

In order to secure the greatest possible number of admissions from opponent's witnesses it is necessary to plan the cross-examination before trial and frequently to block out the questions it is desired to have answered.

Some lawyers claim that cross-examinations cannot be prepared in advance, because they have no knowledge as to what the witnesses will testify. This is not so, however. If the lawyer has thoroughly prepared his case by a full and complete investigation, if he has thoroughly digested the pleadings, if he knows his own theory and case, and knows under the law just what facts must be proved, he cannot help but know just about what the direct examination will be, and know just what admissions he desires to obtain by cross-examination.

10 Quincy Gas Co. v. Bauman, 104 Ill. App. 600; McBride v. McBride, 120 N. W. 709, 142 Iowa 169; Goldman v. Ashkins, 165 N. E. 513, 266 Mass. 374; Peo. v. Considine, 63 N. W. 196, 105 Mich. 149; Foster v. Tannenbaum, 37 N. Y. S. 722, 2 App. Div. 168; Texas, etc., Co. v. Webster, 59 S. W. (2d) 902 (Tex. C. A.).

11 Bistritz v. Star F. Ins. Co., 105 N. Y. S. 116, 55 Misc. 230; Little v. Lichkoff, 12 So. 429, 98 Ala. 321; Atchison, etc., R. Co. v. Hays, 54 Pac. 322, 8 Kan. App. 545.

12 Neff v. Neff, 114 A. 126, 96 Conn. 273.

13 McKivitt v. Cone, 30 Iowa 455; Duncan v. Seeley, 34 Mich. 369; Green v. State, 53 Tex. Cr. Rep. 490, 110 S. W. 920, 22 L. R. A. (N. S.) 706; Harmon v. H. E. Coal Co., 237 Ill. 36.

Cornelius in "Cross-Examination of Witnesses," cites an instance of the method to be followed in planning cross-examination in advance in the following language:

"A careful study of the pleadings and a survey of the evidence which the adverse party will probably introduce in support of his contention almost invariably enables opposing counsel to forecast, with considerable accuracy, the trend which the testimony of the opposing witnesses will likely take. Thus in making a plan, counsel should prepare a statement of these probabilities which he may use advantageously as a foundation for the questioning of any number of adverse witnesses, provided they testify contrary to the probabilities thus worked out. For example, consider the following actual case:

"A. purchased an apartment house from an owner B., for $65,000 and paid $15,000 down, leaving a balance of $50,000 to be paid on the contract, at the rate of $600 per month.

A. claimed that the owner B., from whom he purchased the property, misrepresented the facts in this transaction, in the following particulars:

(a) That the rentals from this property of $700.00 per month had been reduced so that they were at absolute bed-rock at the time the transaction was closed and that all of the tenants were prompt in paying same, and that an expenditure of only about $300 *per annum* was required for heat.

(b) That the owner represented that all of the apartments were in good repair as to decorations; that the buildings would easily carry the contract and pay for itself out of the rentals.

"A. purchased the property, entered into possession and discovered the following facts:

1. That it cost him $250 *per month* for heat.
2. That the tenants were not prompt in paying rent.
3. That heating plant required $500 repairs immediately.
4. That the property lacked approximately $300 *per month* of paying for itself from the rentals.

"A. brought suit for rescission against B. The defendant in his answer denied that he made any such representations as above set out.

"What, now, are the probabilities in this case? The lawyer for the plaintiff, in planning his cross-examination of the defendant and his witnesses, should reach the following conclusions respecting the same:

Statement of Probabilities

A. v. B.

"(1) A. as a purchaser would be vitally interested in knowing what income the apartment produced. B., the owner, had that information. A. did not. The probabilities, therefore, strongly support the contention of A. that he asked for this information. If B. had given him the actual facts he would have refused to purchase the property. So here again, the probabilities support A. that B. misrepresented the income.

"(2) Since heating costs of large apartment buildings vary widely, depending upon the efficiency of the heating plant as well as upon the construction of the building, the probabilities are strongly with A. when he stated that he asked B. what said cost would be and B. told him. If B. made any representations at all about the heating costs of the apartment, it would have to be a representation consistent with the purchase of the building by A. Had B. told the real facts, A. would not have purchased.

"(3) As to the condition of the interior decorations, the individual apartments being all rented, A. did not have access to them and he was compelled to depend on B. for information. Here again a true disclosure would, in all probability, have blocked the deal.

"(4) Since the tenants in the building were none of them prompt paying and since A. naturally would be interested in making inquiries as to their character, the probabilities are that A. did inquire and that B. concealed and misrepresented the real facts.

"Since one of the important objectives in cross-examination is to show that the witness is not testifying truthfully, one forceful method of doing this is to show the improbability of his story by emphasizing facts before the jury which render such story improbable. Counsel, therefore, cross-examined the defendant in this case as follows:

"Q. (Addressed to the defendant on the witness stand.) You, as the owner and operator of this property, knew the annual cost to heat this building?

A. Yes, sir.

Q. The heating costs of apartment buildings vary widely do they not, depending upon the condition and efficiency of the heating plant and the construction of the building?

A. Yes, sir.

Q. You had exact information as to what it cost to heat this building?

A. Yes, sir.

Q. Mr. A., your prospective purchaser, had no information as to what these costs were?

A. No, sir.

Q. And he, as a prospective purchaser of this building, would naturally be very much interested in knowing what these heating costs were?

A. Yes, sir.

Q. You were ready to answer his questions in this regard?

A. Yes, sir.

Q. And yet he asked you nothing about this important subject?

A. No, sir.

"The same general line of questions were successfully applied to all the claimed misrepresentations in the foregoing statement of facts."

§ 556. Preparation for cross-examination.

The best test as to whether or not the lawyer has properly prepared the facts in his case will be determined by the kind and character of cross-examination to which all of opponent's witnesses are subjected. A lack of preparation will result in an ineffective cross-examination. One of the basic requirements for proper cross-examination is a complete knowledge of the facts which the lawyer is seeking to prove. Unless the lawyer knows all of the facts involved, both favorable and unfavorable, he will not be in a position to cross-examine a witness effectively.

It is suggested that in the early experiences of the trial lawyer he block out most of the questions which he expects to use upon cross-examination. Here again the more experienced and successful trial lawyer may disagree. But, as has been demonstrated, the inexperienced trial lawyer is quite apt to forget all questions and plans which he has made when the time comes for him to cross-examine his first half-dozen witnesses.

§ 557. Listen carefully to direct examination.

One of the greatest mistakes of the inexperienced trial attorney is his failure to listen attentively to every detail of the direct examination of the witness he expects to cross-examine. For some reason or another the inexperienced trial lawyer takes the occasion of the direct examination of opponent's witnesses to look through his files for papers, or to carry on a conference with his client. He fails to appreciate that he must be on the alert during such direct examination for the weak spot in that witness' testimony. He must forever watch the witness' face in an attempt to determine whether the witness is telling the truth.

It is suggested that the lawyer make notes of the direct examination so that he can use these notes as a basis for the cross-examination. Many successful trial lawyers who have completely and fully prepared their case do not make notes during the direct examination, except an occasional word or two here and there. Their experience and preparation make it unnecessary to do any more. They usually have so planned their cross-examination that very little comes up in the direct examination which they are not prepared to meet.

It is suggested that the lawyer provide his client with a pad of paper and a pencil to write down any suggestions that he has to offer and to pass the note to the attorney instead of attempting to convey them orally. This will permit the lawyer to give his entire attention to the direct examination.

§ 558. Demeanor.

The manner employed by trial attorneys in cross-examining a witness is of the utmost importance when considered in the light of its effect upon the jury. The bullying manner of the old-time cross-examiner is now entirely obsolete. Successful trial lawyers have come to recognize the fact that juries sympathize with witnesses who are subjected to brow-beating, or to an insulting and sarcastic examination. Jurors recognize the fact that the witness is at the mercy of the cross-examining attorney and quickly resent any attempt to take unfair advantage of the witness. An attitude of fair play and gentlemanly conduct is necessary to secure a favorable verdict. In fact, an attitude of fairness and honorableness must be maintained throughout the entire trial, because the verdict in many cases depends to a great extent upon whether or not the jury likes or dislikes the trial attorney. The sarcastic repeating of answers of a witness to questions propounded on cross-examination is to be avoided. This is considered improper trial tactics and is subject to objection.

§ 559. Never cross-examine unless you know what answer will be.

It has been frequently stated by leading trial lawyers that no question should ever be asked unless the attorney knows just what the answer will be. A blind, haphazard, cross-examination, without a previously planned objective will usually result in more harm than good. The primary purpose of cross-examination should forever be kept uppermost in mind, and admissions should be sought that will tend to corroborate the lawyer's theory of the case.

§ 560. Objective must be hidden.

To derive the greatest benefit from a cross-examination, the purpose of the cross-examiner must always be hidden from the witness. Just as soon as the witness understands the answer that the lawyer actually is seeking, he will immediately attempt to avoid the trap planned for him. Questions should be asked in a casual manner as though the answers are of no particular importance so as not to arouse the suspicion of the witnesses. In most instances a favorable answer may be obtained by indicating in the manner and question the opposite of the real answer that is desired. Some witnesses under cross-examination will always answer just contrary to whatever they feel the cross-examiner desires.

The witness must never be permitted to know just how little the lawyer knows of the subject under discussion. The impression must be conveyed to him that the lawyer is fully prepared and that he knows all about that particular subject. The greatest effect may sometimes be had by leading the witness to believe that the lawyer knows all about the subject under discussion by indicating one or two or three things as evidence of his knowledge, and then permit him to give the balance of the details. For instance, it is the lawyer's desire to know just what conversation took place between the witness and the defendant on a certain occasion. The lawyer has been told that the conversation took place on a certain day and place in the presence of one or two others. He would therefore question the witness somewhat along these lines:

Illustration

Q. Now, Mr. Jones, you had a conversation with the defendant, Ed Thompson, on January 2nd, did you not?

A. Yes.

Q. And at that conversation Henry Michaels and Tom Simmons were also present, were they not?

A. Yes.

Q. And you discussed the matter involved in this case with them, didn't you?

A. Yes.

Q. Now, you just tell us what they said to you and what you said to them.

A. Why, —etc.

§ 561. Determine whether or not to cross-examine at all. In most instances the inexperienced trial lawyer feels that after the witness has testified, it is incumbent upon him to cross-examine every such witness without regard to whether or not the direct examination has been harmful to his case. In a great many instances some attorneys cross-examine where there is absolutely no reason for doing so. Upon statement by opposing counsel that "you may cross-examine," it becomes of the utmost importance to determine whether or not the witness has testified to anything detrimental to the trial lawyer's case. If upon due attention to the testimony of the witness on direct examination and after a quick consideration of such testimony it is found that the witness has not harmed the case he should not be cross-examined. Experience teaches that whenever the lawyer cross-examines in these instances that he usually succeeds in opening up other evidence for investigation not considered by opposing counsel or has by such cross-examination brought out facts which have helped to strengthen the case of his opponent.

§ 562. Never cross-examine a truthful witness as to his direct examination.

It is always bad policy to cross-examine a witness as to his story told on direct examination when it is believed, after due observation of such witness, that he is telling the truth. It is common practice for clients to attempt to get their own attorneys to believe that the adverse party and all of his witnesses are liars and perjurers. Clients color their stories and frequently try to keep their lawyer from learning all of the facts in the case. Therefore, the lawyer must be on guard throughout every trial. As a witness testifies one ordinarily can make up his mind as to whether or not he is telling the truth, and if it is felt that he is the story should be attacked, if possible, through one of the methods recommended under the heading of impeachment; or the lawyer should limit himself to showing some interest in the case, by relationship, payment for services, time spent by witness, etc., rather than to take the chance of going over the whole story again and harming his case by so doing.

§ 563. Do not have story repeated by witness.

One of the most common mistakes made by some trial attorneys in cross-examination is to go over again the story testified to by the witness on direct examination. This type of cross-examination only serves to emphasize the witness' story in the minds of the jury, and also serves to convince the jury that the witness is telling the truth because the cross-examiner was unable to shake his story on cross-examination. *The only time* that a witness should be permitted on cross-examination to retell his story is when the lawyer is in a position to absolutely disprove that witness' story or statement by other witnesses, by some contrary statement, either oral or written, by some contrary sworn affidavit, or by some contrary prior sworn testimony, all of which are discussed under the heading of "Impeachment."

Francis Wellman in the "Art of Cross-examination" relates the instance where that great trial attorney, Max Steuer, cross-examined a witness, and acquitted his clients by having the witness repeat the story a second time and then a third time, and then demonstrated to the jury that the witness had memorized word for word the story to be told on the witness stand, and that during the repetition of the story the witness had left out one or two words which had been included in direct examination. While this method of cross-examination was successfully employed in this particular instance, all lawyers are not Max Steuers, and it is the exception rather than the general rule. In the general trial of cases it is much safer to follow the rule of never having the witness repeat his story unless one is in a position to disprove it absolutely.

§ 564. Plan your traps.

One of the most effective methods of cross-examination is to lead the witness into a trap deliberately and then to destroy his story. This procedure requires the maintenance of a casual attitude and manner as well as control over desires to trap the witness too speedily. Over-anxiety will defeat the purpose and warn the witness of impending danger. The longer the lawyer can keep the witness in the dark as to just what his objective is, the greater will be the destructive effect of the cross-examination. The lawyer should not be in too much of a hurry to confront the witness with the evidence he feels will completely refute his story. He should not be so anxious to make his point that he over cross-examines and permits the witness to nullify the effect of the same. When he is in possession of evidence or written statements which is contrary to the testimony of the witness on direct examination, it should become his purpose to get the witness to repeat such testimony, as suggested and illustrated in the chapter on "Impeachment." For an illustration of the method of laying such a trap see "Expert Witnesses," pages 433 to 437. This illustration also calls attention to the error of counsel in being over-anxious.

The "Indian Joe" Huszar case might serve as a good illustration of laying a trap and also as to preparation of the facts:

"Indian Joe" was well known as the Chief of Police who had been frequently charged with "shaking down" motorists, and also with the fact that he was operating a speed trap in a small village, just outside of Chicago. Prosecutions had been unavailing, resulting in acquittal of the defendant on charges of conspiracy, etc. In this particular case, the complaining witnesses were a young man and his fiancee, who claimed that while they had stopped just outside of the village to eat some popcorn, "Indian Joe" crept upon them, arrested them, drew a gun and threatened to shoot the young man if he did not post a $22.00 cash bond for disorderly conduct. "Indian Joe" was indicted and charged with assault with intent to commit murder. The complaining witnesses testified that these acts occurred in *September,* 1925. Cross-examination by the defense of these complaining witnesses attempted to show that they were deliberately falsifying as to the dates and that the transaction actually took place six months prior, in *February,* 1925. To support this contention, the defendant while being cross-examined produced the public records of the Police Magistrate of the village, showing that the complaining witnesses were tried before the said Judge sometime in *February,* 1925, were found guilty and fined a small sum for disorderly conduct. My associate, Assistant States Attorney Charles J. Mueller, was cross-examining the defendant, and asked for the production by the defense of the Judge's docket. During the progress of the cross-examination, the docket was examined. It was apparently kept in proper order, each case following in consecutive order and on consecutive dates. While my associate proceeded with the examination, I asked him for the docket and looked at it. It seemed to be in order, and yet I could not conceive of any reason why the complaining witnesses could have been mistaken about the facts of the case. I happened to glance at the bottom of one of the pages where the name "Legal Publisher's Company" was printed. By that time, the noon recess was declared by the court. I went downstairs to the State's Attorney's Office with my associate and told him that there must be something wrong. I called up this concern to find out if they had been in business in 1925, they told me that they had been in business since 1899. Still not satisfied, I had an investigator go with me to the office of the Legal Publishing Company, and asked them to show me some of their dockets. The ones they showed me were not similar to the one shown in court. During the conversation, I asked them if they had made any special dockets and they said that they had not for some time. I asked them who they made them for, and they said for this particular Village. I then explained that I was an Assistant States Attorney, and asked them to show me any records they had from this Village. They produced, not only the copy of an invoice, but an original order from the clerk of the Village dated *June,* 1925, with delivery tickets showing that the said dockets had not been delivered until *July,* 1925. With this information we returned to court. The next witness presented for examination was the Police Magistrate, who testified that the transactions involving the complaining witnesses took place in *February,* 1925, as recorded in his dockets, and he was then turned over to me for cross-examination. The cross-examination was as follows:

Q. How long have you been Police Magistrate of the Village?

A. Eight years.

Q. Are you required by law to keep a true and correct record of the cases tried before you?

A. Yes, sir.

Q. Did you keep a true and correct record of all cases tried before you?

A. Yes, sir.

Q. Defendant's Exhibit 1 is one of your records, is it not?

A. Yes, sir.

Q. And you claim that Defendant's Exhibit 1 is a true and correct record of all cases tried by you—is that so?

A. Yes, sir.

Q. I believe you stated that all records were made and prepared under your direct supervision, is that so?

A. Yes, sir.

Q. Defendant's Exhibit 1 was also prepared under your direct supervision?

A. Yes, sir.

Q. How many of the entries in Defendant's Exhibit 1 were made by you personally?

A. Very few of them.

Q. Who made most of the entries in Defendant's Exhibit 1?

A. My son-in-law.

Q. Was he employed by you for that purpose?

A. Yes, he was.

Q. When did he make the entries in reference to any certain case?

A. Just after the trial was completed.

Q. Would that be during the course of the hearings, or afterwards?

A. It would usually be afterwards.

Q. How long afterwards?

A. Usually the next day or the next evening.

Q. From whom would he get his information in reference to these records in Defendant's Exhibit 1?

A. From me.

Q. Are the records of all cases in Defendant's Exhibit 1 true and correct?

A. They are.

Q. Who dictated all of the information contained in Defendant's Exhibit 1?

A. I did.

Q. When was the information dictated by you in reference to the dates of trial of the various cases listed?

A. They were usually dictated by me as I said, the next day or the next evening, to my son-in-law.

Q. In whose hand writing is the record of the case of the Village v. John Doe and Mary Roe?

A. In my son-in-law's hand writing.

Q. Did you give him the information in reference to these two cases?

A. I did.

Q. When?

A. About the day after the cases were tried.

Q. In what month and in what year?

A. In February, 1925.

Q. Does the record of these two cases in your docket, which is Defendant's Exhibit 1, truly and correctly state the findings in those cases?

A. It does.

Q. Now let me see—do you recall these particular cases?

A. I do.

Q. How do you happen to recall these two particular cases?

A. Well, I remember that the man was quite violent and made a lot of nasty remarks about our Chief of Police, Joe Huszar.

Q. So you have a distinct recollection of the dates in these cases which you tried?

A. Well I don't remember the exact date but my docket shows that they were tried on February 16, 1925.

Q. Do you particularly remember the date of February 16, 1925?

A. No, but I do remember distinctly that they were tried in the month of February, 1925.

Q. Do you distinctly remember that you dictated the information in reference to these cases to your son-in-law within a day or so after the cases were tried on February 16, 1925?

A. I do.

Q. And these entries in Defendant's Exhibit 1 in reference to the case of John Doe and Mary Roe were made by your son-in-law on February 17 or 18, 1925, is that so?

A. Yes, sir.

Q. You are sure about that, are you?

A. Yes, sir.

Q. And you have a distinct recollection of both the trial of the cases and the entries in Defendant's Exhibit 1 as having occurred in the month of February, 1925?

A. Yes, sir.

Q. And you still say that the entries in Defendant's Exhibit 1 are true and correct?

A. Yes, sir.

Q. And you have a distinct recollection of everything I have asked you about?

A. Yes, sir.

Q. That the records were made in Defendant's Exhibit 1 in the month of February, 1925?

A. Yes, sir.

Q. Judge, do you happen to know when these particular dockets were ordered?

A. No, I do not.

Q. Who ordered them?

A. The Village Clerk.

Q. Don't you know that that particular docket was not ordered until June, 1925, and that it was not delivered to the Village until *July* of 1925?

A. No, sir.

Counsel: That is all.

I thereafter placed upon the witness stand the gentleman with whom I had spoken at the Legal Publishing Company, introduced the original order of the clerk of the Village dated June, 1925, the delivery tickets with positive testimony that the dockets were not even in existence in *February,* 1925. I followed this up with evidence from the lithographers and printers, all testifying conclusively to the fact that the dockets were not even printed nor prepared until *June* or *July,* 1925. Defendant was convicted.

§ 565. Avoid broad cross-examining.

As stated, cross-examination may prove to be in some instances a two-edged sword, if care is not taken in its planning and use by limiting it to just those things desired to be proved. The lawyer may open the door by his questions to much harmful testimony. Any question, which is so broad in its scope as to permit a witness to explain too much, will prove detrimental. It must be ever kept in mind that the adverse witness will always be seeking an opportunity to interject favorable testimony in behalf of the adverse party and will "jump with glee" at an opportunity that will permit an added explanation which will be the basis for acceptance of his testimony as true by the jury. Such questions as "why," "how do you explain," "how did it happen," etc., will usually result in harm to the case unless the lawyer is in a position to refute the answer absolutely.

§ 566. Do not over cross-examine.

Many trial attorneys in their desire to discredit the witness' testimony before a jury and in their anxiety to make sure that the jury see the point of their cross-examination are bound to over cross-examine with harmful results. Too much persistence in attempting to over-emphasize a point made will usually result in the witness' explaining away favorable aspects of the admission obtained. For instance, in one case where the issue involved was whether or not the defendant had returned certain merchandise for credit, a witness for the plaintiff testified that the defendant had taken the merchandise with him after he had attempted to return it for credit. Upon cross-examination the witness admitted that she was not in a position to see whether or not the defendant had left the merchandise in her employer's room. Instead of resting content with this admission counsel persisted and asked the further question as to how she knew that the defendant had taken the merchandise back with him. The reply was that she saw him come in with the package, and that when he left he had the same package with him. This testimony plus the other in the case was sufficient to earn a verdict for the plaintiff.

One successful trial lawyer has developed a method of making his points both on direct examination and on cross-examination sometimes so inconspicuous that their full import are rarely realized until the final argument and summation. In his summing up he then places point by point, side by side and builds up his case and analysis so as to show that he has successfully proved his contentions.

§ 567. Make your big points.

Some cross-examiners feel that they must go over everything in their "repertoire" with every witness under cross-examination. In most instances, it is a great deal better to secure one or two *big* admissions or to make one or two *big* points and to dismiss the witness rather than to take a chance on nullifying the good effect of such cross-examination by continuing on endlessly. If the one or two big points made have been sufficient to either disprove the witness' story or to discredit him in the eyes of the jury, it is greatly to be desired to "leave well enough alone" and to "quit a winner," as the saying goes. The development of anti-climaxes or the chance that may be taken by the witness' finally turning the tables against the lawyer is not worth the attempt of continuing the cross-examination.

§ 568. Avoid small triumphs.

Sometimes there is the temptation to make too much of admissions received from witnesses on immaterial issues, or in attempting to prove them mistaken on inconsequential matters. The lawyer should not attempt to prove or to call the witness a liar and a perjurer because he has testified incorrectly to some date or fact not really material in the case. The jury will resent any such attempt.

§ 569. Evasions by the witness.

The trial attorney should ever be on the alert to prevent evasions by the witness under cross-examination. He should also be careful that by such evasion the witness does not direct his trend of thought to another and less dangerous subject of inquiry. The clever witness will attempt to avoid answering directly a question, the answer to which might tend to disprove his testimony, and will make an unresponsive answer not related to the question. This should be prevented immediately by an objection and a motion to strike the answer as not responsive, requesting the court reporter to read the original question and requiring the witness to answer that question directly. Should the witness persist in trying to evade answering the question, the jury will be quick to see this unfair attitude on the part of the witness and will give less credence to his story. Every witness should be forced to answer every question on each subject of inquiry before passing on to another subject in order to secure a better psychological effect.

§ 570. Cross-examination of women and children.

The cross-examination of women has always been considered by trial attorneys as rather dangerous. Women are quite prone to evade a direct answer to questions and pay very little, if any, attention to the rules governing the proof of facts. There is ever present the possibility of the witness' resorting to tears and to make comments or answers that may destroy the lawyer before the jury. The demeanor and attitude of the cross-examiner must be overly fair and gentle in cross-examining women, and more so in cross-examining children. The character or reputation of a woman must never be attacked, either directly or by innuendo, unless the absolute necessities of the occasion require it, and then only when the proof of such bad reputation or character is overwhelming. Even then, the trial lawyer should hesitate. Unusual care must be utilized in the cross-examination of witnesses who are ignorant, abnormal or subnormal.

§ 571. Do not allow interruptions by opposing counsel.

It frequently happens that during a cross-examination opposing counsel will interrupt with some question or objection, and in the argument on the same will try to warn the witness of the purpose of the cross-examination, or will utilize that method to signal the witness to be careful. Objections should be made in all such instances with the request that the court admonish opposing counsel not to interrupt or to interfere with the cross-examination. This does not apply in those instances where opposing counsel's objections are well-founded legally.

§ 572. "To whom have you talked about this case?"

Most witnesses in every jury trial are usually asked by either one attorney or another the question "To whom have you talked about this case?" All witnesses before trial should be told about this question and to answer it truthfully. The witness who has never appeared in court before seems to think it is some sort of a crime to discuss his testimony with the trial attorney prior to his taking the witness stand, and even the most truthful of such witnesses usually reply that they have talked to no one about the case, not even the examining attorney. While this is one of the old "trick" questions it is being used continually. Where the attorney has asked this question and the witness has not answered truthfully, he can take advantage of this situation in the arguments to the jury by telling the jury frankly that the answer of the witness to this question are of no real importance excepting insofar as to show the tendency on the part of the witness to change his story whenever he finds it convenient or necessary to do so. This argument has been used to good effect in cases where the evidence has been conflicting and close.

§ 573. "When did you first know you were to be a witness?"

This question should always be asked in those instances where it is sought to show that the story told by the witness is improbable.

Many witnesses claim to remember insignificant details of events happening some years before the trial, when such details or such incidents could not possibly have impressed themselves upon their minds so forcibly as to be able now to remember such details. When such witness is asked the question, "When did you first know you were to be a witness?" and when this question is followed with the further question that "at the time of the happening of these events you did not know that there would be a law suit," "or that these incidents would be the basis of the present law suit," or that "it was of importance to remember the happening of these events so long before the trial," and when the answers are received to these questions that the witness did not know of any pending law suit, and did not know of any reason for particularly remembering these details it will become apparent to the jury that the story told is improbable.

§ 574. Assuming facts in questions.

It is not permitted to assume anything as true in general cross-examination and in the questions, which are not in evidence and which have not been proved in evidence. The only possible exception to this is the cross-examination of doctors in reference to their testimony given in answer to hypothetical questions.

§ 575. "I don't remember."

Where a witness testifies fully on direct examination and remembers everything and then under cross-examination answers that he "does not remember," the more times that the lawyer can make the witness say "I don't remember" to questions propounded, the better will be the psychological effect, and the more forceful the argument that can be made in "summing up." Every juror will view with suspicion the witness who remembers everything on direct examination and can remember nothing on cross-examination.

§ 576. Cross-examination to show story improbable. One of the most effective uses of cross-examination is the method and technique employed in showing to the court and jury that a witness' story is not worthy of belief because it is improbable. The facts testified to by a witness which do not fit in with the documentary evidence and which are not reasonable can be shown when the proper use of cross-examination is made. Neither judge nor jury will believe a witness who testifies to facts which in their experience tell them cannot be so. The use of this form of cross-examination may be utilized in all cases of cross-examination of alibi witnesses, in deliveries of merchandise, incidental conversations, etc. This form of cross-examination should also be used in all cases where the witness tries to exaggerate or "over-testify" in reference to any set of facts. For instance, in one case a young woman, who in company with two young men was charged with stealing from telephone coin boxes. The defense claimed the woman was intoxicated to such an extent that she was unable to form any intent to commit the crime. She was cross-examined in reference to her drinking. She was apparently so anxious to convince the jury that she was drunk that she was willing to testify to having taken an unlimited number of drinks, and apparently to have taken so much throughout the early part of the evening, while she was with the young men, that it would have been impossible for any human being to have taken so much liquor and to have been able to stand, or to have been conscious. This was all rather absurd in view of the fact that when apprehended a few moments later she was fully conscious of what she was doing.

In a civil case, the defendant produced a witness by whom they sought to prove that plaintiff had *not* taken a sample of the first shipment of oil delivered. This particular happening took place almost five years before the trial. The witness claimed to remember that he knocked on the door, handed in the receipt to be signed by the plaintiff and that she did *not* take a sample. The witness was cross-examined along the following lines: He was asked to tell the name of the party to whom he had delivered oil just before he delivered it to the plaintiff, and to whom he next delivered oil; who he had delivered oil to the day before, or any day within a week after delivery of the oil in question. He answered that he could not. He was then made to describe his coming up to the door. He was intent upon giving favorable testimony. When asked "What door?" he said "The back door." "Was the receipt signed in your presence?" he was then asked. He said, "Yes." The lawyer next asked him whether the receipt was signed by pencil or by pen and ink. He said, "Pencil." When asked what kind of a pencil he went on to describe the particular pencil. After making him go through a lot of this detail, the lawyer then showed him the receipt signed in that case, which previous testimony had shown to be signed by another lady and not the plaintiff. When this fact was made known to him, which was already known to the jury, it completely discredited his testimony.

In the same oil case referred to, the burden was on the plaintiff to prove, as alleged, that the oil shipped to the plaintiff by the defendant at the time complained of was *not* straw-colored gas oil of the grade and quality which they had shipped in the first instance and that it was not of the color which had been recommended for use in the oil-burner by Mr. Stanton, Sales Manager of the Oil Burner Company. The defendant placed upon the witness stand the said Mr. Stanton in an effort to discredit plaintiff's testimony by showing that Mr. Stanton had never recommended straw-colored oil or any other particular color or grade of oil. Mr. Stanton, on direct examination, testified that they were not in the habit of discussing oil with purchasers and particularly not in the habit of telling them what color or grade of oil to use; that in the instance of this sale, no special conversation in reference to oil was ever had with the plaintiff; that oil was never discussed between them, and particularly that nothing was said by him in reference to the use of straw-colored oil by her. Mr. Stanton was cross-examined as to whether he knew that the plaintiff had previously been heating her home by furnace and that she used coal. He replied that he did not know that. He was then asked whether he knew that she had never had an oil burner before and knew nothing whatever of the operation of a burner or the use of fuel oil for heating purposes. He replied that she did not. He was then asked whether or not he recommended the use of oil burners in homes for heating purposes and he said he did. The attorney then asked him whether or not he had sought to convince the plaintiff that it would be to her advantage to utilize oil in preference to coal and he said that he did. The next question asked him was whether or not she was interested in determining the relative costs of the operation and the difference in price between oil and coal, and he answered, "Yes." He was then asked whether or not she was not also interested in the various grades of oil with a view to determining the most economical operation of an oil burner. He said "Yes." The next question was: "She told you, did she not, that she knew absolutely nothing about oils?" and he said "Yes, she did." The attorney then asked him, "Do you mean to have this jury understand that she knew nothing about oil burners and that she was seeking to learn about them and about the advisability of replacing the coal furnace with the fuel oil burner and that she did not ask you what kind or grade of oil should be used in the oil burner?" He answered, "No, she did not." However, this was clearly improbable and impossible to believe. This cross-examination coupled with the testimony given by another witness, presented by defendant in this case, completely discredited Mr. Stanton.

A young man, by the name of Duffy, was then presented who testified on direct examination that he had gone to the home of the plaintiff and when he got there, talked with her, examined the home and found nothing particularly wrong or smoky there. He stated on direct examination that she did not make any complaint about the oil, and on cross-examination, keeping in mind Mr. Stanton's testimony, he was asked whether or not in that conversation the plaintiff had said anything to him about the oil that was purchased and the kind and grade of oil recommended to be purchased. Having been excluded during the testimony of Mr. Stanton, Mr. Duffy answered that she had said that Mr. Stanton of the Oil Burner Company had recommended a No. 2 domestic heating oil which was a *dark colored oil* and *not* a straw-colored oil. In view of the fact that Stanton had stated that he had never discussed *any oil* or the kind of oil with the plaintiff, the attorney immediately attempted to convey to Duffy that he wanted him to say that she had not said anything about Stanton's recommending *any* oil, and he, therefore, said to him, "Do you mean to tell this jury that she said Stanton recommended *any* kind of oil to be used in this oil burner, and he said "Yes." The attorney then restated the same proposition again in other words, with the same result. This coupled with the improbability of Stanton's testimony, served to completely discredit Stanton's story.

§ 577. — Testing recollection—Delivery of merchandise.

Illustration

Q. You say you remember delivering this particular merchandise to Mr. Johnson, personally, do you?

A. Yes, sir.

Q. All right, Mr. Jones, will you just give us the name of the person to whom you delivered some merchandise just prior to this delivery you claim you made to Mr. Johnson?

A. I do not recall.

Q. Give us the name of the person to whom you delivered merchandise immediately after you claim you delivered this parcel to Mr. Johnson?

A. I do not remember.

Q. Give us the name of the first person to whom you delivered a package on that day?

A. I do not know who it was.

Q. Well, Mr. Jones, tell the Court and jury the name of any other person to whom you delivered a package the following day after you claim you delivered this package to Mr. Johnson?

A. I cannot do it.

(Note: This method can be continued as to several days before and several days after alleged delivery.)

§ 578. — Real estate broker's commission case.

In one case, a real estate broker sued for commission with reference to the sale of a building formerly owned by the defendant. Both the plaintiff and the defendant were close personal friends. The defendant claimed that he thought the plaintiff was merely doing him a favor in securing a purchaser for the building and that he never agreed to pay any commission of any kind to the plaintiff, nor did he ever expect to pay any.

The cross-examination to discredit this defense by showing it to be unworthy of belief was as follows:

Illustration

Q. You say that you thought the plaintiff was merely doing you a favor in securing a purchaser for your building do you?

A. Yes, sir.

Q. And that you thought he would not require you to pay any commission on the deal, is that so?

A. Yes, sir.

Q. You were a close personal friend of Mr. Jones, were you not?

A. Yes, sir.

Q. And you had known him for a great number of years had you not?

A. Yes, sir.

Q. You have visited frequently at his home?

A. Yes, sir.

Q. You knew he was a married man and had three children?

A. Yes, sir.

Q. You knew that none of the children were employed, did you not?

A. Yes, sir.

Q. You knew Mr. Jones was a licensed real estate broker?

A. Yes, sir.

Q. And you knew that that was his business?

A. Yes, sir.

Q. You also knew, did you not, that he and his family depended upon that business exclusively for their livelihood, did you not?

A. Yes, sir.

Q. Have you ever loaned Mr. Jones any large sums of money?

A. No, sir.

Q. Have you ever done anything for him which would obligate him to pay you $1500.00 or more?

A. No, sir.

Q. You know do you not, that the regular charge and commission for the sale of a building such as yours amounts to $1500.00?

A. Yes, sir.

Q. And knowing that Mr. Jones was not under obligation to give you $1500.00 and knowing that he and his family depend on his commissions as a real estate broker for a living, yet you felt that he secured a purchaser for your building just merely as a favor to you and that you were not to pay any commission, is that right?

A. Yes, sir.

Counsel: That is all.

§ 579. Suit for return of deposit.

In one case the plaintiff sued for the return of a deposit given on the purchase of a store on the grounds of breach of warranty, claiming that the defendant had warranted the gross sales of the business purchased by him to be at least $350.00 per week whereas the actual sales were only $200.00 a week. There was nothing in writing to evidence the warranty.

The defendant on the witness stand denied that he had made any statement whatsoever with reference to the amount of sales.

To show by cross-examination that the defendant's statement was improbable, the following method was utilized:

Illustration

Q. You say that Arthur Simon, the plaintiff in this case, did not ask you anything about your gross sales?

A. No, sir.

Q. And that you did not tell him anything about the sales?

A. No, sir.

Q. Mr. Simon, prior to this deal, was a stranger to you was he not?

A. Yes, that is right.

Q. That is, he did not know you and you did not know him?

A. That is right.

Q. And he knew nothing about your business before that time did he?

A. No, sir.

Q. However, you did have knowledge, did you not, as to the amount of sales?

A. Yes, sir.

Q. And you kept regular records to show how much merchandise you sold every week?

A. Yes, sir.

Q. Well, Mr. Jones, any prospective purchaser of a store would naturally be interested in the amount of your sales, would he not?

A. Well, he might.

Q. The amount of sales has something to do, has it not, with reference to the amount of profits?

A. Yes, sir.

Q. In other words, Mr. Jones, the greater the sales in a store with the same overhead, the more the profits will be, isn't that right?

A. Yes, sir.

Q. And a store showing more sales and more profits is of more value than a store having small sales and small profits, isn't that right?

A. Yes, sir.

Q. In fact, one of the ways of determining the value of a store is by the sales and profits, isn't that right, Mr. Jones?

A. Yes, sir.

Q. And in determining the selling price of your store, Mr. Jones, you naturally took into consideration, did you not, the amount of your sales and the amount of your profits at the store?

A. Yes, sir.

Q. And any prospective purchaser of a store would determine the purchase price and value of that store based upon the sales and profits, would he not?

A. Yes, sir.

Q. Mr. Jones, a store having the same overhead with sales of $350.00 per week would be worth more, would it not, than the same store with the same overhead, doing $200.00 per week business?

A. I guess so.

Q. And yet you say that Arthur Simon in this case did not ask you how much the sales were per week in your store? Is that right?

A. Yes, sir.

Q. That is all.

§ 580. "Alibi" witnesses.

In the examination of so called "Alibi" witnesses who claim to have met the defendant at a certain time and place, the following method can be utilized in most instances to discredit their testimony. It should be kept in mind that the technique employed utilizes the *names* of persons rather than the time and place of events. The witness may be able to recall where he was at a particular time and place on certain days, or even every day, because of habitual and customary procedure. But when he is examined with reference to the *names* of persons, other than that of the defendant in the case whom he met at the same time, the day before the alleged meeting with the defendant and the day after and over a period of time it will be found that he will be unable to recall the *names* of any such persons, particularly when he must fix the *time* he met such persons also.

Illustration

Q. You say you met the defendant John Jones at Fourth Avenue and Maine Street on January 17, 1932 at 4:00 p. m.?

A. Yes, sir.

Q. All right, just tell the Court and jury the name of the person whom you met at 4:00 the day before.

A. Well, I just don't remember right now.

Q. Well give us the name of the person whom you met at 4:00 o'clock on the day after you met the defendant.

A. Well, I just don't remember meeting anyone that afternoon at that time.

Q. Give us the name of any person you met that afternoon and tell us just what time you met him.

A. Well, I just can't do that.

Q. Give us the name of any person you met two days before you met the defendant at 4:00 p. m.?

A. Well, I didn't meet anyone at 4:00 p. m.

Q. Well, at 2:00 p. m. then.

A. I don't remember.

Q. Give us the name of any person you met that week and tell us what time you met him?

A. I don't remember just now.

§ 581. Court's witness.

In some jurisdictions the trial judge in Civil as well as Criminal Cases has a right, in his discretion and in the interests of justice, to call for examination as the Court's witness any person who has knowledge of the facts in dispute whom either party is unwilling to vouch for as to truth and veracity.[14] The Court should, however, require some showing of hostility on the part of the witness before exercising his discretion, particularly in Civil cases.

The Court usually asks the witness his name, address and business and then turns the witness over as for cross-examination to both sides.

§ 582. Cross-examination of adverse party.

The right to call the adverse party for examination *without being bound* by the testimony is available in the trial of cases in many jurisdictions. Every trial attorney should avail himself of this privilege in every possible instance. Its value lies in the fact that the defendant in every case may be cross-examined at the beginning of the trial to secure admissions which will supply deficiencies in the attorney's

14 Merchants' Bank v. Goodfellow, 140 Pac. 759, 44 Utah 349; O'Connor v. National Ice Co., 4 N. Y. S. 537, 56 N. Y. Super. Ct. 410 (aff'd 24 N. E. 1092, 121 N. Y. 662); Roth v. Moeller, 197 Pac. 62, 185 Cal. 415; Townsend v. City of Joplin, 123 S. W. 474, 139 Mo. App. 394; The Kawailani, 128 F. 879, 63 C. C. A. 347; Lycan v. People, 107 Ill. 423; State v. Lee, 80 N. C. 483; Gilhooley v. Columbus R., etc., Co., 20 Ohio N. P. N. S. 545; Lafferty v. State, 35 S. W. 374 (Texas).

case. The admissions thus received will obviate the necessity of calling extra witnesses to prove such admitted facts. This tends to eliminate considerable time in the trial of cases. The right to cross-examine the adverse party without being bound by such testimony is also of value in that it prevents the defendant from changing his story after the plaintiff and his witnesses have testified. This tends to narrow the issues involved. It also helps to eliminate whatever good psychological effect there would have been in the telling of the story by the defendant under the careful guidance of his attorney. Under this right of cross-examination the story of the defendant is given to the jury somewhat brokenly, and interspersed with admissions the lawyer has secured. Then when the defendant later takes the stand to retell the story, it is less interesting because the jury has heard it all before. The adverse party should be cross-examined at the start of the trial whenever it is desired to know which of several possible positions the defendant intends to take.

Some judges, upon objection, limit the cross-examination under the statute to those facts and issues which the examiner is unable to prove by his own witnesses. However, there is nothing in these statutes which limits the cross-examination permitted under these sections only to those facts or issues which the examiner cannot prove by his own witnesses.[15]

In In re Brown, 38 Minn. 112, the court said:

"The object of the statute is to authorize an adversary *to be examined, unprotected by the well-known rules of evidence.* The effect is to compel him to undergo examination as well as cross-examination at the hands of the opposition if it so desires. *It follows that any question which could properly have been asked the witness, were he undergoing the ordinary cross-examination, was legitimate.*

"It hardly seems necessary to add that any evidence so obtained is as legitimate and competent as any other evidence to establish any fact in the case necessary to be proved, not only as against the witness, but any other party in the cause,

15 Malleable Iron Co. v. Brennan, 174 Ill. App. 38 at 43; State v. Jeffrey, 247 N. W. 692, 188 Minn. 476; In re Olson's Est., 223 N. W. 41, 54 S. D. 184.

if the evidence was not inadmissible for some other reason than the mere fact that he was being cross-examined or examined by the use of leading questions."

In the case of Rosenberg v. Miller, 181 Ill. App. 443, the court accepted and passed upon the evidence (*in this case*) where the *only* testimony offered was that of the defendant who was called for examination under Section 33 of the Municipal Court Act. The plaintiff caused the defendant to be examined on all phases of the case without being restricted merely to facts that he was unable to prove by other witnesses. Thus, it would seem that the Illinois Appellate Court, has placed no such restriction on the right of examination of the adverse party.

In truth and in fact there should be no such restriction nor limitation made. After all the courts are interested in passing upon all of the issues involved in the case and to determine wherein the truth lies. The courts should also be interested in saving time in the trial of cases rather than in preventing a plaintiff or a defendant, as the case may be, from proving his case by securing admissions from the adverse party. Technicalities which would prevent admission of evidence as to all facts involved in the easiest and quickest manner should not be tolerated by limiting the scope of the cross-examination of the adverse party.[16]

The value of cross-examination of an adverse party at the beginning of the trial is illustrated in the following instance:

In a case recently tried, suit was instituted on a burglary insurance policy. The defense raised was fraudulent statements as to prior losses. After the insurance adjuster was examined, the plaintiff received permission to file an amended complaint alleging waiver by the insurance company of the defense of fraudulent statements as to prior loss, due to the attempted cancellation of the policy after the loss. The insurance company failed to return the entire premium or at

16 As a general rule a broad range in inquiry is permitted. Guinan v. Famous, etc., Corp., 167 N. E. 235, 267 Mass. 501; Little v. Los Angeles Ry. Corp., 271 Pac. 134, 94 Cal. App. 303; Waller v. Sloan, 196 N. W. 347, 225 Mich. 600; Levin v. Spero, 35 Misc. 792, 72 N. Y. S. 1115; Simon v. Mooney, 22 Ohio Cir. Ct. 21, 12 Ohio Cir. Dec. 73; Knox v. Sandquist, 197 N. W. 733, 183 Wis. 104; Frank Prox Co. v. Bryan, 162 Ill. App. 381.

least the pro-rata premium from the date of the discovery of the false answers, but cancelled the policy as of a date two months later. After the insurance adjuster testified, the case was continued to give the defendant time to file its answer to the amended complaint. (There was no jury.) The insurance company in answer to the amended complaint stated that there had been a rescission of the policy by the adjuster immediately upon his securing the knowledge of the falsity of the statements. Plaintiff denied any such rescission. The insurance adjuster had been called for cross-examination under the statute and testified at the prior hearing as follows:

"My name is Peter Borg. I am representing the Blank Insurance Corporation, as an adjuster. I had charge of the investigation of this case. Mr. and Mrs. Carr were at my office once, on which occasion they brought some bills. I do not recall the date on which they called at my office. I think that Plaintiff's Exhibits 2, 3, 4, and 5 for identification were the bills delivered to me by Mr. and Mrs. Carr. I did not, on that occasion, request Mr. and Mrs. Carr to mail any notice of loss of any kind. I took a notice of loss personally. (Witness produces Plaintiff's Exhibit 6 for identification, which is offered in evidence.) This was signed by Mr. Carr in my presence, on the date it bears. I was given a list of the items claimed to have been lost. Plaintiff's Exhibit 7 is that list. I caused an investigation to be made of the report of the loss to the police department. I do not remember the exact station. I have a copy of that report in my files. Plaintiff's Exhibit 9 is the report that I received from the Police Station. (Plaintiff's Exhibit 9 admitted as evidence.) The first time that I found out that there had been a previous loss from burglary was at the date of the investigation at the police department. I did not find it out from Mr. and Mrs. Carr. Besides Plaintiff's Exhibit 6, which I received from the Carrs, I took a statement from them. Mr. Carr signed said statement. I talked to Mr. Carr on the 17th day of April.

Q. Did you have occasion to talk to Mr. Carr at any subsequent date?

A. I did not see Mr. Carr again until the date I tendered a return premium. I tendered Defendant's Exhibit 1 for identification and the cash to Mr. Carr on October 24, 1932, and he refused it.

Q. Have you that money in court?

A. No, sir.

Q. You are not tendering it to us or rescinding on the policy?

A. We would be glad to if you would like it.

Q. But you haven't?

A. *Not yet.*

Q. At whose request did you decide to offer the full amount of the premium back?

A. That is my position to do so.

Q. You knew about this previous check that had been issued for $65.17?

A. No, I did not.

Q. You didn't know any thing about that?

A. No, sir.

Sometime later the insurance adjuster testified as a witness for the defendant and attempted to change his story to overcome the claim of waiver. He was thereupon cross-examined in this manner:

Q. Do you remember the date of the previous hearing?

A. I don't remember.

The Court: I think the records will show.

Counsel: Yes, I just wanted to ask that question anyway.

Q. Now, Mr. Borg, for the purpose of the record, tell us how long you have been an insurance adjuster?

A. Eighteen years.

Q. That is with all classes of insurance?

A. Yes.

Q. Are you connected with the defendant exclusively, or do you also adjust for other concerns?

A. I adjust for other concerns.

Q. What is your business called in insurance circles?

A. It is classified as "independent adjusters."

Q. That is what I was trying to get, the term. Now, you were familiar with the terms of this policy by reason of your employment with the Blank Co., is that right?

A. Yes, sir.

Q. And you were also familiar with the terms of the policy when you were given this job to investigate and adjust the loss with Mr. Carr, the plaintiff here, is that right?

A. Yes, sir.

Q. Mr. Borg, your job as adjuster has brought you into contact with insurance law and insurance policies to the extent that you make up your mind for the company as to whether or not there is liability on a policy or nor, is that correct?

A. In some cases, yes, and in some cases, no.

Q. I just want to show your familiarity with insurance questions. Now, I take it, you know what is meant by cancellation under a policy of insurance, is that right?

A. Yes, I do.

Q. And that is also true as to rescission of insurance policies?

A. Yes, sir.

Q. You understood in April, 1932, the rights of the Blank Company to claim a rescission under this policy?

A. Yes, sir.

Q. And you are also familiar with the procedure followed in making tender of premiums, return of premiums, is that right?

A. Yes.

Q. You realize the significance of such a tender and you realized it in April, 1932, is that correct?

A. Yes.

Q. Now, you say that on this first occasion when you met Mr. Carr, you rescinded the policy, is that correct?

A. No, sir, the second occasion.

Q. I mean the first occasion you really talked about the terms of the policy. You say on the second occasion, April 19th?

A. Yes.

Q. You recall that very distinctly, I take it?

A. Yes.

Q. On that occasion you say you rescinded the policy?

A. I did.

Q. And you made a tender of how much money?

A. $96.88.

Q. Now, tell us for the purpose of the record, please, how that money was made up?

A. Ones, twos, fives, tens, twenties and silver.

Q. In what proportions?

A. I can't tell you from my memory.

Q. Did you make a note of it any place?

A. I made a list of it somewhere in my files.

Q. I will ask Counsel to produce that list. When did you make that list?

A. I had one list made up in April and it was later copied off, one original and three copies on the typewriter.

Q. Was that list the one you had previously run off on October 24, 1932?

A. Yes.

Q. You realized when you made this tender and the rescission the importance of that particular fact?

A. Yes.

Q. You took particular notice of the fact that you were tendering the premium in cash?

A. Yes.

Q. You realized the significance of what a legal tender was, is that right?

A. Yes.

Q. And you made particular note of the fact that you tendered him ninety-six and how much?

A. Eighty-eight cents.

Q. Was there anybody else present at that time?

A. The young man that worked for me sat across a double desk.

Q. And I take it he was taking note of the fact that you tendered him $96.88?

A. I used him as a witness.

Q. *You had already planned that meeting for the purpose of rescinding that policy of insurance, is that right?*

A. That is right.

Q. So that there is no question about that between us in the record?

A. That is right.

Q. So that everything in that meeting became of importance to you?

A. Yes.

Q. You testified in this case before, haven't you?
A. Yes, sir.
Q. But you don't remember when that was?
A. I don't remember the date, no, sir.
Q. Do you remember the month?
A. I would say it was about five or six weeks ago.
Q. Five or six weeks ago?
A. Possibly.
Q. This is the end of May, it would be about the middle of April?
A. I can't be sure, I don't know.
Q. I am just testing your memory.
A. On that you can't because I dismissed it from my mind.
Q. I will ask you if you have made any contrary statements at any time with reference to planning this meeting for the purpose of rescinding this policy of insurance, any time or any place?
A. Other than my own office?
Q. Other than what you are saying now, have you ever made any statements contrary to that?
A. No.
Q. Do you recall your testimony in the previous hearing of this case?
A. I believe I do, yes, sir.
Q. Now, let us test your memory and see what you said at that previous hearing in reference to this rescission and the tendering of the money.
A. I took the policy and threw it back on the desk and told them that loss wasn't covered on the contract.
Q. What else did you testify in the previous hearing as to rescission or tendering of money?
A. I stated his premium would be returned to him and here it was, in legal tender, which he refused.
Q. That is what you testified to in the last hearing?
A. Yes, sir.
Q. At that previous hearing did you say, "I am rescinding this policy of insurance and I am tendering you this $96.88?"
A. To the best of my recollection, yes.

Q. How long on that occasion in April, 1932, did you converse with Mr. Carr or Mrs. Carr, either one?

A. I would say a matter of three minutes each time.

Q. And you discussed nothing else but that rescission and tender, is that right?

A. At first, I didn't.

Q. I mean when you rescinded and tendered the money?

A. That was the second one.

Q. Calling your attention to your previous testimony in this hearing, I ask you whether or not you were asked whether you had seen Mr. Carr on more than one occasion and did you not answer that you saw him only once?

A. I don't remember that.

Q. At that previous hearing when you were examined by me under Section 33, were you asked as to when you had seen Mr. Carr again and prior to that time you had said nothing at all in the testimony with reference to making any rescission of tender of money, did you say this, "I never saw Mr. Carr again until I tendered his return premium." Were you asked that question and did you make that answer?

A. My answer to that would be I didn't until I made another tender of return premium which was in October.

Q. Is that your recollection now that you did say you had seen him again when you again made a tender?

A. Approximately October 18th, when he came in the office.

Q. Did Mr. Gann ask you, "I show you Defendant's Exhibit 1 for identification," in an effort to refresh your recollection as to the date and did you say, "It was on the October after?"

A. October after what?

Q. After this previous meeting.

A. I don't know what you mean.

Q. Let us see the next question. Then did you say, "On the October after that I tendered him the paper, that and the cash and we still have the tender?"

A. I didn't tender any paper.

Q. You didn't say that?

A. Not that I recollect, no.

Q. Were you then asked by the Court "You mean you tendered him money and that paper?"

A. That was a receipt for the money, yes.

Q. Then you did tender a paper?

A. There was a paper, yes.

Q. Then the Court asked you "What did he do?"

A. He refused it.

Q. Did the Court ask you, "When was that?" and did you answer, "I just don't recall the date, October?" Then I asked you, "Is that the proper date?" and Mr. Gann answered, "October 24, 1932." Were those questions asked and were those answers made?

A. I don't remember.

Q. Do you recall that I asked you this question, *"You are not tendering it to us or rescinding on the policy?" and did you make this answer "We would be glad to if you would like it." Then did I ask you, "But you haven't?" and you answered, "Not yet?"*

A. I don't remember.

Q. You don't remember those questions or those answers?

A. No.

Q. Then did I ask you this question, "At whose request did you decide to offer the full amount of the premium back?" and did you make this answer, "That is my business to do so." "Question. You knew about this previous check that had been issued for $65.17. Answer. No, I did not." Were those questions asked you and did you make those answers?

A. I don't remember the fact coming up in court.

Q. Now, Mr. Borg, don't you know that in your previous testimony you never mentioned one word about rescission or tender prior to October, 1932? Yes, or no, please.

A. I have no answer. You have the testimony.

Counsel: That is all. (Witness excused.)

§ 583. Cross-examination where signature denied.

In instances where the defendant denies signing or executing any note, check or other instrument, the following method of cross-examination can be utilized to good advantage:

Illustration

Q. You say you did not sign this note?

A. Yes, sir.

Q. You never saw it before?

A. No, sir, I did not.

Q. All right, will you please sign your name on this piece of paper which I am marking Plaintiff's Exhibit 4 for identification, and use this *fountain pen,* please?

(Witness does so.)

Q. Now will you please sign your name once more on this piece of paper which I have marked Plaintiff's Exhibit 5 for identification, and use the *pencil* please?

(Witness signs second piece of paper.)

Q. Now will you again sign your name with this *fountain pen* on this paper, which I have marked Plaintiff's Exhibit 6 for identification?

(Witness does so.)

Q. Now will you please sign once more your name on this piece of paper which I have marked Plaintiff's Exhibit 7 for identification and use the *pencil* please?

(Witness does so.)

(Note: It is always good policy to have the witness sign his name several times, using both pencil and pen and ink on different pieces of paper, each piece of paper being put aside without permitting the witness to view any of the signatures, so that he will not be able to copy them. After several such specimens are taken it will be a comparatively simple matter for a hand writing expert to determine whether or not the witness signed the note involved in the law suit.)

The question sometimes arises as to whether or not the court has power to compel the witness to sign his name during cross-examination.[17]

In the event that the witness refuses to sign his name on the ground that it might incriminate him, such refusal will of course destroy his credibility before the jury so that even though the judge refuses to compel him to sign his name all the possible good the trial attorney could possibly desire will have been accomplished.

§ 584. Contributory negligence.

In the defense of all personal injury cases, the cross-examination of the plaintiffs should be planned in such a way as

17 The Court has power to compel signature. Williams v. Riches, 46 N. W. 817, 77 Wis. 569; Bradford v. People, 43 Pac. 1014, 22 Col. Crim. 157; Smith v. King, 26 Atl. 1059, 62 Conn. 515.

to show contributory negligence. In most instances this is the most logical and the most effective defense to be utilized, especially when considered by an appellate or reviewing court. A proper cross-examination, coupled with some effective instructions by the court on the subject of contributory negligence will aid in winning many cases.

In one instance, a woman went into a rest room of a moving picture theatre and slipped on a banana peel, severely injuring herself. The defendant (after suit was started) defended on the ground of contributory negligence.

The plaintiff was cross-examined as follows:

Illustration

Q. You say that you witnessed the show and that after the show you went to the ladies rest room?

A. Yes, sir.

Q. Just where was the ladies rest room?

A. On the left side of the lower floor.

Q. Describe the door to the ladies rest room.

A. It was a swinging door opening in either direction.

Q. Will you tell the Court and jury about what size room it was that you entered?

A. Well, it was about fifteen feet long and about twelve to fourteen feet wide.

Q. Will you describe the room that you entered?

A. It seemed to be a sort of a lounge room with a number of easy chairs and several lamps.

Q. Will you describe to the Court and jury the floor of this room?

A. Well the floor had a sort of a figured linoleum.

Q. Did the linoleum extend to all walls of the room?

A. Yes, it did.

Q. What else did you notice in the room?

A. Well there was an Italian Cut Velvet sofa on one side of the wall.

Q. Will you describe the sofa?

A. It was a long seat with stuffed bottom, back and arms. It had a floral design and was burgundy color.

Q. Will you describe the walls, please?

A. The walls were of a light color. There were several pictures on the walls.

Q. Will you please tell the Court and jury what other furnishings there were in this room?

A. I noticed three or four large lamps, several table lamps and two occasional chairs.

Q. Were the lamps lighted?

A. Yes, sir.

Q. Just where in the room did you fall?

A. About five to ten feet beyond the door.

Q. After you fell, where was this banana peel?

A. It had moved about three or four feet from where I stepped on it.

Q. Were you able to see the banana peel quite clearly after you fell?

A. Yes, I did.

Q. It was in plain sight then, was it?

A. Yes, sir.

Q. Now, going back to just before you fell. Will you tell the Court and the jury just how you walked into the room?

A. Well, I walked in the natural manner, looking straight ahead.

Q. There was nothing beside the banana peel on the floor where you fell, was there?

A. No, sir.

Q. But you did not see the banana peel until you fell, did you?

A. No, sir.

Q. However, if you had looked down at the floor you could have seen the banana peel, could you not?

A. I don't know. I might have been able to.

Q. And if you had seen it on the floor you could have avoided it, could you not, by making a step in another direction?

A. Maybe.

Q. That is all.

(Note: In attempting to prove contributory negligence on the part of the plaintiff in this type of case, the trial attorney should never directly ask the plaintiff whether or not the room was sufficiently lighted to see the object which caused the fall. It is always better to pursue the above indirect method of proving that the room was lighted well enough for the plaintiff to have seen everything in the room.)

In personal injury cases a valuable assistant in planning a cross-examination is Schwartz on "Cross-examination in Personal Injury Cases." It abounds with practical illustrations of what to do and how to do it. It is of value to attorneys for plaintiffs in personal injury cases in preparing clients for cross-examination. As for those attorneys who are engaged in the defense of personal injury cases it is of incalculable value. No attorney can afford to go to trial in this class of case without referring to this commendable work.

§ 585. Slipping on rugs or polished floors.

The following three illustrations (Sections 585, 586 and 587) are from Schwartz's book:

"This type of case often affords an example of how a cross-examiner with a combined knowledge of law and human nature can win a case for the defendant which might otherwise be lost. To take a typical illustration, a customer goes into a store to buy rugs, let us say. While in the store he steps upon a small rug which slips from under him and he falls and is injured. Now the rule of law applicable is that the storekeeper owes the customer the duty to use reasonable care to keep his premises in safe condition, or at least to warn them against dangers which are not known or obvious to any ordinarily intelligent person.[18] By taking advantage of the plaintiff's overzealousness to pin the blame on the storekeeper, he may be led to testify himself out of court.

"Upon the cross-examiner demanding whether the floor was not an ordinary floor, the witness will deny this. It will be described as a "most highly polished and slippery floor," in fact, "the most highly polished floor plaintiff had ever seen." It was so highly polished that it was positively glassy in appearance. Of course, a small rug on a slippery floor is apt to slip. Everyone knows it and the plaintiff will readily admit that he knew it. Next the cross-examiner brings out the fact that plaintiff did not know of certain devices which can keep a rug from slipping or if he did know of such that he had no reason to believe that such device was used on the

18 Kennedy v. Cherry & Webb Co. (Mass.), 166 N. E. 562; Shaw v. Ogden, 214 Mass. 475, 102 N. E. 61; Kelley v. N. Y. Central R. Co., 255 Mass. 124, 150 N. E. 849.

rug in question. Having obtained all of these salient admissions, the cross-examiner can next force the plaintiff to admit that by stepping aside and walking a foot or so out of the way he could have avoided the rug, and the thing is done.

"Plaintiff does not realize it, but he has shown that he knew all of the conditions of which he complains, that he appreciated the danger and voluntarily assumed the risk of the accident and he is out of court.[19]

"If the condition complained of is the placing of wax on a dance floor there can be no recovery for dance floors are intended to be slippery.[20]

Illustration

"Plaintiff was a guest at a wedding and asserted that she was injured while walking across the floor of the dining hall, which was being prepared for further dancing. She had danced theretofore. She said that she stepped upon a small piece of wax which adhered to the heel of her shoe and caused her to fall upon the floor. She claimed she saw an employee of defendant scattering wax upon the floor.[21]

Q. You say you saw men putting a substance out of a can on the floor?

A. Yes.

Q. What did they do after putting that substance on the floor?

A. They left it there.

Q. You saw it left there?

A. Yes.

Q. On what part of the floor did you see that substance?

A. The center of the dance floor.

19 Crone v. Jordan Marsh Co. (Mass.), 169 N. E. 136; Kitchen v. Women's City Club of Boston (Mass.), 166 N. E. 554. See also Miner v. Connecticut River R. Co., 153 Mass. 398, 402, 26 N. E. 994; Rosen-Steinsitz v. Wanamaker, 154 N. Y. Supp. 262; Chilberg v. Standard Furniture Co., 63 Wash. 414, 115 Pac. 837, 34 L. R. A. (N. S.) 1079.

20 Fishman v. Brooklyn Jewish Center, Inc., 234 App. Div. 319, 255 N. Y. Supp. 124.

21 Adapted from cross-examination of plaintiff. Fishman v. Brooklyn Jewish Center, Inc., 234 App. Div. 319, 255 N. Y. Supp. 124, by Frank M. Wilcox, Esq., New York City.

Q. How near were you to those men who were putting the stuff on the floor?

A. About 10 feet away.

Q. Did they come over anywhere near to where you were standing?

A. No.

Q. You didn't see them put any wax over near where you were standing?

A. No.

Q. And you didn't see them put any wax over near the chair where you went to sit down?

A. No.

Q. You don't know where you got this piece of substance on your heel?

A. Well, I got it.

Q. You don't know where you got the substance on your heel, yes or no?

A. I do know.

Q. When did you first notice you had it on your heel?

A. After I took the shoe off.

Q. Now, when you walked over to sit down on this chair, you could see the floor?

A. I don't look down on the floor to see whether there is anything there or not.

Q. You were looking down toward the chair weren't you?

A. I was not looking at the chair.

Q. You were going to sit down in this chair, weren't you?

A. Yes.

Q. And did you look down on the floor as you went to sit down?

A. I didn't look down on the floor.

Q. Then you don't know what made you slip?

A. I noticed after I took off my shoe there was something stuck on it.

Q. That was after you took off your shoe, you noticed something stuck to your heel?

A. Yes.

Q. When it got there, or where you were when it got there you don't know, is that right?

A. That is right.

Q. How near did you get to this chair before you slipped?
A. About four feet.
Q. You didn't see them throwing any wax or any hard material over in the vicinity of the chair where you went to sit down?
A. No, I didn't.
Q. You had been dancing earlier that evening on that very floor, hadn't you?
A. Yes.
Q. Now, these chairs in this place, at the time this happened were all pushed back against the wall, weren't they?
A. Yes, they were.
Q. So that, whatever there was on the floor, was free from the chairs, is that correct?
A. Yes.
Q. And you say you didn't look on the floor when you went over to sit down?
A. No, I was not looking for any particular thing.
Q. You didn't notice anything?
A. No.
Q. Now did you have high heels on?
A. Not too high heels.
Q. Did you have high heels?
A. Medium.
Q. You had dancing shoes on?
A. Yes, evening shoes.
Q. And they were fairly high shoes, is that right?
A. I can bring the shoes here.
Q. I don't care about bringing the shoes here. They were fairly high shoes?
A. They were high heels.

"The complaint was dismissed on the ground that it is not negligence to put wax on a dance floor. A dance floor is intended to be slippery, and plaintiff with knowledge of the conditions, took the chance of slipping."

§ 586. Length of time confined to bed.

"Another claim commonly and easily exaggerated is the length of time plaintiff was confined to bed and home as a result of the accident. A prompt and thorough investigation will often furnish material with which to discredit the plaintiff's claim on this score. An investigator sent to plaintiff's home a few days after the accident may find that he is not at home. A check-up on the plaintiff's employment and an interview with his employer may disclose that plaintiff was back at work during the period he claims to have been disabled. School records are helpful if the plaintiff be a child. Where definite proof of the falsity of plaintiff's claim is at hand, the course on cross-examination is simple. Have the plaintiff reiterate his claims, and have him deny specifically being out of his home on the date to which your own proof relates—then present that proof.

Illustration

Q. Now you say that you were in bed for nine weeks, is that correct?

A. That is right.

Q. Is that just exactly what you mean, that you were in bed?

A. Absolutely.

Q. Actually, physically in bed throughout those entire nine weeks?

A. Nine weeks, yes, sir.

Q. You never went out during that time?

A. No, sir. Not until after the nine weeks.

Q. Let us figure out the exact dates—you were in bed for nine weeks from September 14th, the date of the accident?

A. Yes.

Q. So that you were in bed from September 14th to November 21st, or two months and one week later, is that correct?

A. Yes, nine weeks.

Q. Now, Miss—did you, for instance go out of your house on October 7th?

A. That is less than nine weeks—no, sir, I was in bed nine weeks.

Q. You are positive that you were not out of your house on October 7th?

A. I was not out of my house before the nine weeks; I couldn't walk. I couldn't step on the leg.

Q. Are you as sure of that as you are of anything else in this case?

A. I am.

Counsel then obtains a book from a witness in the courtroom and hands it up to the witness.

Q. (Showing same to witness) Will you tell us whether this is your signature?

A. Yes, it is.

Counsel: I offer this entry in evidence.

The Witness: What is this entry?

Q. That is your signature, isn't it?

A. Yes.

The Court: You may read the entry.

(The entry was one made by the plaintiff on October 7th when she registered as a voter at the regular registration place.)"

§ 587. When case given to attorney.

"The date when the action was commenced may have no significance and then again it may take on importance. At any rate, be sure to notice the date on the summons. If issued very soon after the accident that fact may give the impression of undue haste and greed on the part of the plaintiff and possibly 'ambulance chasing' by his attorney. On the other hand, if the action was delayed too long, that may cast some doubt upon the *bona fides* of the claim. In such a case the argument may be advanced that the case was purposely delayed so that the defendant would not be afforded an opportunity to check upon plaintiff's physical condition by a physical examination. (True in some states.)

It frequently happens that the action is commenced at a time when plaintiff claims he was confined to bed. In such event it becomes interesting to know how his lawyer got the information necessary to start suit, for clients usually go to their attorney's office, to retain them. So, in one case, the plaintiff claimed she was confined to bed for nine weeks, yet the summons was dated six days after the accident. Plaintiff was a shrewd woman and a direct question would have put her on her guard. The question asked was:

Q. Who accompanied you down to your lawyer's office when you gave him your case?

A. My mother took me in a taxi.

This question really assumed a fact not in evidence, but no objection was made to it and the witness was intent on showing that she needed help of her mother and a taxicab in order to get her to the lawyer's office and quite forgot that she was supposed to have been confined to her bed at the time."

§ 588. Discrediting story of one witness by cross-examination of another.

An effective method of discrediting the story of one witness is by cross-examining another witness and securing admissions from the second witness which refutes the story of the first witness.

For instance, in one case where it was claimed that the plaintiff was incompetent when he signed and executed a certain deed, a member of the plaintiff's family testified that in his opinion the plaintiff was not competent to transact his business affairs. The witness was turned over for cross-examination which showed that the plaintiff had cared for the real estate and that his mental condition was such that he knew just what had to be done.

Cross-examination (in part):

Q. Prior to the time that this paper was signed there by your father, were you there once, twice or three times?

A. When?

Q. Before this time that you are telling about when the paper was signed and thrown in the wastebasket.

A. Yes.

Q. Yes, what?

A. I went there before the papers were signed.

Q. More than one time?

A. Yes.

Q. How long before the second time was the first time?

A. I don't know, but I was there.

Q. You were there?

A. Yes.

Q. All right, let's see. Who else went with you over there this time?

A. Not anyone, just my father and I went.

Q. Now, the first time that you ever went to Gardner's office, who went?

A. Not anyone. We went there by ourselves all the time.

Q. Then every time you were there your father was there, is that right?

A. Yes.

Q. Now, your father was taking care of his property, isn't that right?

A. Yes.

Q. Collecting rents and everything?

A. Yes.

Q. And taking care of the repairs?

A. Yes.

Q. And he took care of his property after that visit there in July, 1926, didn't he?

A. Yes.

Q. And he was getting around all right, was he?

A. Yes.

Q. He was able to walk?

A. Yes.

Q. Did he walk over to Cannon Gardner's office?

A. Sure.

Q. He was all right and well?

A. Yes.

Q. And how long after that did he take care of his own property?

A. Well, after he got away from Gardner he had it in a different real estate's hands.

Q. Did he check over the reports from the real estate people?

A. Yes.

Q. And check up the amount of money he received from the property?

A. Yes.

Q. He put it in the bank? He didn't have any trouble doing that, did he?

A. No.

Q. Now, how long after Gardner was interested? That would be a year and three months?

A. Yes, sir.

Q. Now, then, did he ask you to speak about the farm at that time?

A. Yes, we talked over the farm.

Q. Well, did you tell him how you were taking care of his farm for him?

A. Yes, sir.

Q. What did he ask you about it?

A. He told me that was all right.

Q. Well, what did he ask you?

A. He asked me about the farm.

Q. Yes?

A. Well, he asked me how come I wasn't making any more than I was, and try to keep it from washing away.

Q. He what?

A. He asked me not to let it wash away.

Q. What else?

A. And he asked me to keep up the taxes on it.

Q. Yes?

A. And build it up.

Q. Yes?

A. And make all I could.

Q. Yes?

A. And try to make myself a home; that he would give it to me.

Q. Yes, and he would give it to you?

A. And make me a deed to it.

Q. Did he?

A. Yes, sir.

Q. I mean did he give you the deed to it?

A. No, sir, he hasn't yet.

Q. How big is the farm down there?

A. Two hundred and two and a half acres.

Q. Did he go over the whole farm with you?

A. No, sir.

Q. Do you keep records there as to what you were making and what you were not making?

A. No, sir.

Q. Well, now what did you show him when he came down?

A. I showed him the building I have built since I have been there.

Q. What did he say about that?
A. He said it was all right.
Q. Did he look it over?
A. Yes, sir. He told me to build right on and fix up the place and get hands to help me.
Q. To what?
A. To get tenants.
Q. Did you?
A. Yes.
Q. And you thought it was all right when he told you to do that?
A. Yes.
Mr. Webster: I object to that. That is not cross-examination. It is invading innumerable fields here that we did not go into at all.
The Court: Why didn't you object to it before?
Mr. Webster: Well, I just thought I would give him plenty of liberty.
Counsel: I am testing this man.
Q. What else did he ask you down there about the farm?
Mr. Webster: I object to that as not material.
The Court: Objection sustained.
The Witness: Ask me about the farm?
Mr. Webster: You need not answer the question.
The Court: Well, wait a minute. I will reverse my ruling. It may go to the motive. He may answer. Answer the question.
The Witness: Well, I don't know that he asked me any more than that, only to see that nobody did not trespass on it.
Counsel: To what?
A. Nobody shouldn't take nothing off of the place.
Q. Did you ever send him any money from the farm?
A. No, sir.
Q. Did you ever make any money on the farm?
A. Very little.

The preparation necessary to be made in the cross-examination of "Expert Witnesses," the planning of the cross-examination in advance, the advisability of such cross-examination and the technique to be employed have all been discussed in the chapter on "Expert Witnesses."

Cross-examination of investigators in personal injury cases will be found under "Impeachment" commencing on page 559.

Cross-examination of doctors in personal injury cases will be found under "Expert Witnesses."

Cross-examination in reference to hypothetical questions is treated under the subject heading "Hypothetical Questions."

CHAPTER XII

IMPEACHMENT

§ 589. In general.

The function of cross-examination utilized to discredit witnesses and their stories is usually designated as "*impeachment.*" This is one of the most important uses of cross-examination and frequently very effective. In the so-called "close" case where the evidence is conflicting, a proper use of cross-examination for the purpose of laying a foundation for impeachment of the witness will often result in a favorable verdict. However, the injudicious use of cross-examination for impeachment purposes may sometimes place the attorney in a rather poor light. Unless he has a knowledge of the law in reference to impeachment and knows when and how a foundation for impeachment must be laid and what proof is necessary to complete the impeachment legally, all of his efforts will be of no avail.

There are a few general rules which must be known to every trial attorney in reference to impeachment. A proper foundation must be laid for impeachment of every witness during his cross-examination.[1] There is one exception to this rule in some jurisdictions. No foundation is necessary where impeachment of *one of the parties* to the law suit, either plaintiff or defendant, is attempted.[2] It is suggested, however, to attain a good psychological effect it is better to lay a foundation for impeachment even in cases involving the parties

1 Peo. v. Babcock, 117 Pac. 549, 160 Cal. 537; Benedict v. Dakins, 90 N. E. 712, 243 Ill. 384; Jerboe v. Kepler, 8 Ind. 314; State v. McCook, 221 N. W. 59, 206 Iowa 629; McCulloch v. Dobson, 30 N. E. 641, 133 N. Y. 114; Radke v. State, 140 N. E. 586, 107 Oh. St. 399; International, etc., R. Co. v. Boykin, 89 S. W. 639, 99 Tex. 259.

2 Keating v. U. S. Light, etc., Co., 125 N. Y. S. 512; Streblow v. Sylvester, 191 N. W. 788, 195 Iowa 168; Edwards v. Osman, 19 S. W. 868, 84 Tex. 656; Hunter v. Gibbs, 48 N. W. 257, 79 Wis. 70; Johnson v. Peterson, 166 Ill. App. 404. (Some states contra.)

themselves. This will be recognized when the technique to be used in laying the foundation is studied. When counsel has impeaching evidence in his possession that he is sure he can prove, it is a great deal more effective to cause the party to deny the existence of such fact, statement or instrument. Then when the impeaching fact, statement, instrument or witness is produced, greater weight is given to this evidence by reason thereof.

§ 590. Own witnesses generally.

Where a party offers a witness in proof of his cause, he thereby, in general, represents him as worthy of belief. He is presumed to know the character of the witness, and having thus presented him in the court, the law will not permit him to impeach his general reputation for truth, or impair his credibility by general evidence tending to show him unworthy of belief.[3]

While a party may not discredit his own witness by general evidence, he is not precluded from putting in evidence contrary to the testimony of one of his own witnesses even though the incidental effect of such testimony is to impeach or discredit a witness already examined in his behalf.[4]

§ 591. Adverse party.

A party who calls his adversary as a witness cannot question the latter's credibility.[5] This is not true, however, where

[3] In re Relph's Est., 221 Pac. 361, 192 Cal. 451; Carney v. Hennessey, 60 Atl. 129, 77 Conn. 577; Est. of Ramsey v. Whitbeck, 81 Ill. App. 210; Pittsburgh, etc., R. Co. v. Carlson, 56 N. E. 251, 24 Ind. App. 559; Homesteader's Life Ass'n v. Salinger, 235 N. W. 485, 212 Iowa 251; Whitaker v. Salisbury, 15 Pick. 534 (Mass.); Barker v. Citizen's Mut. F. Ins. Co., 99 N. W. 866, 136 Mich. 626; Potts v. Pardee, 116 N. E. 78, 220 N. Y. 431; Ettinger v. Goodyear, 165 N. E. 862, 30 Ohio App. 572; Evans v. Bryant, 29 S. W. (2d) 484 (Texas); Collins v. Hoehle, 75 N. W. 416, 99 Wis. 639.

[4] Froeming v. Stockton El. R. Co., 153 Pac. 712, 171 Cal. 401; Wells v. Lavitt, 160 Atl. 617, 115 Conn. 117; Chicago City R. Co. v. Gregory, 77 N. E. 1112, 221 Ill. 591; Parker v. State, 149 N. E. 59, 196 Ind. 534; Com. v. Turner, 112 N. E. 864, 224 Mass. 229; Quick v. Amer. Can Co., 98 N. E. 48, 205 N. Y. 330; State, etc. v. Friedman, 171 N. E. 419, 34 Ohio App. 551; Paxton v. Boyce, 235 S. W. 975 (Tex. C. A.).

[5] Hopkins v. White, 128 Pac. 780, 20 Cal. App. 234; Luthy & Co. v. Paradise, 132 N. E. 556, 299 Ill. 380; Labrie v. Midwood, 174 N. E. 214,

the adverse party is called as for cross-examination under practice act or statutory provisions.

§ 592. Refreshing memory.

If a witness gives testimony different from previous statements, so that his testimony is a matter of surprise to party calling him, the party may refresh his memory by calling his attention to the former statements, either to refresh his memory, or to awaken his conscience.[6]

§ 593. Immaterial issues.

Impeachment will not be permitted on an *immaterial* issue[7] and therefore the trial attorney must question himself as to whether or not the matter which he seeks to impeach is material and relevant to the issues involved in the trial. While it must be remembered, as suggested in the chapter on "Cross-examination," that the lawyer must not attempt to discredit the witness' story in every detail for fear of losing whatever value might be obtained, yet if it is desired and where indicated, impeachment on *immaterial* issues may be shown by searching *cross-examination* of the witness in an effort to secure admissions of error or mistake.

§ 594. Must be impeaching evidence.[8]

Some trial attorneys attempt to lay a foundation for impeachment only to find an objection made on the ground that

273 Mass. 578; Hawkinson v. Valentine, 46 N. E. 292, 152 N. Y. 20; Paxton v. Boyce, 235 S. W. 975 (Tex.); but he may be contradicted by other witnesses: Chance v. Kinsella, 142 N. E. 194, 310 Ill. 515; De Meli v. De Meli, 24 N. E. 996, 120 N. Y. 485.

6 Latham v. Jordan, 17 S. W. (2d) 805 (Tex.); Peo. v. Durrant, 58 Pac. 75, 116 Cal. 179; Niell v. Brackett, 135 N. E. 690, 241 Mass. 534; Peo. v. Hallas, 241 N. W. 193, 257 Mich. 127.

7 Nau v. Standard Oil Co., 154 Ill. App. 421; Peo. v. Tiley, 24 Pac. 290, 84 Cal. 651; Talburt v. Berkshire Life Ins. Co., 80 Ind. 434; State v. Roscum, 93 N. W. 295, 119 Iowa 330; Kaler v. Builders' Mut. F. Ins. Co., 120 Mass. 333; Thomas v. Byron, 134 N. W. 1021, 168 Mich. 593, 38 L. R. A. (N. S.) 1186; Peo. v. Van Tassel, 50 N. Y. 556, 26 App. Div. 465; Toledo R., etc. v. Prus, 28 Ohio Civ. App. 369; Liverpool, etc., Co. v. Ende, 65 Tex. 118.

8 The evidence must actually contradict or be inconsistent. State v. Davis, 234 N. W. 858, 212 Iowa 582; Peo. v. Powell, 194 N. W. 502, 223 Mich. 633; Worley v. Spreckels, etc., Co., 124 Pac. 697, 163 Cal. 60; Peo. v. Youngs, 45 N. E. 460, 151 N. Y. 210; Godair v. Ham. Nat. Bank, 225 Ill. 572; Old Colony Trust Co. v. Di Cola, 123 N. E. 454, 233 Mass. 119; Bailey v. Look, 174 S. W. 1010 (Tex. C. A.).

the matter they are attempting to present is not in reality impeaching nor contradictory to the statements made by the witness on the witness stand. When an objection is sustained on this ground it may prove harmful. The trial lawyer must in each instance, consider seriously, whether or not the matter which he wishes to present is in fact contradictory so as to be available for use for impeachment purposes.

§ 595. Impeachment proof available unless direct admission made.

An important fact to keep in mind is this: when the witness is asked whether he has ever made statements contrary to his testimony on the trial and the time and place and language are specified, and he states he "does not recollect," or where the witness says he "does not remember," "don't think I did," "maybe I did," or where he makes any statement which is just short of an out and out denial or a straight-forward admission that he did make such contradictory statement, the other party may and should call witnesses to prove that he did make such statements and it is error for the court to reject such impeaching evidence.[9]

§ 596. Disinterested witnesses—To prove contrary facts.

The best method of impeachment and of discrediting the story of a witness is by the introduction of contradictory testimony through other and disinterested witnesses. The overwhelming proof of facts by the trial attorney's own witnesses carries more weight, of course, than any other method of impeachment. Too much emphasis, therefore, cannot be placed upon the suggestion that a full and complete preparation be made with a view to securing as many witnesses as possible to corroborate and to testify to the facts as stated by the client.

9 Peo. v. Vatck, 236 Pac. 163, 71 Cal. App. 453; Peo. v. Preston, 173 N. E. 383, 341 Ill. 407; Anthony v. Cass, etc., Co., 130 N. W. 659, 165 Mich. 388; Sloan v. N. Y. C. R. R. Co., 45 N. Y. 125; Cincinnati Terminal Co. v. Banning, 27 Ohio N. P. (N. S.) 548; Johnson v. Brown, 51 Tex. 65; Heddles v. Chicago, etc., R. Co., 46 N. W. 115, 77 Wis. 228. But, contra, Mendenhall v. Banks, 16 Ind. 284; Labrecque v. Donham, 127 N. E. 537, 236 Mass. 10. (Some states contra.)

§ 597. When impeachment available.

Impeachment may be used in the following instances:

(1) Where witness has made a former contradictory oral statement.

(2) Where witness has made a former contradictory written statement either sworn or unsworn.

(3) Where witness had made a contradictory statement during some previous trial or hearing.

(4) Where witness has made a contradictory statement in the pleadings of either the same or another law suit, either sworn or unsworn.

(5) Where proceedings instituted by witness or participated in by witness in another law suit contradict his present testimony.

(6) By proof of the witness' conviction of an infamous crime, in some states. (In other states conviction of a felony is only necessary.)

(7) By proof that witness' general reputation in the community in which he resides is bad for truth and veracity or for honesty and integrity.

(8) By introduction and proof of official certified copies of public records showing the witness as incompetent or insane.

(9) By cross-examination and proof to show that the witness is interested in the outcome of the law suit as a relative, a close friend, a business associate or an enemy.

§ 598. Keep object hidden.

It must be remembered that in every instance where a foundation for impeachment is laid that the witness must never be allowed to guess the trial lawyer's intention. Questions should be casually asked, commencing with rather vague general questions with a view to getting the witness to deny the existence of any impeaching statement and to deny generally having ever made any contradictory oral statement. Illustrations of this are shown in the technique suggested under each of the several instances where impeachment may be used.

§ 599. Impeachment proof necessary.

The trial attorney is also cautioned ever to keep in mind the fact that *further proof is necessary* in every instance where the foundation for impeachment is made, except where the witness admits having made the contradictory statement. He must also keep in mind, of course, that impeaching proof must be made in his direct case.[10]

§ 600. Objection should be made whenever cross-examination improper.

Some lawyers proceed with laying the foundation for impeachment, well knowing that they have no impeaching evidence nor proof and also that they are unable to prove such impeaching facts. Therefore, whenever the cross-examination goes beyond the scope of the direct examination and opposing counsel examines in reference to matters that apparently are not material to the issues, an objection should be made in this suggested form:

Illustration

Counsel: I object to any further cross-examination along this line. It goes beyond the scope of the direct examination and unless counsel assures the court that he is laying a foundation for impeachment *and will offer proof of said purported impeachment,* I object to it.

If after laying the foundation for impeachment, opposing counsel fails to follow up with the necessary proof sufficient to constitute a legal impeachment, but instead rests his case, a motion to strike out all of the testimony in reference to said purported impeachment may be made to the court with the further suggestion that the jury be ordered to disregard it. A great deal of advantage can be taken of this unfair procedure by proper reference to it during the final arguments.

§ 601. Former contradictory oral statements.[11]

In those instances where the lawyer is in possession of information as to verbal statements made by the witness which

10 Chicago City Ry. Co. v. Matthieson, 72 N. E. 443, 212 Ill. 292; Cole v. Drum, 197 Pac. 1105, 109 Kan. 148; Washington v. Smith, 53 App. D. C. 184, 289 Fed. 582; Peo. v. Oblaser, 62 N. W. 732, 104 Mich. 579.

11 The attention of the witness must be called to the statement.

are directly contrary to his present testimony, the following procedure is suggested: First—get the witness to repeat upon cross-examination the statements that he has made on direct examination, then put a casual and general question as to whether or not he has ever made a statement to the contrary, at any time or place, then identify the person to whom the contradictory statement is purported to have been made, then direct his attention to the time,[11a] the place,[11b] and the exact language used or in substance, and again ask him whether or not he had made such contradictory statement. Upon his denial he might again be interrogated on the same question for psychological effect and upon a similar denial the witness should be excused.

After opponent's case is in and he rests, the lawyer should then produce the impeaching witness and prove the contradictory statement by him.

For illustration, suppose the witness Henry Jones on direct examination claims that he saw the defendant hit the plaintiff on the head *with the butt of a gun.* Investigation has disclosed that he, Henry Jones, had told George Turner that the defendant had hit the plaintiff *with a black jack* and *not the butt of a gun* and that this statement was made in a pool room at 927 Blank Street on January 4, 1932, at about 9:00 P. M.

The suggested cross-examination would be about as follows:

Illustration

Q. You *say* that Tom Brown (the defendant) hit Sam Sharp (the plaintiff) on the head with the butt of a gun?
A. Yes.

McKiernan v. Hall, 121 N. Y. S. 87, 65 Misc. 138; Radke v. State, 140 N. E. 586, 107 Ohio St. 399; Miller v. State, 81 N. W. 1020, 106 Wis. 156; Miner v. Phillips, 42 Ill. 123.

11a Loughlin v. Brassel, 79 N. E. 854. 187 N. Y. 128; International, etc., R. Co. v. Boykin, 89 S. W. 639, 99 Tex. 259.

11b Peo. v. Lenhart, 173 N. E. 155, 340 Ill. 538; Houston v. State, 180 N. E. 582, 203 Ind. 409; Peo. v. Rulia Singh, 188 Pac. 987, 182 Cal. 457 (Massachusetts, contra: Carville v. Watford, 40 N. E. 893, 163 Mass. 544).

Q. And that you were standing right there and could plainly see the gun?
A. Yes.
Q. What kind of a gun was it?
A. It was a large blue steel gun.
Q. Have you ever made a statement to the contrary?
A. What do you mean?
Q. Have you ever told anybody that it was not a gun, that was used?
A. No, sir.
Q. Did you ever tell anyone at any time that Tom Brown hit Sam Sharp with a black jack and not with a gun?
A. No, sir, I did not.
Q. Do you know George Turner?
A. Yes, I do.
Q. How long have you known him?
A. Two or three years.
Q. Ever talk with him about the case?
A. No, sir.
Q. Did you ever tell him that you saw Tom Brown hit Sam Sharp with a black jack?
A. No, sir.
Q. Do you know where a pool room is on Blank Street?
A. Yes, I do.
Q. The one at 927 Blank Street?
A. Yes.
Q. Did you ever meet George Turner there?
A. Yes, I have.
Q. Have you ever talked with him there?
A. Yes.
Q. Did you talk with him on January 4, 1932, at about 9:00 P. M. in the pool room at 927 Blank Street?
A. I don't remember.
Q. Did you at that time and place tell George Turner that you saw Tom Brown hit Sam Sharp *with a black jack?*
A. No, I did not.
Q. You say you did not say that?
A. No, I didn't.
Q. Didn't you say that to him in the presence of Charlie Small and Hank Brooks?
A. No, I did not.

Q. Are you sure?
A. Yes, I am.
Q. Now, Mr. Witness, I want you to know that we intend to bring George Turner, Charlie Small and Hank Brooks in here.
A. I don't care.
Q. Do you still insist that you did not say that at that time and place and in the presence of those men?
A. Yes, I do.
Q. All right, that is all.

After opposing counsel has rested his case, the trial attorney should then place all three impeaching witnesses on the stand and prove the contradictory statement in words as closely as possible as used in laying the foundation for such impeachment.[11c]

Illustration

Q. What is your name, please?
A. George Turner.
Q. Where do you live?
A. 917 Blank Street.
Q. What is your business?
A. I am an automobile mechanic.
Q. Do you know Henry Jones?
A. I do.
Q. How long do you know him?
A. Two or three years.
Q. Do you know Sam Sharp the plaintiff here?
A. I do.
Q. Do you know Tom Brown, the defendant?
A. I do.
Q. Directing your attention to January 4, 1932, at about 9:00 P. M. did you see Henry Jones?
A. I did.
Q. Where?
A. At the pool room.

11c In re Champion's Est., 180 N. W. 174, 190 Iowa 451; Richard Cocke & Co. v. New Era, etc., Co., 168 S. W. 988 (Tex. C. A.); Peo. v. Lee Ah Yute, 60 Cal. 95; State v. Noyes, 36 Conn. 80.

Q. Where is that?
A. 927 Blank Street.
Q. Who was present at that time?
A. Henry Jones, Charlie Small and Hank Brooks and myself.
Q. Did Henry Jones at that time and place say he had seen the fight between Sam Sharp and Tom Brown and that Tom Brown hit Sam Sharp on the head with a black jack?
A. He did.

The same procedure would be followed in the case of the witnesses Charlie Small and Hank Brooks.

§ 602. Former contradictory written statements.

Under this heading comes all written statements or documents of every kind and description. It includes signed or initialed unsworn statements given to investigators in all personal injury, medical, chemical and insurance cases, as well as any other type of case, all letters, unsigned but readily identified statements shown to be in the handwriting of the witness, in fact, any signed or written document or instrument.

In order to impeach a witness by former contradictory written statements, a foundation must first be laid.[12] The attention of the witness must be directed to the writing,[12a] and he must then be asked whether or not he made the statement[12b] and given an opportunity to answer.[12c] The statement should be produced at that time,[12d] and shown to the witness.[12e]

[12] Froeming v. Stockton El. R. Co., 153 Pac. 712, 171 Cal. 401; Morrison v. Meyers, 11 Iowa 538 (letter); Lorain Steel Co. v. Hayes, 27 Ohio Cir. Ct. 407 (written statement of accident); St. Louis W. R. Co. v. Bishop, 291 S. W. 343 (Texas) (affidavit).

[12a] Helgeson v. Chicago, etc., Co., 156 Ill. App. 541.

[12b] Peck v. Parchen, 2 N. W. 597, 52 Iowa 46; Parker v. Schrimser, 172 S. W. 165 (Texas).

[12c] Helgeson v. Chicago, etc., Co., 156 Ill. App. 541; Parker v. Schrimser, 172 S. W. 165 (Texas).

[12d] Gaffney v. People, 50 N. Y. 416.

[12e] Ill. Cent. R. Co. v. Wade, 69 N. E. 565, 206 Ill. 523; Peck v. Parchen, 2 N. W. 597, 52 Iowa 46; Larkin v. Nassau El. R. Co., 98 N. E. 65, 205 N. Y. 267; Peo. v. Orosco, 239 Pac. 82, 73 Cal. 580.

The statement may be read to the jury in whole. Peo. v. Sweeney, 22 N. W. 50, 55 Mich. 586; Larkin v. Nassau El. R. Co., 98 N. E. 465, 205 N. Y. 267.

. . . or in part, where only a portion of the writing is impeaching. Peo. v. Cole, 59 Pac. 984, 127 Cal.

The following is a narrative form illustration of the direct examination (in part) and the cross-examination of a witness who had made a purported contradictory written statement. Also shown is a cross-examination of the investigator who took the statement.

Direct examination (in part)

My name is Lester Johnson. I live at 206 West Avenue. I am twenty years old and my trade is upholstery work for the Wright Furniture Company at 500 North Western Avenue. I was an eye-witness to the accident on New Year's Eve, 1931, when Officer Hemrick was hurt. I was standing right next to Officer Hemrick and Mr. Jensen.

Officer Hemrick was taking the witnesses' names to the first accident and writing them down in a note-book. Mr. Jensen was talking to Officer Hemrick who was on the south side of Grand Avenue. He was standing a few feet away from the curbstone. He was taking down the name in front of a Chevrolet, under the lights of the Chevrolet, standing in front of the Chevrolet which was parked directly across from the other accident, about 175 feet from Keeler Avenue. The Chevrolet was standing even with the curb. Officer Hemrick, Jensen and I were standing right in front of the headlights of the Chevrolet. I was standing in front of Officer Hemrick and Jensen as he was writing down the names, and just then that machine came along and hit Officer Hemrick in the back and knocked him down. Jensen hollered for him to jump,

545; E. Alkemeyer Co. v. McCardell, 183 S. W. 416 (Texas).

The contrary or inconsistent statement may be explained. Sichterman v. R. M. Hollingshead Co., 4 Pac. (2d) 181, 117 Cal. 504; Grayson v. Hays, 295 S. W. 289 (Tex. C. A.); Peo. v. Mills, 54 N. W. 488, 94 Mich. 630; Butler v. Lohn H. Leadley Co., 247 N. Y. S. 81, 231 App. Div. 474; Baum v. State, 27 Ohio Cir. Ct. 569; Cal Hirsch, etc., Co. v. Coleman, 128 Ill. App. 245, 81 N. E. 21.

Introduction of impeaching writing. The court may permit it to be introduced on cross-examination, if the witness admits his signature. Cole v. Drum, 197 Pac. 1105, 109 Kan. 148; Chicago City R. Co. v. Matthieson, 72 N. E. 443, 212 Ill. 292 (improper, but not reversible error); Perine v. Interurban St. R. Co., 86 N. Y. S. 479, 43 Misc. 70.

Letters written by witness may be used to inpeach him. In re De Laveaga's Estate, 133 Pac. 307, 165 Cal. 607; Pirek v. Scott, 206 Ill. App. 44; Aldridge v. Aetna Life Ins. Co., 97 N. E. 399, 204 N. Y. 483.

and he just hollered too late, I suppose. Jensen came to pick him up. He hollered to Hemrick to jump and Jensen, I believe, jumped on the side, or he just stood there.

Officer Hemrick was standing still when he was hit.

He was standing there in a slightly bent over position, bent toward the south of the car line, under the glare of the headlights. I mean toward the south curb. *I did not see the automobile that hit him coming.* I just turned around and I just seen Officer Hemrick get hit, right then and there. I did not hear any horn or bell or warning sounded by the car at all. The right fender of the car hit Officer Hemrick. When he was hit he rolled over, laid there, and the other witnesses and myself and Jensen picked him up. The car that hit the officer was going east on Grand Avenue, on the south side of the street going east.

Cross-examination (in part)

Q. Where were you standing at the time of the accident?

A. I was standing in front of the Chevrolet, talking to Officer Hemrick.

Q. Just where were you?

A. About five feet with the light shining on the Chevrolet.

Q. Where was Officer Hemrick?

A. He was in front of the Chevrolet, in front of the left front headlight.

Q. Just before the impact, where did you come from?

A. I came about the same time with Officer Hemrick.

Q. Where was Jensen at that time?

A. He was already across the street.

Q. Where were you just before the accident?

A. I was also in front of the Chevrolet, we couldn't have been more than two feet in front. We were just east of the front headlight.

Q. Where was Officer Hemrick?

A. He was just a little bit to the left in a stooping position, writing in his note book in front of the light.

Q. Now, did you see this automobile as it came down from the west before the accident happened?

A. No, sir, I don't recall.

Q. Didn't see it at all? You didn't see it before the accident, did you?

A. I am not sure if I did.

Q. When the automobile came to a stop where was it, after the accident?

A. I know Officer Hemrick was about even with the back of the car when it stopped.

Q. In other words, the automobile went probably 15 feet after, 12 or 15 feet after the impact?

A. Well, about 10 or 15 feet.

Q. You say you did not see the automobile that hit Officer Hemrick coming?

A. No, sir.

Q. Have you ever made any statement to the contrary?

A. No, sir.

Q. At any time?

A. No.

Q. At any place?

A. No, sir.

Q. To any person?

A. No, sir.

Q. Do you remember an investigator who came out to see you about this accident?

A. Yes, sir.

Q. Did you talk to him about it?

A. Yes, I did.

Mr. Hawk (to Court Reporter): Will you please mark this Defendant's Exhibit 1 for identification consisting of two pages?

(To Witness):

I will ask you to examine Defendant's Exhibit 1 for identification and each page thereof and state whether or not your signature appears on each page?

A. Yes, that is my signature.

Q. On each page?

A. Yes, sir.

Q. Did you sign it on or about the date it bears?

A. Yes, sir.

Q. Where were you working at that time?

A. At the Majestic Radio Shop.

Q. Do you work there now?

A. Now I work somewhere else.

Q. Is Defendant's Exhibit 1 for identification in the same condition now as when you signed it?

A. Yes, sir.

Q. Have there been any changes in Defendant's Exhibit 1 since you signed it?

A. No, sir.

Q. Were the statements contained in Defendant's Exhibit 1 for identification true and correct at the time you signed it?

A. Yes, sir.

Q. Now, I will ask you if on the 9th day of August, 1931, you did not make this statement: "in a minute or so when I saw that Hemrick was getting some information from this Chevrolet driver, I started also to cross southwesterly from the damaged car as Hemrick had done, and I saw the headlights of an eastbound sedan in the eastbound tracks." You made that statement, didn't you? Just read it.

Counsel: Let the record show that witness is now examining Defendant's Exhibit 1 for identification.

A. I am not positive it was that car though.

Q. Just read it. That wasn't the same car that struck him?

A. I wouldn't swear that it was.

Q. Were there many cars coming east?

A. There was quite a few cars that early in the morning, there was quite a few.

Q. Traffic was quite heavy along there?

A. It was not too heavy, just now and then an automobile would pass.

Q. About how far apart would you say the automobiles were as they went east?

A. It is hard to say.

Q. Did you say in the statement, "Well, it was a big sedan, light tan colored. It was possibly a Graham-Paige. I stopped in about the center of the westbound rails to wait for it to pass so I could cross. I had noticed the lights as I left the curb, and it was then just east of Keeler. It was going about 20 or 25 miles an hour, and slowed up to about

12 to 15 miles an hour, as he probably saw the crowd gathered at the accident."

"If I am not mistaken, he sounded his horn, but I don't know whether for me or for Hemrick. I don't know if other autos had passed between the two accidents, I know that the street was clear for traffic both ways. There was no one flagging down traffic, though possibly some one should have been. This car proceeded cautiously and under control. The policeman Hemrick had been facing westward, and I don't see how he didn't see the headlights. I think that he probably turned his face southward and in the conversation with his witness he was talking to, and therefore didn't see the auto. I heard some one holler 'jump.' "

Q. Did you make those statements?

A. If my name is on the bottom there, it must be.

Q. Then you did see this automobile?

A. I am not sure if that was the automobile, though.

Q. It is the same automobile mentioned all through here.

A. There was quite a few autos passing and I am not sure if it was the one.

Q. "The right front fender struck his hip." Now, that is the same automobile you were talking about, isn't it?

A. Sure, but they all have right front fenders.

Q. Yes, but you are talking about this automobile that you saw the headlights of.

The Court: Was the officer hit more than once?

A. No, sir, just once.

Q. "The auto involved stopped on a dime, making a good quick stop. It stopped with its front end about 1 foot westerly of him, still in the car tracks." Is that correct?

A. I don't know, I must have been excited when I made that statement.

Q. You weren't very excited on the 5th of August, 1931, were you?

A. Well, I know if that was my dad I know how I would feel about it. I felt that way toward anybody else.

Q. Just answer my question.

The Court: Mr. Witness, it is not how you felt or how your dad feels, the question is is that true or not?

A. I wouldn't say it stopped within 1 foot.

Mr. Hawks: All right. But it stopped with its front end still on the car tracks, that is true isn't it?

A. Yes, sir.

Q. In other words, this eastbound car that Hemrick and the car collided with was in the car tracks at the time of the collision?

A. Yes, sir.

Q. Was it wholly in the car tracks? By that I mean both wheels right in the car track?

A. I did not notice that.

Q. You did not notice that?

A. No, sir.

Q. "The automobile stopped within about 3 feet, without swerving or skidding" is that correct?

A. Yes, sir, he had it under control.

§ 603. —Direct examination of impeaching witness–investigator.

Illustration

(On defendant's direct case)

Q. Will you state your name, please?

A. Harold F. Carey.

Q. Where do you live?

A. 1676 Emerald Avenue.

Q. What is your business?

A. Investigator.

Q. With whom are you associated?

A. G. R. Barnett.

Q. And how long have you been connected with him?

A. Since about January or February, 1932.

Q. 1931?

A. Of this year, or of 1931, yes.

Q. And previous to that where did you work?

A. Armour & Company.

Q. How long were you with Armour & Company?

A. About five years or so.

Q. Now, Mr. Carey, at my request did you investigate an accident in which Officer Hemrick was injured by an automobile?

A. I did.

Q. And when were you requested by me to make that investigation?

A. In about July of 1931.

Q. Following that did you go to the scene of the accident?

A. I did.

Q. Tell us what you did out there, briefly?

A. I looked over the street where the accident was alleged to have occurred and found that it was in between a couple of intersecting streets, Kedvale and Keeler, I believe, on, as I recall it, Grand Avenue. I also canvassed the neighborhood through in there to locate any witnesses, trying to determine as well as I could how the accident occurred, find witnesses.

Q. What else did you do, if anything?

A. I examined the police reports.

Q. With what result?

A. I found the names of three or four witnesses.

Q. Now, I will ask you if you learned the name of a witness by the name of Lester Johnson?

A. I did.

Q. Did you call upon Mr. Johnson?

A. I did.

Q. When?

A. On or about August 5, 1931.

Q. And do you recall where you interviewed him?

A. I think it was at his home.

Q. At that time did he tell you how the accident happened?

A. Yes, he did.

Q. And did you take a statement from him?

A. I did.

Q. In what form was that statement?

A. Written down.

Q. Who wrote it down?

A. I did.

Q. I will show you an exhibit, marked for identification Defendants' Exhibit 1. Glance at it. Is that the statement you have referred to?

A. That is the statement I wrote of the accident as described to me by Lester Johnson.

Q. Have there been any changes in the statement from the time you wrote it down to the present time?

A. No.

Q. What did Mr. Johnson then do, if anything?

A. He signed his name on each page, on each sheet.

Q. Do you know whether he read the statement over?

A. Yes, he read the statement over.

Q. Did you write down just what he told you?

A. Yes, I did.

Q. Did you make any insertions or corrections or write down anything that he did not tell you?

A. No, I didn't write anything except what he told me.

Q. Was there any inducement or monetary offer given to him for signing the statement?

A. None whatever.

Q. Now I will ask you at that time and place if Mr. Johnson made this statement to you (reading): "In a minute or so when I saw that Hemrick was getting some information from this Chevrolet driver, I started also to cross southwesterly from the damaged car, as Hemrick had done, and I saw the headlights of an eastbound sedan in the eastbound tracks." Did he make that statement to you?

A. Yes, he did.

Q. (continuing reading): "It was a big sedan, a light tan color, possibly a Graham-Paige. I stopped in about the center of the westbound rails to wait for it to pass so I could cross. I had noticed the lights as I left the curb." Did he make that statement?

A. Yes, he did.

Q. "It was then just east of Keeler. It was going about twenty to twenty-five miles an hour and slowed up to about twelve or fifteen miles an hour." Did he make that statement?

A. Yes, he did.

Q. "I know the street was clear for traffic both ways, there was no one flagging down traffic." Did he make that statement?

A. Yes, he did.

Q. "This car proceeded cautiously and under control." Did he make that statement?

A. Yes, he did.

Q. "The automobile stopped with its front end about one foot westerly of him still in the car tracks, and it stopped in about three feet, without swerving or skidding." Did he make that statement?

A. Yes, he did.

Q. And he read it over afterwards, you say?

A. Yes, he read it.

Q. I now offer in evidence those statements. For the sake of brevity, if the Court please, can those statements I have just read, be considered as read to the jury without repeating them? Can I offer them in evidence, is that agreeable to you, Mr. Todd?

Mr. Todd: You mean the whole statement?

Mr. Hawks: No, just the impeaching questions I have just put in.

Mr. Todd: Why don't you put the whole statement in evidence?

Mr. Hawks: I would be very glad to, if you have no objection to it.

Mr. Todd: Let the jury have the whole statement.

Mr. Hawks: I don't believe it is proper, but I would be glad to, with your approval.

Mr. Todd: The only part you want is what you read?

Mr. Hawks: That is all that is competent.

Mr. Todd: You want to consider that as read into the record?

Mr. Hawks: Yes.

Mr. Todd: I won't object to that.

Mr. Hawks: If you want to put the whole statement in, I am perfectly willing to.

Mr. Todd: That is all right, as long as that is the only part you are interested in we will have it considered as read into the record.

§ 604. Cross-examination of impeaching witness–investigator.

Q. Mr. Carey, whom did you say you worked for?

A. Mr. G. R. Barnett.

Q. And where is G. R. Barnett located?

A. 330 South Main St.

Q. And the business of the outfit that you work for is to investigate automobile accidents and various kinds of accidents, is that correct?

A. Various kinds of accidents, also other legal claims of various kinds.

Q. And you have had many years experience as a private detective or investigator?

A. I am not a detective.

Q. Well, whatever you call yourself, how many years have you had?

A. Well, about five or six years altogether.

Q. And your purpose in going out to get signed statements from these boys was to try to get signed statements so they could be impeached when they came to court, isn't that it?

A. No, just to get an accurate description of the accident so I could make a report of it.

Q. You knew there was a law suit pending when you went out there, didn't you?

A. Yes, I believe it was pending at that time.

Q. And you were hired and employed by the parties interested in the defense of this case to get statements from everybody you could, with orders to tie them all up on signed statements, isn't that right?

A. Not to tie them up exactly, but to get what happened.

Q. Why did you take the precaution of having every one of the people you saw sign every sheet of paper, why did you do that?

A. I do that in every case I investigate.

Q. Why is that done, what is the purpose of that?

A. I don't know; I suppose so they can't change their story.

Q. In other words, that is just what I say, you go out and get a signed statement for the purpose of trying to use that signed statement as an impeachment in court?

A. Not impeachment. I get it from all parties concerned whether they are favorable or not.

Q. When you go out, Mr. Carey, you don't have the Court with you to watch what questions you put to the people, do you?

A. No.

Q. You don't have a stenographer there to take down word for word what they say, do you?

A. No.

Q. You don't have any one to advise them or to safeguard them in their statements that they make to you, do you?

A. No.

Q. You don't put the questions that you ask them and the answers down, in question and answer form, like they do in a court of justice, do you?

A. Not written out in shorthand.

Q. In other words, what I am getting at, you don't say to the boy that you are wanting to question, "where was the police officer standing?" And then write down your question, "Where was the police officer standing?" And then they may answer it, "He was standing on the north side of the street." You don't get your statements that way, do you?

A. No, that takes too much writing if you are doing it every day.

Q. What you do is to carry on a general conversation with him, you interpret what he says in your own language, don't you, and write it down on a sheet of paper?

A. No, I put it down as he tells it to me.

Q. And you know very well you didn't have these boys read over the statements, don't you?

A. I did.

Q. What you were interested in was getting down the particular phase of their story that would be favorable to the parties you were representing, getting their signature and getting out of there, weren't you?

A. No, I am as much interested in getting any points that are unfavorable as well as favorable, because it doesn't do any good—

Q. Why are you as much interested in getting down what is unfavorable as well as favorable?

A. It is the only way you can properly hand in a report of exactly what happened.

Q. But you didn't put in your report anything unfavorable to you?

A. I don't know what you call it. I put down exactly what happened, no matter what it is.

Q. During all the time, that you have been an investigator you were always interested in the defendant's end of the investigation, weren't you, as distinguished from the plaintiff, I mean?

A. I have always been interested—

Q. I mean, you were always interested in cases where somebody made a claim against your client?

A. Oh, sure.

Q. The man being sued is called the defendant, the man suing is called the plaintiff. That is true, isn't it?

A. Well, I don't believe I understand your question. I am always interested, yes.

Q. I mean, you as investigator always go out for Barnett to investigate cases for defendants?

A. That is part of my work.

Q. And you consider yourself as a pretty good investigator?

A. Well, five years' experience.

Q. Well, a good investigator would be expected to bring in reports favorable to the defendant?

A. No, I wouldn't say that.

Q. Have you ever studied law?

A. Yes, I have.

Q. Well, suppose you had gone out to see someone who was hurt and he told you a lot of immaterial things in connection with the accident. Would you put all those immaterial issues in it?

A. Well, I consider everything connected with the accident as material.

Q. Who is the judge of a certain thing or statement whether it is pertinent to the accident, or material to the accident, you or the person giving the statement?

A. Why, I am.

Q. If you call on a woman about an accident and she tells you about a divorce a year before, would you put that in the statement?

A. Certainly not.

Q. Well, you wouldn't put it in because it wasn't material; is that right? Isn't that true?

A. No, it wouldn't be material to that.

Q. Now, I want to know who judges whether any statement said about a divorce or love affair or anything else is or is not material to the accident? You or the person making the statement?

A. *I do, of course.*

Q. You told us a little while ago you asked questions and write down their answers: Is that right?

A. I ask people what they know about the accident.

Q. You have seen a great number of people since, haven't you?

A. Oh, yes.

Q. And you have seen a great number before that?

A. Certainly.

Q. It would run into the thousands, wouldn't they?

A. I wouldn't say thousands.

Q. In five years?

A. Possibly.

Q. You haven't any distinct recollection of any conversation with this man any more than any other people you say?

A. I have no independent recollection of any witness a year and a half ago.

Q. So that everything you told us is what you have refreshed your memory from the document shown you?

A. I remember writing the document.

Q. I say, whatever happened, from that document you refreshed your memory?

A. I refreshed my memory to the extent I remembered he signed it.

Q. Your handwriting is there and his signature?

A. Yes.

Q. But outside of that, that is just one of the many you saw?

A. Just one of the witnesses.

Q. In other words, if you were put on the stand, tomorrow, say, you would give the same version of it?

A. Assuming it was in proper form.

Q. I am assuming everything you do is in proper form, but you would give the same answer to it?

A. I assume so.

Q. How long did you spend with Mr. Johnson?

A. About two hours.

Q. That is, your interview took two hours?

A. Yes.

Q. This statement you took consists of two short pages, does it not?

A. Yes.

Q. That is all you wrote in two hours?

A. Yes.

Q. That is all.

Re-direct examination

Q. You have been in the business five years?

A. Yes, sir.

Q. You have gone to law school?

A. Yes, sir.

Q. I gather from your answer to Mr. Todd you aim to put in everything that is material to the accident?

A. Yes, sir.

Q. Is there any doubt in your mind or has there been any doubt in your mind in the last five years the question of whether or not (so and so ———) would be material?

A. I would consider it very material.

Q. And you aim to put in everything that is material.

A. Certainly.

Re-cross examination

Q. Would you think that would help constitute a defense, from your experience as a lawyer and an investigator?

A. I am not the judge of that.

Q. Give us your opinion. Would you consider that element as a help in the defense of the case?

A. I wouldn't say that I would.

Re-direct examination

Q. But you would know if they told it to you at that time they would certainly tell it on the stand, too?

A. Yes, sir.

Q. So that you would know the best thing to do for your outfit would be to—

Mr. Todd: Judge, that is leading.

Mr. Hawks: All right, that is all.

§ 605. Cross-examining opponent's witnesses as to statements signed.

A rather *dangerous* expedient that may sometimes be resorted to in those instances where you feel that the witness is now testifying untruthfully is to seek to have opposing counsel produce from his files the signed statement which the witness had given him prior to trial. This may be accomplished by asking the witness in a casual manner as to whether he signed a statement for opposing counsel or for his investigator at any time. If he answers that he did, a request to opponent openly and in the presence of the jury to produce it will usually result in its production. A glance through it will soon disclose any discrepancies or exaggerations. If it contains any contrary statements, it can then be used for impeachment purposes to discredit the witness entirely.

If the examination does not disclose any contrary statements, the document may be handed back to the opponent without any remark or the witness may be asked some unimportant or casual question and then hand the document back to counsel later. It is sometimes more advisable to jump to some other phase of the case with the witness so that no undue importance will attach to the incident, and then unobtrusively return the document.

The main objection to this very dangerous procedure is that it tends to strengthen the witness' story if the lawyer is unable to point out any differences between the statement and his testimony. This method should only be resorted to in desperate cases. Another objection is that opposing counsel may then seek to introduce the statement as corroboration of his witness.

§ 606. Former contradictory sworn statements, pleadings, and affidavits.

Francis Wellman in his "Art of Cross-examination" makes this comment and cites the following illustration of one method of cross-examination:

"A difficult but extremely effective method of exposing a certain kind of perjurer is to lead him gradually to a point in his story, where—in his answer to the final question, 'Which?' he will have to choose either one or the other of the only two explanations left to him, either of which would degrade if not entirely discredit him in the eyes of the jury.

"The writer once heard the Hon. Joseph H. Choate make very telling use of this method of examination. A stockbroker was being sued by a married woman for the return of certain bonds and securities in the broker's possession, which she alleged belonged to her. Her husband took the witness stand and swore that he had deposited the securities with the stockbroker as collateral against his own market speculations, but that they did not belong to him, and that he was acting for himself and not as agent for his wife, and had taken her securities unknown to her.

"It was the contention of Mr. Choate that, even if the bonds belonged to the wife, she had either consented to her husband's use of the bonds, or else was a partner with him in the transaction. Both of these contentions were denied under oath by the husband."

Mr. Choate: "When you ventured into the realm of speculations in Wall Street I presume you contemplated the possibility of the market going against you, did you not?"

Witness: "Well, no, Mr. Choate, I went into Wall Street to make money, not to lose it."

Mr. Choate: "Quite so, sir; but you will admit, will you not, that sometimes the stock market goes contrary to expectations?"

Witness: "Oh, yes, I suppose it does."

Mr. Choate: "You say the bonds were not your own property, but your wife's?"

Witness: "Yes, sir."

Mr. Choate: "And you say that she did not lend them to you for purposes of speculation, or even know you had pos session of them?"

Witness: "Yes, sir."

Mr. Choate: "You even admit that when you deposited the bonds with your broker as collateral against your stock speculations, you did not acquaint him with the fact that they were not your own property?"

Witness: "I did not mention whose property they were, sir."

Mr. Choate: (in his inimitable style) "Well, sir, in the event of the market going against you and your collateral being sold to meet your losses, whom did you intend to cheat, your broker or your wife?"

This method has been utilized with some variations as the technique to be employed in all instances where the lawyer has been able to secure an admission from a witness that he has made a contrary sworn statement at some prior time and where impeachment is sought involving either sworn statements, sworn pleadings, or sworn testimony in previous trials or in prior hearings. When properly used this technique has proved to be quite destructive. It has the greatest psychological effect in discrediting a witness and his testimony. Instead of concluding as does the "Choate instance" with the query, "Whom did you intend to cheat, your broker or your wife?" the concluding question is *"Were you swearing falsely then or are you swearing falsely now?"*

In the case of an unsworn written statement or instances of unsworn verbal statements, the concluding question *can* be "Were you telling the truth then or are you telling the truth now?"

§ 607. Laying the foundation.

In most instances those concluding questions remain unanswered and usually the witness as well as his story is completely discredited and destroyed.

Sometimes the effective use of this technique might be lost if the witness is given an opportunity to *deny* that he swore to the statement, especially if he begins to suspect a trap. To avoid this possibility it has been suggested that this question be put to the witness:

Q. You signed this *sworn statement* did you not?

The answer will be "yes" if he did sign it and the basis is laid then for the concluding question. The lawyer then has an admission that he has sworn to a contradictory statement prior to his testifying. Someone may object to the form of this question on the grounds that it assumes that it is sworn to, but if it has a jurat with a notary public signature and seal, one can with propriety claim it is a sworn statement or at least that it purports to be a sworn statement.

In those instances, such as in former testimony, where there is no doubt but what the witness had previously testified to facts contrary to his present testimony, there should be no hesitancy about going through all the preliminary questions as to his having been previously sworn in the prior hearing.

Illustration

Q. Now, Mr. Jones, you testified at a previous hearing of this case, did you not?

A. Yes, sir.

Q. And you were sworn as a witness at that time to tell the truth were you not?
A. Yes, sir.
Q. And you are now testifying under oath?
A. Yes, sir.

These questions and answers will give the foundation for the use of the suggested concluding question *in every instance where the lawyer is able to secure an admission from the witness* that at some prior date he has given sworn testimony or a sworn statement directly contrary to his present testimony.

§ 608. Use of sworn applications to disprove denial of ownership.

In one case where the witness denied ownership of an automobile and claimed on direct examination that the automobile belonged to his wife, the following technique was used with very good results:

Illustration

Q. You say your wife owns this Buick automobile?
A. Yes.
Q. How long has she owned it?
A. About ten months.
Q. That is since the first of the year, is that correct?
A. Yes.
Q. But you drive the car all day, do you not?
A. Yes, I do.
Q. You use it in your business also, do you not?
A. Yes.
Q. Does your wife know how to drive a car?
A. No, she does not.
Q. And she has never driven this Buick then, has she?
A. No.
Q. What is the license number of this car?
A. 277642.
Q. I show you Plaintiff's Exhibit 10 for identification and ask you whether or not your signature is on that document? (Application for license.)
A. It is.

Q. You swore to that before a Notary Public?

A. Yes.

Q. In Plaintiff's Exhibit 10 for identification you state that you are the owner, do you not?

A. Yes.

Q. And you swore at that time that you were the owner did you not?

A. Yes.

Q. And the Secretary of State issued a license to you upon your sworn representation, did he not?

A. Yes.

Q. Well, were you swearing falsely then or are you swearing falsely now?

A. (No answer.)

Q. That is all.

The same technique can and should be used in all instances where contradictory statements have been made in sworn pleadings in all law suits, in all sworn affidavits, sworn proofs of loss in insurance claims, all kinds of sworn applications for licenses and the like.

§ 609. Former contradictory sworn testimony in a previous trial or preliminary hearing.[13]

The general technique to be employed in those instances where impeachment of a witness is desired and attempted by reason of some contradictory sworn testimony given on a previous trial or hearing is similar to that used in cases of sworn statements, sworn pleadings, and affidavits with a few differences. The foundation is laid by calling attention to the exact question asked and the answer given by the witness, first—stating the time and place of the hearing, the

13 At inquest. Bolden v. State, 178 S. W. 533, 77 Tex. Cr. 274; Hickey v. Detroit United Ry. Co., 168 N. W. 517, 202 Mich. 496. But see as to form of question. Math v. Chgo. City Ry. Co., 243 Ill. 114 at 121; Novitsky v. Knickerbocker Ice Co., 180 Ill. App. 188 at 192; People v. Goehringer, 196 Ill. App. 472 at 479.

At grand jury. Burdick v. Hunt, 43 Ind. 381; Com. v. Homer, 127 N. E. 517, 235 Mass. 526.

At former trial. Peo. v. Fitzgerald, 70 Pac. 1014, 138 Cal. 39; Savich v. Amer. St. Bank, 225 N. W. 566, 247 Mich. 164; Hanlon v. Ehrich, 71 N. E. 12, 178 N. Y. 474; Dady v. Condit, 104 Ill. App. 507.

Extent of cross-examination within court's discretion. Sandra v. Times Co., 155 Atl. 819, 113 Conn. 574; Peo. v. Kramer, 215 N. W. 62, 240 Mich. 98.

name of the judge and then asking him if he testified at that hearing, whether he was under oath just as he is now, and then asking this question, "At that hearing were you asked this question by me (or name the person) and did you make this answer, question, "What time did you get there? Answer—Oh, about ten o'clock." "Were you asked that question and did you make that answer?"

Upon an outright denial of having made any such answer or where the witness says he "does not remember," "I don't think so," or "I do not recall," counsel should follow up with the impeaching witness after opponent has rested.

Illustration

Cross-examination (in part)

Q. Where was he when he jumped?

A. He was on the fire escape.

Q. Where on the fire escape?

A. On the running part, where it goes down.

Q. What do you mean, on the movable part of the fire escape?

A. Yes.

Q. He was not on the permanent part of the fire escape?

A. On the movable part.

Q. He was on the movable part, you saw that?

A. Yes.

Q. You saw that?

A. Yes.

Q. Now, that is right, is it?

A. Yes.

Q. You saw that at that time, did you?

A. Yes.

Q. Well, the next day or so after that, you went to the coroner's inquest, didn't you?

A. Yes.

Q. And you were sworn to tell the truth as a witness and you testified at the coroner's inquest, didn't you?

A. Yes.

Mr. Bloomingston: Now, was this question asked you by the deputy coroner at the inquest and did you make this answer: "Q. Go ahead." And did you answer: "Oh, we heard an explosion and we woke up and we looked out the window and we saw the fire, so we ran." Were you asked that question and did you make that answer?

A. No, sir.

Q. You did not say that?

A. No, sir.

Q. Then was this question asked you and did you make this answer: Question, "Where was the fire coming from then when you looked out of the window?" And did you answer: "It was on the second floor of the place at the front and we ran back and we opened the door and we couldn't use it on account of the smoke there, so we came to the fire ladder and there is a little place like where you put your body through to get down and I came across and my brother Joseph was paralyzed and he was dizzy and he went to get across and he stepped off, and his foot slipped and he fell to the second floor where the place was." Did you make that answer to the question at the coroner's inquest?

A. How do you mean, did I?

Q. Did you say that under oath at the coroner's inquest, did you make that answer to the coroner's question?

A. Not some of it.

Q. Was this question asked you, and did you make this answer: Question, "On the fire escape?" and did you answer, "Yes." And was the question asked, "He fell then from the third floor to the second on the fire escape? Answer: Yes." Were those questions asked you and did you make those answers?

A. I didn't get that straight.

Q. Were these questions asked you and did you make these answers?

A. Yes, I answered.

Q. Then was this question asked you, and did you make this answer: Question, "he fell from the third to the second? Answer, He fell from the third to the second." Did you make that answer at the coroner's inquest in response to that question?

A. Yes.

(Note: Where witness admits making contrary statements it is not necessary nor permitted to prove these contrary statements by the court reporter.)

Q. "On the fire escape? A. Yes, he fell down the fire escape, yes, and I went to the hospital?"

A. He fell on the fire escape again and I went to the hospital.

Q. Was this question asked you—Just a moment, "Did you go down first on the fire escape?" And did you answer, "No, sir." Did you make that answer?

A. Well, —

Q. Did you make that answer? Yes or no.

A. No.

Q. Then was this question asked you, "Did you see him after he was down on the sidewalk? A. No, sir, I saw a doctor jump from the window. Q. What did he do? A. He jumped right out of the window, right after my brother and he took care of my brother and took him to the hospital." Did you make those answers in response to those questions?

A. No, sir.

Q. Now, the doctor, do you remember there was a doctor there?

A. How do you mean, I remember?

The Court: Do you remember there was a doctor there that day, we are talking about the fire, did you see a doctor there?

A. I didn't see nothing about a doctor till I was—

Counsel: Did you see Dr. Daro jump out of the window?

A. No, sir.

Q. Did you see him on the sidewalk taking care of your brother?

A. No, sir.

Q. Did you see him around there at all?

A. No, sir, I seen him at the hospital.

Q. Well, then, you say you did not tell about the doctor jumping out the window?

A. No, sir.

Q. So that if you said that at the coroner's inquest you told something there that was not true?

A. Sir?

Q. If you told that at the coroner's inquest, that was not true?

A. I told the truth in there.

Q. Then if you told them at the coroner's inquest: "Q. Did you see him after he was down on the sidewalk? A. No, sir, I saw a doctor jump from the window. Q. What did he do? A. He jumped right out of the window right after my brother, he took care of my brother." If you said that at the coroner's inquest, that was true, was it?

A. I never said that at the coroner's inquest.

Q. Was the question asked you, "Where was the doctor, what number? A. He was on the second floor. Q. What was he doing there? A. He lives there. Q. He jumped from the fire escape, did he? A. He jumped from the window. Q. Did he get hurt at all? A. Yes, he got a cut on the leg. Q. He took your brother to the hospital?" Did you make those answers in response to questions at the coroner's inquest?

A. I don't get you.

Q. Did you make those answers in response to the questions at the coroner's inquest, did you or didn't you?

A. No, sir.

Q. Now, was this question asked you, "Did anybody else go down the fire escape and try to push it? A. Nobody else came. Q. Did the doctor try to get down there? A. No, sir, he jumped right out of the window." Did you make those responses to those questions at the coroner's inquest?

A. No, sir.

Q. Were you then asked this question and did you then make this answer: Q. "The firemen came up and took you down? A. Yes. Q. Did they take your brother down also? A. No sir, he jumped before the firemen got there. Q. He jumped from the second floor to the first floor? A. Yes. Q. What did he fall on, on the sidewalk? A. I am not sure what he fell on." Did you make those answers in response to those questions?

A. Well, —

The Court: Yes or no, or don't you remember?

Mr. Bloomingston: Q. (Reading) Did you make those answers in response to those questions at the coroner's inquest?

A. Yes.

(Note: At this point, where witness admits that he testified at the inquest under oath contrary to what he now testifies to, the suggested concluding question could be used with deadly effect.)

Q. Were you swearing falsely there or are you swearing falsely now?

(Witness' story and credibility will be destroyed whichever way he answers.)

§ 610. — Impeaching witness—Court reporter.

In almost all of these cases the impeaching witness will be the court reporter who reported the trial at the previous hearing.

The court reporter should be requested to bring with him his *original* shorthand notes. Counsel should go over the notes with him to locate the impeaching testimony and mark the place so that ready reference may be had without undue delay. If possible that portion of the impeaching testimony should be transcribed so that the lawyer is in a position to refer to the exact questions and answers.

After properly qualifying the shorthand or court reporter as an expert in his line he should be referred to the contradictory testimony. He should testify to the fact that the witness sought to be impeached had been sworn and testified at the previous hearing. Then the following procedure is suggested:

Illustration

Q. Now, Mr. Johnson, will you please refer to your original shorthand notes and tell the Court and jury whether or not this question was asked of the witness Henry Smith by me and did he make this answer: Question. What time did you get there? Answer. Oh, about ten o'clock.

The court reporter will or should make this reply: "That question was asked and that answer was made (or given)."

§ 611. — Qualification and examination of court reporter.

Direct examination

Q. What is your name and where do you live?

A. Earl Waller, 901 Winthrop Avenue.

Q. Business or profession?

A. Court reporter.

Q. How many years have you been a court reporter?

A. Over twenty-one years.

Q. You understand the method of transcribing and taking down in shorthand, don't you?

A. Yes, I do.

Q. Did you take the testimony at the inquest held over the body of a boy named Sam Dunn, August 13, August 30, and September 13, 1928?

A. Yes, I did.

Q. Did you bring your original shorthand notes with you?

A. Yes.

Q. Turn to the testimony of Joe Dunn, the second witness who was heard at that proceeding.

A. Yes.

Q. Very shortly after the beginning there is a question: "Q. Go ahead? A. And we heard an explosion and we waked up and we looked out the window and we saw the fire, so we ran." Was that question asked and was that answer made?

A. Yes, that question was asked and that answer was made.

Q. Was this question then asked, and was this answer made by the witness: "Q. Where was the fire coming from then when you looked out the window?" And did he answer, "It was on the front door on the second floor of the place. We ran to go to the back and we opened the door and we could not use it on account of the smoke there, so we came to the fire ladder and it was a little place like where you put your body through to get down, and I came across and my brother Joseph was paralyzed and dizzy and he went to get across and he stepped on it and his foot slipped and he fell to the second floor where the place was." Was that question asked and was that answer made?

A. Yes, that question was asked and that answer made.

Q. Was this question asked, "Was he on the fire escape? A. Yes. Q. He fell then from the third floor? A. Yes, to the second on the fire escape, yes." Were those questions asked and the answers made?

A. Yes, those questions were asked and those answers were made.

Q. The question following: "He fell down on the fire escape? A. And I went to the hospital, yes." Were those questions asked and that answer made?

A. Yes, those questions were asked and those answers were made.

Q. That is immediately following, then skip a question, no, this follows: "Just a moment, did you go down first, down this fire escape? A. No, sir." Did he make that answer?

A. Yes, that question was asked and that answer was made.

Q. "Q. Didn't you go down the fire escape? A. I stayed up there and I was trying to get down because I knew my brother was paralyzed and couldn't help himself, when I seen that he could not get up, but he tried to help himself to go down through that thing. Q. He was standing on that, was he, or was he lying down, did he go down any of these steps, were there steps going down the fire escape? A. The steps is lost." Did he make those answers in response to those questions?

A. Yes.

Q. Then was he asked these questions: "Q. You say he came through the window on the fire escape? A. Out of the window onto the fire escape. Q. Then he fell down to the platform below? A. Yes, on the second floor." Were those answers made in response to those questions?

A. Yes, those questions were asked and those answers were made.

Q. Was this question asked: "Couldn't you have got down there to help pull down that ladder?" And was the answer made, "The steps was too hard to get down." Did he make that answer?

A. Yes, that question was asked and that answer made.

Q. "Q. Understand you said down on the third floor? A. On the third floor." Did he make that answer in response to that question?

A. Yes, that question was asked and that answer was made.

Q. Then was this question asked, "The firemen came up and took you down, did they take your brother down there? A. No, he jumped before the firemen got there." Was that question asked and was that answer given?

A. Yes, that question was asked and that answer made.

Q. Was this question asked, "He jumped from the second floor down to the first floor? A. Yes. Q. What did he fall on, on the sidewalk? A. I am not sure what he fell on.

Q. Did you see him after he was down on the sidewalk? A. No, sir, I saw a doctor jump from the window. Q. What did he do? A. He jumped out of the window right after my brother and he took care of my brother and took him to the hospital. Q. Where was the doctor at the time? A. He was on the second floor. Q. What was he doing up there? A. He lived there. Q. He lived there? A. Yes. Q. He jumped from the fire escape did he? A. From the window. Q. Did he get hurt at all? A. Yes, he got a cut on the leg." Were those questions asked and were those answers given by the witness Joe Dunn under oath at the coroner's inquest?

A. Yes, those questions were asked and those answers were made under oath. (Witness excused.)

(Note: If in some rare instance it is not possible to secure the testimony of the court reporter or if the lawyer has made the mistake of going to trial without a court reporter in the previous trial or hearing, it would be permissible to prove the impeachment by any person who heard the purported contradictory testimony at the previous hearing. This sort of impeachment is far from satisfactory, and weakens a case considerably, but in an emergency it should be resorted to for what it is worth.)

§ 612. Impeachment by proof that the witness' general reputation is bad.

While care must be exercised in attempting to impeach a witness because of the bad reputation he has in the community in which he resides for truth and veracity and for honesty and integrity, yet, by the proper and judicious use of this form of impeachment, verdicts have been obtained, which, without this proof could never have been won. Sometimes there seems to be no way of attacking or destroying a witness' story. In that event, if to the lawyer's knowledge the witness has a poor reputation among his reputable neighbors, then this method of impeachment is positively indicated.

§ 613. — Good reputation.

In criminal cases, character witnesses as to the defendant's *good* reputation should always be presented in behalf of a defendant.

§ 614. — Selection of character witnesses.

Care must be shown, of course, in the selection of character witnesses when they are presented for the purpose of proving a client's good reputation. Only upright, outstanding business, professional men or public officials should be used. Unless character witnesses are the type who themselves command respect and confidence, the jury will not give their testimony much weight or credence.

The same is true in those instances where it is desired to impeach a witness by proof of *bad* reputation. The attorney must select the highest type of witness possible under the circumstances. In all instances where character and reputation become involved such testimony should be followed by *appropriate instructions* to the jury on that subject.

The lawyer should always searchingly examine proposed impeaching character witnesses as to whether or not they have had any trouble with the party whom it is sought to impeach. An out and out enemy will be of little help before the jury; neither will one who is closely related to client; nor one who is closely associated with him in business. No one, who is or will have some interest in the outcome of the case, should be used to impeach the character of opponent.

Where the witness it is desired to impeach has been convicted of some minor crime or crimes not included in the list of "infamous crimes" or "felonies" so that counsel is unable to prove such criminal record, it is suggested that he secure the complaining witnesses in those cases who will be most familiar with the bad reputation of the opposing party. Such complaining witnesses will make the best type of impeaching witnesses. The opponent will hardly dare to cross-examine them.

§ 615. — Proving reputation.

The technique to be used in proving good and bad reputation is as follows: The witness' business, profession and titles (public officials) should be ascertained, his acquaintance with the witness or party should be shown, his association and contact with him, the frequency of their meetings, how close to each other they live, or their business, social or professional relationships, the length of time the witness resided in the community,[14] then inquire whether he knows the witness' reputation in the community [15] in which he resides or among his business associates [16] and neighbors and general associates [16a] for truth and veracity (or for honesty and integrity.) [17] *In some states in criminal cases the question must be limited to the time prior to the indictment.*[18]

The details upon which the witness bases his answer as to the good or bad reputation of the party in question cannot be inquired into either on direct examination or on cross-examination.[19]

§ 616. —Discussing reputation.

Sometimes a character witness is cross-examined, as to "whom he has discussed the party's reputation with," and if

14 Witness must have resided in the community a reasonable time. Kennedy v. Modern Woodmen, etc., 90 N. E. 1084, 243 Ill. 560; Kator v. Peo., 32 Mich. 484; Rathbun v. Ross, 46 Barb. 127 (N. Y.); Mynatt v. Hudson, 17 S. W. 396, 66 Tex. 66; Pape v. Wright, 19 N. E. 459, 116 Ind. 502; State v. Norman, infra.

15 Ramsey v. State, 65 S. W. 187 (Texas); Foreman v. State, 180 N. E. 291, 203 Ind. 324; Miller v. Assured's, etc., Co., 184 Ill. App. 271, 106 N. E. 203, 264 Ill. 380; Peo. v. Lyons, 16 N. W. 380, 51 Mich. 215; McGuire v. Kenefick, 82 N. W. 485, 111 Iowa 147.

16 Barker v. Ford, 152 Ill. App. 12. (Some cases contra.)

16a Khan v. Zemansky, 210 Pac. 529, 59 Colo. App. 324; Hays v. Johnson, 92 Ill. App. 80; Com. v. Rogers, 136 Mass. 158; Peo. v. Griffin, 189 N. W. 5, 219 Mich. 617; Carlson v. Winterson, 42 N. E. 347, 147 N. Y. 652.

17 In most jurisdictions, impeachment cannot go beyond attack on reputation for truth and veracity. Dore v. Babcock, 50 Atl. 1016, 74 Conn. 425; Frye v. State Bank, 11 Ill. 367; F. W. Stock & Sons v. Dellapenna, 105 N. E. 378, 217 Mass. 503; Craig v. State, 5 Ohio St. 605; Missouri, etc., R. Co. v. Creason, 107 S. W. 527, 101 Tex. 335.

But in some jurisdictions it is permissible to show bad moral character. Carlson v. Winterson, 31 N. Y. S. 430, 10 Misc. 338; Heath v. Scott, 4 Pac. 557, 65 Cal. 548; Dotterer v. State, 88 N. E. 689, 172 Ind. 357, 30 L. R. A. (N. S.) 846; State v. Blackburn, 114 N. W. 531, 136 Iowa 743; Indianapolis, etc., R. Co. v. Anthony, 43 Ind. 183.

18 Peo. v. Lehner, 326 Ill. 216.

19 The attack cannot be directed to any particular trait of character. The rule applies in both civil and criminal cases. Gates v. Bowers, 61 N. E. 993, 169 N. Y. 14; Conway v. State, 26 S. W. 401, 33 Tex. 327; State v. Gregory, 126 N. W. 1109, 148 Iowa 152; Dore v. Babcock, 50 Atl. 1016, 74 Conn. 425; Massey v. Bank, 104 Ill. 327; Dunn v. State, 70 N. E. 521, 162 Ind. 174; King v. Chicago, etc., R. Co., 116 N. W. 719, 138 Iowa 625; F. W. Stock & Sons v. Dellapenna, 105 N. E. 378, 217 Mass. 503; Leedy v. Hoover, 125 N. W. 394, 160 Mich. 449; Boon v. Weathered's Admr., 23 Tex. 675; Steen v. Santa Clara, etc., Co., 66 Pac. 321, 134 Cal. 355.

the witness admits that he cannot recollect having discussed it with anyone, there have been occasions when the cross-examiner would thereupon move to strike out all of the character testimony on that ground. In some states it has been held in several criminal cases that it is not necessary to discuss a man's reputation with others before such testimony is admissible, for the reason that a lack of discussion raises the *presumption* that the person's reputation must be good for lack of any bad qualities to discuss. Therefore a motion to strike such testimony on that ground should be denied.[20]

§ 617. — Preparing character witnesses.

In preparing character witnesses for their testimony the lawyer should always see that they are able to define the words "veracity," "integrity," "character" and the like, as one of the common methods of cross-examining character witnesses, is to discredit their testimony by showing that they do not know the meaning of the words they are testifying to. (See note 22.)

§ 618. — "Would you believe him under oath?"

In some states it is permissible to ask witnesses who are testifying to a person's *bad* reputation as to whether or not they would believe that person under oath.[21] In other states

20 Peo. v. Okopske, 321 Ill. 32; Peo. v. Savage, 325 Ill. 313.

21 Wise v. Wakefield, 50 Pac. 310, 118 Cal. 107; Laclede Bank v. Keeler, 109 Ill. 385; Peo. v. Ryder, 114 N. W. 1021, 151 Mich. 187; Peo. v. Revtor, 19 Wend. 569 (N. Y.); Hillis v. Wylie, 26 Oh. St. 574, Duffy v. Radke, 119 N. W. 811, 138 Wis. 38. But contra: Weldon v. State, 88 Ind. 9; Eastman v. Boston El. R. Co., 86 N. E. 793, 200 Mass. 412; Griffin v. State, 255 S. W. 173, 95 Tex. Cr. 588.

Time to which inquiry extends: Primarily it extends to the time when the witness testifies. Bills v. State, 119 N. E. 465, 187 Ind. 721; Calkins v. Colburn, 10 N. Y. St. 778, 46 Hun 675.

Or to a reasonable time thereto. Radke v. State, 140 N. E. 586, 107 Oh. St. 399.

As a rule there is no definite time limit as to the time prior to the trial to which the impeaching testimony refers. State v. Norman, 113 N. W. 340, 135 Iowa 483; Stevens v. Rodger, 25 Hun 54 (N. Y.); Bills v. State, 119 N. E. 465, 187 Ind. 721.

The rule is the same in criminal cases. State v. Dillman, 168 N. W. 204, 183 Iowa 1147; Peo. v. Bastian, 272 Pac. 756, 95 Colo. App. 249.

Sustaining character of impeached witness. Reputation of witness first must be attacked. San Antonio, etc., R. Co. v. Nappier, 141 S. W. 564 (Tex. C. A.); Leseur v. State, 95 N. E. 239,

this is not permitted. The trial attorney should check the law on this subject in his particular state.

Illustration (proving bad reputation)

Q. What is your name, please?
A. Bart Hogan.
Q. What is your address?
A. 2027 Palmer Ave.
Q. What is your business or profession?
A. Accountant.
Q. Do you know John Simpson?
A. Yes.
Q. How long do you know him?
A. About ten years.
Q. Do you know where John Simpson lives?
A. Yes, I do.
Q. Where?
A. About a block away from my home.
Q. Have you had occasion to meet him socially?
A. Yes, I have.
Q. How frequently?
A. About a couple of times a week *until two years ago.*

Q. Are you acquainted with and do you know the general reputation of John Simpson for truth and veracity (or honesty and integrity where those questions are involved) in the community in which he lives (if in a criminal case and in

176 Ind. 448; Com. v. Ingraham, 7 Gray (Mass.) 46; Rogers v. Moore, 10 Conn. 13; Peo. v. Hulse, 3 Hill (N. Y.) 309.

Sustaining witness must be acquainted with the general reputation of the impeached witness. Lee v. Andrews, 114 N. W. 672, 151 Mich. 5; Wolff v. Western Union Tel. Co., 94 S. W. 1062, 42 Tex. C. A. 30; Adams v. Greenwich Ins. Co., 70 N. Y. 166; Gifford v. Peo., 35 N. E. 754, 148 Ill. 173.

The evidence must be of the witness' good character and reputation. Hofacre v. Monticello, 103 N. W. 488, 128 Iowa 239; Stacy v. Graham, 14 N. Y. 492; Beeson v. State, 130 S. W. 1006, 60 Tex. Cr. 39; Gifford v. Peo., 35 N. E. 754, 148 Ill. 173.

Time and place to which evidence may relate. A wider range as to time and place is permitted in the case of the sustaining witness as compared to that of the impeaching witness. Stratton v. State, 45 Ind. 468; State v. Knight, 118 Wis. 473, 95 N. W. 390; Graham v. Chrystal, 2 Abb. Dec. 263 (N. Y.); Woodman v. Churchill, 51 Me. 112.

some states would add "prior to January 17, 1932" (the date of the indictment).)

A. Yes, I do.

Q. Is that reputation good or bad.

A. It is bad (or good as the case may be.)

(Note: If permissible in the local jurisdiction this additional question may be added.)

Q. Would you believe him under oath?

A. No.

§ 619. — Cross-examining adverse character witness.[22] Cornelius in "Trial Tactics" suggests a very good method of cross-examining an *adverse* character witness as follows: "Where a witness has been called by the adverse party to impeach one of your witnesses or your client, you are usually safe in assuming that such witness is hostile to your client, but in nine cases out of ten he will deny any hostility or any unfriendliness. It is well in cross-examining a witness who takes such a position, to adopt a course that will drive him to state that he is friendly to the witness or party he is assailing. A plan I have found to be workable is first to ask an extreme question of the witness which you may be quite certain he will answer in the negative. For example:

Q. You are a very bitter enemy of the witness (naming him)?

A. No, sir.

Q. You are an enemy though?

A. I have nothing against him.

Q. Are you friendly to him?

A. I am not an enemy.

Q. Please answer the question. Would you say that you are a friend or an enemy?

A. I am a friend.

22 Generally, a liberal cross-examination as to the witness' means of knowledge is permitted. Peo. v. Bartley, 108 Pac. 868, 12 Cal. App. 773; Weeks v. Hull, 19 Conn. 376; Dowie v. Black, 90 Ill. App. 167; Bates v. Barber, 4 Cush. 107 (Mass.); Annis v. Peo., 13 Mich. 511; Fulton Bank v. Benedict, 1 N. Y. Super. 480–529; Ft. Worth, etc., Co. v. Cabell, 161 S. W. 1083 (Tex. C. A.). . . . may show bias of witness, Knight v. Seney, 124 N. E. 813, 290 Ill. 11; Burt v. Long, 64 N. W. 60, 106 Mich. 210; Matthews v. State, 189 S. W. 491, 80 Tex. Cr. 177. . . . may ask witness as to meaning of terms, Bullard v. Lambert, 40 Ala. 204 (meaning of "character").

Q. Were you subpoenaed to come to court today?

A. No, sir.

Q. You came down here, did you, to testify against your friend without any subpoena?

A. Yes, sir.

Q. You consider that you are doing your friend a brotherly act by coming down here and besmirching his character?

A. No.

Q. You are a friend but you are not acting friendly?

A. No, sir.

"At this point, let me say that, if you are representing a party and adverse counsel attempts to impeach him and *you know his reputation is bad,* it is a very excellent plan not to cross-examine the impeaching witnesses at all. If you do, such witness will undoubtedly enlarge and amplify his testimony, and he may be loaded with a wealth of detail which will certainly damn your client in the eyes of the jury. The worst possible trial tactics *in such a case* (where the client's reputation is bad) is for the cross-examiner to ask the witness, 'Who have you heard say anything against him?' This procedure opens the door at once for the witness to tell all the things he has heard detrimental to your client.

"In cross-examining the character witness who has impeached your client or any other witnesses (who really bear good reputations), I have seen the following formula used with excellent effect. We will say that the trial is being held in Cleveland, Ohio. Counsel in cross-examining the impeaching witness, interrogates him somewhat as follows:

Q. Who have you heard speak ill of him?

A. Well, I have heard John Doe.

Q. Well, John Doe and he have had some trouble, had they not?

A. I don't know.

Q. Well, John Doe was an enemy of his?

A. Yes, I think so.

Q. Who else did you hear say his reputation was bad?

A. R. Roe.

Q. He was an enemy, too?

A. I don't know.

Q. Well, he was not a friend?

A. I don't think so.

Q. Who else?
A. I can't think of anybody else.
(And two persons are usually the limit.)
Q. How large a city is Cleveland, Ohio?
A. I don't know, better than a million.
Q. How long have you lived in this city?
A. Eighteen years.
Q. During all of that time you say you heard two people speak ill of him?
A. Yes, sir. Two different people said that they would not believe him under oath, or words to that effect.
Q. Now, covering a period of fifteen years and out of more than one million living in this city, you have only heard three out of a million say anything against this man?
A. Yes, sir."

§ 620. —Using opponent's witness.

In some instances particularly in criminal cases, the State's witnesses may be friendly to the client, but circumstances force them to testify against him. It is always good policy for the trial lawyer to request the court to permit him to use this same witness (out of turn) at the conclusion of his testimony, and then proceed to have him testify to client's good reputation. When a supposedly adverse witness thus testifies to a client's good reputation, it will help to nullify his adverse testimony. It will also have a wonderfully good psychological effect as far as the jury is concerned.

§ 621. Former conviction of infamous crime.[23]

In some states, impeachment of a witness by the record of a former criminal conviction can only be done in those instances where the party has been convicted of *"an infamous crime"* as defined by Statute which reads as follows:

"Every person convicted of the crime of murder, rape, kidnapping, willful and corrupt perjury or subornation of perjury, arson, burglary, sodomy, or other crime against nature,

23 Where crime of which witness has been convicted was not an infamous crime within section, neither record nor evidence of conviction or imprisonment was admissible to discredit him. People v. Parks, 321 Ill. 143, 151 N. E. 563.

incest, forgery, counterfeiting, bigamy or larceny, if the punishment for said larceny is by imprisonment in the penitentiary, shall be deemed infamous, and shall forever thereafter be rendered incapable of holding any office of honor, trust, or profit, of voting at any election, of serving as a juror, unless he or she is again restored to such rights by the terms of a pardon for the offense or otherwise according to law."

§ 622. — Arrests, indictments, etc.

It is improper to show that the witness has been accused of a crime,[24] or arrested [24a] or indicted.[24b] Nor is it proper to show conviction of a misdemeanor.[24c]

§ 623. — Conviction of felony.

In other states, impeachment is limited to conviction of *felonies* and the law in reference thereto in each particular jurisdiction should be investigated.[24d]

§ 624. — Proof of conviction where probation granted.

It should be remembered that proof of a conviction of an infamous crime is permissible even though the person was

24 Petro v. State, 184 N. E. 710; Peo. v. Malkin, 164 N. E. 900, 250 N. Y. 185; Peo. v. Green, 292 Ill. 351.

24a Peo. v. Gray, 83 Pac. 707, 148 Cal. 507; Peo. v. Joyce, 134 N. E. 836, 233 N. Y. 61; Clark v. State, 156 N. E. 219, 23 Ohio App. 474.

24b Peo. v. Moshiek, 153 N. E. 720, 323 Ill. 11; Dotterer v. State, 88 N. E. 689, 172 Ind. 357, 30 L. R. A. (N. S.) 846.

But in Texas it may be done. See, Sherman v. State, 62 S. W. (2d) 146 (indicted); Willis v. State, 90 S. W. 1100, 49 Tex. Cr. 139 (accused of crime); Collier v. State, 1 S. W. (2d) 295, 108 Tex. Cr. 339 (arrested).

24c Kennedy v. Lee, 82 Pac. 257, 147 Cal. 596; Lingle v. Bulfer, 153 N. E. 589, 322 Ill. 606; In re Osborn's Estate, 168 N. W. 288, 105 Iowa 1307.

But in some states it is within the discretion of the court whether or not conviction of misdemeanor can be shown. Fritch v. State, 155 N. E. 257, 199 Ind. 89; Quigley v. Turner, 22 N. E. 586, 150 Mass. 108; Ahart v. Stock, 27 N. Y. S. 301, 6 Misc. 579.

24d Witness may be impeached both in civil and criminal cases by showing conviction of felony. State v. Johnson, 245 N. W. 728, 215 Iowa 483; McMurray v. State, 45 S. W. (2d) 606, 119 Tex. Cr. 446; Peo. v. Spain, 157 Ill. App. 49 (infamous crime); Peo. v. La Verne, 297 Pac. 561, 212 Cal. 29; Hackett v. Freeman, 72 N. W. 528, 103 Iowa 296; Conkey v. Carpenter, 69 N. W. 990, 106 Mich. 1; Cook v. Glassheim, 202 N. Y. S. 599, 207 App. Div. 592; In re Abrams, 173 N. E. 312, 26 Oh. App. 384; Bernard's Inc. v. Austin, 300 S. W. 256 (Tex. C. A.); Bruno v. Heckman, 182 N. W. 356, 174 Wis. 63.

not sentenced to the penitentiary but was placed on probation as the conviction is the thing of importance and not the sentence.[25]

§ 625. — Admission as to conviction.

If the witness admits on cross-examination that he has been convicted of an infamous crime no further proof is necessary or permitted.[26]

§ 626. — Cross-examination as to former conviction.

It is advisable, as has been previously suggested, in order to secure a better psychological advantage, not to allow the witness to realize that the lawyer knows of his previous conviction. However, this is sometimes difficult to do, since in many jurisdictions, trial court's will not permit the cross-examiner to ask a witness or a party to the case, as to whether or not he has ever been convicted of *any* crime, or whether he has ever been convicted of a *felony,* or whether he has ever been convicted of an *infamous* crime. Of course, if no objection is made to the form of these particular questions the objection will be waived.[27] If the witness thinks counsel does not actually know of the former conviction, he may deny it. He then can be questioned further about it. Care must be taken not to arouse the sympathy of the jury in behalf of the witness by a too violent or bullying examination. In many instances, local authorities only permit the impeachment of a witness by former conviction by the introduction in evidence of the record of such conviction. Therefore, the laws of the attorney's state should be investigated to determine the extent of the proposed examination.

25 Webb v. Dale & Cain, 179 N. Y. S. 957; Hunter v. State, 45 S. W. (2d) 969, 119 Tex. Cr. 558; Comm. v. Sacco, 151 N. E. 839, 255 Mass. 369; People v. Andrae, 295 Ill. 445.

In California, by statute, where witness is placed on probation, conviction cannot be shown. Peo. v. Mackay, 208 Pac. 135, 58 Cal. App. 123.

26 If the witness admits the conviction, the record will not be permitted to go in evidence. State v. Hamilton, 176 N. W. 773, 171 Wis. 203; Peo. v. Chin Mook Sow, 51 Cal. 597; Dotterer v. State, 88 N. E. 689, 172 Ind. 357, 30 L. R. A. (N. S.) 846; Peo. v. Cascone, 78 N. E. 287, 185 N. Y. 317; Andrews v. State, 33 Oh. Cir. Ct. 564; Keaton v. State, 57 S. W. 1125, 41 Tex. Cr. 621.

27 Peo. v. Fisher, 340 Ill. 216.

Illustration

Q. Were you convicted of burglary in the Criminal Court of Cook County in 1924?

A. No.

Q. Were you the defendant in case No. 32561 entitled People of the State of Illinois v. John Jones?

A. No, I was not.

Counsel: That is all.

§ 627. —Proof of former conviction.[28]

The Clerk of the Criminal Court would then be subpoenaed with his files and records and the following technique would be employed:

Illustration

Questions to be asked the Deputy Clerk

Q. What is your name, please?

A. Ben Smith.

Q. What is your business?

A. Deputy Clerk of the Criminal Court of ——— County.

Q. Have you with you the official records of the Clerk of the Criminal Court of ——— County to prove the record of the conviction of John Jones?

A. Yes, sir.

Q. Have you the return of an indictment against John Jones for Burglary by the January Term 1924 Grand Jury?

A. Yes, sir.

Q. Read it, please.

(Witness does so.)

Q. Have you the files in Cause No. 35261?

A. Yes.

28 Proof of the conviction of crime may be by the record of the conviction. Peo. v. Spain, 157 Ill. App. 49; Peo. v. Chin Mook Sow, 51 Cal. 597; Peo. v. De Camp, 109 N. W. 1047, 146 Mich. 533; Peo. v. Cascone, 78 N. E. 287, 185 N. Y. 317; Huff v. McMichael, 127 S. W. 574; Peo. v. Novak, 175 N. E. 551; Deigel v. State, 33 Oh. Cir. Ct. 82, 99 N. E. 1125; Kirschner v. State, 9 Wis. 140.

The witness must be identified as the person named in the record. Peo. v. Schanda, 185 N. E. 183, 352 Ill. 36; Ayers v. Ratshewsky, 101 N. E. 78, 213 Mass. 589; Colbert v. State, 104 N. W. 61, 125 Wis. 423.

Q. Have you the record of the plea of not guilty to the indictment entered January 29th, 1924?

A. Yes, sir.

Q. Have you the record of the trial and judgment before his Honor, Judge ———, on April 18th, 1924?

A. Yes.

Q. Will you produce the verdict, please?

A. Yes, sir.

Q. Please read it.

(Witness does so.)

Q. Will you read the sentence, please?

(Witness does so.)

Then the identifying officer should be called as a witness and examined in the following manner:

Illustration

Q. What is your name?

A. Officer Dan Donahan.

Q. What is your occupation?

Q. How long have you been a police officer?

Q. Did you make the arrest of one John Jones in 1923 or January, 1924?

Q. Were you in Judge ———'s courtroom on April 18th, 1924, when he was convicted by a jury?

Q. Do you see him in this court?

A. Yes, sir.

Q. Point him out.

§ 628. — Old convictions.

Where the attorney knows that since a prior conviction the witness has reformed and is now considered honorable, he is advised not to attempt to bring out evidence of the former conviction for fear of prejudicing the jury against him. In any event extreme caution should always be used in impeachment of this sort. *This is particularly true when the conviction was had many years before and is an old record.*

Harris in "Hints on Advocacy" has the following to say in reference to impeaching the character of witnesses:

"Cross-examination as to character is at most times an uncertain performance. You never can be sure as to the view the jury will take. It is the part of an advocate's duty which they least like. A personal suspicion arises that their own characters would not be secure from attack if once they were compelled to enter the witness-box. Every delinquency might be laid bare, and his most tender feelings outraged by an unscrupulous and unfeeling advocate. All this might be quite unfounded as a suspicion, but that matters little if the suspicion exists. I need not say it is your bounden duty to protect your witness to the utmost of your power. Sometimes you may do it by way of objection, but if not, you must exercise your best skill to effect your purpose by re-examination.

"I will give one instance out of many where character was once in my hearing cruelly assailed in cross-examination by an inexperienced advocate, and upon whom it recoiled with crushing severity. He asked a witness if he had not been convicted of felony. In vain the unfortunate victim in the box protested that it had nothing to do with the case. 'Have you not been convicted of felony?' persisted the counsel. 'Must I answer, my Lord?' 'I am afraid you must,' answered his lordship. 'There is no help. It will be better to answer it, as your refusal in any event would be as bad as the answer.' 'I have,' murmered the witness, under a sense of shame and confusion I never saw more painfully manifest. The triumphant counsel sat down. Not long, however, was his satisfaction.

"In re-examination the witness was asked: 'When was it? A. Twenty-nine years ago!'

"The Judge: 'You were only a boy?' Witness: 'Yes, my lord.'

"It need scarcely be added that just and manly indignation burst from all parts of the Court, and the comments of the learned judge were anything but complimentary to the injudicious advocate."

§ 629. Showing relationship to parties or interest in the outcome of case.

It is always competent as well as good policy to show that a witness is either related to the parties,[29] is a close friend

29 Holloway v. Griffith, 32 Iowa 409; Govin v. De Miranda, 35 N. E. 628, 140 N. Y. 662.

or business associate [30] or expects some financial return out of a favorable verdict and collection of a possible judgment. It always affects the weight and credence to be given to that witness' story. It should be shown that the witness has not been subpoenaed but has volunteered his services, that he expects to be paid for his time in court, and the amount of compensation he expects to receive.

It is also proper to inquire as to the witness' motive in testifying,[31] friendliness or animosity,[32] mental capacity of witness [33] and intoxication of witness at the time of the events testified to.[34] Generally, a wide range of cross-examination is permitted.[35]

In one instance a doctor had given very damaging testimony in a case and could not be shaken on cross-examination. The cross-examiner suddenly "took a chance" and asked if the witness was related to the plaintiff, a fact which had been studiously avoided by the plaintiff's attorney in direct examination. When this was pointed out on cross-examination and later in the arguments to the jury, it helped to turn the scales in the defendant's favor, especially since the medical testimony of the defendant directly contradicted that of the plaintiff's doctor.

Illustration

Mr. Jacker: Q. You are not related to the plaintiff in any way are you?

A. Yes.

Q. Oh! You are related?

A. Yes.

30 Northern Assur. Co. v. Melinsky, 213 N. W. 70, 237 Mich. 665.

31 Reynolds v. Struble, 19 Pac. (2d) 690, 128 Cal. App. 716; Metzer v. Doll, 91 N. Y. 365; Tosser v. State, 162 N. E. 49, 200 Ind. 156; Sovereign, etc. v. Jackson, 138 S. W. 1137 (Tex. C. A.).

32 In re Martin's Est., 151 Pac. 130, 170 Cal. 657; Peo. v. Turner, 107 N. E. 162; Hemler v. Hucony Gas Co., 18 S. W. (2d) 942 (Tex. C. A.).

33 State v. Alberts, 202 N. W. 519, 199 Iowa 815; Roberts v. State, 35 S. W. (2d) 175, 117 Tex. Cr. 418.

34 Com. v. Barber, 158 N. E. 840, 261 Mass. 281; Smith v. State, 51 S. W. (2d) 686, 121 Tex. Cr. 231.

35 Blanchard v. Blanchard, 191 Ill. 450; Bond v. Lotz, 243 N. W. 586, 214 Iowa 683; Pyne v. Broadway, etc., R. Co., 19 N. Y. S. 217, 33 N. E. 1083.

Q. What is the relationship?

A. He is my brother-in-law.

Q. Oh, I see. This was sort of a family affair. That is all.

It is, therefore, suggested that in every case where a witness is related to the client, it is better policy to make that fact known casually and as early as possible *in the direct examination* in order to minimize the bad effect of the relationship. Counsel should never wait for his opponent to bring out that fact on cross-examination. It will cast more suspicion on all of the witness' testimony.

Another method of showing financial interest in the outcome of a case:

Illustration

Q. Have you an interest in this lawsuit?

A. No.

Q. Do you know a Mr. Green?

A. No.

Q. J. N. Green, an attorney?

A. I may know him.

Q. Did you talk with him in the Municipal Court about six months ago?

A. Possibly I did.

Q. Did you tell Mr. Green at that time that there was a case pending in court of John Moulton v. Builders Agency in which you had an interest?

A. I don't remember that I did.

Q. Did you or did you not?

A. I don't know who Mr. Green is. I was questioned by a lawyer, but I don't remember his name.

Q. Did you tell that lawyer that you had an interest in that litigation?

A. A financial interest?

Q. A financial interest?

A. I don't believe I did. The case was mentioned, I remember that, I believe I mentioned it. Mr. Green didn't mention anything about my interest in that lawsuit, but I mentioned it.

Q. You said pending the result of this lawsuit that as soon as you had the money you would pay it?

A. At that time?

Q. After this present lawsuit was over?
A. I said if I had the money I would pay it.
Q. You expected to get it from this lawsuit if there was a judgment in favor of Mr. Moulton?
A. I don't know that I said anything of the kind.
Q. Was that your hopes in saying that?
A. Possibly.

§ 630. Impeachment by public records.

The most common form of impeachment by public records occurs in the use of weather bureau reports as to weather conditions. Whenever a witness testifies to weather conditions and by telephone call or previous preparation the lawyer has obtained a *certified copy* of the weather reports for the month in question, the certified report should be introduced in evidence to impeach the witness after having the witness repeat his statements as to the condition of the weather.

In some instances records of courts in reference to the insanity of witnesses have been introduced to impeach such witnesses. Care must always be exercised in this type of impeachment or the sympathy of the jury will be aroused in favor of the witness.

CHAPTER XIII

RE-DIRECT EXAMINATION AND REBUTTAL

§ 631. In general.

Re-direct examination or re-examination of a witness, as it is sometimes called, like direct examination, has been sadly neglected in so far as due consideration on the part of writers on trial practice is concerned. Very little attention has been given to this important phase of trial technique. Not only is re-direct examination a fairly good indication of a trial lawyer's general ability, but it is a true test of his preparation of the facts. A failure to make telling use of his right to re-examine witnesses where necessary is a clear indication of the trial lawyer's lack of preparation of the facts in his case.

As he views the wreckage which remains after his opponent has completed his cross-examination of the most important witness in the case, it is only the trial lawyer's most painstakingly complete and thorough preparation of the facts that will make it possible for him to restore the witness in the confidence of the court and jury, especially in those instances where the opponent's telling cross-examination has apparently resulted in the witness' making so-called damaging admissions and contradictions. Suspicion has been cast upon his story by innuendo and insinuation. The beautifully interesting and connected story told by the witness on direct examination has all been disarranged. All connecting links apparently have been scattered to the four winds. Hardly anything seems to remain that would warrant the jury in giving any credence to the story told by the witness.

All seems to be lost to the average on-looker and even to the jury.

Then the able trial lawyer commences his re-direct examination, and in a few moments order appears out of chaos. The jumbled disarranged "mess" begins to take shape once again. The jury and audience breathe a sigh of relief as they watch the master "re-build" and "repair" all the damage done by the merciless and destructive cross-examination. All humans naturally respond to the constructive re-creation and restoration of re-direct examination rather than the destruction and havoc occasioned by a cruel and gruelling cross-examination. Their natural sympathies are in favor of the helpless witness who is at the mercy of a supposedly merciless inquisitor. They are always pleased to have the good impression the witness made upon them during his direct examination restored during the re-direct examination.

The purpose of re-direct examination is to clarify and explain all apparent contradictions, fallacies and improbabilities brought out on cross-examination.

This can be successfully accomplished only by the lawyer who knows all the facts in the case. When he is fully and completely prepared, it is a comparatively simple matter for him to recognize where an unjustified insinuation is utilized by his opponent and one or two questions on re-direct examination will serve to bring out the true facts.

An appreciation of the importance and value of re-direct examination will always cause the trial lawyer to be on the alert every moment of the cross-examination so as to be able to note, either mentally or by a quickly scribbled word on a piece of paper, the various subjects he wishes to cover on re-direct examination.

This applies with equal force to the "layman fact" witness and to the expert witness, alike. It may be said in some instances, the re-direct examination of an expert witness assumes greater importance than that of a "lay" witness for an admission received by opponent from an expert witness on cross-examination may serve to nullify such expert's testimony unless the trial lawyer's knowledge of the subject in question is sufficient to enable him to re-establish his expert by proper re-direct examination. The trial lawyer who does not know or realize that when the expert admits on cross-examination that a certain thing is true but adds "under certain conditions" that he must on re-direct examination ask the expert to "tell the Court and jury under what conditions the admitted fact will be true," has failed to give the expert proper co-operation, and stamps himself as either unprepared or incompetent or both. It may also indicate that his mind was occupied with other things that took his attention away from the matter at hand, namely, the cross-examination of his witness.

§ 632. Signals.

The expert witness will usually give some signal or indication to the attorney which will call his attention to the fact that the answer to a question propounded on cross-examination can be satisfactorily explained. Just as the lay witness will not say "that is all that happened," but will usually reply in such an instance *"that is all I can recall,"* so as to permit a direct or leading question to be utilized for the purpose of refreshing his recollection, so will the experienced and expert witness indicate in his answer to a question on cross-examination that an apparently harmful admission when fully explained is not actually so. Some oft used responses may include "that is true under certain circumstances," "that is not always so," "it was not exactly so," "it did not happen in just that way," "that depends on other factors also," "there were other things said also," and "that is not all that took place there."

While re-direct examination may be used by the trial lawyer as an effective instrument for good, it must always be remembered that its effectiveness is dependent upon the discretion shown in its employment. Not every cross-examination indicates the necessity for its use. If the cross-examination has failed to reach any *material* part of the story on direct examination, the better policy would be to waive re-direct examination. There is always the possibility that an injudicious question on re-direct may open the "door" to a truly effective re-cross-examination that may really harm the trial lawyer's case. "Let well enough alone" still holds good in reference to re-direct examination. Every immaterial matter raised by opponent's cross-examination does not require attention on re-examination. It is never wise to distract the attention of the jury away from the really material issues by creating and taking issue on some immaterial fact. This may be part of opponent's plan, and is good tactics from his view-point, especially where he has been unable to "shake" the witness on cross-examination.

One of the important things for the trial lawyer to keep in mind during the cross-examination and in fact throughout the entire trial is to show no concern in the presence of the jury as to the damaging effect of such cross-examination. He must maintain the proverbial "poker face" and never for a moment indicate the "sinking heart" feeling which every trial lawyer experiences at least once or twice throughout every trial. An attitude of absolute calm and unconcern must be maintained not only for the benefit of the jury, but also for the witness. If any indication of the trial lawyer's perturbation appears, it will only serve the purpose of increasing the nervousness and confusion of the witness to the point where he will "destroy" himself altogether.

The first thought in the attorney's mind as he rises to commence his re-direct examination (where indicated) should be to restore the confidence of his witness. This can be accomplished by adopting a slow, easy, "calming" manner. A few simple, unimportant questions asked in a soothing, friendly manner and voice concerning some immaterial matter will give the witness a chance to "pull himself together."

When the witness' confidence has been restored, then the work of repair can be undertaken. It should ordinarily start at the point where the witness first proved to be vulnerable, or apparently so, under cross-examination. This suggestion pre-supposes that the trial lawyer will only consider material matters and not some minor detail which will not make any real difference. The story should then be re-built, clarified and explained until it is once more probable and worthy of belief.

§ 633. Leading questions.

The same rules apply as to leading questions on re-direct examination as govern the use thereof during direct examination. In general, leading questions are not permissible on re-direct examination, but in the main, it is discretionary with the court to permit the use of leading questions where indicated.

§ 634. Cannot repeat direct examination.

It is, of course, elementary that only facts which explain matters brought out on cross-examination are permitted on re-direct examination. Not only is the repeating of the direct examination legally improper, but from a psychological standpoint, should rarely be resorted to.

§ 635. Let well enough alone.

The trial attorney has been frequently warned not to attempt to prove his case too well for fear that he may open the door to dangerous testimony. It is not necessary on re-direct examination to have the witness reiterate or repeat some favorable testimony which opposing counsel brought out. The attorney can be sure that most of the jurors heard the testimony, and will recall whatever favorable aspects appear in the statement; repeating it serves no good purpose. On the other hand, it may be possible that the witness may volunteer something further which will permit opposing counsel, on re-cross-examination, to eliminate whatever there is favorable in the testimony. Again, the repetition of this testimony may suggest a new train of thought to the opposing counsel with a dangerous result. It is, therefore, suggested that the trial lawyer should not try to make his case "too good." Unimportant discrepancies should never be seized upon for a detailed re-direct examination. It may only serve the purpose of creating a false issue upon the new immaterial matter.

§ 636. Be careful of traps.

It sometimes happens that the clever opponent, on cross-examination, will touch upon a particular subject and then suddenly drop the matter in the hope that the trial lawyer will, on re-direct examination, go further into the same subject and bring out something that may prove harmful to his case. However, the trial attorney, who has made a complete preparation of the facts and is familiar with the entire subject matter upon which opponent has touched, will know from that preparation whether or not the subject is one which he will care to examine further in re-direct examination.

If the matter is something which is not familiar to the trial attorney, he should seriously consider whether or not to follow up the subject, always keeping in mind the possible harm which may result therefrom.

§ 637. Refreshing recollection.

Where, in cross-examination, the witness has become confused in reference to conversations, dates or events, it becomes very important that the trial attorney, on re-direct examination, refresh the recollection of the witness so that the true state of affairs can be ascertained.

If the witness has forgotten a certain part of a conversation involving a third person, and has forgotten either the statement by the third party or the fact that the conversation involved such third person, a good method to employ would be, first, to ask him if he knows this particular third party, and then to direct his attention to this conversation. It will be found that this preliminary question in reference to the identity of this third person, will immediately recall to the witness that such third party was present at the conversation or the fact that part of the conversation involved such third person. The same method can be utilized in an effort to refresh the recollections of the witness in reference to dates or events. A general suggestion as to some happening or time which will be associated in the mind of the witness with the conversation or event will almost always awaken his memory sufficiently to then detail and testify as to the correct date of the event. Should the witness testify incorrectly, under cross-examination, as to the date or event involved, it is always a good policy on re-direct examination to take up the happening of the various events or conversations in logical sequence. This will refresh his memory as to the true date or event. It is usually possible to arrive at the correct time or date by having the witness tell that the event took place a certain length of time, either before or after some other date or event which he clearly remembers.

In this way, the jury will know that he is probably mistaken as to the exact date, but that his testimony is true in all other respects when viewed in the light of his fixing the time in relation to other happenings or events correctly proved in the case.

When opposing counsel adopts the method of cross-examination which shows that the witness is unable to recall the name of other persons or happenings on the same day, the day before, or the day after, re-direct examination should be utilized for the purpose of showing that as to the particular date or event in question, to which the witness has testified, that he is able to recall such date or incident by reason of the fact that he has refreshed his recollection just prior to his testifying in court under the instructions of the trial attorney. The witness should always be told, before he takes the witness stand, that it is legally proper for him to refresh his memory as to certain dates and events before he takes the witness stand, and that, in respect to any general question on cross-examination by opposing counsel as to how he happens to recall this particular date or event, he should reply that he refreshed his recollection just before taking the witness stand.

§ 638. Opening the door.

Every trial attorney, in determining whether or not he will re-examine the witness, must always keep in mind the danger of "opening the door" to the admissibility of harmful testimony. Some young attorneys will object to an opponent's cross-examining in reference to certain subjects on the ground that such subject is beyond the scope of the pleading or immaterial to the issues, and then will fall into the error of examining in reference to the same subject on re-direct examination. This error makes it possible for opposing counsel to go into the same subject on re-cross-examination, and in a few moments an entirely new issue has become involved in the case, sometimes so damaging as to result in an unfavorable verdict.

§ 639. Planning traps.

In some instances, it is possible to plan a trap for opposing counsel that may result in a great deal of value to the attorney's case. This is particularly true in those cases involving expert witnesses who are not permitted to testify or who do not desire to produce certain evidence on direct examination, but wish to lead opposing counsel into calling for such evidence, or at least, making it possible to cover that subject on re-direct examination. In one case involving silicosis (an occupational disease), an X-ray expert was placed on the witness stand to testify in reference to his findings. It was generally known that one of the outstanding authorities in this field had published an article with statements and findings contrary to those testified to by the witness. However, this outstanding authority, just prior to the trial of the case, had announced at a certain medical meeting that he had arrived at findings which were directly contrary to those published by himself in the past. This witness had secured a letter from this authority citing his changed views on the subject. The trial attorney and the witness both believed that opposing counsel would resort to the published works of this authority in cross-examination, on the theory of contradicting the witness' findings. When the witness was turned over for cross-examination, the opposing counsel did that very thing. When examined in reference to the supposedly contrary views found by this outstanding authority, the witness was able to state that this authority had changed his mind in reference to his views on the subject. The cross-examiner asked him what proof he had of this fact and the witness replied that he had a letter in his pocket, addressed to himself, and signed by this authority stating that from recent experiments he had arrived at a contrary conclusion and that this contrary conclusion was in harmony with the witness' own findings. When it came time for re-direct examination, the trial attorney requested the witness to produce the letter, and offered it in evidence. Opposing counsel did not dare to offer any objections thereto.

§ 640. Forgotten questions.

It sometimes happens that during the cross-examination of a witness, the lawyer suddenly remembers some question or field of inquiry which he has failed to touch upon in direct examination. As has been previously stated, it is discretionary with the court to permit the trial attorney to ask questions on re-direct examination or during the cross-examination that he forgot to ask before. Some attorneys try to avoid requesting permission to ask such questions, and proceed to ask the question as though properly a part of re-direct examination, only to be met with an objection which is usually sustained. Some judges resent the effort thereafter to secure permission to ask the questions on the grounds that counsel forgot to ask them during direct examination. It is much better and less subject to objection to admit inadvertent failure to ask the question on direct examination. Such open admission in the first instance, coupled with the request for permission to ask the questions, will usually be granted, and appeals more to both the court and the jury.

§ 641. Scope of re-direct examination.

The proper function of re-direct examination is to explain, rebut, or avoid the effect of new matter brought out on cross-examination.[1]

Generally testimony on re-direct examination of a witness which tends to rebut or avoid the effect of matter brought out on cross-examination is properly received. Testimony of this character in support or corroboration of that brought out on direct examination is proper.[2]

A witness may be questioned to test his capacity to measure distances, or he may be questioned to test his recollection and to bring out facts showing on what his recollection is based. Where a witness has on cross-examination materially modified his statements on direct, it is proper to attempt to show on re-direct that his first version was the correct one. The scope and extent of the re-direct examination are in the discretion of the court, and no error can be predicated where the discretion has not been abused.[3]

To rebut and to avoid the effect of the cross-examination, a witness is properly examined as to matters concerning which he was cross-examined,[4] such as facts which the cross-examination brought out or elicited,[5] or injected in the case,[6] or new matter which was first introduced on cross-examination,[7]

1 70 C. J. 698–717. Richardson v. State, 268 Pac. 615, 34 Ariz. 475.

2 Moran v. State, 11 Ohio Cir. Ct. 565, 5 Ohio Cir. Dec. 234; Gray v. State, 108 So. 658, 21 Ala. App. 409.

3 Heidler Hardwood Lumber Company v. Wilson & Bennett Mfg. Co., 243 Ill. App. 89; Commonwealth v. Sacco, 151 N. E. 839, 255 Mass. 369; People v. Tubbs, 110 N. W. 132, 147 Mich. 1; People v. Majoine, 77 Pac. 952, 144 Cal. 303.

4 Pedley v. Doyle, 170 Pac. 602, 177 Cal. 284; Rommel Bros. v. Wenks, 186 Ill. App. 369; Kreutzer & Wasem v. Reese, 174 N. W. 935, 187 Iowa 1100; Nute v. Boston & M. R. R., 100 N. E. 1099, 214 Mass. 184; People v. McArron, 79 N. W. 944, 121 Mich. 1; People v. Buchanan, 39 N. E. 846, 145 N. Y. 1; Pardue v. Whitfield, 115 S. W. 306, 53 Tex. Cov. App. 63; Hupfer v. National Distilling Co., 106 N. W. 831, 127 Wis. 306.

5 People v. Klopfer, 214 Pac. 878, 61 Cal. App. 291; Mayer v. Brensinger, 54 N. E. 159, 180 Ill. 72, 110; Luin v. Chicago Grill Co., 115 N. W. 1024, 138 Iowa 268; People v. Gross, 203 N. W. 534, 230 Mich. 653; People v. Bertini, 113 N. E. 541, 218 N. Y. 584; Rhea v. State, 275 S. W. 1021, 101 Tex. Cr. 298.

6 Stover v. State, 143 So. 239, 25 Ala. App., 222.

7 California Electric Light Co. v. California Safe Deposit, etc., Co., 78 Pac. 372, 145 Cal. 124; Jeffrey v. Keokuk, etc., R. Co., 9 N. W. 884, 56 Iowa 546; Mahoney v. Cooch, 141

although the testimony would not have been admissible on direct examination.[8] Similarly on direct the same line of inquiry or course of questioning followed on cross may be pursued.[9] Where incompetent testimony is elicited on cross-examination, it has been held that the matters so brought out can be gone into on re-direct,[10] but there is other authority to the contrary.[11] Re-examination generally should be confined to the scope of the cross-examination, and testimony beyond this is properly excluded,[12] but the court, in the exercise of its discretion, may permit the re-examination to go beyond the scope of the cross-examination.[13]

§ 642. Rebuttal.

As a general proposition, most lawyers appreciate their legal right to offer evidence in rebuttal, but many fail to appreciate the psychological importance of offering evidence in rebuttal where properly indicated. Legally, either party is entitled to introduce evidence to rebut that of his adversary, and for this purpose, any competent evidence to explain, repel, counteract or disprove the adversary's proof is admissible. Psychologically, the determination and decision as to whether or not to offer evidence in rebuttal in the main, depends upon the attorney's ability to disassociate himself impersonally from his client's cause in an effort to weigh the

N. E. 605, 246 Mass. 567; People v. Robinson, 98 N. W. 12, 135 Mich. 511; People v. Noblett, 89 N. Y. S. 181, 96 App. Div. 293, 18 N. Y. Cr. 476 (aff'd 77 N. E. 1193, 184 N. Y. 612); Bassham v. State, 38 Tex. 622; Tuckwood v. Hanthorn, 30 N. W. 705, 67 Wis. 326.

8 People v. Buchanan, 39 N. E. 846, 145 N. Y. 1 (error den. 39 S. Ct. 884, 158 U. S. 31, 39 L. Ed. 886).

9 Fowles v. Joslyn, 97 N. W. 790, 135 Mich. 333; People v. Buchanan, 39 N. E. 846, 145 N. Y. 1 (error den. 39 S. Ct. 884, 158 U. S. 31, 39 L. Ed. 886); Washington v. State, 125 S. W. 917, 58 Tex. Ct. 345.

10 In re Wharton's Will, 109 N. W. 492, 132 Iowa 714; People v. Barone, 55 N. E. 1083, 161 N. Y. 451.

11 Glascoe v. State, 210 S. W. 956, 85 Tex. Cr. 234; see Wagner v. People, 30 Mich. 384.

12 Hotaling v. Hotaling, 203 Pac. 745, 187 Cal. 695; Finley v. West Chicago St. R. Co., 90 Ill. App. 368; State v. Beeson, 136 N. W. 317, 155 Iowa 355; Chase v. Chase, 171 N. E. 651, 271 Mass. 485; Robinson v. New York El. R. Co., 67 N. E. 431, 175 N. Y. 219; Donohue v. State, 236 S. W. 86, 90 Tex. Cr. 541.

13 Majors v. Connor, 121 Pac. 371, 162 Cal. 131; Commonwealth v. Patalano, 149 N. E. 689, 254 Mass. 69; Manufacturers', etc., Bank v. Koch, 12 N. E. 9, 105 N. Y. 630.

effect of the opponent's evidence on the jury. The trial attorney frequently becomes so immersed in his client's cause that he loses his perspective. He easily becomes convinced of his client's truthfulness and that of his witnesses in a desire to justify his representing the client. It may also be a fact that his client and witnesses are telling the truth, but sometimes he fails to appreciate that the jurors, who know nothing about either of the parties or the witnesses involved, and who do not have any desire to color their belief, may come to the conclusion that the opponent's witnesses are telling the truth. It is, of course, impossible for the jurors to determine absolutely where the truth lies, and because of that fact, the failure of counsel to offer proper rebuttal evidence, though it may only be putting his client on the stand to deny certain statements of the adversary, may result in an unfavorable verdict, because the jury was at a loss to understand such failure to deny. They then feel that the statements made by the opposition must be true; otherwise, in their opinion, so-called "outraged innocence" would require a refutation of such statement. It frequently happens that the trial lawyer considers such statement preposterous, and feels that rebuttal may dignify it. However, the failure to offer rebuttal evidence may result in a great deal of harm.

§ 643. Direct questions.

On rebuttal, it is legally permissible to use direct and leading questions. Direct or leading questions in reference to denials may and should be utilized. If it is desired to refute a certain statement made by the defendant, the plaintiff's attorney should directly ask the witness, in rebuttal, whether or not he made that particular statement. If a question of impeachment is involved, the leading statement or question should be put directly to the witness. (See illustration "Impeachment," page 550.)

§ 644. Witnesses.

Any witness may be used in rebuttal whether or not he has testified during the direct case of the plaintiff. It may sometimes become necessary, in order to refute the statements of expert witnesses offered on behalf of the defendant, for the plaintiff to produce a number of other experts, who will testify directly contrary to the testimony offered by the defendant wherever indicated. The trial attorney should not hesitate to utilize experts for this purpose in rebuttal where indicated.

Sometimes the attorneys offer witnesses to prove the bad reputation of the defendant or of some of the defendant's witnesses on rebuttal. This testimony is, of course, admissible.

§ 645. Scope of rebuttal.[14]

Either party is entitled to introduce evidence to rebut that of his adversary,[14a] and for this purpose any competent evidence to explain, repel, counteract, or disprove the adversary's proof is admissible,[15] although it tends to support his case in chief.[16]

Rebuttal testimony is, generally speaking, receivable only where new matter has been developed by the evidence of one of the parties [17] and is generally limited to a reply to new points.[18] Matters adduced by cross-examination may be rebutted.[19] It is not competent for a party to go into a collateral matter on cross-examination and afterward rebut the testimony so called out,[20] or to introduce evidence to rebut matters which are not proved but merely attempted to be proved,[21]

14 64 C. J. 152–157.

14a Robinson v. McKnight, 284 Pac. 1056, 103 Cal. App. 718; Presley v. Kinlock-Bloomington Telephone Co., 158 Ill. App. 220; Ordway v. Buckingham, 152 Ill. App. 45; Wallis v. Randolph, 81 N. Y. 164 (aff'g 16 Hun 331); American Automobile Ins. Co. v. Struwe (Civ. App.) 218 S. W. 534.

15 Conlon v. Osborn, 120 Pac. 755, 161 Cal. 659; Pittsburgh, C. C. & St. L. Ry. Co. v. Gage, 121 N. E. 582, 286 Ill. 213; Pronskevitch v. Chicago, etc., R. Co., 83 N. E. 545, 232 Ill. 136; Schevers v. American Ry. Express Co., 192 N. W. 225, 195 Iowa 423; Gorgol v. Michigan Cent. R. Co., 211 N. W. 50, 236 Mich. 646; McAleenan v. Massachusetts Bonding & Insurance Co., 232 N. Y. 199, 133 N. E. 444; N. W. Graham & Co. v. W. H. Davis & Co., 62 Am. D. 285, 4 Ohio St. 362; Bounds v. Little, 15 S. W. 225, 79 Tex. 128.

16 Baillargeon v. Myers, 182 Pac. 37, 180 Cal. 504; Lane v. Butler, 225 Ill. App. 382; Ankersmit v. Tuch, 20 N. E. 819, 114 N. Y. 51; Gulf, etc., R. Co. v. Holliday, 65 Tex. 512; Waterman v. Chicago, etc., R. Co., 52 N. W. 247, 1136, 82 Wis. 613.

17 Pontecorvo v. Clark, 272 Pac. 591, 95 Cal. App. 162.

18 Graham & Co. v. Davis & Co., 4 Ohio St. 362, 62 Am. D. 285; Wade v. Galveston, etc., R. Co. (Civ. App.), 110 S. W. 84.

19 Gifford-Wood Co. v. Western Fuel Co., 209 Ill. App. 357; Cobb, Bates & Yerxa Co. v. Hills, 94 N. E. 265, 208 Mass. 270; City of Ft. Worth v. Lopp (Civ. App.), 134 S. W. 824.

20 Buckley v. Silverberg, 45 Pac. 804, 113 Cal. 673.

21 Chicago, etc., R. Co. v. Ryan, 57 Ill. App. 612.

or on which no evidence has been offered,[22] to prove matters not in issue,[23] or collateral to the issues,[24] or matters admitted by the other party,[25] or to introduce testimony which is not in rebuttal of and does not tend to dispute the adverse party's evidence.[26] New matter, to which the adverse party is denied the right to introduce evidence is inadmissible on rebuttal.[27] Evidence given on cross-examination need not be given again on rebuttal.[28]

Although the Court may, in its discretion, allow it,[29] evidence in rebuttal which is merely cumulative to that offered in chief is not generally admissible,[30] and the witnesses should not be permitted to reiterate their testimony under the guise of rebuttal;[31] but a witness may, during the course of rebuttal, correct his testimony giving proof of the case in chief.[32]

The admission of improper or immaterial evidence on behalf of one party without objection will not justify a resort by the other party to immaterial and irrelevant evidence to rebut it.[33] The general rule is that parties cannot create a right to try an immaterial issue or introduce irrelevant evidence by mere silence or consent, when they might have had the adverse evidence kept out or stricken out.[34]

22 Brodsky v. Brodsky, 215 N. W. 181, 172 Minn. 250.

23 Marshall v. Partyka, 120 Atl. 507, 98 Conn. 778.

24 Stanton v. Lapp, 77 Atl. 672, 113 Md. 324.

25 Caldwell v. Richards, 267 Pac. 127, 91 Cal. App. 428.

26 Hanton v. Pacific Electric Ry. Co., 174 Pac. 61, 178 Cal. 616; Patterson v. Patterson, 95 N. E. 1051, 251 Ill. 153; Bartlett v. City of Medford, 147 N. E. 739, 252 Mass. 311; Rhodes v. Meloy (Civ. App.) 289 S. W. 159.

27 Hermann v. Combs, 85 Atl. 1044, 119 Md. 41.

28 Gunn v. McCabe, 139 Atl. 916, 49 R. I. 53.

29 New Jersey Zinc Co. v. American Zinc, Lead & Smelting Co., 284 F. 305 (aff'g 276 F. 733).

30 Scheerer v. Deming, 97 Pac. 155, 154 Cal. 138; Falvai v. Calumet & South Chicago Ry. Co., 177 Ill. App. 125. See Abt v. Chicago Rys. Co., 207 Ill. App. 314; Poole v. Boston & M. R. R., 102 N. E. 918, 216 Mass. 12; Reiche v. Gleicher, 172 N. Y. S. 200; Weinberg v. Hartzell, 153 N. E. 106, 21 Ohio App. 93.

31 Pontecorvo v. Clark, 272 Pac. 591, 95 Cal. App. 162.

32 Omaha Beverage Co. v. Temp Brew Co., 171 N. W. 704, 185 Iowa 1189.

33 Donelly v. Curran, 54 Cal. 282; Maxwell v. Durkin, 57 N. E. 433, 185 Ill. 546; Wickenkamp v. Wickenkamp, 77 Ill. 92; People v. Dowling, 84 N. Y. 478.

34 Maxwell v. Durkin, 57 N. E. 433, 185 Ill. 546.

§ 646. Evidence in chief.

One cannot, as a matter of right, offer in rebuttal, evidence which was proper or should have been introduced in chief,[35] even though it tends to contradict the adverse party's evidence,[36] and, while the court may in its discretion admit in rebuttal evidence which more properly should have been introduced in chief,[37] it may, in its discretion, and generally should decline to permit either party to introduce evidence in support of his case in chief on rebuttal,[38] especially upon a subject fully covered in his case in chief,[39] unless sufficient reason is offered for not introducing it at the proper time.[40]

§ 647. Reply or surrebuttal. When plaintiff in rebuttal is permitted to introduce new matter, defendant should be permitted to introduce evidence in surrebuttal,[41] and to decline to permit him to do so is error,[42] especially where the evidence offered in surrebuttal is for the first time made competent by the evidence introduced by plaintiff in rebuttal.

35 Yankee Jim's Union Water Co. v. Crary, 25 Cal. 504, 85 Am. D. 145; Marshall v. Davies, 78 N. Y. 414, 58 How. Pr. 231 (rev'g 16 Hun 606); Speyer v. Stern, 32 N. Y. Super. 516; N. W. Graham & Co. v. W. H. Davis & Co., 4 Ohio St. 362, 62 Am. D. 285; Bass v. Receivers of Kirby Lumber Co. (Civ. App.), 146 S. W. 658.

36 Light v. Toledo, St. L. & W. R. Co., 208 F. 158.

37 Dawson v. Pacific Electric Ry. Co., 170 Pac. 603, 177 Cal. 268; Wunderlich v. Buerger, 122 N. E. 827, 287 Ill. 440; In re Swain's Estate, 174 N. W. 493, 189 Iowa 28; Young v. New York, N. H. & H. R. Co., 174 N. E. 318, 273 Mass. 567; Zylstra v. Graham, 221 N. W. 318, 244 Mich. 319 (aff'd 224 N. W. 343); Gishwiller v. Dodez, 4 Ohio St. 615; N. W. Graham & Co. v. W. H. Davis & Co., 4 Ohio St. 362; San Antonio, etc., R. Co. v. Robinson, 15 S. W. 584, 79 Tex. 608; Brockman v. Wisconsin Power & Light Co., 222 N. W. 239, 197 Wis. 374.

38 Young v. Brady, 29 Pac. 489, 94 Cal. 128; Hoopeston First Nat. Bank v. Lake Erie, etc., R. Co., 50 N. E. 1023, 174 Ill. 36; Manning v. Burlington, etc., R. Co., 20 N. W. 169, 64 Iowa 240; McDonough v. McGovern, 135 N. E. 128, 241 Mass. 236; Shearer v. Middleton, 50 N. W. 737, 88 Mich. 621; Ankersmit v. Tuch, 20 N. E. 819, 114 N. Y. 51, 23 Abb. N. Cas. 87; Toledo, etc., R. Co. v. Wales, 11 Ohio Cir. Ct. 371, 1 Ohio Cir. Dec. 168; Rhodes v. Meloy (Civ. App.), 289 S. W. 159; Brockman v. Wisconsin Power & Light Co., 222 N. W. 239, 197 Wis. 374.

39 Kuznik v. Orient Ins. Co., 73 Ill. App. 201; Runge v. Schroeder, 218 N. W. 455, 174 Minn. 131; Gibson v. Johnson, 46 N. Y. S. 870, 21 Misc. 59.

40 Hills v. Ludwig, 24 N. E. 596, 46 Ohio St. 373.

41 Rock Island v. Starkey, 59 N. E. 971, 189 Ill. 515, rev'g 91 Ill. App. 592; Foster v. Newbrough, 59 N. Y. 481 (rev. 66 Barb. 645).

42 Anderson v. Anderson, 117 N. W. 801, 136 Wis. 328.

CHAPTER XIV

ARGUMENTS TO THE JURY

§ 648. In general.

It is generally known that there has been an evolution in the type of oratory used in arguments to the jury. Perhaps the better way to put it is to say that it should be generally known. The loud, noisy, flowing oratory of the past, if attempted today, would be totally unavailing. Dramatic appeals without regard to the facts in each case no longer result in favorable verdicts. The average juror today is a fairly well read business man of experience, with ability to analyze situations in the light of that business experience and knowledge. Today the arguments to jurors must appeal to their reason. The ability to do this when coupled with a proper emotional appeal would today constitute the best type of argument. The argument which today results in a favorable verdict is the one delivered in a manner denoting sincerity, earnestness and confidence in the righteousness of the attorney's cause. It is more of a friendly discussion with the jurors in attempting to convince them by logic and reason of the right to a verdict in the case.

Donovan in "Modern Jury Trials" says, "The most successful trial lawyers of to-day studiously avoid bombastic argument in their summation. Their appeal to the jury is made in conversational tones. They use just simple words to express their meaning in a brief speech. They seek to create the impression that they are taking the jurors into their confidence. Their statements are forceful, logical, statements of facts. The voice should very rarely be raised. It is only when one has reached a climax that the raising of the voice is necessary. Shrieking at the top of your voice from the opening of the argument to the conclusion is certainly no aid to the jury. It becomes monotonous, distracts the attention of the jury from the context, and very often the reaction is decidedly unfavorable. The standards here recommended are, of course, by no means easy to adopt. Ever since the days of Demosthenes oratorical excellence has been purchased at the price of great labor.

"The average jury of today seems quite able to separate the chaff from the wheat and to arrive at the truth fairly and impartially. More often the blunders that the jury commits are due to the errors that counsel have been guilty of than to any other cause."

§ 649. Preparation for argument.

A well prepared and a well tried case deserves a well delivered and a thoroughly prepared argument. The same theory applies in arguments as applies to all other parts of the trial. The lawyer must ever keep in mind that his object is to *prove his side of the case* rather than to disprove his opponent's case. Therefore, in preparation for the argument in each case he must decide the theory upon which he intends to argue. This does not mean that the lawyer should "rehash" or go over the entire testimony as presented in the case before the jury, but rather that he should adopt a subject for discussion, and then prove that subject as entitling him to a verdict. For instance, instead of the procedure followed by some attorneys in stressing to what each witness has testified, it is better practice to picture the situation which is testified to or corroborated by certain witnesses. In other words, he should *stress pictures rather than witnesses.* For, after all, the main thing that the lawyer is concerned with is securing the approval and verdict of the jury as to the cause of action and not merely as to certain witnesses and to what they have testified. This makes it a lot more interesting to the jury and much more easily followed and understood. This is especially true in some long drawn out cases which have not been properly planned, and as a consequence the jury is at a loss to understand just what the case is about.

George Gordon Battle of the New York Bar in an address before the New York Bar Association stated in part as follows:

"That leads me to say that if there is in my judgment any one cardinal fault of all trial lawyers, both the best as well as the worst, it is the fact that they are not sufficiently explicit; the fact that they don't make sufficiently clear just what they wish to impress upon the minds of the jury. It is almost impossible for a man who knows his story pretty well and who is accustomed to dealing with and understanding more or less complicated statements of facts—I say it is almost impossible for him to remember that it is all a new story to the jury, and that they are not as skilled as he is, and as experienced as he is in digesting and understanding more or less complicated statements of facts. So that in very many instances very often the jury have a very vague notion of what it is all about. I often think that to a jury sitting in a box the progress of a case must be like one of those mirages in the desert where there is a mingling of forms and shapes without any definite outline, without producing any definite impression as to what the meaning and significance of it all is, so that in many cases the juries do not understand what it is all about. They don't understand the points that counsel is making, and the result is that when they retire to their room after the trial they render a verdict more or less by chance.''

§ 650. Adopt a theory of case.

This is true in those instances where the trial lawyer has failed to adopt a certain theory in the case, and fails to direct all of his efforts towards proving that theory.

If a lawyer can picture to the jury his theory of the testimony of the witnesses, and, thereafter, point out to them the various witnesses in cumulative or corroboratory fashion who have testified to this picture as well as the witnesses or exhibits which corroborate that particular testimony, it would seem to be a great deal more effective and desirable. This does not mean that each witness' story must then be repeated in detail. The attorney may merely point out that the witnesses (by name) have corroborated the general theory of the case.

§ 651. Models or hands.

One method usually employed in the attempt to picture the happening of an accident is through the use of models,[1] or

1 It is within the discretion of the court to permit counsel to use physical objects in illustrating remarks. Billett v. Mich. Bonding & Surety Co.,

where no models are available, through the use of the hands. This would be particularly true in an automobile collision case where the lawyer can demonstrate with the left hand one car approaching the intersection in one direction and then use the other hand to demonstrate the defendant's car approaching from the other direction. Through these means the jurors can almost visualize just how the collision took place. When this procedure is followed it is quite evident that it requires less effort on the part of the jury to understand.

§ 652. Word pictures.

It is frequently asked as to how one may acquire the ability to "picturize" situations in arguments to the jury. This power to arouse the emotions by a dramatic or moving "word picture" of a certain event or happening can be attained by the reading of the outstanding works of fiction, both past and present. If it is desired to detail the permanent effect of some personal injury which has crippled or deformed a client, the collection of a number of vivid descriptions by various authors as to similar characters in their stories who have been crippled or deformed will give the lawyer the basis of a dramatic appeal to the jury.

Almost every happening or situation in life which confronts the lawyer in the average law suit today has been portrayed and described by some author in some work of fiction.

An effort to find and classify these descriptions will more than repay the trial lawyer throughout his career.

It is suggested that lawyers should read and thoroughly digest all the arguments made by famous trial lawyers of the past as reported in Sellers' Classics of the Bar, American State Trials, Hicks' Famous Jury Speeches, Erskine's Speeches, and Notable British Trials.

While many of the expressions and some of the styles might not be used today, yet they may all be utilized as a basis for worth-while legal oratory.

161 N. W. 908, 195 Mich. 202; Cincinnati H. & D. Ry. v. Tafelski, 31 Ohio Cir. Ct. 643, 94 N. E. 1103; Mizner v. Lohr, 238 N. W. 584, 213 Iowa 1182.

The following newspaper article tells of one method of picturing and explaining a supposedly complicated situation:

EXPLAINS BANK DEAL WITH AID OF PAPER CUPS

DEMONSTRATION PUT ON FOR JURY

New York, Sept. 19. The white-haired John W. Davis solemnly made use of a drinking glass and eight white paper drinking cups this afternoon in "an elementary demonstration" before the jury which is trying a defendant on charges of misapplying the funds of the Safe Deposit Company, an affiliate of the now defunct Bank of United States. Mr. Davis is counsel for the defense.

The defendant, who was counsel to and a director of the bank, is on trial in the criminal branch of the Supreme Court.

Mr. Davis made his demonstration during his address to the jury to prove, he said, that not one cent was lost or gained by the Bank or any of its subsidiaries as a result of an intricate security switching transaction on which the indictment is based.

From the glass Mr. Davis poured water into a paper cup and then transferred the water from the cup to cup and back to the glass again.

"Now you see," he said, "not a drop was spilled in the transaction—not even as much as I have spilled here in my elementary demonstration. Not a cent was lost or gained by the transaction which has been described."

In making the demonstration Mr. Davis had explained that three of the cups represented financial subsidiaries of the bank, two represented development companies, three represented safe deposit companies, and the glass represented the bank itself.

"If there ever was a technical crime committed," Mr. Davis said, "You'll find that this was that sort of crime."

He went on to say that "the transaction had nothing to do with the failure of the bank in December, 1930. . . ."

§ 653. Exhibits.

It is also suggested, in accordance with the theory of presenting "pictures" to the jury, that exhibits be read to the jury during the course of the argument rather than just merely referring to the exhibit, and requesting the jury to read it when they have retired to the jury room for deliberation. If there is something of importance in any exhibit, agreement, or letter which tends to prove the attorney's theory of the case, it should be read to them at that particular time so as to receive the most effective use and benefit of it.

§ 654. Making speech.

The greatest difficulty of the trial lawyer is to *"forget"* that he is making a speech. If he could only keep uppermost in his mind the fact that the mode of today is towards conversational oratory with a conversational manner which must be natural, he will have gone a long way towards creating good will both for his client's cause and for his own ability as a trial lawyer.

§ 655. Demeanor and attitude.

The lawyer's *attitude* should be friendly, conversational and direct. This may be somewhat illustrated in this manner. The lawyer actually is saying "Gentlemen of the Jury," but his meaning and attitude should be saying "friends," "folks" or "fellows." He must look straight at them and speak directly to them as though they were all sitting and conversing together. The moment he forgets this attitude and seems to be making a speech, he starts to fail. He must forever keep in mind that his purpose is to have a little friendly conversation with them in an effort to convince them of his theory of the case and to point out why opponent is wrong in his contentions. This attitude may be attained partially through the use of short sentences. A long drawn out sentence will serve merely to make the jury forget what the lawyer started to say in the beginning, and they will lose his thought before he gets to the end. It must ever be kept in mind that the jury must understand every word the moment it is uttered. The voice should be well modulated and care should be taken not to permit the voice to become too loud, shrill nor irritating. In every instance when the natural inclination is to raise the voice, it is more effective to lower it; in other words to talk down towards the chest (but not in the chest) rather than up into the head. Care should be taken not to deliver the argument in a continuous monotone.

§ 656. Convey thoughts, not words.

Do not try to select words particularly. The main purpose is to convey thoughts and ideas. It is the thought and the idea that must be acceptable to the jury and not three or four syllable words. If the lawyer has the thought of what he desires to convey well in mind he will find that the words with which to do so will always be available.

§ 657. Planned argument.

As before stated, the argument should be planned in advance (not memorized), and should be very carefully considered. Stress should be laid on the one important theory upon which the lawyer relies for a recovery in the case or upon the defense which he feels will entitle him to a verdict. In many instances, he will be tempted to rely for a verdict upon a number of different theories, with the result that he actually proves none of them. It is, of course, permissible to argue incidentally, as a sort of sub-head one, or two other theories of defense, but the main subject and theme of his argument should be towards proving his main contention. For instance, in a case involving a suit on a life insurance policy, the insurance company defended on the theory that the assured made false answers as to her condition of health in the application and medical report given prior to the issuance of the policy. The theory of the defendant might be in this type of case that their company does business almost exclusively upon the good faith and honesty of the answers made by the applicant. This would be the main theory of defense, and a good portion of the argument should be directed towards that end. The insurance company's attorney would argue that the medical examination made by their medical examiner was merely cursory and casual. If the assured in this case died, say, some four months after the issuance of the policy of an advanced case of pulmonary tuberculosis, they would try to picture before the jury that she knew, as shown by the evidence, that she had pulmonary tuberculosis, that if she had answered the questions in reference to her medical condition truthfully, they would never have issued this policy, that no other company would have issued a policy, and, therefore, there should be a verdict for the defendant. The various questions in the medical report would be taken up individually in cumulative fashion in the argument. All questions and untruthful answers would be stated, and then the evidence would be commented on as showing proof of her prior ill health and of the falsity of her answers by calling attention to the testimony of the various doctors who had treated her at the medical dispensaries and clinics, and to show that she had knowledge of her condition. This would all be done without applying any epithets to the assured who is now deceased, but would be done indirectly by allowing the jury to arrive at their own conclusion that the deceased had untruthfully answered these various questions. The attorney for the insurance company would also argue that it is common knowledge, and they would have also placed upon the witness stand, doctors to prove that in many cases it is impossible to detect, merely by a stethoscope examination, that a person has pulmonary tuberculosis, but that in order to really determine it, it would be necessary to take x-rays of the chest as well as laboratory tests of the sputum; that this was not done in the case of the assured; that merely a casual examination was made, and that the jurors as men of reason and of business experience can very readily see that this insurance policy was only issued in reliance upon the believed truthful answers made in the application and in answer to the medical examiner's questioning. The answers being untrue, the policy is void, and they should return a verdict in favor of the defendant.

On the other hand, if representing the plaintiff, the main theory of the argument would be that if assured had pulmonary tuberculosis, that the medical examiner of this *big* insurance company, who certainly would not have employed anybody but an expert in such medical examinations, would very easily have known and recognized the fact that the assured had pulmonary tuberculosis, if she did have it in such an active and advanced stage that four months later she died as a result thereof. In this particular case that we have in mind, the insurance company failed to put such medical examiner on the witness stand, and therefore, the plaintiff would argue quite strongly that the failure of the insurance company to put the said medical examiner on the witness stand is a presumption in favor of the plaintiff and against the defendant. This would carry a great deal of weight as counsel would argue that it is quite evident that the insurance company, in issuing the policy based upon the medical report of that medical examiner, conclusively shows that the medical examiner had found her in sufficiently good health to warrant the acceptance of her insurance application, and that, therefore, if she was suffering from pulmonary tuberculosis, the evidence shows that she did not know it, that she was not sick enough for the medical examiner to have recognized it, and, therefore, she had kept her end of the bargain. The plaintiff's attorney would then ask that the jury by their verdict insist upon the defendant insurance company keeping their end of the bargain by paying the sum sued for.

§ 658. One issue.

If there is only one phase of the case actually in controversy, the arguments should be directed to that one question almost wholly. Incidental reference can be made to the case in general, but in the main, all arguments should be directed towards the point in controversy. For instance in a case involving, among other things, the question of whether or not fraudulent representations were made to induce the defendant to execute a certain agreement of indemnity, while there might be several other defenses which should be incidentally referred to as proved by the evidence, the attorney should take the position that there is only one real question involved, and that is "Was he fraudulently induced to sign this agreement?" A picture should then be presented to the jury as to just what occurred. The grounds of claimed fraud should be "pictured" to them, and then shown that this "pictured" fraud has been proved and corroborated by various witnesses. An appeal to the emotions might be made showing the relationship of the parties, that the client depended upon the honor, integrity and good faith of the opposing party, that he relied upon the misrepresentations made, that he would never have signed the agreement except for that, and that the evidence having so shown, he is entitled to a verdict.

§ 659. Outline.

In preparing an argument, a definite outline should be made, keeping in mind the logical sequence and the best dramatic climax hoped to be obtained. As the lawyer marks down each thought or idea he should question himself as to whether or not it tends to prove the main theme or subject of his address. If he does not follow this procedure he will find himself rambling in every direction and finally proving nothing.

It is suggested that good practice and worthwhile achievement in delivering arguments to the jury may be made by intensive study of the art of effective speaking with a general study of the rules of psychology underlying effective speech.

§ 660. Improbabilities.

Some cases may be argued to the jury on the basis of improbabilities; that the other side's contentions are not probable nor reasonable in the light of general business experience. In other words, just because a man swears that a fact is so does not mean that one must accept it as so, if, from one's general experience in life and that of the jurors, no one would believe that the happening of the events claimed could be possible or probable.

§ 661. Avoid personalities and epithets.

The trial attorney is strongly cautioned to ever keep foremost in his mind the thought that he must be absolutely fair, honest and gentlemanly in his conduct before the jury. There is no occasion to engage in bitter verbal combats with the opposing attorney. There is no occasion in the arguments to call anyone a liar or perjurer directly. The same result can be obtained by indirection. As business men, if the testimony proves certain witnesses to have testified falsely, the jury will be quick to arrive at that conclusion themselves, and a reference to such testimony with a generous statement that the witness might have been mistaken or was clearly mistaken, as proved by the testimony will do a lot more good than to loudly proclaim that they are liars and perjurers. It is a mistake to attempt to prove all of opponent's witnesses as perjurers and to claim that only counsel's own witnesses are telling the absolute truth.

§ 662. Misstating evidence.

One of the greatest mistakes that can be made in arguments to the jury is to misstate the evidence intentionally and deliberately. After opposing counsel, by objection, has called the jurors' attention to this grievous error several times, the lawyer will be completely discredited before the jury. He will have harmed his client's case to the point where the jury may return an unfavorable verdict against him.

§ 663. Objections.

Objections and exceptions should be made and preserved to any improper, inflammatory or prejudicial remarks of an opponent during the course of his arguments to the jury.

§ 664. Plaintiff's opening argument—Full or incomplete.

It is often a mooted question among trial attorneys as to whether the plaintiff in his opening argument should make out a full and complete case entitling him to a verdict, or whether he should cover all of the testimony casually in his opening argument and wait until his closing argument for the full force of his talk. This question has been covered in Cornelius on "Trial Tactics" as follows:

"Another problem that will frequently confront you when representing the plaintiff is this. Shall I develop my argument on all the facts of the case fully in my opening, thereby giving opposing counsel a full opportunity to reply thereto, or shall I merely touch the high spots in the case, and then after counsel for the defendant has closed his argument, develop my argument fully on the final and closing argument, when my adversary will have no opportunity to reply to me?

"I have noticed very many lawyers who have had some considerable experience, make a rather brief opening argument, saving for their closing, the strongest points in the case. My personal opinion, however, is that such a course is not advisable. The danger in pursuing such a course lies in the fact that the jury may detect your strategy, and feel that you are acting unfairly towards the opposition.

"On this point, William Henry Gallagher, one of the foremost trial lawyers in Detroit, makes the following statement:

"I have always had but one policy in my opening argument, that is to make a full presentation of the plaintiff's case. But that policy is dictated by a sense of decency and fairness rather than strategy.

"I feel the defendant is entitled to have the plaintiff's theory and the arguments justifying it fully expounded in the opening in order that he might have an opportunity of meeting it in his argument . . .

"But one does then have the advantage of being able to emphasize before the jury defendant's failure to meet and answer one's argument.

"On those occasions when the plaintiff has failed to make a full and fair opening, and where I have appeared for the defendant I have never failed to point out to the jury that plaintiff's failure to develop his case fully in the argument must be the result of a desire to take advantage of the defendant by not giving him the opportunity of answering or of the consciousness that his arguments if fully developed were capable of ready answer. And I then caution the jury that they must analyze the closing argument carefully without any aid from me, and make certain that no advantage is taken of them as well as of me. .

"It seems to me that an incomplete opening which is met with such strategy will defeat its own purpose.

"If there were alert counsel for the defense, therefore, strategy as well as fairness should dictate that a fairly comprehensive opening argument be made."

"Where the defendant is making an argument to the jury and the plaintiff has the closing argument, counsel for the defendant will of course be permitted to address the jury only once. He will not be able to reply, to the plaintiff's closing argument. I have heard many seasoned trial lawyers closing their argument something like this: 'Now, gentlemen of the jury, I have discussed this case but I will not be permitted to address you again on this subject. My brother at the bar has the closing argument but I should like to impress upon your mind that there is no evidence in this case and there is no contention that he may make to support his theory that could not be met by me had I the opportunity to reply. I have discussed all that now occurs to me and all the contentions that counsel has advanced. If the opposing counsel should bring forward any argument in his closing which I have not touched upon in my discussion of this case, I want you to remember that there is no argument that he can urge that could not be fully met by me if I had the opportunity to reply.' "

In reference to instances where the plaintiff has made an insufficient opening the above suggestions should be adopted. In addition the trial lawyer can urge the jurors, as men of intelligence and men of business experience, to answer themselves each and every argument advanced by plaintiff's attorney in his closing argument from the evidence, with the statement that he (the attorney) is sure that their memory will call to mind all the testimony that completely refutes counsel for the plaintiff's argument.

Sometimes in making a full, fair and complete opening argument for the plaintiff, it is advisable to state the theory of the case, and leave for the closing argument the attempt to dispose of the theories and arguments of the defendant. This, however, is not recommended. This procedure may be resorted to in those instances where the court has unusually limited the amount of time for arguments. In such an event, it may be better to leave those matters for the closing argument.

§ 665. Damages in personal injury cases.

In personal injury cases, and in those classes of cases where the amount of damage is to be fixed by the jury, it is permissible, and it is suggested, that the attorney for the plaintiff state to the jury what *the evidence shows* he has proved in the way of damages, and, in general, the amount that the plaintiff is entitled to recover. If it should happen that the damages proved fall far short of the ad damnum claimed, as in some instances where but one or two thousand dollars of damages is shown and a general ad damnum is stated of fifty thousand or one hundred thousand dollars, it should be explained to the jury during the argument, or shown by the evidence, that the case was started before a complete recovery had been made; that no one could say what the actual damage would be at the time the suit was instituted; and for that reason a large ad damnum was pleaded. However, this procedure is subject to the objection of admitting the weakness of the case.

§ 666. Argument based on instructions.

Some attorneys, in planning the argument to the jury, build the theory of their talk in part, if not entirely, on the instructions to be given by the court. For instance, it may be based on an instruction as to the determination of the credibility of witnesses. Each of the elements involved is shown as applying favorably to counsel's witnesses and unfavorably to opponent's witnesses. If a number of disinterested witnesses testify, it is, of course, important to stress before the jury the value and weight to be given to such testimony.

§ 667. Negligence, due care and contributory negligence.

Many trial attorneys build the theory of their argument, especially in personal injury cases, on the question of the negligence of the defendant, with the incidental requirement of due care and caution for the safety of the plaintiff. In these instances, they stress the duty that the defendant owed to the plaintiff, and show by the evidence how the defendant failed to perform that duty; that, as a result thereof, the plaintiff was injured and damaged permanently, and is therefore entitled to a verdict. The defendant on the other hand, if the evidence warranted, would build his theory on the basis of contributory negligence. He would emphasize those things that the plaintiff should have done in the exercise of due care and caution for his own safety; that the evidence shows that the plaintiff did not exercise due care and caution and was guilty of contributory negligence, and therefore the defendant should be entitled to a verdict of not guilty.

§ 668. Questions for counsel to answer.

Sometimes attorneys in arguments to the jury will make requests of opposing counsel to answer his argument. In many particulars he will say before the jury, "And I want counsel to answer this question. . . . And I want counsel to tell you gentlemen of the jury why his client did so and so. . . .", and will demand of counsel a reply to many such questions and statements. This is frequently done for the purpose of breaking up the original theory upon which opposing counsel would have argued his case to the jury. In attempting to answer all of these questions and propositions, so much time is taken that before he realizes, the entire time is taken with answering these questions, and little attention is given to his own side of the case. If opposing counsel merely asks an answer to one or two questions, which are important in the case, they should, of course, be replied to, if possible; otherwise the jury will be quick to believe that he is afraid or unable to answer them. If there are a great number of such questions, however, they can usually be disposed of by calling attention of the jury to the fact that this is merely a trick on the part of counsel; the lawyer then proceeds to dispose of one or two of the questions for illustration purposes to show the jury that, if time was had, all questions could be answered; and, finally, a statement that all propositions and questions will be answered, if time permits, after the true issues involved have been presented. In this manner he can dispose of questions so put by opposing counsel, and go directly to his theory of the case.

§ 669. Unfavorable instructions.

It is sometimes advisable during the course of the arguments to the jury to take cognizance of the instructions which the court may give to the jury that are particularly favorable to opponent's case. One method usually followed is to tell the jury that the court in its instructions does not intend to give any opinion as to how the jury should decide the facts, but that the instructions given shall only be applied by them in the event they find the facts in favor of one side's theory or the other. Then counsel should point out one such instruction, and show how, under his theory of the case, that instruction will not apply, because the facts are to the contrary.

§ 670. Evidence answers every argument.

Where it is felt that the case has been proved in accordance with the law, and counsel has the opening and the closing argument, it is sometimes good policy to ask the jury to follow opponent's arguments closely and then see if the evidence that they have heard and the arguments do not conclusively answer every material point raised.

§ 671. Names rather than parties.

It is suggested to refer to parties by name rather than to designate them as plaintiff and defendant. The attorney should say, that "*John Jones,* the plaintiff on a certain day did so and so," instead of saying, "the *plaintiff* on a certain day did so and so." It is more intimate and effective, and not so legally distant.

§ 672. Exaggerated opening statement.

In those instances where opposing counsel *has overly exaggerated* his opening statement and *his evidence falls far short* in the way of proof, this method has been utilized successfully, "In counsel's opening statement he told you that he would prove so and so. . . . Did he prove it? No. He also told you that he would prove that so and so. . . . But did he prove it? No." This technique can be followed as to each fact which the defendant failed to prove.

§ 673. Framing the argument.

The first step in the preparation of the argument to the jury necessarily entails a thorough analysis of the case. The evidence should be analyzed to determine the main question or issue involved, and when once determined, that issue should become the subject of the lawyer's address to the jury.

The argument to the jury will consist of:

(1) The introduction.
(2) The issue.
(3) The picture of the cause of action.
(4) The corroboration and cumulation.
(5) The opponent's contentions.
(6) The refutation.
(7) The appeal and conclusion.

§ 674. (1) The introduction.

The introduction may consist of just a few words; it may consist of a number of sentences; or it may consist of a paragraph or two. The function of the introduction is to secure the good will of the jury towards the lawyer, the client, the cause of action, and to secure the undivided attention of the jurors. The good will towards the speaker is secured by a friendly attitude, coupled with a friendly ring in the voice. This good will should be progressively attained throughout the entire trial. The few introductory remarks may be in the nature of thanking the jury for their attention and consideration throughout the trial, or counsel may inform them of his appreciation for the careful manner in which they have followed all of the evidence.

The introduction may also include a reiteration of faith in their fairness and impartiality as stated by them during the selection of the jury, with the possible compliment to them that the attorney still feels that they will be fair and impartial to the end of the trial no matter what their verdict may be.

Sometimes attorneys commence their opening arguments with this statement, "At the opening of this trial we told you that we would prove so and so. . . . Now let us see whether or not we have proved all of these facts." Then they proceed to give a picture of the testimony proved on the trial.

§ 675. (2) The issue.

Following the introduction, the issue involved in the case should be called to their attention. If the only issue in a certain case is whether or not the defendant signed a certain agreement or a certain document, that should be the subject of the address. For illustration: Immediately after the few introductory remarks one might say: "Gentlemen of the jury, there is only one real issue in this case and only one. The question which you are called upon to decide is whether or not the defendant signed the agreement which is the basis of this law suit. If this evidence shows that he did sign it, then your verdict should be in our favor."

If there are one or two other or minor issues involved they should be stated at this time and called to the attention of the jury as being only minor.

§ 676. (3) The picture of the cause of action.

For instance, in a personal injury case, by the "picture" is meant a clear, logical "word picture" description of the scene of the accident and showing just how the accident occurred. This is done *not* by saying that the plaintiff, John Jones, *testified* that a certain thing happened on a certain day, but rather a statement to the jury somewhat to this effect, "Now gentlemen, let us see just what did happen on January 6, 1932. At about 5:00 o'clock, John Jones was driving his car west on John Street close to the intersection. Another car, a big black limousine, was speeding from a southerly direction on Blank Street. . . ." Then would be related the speed and a graphic description of the collision. If it was a question of the right of way it should be shown how the accident happened, that client had the right of way, picturing where client's car was, and that it had arrived at the intersection first, while the defendant's car was approaching from the left.

§ 677. (4) The corroboration and cumulation.

The above "word picture" description of how the accident happened and showing the right to recover should then be pointed out to the jury as being corroborated in various ways.

(a) *By the plaintiff* (or defendant as the case may be). It may be done in this way: "Now gentlemen, let us see whether or not this accident happened as we claim it did. In the first place John Jones, the plaintiff, told you that it did."

At this point a word picture should be presented to the jury of the client. Everything good that can be said about him, that will create respect for him as a man and that will add to the credence to be given to his story should be stated. His position in life, his appearance and demeanor while on the witness stand should all be commented on as showing him worthy of belief.

(b) *By the witnesses.* Here counsel would point out that client's version of the story is corroborated by a number of disinterested witnesses who have no interest in the outcome of the case and who have not been impeached. It may be stated in this manner, "One of those witnesses is James Wilson who is a . . . (build up each witness) . . . and who told you that it happened that way. Our case is further corroborated by Mrs. Anna Clark, who made such a wonderful impression while testifying and who is . . . She told you that it happened in the same way." (It is not necessary to detail, however, each witness' story. Just show that they corroborated the plaintiff.)

All further corroborating witnesses would be treated in the same manner. The lawyer will find that this procedure will carry a great deal more weight with the jury.

(c) *By the documentary evidence.* Whenever there is an exhibit or instrument admitted in evidence, which corroborates the lawyer's position in the case, that should be pointed out to the jury and read in support of the picture presented. This written or documentary evidence should be pointed out as worthy of more weight and credence than any verbal testimony of any witness, in accordance with the statement in the case of Miller v. Cotten in 5 Ga. 341 on page 349, which states as follows: "I would sooner trust the smallest slip of paper for truth than the strongest and most retentive memory ever bestowed on mortal man."

This corroboration, when presented in cumulative fashion, will build up a picture of the case in a way that will secure acceptance by the jury, and will help to secure a favorable verdict.

§ 678. (5) The opponent's contentions.

The next step in the preparation of the argument is the consideration of the opponent's contentions. The opponent's theory should be stated and analyzed.

§ 679. (6) The refutation.

It should then be pointed out to the jury that the opponent's theory is untenable, and is refuted by the law, the facts, and circumstances in the case. The improbabilities of the defendant's story, as well as the stories of his witnesses, should be shown; that it is unlikely, in view of the physical facts and the true situation as propounded by counsel, that the opponent's story can be true.

If the opponent and his witnesses, or any of them, have been impeached, that fact should be brought out as disposing of the opponent's contentions.

§ 680. (7) The appeal and conclusion.

The argument should be closed with an appeal to the jury to return a favorable verdict based upon logic, reason, and justice; that the attorney has proved his contentions under the law and under the evidence, and that he is therefore entitled to a verdict. If, in a personal injury case, the evidence discloses some basis upon which it can be indicated to the jury what is believed (*from the evidence*) the amount of the verdict should be, the conclusion and appeal should so state.

§ 681. General suggestions.

The following are some general suggestions by various writers on trial practice:

Norbert Savay in the "Art of Trial" writes:

"The proper function of the summing up is to aid the Court and the jury in arriving at a just judgment or verdict on the basis of facts. Therefore, to analyze the evidence presented by the speaker's side and to contrast this with that of the opposition is the prime requisite to this end. This analysis should include the conduct of witnesses, their relationships to the case, their bias and credibility, and the natural probability or improbability of the facts and circumstances developed at the trial. Also it may contain an explanation of any contradictions that may have occurred on the speaker's side of the case.

"Finally, the summing up may include, and frequently should, the propositions of law which tend to support the speaker's cause, such, for instance, as the principle of reasonable doubt in criminal cases.

"There are many attorneys who spend much time on the points they expect their adversary to urge against them. This is often a mistake if for no other reason than that these points are thereby unduly emphasized, and strengthened by double exposure, so to speak.

"What the jury wants is to have their doubts cleared, convictions strengthened, the weaknesses of the claim he advocates explained, its strong points brought out, and correlations established unmistakably. In a word, they want to be aided in arriving at a just verdict.

"In conclusion, there are certain things connected with the summing up that should be wholly clear to every trial lawyer wishing to excel in his craft:

"First, that an effective summing up depends primarily upon a plausible theory of the case.

"Second, that both sides of the case should be mastered thoroughly before the trial, as an essential part of the strategic course mapped out in advance.

"Third, that the salient points developed during the trial should be digested and absorbed with such thoroughness, and assimilated so completely that automatically they stand out; rising above masses of detail, to guide the speaker toward a convincing climax.

"Fourth, that before or during the trial the counsel should work out a pattern, an ascending scale punctuated with pauses, each marking a climax both of rhetoric and reason."

Hirshl in "Trial Tactics" suggests:

"As a mere matter of policy it is best to be honest with the jury for they are quick to detect sham. The fundamental principles of right and wrong that they all can understand must be adhered to. If there is an exception upon which the advocate relies he must see that the jury clearly understands it. If, for instance, he relies upon the statute of limitations he must see that the jury understands that there is reason and justice in the statute of limitations. Otherwise they will think it merely a shrewd technicality and will disregard it. . . .

"Even the lawyer with the last speech, however, must anticipate that the court is going to charge the jury, and in general what he will say. For instance an instruction is very apt to be given that preponderance of the evidence depends not alone upon the number of witnesses but upon the credibility of the witnesses and other circumstances in the case. That is a very important instruction for a lawyer who happens to have two witnesses against his opponent's six and he should not only see that it gets into the case but should argue upon it and impress upon the jury the reason why the two witnesses may be as strong as the six. The jury generally pays attention to the utterances of the court because they understand that the court is impartial and is endeavoring to do his duty to both sides. . . .

"Frequently the advice is given a lawyer to address himself to one juror, to pick out one strong man in the jury box and convince him beyond question, relying upon him to carry the other jurors. It is barely possible that this is a good plan for the defense to follow because it may result in a hung jury, but as a general rule it is not advisable for the plaintiff, for even if that one man is convinced and made the advocate with the jury it will make the other jurors jealous, feeling that they have been slighted and the chances are that it would do more harm than good. The plaintiff must have the whole twelve jurors and not one. . . .

"Care must be taken not to couple a weak argument with a strong one. If a weak argument and a strong one are joined the opponent will cast ridicule upon the weak argument to such an extent that the jury will ignore the strong one. They will forget it and in a general way get the impression that the entire speech and that side of the case are weak. If there is a good, clear strong point that and nothing else should be insisted upon and emphasized to the jury. They will take that with them into the jury room and even if the opponent has the last speech he will not be able to overcome it. But if two arguments are put in, a strong one and a weak one, the opponent will gloss over the strong one and emphasize the inaptness of the weak one until the jury will retire to the jury room with the impression that that side of the case has no argument at all. . . .

"In a will controversy the contestants may speak of the injustice of disinheriting the wife or children who have by a lifetime of assistance, of self-denial and economy aided the testator in accumulating the estate, while the proponents on the other hand may dwell upon the importance of the power of disinheriting. They will show that it stands as an inducement to the direct heirs to treat the testator kindly and properly, if not actuated by affection at least under fear of disinheritance, for filial gratitude and devotion alone are not always sufficient to insure respect and attention. . . .

"To a layman, particularly the small wage earner, the demand by a plaintiff for a brokerage "commission" of a large amount, say $50,000, especially where the negotiations were carried through in a comparatively short period seems so enormous that his mind must be thoroughly prepared in advance for a comprehension of the merits and the justice of the demand. It should be pointed out to him that a broker is not like a merchant or a professional man; that these have a somewhat steady stream of daily business, the moderate profits from which pay the current expenses and yield the net profit. But the broker, while under a similar current expense may have but an occasional success in his negotiations and long periods must intervene in which he has no income whatsoever, hence the necessity and consequently the justice of the larger compensation on the successful negotiation. Moreover, the party who benefits from the broker's efforts is in this way and this way only enabled to find a market at perhaps a very great profit for his large holdings. Unless he were through the agent to dispose of them or even to carry them further, he might be deprived of them at a ruinous sacrifice. . . .

"*When one has the intermediate speech,* he must anticipate everything that his opponent is apt to say so that the jury will have some answer to it when he does say it. In addition he must call attention to the fact that the opponent does speak last and of the great advantage that this gives him. As the great majority of humanity loves fair play the jury should be given to understand that it would have been the part of fairness for the opponent to have advanced in his first argument every proposition that he expects to advance in his last argument and that it would not be fair for him in his last speech to advance any argument to answer which no opportunity is given.

"Every phase of the case that the opponent advances should be covered. No point should be left unanswered or unprotected because sometimes a very small point that may seem trivial may have its effect upon either the whole jury or upon some member of the jury. If it is trivial its weakness should be shown.

"At all times it must be borne in mind that mere abuse is not argument, mere rhetoric is not reason, and that eloquence is not evidence. They may all be very useful but the substantial framework and foundation of the case must be argument, reason, and evidence.

"Where there is a sharp conflict of evidence the lawyer must by summary show that his own evidence is not inconsistent with the possibilities or the probabilities, or the actualities of the case. Of course that line of evidence is most convincing which is fully in accord with the conceded circumstances. Next comes the probable and last the possible.

"One of the most skillful moves in a case is to harmonize everything as much as possible. It is much easier to swim with the current than against it. So the lawyer must try to turn so much of the evidence as he can into the channel leading to his side of the case rather than try to oppose it."

Elliott in the "Work of the Advocate" has this to say:

"Where arguments are plainly irrelevant or immaterial, it is enough to direct attention to their immateriality, or irrelevancy, in a few words, and to waste no time in refuting them. When this course is resolved on, the fewer the words, and the more positive the manner in which such arguments are put aside, the better. It is often a delicate work to decide how far arguments perceived by the advocate to be wholly immaterial and totally irrelevant are supposed by the jury to be material and relevant. It must not be assumed, where there is reason for doubt, that jurors will perceive irrelevancy of the arguments; but, on the contrary, it must as a general rule, be assumed that they do not perceive the infirmity in the argument, and, acting upon this assumption, the advocate must lay bare the infirmity so that it may be clearly perceived by every juror, or at least by the 'master minds' of the jury. Men are more apt to be misled by irrelevant arguments than the careless thinker suspects. The advocate himself, if he be not wary and vigilant, is in danger of being led astray by irrelevant arguments, and drawn into a path that may lead him far from the merits of the controversy. It is always unwise to attack with severity where there is cause to believe that the argument upon the other side has made a favorable impression upon the minds of the jury. The reason why such a course is unwise is not far to seek. . . . Lord Abinger's statement of his own practice is better than a code of rules. . . . 'Very often, when the impression of the jury, and sometimes of the judge, has been against me on the conclusion of the defendant's case, I have had the good fortune to bring them entirely to adopt my conclusions. Whenever I observed this impression, but thought myself entitled to the verdict I made it a rule to treat the impression as very natural and reasonable and to acknowledge that there were circumstances which presented great difficulties and doubts, to invite a candid and temperate investigation of all the important topics that belonged to the case, and to express rather a hope than a confident opinion that upon a deliberate and calm investigation I should be able to satisfy the court and jury that the plaintiff was entitled to the verdict. I then avoided all appearance of confidence, and endeavored to place the reasoning on my part in the strongest and clearest view, and to weaken that of my adversary; to show that the facts for the plaintiff could lead naturally but to one conclusion, while those of the defendant might be accounted for on other hypotheses; and when I thought I had gained my point, I left it to the candor and good sense of the jury to draw their own conclusion. This seems to me not to be the result of any consummate art, but the plain and natural course which common sense could dictate.' "

§ 682. Right to open and close.

The right to open and close the arguments is something frequently overlooked by trial attorneys when representing the defendant. Attorneys are sometimes prone to believe that because they represent the defendant, the plaintiff has the right to make the opening and closing argument. This is not true in all instances, and the local law should be investigated in all instances where the defendant seeks to establish an affirmative defense, and in all instances where he has the burden of proof. The right to open and close is a very important one, and most attorneys seek the additional benefits to be derived from having the last word to the jury in the final and closing arguments. The right to open and close should, therefore, be requested and demanded by the attorney for the defendant in all instances where indicated.

The right to the opening and closing is a very valuable right. It is often a matter of as much consequence to a party to have the closing argument as it is to have questions of law ruled in his favor.[2]

§ 683. — In criminal cases.

In a criminal case the people are entitled to open and close arguments.[3]

2 Shugart v. Halliday, 2 Ill. App. 45.

3 State v. Novak, 109 Iowa 717, 79 N. W. 465; People v. Bundy, 295 Ill. 322.

In Texas the right to open is discretionary with court. but the State always has the right to close. Vines v. State, 31 Tex. Cr. 31, 19 S. W. 545.

§ 684. — Determination of right.

Because one is plaintiff does not establish the right to open and close.[4]

The rule is that where the plaintiff has anything to prove in order to get a verdict, whether in an action *ex contractu* or *ex delicto* and whether to establish his right of action or to fix the amount of his damages, the right to open and close belongs to him.[5]

The burden of proof is upon the party who substantially asserts the affirmative of the issue, and, as a consequence, that party is entitled to open and close, regard being had to the substance and effect of the issue rather than to the form of it.[6]

The party offering the issue has the burden of proof to establish it, and has the right to open and conclude.[7]

The test is that the party entitled to begin is he who would have a verdict against him if no evidence were given on either side.[8]

§ 685. — Defendant's right.

A defendant can only be allowed to open and close a case when the state of the pleadings is such that the plaintiff or complainant has nothing to prove in order to be entitled to a verdict.[9] And where defendant, by stipulation, admits plain-

4 Harvey v. Ellithorpe, 26 Ill. 418; Nagle v. Schnadt, 239 Ill. 595.

5 Burke v. Nat. Liberty Ins. Co., etc., 209 N. Y. S. 608, 212 App. Div. 738; Lexington, etc., Co. v. Paver, 16 Ohio 324; Producer's Oil Co. v. State, 213 S. W. 349 (Texas); Gardner v. Meeker, 169 Ill. 40.

6 Ladany v. Assad, 99 Atl. 762, 91 Conn. 316; Walsh v. West Baden Springs Co., 125 N. E. 727, 291 Ill. 34; Long, etc., Co. v. Barnes, 69 N. E. 454, 162 Ind. 22; Continental Bank, etc. v. Greene, 203 N. W. 9, 200 Iowa 568; Hurley v. O'Sullivan, 137 Mass. 86; In re Murray, 188 N. W. 381, 219 Mass. 70; Bender v. Terwilliger, 59 N. E. 118, 166 N. Y. 590; Beatty v. Hatcher, 13 Ohio St. 115; Willis & Conner v. Turner, 25 S. W. (2d) 642 (Texas).

7 Walsh v. West Baden Springs Co., 291 Ill. 35; Kells v. Davis, 57 Ill. 261.

8 McReynolds v. Burlington & O. R. Ry. Co., 106 Ill. 152; Chicago, B. & Q. Ry. Co. v. Bryan, 90 Ill. 126.

9 Razor v. Razor, 42 Ill. App. 504; Mason v. Seitz, 36 Ind. 516; Kotlowitz v. Selberstein, 144 N. Y. S. 766, 83 Misc. 82; J. W. Carter, etc. v. Bailey, 179 S. W. 547 (Texas); Convert v. Bishop, etc., 152 Ill. App. 516; Neff v. Cincinnati, 32 Ohio St. 215; Farmer v. Norton, 105 N. W. 371 (Iowa), where it was held that putting the pleadings in affirmative form will not give the defendant the right, if the effect is to merely deny plain-

tiff's *prima facie* case, he is entitled to open and close.[10] But if plaintiff, after general issue is withdrawn, has something to prove to establish his right or to show the extent of his damages, the right to open and close remains with him.[11] Where the defendant pleads in confession and avoidance and relies solely on affirmative pleas, he has the right to open and close;[12] as on plea of payment,[13] or usury,[14] or illegal consideration for note sued on.[15]

Where it is necessary for plaintiff to prove the amount of his damages he has the right to open and close.[16]

A party claiming judgment by confession to be fraudulent has right to open and close argument.[17]

§ 686. Waiver.

If party entitled to open and close wrongfully assumes that his adversary has the burden of proof and trial is so had, he waives his right.[18]

Or if the trial is conducted on the theory that the issues require proof in the first instance by the plaintiff, defendant can not insist as of right to close the argument.[19]

§ 687. —Discretion of court.

Whether a plaintiff or defendant shall have the opening is generally deemed a matter of discretion to be ordered by the judge of the trial as he may think most conducive to the ad-

tiff's allegation. See Carmody v. Kolecheski, 194 N. W. 584, 181 Wis. 394, where the court held that the party having the burden as made out by the evidence, has the right to open and close the final argument.

10 Fain v. Nelms, 113 S. W. 1002 (Tex.); Cilley v. Preferred, etc., Co., 96 N. Y. S. 282, 109 A. D. 394; Merchants Life Ins. Co. v. Treat, 98 Ill. App. 59.

11 Geringer v. Novak, 117 Ill. App. 160.

12 Silvius v. Mordoff, 192 Pac. 289, 183 Cal. 628; City Bank, etc. v. Alcorn, 176 N. W. 628, 188 Iowa 592; Swift v. Henry, etc. Co. v. Mounts, 295 S. W. 932 (Texas); American Union Line v. Oriental Nav. Corp., 192 N. Y. S. 154, 199 App. Div. 513.

Where set-off or counterclaim filed. Truesdale Mfg. Co. v. Hoyle, 39 Ill. App. 532; Schee v. McQuilken, 59 Ind. 269; Bonnell v. Jacobs, 36 Wis. 59.

13 Kent v. Mason, 79 Ill. 540.

14 Harvey v. Ellithorpe, 26 Ill. 418.

15 Gardner v. Meeker, 160 Ill. 40; Carroll v. Holmes, 24 Ill. App. 453.

16 Gardner v. Meeker, 169 Ill. 40; Geringer v. Novak, 117 Ill. App. 160.

17 Chronister v. Anderson, 73 Ill. App. 524.

18 Kassing v. Walter, 65 N. W. 832 (Iowa); Atkinson v. National Council, 193 Ill. App. 215.

19 Nagle v. Schnadt, 239 Ill. 595.

ministration of justice;[20] and error in practice would not be sufficient to reverse a judgment just in itself when a fair trial has been had upon the merits and upon proper instructions.[21] It has been held, however, in some jurisdictions, that the right does not merely rest with the discretion of the court, and a denial of the right would constitute reversible error;[22] but not where no harm results.[22a]

§ 688. —Right to make closing argument.

The right of a party litigant to address the jury by his counsel is absolute, when there is an issue to be submitted to the jury;[23] but not where the issue is of law only.[23a]

§ 689. —Purpose of reply argument.

The purpose of a reply argument is to explain or refute anything that may have been erroneously said or improperly argued by opposing counsel. Its office is simply that of a reply and it would not be proper for the counsel for plaintiff to argue the case in chief in a reply argument.[24]

§ 690. —Time limit.

It is clearly within the legal discretion of the court to limit the time for argument.[25]

20 Carpenter, et al. v. First Nat. Bank of Joliet, 119 Ill. 352; Morse v. Fuller, 164 Ill. App. 85.

21 Salt Springs Nat. Bank v. Schlosser, 171 N. E. 202, 91 Ind. App. 295; Dillie v. Lovell, 37 Ohio St. 415; Winn v. Itzel, 103 N. W. 220, 125 Wis. 19; Huddle v. Martin, 54 Ill. 258.

22 Brink's Express Co. v. Burns, 245 N. Y. S. 649, 230 App. Div. 559; Ney v. Rothe, 61 Tex. 374; Porter v. Still, 63 Miss. 357.

22a Nagle v. Schnadt, 239 Ill. 595; Salt Springs Nat. Bank v. Schlosser, 171 N. E. 202; Huntington v. Conkey, 33 Barb. 218 (N. Y.); Dille v. Lovell, 37 Ohio St. 415.

23 Lana v. Hibbard Co., 63 Ill. App. 54; Lyman v. Fidelity, etc., Co., 72 N. Y. S. 498, 65 App. Div. 27; Shippy v. Peninsula, etc., Co., 240 Pac. 785, 197 Cal. 290; Sando v. Smith, 237 Ill. App. 570.

23a Heagy v. State, 85 Ind. 260; Bradish v. Grant, 9 N. E. 332, 119 Ill. 606.

24 Creager v. Blank, 32 Ill. App. 615.

25 Bisinger v. Sacramento Lodge, etc., 203 Pac. 768, 187 Cal. 578; Miller v. Perlroth, 95 Conn. 79, 110 Atl. 535; Rehberg v. N. V., 2 N. E. 11, 99 N. Y. 652; Cornelison Motor Co. v. Morris, 30 S. W. (2d) 509 (Texas); People, etc., Co. v. Darrow, 49 N. E. 1005, 172 Ill. 162.

§ 691. Limitation on number of attorneys.

It is also discretionary with the court to limit the number of attorneys who may argue.[26]

§ 692. —Waiver of right.[27]

Under the practice in some states, the complainant may waive the opening argument if he desires; then if the defendant waives argument on his part, the case will go to the jury without any argument. But when plaintiff waives the opening and defendant makes an argument, plaintiff has the right to close, although he has made no opening argument.[28]

§ 693. —Right to interrupt improper argument.

It is the unquestionable right of counsel to interrupt an improper argument by opposing counsel for the purpose of stating his objection and moving the court to take proper action.[29] And counsel waives legal rights when he fails to make them, though at the request of the court.[30]

§ 694. —Scope of arguments—Generally.

Subject to regulation, counsel is allowed a reasonable latitude in his arguments.[31]

26 In re Gird's Est., 108 Pac. 499, 157 Cal. 534; Carruthers v. McMurray, 39 N. W. 255, 75 Ia. 173; Lovas v. Independent Breweries Co., 199 Ill. App. 60.

27 Waiver by failure to assert right. Haas v. King, 215 N. Y. S. 641, 216 App. Div. 821; Herrington v. Pouley, 26 Ill. 94.

28 Trask v. People, 151 Ill. App. 674. Contra, Jewell v. Wisconsin, etc., Co., 194 N. W. 31, 181 Wis. 56.

The court may refuse to permit the party entitled to the right to make a second argument when the opponent declines to make any argument at all. Beaver v. Emry, 149 N. E. 730, 84 Ind. App. 581; Oden v. Texas & P. Railway Co., 9 S. W. (2d) 367.

But it has been held that it is within the court's discretion so to do. Bisinger v. Sacramento Lodge, etc., 203 Pac. 768, 187 Cal. 578; Pittsburgh, etc., Railroad Co. v. Martin, 82 Ind. 476; Fred W. Albrecht Grocery Co. v. Overfield, 168 N. E. 386, 32 Ohio App. 512.

29 West Chicago St. Ry. Co. v. Sullivan, 165 Ill. 302; People v. Hamilton, 268 Ill. 390.

30 Brant v. Chicago & Alton R. R. Co., 294 Ill. 606; Roberts v. People, 226 Ill. 296.

31 Stadler v. Chicago City Railway Co., 159 Ill. App. 617; Spry v. Logansport, etc., Co., 133 N. E. 827, 191 Ind. 522; Mitchell v. Mystic Coal Co., 179 N. W. 428, 189 Ia. 1018; Suhr v. Hoover, 15 Ohio Cir. Ct. 690; O'Neill v. Larkin Carey Co., 137 Atl. 721, 106 Conn. 153; O'Neill v. Ross, 145 N. E. 60, 250 Mass. 92; Houston Ice, etc.,

Counsel should be free to argue a case, make illustrations and draw any legitimate deduction and inference from the testimony.[32] It is never allowable for counsel to state in their arguments to the jury, the facts that are not in the record.[33]

§ 695. — Matters within counsel's personal knowledge.

An attorney should not be permitted to state matters as of his own personal knowledge.[34]

§ 696. —Reading authorities.

The correct practice in civil cases is not to permit counsel to read authorities to the jury. Such a practice would be to appeal to the jury to determine what the law is, which is beyond their province, and would be calculated to render the administration of justice uncertain and should therefore not be permitted.[35]

Co. v. Harlan, 212 S. W. 779 (Texas); Andrews v. U. S. Casualty Co., 142 N. W. 487, 154 Wis. 82; Williams v. Brooklyn El. R. Co., 26 N. E. 1048, 126 N. Y. 96.

Counsel is permitted to use oratory, Bohen v. North American Life Insurance Co., etc., 177 N. W. 706, 188 Ia. 1349; or use picturesque language, Norton v. Atlantic, etc., Co., 143 Atl. 469, 83 N. H. 407; or use poetry, Colorado, etc., R. Co. v. Chiles, 114 Pac. 661, 50 Colo. 191; or shed tears. Ferguson v. Moore, 39 S. W. 341, 98 Tenn. 342.

32 All proper inferences from the evidence may be stated. Shephard v. Platt, 122 N. W. 539, 158 Mich. 181; Heard v. Heard, 272 S. W. 501 (Texas); Metz v. Yellow Cab Co., 248 Ill. App. 609; Wheeler v. Lawler, 110 N. E. 273, 222 Mass. 210; Moore v. Chicago, etc., Ry. Co., 131 N. W. 30, 151 Ia. 353; Hubb Diggs Co. v. Bell, 293 S. W. 808, 116 Tex. 427.

33 Indianapolis, etc., Co. v. Pugh, 33 N. E. 991, 6 Ind. App. 510; Menard v. Boston, etc., R. Co., 23 N. E. 214, 150 Mass. 386; Gagush v. Hoeft, 175 N. W. 170, 171 N. W. 437, 208 Mich. 147; Williams v. Brooklyn El. R. Co., 26 N. E. 1048, 126 N. Y. 96; Cincinnati Traction Co. v. McKim, 13 Ohio App. 108; Davis v. Hill, 298 S. W. 526 (Texas); Wolczek v. Public Service Co., etc., 174 N. E. 577, 342 Ill. 482; Effron, etc., Co. v. American Ry. Express Co., 193 N. W. 539, 195 Ia. 1168; Schoefer v. Fond du Lac, 80 N. W. 59, 104 Wis. 39.

34 Kenna v. Calumet, H. & S. E. R. Co., 284 Ill. 301; People v. McCann, 247 Ill. 130.

35 Chicago v. McGiven, 78 Ill. 347; Johnson v. Culver, 19 N. E. 129, 116 Ind. 278; Griebel v. Rochester Printing Co., 48 N. Y. S. 505, 24 App. Div. 288; Boltz v. Sullivan, 77 N. W. 870, 101 Wis. 608; Stone v. Com., 63 N. E. 1074, 181 Mass. 438; but, contra, Miles v. Strong, 36 Atl. 55, 68 Conn. 273; Springfield, etc., Co. v. Hubbs, etc., Co., 28 S. W. (2nd) 1088 (Texas).

§ 697. — Reference to previous trial.

Counsel should not try to get before the jury the fact that there were other trials of the cause or the number of them.[36]

It is not in order to attempt to bring before the jury the result of any former trial in the same case.[37]

§ 698. — Reference to instructions.

Counsel have the right to state to the jury the propositions of law upon which they rely, and predicate the argument upon such propositions. If this may be done, upon the same principle there is no good reason why counsel, in the argument, may not read to the jury the instructions which he intends to ask[38] and insist before the jury that such instructions contain the law involved in the case. Where this course is pursued, the attorney takes the risk of having his argument condemned by the refusal of the court to give the instructions.

It is improper for an attorney to explain the procedure of procuring instructions and that he was not going to ask for instructions or that the case was not one that needed instructions.[39]

§ 699. — Reading of pleadings.

As a general rule it is permissible to read the pleadings to the jury,[40] but there is authority to the contrary.[41]

36 Chicago Union Trac. Co. v. Lawrence, 211 Ill. 373.

37 Chicago & A. R. Co. v. Bragonier, 13 Ill. App. 467; Hennies v. Vogel, 87 Ill. 242.

38 Humbarger v. Carey, 42 N. E. 749, 44 N. E. 302, 145 Ind. 324; Southwestern, etc. v. French, 245 S. W. 997 (Texas); Boreham v. Byrne, 23 Pac. 212, 82 Cal. 23; Cayne v. Arvey, 59 N. E. 788, 189 Ill. 378.

But it is improper to comment upon the refusal of the court to give a certain instruction. Philpot v. Fifth Avenue Church, 128 N. Y. S. 35, 142 App. Div. 811.

39 Paige v. Illinois Steel Co., 233 Ill. 313; Illinois Central R. Co. v. Leiner, 202 Ill. 624.

40 Dyas v. Southern Pacific Co., 73 Pac. 972, 140 Cal. 296; Pullin v. First National Bank, 158 N. E. 579, 86 Ind. App. 473; Holmes v. Jones, 24 N. E. 701, 121 N. Y. 461; Luginbyhl v. Thompson, 11 S. W. (2nd) Pac. 380; Zeidler v. Gollyer, 195 N. W. 849.

It is improper to comment on pleadings that have been stricken, Heard v. Heard, 272 S. W. 501 (Texas); or withdrawn, Riley v. Iowa Falls, 50 N. W. 33, 83 Ia. 761; Gesualdi v. Personeni, 128 N. Y. S. 683; Moore v. Murphy, 183 Ill. App. 499; or superseded by amendement. Buhrmaster v. N. Y. C. and H. R. R. Co., 158 N. Y. S. 712, 172 App. Div. 62.

41 Locander v. Joliet, etc., Co., 225 Ill. App. 143.

§ 700. — Objections by opponent.

It is improper to comment upon opponent's objections to evidence where the objections were proper.[42]

§ 701. — Excluded evidence.

No discussion of evidence excluded should be permitted.[43]

§ 702. — Conduct of parties.

Counsel may arraign the conduct of the parties and impugn, excuse, justify, or condemn motives so far as they are developed and sustained by the evidence.[44]

§ 703. — Vouching for witnesses.

Counsel should not personally vouch for his witnesses. He has no right to throw the weight of his character and standing into the scale in favor of the witnesses on his side.[45]

§ 704. — Failure to produce witnesses.

It is permissible for counsel to comment upon the failure of opponent to bring in witnesses.[46] It is unfair for an attorney to predicate an argument on the failure to testify by a party who is incompetent as a witness, and against whom he has made an objection.[47] Counsel may properly comment

[42] Phillips v. Chase, 87 N. E. 755, 201 Mass. 444; Cleveland, etc., R. Co. v. Pritschan, 69 N. E. 663, 69 Ohio St. 438.

[43] De Lucia v. Kneeland, 142 Atl. 742, 108 Conn. 191; Anderson v. Chicago, R. I. & P. Ry. Co., 243 Ill. App. 337; Estes v. Davis, 28 S. W. (2nd) 565, 44 S. W. (2nd) 952 (Texas).

[44] Commonwealth El. Co. v. Rose, 214 Ill. 545. But improper when not sustained by the evidence, Chicago, etc., R. Co. v. American McKenna Process Co., 200 Ill. App. 166; Riggins v. Chicago, etc., Ry. Co., 186 N. W. 856, 193 Ia. 266; Scofield v. Clarke, 146 N. W. 377, 179 Mich. 681; Beville v. Jones, 11 S. W. 1128, 74 Texas 148; Manol v. Moskin, etc., Co., 233 N. W. 579, 203 Wis. 47.

[45] Appel v. Chicago City Ry. Co., 259 Ill. 561.

[46] Sesler v. Montgomery, 19 Pac. 686, 21 Pac. 185, 78 Cal. 486, 3 L. R. A. 653; Cincinnati, etc., Co. v. Gross, 114 N. E. 962, 186 Ind. 471; Dykstra v. Grand Rapids, etc., Co., 130 N. W. 320, 165 Mich. 13; Houston, etc., Co. v. Boone, 146 S. W. 533, 105 Texas 188.

Particularly when opponent fails to call his own physician, Freeman v. Vetter, 130 S. W. 190, 61 Texas C. A. 569; but not when the witness is equally accessible to both sides. Jones v. Boston, etc., Ry., 98 N. E. 506, 211 Mass. 552.

[47] Ravenscroft v. Stull, 117 N. E. 602, 280 Ill. 406.

upon the fact that party did not call an employee who has special knowledge of the matter in controversy.[48]

§ 705. — Failure to produce evidence.

It is proper to comment upon opponent's failure to produce evidence that naturally should be produced.[49]

§ 706. — Well known facts — History.

Illustrations drawn from well-known historical facts are not out of place when used merely for the purpose of explaining or emphasizing the bearings of the evidence.[50]

§ 707. — Reference to jurors by name.

Reference to jurors by name is highly improper.[51]

§ 708. — Requesting jurors to make notes prohibited.

Courts should not countenance the practice of permitting attorneys in arguing a case, to get jurors to take paper and pencil and take down his calculations of amounts and to permit such memoranda to be taken to the jury room to be used in finding their verdict.[52]

§ 709. — Appeals to passion and prejudice — Violent language.

Attorney has no right to indulge in violent or inflammatory language, for the purpose of arousing the prejudice and pas-

48 Consolidated Coal Co. of St. Louis v. Scheiber, 167 Ill. 539; Lebanon C. M. Ass'n v. Zerwick, 77 Ill. App. 486.

49 Freeman v. United Fruit Co., 111 N. E. 789, 223 Mass. 300; Stoddard v. Grand Trunk, etc., Ry. Co., 158 N. W. 7, 191 Mich. 321; Texas El. Ry. v. Gonzolis, 211 S. W. 347 (Texas); Brotherton v. Barber, etc., Co., 102 N. Y. S. 1089, 117 App. Div. 791; but not when defendant rests and offers no evidence at all. Sandberg v. Chicago Rys. Co., 191 Ill. App. 199.

50 Sanders v. People, 124 Ill. 218; Western, etc., R. Co. v. York, 58 S. E. 183, 128 Ga. 687. Reference to science and literature is permissible. Conn v. Seaboard Air Line Ry. Co., 159 S. E. 331, 201 N. C. 157. It is permissible to comment on matters of common knowledge. Pioneer, etc., Co. v. Washburn, 201 Ill. App. 361; Texas, etc., Co. v. Bell, 28 S. W. (2nd) 853 (Texas).

51 Poole v. Lamsden, 183 Ill. App. 609; Orchin v. Ft. Worth, etc., Co., 43 S. W. (2nd) 308.

52 Indianapolis & St. L. R. Co. v. Miller, 71 Ill. 463; Ettelsohn v. Kirkwood, 33 Ill. App. 103.

sions of the jury.[53] Appeals to patriotic or religious prejudice are improper.[53a]

Remarks that "the defendant spares no money, no means, nothing, to defend its cases," are objectionable.[54]

As a rule such epithets as "sham," "fake" and "frame-up" are improper.[55]

§ 710. —Personal animosity.

Counsel should suppress exhibitions of personal animosity.[56]

§ 711. —Prejudice against corporations.

Remarks attacking corporations generally in such a manner as to incite prejudice in minds of jury are improper.[57]

§ 712. —Reference to insurance.

It is highly improper for counsel to comment upon insurance or any other indemnity that the defendant may have. Whether done directly or by insinuation, it is reversible error.[58]

[53] Chicago & A. R. Co. v. Scott, 232 Ill. 419; Aydlott v. Key, etc., Co., 286 Pac. 456, 104 Cal. App. 621; U. S. Cement Co. v. Cooper, 88 N. E. 69, 172 Ind. 599.

As a rule, counsel cannot make any statements which are not sustained by the evidence, and are injected to cause prejudice, Gregory v. Rickey, 138 N. E. 669, 307 Ill. 219; Gulf, etc., Ry. Co. v. Dooley, 131 S. W. 831, 62 Texas 345; but if predicated on the evidence it may be permissible. Mohoney v. Goldblatt, 163 Ill. App. 563; Winters v. Duncan, 220 S. W. 219 (Texas).

[53a] Pantelis v. Arsht, 227 Ill. App. 488; Dowdell v. Wilcox, 21 N. W. 147, 64 Ia. 721; Solomon v. Stewart, 151 N. W. 716 (Mich.).

[54] Chicago & Joliet El. R. Co. v. Herbert, 115 Ill. App. 248.

[55] Dunham v. Chicago City Ry. Co., 178 Ill. App. 186.

[56] Hawes v. People, 129 Ill. 123.

[57] Masterson v. Chicago, etc., R. Co., 78 N. W. 757, 102 Wis. 571; Galveston, etc., R. Co. v. Kutac, 11 S. W. 127, 72 Texas 643; Aydlott v. Key, etc., Co., 286 Pac. 456, 104 Cal. 621; Quincy, G. & E. Co. v. Baumann, 203 Ill. 295.

[58] Fuller v. Darrogh, 101 Ill. App. 664; Emery Dry Goods Co. v. DeHart, 130 Ill. App. 244; Flamion v. Dawes, 169 N. E. 60, 91 Ind. App. 394; Berridge v. Pray, 210 N. W. 916, 202 Ia. 663; Tremblay v. Harden, 38 N. E. 972, 162 Mass. 383; Ritacco v. New Rochelle, City of, 168 N. Y. S. 190, 180 App. Div. 559; Morrison v. Carpenter, 146 N. W. 106, 179 Mich. 207; D. & H. Truck Line v. Lavelle, 7 S. W. (2nd) 661 (Texas).

§ 713. — Appeals to sympathy.

Appeals to sympathy are permissible when based on the facts,[59] but not otherwise.[59a]

In an action for personal injuries, it is improper for counsel for plaintiff to speak of him as a man with a wife and a large family of children.[59b]

§ 714. — Wealth or poverty of parties.

In the argument of an action for personal injury, the financial condition of the parties to the suit is not a question for the jury, and remarks of comparison in that behalf, in argument, are improper and deserving of condemnation.[60]

§ 715. — Requesting jurors to put themselves in plaintiff's place.

It is improper, particularly in personal injury suits, to ask the jurors to put themselves in plaintiff's place.[61]

A jury should not be urged to give as their verdict such a sum as might be based upon what the jury or any other man might base it, if he had sustained the damages that the plaintiff had.[62]

§ 716. — Amount of damages.

There is no valid objection to counsel, in argument, telling the jury what, under the evidence, counsel considers a fair compensation for injuries received.[63]

59 Hale v. San Bernardino, etc., Co., 106 Pac. 83, 156 Cal. 713; Mitchell v. Mystic Coal Co., 179 N. W. 428, 189 Ia. 1018.

59a McCarthy v. Spring Valley Coal Co., 83 N. E. 957, 232 Ill. 473; West Texas Utility Co. v. Penner, 53 S. W. (2d) 451 (Texas); American, etc., Co. v. Pierce, 18 Ohio Cir. Ct. (N. S.) 278.

59b McCarthy v. Spring Valley Coal Co., 232 Ill. 473.

60 Monmouth v. Erling, 148 Ill. 521; Perez v. Wilson, 260 Pac. 838, 86 Cal. App. 288; Appel v. Chicago City Ry. Co., 102 N. E. 1021, 259 Ill. 561; Walsh v. Frankenthaler, 173 N. Y. S. 764, 186 App. Div. 62; Urbanowicz v. Roman, 18 Ohio Cir. Ct. (N. S.) 61; Smith v. Jennings, 80 N. W. 236, 121 Mich. 393.

61 Gungrich v. Anderson, 155 N. W. 379, 189 Mich. 144; Larson v. Hanson, 242 N. W. 184 (Wis.); Eagle Star, etc., Co. v. Head, 47 S. W. (2d) 625 (Texas); Thomas v. Illinois Power & Light Corp., 247 Ill. App. 378.

62 West Chicago St. Ry. Co. v. Dedloff, 92 Ill. App. 547.

63 Ledwell v. Chicago City Ry. Co., 160 Ill. App. 596; International, etc., Ry. Co. v. Jones, 175 S. W. 488 (Texas).

§ 717. — Comments as to the law.

Counsel may state the position of the law he relies upon.[64] It is the privilege of counsel to state what he believes the law to be and to base arguments thereon.[65]

§ 718. — Retaliatory remarks.

A party can have no just ground of complaint on account of improper remarks which have been used in reply to like remarks on his side. The law does not permit him to avail of errors of his own creation.[66]

§ 719. — Arguments in suit on insurance policy.

Plaintiff's opening argument

"May it please the Court and Gentlemen of the Jury:

Everyone connected with this case, including the parties and the attorneys, must appreciate the close attention you have paid to all of the witnesses and the evidence as it has been presented before you. From the close consideration you have given to all of the testimony, I am sure you are in a position to render a proper verdict without the aid of arguments from either counsel or myself. Personally, I would be content to submit this matter to you without any further argument were it not for the fact that client might feel that I had not fulfilled my entire duty toward him. Part of my duty in this case, of course, is to give you my analysis of the evidence to assist you as best I can in arriving at a verdict. May I, then, for this purpose ask you kindly to follow the arguments for just a little while longer. I would appreciate it also if you will grant opposing counsel the same consideration. Then see whether or not his every argument and con-

64 Hardy v. Schermer, 124 Pac. 993, 163 Cal. 272; Rose v. Chicago City R. Co., 199 Ill. App. 600; U. S. Fidelity & Guaranty Co. v. Poetker, 102 N. E. 372, 180 Ind. 255, L. R. A. 1917 B 984; Terrill v. Michigan, etc., Co., 183 N. W. 46, 214 Mich. 478; American, etc., Co. v. Maynahan, 36 S. W. (2d) 555 (Texas).

65 Voche v. City of Chicago, 208 Ill. 192.

66 Kenna v. Calumet, H. & S. E. R. Co., 284 Ill. 301; Lawton v. Oglesby Coal Co., 154 Ill. App. 368; Wallden v. Market St. Ry. Co., 9 Pac. (2d) 602 (California); Chase v. Boston El. R. Co., 122 N. E. 174, 232 Mass. 133; Paschal v. Owen, 14 S. W. 203, 77 Tex. 583.

tention is refuted by the evidence in this case. I am sure you will agree that it is and return a verdict in favor of the plaintiff.

Now let us see just what the issues are in this case. Suppose we consider first all of the admitted and non-disputed facts. First, it has been admitted and the evidence shows that a burglary insurance policy was issued on March 4th, 1932 by the Blank Insurance Co. to Howard Wright, the plaintiff in this case. It is undisputed that the premium of $96.88 has been paid. There is no serious claim made but that Howard Wright had a burglary at his home April 5, 1932 and lost clothing and jewelry amounting to $2,150.00. We do not dispute the fact that he had a prior burglary loss about a month before he took out this policy. There is also no doubt but what the policy in this case states that he had had no prior losses but the testimony shows that Howard Wright did not know that provision was in the policy. The proof also shows that he never read the policy until after the burglary occurred.

That brings us down to the main issues in this case. The main issues are two; the first one is — Did the Blank Insurance Co. through its duly authorized agents, have knowledge of Howard Wright's prior loss? If they did have this knowledge *before* the policy was issued, then they are liable under this policy for the loss sustained. The second issue is — Did the Blank Insurance Co. have knowledge of the prior loss *after* the policy was issued and did they do anything to waive their right to avoid liability under the policy? In other words, did the Insurance Company do anything after they learned Howard Wright had a prior burglary loss to indicate that they did not intend to deny liability under the policy on that ground. If they did, and you so find from the evidence, then your verdict must be for the plaintiff.

Let us consider the first of these issues in the light of all the evidence in this case.

In February 1932 Howard Wright's home was burglarized. Jack Simpson, an insurance agent, heard of Howard Wright's loss and solicited him to purchase some burglary insurance. He convinced Mr. Wright to take out the insurance policy sued on in this case. Howard Wright had explained all about this prior loss to Jack Simpson. He ordered the insurance and several days later the policy was delivered. Howard Wright took the policy but did not read it. He assumed that Jack Simpson had given this company all information as to his prior loss. He had a right, under the law to assume that Jack Simpson had done everything he should have done. He assumed, as he had a right to assume, that Jack Simpson was the direct agent of the Blank Insurance Co. Simpson delivered the policy, received the report of the loss sued on and also collected the premium. As far as Howard Wright is concerned, he believed that Simpson was the agent of the Blank Insurance Co. He knew nothing to the contrary until this loss occurred.

I am going to leave it to you, as men of business experience, whether he should have done anything further—whether he did not have full right to feel that he was doing business with an agent of the Blank Insurance Co.

After the loss, for the first time, Simpson brought Jackson over. He told Wright that he had placed the insurance through Jackson and that Jackson was the real agent. Now it turns out that Jackson placed the insurance through a third party.

It is our contention that as far as we are concerned Simpson was the direct agent of the company—that he had knowledge of our prior loss and that as to us the Insurance Company is liable under this policy.

The next issue and probably the most important one in this case is whether the insurance company has waived its right to deny liability on account of this prior loss. If this evidence shows, as it does, that after the insurance company learned of the prior loss it did anything to indicate they intended to overlook the fact that Howard Wright had a prior loss, then under the law it will be presumed they have waived their right to deny liability on that ground.

I believe the Court will instruct you that under the law waiver can be shown in many ways—and that an insurance company or anyone else can waive almost any defense they may have if they desire to do so. I believe you will also be instructed that if an insurance company or anyone else once waives its rights, it cannot later retract the waiver. I believe you will also find, under the instructions of the Court, that it is not necessary for the defendant to state or indicate specifically that it expressly waives its rights under an insurance policy. The waiver is absolute under the law if by its conduct it does anything which will amount legally to a waiver. In other words, the defendant may say that the company did not waive its rights, yet, if under the law this evidence shows that it did, you are justified in finding that it did.

Let me make one further observation in reference to the law. Under the law, as I believe, the Court will give it to you in his instructions, an attempted cancellation by an insurance company after a loss has been sustained recognizes the fact that the policy has been in force legally until the date of the attempted cancellation. In other words, if this defendant had a right to cancel this policy on the grounds of Howard Wright's prior loss at the time they learned of it, they should have cancelled the policy on that ground at once. If after learning of the prior loss they failed to cancel the policy or went right ahead considering the policy in full force and effect, under the law, it will be held that the defendant has waived all of its claims as to the prior loss.

Now let us review the evidence in reference to the issue of waiver. On April 18, 1932, Howard Wright and his wife went to the office of Peter Borg, the insurance adjuster to deliver the various duplicate paid bills demanded by Borg. These bills covered all of the important items of jewelry and clothing that were stolen in this burglary. When Borg looked over the bills he told Wright that all of the items seemed to have been purchased during the month of February, 1932. He said 'that's funny, how does it happen that all of the clothing is practically new.' Howard Wright said, 'Why, I had to purchase everything new after my other burglary.' Borg wanted to know when they had the other burglary. Wright told him about a month before he took out the insurance policy. Borg looked at Wright's policy. He then threw the policy at Wright and told him 'you have no claim. The policy states that you had no prior losses and you just admitted that you did have a prior loss. The company does not have to pay you anything.' Wright looked at the policy also and said, 'I don't understand how the policy can state that, your agent, Simpson, knew I had this other burglary, I told him all about it. I never read the policy. If he put it in this way it is his fault.'

Now if the company had cancelled the policy then and there, the only question you would have to decide is whether or not Simpson was the agent of the defendant, actually or apparently, so that his knowledge of the prior loss would also be the legal knowledge of the Blank Insurance Co.. But that is not all that happened. The insurance company did not cancel the policy but several days later on April 23rd, 1932 they accepted the full premium of $96.88. Instead of refusing the whole premium they accepted the entire amount due. This in itself was a clear indication that they considered the policy was in full force and effect. All this took place after Borg had found out that Howard Wright had suffered a prior loss. This would constitute a waiver. However that was not all that showed the company intended to overlook the prior loss. On June 16th, 1932, three months later, the defendant, through its general agent sent a letter to Howard Wright which clearly proves the waiver. This letter which is very important is marked Plaintiff's Exhibit 13. You will want to consider it fully when you are deliberating in the jury room. Let me read it to you:

'Dear Sir: This corporation hereby notifies you that it elects to cancel its policy No. 4399 in accordance with the terms and conditions therein provided. Said policy was issued to you through its Agency at Chicago, Illinois.

In accordance with the conditions referred to all liability of this corporation under this policy will cease and terminate at the expiration of five days from the receipt by you hereof. Check for Return premium of *$67.15* is enclosed.

Yours very truly'

You will notice that there is not one word in this letter with reference to a prior loss. There is nothing to indicate in the letter three months after the Company received knowledge of the fact that Howard Wright had had a prior loss, that they were cancelling the policy on that ground. There was not one word heard from the Company during these three months to indicate in any way that they expected to take advantage of their rights under the policy because of this prior loss. Their entire attitude as well as this particular letter shows that they considered the policy in full force and effect from the date of its issuance until the date of cancellation which was on June 21, 1932. One very important and significant fact in this letter is the return premium of $67.15. Instead of claiming that the policy was void from its inception because of the fact that the plaintiff had suffered a prior loss *they returned only part of the premium,* that is the unexpired portion from June 21st on. The full premium was $96.88. This clearly indicates again that the Company considered the policy in full force and effect from the date of its issuance and also indicates a legal waiver on their part now to declare the policy cancelled and void because of such prior loss. You will remember, of course, that this loss took place on April 5, 1932; just about two weeks later on April 18, 1932 the Insurance Company through Peter Borg had full knowledge as to the prior loss. Having this knowledge they did nothing about it until June 21, 1932 and then they did not cancel the policy on the grounds of the prior loss but cancelled it at their option under their policy as to the future. That is, from June 21, 1932 to March 3, 1933. This letter, which is marked Plaintiff's Exhibit 13 is dated June 16th, 1932 corroborating the theory of the plaintiff that the defendant waived its rights to deny liability under the policy by reason of Howard Wright's prior loss. This is further corroborated by the partial return of premium and further by the Company's failure to return the entire premium from April 18, 1932 almost down to the date of this trial. Of course, gentlemen, the defendant contends in this case that he rescinded the policy on April 18, 1932 and that having rescinded it at that time, anything that occurred thereafter would have no legal effect. Now that is the defendant's contention but it is completely refuted by all of the evidence and the circumstances in this case. Borg, when cross-examined at the beginning of the trial under the statute, never mentioned one word about rescinding the contract or making a tender of the entire premium of $96.88. However, after we filed the amended complaint during the course of the trial alleging a waiver of the right of the defendant to deny liability, then, for the first time, Mr. Borg decided that he had rescinded the contract on April 18, 1932 and had tendered the sum of $96.88 back to Howard Wright. Borg evidently considered it all so important that he even brought in his assistant to swear to the same thing. However, both Borg and Hoeger have been impeached and discredited by the documentary evidence in this case, including Defendant's Exhibits A and B, which you will take with you to the Jury room and examine. Gentlemen, from all of the facts, from all of the evidence in this case, from a consideration of all of the witnesses that we have heard, there is only one conclusion that you can arrive at and that is a verdict in favor of the plaintiff in the sum of $2,150.00.

Thank you.''

Defendant's argument

''May it please the Court and Gentlemen of the Jury:

I also wish to express my appreciation for the close attention you have paid throughout this entire case. We, for the defense, are just as confident now as we were at the beginning of the trial that you could and would return a favorable and just verdict in this case and no matter what your verdict will be at the conclusion of the trial, we will still feel that your verdict represents your honest opinion based upon the law and the evidence in this case.

Counsel for the plaintiff has told you that the issue in the case is whether or not we have waived our right to deny liability by reason of the false statement in reference to prior losses of the plaintiff and also that another issue is whether or not Simpson was our agent in this transaction. In so far as the question of agency is concerned there can be no issue on that question. This evidence shows conclusively that Simpson was not our agent but was the agent of the plaintiff. The issue as to waiver is not the true issue in this case but the true issue is whether or not the defendant rescinded the policy of insurance on April 18, 1932 and made a tender of the premium.

On the statement of counsel as to the agency of Simpson, let us consider the evidence. In the first place there has been no evidence whatever to the effect that Simpson was ever the agent of the Blank Insurance Company. On the contrary, the evidence shows that Simpson is a general insurance broker, having absolutely no direct connection with us at all. The evidence shows that Simpson had written an insurance policy for the plaintiff in a different company before the one in question; that the plaintiff was recommended to Simpson by Golden, the furrier, who made the fur coat for Mrs. Wright. The plaintiff called Simpson in reference to the policy and asked him to secure coverage for him against burglary. Now, this would make Simpson the plaintiff's agent. You want to remember, gentlemen, that the plaintiff in this case has been in the insurance business for twenty-two years. He knows the difference between a direct agent for an insurance company and a general insurance broker. From his experience and knowledge in the insurance business he knew, or should have known, that Simpson was a general insurance broker and not a direct agent of this company.

The plaintiff claims that by reason of the fact that Simpson got part of the commission and delivered the policy and received payment of the premium, that that would make Simpson our agent but I am sure the Court will instruct you that under the law this fact would not make Simpson our agent. The evidence also shows that, Simpson was not only *not* our agent but the man through whom he placed this order for insurance was also not our agent. Simpson gave this order to Harry Jackson and he, in turn, placed it with Julius Frenz, who did have some connection with our Company. Frenz testified that he was told nothing whatever about any prior loss, that on the contrary, he was told there had been no prior losses. Jackson has not testified; for some reason or other the plaintiff has failed to produce him. Simpson said he knew of the prior losses and had told Jackson but he also admitted that he knew Jackson had no connection with our company. Frenz was the only agent we had and he testified that Jackson told him nothing whatever about any prior losses. The very fact that it required three different persons to place this insurance policy shows conclusively to any man of reasonable intelligence that the plaintiff was unable to place this policy of insurance with anybody as long as his agents made known to the companies the fact of this prior loss. You know as well as I do that after making three attempts somebody in the chain decided to tell the company's representative that there had been no losses and that is how the policy came to be issued by us. I am sure that after you have heard the instructions of the Court and considered the evidence offered by the plaintiff with reference to what they claim is the agency of Simpson you can arrive at only one conclusion and that is that Simpson was *not* the agent of the Blank Insurance Company in this case and that even if he did have knowledge of a prior loss that that knowledge was not repeated to this defendant.

Now why is the plaintiff so interested in proving, or in trying to prove that Simpson was our agent. Because under the law, as I believe the Court will instruct you, a false statement as to prior losses will avoid liability on our part under the policy. There can be no doubt in this case, under the evidence, but what the plaintiff suffered not only one prior loss but two, a burglary just a month before of his home and two months before the issuance of this policy he suffered another loss of theft of clothing from his automobile. As an insurance man, he knew that a declaration of these prior losses would in all probability prevent him from getting this insurance. I say that he knew, or should have known, this, and if he did not know it then his agents in trying to place this policy soon learned that this was true and the fact that they went in such a round about method in securing this policy and finally made false statements as to prior losses, proves this point.

The real issue in this case, gentlemen, is the fact of having suffered the prior losses and that Peter Borg for the company rescinded the insurance policy on April 18, 1932. We do not have to spend any time as to the fact of prior losses because they have been admitted by the plaintiff. There can be no question in your mind but that we did not know anything about any prior loss until the conversation between Howard Wright and Peter Borg when the plaintiff presented the bills for clothing and jewelry which he claimed were lost. Peter Borg was quite surprised when he looked at the bills to see that they were all dated approximately a month before the policy of the insurance was issued. This to him, as an adjuster, of course, was suspicious so he asked the plaintiff how it happened and then much to his surprise the plaintiff admitted having had a prior burglary about a month before the policy was issued. Borg immediately looked at the policy and saw the statement that the applicant claimed to have sustained no prior losses. He immediately disclaimed liability and as an adjuster of many years' experience, he immediately rescinded the policy and tendered back to the plaintiff the premium he had paid, namely, $96.88. The fact of this rescission and the tender has been corroborated by the witness Hoeger in every detail as to what happened on that occasion but the plaintiff now denies that Borg rescinded the contract or made a tender of the full payment.

You have seen Peter Borg on the witness stand, you know that he has been in the business for a long time, and you know that he would appreciate the importance of rescinding the policy and making the tender when he learned of the false statement as to prior losses. Do you believe for one instant that with his background, with his experience and with his knowledge of insurance law that he would have done anything other than what he has sworn to you under oath that he did? It was the only natural thing for him to do. When the plaintiff tells you that Borg did everything he said he did with the one exception of rescinding the contract and making the tender you can be sure that the rest of it happened also. The plaintiff is also an insurance man. He is financially interested in the outcome of this case and naturally would deny the rescission and the tender. He knows that he must deny it in an effort to get a verdict here. Gentlemen: there can be no question whatever but what Peter Borg rescinded the policy on April 18, 1932 and made a tender of the $96.88. In rescinding the contract and in making this tender he absolutely absolved, as he had a right to do, this company from any liability. The false statement in reference to prior loss was made by either the plaintiff himself or his agents and being so made he must suffer the consequences.

The plaintiff tells you that he never read his policy in this case. Can you believe that any man who has been in the insurance business for twenty-two years who is repeatedly and continuously telling others that they must read their insurance policy, can you believe for one moment that any such man would fail to read his policy? You know and I know that he either read this policy or if he did not, as an insurance man he knows, he will be bound by the terms and provisions thereof. This is also another feature of the case that becomes important to the plaintiff. He knows from his experience that if he would admit having seen the policy or the contents he would be precluded from recovering in this case. So when the fact of the prior loss becomes known to us, he decides that he never read the policy. I am sure that you will not give much credence to any such claim by a man having twenty-two years of experience in insurance matters.

Since the commencement of the trial a most interesting and peculiar thing happened. After most of the evidence was in, counsel for the plaintiff suddenly realized that he had no case and as an afterthought amended his complaint by setting out a claim of waiver of our right to avoid liability on the ground of false statements. The plaintiff in this case, after attempting to prove the agency of Simpson and absolutely failing to do so then decided to try to recover in this case on the ground of waiver. I am sure, however, that this last minute procedure on their part will prove unavailing. They are basing their claim of waiver on the letter of June 16, 1932. This letter as has been shown to you by the evidence was sent out by mistake. It can have no legal effect because Peter Borg on April 18, 1932 had already rescinded the policy in this case and had made a tender of the premium. Whatever happened after that could have no legal effect on the question of waiver. When the policy has been once rescinded and the tender made, that ends the liability of the company once and for all. A subsequent letter which was sent out by mistake could not revive the policy in any way. I believe the Court will instruct you that if you find from the evidence that the policy was rescinded on April 18, 1932 and a tender of the premium made, that the subsequent letter can do nothing towards reviving any liability.

Gentlemen, we are sure that you will not permit the plaintiff to blow hot and blow cold. Their original claim here was that Simpson was our agent and knew of the prior loss. They have practically abandoned that claim as this evidence shows they must. Now, as an afterthought, they are depending upon a claimed legal waiver. But the proof does not sustain any such afterthought. They must prove such claim by a preponderance of the evidence and they have failed to do so. They are basing this last claim and their last hope on a letter which was sent out by mistake. I am sure you will not permit them to take advantage of the situation but will return a verdict in favor of this defendant.

Thank you."

Plaintiff's closing argument

"May it please the Court, Counsel for the defense and Gentlemen of the Jury:

The defendant in this case claims that the real issue here is the question of rescission and the tender of the premium. While we insist, that is not the real issue, we are prepared to meet him even on this ground.

Every bit of credible evidence in this case conclusively proves that Peter Borg did not rescind the policy of insurance on April 18, 1932 and did not tender to Howard Wright the sum of $96.88 on that day. If this evidence proves, as it does, that Peter Borg did not rescind the policy on April 18th and that he did not make the tender of the money, then there is absolutely nothing left for the defendant to stand on because counsel based his whole argument and claim on such supposed rescission and tender. Of course, Peter Borg says that he did rescind it and that he did make a tender and, of course, Hoeger states almost the same, but every other detail of this evidence, almost every other statement of Peter Borg himself shows that he did not rescind and did not make a tender. It was very fortunate for us in this case that the statute makes provisions for the examination of the agents of the defendant at the beginning of the trial and that such examination is to be conducted as though the agent was under cross-examination. It was also particularly fortunate for the plaintiff that we did not amend our complaint until after Peter Borg had been examined first. It is quite easy to see what would have happened if we had amended our complaint on the grounds of waiver before Peter Borg testified. You know what did happen. You heard him testify when he was put on the stand later by the defendant, when he began to realize the importance and the necessity for claiming that a rescission and a tender had been made on April 18, 1932.

When we filed the amended complaint claiming waiver, then, for the first time Peter Borg remembered that he had rescinded the policy and made a tender of the premium on April 18, 1932. But, what did he say when he was examined by me at the beginning of the trial. You will remember that I asked him this question:

'Have you that money in court?'

The answer was

'No Sir.'

The next question was

'You have not tendered it to us or rescinded the policy?'

Answer

'We would be glad to if you would like it.'

Question

'But you have not done so as yet?'

Answer

"No Sir."

Now, when was Peter Borg telling the truth—at the beginning of the trial or after we filed our amended complaint alleging waiver. He was under oath both times. Can you imagine a man of his experience—18 years as an insurance adjuster, who admitted under cross-examination that he realized the importance of rescinding the policy as well as the legal significance of a tender on April 18, 1932 failing to tell you about rescinding that policy if he did so on April 18th. Not only did he realize it then but he more *forcibly* realized it after we filed our amended complaint alleging waiver. No man of his experience, with the realization of the importance and legal effect of the rescission and tender, would have failed to have made known such fact when he was cross-examined by me at the beginning of the trial, but he did not say a word about the tender at that time. Later in the trial he told you that he had planned that meeting with Mr. Wright for the express purpose of rescinding that policy of insurance. If that were true, he surely would have told you about it at the beginning of the trial. However, this evidence shows that even that statement is not true, because his assistant Hoeger said that as far as he knew that meeting had not been planned for the purpose of rescinding the policy. There can be no question, Gentlemen, but that Peter Borg did not rescind the policy on April 18.

Peter Borg did not make a tender to Howard Wright of the sum of $96.88. This is further proved by two other very important pieces of evidence in this case. Every lawyer sooner or later comes to realize that it is some written document that proves or discredits the oral statements made by some witnesses. As one judge stated, he 'would rather trust the smallest slip of paper for truth than the strongest and most retentive memory ever bestowed on mortal man.' So, if you will look over all the documentary evidence in this case you will not find one word tending to prove the fact that Peter Borg rescinded the policy or made the tender in April, 1932. On the contrary, everything in this case shows that he did not rescind or make the tender. In the letter of June 16, 1932 not one word of rescission is mentioned nor is there a word with reference to the fact that a full and complete tender of $96.88 had been made. On the contrary, they return a check for a part of the premium in the sum of $67.15.

Now counsel tells you that that letter of June 16, 1932 was sent out by mistake and Peter Borg claims that he had no knowledge that that letter was sent out until the trial of this case. Now let us see whether that is true.

Defendant's Exhibit 1 which they put into evidence themselves is dated October 14, 1932 and purports to set out a list of the various pieces of money which Peter Borg tendered to Howard Wright. Peter Borg told you that he prepared that instrument in his own office. Now you will recall that he swore under oath that he did not know that the letter of June 16 had been sent out.

Let us refer to this Defendant's Exhibit 1 and we find at the bottom the following words:

'Received of Blank Insurance Corporation Limited by its agent, Peter Borg the above captioned currency, being return premium on policy *which was cancelled, as of June 21, 1932.'*

Can you now say that Peter Borg did not know of the letter sent out under date of June 16, 1932? Do you believe that he could now take the stand and in the face of this written instrument prepared by himself claim that he did not know of that prior letter?

In the face of all of this how can you give any credence whatever to the statements of Peter Borg? In the face of all of this what happens to the issue of rescission? There is none. The main issue is that of waiver. The attempted cancellation, the failure to set out a denial of liability on the grounds of such prior loss, the long time that intervened since knowledge of the prior loss came to the defendant show conclusively that we are entitled to a verdict at your hands.

May I make this one closing observation which I forgot to mention? Another conclusive fact proving that Peter Borg made no tender on April 18, 1932 is that the premium was not even paid by Howard Wright until April 23, 1932 as shown by the check which has been introduced here as Plaintiff's Exhibit 4. How could Peter Borg make a tender of a premium before he had even received it? Gentlemen, every fact, every circumstance, every bit of credible evidence in this case shrieks aloud the defendant's guilt. The damages have been proved, common sense and justice argue that we are entitled to a verdict and we ask you to return a verdict in favor of the plaintiff for the sum of $2,150.00. Thank you."

§ 720. — Arguments in suit against husband for jewelry sold to wife as necessaries.

Opening argument for the plaintiff

"May it please the Court and Gentlemen of the Jury:

At the completion of all this evidence you must be wondering, as I am wondering, just what the defense is in this case. Defendant's counsel failed to tell you what he expected to prove in his opening statement. Now we can see just why he waived his opening statement. Not only did he fail to tell you what he expected to prove, but he has also failed to prove anything throughout the trial of this case. He has not offered one witness. He has failed to even produce the defendant. It is quite easy to understand counsel's failure, because this evidence shows conclusively that they have no defense.

In my opening statement, I told you what we expected to prove. Now let us see whether or not we have proved our right to a verdict against the defendant, James N. Stanley, for the sum of $16,738.50.

The questions presented in this case are threefold—first, does the jewelry purchased by Mrs. Stanley come within the class known as necessaries;—second, did James Stanley know of the purchase, and did he expressly authorize its purchase; third, if he did not learn of its purchase at the time, did he ratify the purchase subsequently and is therefore estopped from questioning Mrs. Stanley's authority to buy the jewelry?

If you can, from this evidence, answer any of the three questions in the affirmative, your verdict must be for the plaintiff.

The first thing that you will have to decide in this case is whether or not the jewelry purchased by Mrs. James N. Stanley were necessaries. I believe the Court will instruct you that the term 'necessaries' is not confined merely to what is requisite barely to support life, but includes many of the conveniences of refined society. It is a relative term which must be applied to the circumstances and conditions of the parties.

It will be a question for you to decide from this evidence as to whether or not the wife of the defendant, from his station in life, would be permitted to purchase jewelry of the type and price involved in this case. I believe the Court will further instruct you that when a wife is living with her husband, it is presumed that she has his assent to pledge his credit for necessaries. The evidence in this case conclusively shows that James Stanley is now engaged in business from which he makes a large profit; that he owns large tracts of timber land, manufactures lumber, owns railroad property, as well as stocks and bonds of various kinds, of a value of more than two and one-half million dollars. It is admitted by the attorney for the defendant that this situation is true. So, we start in this case with a man, who is a millionaire twice over, who maintains homes in Chicago and in Miami, Florida, has three or four automobiles, who provides automobiles for his caretaker and for his employees; who, in 1926, provided his wife with $1,000.00 a month for her personal expenses; who, in 1927, gave her for her personal expenses $19,000.00, in 1928, $18,500.00, and the same amount in 1929. He provided her, in addition thereto, with an automobile; in 1926 he gave his wife an emerald and diamond bracelet costing $8,550.00, and a year later he reset this bracelet at an additional cost of $8,500.00. In May, 1927, he gave his wife a diamond ring worth, with the setting, $23,800.00. This evidence of wealth coupled with the evidence that they moved in the highest type of society and taking into consideration the gifts which the defendant presented to his wife, how can any reasonable man claim that the purchase of these two bracelets in April, 1928, one for $9,500 and the other for $12,500.00, was not necessaries, that they were not the type of jewelry to which Mrs. Stanley was accustomed. There can be no question whatever in your minds, gentlemen, that these purchases of jewelry, in addition to the one on October 14th of a brooch for $6,500.00, were all within the means of the defendant, and were not unusual. There can also be no question and there has been no denial, but that Mrs. Stanley was living with her husband at the time she purchased these articles of jewelry. Being so married, under the law she had a right to pledge the credit of the husband to the plaintiffs in this case, and the plaintiffs had a right to assume the defendant's consent to his wife's pledging of his credit.

The defendant claims that he did not know that his wife had purchased these articles of jewelry, but everything in the case shows that he did. The defendant came to New York shortly after his wife had purchased these jewels. He saw her wearing them; he must have known she had them. He knew she did not have them before. He has not taken the stand, nor seen fit to appear here to deny that he knew his wife had purchased these articles of jewelry. Gentlemen, you know and I know that if there had not been domestic difficulties between James Stanley and his wife there would be no question about this bill. He would have paid it in the regular course of business.

This evidence shows that he did know of these purchases, because he made payments on account of this balance on several occasions. His man, John P. Gregg, testified that he had discussed the payments on account of this bill with the defendant, and the defendant, James Stanley, personally signed one or two of the checks. The other was signed by John P. Gregg for and in behalf of the defendant. Statements were rendered regularly, and then another payment was made by check, signed by James Stanley. How can any reasonable man claim that James Stanley had no knowledge of these purchases?

The defendant's knowledge of these purchases is further established by the fact that he later took out an insurance policy covering articles of jewelry which included the three items involved in this suit. The insurance policy was taken out by John P. Gregg upon the express authorization of James Stanley. His knowledge of the purchase is further proved by the statements of his estranged wife, Mrs. Nellie Stanley. She told you under oath that she had discussed the purchase of the bracelet and the brooch with her husband before the deal was consummated. She had told him about it over the telephone, and requested his permission to purchase these as a birthday gift. Stanley must have seen his wife wearing these bracelets and the brooch for many months thereafter, and he has ratified the purchase of them by Mrs. Stanley. The fact that he has made payments on this account, the fact that they were necessaries in view of the position and station in life of Mrs. Stanley, the fact that it was upon the direct authorization of the defendant to her to purchase it and the defendant's failure to appear here to deny his liability, shows that we are entitled to a verdict in favor of the plaintiff in the sum of $16,738.50. Thank you."

Argument for the defendant

"May it please the Court, Counsel for the plaintiff and Gentlemen of the Jury:

The attorney for the plaintiff has placed a great deal of stress on the fact that the defendant is not present in court and that we have not offered any witnesses in his behalf. This case from the view point of the defendant requires no witnesses. Our complete defense has been proved by the plaintiff's witnesses. Therefore, there is no necessity for any witnesses on the part of the defense. This is a plain open and shut case. The testimony of the plaintiff shows without doubt that the defendant is not liable. The issue here is not whether the jewelry were necessaries; it is not whether there was direct authority to purchase; it is not whether there was ratification and estoppel. The main question involved in this case is to whom was the credit extended. That is the main issue. Gentlemen, the credit in this case was extended to Mrs. Nellie Stanley and not to the defendant.

Everything in this case corroborates the defendant's contention that E. M. Grey & Co. sold this jewelry to Mrs. Stanley, and extended the credit to her exclusively. Now, when trouble arises between Mr. & Mrs. Stanley, for some reason or another, they are resorting to the second best guess, and are attempting to collect from Mr. Stanley. The original invoice was made out to Mrs. Nellie Stanley. The jewelry was purchased by Mrs. Stanley; no question was ever raised by the plaintiff or any of the representatives in reference to extending credit to Mr. Stanley. All letters asking for payments on this account were originally addressed to Mrs. Stanley. Even the payments that were made by Mr. Stanley were made by and for and on account of Mrs. Stanley. The books of account of the plaintiff were all carried in the name of Mrs. Nellie Stanley. Where is there anything in this case, until the domestic difficulties appeared, to show that the plaintiff was extending credit to Mr. Stanley and not to Mrs. Stanley? Counsel for the plaintiff cannot point to one single item during the entire discussion of this transaction to show that the plaintiff was looking to the defendant, James Stanley, for payment of this account.

Plaintiff's Exhibit 1 in evidence, the original invoice dated April 8, 1928 reads as follows:

'Mrs. Nellie Stanley to E. M. Grey & Co., Debtor
April 5, 1928.
Bracelet $9,500
Bracelet 12,500'

At that time Mrs. Stanley also turned in for credit on this original purchase, a bracelet valued at $4,000. This certainly was not turned in by Mr. Stanley, nor had he any knowledge of it. The letter of August 8, 1928 acknowledging the payment of $2,000 signed by the plaintiff in this case reads as follows:

'Mrs. Nellie Stanley,
Chicago, Ill.

Dear Mrs. Stanley:

We hereby acknowledge receipt of check for $1,000 which has been credited to your account, with thanks.' At this point, let me say a few words with reference to the insurance to which counsel has called attention. He says that

Mr. Stanley took out that insurance. Certainly he did, but how does the insurance run. This policy covers James Stanley and/or Nellie Stanley. This was a double barreled policy covering either or both, and the jewelry listed and purchased by Mrs. Stanley would be covered in her name only.

There has been no proof that the plaintiff knew as a fact that Mrs. Stanley was married to James Stanley. They merely took her word for it, and apparently were not concerned with the credit of Mr. Stanley. They made no inquiry of him as to whether or not he would consent to this purchase by his wife. They made no inquiry to determine whether or not she had more than sufficient jewelry. They made no effort to ascertain whether she was acting as Mr. Stanley's agent in the transaction, but apparently took it for granted that her personal allowance would be sufficient upon which to base this credit. The evidence shows that Mrs. Stanley had an allowance of $18,000.00 or more per year. This was more than sufficient to take care of her personal expenses and requirements. Evidently the plaintiff thought so, because they billed and extended the credit to her. Having extended the credit to her in the first instance, there is no reason nor right on their part to now claim this money from Mr. Stanley. The evidence shows that their claim is against Mrs. Stanley, and, therefore, we ask you to return a verdict in favor of the defendant, finding him not liable in this suit. Thank you."

Plaintiff's closing argument

"May it please the Court, Counsel for the defense and Gentlemen of the Jury:

Apparently the defense is now relying on the rather flimsy claim that the original invoice happened to be made out to Mrs. James N. Stanley rather than to Mr. James N Stanley. The defendant now claims that the credit was extended to the wife and not to the husband, in the face of the direct unimpeached and uncontradicted evidence that E. M. Gray & Co. had been doing some business with Mrs. Stanley before she was married and that her credit with that concern never amounted to more than $50.00. Do you, as men of business experience, believe for one moment that E. M. Gray & Co. would suddenly jump from a credit basis of $50.00 to that of

$22,000 unless it was based upon her marriage to the defendant, James Stanley?

The only time that the name Mrs. Stanley is mentioned is on the original invoice. Counsel is mistaken when he tells you that the letter of December 13th, 1928 was addressed to Mrs. Stanley. Let us look at it. You will see that it is addressed to Mr. James Stanley, and acknowledges receipt of a check from him crediting his account. Every letter after that was addressed to Mr. James Stanley. Every payment on account was made by James Stanley. The insurance policy which counsel objects to on the grounds that it insures James Stanley and/or Mrs. Nellie Stanley was paid for solely and wholly by James Stanley. It was his insurance policy covering the items which he had permitted to be purchased. If James Stanley had not intended to be bound by the purchase of his wife when he first received a notice from the E. M. Gray & Co., he would have immediately written, wired or telephoned to the effect that he would not be liable and that they should look to his wife for payment. Isn't that what any honest, fair minded business man would do? But what did James Stanley do. By his subsequent actions, he not only acknowledged to E. M. Gray & Co. but to the world at large, liability for his wife's purchases. He made all of the subsequent payments; one for $1,000 and one for $2,500.00 with never a word denying liability. He had seen his wife nearly every day during the one and a half years since the jewelry was purchased. Have you heard one word of protest or inquiry as to when or where she got this jewelry? Have you heard one word of denial that he would pay for it? Now, gentlemen, James Stanley did not have the courage to come here and try to face you and tell you, under oath, that Mrs. Stanley never asked him for permission to purchase these items. Apparently all that we have here is a millionaire's whim, trying to take out his spite against his wife on the plaintiff, my client. (Objection to this statement sustained.)

Stanley knew that his wife was going to purchase these bracelets for a birthday gift, and he authorized her to purchase them. By doing so he constituted her his agent for that purpose, and he is liable for the purchases so made.

Gentlemen, we ask you to return a verdict in favor of the plaintiff for the sum of $16,738.50. Thank you for your kind attention."

§ 721. Disputed document case.*

"Gentlemen of the Jury:

The interpretation that the opposition has attempted to put upon some of the evidence before you makes it necessary for us to consider for a few minutes its nature and purpose. The Court will instruct you in the law of this case; I do not attempt to do that, but there have been some changes made in the methods employed in cases of this character that throw light on an investigation of this kind. These changes, like many technical legal rules, are not known to the general public. I am quite sure that a knowledge of them will not only assist you in your investigation of the facts in this case, but will show you that the contention of the opposition regarding this testimony is not correct.

From some of the arguments made here, during the progress of this trial, and now at its close, one might be led to think that you had not seen and were not to be permitted to see for yourselves this disputed writing. Strange to say, in the old days in many cases you would not in fact have been allowed to compare it with any standard or genuine writing for you to look at, unless it had gotten into the case by accident. It could not have been put in evidence for the purpose of comparison. You will be astonished to know that this old practice continued in your courts down almost to the present day. Jurors were not supposed to be sufficiently qualified to examine certain subjects for themselves, and were asked to listen to what others said and then, if possible, determine from the conflicting evidence before them which witnesses were telling the truth. Long ago there was some reason for this practice, because many a jury would have had men who could not read writing, but the old practice continued long beyond the time when jurors could read.

The evidence in cases of this kind at the present time, as you have seen, and this is the vital point of application in this case, differs from most evidence in trials at law, because

* Osborn, Problem of Proof.

it appeals to the mind through the eye as well as through the ear. In any case of disputed handwriting, no matter how plain, or how bold, or bad the facts may be, some witnesses may possibly be found, as in this case, who will testify against the facts. This testimony in the old days would offset the mere opinion of another witness who had given an opposite opinion, and, with a juror who was a hearer only, the condition was practically as if the testimony had not been given. But when the writings themselves are examined, and full and detailed reasons are given for the opinion expressed, then the old order is totally changed.

You have already heard, or will hear, criticisms in this case of expert testimony as expert testimony. The old books have many such criticisms, and it is not strange that in the old days abuses of various kinds were common. Up to 1913 it was against the law in every United States Federal Court of this progressive country, to put in evidence any standard writing whatever for purposes of comparison, and, as stated before, this same practice continued in nearly all the state courts up to a recent time and was only changed in this state by a recent statute.

Handwriting witnesses were supposed to remember how a man's writing looked from having seen it sometime, and then were asked to look at a signature on a will, or a note, or a contract, and say offhand, from memory alone, that it was genuine or not genuine. During these old days the abuse of expert testimony regarding documents was common and inevitable, and under the old rules there was no adequate remedy; but the remedy now is to ask for reasons and illustrations and then to ask the jurymen themselves, with their own eyes and their own minds, to review the conflicting testimony with the actual documents before them. The Court will tell you that you are not obliged to take anybody's opinion here regarding these documents.

While we think the opinions of our qualified, experienced and reputable witnesses are reliable and correct, you can review all that testimony and determine whether or not it is logical and credible. You have heard the witnesses and have seen the witnesses, and can see the papers and see them in enlarged form in photographs. The appeal then is not to your credulity, as to whether you would *believe* this witness or that witness, but rather to your intelligence as to whether the witnesses have presented the testimony to you in a reasonable and convincing manner and whether their interpretation of the physical facts before you is a correct interpretation. This practice with the illustrations, you see, takes their testimony entirely out of the class of mere opinion testimony, and when my distinguished opponent talks generalities about the dangers of 'mere expert testimony,' or about old abuses, you will please to remember that he is *not referring to this case.*

He even objected to their admission as evidence, and now seems unhappy, when we use the photographs. Now let us see for just what purpose they are here under the present practice. They show more distinctly than the originals, and put in more convenient form, the physical facts upon which a conclusion must be based. Their value and use, in your hands and before your eyes, are thus perfectly evident, and an objection to their use is an objection to your seeing clearly and distinctly the very evidence upon which you must finally base a verdict. Is that fair to you or to the case? To be really consistent, those opposed to us here should endeavor to darken this room so that you could not see these documents clearly or should attempt to produce some kind of an actual fog there, instead of a mere verbal and mental fog, and thus prevent or make it difficult for you to see the physical facts.

We have asked our witnesses to give full and detailed reasons for their opinions on direct examination. We are permitted to do this by a decision of the highest court of this state. This procedure also is a result of a revolution in the practice of law brought about undoubtedly by the advance in education and general intelligence. You can readily see that in making an attack upon our case it is a very different matter to attack the opinions of the witnesses instead of the reasons for their opinions. Cross-examination to the point is cross-examination on the reasons given for the testimony presented here. If these reasons are not reasonable to you, and if you cannot follow and understand, and if the interpretation does not seem to you correct, then you are not bound by it in any way. We confidently think that the more you see and the better you understand, the better it will be for our contention.

You see how different all this makes a case involving what we call opinion testimony with reasons from that class of expert testimony relating to the injury, let us say, of some man who fell from a street car. One doctor comes forward and testifies that the man will never be well again, and another doctor, who seems to know as much as the first, says that in a few months he will be as well as ever. When expert testimony of this class is presented to a jury and there is a conflict in the testimony, the jury is helpless. It is practically as though there had been no testimony given on the subject; but this is not true when reasons can be given and illustrations shown that can be understood and appreciated by intelligent men. This, you see, sweeps away all of that fine rhetoric, bitter sarcasm, and inconclusive logic which assumed that a ready-made opinion was being brought in here to be foisted upon you men for your adoption.

When the opposition argues, thus slurring and attacking the testimony of his own witnesses as well as ours, that if there is any conflict then the testimony is all to be of no value, you will see that this is not a good argument. The primary question is whether the physical things are here that we say are here, and whether the interpretation of these things is the correct interpretation. You are not to be misled by any of these general criticisms of expert testimony, for here you not only have the opportunity, but it becomes your duty to examine this testimony for yourselves and see just what it is and what it signifies. We are confident that you will not be misled, but will see and understand as we desire and expect you will see and understand.

Referring again to the photographs it should be said that these illustrations, these tangible, visible enlargements that you can hold in your own hands and look at with your own eyes and reason about with your own brains, are the very effective reasons for the opinions in this case. That is what they were made for, and the real objection to them by the opposition is that they do well just exactly what they are intended to do, that is, make clear and distinct to you the facts in this case. Our opponent has especially objected to the photographs because they are enlarged, and this objection exposes the real purpose of the opposition. The illustrations are of course more plain and useful when enlarged, more effective in illustrating the facts, and therefore the more damaging to the claims of those who are against the facts.

All this, it is evident, is far removed from the kind of testimony that is weighed by counting the witnesses. One good witness with good reasons and good illustrations will prevail against a whole omnibus load of those who merely give opinions, or give some incredible, visionary reasons which neither you nor I can understand. We ask you to examine the facts for yourselves in the light of all the testimony we have presented, and then we think you will render a verdict in accordance with the facts which will be in our favor."

§ 722. —Another illustration.

"Gentlemen of the Jury:

You have heard the violent general criticism of expert testimony, but it has not been so much criticism of the testimony in this particular case as of expert testimony as a whole. We desire especially that you should carefully consider this testimony. We have brought this expert testimony here for the purpose of assisting you in seeing, and correctly interpreting the physical facts in connection with these documents. That is its purpose, to assist in showing the facts. In this connection it is highly important that you should not be deceived as to just what this testimony is. From the reference made to it by the opposition one might be led to think of it as something brought in here to deceive you or be foisted upon you, and it is suggested at least that you would be helpless in the matter and could not in any way understand the significance of the special testimony, or be able to recognize its value or discover its worthlessness.

What relation does this expert testimony have to this particular case and to the problem that you have to solve, is the real question for us. The deceptive nature of the criticisms of this testimony becomes quite apparent when it is clearly understood just what it aims to do. Let us see what it is.

On this particular subject a qualified specialist comes before you and is permitted by the law to give an opinion for your assistance, but not necessarily for your adoption. In the old days this testimony ended with the opinion, but as education became more general and intelligence increased, the law has said that a witness of this kind can not only give an opinion but he can give the reasons for the opinion to those who are to decide the case. This at once distinguishes this testimony from testimony regarding insanity and medicine and various questions where it is impossible for those of us not technically trained to follow the witness.

When we are told by one witness that the heart of a living man has a thin wall on one side which is gradually growing thinner, or that some valve is defective in some way and that the health of the patient never will be any better, it is impossible for you and me, by looking at this man or even by listening to his heart, to say whether the statements made about him are correct or not. And then when another witness appears, of equally good appearance, and gives his opinion that his heart is really better than the average heart, you and I are not aided by this testimony in reaching a conclusion about the question at issue because we cannot follow and check up the statements of the witnesses.

But this is not the condition in this case where a disputed document itself is before the court and before you. We in fact have, in these disputed papers, as it were, this 'heart' under investigation out here before us where we can see it and examine it and test it by these standard writings and the enlarged photographs, which are really the illustrated 'reasons' for the opinion here expressed.

It would be perfectly proper for the opposition in this case to attack with all the skill and vigor available the reasons for the opinion expressed here, but his eloquent and ingenious attack has not been against the reasons but mainly against the opinion. We think the opinion of this experienced and reputable witness has force and is worthy of consideration; but you are not asked to take the opinion unless the reasons for that opinion appeal to you as reasonable men. These reasons we contend are conclusive and are given here because the Court of Appeals of this state in a recent case has said that an expert can give reasons for an opinion on direct examination. On this subject the court says, with a good common sense that appeals to any man, that testimony with reasons may be controlling but without reasons may have little weight. Now you see how superficial and deceiving it is to attack this testimony without attacking the reasons and illustrations on which it is based. We want you to see and appreciate the facts as shown by these documents for the reason that the facts themselves argue for our contention.

We are confident that when you have considered the testimony in these three ways, or under these three heads of the opinion, of the physical facts, and the interpretation of the facts, that you will not be misled, but will see and understand as we desire and expect you will see and understand."

§ 723. Personal injury case.

Opening argument for plaintiff

"If your Honor please, and Gentlemen of the Jury: It is the privilege of the lawyers at this stage of proceedings, and at the conclusion of all the evidence, to sum it up and point out to you wherein they have sustained the issues involved in the case, the controverted issue.

Gentlemen, at the outset I told you, in my opening statement, that Mr. Prince, the plaintiff, became a passenger on a bus operated by the Grey Lines, paid his fare, received a ticket, and that under the circumstances it became and was the duty of the defendant to exercise the highest degree of care consistent with the practical prosecution of the business, to carry him safely. That is a duty imposed by law upon all common carriers of passengers.

You gentlemen told us that you would listen carefully to the Court's instructions relative to the obligations imposed by law upon the respective parties. It was explained to you somewhat in detail by both sides that it was incumbent upon the plaintiff in the first instance to prove the material allegations of his declaration, which is a document filed in every case, by the plaintiff setting forth his cause of action and apprising the defendants of what they are required to meet when they go to court.

The Plaintiff set forth all these facts in his declaration, set forth that he was a passenger for hire and reward, and it became the duty of the defendant to carry him safely; that he was seated, as a passenger, in the exercise of ordinary care for his own safety, and was thrown from his seat and injured by the negligent manner in which the bus was operated.

Now, the issue is very simple, gentlemen. It is true that the burden of proof is on the plaintiff to prove that he was a passenger; it is true that he must prove that he was in the exercise of ordinary care; it is true that he must prove the negligent operation of the bus as charged in the declaration; and gentlemen, when this is shown, when it is proved conclusively that he was a passenger in that bus, doing what any reasonably prudent man would do in reliance on the belief and assumption that this common carrier would perform the duty imposed by law upon it or them to carry him, safely, I say to you, that there is no basis for any claim that Prince was not exercising ordinary care for his own safety. Why, gentlemen, as this case progressed, and as witness after witness went on, it was really astounding how the proof all demonstrates that Prince's story is true, virtually true almost in minute detail, making due allowances for the condition of the man and for the lack of memory, being not only called upon to recite exactly what occurred in a mishap such as he has gone through, his testimony is supported by every reliable witness in the case.

I submit, gentlemen, you could sit in cases for a thousand years, and you would never have such an experience perhaps again, or a case where there is so little real conflict in the evidence.

What are the undisputed facts? Prince became a passenger and paid his fare, that is number one. Number two, that the law imposes upon these carriers the duty to exercise the highest degree of care to carry him safely, and they are responsible for the slightest neglect if it results in injury to the passenger, or to Prince, who was a passenger; that he was injured, number three is undisputed.

There is not a scintilla of evidence or a scintilla of a suggestion to show that Prince was not a strong, vigorous, healthy man prior to his taking passage on that bus on the day in question.

Now, gentlemen, let us review the evidence briefly, let us consider the conflict and wherein it arises.

Prince told you that as this bus was going along there that day, and as it started to descend this grade, it was going over a rough roadway, that there was a little jolting and jarring, and that some of the passengers in the rear of the bus complained; finally someone shouted; there was a commotion, and just about that moment this bus ran into a large rut or depression or against something that caused an unusual swerve or jolt of the bus, crushed his hat, and was thrown down on the opposite side of the bus, doubled up in such manner as to break his back, and inflict this injury. He told you the bus went a considerable distance following this, that somebody finally shouted, got up on the seat and pulled the bell cord before the bus came to a stop.

Prince was a stranger on the bus. There he was, following this accident, helpless, suffering pain. The people around him perhaps did not realize, appreciate or understand the nature and extent of his injuries, he did not himself, of course, but you gentlemen know now, Prince knows now how seriously he was hurt; he knows what he has gone through. He was a stranger on that bus, had no opportunity to obtain the names of the passengers. He was suffering so much that they had to place him on the back seat, and this lady who took the stand this morning, told you something that he did not even remember, that she came back and put a garment under his head and fanned him on the way to the town of Auburn.

He was taken out of there with the assistance of a man on either side of him, put into a car of a doctor for the bus company, taken to a hospital where they did not have the equipment to X-ray him, and no doubt the doctor in good faith believed that he was not so seriously hurt, as he thought, gave him morphine and other narcotics, put him in bed, strapped up his back, and the pain continued and continued, and they decided he had better go to Kansas City, the headquarters, and have medical advice.

Gentlemen, as this case unfolds itself, it is clear as day what happened.

You know his condition since that time, I don't have to dwell upon it in my opening argument.

Now, as I started out to say to you gentlemen, where is the conflict in the evidence? Out of ten or fifteen passengers on the bus, you have heard the sworn testimony of five witnesses.

Mrs. De Vore and her fifteen year old daughter, whose depositions have been read to you, I just wish to call your attention to the fact, that those people, not knowing or appreciating the nature or extent of the man's injuries, no doubt after the lapse of time were led to believe that there was nothing extraordinary in the movement of the bus. In the bus they were seated up near the front where they did not get the shock and jar. They were so willing to testify to facts that would help the Grey Lines, that it is a matter of comment, it is most extraordinary. The mother, goes on the stand and tells you that there was a commotion, that she looked back and saw the man suffering pain and saw him lying on the seat where he was, and out of a clear sky the lawyer asks her if there were any cushions dislodged, and she said absolutely not, and in the next breath she tells you the man was surrounded with passengers where she couldn't possibly see if a cushion had been dislodged. We have her telling this extraordinary story that the bus during the entire trip was going along twenty-five miles an hour, yet they must admit, they all have to admit the man was thrown and injured, and then the little daughter telling you that the man she saw was seated up in the forward part of the bus, sitting there. Their stories do not coincide, they do not carry any weight, gentlemen, and could not.

Mr. Prince was on the back seat, lying down just as Mrs. Wolfe told you, and you know that his back was broken, you know this talk about there being no jerk or jolt has been disproved by the defendant's own witnesses.

Now, gentlemen, they got this woman, this mother and a nurse and daughter, to tell you the bus was traveling along as smooth as if on this courthouse floor, just as the driver told you; yet they put on two passengers, Mr. and Mrs. Wolfe, who sat, not in the back where the force of the jar of the bus would occur, but up in the center of the bus or beyond. They told you that there was a violent jolting, jarring and jerking, then extremely violent jerking at the time Prince was hurt. Gentlemen, I would have been delighted to call these people to the witness stand as my witnesses, had I known who they were.

This estimate of speed is of no importance. What difference does it make if the bus was going thirty-five miles, forty miles, or twenty-five miles an hour? It was the duty of that driver to drive the bus carefully, so that he would not injure his passengers, and his story told on the witness stand that it was a clear, gravel road is rebutted by the defendant's own evidence, every one with the exception of the nurse and daughter, the daughter from Missouri Valley and the driver, are the only witnesses in this case who attempted to tell you that there was not any severe lurching, jolting or jarring of this bus, the only witnesses who attempted to tell you the bus was going along twenty-five miles an hour.

We have proved the distance that the bus traveled and the time it was due, 3:05 and it was half an hour late. Gentlemen, use your common sense, don't you know that this driver was trying to make up time when he struck this gravel road, and was going just as Prince said he was, going at least fifty miles an hour down the hill, and he ran into the ruts and threw this man from the seat, and injured him for life. That is the truth, and it has been proven by the great overwhelming preponderance of the evidence.

I don't care about these little fly specks, gentlemen, the little contradictions, they are on immaterial matters. How do they account for this man breaking his back, twisting his back out of place, receiving a compression fracture and twisting the back out of alignment? What nonsense to claim he was not thrown from the seat. They knew what his claim was going to be, the doctors had it, their representatives saw him, all the facts were seen. If there was no bell cord on that bus, they could prove it by merely taking a photograph of the interior of it. If the road was not a rough road, or in bad condition at the point of the accident, they had every opportunity to take a picture of that roadway.

They come here glibly with their driver in contradiction of all the testimony in the case except the nurse and this small daughter, and tell you the road was a smooth gravel roadway, but for some unknown reason a man breaks his back on the bus. Silly, isn't it? No serious attempt has been made here to prove that these defendants fulfilled its obligations that they owed to this man as their passenger.

Of course, in every lawsuit each side is entitled to have his view of the law given to the jury. I believe his Honor will instruct you that the burden of proof is upon the plaintiff to prove he was in the exercise of ordinary care and was injured through the negligence of the defendant. He will tell you if you believe from the evidence he was not in the exercise of ordinary care, then he cannot recover. I believe he will tell you if the defendants were not guilty of negligence, that if they were using the proper degree of care and foresight and the accident was unavoidable, or a mere accident, that the plaintiff cannot recover; but the Court does not intimate by giving any of the instructions that those are the facts. If these are not the facts the rules of law given are inapplicable.

You know the very thing speaks for itself. The very fact that the man was thrown from the seat, and the mere fact that his back was broken in this terrible fashion, demonstrates it was violent. If they brought every passenger in the bus to tell the story that the bus driver told, I would still insist they were mistaken or testifying to a falsehood, because Prince was a hale, hearty, physical man when he entered that bus and he came out an invalid for life.

What are you going to do with it? Counsel in the examination of the jury stated we had sued for $100,000 damages. I said to one or two of you gentlemen after that intimation was disclosed to you that if the evidence warranted that, that you would not be influenced by the amount sued for, if it was a fair amount, you would be guided by the evidence in arriving at your verdict. All right, gentlemen, what are the elements of damage in this case?

The evidence is undisputed that this man for ten years earned virtually $10,000 a year. It is not disputed the corporations and their astute lawyers had every opportunity to investigate this man, and look into his past history, and you know if it was not Gospel truth that John Prince was earning $800 a month for nine years, it would have been disproved here. You know when he quit that job, he took one with better prospects in view of the drawing account in all probability he thought it would better his condition in life, and he would have bettered it. Is there any contradiction of that evidence? Why, gentlemen, his loss of earnings today, or for a year, are such that his hospital bills and doctors' bills, are mere drops of water in this great subject of damages. They are infinitely small when you consider what this man has to go through the rest of his life. Treat it as a common horse sense proposition, this man's loss of earnings alone in the past and in the years to come would aggregate double the amount of damages we have sued for in this lawsuit, his loss of earnings alone, if you consider his age, his expectancy in life, and the fact that we know that men nowadays live to be much older than in our early youth. Science and our modern way of living have had a great tendency to prolong life, as everyone knows; you read occasionally in the papers of men along past the eighty mark playing golf and enjoying life, and doing things for the community; but suppose this man at forty-six years of age had only twenty years' expectancy, and if you say twenty years, and multiply his actual earnings by the expectancy of twenty years of life, you have double the amount of damages that is sued for here, and that is just a small portion of the damages; infinitely more is the loss of health, the loss of strength, the pain and suffering, the knowledge that during the rest of his life he goes about crippled, wearing a brace, with the alternative staring him in the face of undergoing an operation which might result in his death and would unavoidably result in the stiffening of his back.

Gentlemen, what are you going to do about it? Talking about suing for $100,000, perhaps we made a mistake and we didn't make the ad damnum large enough; but, gentlemen, can any reasonable man say that the amount of damages here that we demand is not conservative and fair.

I want counsel in his argument to tell you men what he believes the evidence would warrant in event these defendants are liable.

I will have an opportunity to speak for a short time when he is through.

I say to you, gentlemen, that when you consider all things, the age of this man, his former good health, his earning capacity, his pain and suffering, past, present, and prospective, and the knowledge that he has to go through life in this crippled condition with his nerves shattered, I don't care what the doctors say about it, this man is a physical wreck, and he will go through life that way, gentlemen, and this is his opportunity for justice. He has waited for this.

The responsibility is yours, gentlemen. When we lawyers sit down, it is up to you to say what would fairly, adequately and fully compensate this man for his injuries."

Argument for defendant.

"If your Honor please, and gentlemen of the jury, with an eloquent adversary such as I have, I cannot hope to compete in attempting to stir your emotions and thereby attempt to overcome your reason.

You gentlemen, when I examined you at the outset, all said to me that you would not allow any sympathy which you might have for this plaintiff, or for any person who is injured, to interfere or affect in any way your judgment on the question of whether the defendant in this case was guilty or not guilty. Now, I expect you gentlemen to discharge your duty as jurors, and pass upon the question of liability in this case irrespective of how sorry you may be for Mr. Prince. I am not telling you not to feel sorry for him, I feel sorry for him myself; any person who had undergone a severe injury, any person who has suffered such as he has, is entitled to sympathy; but that does not mean, gentlemen, that it is your duty or your province to award him one cent of damages unless you are satisfied under the evidence and under the law as his Honor will give it to you, that there is a liability in this case so far as the defendant is concerned.

Now, Mr. Prince was not a passenger on a railroad train. Don't forget that, that is important. When a man gets on a railroad train, the tracks belong to the railroad, the tracks are smooth, or supposed to be smooth, and the train is supposed to be operated in such a way as to not create any serious jolts for the passengers, or to injure the passenger while he is riding on that train. This is a case where the highways were highways that belonged to the public, they were highways that crossed the State of Nebraska, and were under the care and control of the State of Nebraska, and the bus line was in no way responsible for the condition of that highway. That is very, very important, whether the highway was smooth or whether the highway was rough, it was Nebraska's highway and not the bus line's highway.

Now, there cannot be any recovery in this case, gentlemen, as the Court will instruct you, unless there is a failure on the part of the bus line to exercise a degree of care, a high degree of care too, consistent with the practical operation of its business, but a common carrier is not an insurer of its passengers; it does not give a guaranty policy to everybody that buys a ticket that they won't be hurt. A common carrier has to operate its bus and has to give service to the public as the law requires it to do; it has to operate its busses so as to keep up according to the schedules or times fixed by the laws and regulations of the state, and has to go from place to place as required by schedule.

Now, a man who takes passage on a carrier such as a bus line knows before he begins that that bus line is going over the highway, and it is going to take the same identical road that he takes when he drives his car, that it is going to meet with the same kind of ruts an automobile meets when a private driver operates the car, and he knows he is going to be exposed to the same jolts and bumps that anybody driving over that highway is going to be exposed to. He knows that the carrier is not guaranteeing him that there are going to be no bumps on that road.

He knows, or he ought to know, that there are certain parts of the bus itself that ride more comfortably than other parts. The back end, of course, is subject to greater sways if you happen to hit a little depression in the road; everybody knows that from experience, that if you come to a little rut in the road, the back end goes down a little more. Everybody that gets in a bus and sits in the back seat knows that. He knew it, or he should have known it, if he was exercising ordinary care for his own safety.

According to his testimony, there were some jolts before the one that took place where he says he got hurt. Well, he didn't have to sit back there. Nobody told him to sit back there. He could have got out of the back seat and gone to the front seat. He hadn't any right to sit back there until he got hurt and try to make the bus line pay for it.

There isn't any duty on the part of the bus line. His legs were good before that, he could walk before that. All he had to do was get up where the other passengers were and sit there. If the road was rough he had to exercise care for his own safety, he couldn't put himself in a place of danger, and try to get the bus line to compensate him if he was injured.

Don't make any mistake about one thing in this case, gentlemen. We are not claiming he was not hurt. He was. The witnesses testified to it. Nobody is trying to pull any wool over your eyes, so far as the defendant is concerned. We brought in all the witnesses who testified. We let them testify. One witness said the road was rough, another witness said the road was not. If we were attempting to pull the wool over your eyes, we would have had them testify the same way, that the road was perfectly smooth, that there wasn't a wrinkle in it, and the bare fact that they testified in certain particulars then, stamps their testimony as truthful, instead of indicating that they were not telling the truth.

Now, what is the situation. You have got a man riding on a bus, who is a passenger. He is a well man. He sits in the back seat, whether he sat there first or whether he sat in some other seat first and moved back doesn't make a particle of difference, I don't care where he sat, except that he sat in the back seat. Now, he got a bump. The back end of that bus went down, and his back was hurt and he was injured and has a case. We did not waste a minute's time in the examination of the doctors, because we are not contesting the claim that the man was hurt. Get that. We are not claiming that he was not hurt; we are claiming we were not responsible for his hurt. We are claiming, if anybody was responsible, it is Mr. Prince.

You saw the young driver on the stand, he had the appearance of an honest, intelligent, careful driver of a bus. He told you how he was driving that bus, and he told you he was familiar with the road, and he is backed up by every other passenger who testified in this case, except the plaintiff, as to how fast he was going.

Now, assuming that he was going at a reasonable rate of speed as required by his schedule, but notwithstanding the fact that he was going at a reasonable rate of speed, the bus came to a place where there was a little wearing out, and some rain or something washed a little of the highway out, and the back end sank and came back up and this fellow got a crick in his back, and sustained injuries to the back, how is the bus company liable? They are no more liable than the driver. If they are liable at all they are liable because he was liable, he was operating the bus. What did he do that was not proper? What did he fail to do that he should have done? That boy, as you see from his appearance, his conduct and demeanor on the stand, was telling the Gospel truth about how he was operating the bus, and he is the one most likely to give you gentlemen an accurate description of just what happened at or about the time of that accident. You don't expect this man to give it to you, Mr. Prince.

Now, making all due allowances for this plaintiff, with all regard for his condition, and all due sympathy for his condition, the man is hurt. His need is great, and you may assume at the outset that he is going to testify in such a way as to make out a case so that you gentlemen will give him a verdict because you are sorry for him, because you sympathize with him.

Now, he knows that bus was not going fifty miles an hour. He knows it very well. That testimony is given to you gentlemen so that maybe he will have a chance with you to get some money, in other words that you will take it from the bus company, and give it to him because you feel sorry for him.

Put yourself in the situation back at the time this accident happened. Let us suppose he got a serious jolt, let us suppose the bus went down in a little depression of some kind and his back was injured, let us suppose his pain was terrible. What would be the natural effect of that? Do you suppose he would be paying any attention as to who was pulling a cord? Do you suppose he would be paying any attention as to who was shouting or making any commotion?

We all know when we are in great pain our interest is in ourselves. We relinquish attention to surrounding circumstances. He never paid any attention at the time he sustained the injury. Therefore his testimony that he gave on the witness stand is given here for the purpose of making out a case.

Opposed to that you have the disinterested testimony of the postoffice supervisor, Mr. Castberg, who testified that he was watching that speedometer. Whether you believe that he watched it all the time or not, does not concern me. He is a man who has idiosyncrasies. He is the type of a man who gets an idea and carries it out. We have all seen men like that. We have seen a man watch a speedometer, because he was interested in determining his ability to judge speed. Now, he watched that speedometer, and was sitting in the seat opposite the driver. The seat right next to the driver was turned over. The driver testified to that himself, that it was an emergency seat which was used only in the event that the bus was crowded. The bus was not crowded, there were only about ten passengers on the bus, I don't recall the exact number, but it had seating capacity of twenty-nine, so that that emergency seat immediately back of that was occupied by Mr. Castberg, who was watching the speedometer alongside of him, and he said 'no.' He was then asked if there was anybody in the seat immediately behind that, and he said he didn't know. Mr. Castberg says he was in that front seat watching that speedometer.

We have the testimony of Mr. Castberg on speed. We have the testimony of Mr. and Mrs. Wolfe from Quincy, Illinois on the speed of that bus. We have the testimony of Mrs. De Vore and her daughter on the subject of the bus and the testimony of the driver of the bus himself.

We have the testimony of these witnesses. Mr. and Mrs. Wolfe are absolutely disinterested. Mr. Castberg is absolutely disinterested. Mrs. De Vore and her daughter are absolutely disinterested, and those are the witnesses from whom you may expect to get the absolute truth.

Now, there isn't any real conflict in the evidence, I agree with my distinguished adversary. The only place there is a conflict is on the speed of that bus. He swears it was fifty miles an hour. Why? To get a verdict, of course; but the overwhelming weight of the evidence is that it was not over thirty-five miles an hour. There isn't any other substantial conflict in the evidence. Some witnesses testified the road was smooth, some testified it was rough, I don't care whether if was smooth or rough, keep that in mind. I am perfectly willing to agree with you gentlemen there was some little depression in the road that was struck by the back end of the bus. The bus sank, this man got a jolt and was hurt; but I say, gentlemen of the jury, that there wasn't any duty on the part of the carrier to protect this man against the ordinary risks that an ordinary automobile would have to undergo in going over the road.

The duty of the driver of a private car toward an occupant is not as great as the duty of a carrier to a passenger, but in determining what the driver of a bus could do and what the driver of a private car could do, you must realize that they both have to travel the same roads, and they have to conduct themselves, if they want to insure the safety of the occupants of their care, just exactly the same.

Gentlemen, there isn't any need of talking about damages in this case.

My adversary very adroitly said he would like to hear from me on the amount, the question of damages in this case, and what I think would be a fair amount to allow this man. Of course, the purpose of that question and invitation was to get me involved in a discussion as to how much he ought to get. He ought not to get anything. That is my answer to that question. He ought not to get five cents, because we did not fail to do anything we should have done. There is no use of talking any $100,000, $50,000 or $10,000. You shouldn't give him $500.00.

It is unfortunate that the plaintiff sustained an accident. It is always unfortunate when anybody sustains an accident. If a man is struck by lightning, it is unfortunate. If you drive your car in a ditch, that is unfortunate. Therefore I say to you gentlemen, there is only one thing for you to do. Consider this from the standpoint of the practical operation of that bus, and in the practical operation of that bus, was that man carried with the proper degree of care? I leave it to you gentlemen to determine from the testimony of these witnesses whether that bus was operated carefully, whether you say the road was rough or was not rough.

I am not going to enter into any discussion whether there was a bell cord or not. The driver's testimony is certainly more reliable than that of the man who was injured as to whether there was a bell cord on this bus, and all those things are by the wayside.

Gentlemen, I am going to ask you to give this case your dispassionate consideration, and I will ask you to consider the question of liability, which is the real question. Don't get sidetracked on the question of giving this man money, because you feel sorry for him. I thank you.''

Closing argument for plaintiff

''May it please your Honor and gentlemen, this argument made by counsel for these defendants, is a most extraordinary one if you stop to analyze it. I made a few notes while he was talking.

I assume that he is claiming that there is some element of sincerity in his makeup, and he is giving you some plausible reason why the defendants are not liable, but I am frank to concede that I cannot discover any logic or fairness in his argument. I will tell you why.

He takes credit for bringing in some passengers whose testimony was in irreconcilable conflict, and he therefore says, because Mr. and Mrs. Wolfe happened to agree with the bus driver or with the ladies they picked up down in Missouri Valley, that the motor bus company should be entitled to a lot of credit in presenting to you the whole truth.

Now, just analyze that for a minute, gentlemen. It is the facts you are after, isn't it? Who is right and who is wrong? Was this highway in a dangerous condition? Was it full of ruts and was there a bad rut in the highway that threw Prince out of his seat and broke his back, or wasn't there? All right, Mr. and Mrs. Wolfe says there was. The driver says there wasn't. What is the last answer? What is the final analysis to a specious argument, where he said you should believe all of them? How can it be done? Somebody is wrong. You can't possibly reconcile the testimony of the driver with the testimony of Mr. and Mrs. Wolfe. You cannot possibly reconcile this evidence, even with the testimony of Castberg, the man who has been here since July 5th, who had the mania, or idiosyncrasy which impelled him to gaze upon that speedometer all the way from Omaha, to where this accident happened; but he could not tell you about anything else, the man who told you he sat in a little seat right opposite the driver. But it developed on trial that he was not sitting there at all. The driver said nobody sat in that seat. They got their wires crossed in one instance, the man who tells you he rode so cheap, he had to admit that; but he wouldn't admit there was any violent lurch or jerk, after saying in one breath that he didn't know, the man who told you that he came here from Omaha at the behest of counsel for the Grey lines and remained here since July 5 at their expense, that his railroad fare was paid, that he never talked to counsel about what his testimony was going to be.

Now, gentlemen, what would you think of a witness that the Plaintiff's lawyer called to the stand, who told you that we sent to Omaha for him, paid his fare here, agreed to pay his expenses and his time while he was here, and have that witness take the stand and say that nobody for the plaintiff, his lawyer or anyone else ever knew what his testimony was going to be? You would know that witness was not telling you the truth, and when that man insisted throughout his cross-examination that he never talked to a living soul about the speed of that bus or the character of the highway or whether there was a violent lurch or jerk, you know he was not telling the truth, and I say that without hesitation.

Counsel takes credit for bringing in Mr. and Mrs. Wolfe. Let me show you something. Just use your thinking apparatus as man to man. They had to make some sort of a defense here in this case, didn't they? They could let the Plaintiff's story go unchallenged, it is true, but they could not let it go unanswered. His story shows that the driver of the bus was grossly negligent. He didn't even exercise ordinary care for the safety of the passengers in the back of that bus, if he drove over the highway full of ruts thirty-five miles an hour, or with sufficient speed to throw the passengers against the roof and injure them, and they bring in Mr. and Mrs. Wolfe. Gentlemen, sometimes witnesses suddenly become inspired with the sense of justice, decency and fair play, and they may casually say, 'I was not much impressed with that at the time,' yet they take the witness stand, and they see the surroundings and they note the presence of the judge and their consciences smite them. It seems to me that when Mr. Wolfe went on the stand and when counsel brought out that he was a brother of the Judge down-state, it seemed to me that the goodness in his heart and the fairness was aroused, and he decided that he would tell the jury the truth, as he remembered it, and he told it. I think it was just as big a surprise to counsel as it was to me, that he would put on such evidence. I will tell you why. The undisputed evidence in this case showed there were ten or twelve passengers on the bus. They brought the people from the center, the front of the bus where the force of this reckless conduct would be felt the least, and the truth is that they took the names of every solitary passenger on the bus, and why haven't they produced them. Was Prince able to get them here? Where are the passengers in the back of the bus who shouted and who made the commotion? Where is the passenger who jumped on the seat and pulled the bell cord? What plausible explanation or excuse has been made to you gentlemen as to why they would select five passengers in the front of the bus and not produce the other five or seven? What would you think of me, gentlemen, if it developed on this trial that Mr. Prince had friends or acquaintances on that bus, or men that he knew and he had their names and addresses, whom he knew would know about this violence or screaming and shouting and swearing, if you please, and the shouting to the driver to slow down before this accident happened, and even after it followed when he heedlessly went on for more than a thousand feet, suppose Mr. Bach said to Mr. Prince, 'You knew three or four men in the back of that bus that could affirm or verify your statement here, you knew where to get them, how to get them, what is your excuse for not bringing them here, Mr. Prince'? Well, the inevitable conclusion, gentlemen, follows that if he did that thing he was not telling you the truth when he told you about the movement of this bus, he was not telling the truth when he told you that he was thrown off the seat, as all the other passengers and the little girl screamed, and the mother complained, and the men shouted at the driver and he didn't hear them because of the noise, you would know that story was not true; and I say to you gentlemen, that when these defendants come into the court and select certain of their passengers in the front of the bus, but do not bring the others who knew actually what happened, and who were in a position to see that the man was thrown from the seat, then they are deliberately withholding from you evidence in their possession, and the irresistible conclusion follows that that evidence would be unfavorable to their defense, or they would have produced it.

Why do you suppose they would bring this man all the way from Omaha who sat up in the front seat, and never knew anything about the accident, never went back to see this man, never knew anything about it, he tells you he was gazing at the speedometer and the silly tale that it went at the same speed? That shows you how fair counsel it. He wants to leave the impression that they are not interested in the damages in this case. He unfairly made this statement to you, he said, 'You are not a passenger on a railroad where you are running on fixed steel rails, you are running on a public highway and the bus company doesn't own the highways, and they have to keep up their schedules in accordance with time tables fixed by the state.' Is there any warrant or basis for that statement in the evidence? Have you heard anybody tell you that the state of Nebraska or any other state is interested in the time tables of the Grey Lines or that they can control their time schedules or require them to operate at any given rate of speed? What an absurdity that is, gentlemen. These bus companies running throughout the United States are required to operate carefully, and for the slightest neglect they are responsible in law, but counsel stands up here and glibly tells you, 'We don't owe this man anything, when he got on the bus he assumed the risk.' There isn't any such thing as assumption of risk. The plaintiff must exercise ordinary care. This man had never been over the highway before. Never rode in their bus before. Did he have a right to assume that the carrier would perform the duty imposed by law on it? Was the driver who made the trip day after day and year after year, chargeable with knowledge of the condition of the pavement down this decline when this accident happened? Why, you know he was. When we take guests in our car and invite them to ride, we are not carrying them for hire, and we owe them no duty except, perhaps not willfully to injure them. At least we owe them nothing more than the duty to exercise ordinary care for their safety. What a far fetched conclusion to urge to twelve intelligent men that when John Prince got on the bus he had to look out for himself and anticipate this driver was going to run down hill thirty-five, forty, or even fifty miles an hour at such speed that he would throw him out of his seat and break his back?

Gentlemen, I say when they are forced to make that kind of argument, it demonstrates again that they have no defense to this lawsuit.

He says that he could have gone to a place of safety; is there any warrant or basis for that in the evidence? Suppose any one of you men were seated as a passenger on the bus. Put the shoe on the other foot, suppose you paid your fare and got a ticket and you said to the driver, 'Where can I smoke?' and the driver said, 'The back seat.' When you got in there would you have a right to expect them to carry you safely, and would you like it if they threw you and broke your back to have counsel for the Grey Lines say 'Why didn't he get into a safe place?'

Counsel has the audacity to say to you that he personally did not care whether the road was rough or smooth. Gentlemen, his conception of the law, if he has such a conception of it, is not only erroneous and unsound, but it is absolutely unscientific and contrary to what the law is and always has been.

Listen to his Honor's instructions. That is all I have to say to you on that subject.

For instance, here is another one of his facetious illustrations. He said the bus company is no more liable than its driver. Where is the analogy? We are not suing the driver, that is not true as a matter of law or a matter of fact. The driver was late, he was making up time. Whether that was true or not, how does that affect John Prince? We have not sued the driver. We have sued the Grey Lines, this company that is operating buses all over the United States, common carriers of passengers for hire. You are entitled to just as great safety if you pay your fare and get into one of these buses as you would be if you stepped into one of the limited trains for New York City. You are entitled to the same degree of care from these companies as you would get from any railroad company in the land.

Counsel says they are no more liable than this driver, and he is a truthful man, that he wouldn't lie to you, the very man that is charged with negligence, whose negligence and grossly careless conduct generally resulted in this terrible injury to Prince. He has the nerve to tell you that Prince is lying, but the driver is telling you the truth. He says the driver has no incentive to tell anything but the truth. Let us see about that. Suppose he told his employers he was driving down this hill at forty miles an hour or fifty miles an hour, and he didn't realize the road was rough, or forgot about the bumps and ran into it at a terrific speed trying to make up time, and he didn't stop until there was a great commotion, until somebody rang him down, afterward, and he went back and found the man with a broken back through his negligent conduct, how long do you suppose he would remain driving a bus for the Grey Lines? He doesn't hesitate to say to you that Prince's needs are great, therefore he sees fit to invent this story in order to get money from the bus company, and yet, gentlemen, mark you, the same man that tells you that the plaintiff is not telling the truth did not dare bring in the passengers on the bus that the plaintiff said was on there and shouted and swore at the driver. He says you can't take money out of the box of the company and give it to him because you are sorry for him. Gentlemen, have I by word or deed or look appealed to you for sympathy for this man? Has Prince done it? Why gentlemen, sympathy has nothing to do with this lawsuit. Let me demonstrate to you why it has not. If these defendants are not liable here under the law and the evidence, you should not find them guilty. If these defendants are not liable here under the law and evidence, you should not give Prince anything out of sympathy. I said that to you once before, and I repeat it. If they are liable, we don't need your sympathy. My God, if this man is not entitled to something more than sympathy in the condition he is now in as the result of their gross negligence, what does justice mean? Sympathy? Who is talking sympathy? Mr. Bach is so sorry for him. Who asked Bach for sympathy in this case? Why I expected that he was going to shed a few tears here for you before he got through talking sympathy. Tears, yes, pecuniary tears no doubt they would be; you would find the dollar mark on every tear if you analyzed them. Who is asking for sympathy? We are asking for justice, gentlemen.

He says, 'We let them show you all about this man's condition without objection.' Why they wouldn't meet the sworn testimony of men like Doctor Magnuson, Tenney, and Blaine.

Sometime gentlemen, after this lawsuit is over, just make a few inquiries about Doctor Magnuson, the greatest bone surgeon in the western states, conceded to be all over the United States, a man who performed an operation on this man and saved his life and gave him a back that perhaps no other surgeon in the western states could perform. Yet Mr. Bach says 'We let you show that without objection.' But did he? Did you hear the struggle we had to get in the X-ray films that the Roentgenologist, Doctor Blaine, at Wesley Hospital took, on some technical objection that he did not pull the switch.

Mr. Bach: I object to that.

The Court: He may make the argument.

But counsel let us show that without objection, how badly Prince was hurt. That is just too bad, isn't it? They didn't cross-examine him, there was nothing to cross-examine him about. The film shows his condition. The operation speaks for itself. The man was before you, you saw him, you heard him, you know whether he is a truthful man or not. You are judges of the weight and credibility of the testimony, of every witness in the case, and I say to you, John Prince told you substantially the truth. He did not exaggerate a thing. When he was first on the stand, in his excitement he forgot to tell you about the brace he was wearing and will have to wear the rest of his life. He forgot to tell you about the blood transfusion. He told his story in his simple, truthful way, gentlemen. It was the God's truth, gentlemen, you men know it. This defense here is simply camouflage from start to finish.

Why gentlemen, I don't believe it is necessary for me to burden you with a review of this evidence again. I will take their own testimony and accept it as mine; I will take the testimony of Mr. and Mrs. Wolfe. I will place it alongside of the plaintiff's and it demonstrates that these companies were grossly negligent on the occasion in question.

I told you gentlemen I wanted to be fair in my argument. I wanted to give counsel an opportunity to tell you, or argue to you, or show you by some argument that this man was not entitled to the amount we sued for. Hear what his answer to that is: 'I refuse to discuss it because we don't owe this man five cents.' Just think of that, gentlemen, a passenger on a bus injured through reckless driving, his back broken, crippled for life, a man earning ten thousand a year, forty-six years old, and counsel walks up in front of the jury and says he has no business to be sitting in the back seat, he should have gone where he would be safe, we won't pay him a nickel. I am glad he said that. I just was pleased when I heard him give that expression, that that was the attitude of the Grey Lines when they carry passengers all over the country. I say to you, gentlemen, that the reason he did not answer my argument on damages is that it is unanswerable. It was just as hard to answer the facts I placed before you with reference to this man's earnings and losses as it would have been to answer Doctor Magnuson or Tenney, therefore he kept still; he couldn't answer.

Gentlemen, I say this to you in conclusion: John Prince was forty-six years old, a strong, vigorous, healthy man, he unfolded before you his life's history, told you where he was born, went to school, worked on a farm, through his own efforts and self-education he became a man of standing in the community and obtained a position that paid him $800.00 a month for years. He was a registered pharmacist, and was manager of a chain store; and he left a ten thousand a year job to take one with the financial company because the prospects were greater for him.

What happened on August 10, 1929? His back was broken by the negligent conduct of this bus company and he will have to go through life a helpless cripple.

Now, gentlemen, just think about it. I don't have to dwell on his loss of earnings, because you can take out your pencil and paper and add it up yourselves. But think what it is worth to a man to lie in a hospital day after day, long weeks in a bucky extension, trying to straighten the back, with his legs partially paralyzed, his bowels not functioning, suffering intensely day and night, injecting morphine all the time. Then on the 10th day of September an operation was performed on him, a piece of bone seven inches long, almost an inch wide and three-quarters of an inch thick is cut out of his leg and welded into his back to weld the broken back and bridge the broken chasm so that the man can live; for two weeks he hovers between life and death, and regains full consciousness only at the end of that time; and when he awakes, he suffers, you know what he suffers. He didn't cry about it, he didn't exaggerate it. I brushed it over myself. You saw this man, you see him when he sits here. I am glad he is not listening to me now. You saw him sit there with pain racking his poor, weak body, as long as he could, when he had to walk into that room and sit down. You see that condition staring him in the face for the rest of his life. Gentlemen, you happen to see him today, five years from now, ten years, twenty years from now, you will see poor John Prince, if he is that old, hobbling along as you see him today with his cane, and as the years grow and the shadows darken, you know that he will not get any better. Think of the pain and suffering alone.

Gentlemen, suppose this was a lawsuit brought in behalf of a woman, a woman who never earned a penny in her life, a strong, vigorous woman forty-six years of age, wouldn't you say she was entitled to what we have sued for here?

The pain and suffering that this man has endured and will endure the rest of his life is infinitely of more value than any sum he could earn. You know, men, the most valuable possession of mankind is good health. A man of almost any age of his life, if he is strong, vigorous and possessed of good health and constitution may lose every cent he has in the world, yet go out with a stout heart and make his money over again. You know there is not a millionaire in Chicago today who is crippled or an invalid who would not give every cent that he has for his good health. You know it is the most valued possession in life.

Prince, mark you, has to go through life in this condition. Why gentlemen, if this were a mere suit on a promissory note, chattel mortgage or an insurance policy for the destruction of a building, if the building was worth a hundred thousand dollars and lightning struck the building and destroyed its value, would you say the man who owned it was not entitled to a hundred thousand dollars? Are you going to say that property rights are more sacred than human rights? Was John Prince worth a hundred thousand dollars to himself on August 9, 1921? Yes, and several hundred thousand dollars.

What is he worth to himself today, or anybody else? A physical wreck, suffering the rest of his life. Why, gentlemen, this is his last day in court. As I said to you before, we are not asking for sympathy, we are asking for justice, just plain, ordinary justice. And gentlemen, when you do that and sign your name to that verdict, I am sure you are not going to cut it. I am sure you are not going to say that a hundred thousand dollars is too much for a man who has gone through a loss such as his loss, and who will suffer and endure the pain and torture that faces him the rest of his life.

I thank you."

TABLE OF CASES

[REFERENCES ARE TO PAGES]

A

Abbott ads. Gulf, etc., R. Co., 457.
Abbott v. Lee, 272.
Abrams, In re, 585.
Abt v. Chicago Rys. Co., 605.
Adams ads. Cincinnati St. Ry. Co., 214.
Adams ads. Oakland, 435, 437.
Adams ads. Taylor, 346.
Adams v. Foley, 363.
Adams v. Greenwich Ins. Co., 581.
Adams v. Sullivan, 425.
Ader ads. Paparone, 95.
Adler ads. Chicago, etc., R. Co., 200.
Adrian ads. Davis, 327.
Aetna Ins. Co. ads. McDowell, 303.
Aetna Ins. Co. v. Paul, 350.
Aetna Life Ins. Co. ads. Aldridge, 551.
Ahart v. Stock, 585.
Ah Quong ads. Cameron, 289.
Ahrends ads. Langdon, 386.
Albany R. Co. ads. Piehl, 388.
Albaugh v. Shrope, 489.
Alberti v. N. Y., etc., R. Co., 326.
Alberts ads. State, 590.
Alberty ads. McMurrough, 219.
Albrecht Grocery Co., 635.
Alcorn ads. City Bank etc., 633.
Aldridge v. Aetna Life Ins. Co., 551.
Alkemeyer Co. v. McCardell, 551.
Allemania F. Ins. Co. ads. Hall, 489.
Allen ads. Brittain, 198.
Allen ads. Fowles, 373.
Allen ads. H. C. King Motor Sales Corp., 150.
Allen ads. Peo., 199.
Allen v. Boston El. R. Co., 475.
Allendale Tp. ads. Hock, 350.
Allgood ads. Botwinnes, 458.
Allyn ads. Hubbard, 363.
Alminowiez v. People, 374.
Alsabrook v. Bishop, 489.
Althoff v. I. C. R. Co., 328.
Aluminum Ore Co. ads. Clay, 324.
Amarillo First Nat. Bk. ads. Rush, 371.
Ambrason ads. Carpenter, 258.
Am. Surety Co. v. N. S., 335.
Amer. Can Co. ads. Quick, 542.
Amer. Express Co. v. Spillman, 285.
Amer. Food Co. v. Halstead, 370.
Amer. Malt Co. ads. Globe Brewing Co., 370.
Amer. St. Bank ads. Savich, 569.
American Automobile Ins. Co. v. Struwe, 604.
American Cereal Co. ads. London, etc., Co., 289.
American Fire Ins. Co. v. First Nat. Bank, 314.
American McKenna ads. Chicago etc., R. Co., 638.
American Motor Car Co. v. Robbin, 287.
American Ry. Express Co. ads. Effron etc., Co., 636.
American Ry. Express Co. ads. Schevers, 604.
American Tube, etc., Co. ads. Gilmore, 385.
American Union Line v. Oriental Nav. Corp., 633.
American Zinc, Lead & Smelting Co. ads. New Jersey Zinc Co., 605.
American & British Mfg. Co. ads. Stove Carriage Co., 286.
American, etc., Co. v. Maynahan, 642.
American, etc., Co. v. Pierce, 641.

Amphett ads. Peoples Gas Light Co., 328.
Ampt ads. State, 279.
Anchor ads. Love, etc., Co., 349.
Anderson ads. Chronister, 633.
Anderson ads. Gungrich, 641.
Anderson ads. Sloan, 334.
Anderson v. Anderson, 606.
Anderson v. Chicago, R. I. & P. Ry. Co., 638.
Anderson v. Crane, 350.
Anderson v. State, 194.
Andrae ads. People, 586.
Andre v. Hardin, 425.
Andrews ads. Edmandson, 348.
Andrews ads. Lee, 581.
Andrews ads. Peo., 488.
Andrews v. State, 282, 586.
Andrews v. U. S. Casualty Co., 636.
Ankersmit v. Tuch, 604, 606.
Ann Arbor R. Co. ads. Close, 283.
Ann Arbor R. Co. ads. Wells, 214.
Annis v. Peo., 582.
Ansbro ads. Dameron, 349.
Anthony ads. Indianapolis etc., R. Co., 579.
Anthony ads. Mutual L. Ins. Co., 289.
Anthony v. Cass, etc. Co., 544.
Appel v. Chicago City Ry. Co., 638, 641.
Appelton ads. Smalley, 386.
Arakelian v. San Pacific Co., 285.
Archer v. N. Y., etc., R. Co., 326.
Armistead v. Com., 199.
Arndt v. Burghardt, 331.
Arnold ads. Cheeney, 259.
Arnold ads. People, 283, 284.
Arnstine v. Treat, 303.
Arpo v. Ferguson, 370.
Arsht ads. Pantelis, 640.
Arvey ads. Cayne, 637.
Aschenbrenner ads. Book, 287.
Ashdown v. Ely, 350, 351.
Ashkins ads. Goldman, 491.
Ashland Water Co. ads. Green, 332.
Ashley v. Root, 331.
Assad ads. Ladany, 632.
Assoc. Realty Corp. ads. Carlson, 283.
Assured's, etc., Co. ads. Miller, 579.
Astoria Box & Paper Co. ads. Rorvick, 219.
Atchison T. & S. F. Ry Co. ads. McComb, 278.
Atchison, etc. R. Co. ads. Richmond Dredging Co., 387.
Atchison, etc. R. Co. v. Hays, 491.
Atherton v. Shelly, 372.
Atkinson v. National Council, 633.
Atlanta ads. Bevan, 315.
Atlanta, etc. R. Co. v. Gardner, 385.
Atlantic Ricemills Co. ads. Bouldin, 309.
Atlantic etc., Co. ads. Norton, 636.
Atwood v. Atwood, 386.
Augusta ads. Tebo, 457.
Aurora etc. R. Co. ads. Krakowski, 386.
Austin ads. Bernard's Inc., 585.
Austin v. Dungan, 288.
Automobile Ins. Co. of Hartford, Conn. ads. Hart, 119.
Avakian ads. Pierce, 369.
Aydlott v. Key, etc., Co., 640.
Ayers ads. Cameron, 383.
Ayers v. Harris, 328.
Ayers v. Ratshewsky, 587.
Ayers Ice Cream Co. ads. Texas Mach. etc., Co., 282.
Ayrault v. Chamberlain, 215.

B

B. A. Building Ass'n ads. Trainor, 310.
B. & O. R. Co. v. Fouts, 282
Babcock ads. Dore, 579.
Babcock ads. Peo., 541.
Babcock v. People, 258.
Bachner ads. Nedlin Realty Co., 96.
Bacon ads. Tooley, 349.
Bailey ads. J. W. Carter, etc., 632.
Bailey v. Centerville, 387.
Bailey v. Look, 543.
Bailey v. Turner, 195, 196.
Bailey v. Woodrum Trunk Lines, 283.
Baillargeon v. Myers, 604.
Bainley ads. Carpenter, 459.
Baird ads. Clark, 408.
Baird ads. Newell, 363.
Baker ads. Bayard, 332.

Baker ads. Dubois, 404, 406.
Baker ads. N. Y. Mut. L. Ins. Co., 350.
Baker Matthews Lumber Co. v. Lincoln Furniture Mfg. Co., 205.
Bakin ads. Benedict, 490.
Balbo v. Peo., 197.
Baldridge v. Penland, 309.
Baldwin ads. Roche, 457.
Balfour v. Fresno, etc., Co., 371.
Ballard v. Breigh, 282.
Balsbaugh v. Frazer, 195.
Banca Nazionale di Credito v. Equitable Trust Co., 116.
Bancroft ads. Kibbe, 309.
Bancroft-Whitney Co. v. McHugh, 489.
Bank ads. Des Noyers Shoe Co., 334.
Bank ads. Massey, 579.
Bank of Commerce v. Elkins, 363.
Bank of Lafayette ads. Patton, 315.
Bank of Utica v. Hilliard, 129.
Banks ads. Mendenhall, 544.
Banks v. Connecticut, etc., Co., 129.
Banning ads. Cincinnati Terminal Co., 544.
Baptist Temple, Inc. ads. Schmitt, 96.
Barber ads. Bates, 582.
Barber ads. Com., 590.
Barber ads. Phares, 259.
Barber v. Merriam, 385.
Barber, etc., Co. ads. Brotherton, 639.
Barber's App., 457, 458, 459.
Barbour Brown & Co. v. Canty, 256, 363.
Barclay v. Peo., 196.
Barden ads. Gardner, 362.
Baretti v. Theurer, 309.
Barker v. Barker, 126.
Barker v. Bushnell, 373.
Barker v. Citizen's Mut. F. Ins. Co., 542.
Barker v. Ford, 579.
Barker v. St. Louis, etc. Co., 458.
Barlow ads. Sipes, 373.
Barnes ads. Long, etc., Co., 632.
Barnes ads. Michigan Air Line R. Co., 194.
Barnes ads. Sargeant, 458.
Barnett v. Chicago City Ry. Co., 366.
Barney v. Forbes, 371.
Barone ads. People, 602.
Barr ads. Milliken, 295.
Barrett ads. Kircheimer, 272.
Barrett ads. Morwich Pharmacal Co., 149.
Barrie v. Quimby, 384.
Barthal ads. City of Indianapolis, 283.
Bartholomew v. Davis, 357.
Bartholomew v. Farwell, 336.
Bartlett v. City of Medford, 605.
Bartley ads. Peo., 582.
Barto v. Detroit Iron, etc., Steel Co., 205.
Bass v. Receivers of Kirby Lumber Co., 606.
Bass v. State, 197.
Bassham v. State, 602.
Bastian ads. Peo., 580.
Bates v. Barber, 582.
Batesole ads. Becvar, 287.
Battele ads. Lincoln, 341.
Bauerlee ads. Redlich, 309.
Baughman v. Metropolitan St. Ry. Co., 217.
Baum v. State, 551.
Bauman ads. Quincy Gas Co., 491.
Bauman ads. Wilson, 279.
Baumann ads. Quincy G. & E. Co., 284, 286, 346, 640.
Baxter v. Chicago, etc., R. Co., 328.
Bay, etc., Co. v. Susman, 127.
Bayard v. Baker, 332.
Beach v Seattle, 197.
Beall ads. Bruce, 323.
Beaman Mach. Co. ads. Chisholm, 309.
Bearden ads. Continental Fire Ass'n, 303.
Beatty v. Hatcher, 632.
Beaver v. Emry, 635.
Bechat v. Knisley, 272.
Beck v. Hanline, 458.
Becvar v. Batesole, 287.
Bedford ads. Blake, 459.
Beecham v. Burns, 127.
Beeson ads. State, 602.
Beeson v. State, 581.
Behrman ads. State, 334.
Bekans, etc., Co. ads. Hood, 291.
Beland ads. O'Neill, 386.

Belknap v. Stewart, 259.
Bell ads. Hubb Diggs Co., 636.
Bell v. State, 489.
Bell v. Toluca Coal Co., 274.
Bender v. Terwilliger, 632.
Bendy ads. Glen Falls Ins. Co., 346.
Benedict ads. Fulton Bank, 582.
Benedict v. Bakin, 490.
Benedict v. Dakins, 541.
Benham ads. Sheldon, 387.
Bennet v. State, 196.
Bennington ads. Gross, 205.
Bennington ads. Merkle, 366.
Benson v. Superior Mfg. Co., 285.
Berens ads. I. C. C. R. R. Co., 282, 284.
Berkshire Bldg. Corp. ads. Kellogg, 151.
Berkshire Life Ins. ads. Talburt, 543.
Bernard's Inc. v. Austin, 585.
Berridge v. Pray, 640.
Berry v. Ingalls, 291.
Bertini ads. People, 601.
Bertolami v. United Eng., etc. Co., 345.
Best ads. Union Trust Co., 370.
Bestmor Realty Corporation ads. Jannotta, 96.
Bettel ads. Ripon, 476.
Bevan ads. Presbyterian Church, etc., 457, 458.
Bevan v. Atlanta, 315.
Bever v. Spangler, 477.
Beverley v. Boston El. R. Co., 385.
Beville v. Jones, 638.
Bias v. Reed, 204, 205.
Bidwell v. Los Angeles, 387.
Biles & Ruby ads. International, etc., R. Co., 489.
Bilger ads. Rosenthal, 258.
Billett v. Mich. Bonding & Surety Co., 609.
Billings Appeal, 295.
Billmeyer v. St. Louis Transit Co., 198.
Bills v. State, 580.
Birdsong ads. McLaten, 198.
Birdwell ads. Texas Employers Ins. Ass'n, 256.
Bishop ads. Alsabrook, 489.
Bishop ads. St. Louis W. R. Co., 550.
Bishop, etc. ads. Convert, 632.
Bisinger v. Sacramento Lodge, etc., 634, 635.
Bistritz v. Star F. Ins. Co., 491.
Black ads. Dowie, 582.
Blackburn ads. State, 579.
Blackwell v. St. Louis, etc. R. Co., 384.
Blackwell v. State, 195.
Blair ads. Mann, 476.
Blake v. Bedford, 459.
Blanchard v. Blanchard, 590.
Blank ads. Greager, 634.
Blanton ads. Texas Cent. R. Co., 199.
Blauner ads. McAnsh, 149.
Bliss ads. Lowe, 351.
Bliss ads. Satterlee, 349.
Bloom Co. v. U. S. Casualty, 284.
Bloomington v. Schrock, 476.
Bloomington Canning ads. Hammond, 460.
Blue ads. Reddington, 371.
Blume v. State, 458.
Blumenthal ads. Nat. Cash Register Co., 285.
Blydenburg ads. State, 385.
Board of Education ads. Nat. Bank of Decatur, 362.
Board of Ed. v. Keenan, 363.
Boehm ads. Riley, 309.
Boehm v. Detroit, 386.
Boerner Fry Co. v. Mucci, 282.
Bohanan v. Hans, 347.
Bohen v. North American Life Insurance Co., etc., 636.
Bolden v. State, 569.
Bolt ads. Dennis, 373.
Bolton ads. Peo., 489.
Boltz v. Sullivan, 636.
Bond v. Lotz, 590.
Bonker ads. Spicer, 205.
Bonnell v. Jacobs, 633.
Bonner ads. San Miguel Consol. Gold Min. Co., 217.
Bonner v. Mayfield, 459.
Book v. Aschenbrenner, 287.
Boon ads. Stone Land, etc., Co., 335.
Boon v. Weathered's Admr., 579.
Boone ads. Houston, etc., Co., 638.
Bordacov ads. Braverman, 127.
Boreham v. Byrne, 637.

Borilli ads. Com., 275.
Borstelman v. Brohan, 321.
Boston ads. Menard, 636.
Boston El. R. Co. ads. Allen, 475.
Boston El. R. Co. ads. Beverley, 385.
Boston El. R. Co. ads. Boyle, 362.
Boston El. R. Co. ads. Chase, 642.
Boston El. R. Co. ads. Eastman, 580.
Boston El. R. Co. ads. Green, 477.
Boston El. R. Co. ads. Loban, 386.
Boston El. R. Co. ads. Romania, 383.
Boston El. R. Co. ads. Root, 477.
Boston, etc. Co. v. Pontiac Clothing Co., 369.
Boston & M. R. R. ads. Nute, 601.
Boston & M. R. R. ads. Poole, 605.
Boston, etc., Ry. ads. Jones, 638.
Boston, etc., R. Co. ads. McKarren, 326.
Boston Food Co. v. Wilson & Co., 349.
Boston Realty Co. ads. Gilson, 370.
Botsford v. Wallace, 274.
Botwinnes v. Allgood, 458.
Bouldin v. Atlantic Ricemills Co., 309.
Bounds v. Little, 604.
Bowe v. Wright, 204.
Bowen ads. Peo., 457.
Bowers ads. Gates, 579.
Bowers v. Hanna, 374.
Bowery Savings Bank ads. Noah, 279.
Bowman v. Seaman, 218.
Boyce ads. Paxton, 542, 543.
Boyce v. Manhattan R. Co., 350.
Boyd ads. Dunham, 293.
Boykin ads. International, etc., R. Co., 541, 547.
Boyle v. Boston El. R. Co., 362.
Brackett ads. Niell, 543.
Bradford v. People, 527.
Bradish v. Grant, 634.
Bradley v. McDonald, 373.
Brady ads. Young, 606.
Brady v. Cassidy, 370.
Bragonier ads. Chicago & A. R., 637.
Brainerd ads. Laine, 289.
Brannan v. Henry, 258.
Brant v. Chicago & Alton R. R. Co., 635.
Brassel ads. Loughlin, 547.
Braverman v. Bordacov, 127.
Brazleton v. State, 194.
Brechler ads. Govier, 283.
Breigh ads. Ballard, 282.
Brelsford ads. Com., 284.
Bremer v. Hoag, 345.
Brennan ads. Malleable Iron Co., 518.
Brensinger ads. Mayer, 601.
Brewer ads. Tabor State Bank, 256.
Brewster v. Forney, 457.
Bride v. Clark, 331.
Bridges ads. Young, 198.
Brier ads. Burns, 348.
Briggs ads. Moorhead, 275.
Brill v. Flagler, 295.
Brink's Express Co. v. Burns, 634.
Bristol ads. Mortimer, 352.
British, etc., Co. v. Wilson, 126.
Brittain v. Allen, 198.
Broadhead v. Wiltse, 476.
Broadway, etc. ads. Byne, 590.
Brocamp ads. Peo., 287.
Brockman v. Wisconsin Power & Light Co., 606.
Brodsky v. Brodsky, 605.
Brohan ads. Borstelman, 321.
Brooklyn ads. Van Wycklen, 458.
Brooklyn City R. Co. ads. Cannon, 386.
Brooklyn El. R. Co. ads. Williams, 636.
Brooklyn El. R. Co. ads. Woodworth, 458.
Brooklyn Hebrew Orphan Asylum ads. Goodman, 204.
Brooklyn Heights R. Co. ads. Clark, 285.
Brooklyn Heights R. Co. ads. Rowe, 271.
Brooklyn Heights R. Co. ads. Swensen, 462.
Brooklyn Jewish Center, Inc. ads. Fishman, 531.
Brooks ads. State, 197.
Brotherton ads. Peo., 199.
Brotherton v. Barber, etc., Co., 639.
Brown ads. Johnson, 334, 544.
Brown ads. Marshall, 476.
Brown ads. St. Louis, etc. R. Co., 278.
Brown ads. Weitzel, 334.
Brown ads. Williams, 458.
Brown v. Wakeman, 346.

Brownlee v. Reiner, 126.
Brownlie v. Brownlie, 328, 489.
Bruce v. Beall, 323.
Bruce v. Western Pipe, etc., Co., 323.
Bruno v. Heckman, 585.
Brush v. Scribner, 331.
Bryan ads. Chicago, B. & Q. Ry. Co., 632.
Bryan ads. Frank Prox. Co., 519.
Bryant ads. Eckels, 385.
Bryant ads. Evans, 542.
Buchanan ads. People, 601, 602.
Buchanan ads. State, 272.
Buckingham ads. Ordway, 604.
Buckley v. Silverberg, 604.
Buckman v. Missouri, etc., R. Co., 425.
Bucyrus Co. ads. Chybowski, 200.
Budd v. Meridian El. R. Co., 351.
Budd Co. ads. Kimball, 96.
Buerger ads. Wunderlich, 606.
Buffalo Structural Steel v. Dickson, 283.
Buford ads. State, 197.
Bugg v. Houlka, 332.
Buhrmaster v. N. Y. C. and H. R. R. Co., 637.
Builders' Mut. F. Ins. Co. ads. Kaler, 543.
Bulfer ads. Lingle, 585.
Bulfinch ads. Dow, 285.
Bullard v. Lamberg, 582.
Bumsted v. Hoadley, 319.
Bundy ads. People, 631.
Burdick v. Hunt, 569.
Burdick v. Raymond, 350.
Burggraf ads. Graham, 315.
Burghardt ads. Arndt, 331.
Burke ads. Allen B. Wrisley, 349.
Burke ads. Crawford, 350.
Burke v. Nat. Liberty Ins. Co., etc., 632.
Burlington & O. R. Ry. Co. ads. McReynolds, 632.
Burlington, etc., R. Co. ads. Manning, 606.
Burnett v. Freeman, 415.
Burnham ads. Marsh, 353.
Burns ads. Beecham, 127.
Burns ads. Brink's Express Co., 634.
Burns v. Brier, 348.
Burt v. Long, 582.
Bush ads. Studwell, 370.
Bushnell ads. Barker, 373.
Butler ads. Lane, 604.
Butler v. Hamburg etc., Bank, 372.
Butler v. Lohn H. Leadley Co., 551.
Buttolf ads. Chicago, etc., R. Co., 200.
Butts v. Purdy, 334.
Byalos v. Matheson, 338.
Byerley v. Sun Co., 294.
Byers v. Nashville, etc. R., 476.
Byington ads. McGarrity, 293.
Byne v. Broadway, etc., 590.
Byrene ads. Boreham, 637.
Byrne ads. Peo., 284.
Byron ads. Thomas, 543.

C

C. C. C. & St. Louis Ry. Co. v. Monaghan, 327.
C. M. Ass'n v. Zerwick, 639.
C. & E. I. R. Co. v. Wallace, 457, 458, 477.
C. & N. W. Ry. Co. ads. Grant, 327.
C. & N. W. R. Co. ads. Kreuziger, 350, 351.
C. & O. R. Co. v. Fultz, 490.
Cabell ads. Ft. Worth, etc., Co., 582.
Cadigan v. Crabtree, 272.
Cadwaller v. Martin, 363.
Cady Lumber Co. v. Wilson etc. Co., 349.
Cal. Mut. L. Ins. Co. ads. Wilmarth, 279.
Cal. Power Co. ads. Foley, 282.
Caldwell ads. Scott, 346.
Caldwell v. Richards, 605.
Caledonia ads. Teegarden, 348.
Caledonian Ins. Co. ads. Goodman, 383.
Cal Hirsch, etc., Co. v. Coleman, 551.
Calhoun v. Ross, 341.
California Electric Light Co. v. California Safe Deposit, etc. Co., 601.
California Safe Deposit, etc., Co. ads. California Elec. Light Co., 601.
California St. R. Co. ads. Lombardi, 198.
California, etc. ads. McCann, 477.
Calkins v. Colburn, 580.

Call ads. Wrobel, 149.
Callahan ads. Pine, 199.
Callanan v. Keeseville, 371.
Callen v. Collins, 385.
Calumet & South Chicago Ry. Co. ads. Falvai, 605.
Calumet, etc. R. Co. ads. Kenna, 477, 636, 642.
Cameron v. Ah Quong, 289.
Cameron v. Ayers, 383.
Campbell ads. J. P. Watkins, etc. Co., 408.
Campbell ads. Lee, 217.
Campbell ads. Wightman, 283, 347.
Campbell v. Campbell, 200.
Campbell v. Germania Fire Ins. Co. of N. Y., 363.
Campion v. Downey, 363.
Cannon ads. El Paso El. Co., 292.
Cannon v. Brooklyn City R. Co., 386.
Canty ads. T. Barbour Brown & Co., 256, 363.
Carey ads. Humbarger, 637.
Carley v. N. Y., etc. R. Co., 425.
Carlson ads. Pittsburgh, etc. R. Co., 542.
Carlson v. Assoc. Realty Corp., 283.
Carlson v. Winterson, 579.
Carlton ads. Finch, 338.
Carmody v. Kolecheski, 633.
Carney v. Hennessey, 542.
Carpenter ads. Conkey, 585.
Carpenter ads. Morrison, 640.
Carpenter v. Ambrason, 258.
Carpenter v. Bainley, 459.
Carpenter v. Markham, 372.
Carpenter, et al. v. First Nat. Bank of Joliet, 634.
Carpenter-Morton Co. ads. Thornhill, 282.
Carr ads. West Chicago St. Ry. Co., 385.
Carr & Brannon ads. Ingwerson, 258.
Carrol ads. Chicago Rys., etc., 361.
Carroll v. Holmes, 633.
Carroll v. Palmer Mfg. Co., 274.
Carroll County v. O'Connor, 364.
Carruthers v. McMurray, 635.
Carter v. King County, 205.
Carter, etc. v. Bailey, 632.
Carville v. Watford, 547.
Cascone ads. Peo., 586, 587.
Caskie v. International Ry. Co., 97.
Cass, etc. Co. ads. Anthony, 544.
Cassen v. Galvin, 258.
Cassidy ads. Brady, 370.
Cassidy ads. Peo., 256.
Casteel v. Millison, 294.
Castelli ads. State, 259.
Castree ads. People, 286, 287.
Casualty Co. of America ads. Everson, 282.
Catlin v. Traders Ins. Co., 342, 459.
Cauble v. Worsham, 369.
Caulfield v. Hermann, 370.
Cayne v. Arvey, 637.
Centerville ads. Bailey, 387.
Central Shoe Co. v. Rashid, 271.
Central, etc., Assoc. v. Seeley, 274.
Century Publishing Co. ads. Huling, 350.
Cepak ads. Chicago Rys., 363.
Chadwick v. U. S., 126.
Chamberlain ads. Ayrault, 215.
Chamberlain v. Lowenthal, 275.
Chambers ads. Dundee, 315.
Chambers ads. Hester, 196.
Champion ads. Chicago, etc., R. Co., 285.
Chan Tin Pen ads. Roberts, 351.
Chance v. Kinsella, 543.
Chandler v. Prince, 279.
Chang Sim v. White, 298.
Chapman v. Strong, 489.
Chase ads. Phillips, 638.
Chase ads. Pool, 372.
Chase v. Boston El. R. Co., 642.
Chase v. Chase, 602.
Cheeney v. Arnold, 259.
Cherry & Webb Co. ads. Kennedy, 530.
Chicago ads. Gage, 332, 335.
Chicago ads. Goodrich, 362.
Chicago ads. McChesney, 301.
Chicago ads. Ouimette, 330.
Chicago ads. Sobieski, 274.
Chicago ads. Springer, 284.
Chicago v. McGiven, 636.
Chicago, B. & Q. Ry. Co. v. Bryan, 632.

Chicago City Ry. Co. ads. Appel, 638, 641.
Chicago City Ry. Co. ads. Barnett, 366.
Chicago City R. Co. ads. Dooley, 397.
Chicago City Ry. Co. ads. Dunhaw, 640.
Chicago City Ry. Co. ads. Ledwell, 641.
Chicago City R. Co. ads. McMahon, 414.
Chicago City Ry. Co. ads. Math, 348, 569.
Chicago City R. Co. ads. Rose, 642.
Chicago City Railway ads. Stadler, 635.
Chicago City R. Co. ads. Ullrich, 475, 476.
Chicago City R. Co. ads. Ward, 387.
Chicago City Ry. v. Douglas, 476.
Chicago City R. Co. v. Enroth, 353.
Chicago City R. Co. v. Gregory, 542.
Chicago City R. Co. v. Hagenback, 278.
Chicago City Ry. Co. v. Hyndshaw, 351.
Chicago City Ry. Co. v. Matthieson, 546, 551.
Chicago City R. Co. v. Smith, 323.
Chicago City R. Co. v. T. W. Jones, etc., Co., 291.
Chicago Great Western R. Co. ads. Upthegrove, 285.
Chicago Grill Co. ads. Luin, 601.
Chicago R. I. & P. Ry. Co. ads. Anderson, 638.
Chicago R. I. & P. Ry. Co. ads. Stillman, 256.
Chicago Rys. Co. ads. Abt, 605.
Chicago Rys. Co. ads. Griswold, 349.
Chicago Rys. Co. ads. Sanderg, 639.
Chi. Rys. Co. ads. Sorenson, 347, 348.
Chicago Rys. Co. ads. Walsh, 256.
Chicago Rys., etc. v. Carrol, 361.
Chicago Rys. v. Cepak, 363.
Chicago San. Dist. v. Corneau, 477.
Chicago Tel. Supply Co. v. Marne, etc., Tel. Co., 285.
Chi. Union Trac. Co. ads. Lauth, 386.
Chicago Union Tract. Co. v. Ertrachter, 435.
Chicago Union Trac. Co. v. Lawrence, 637.
Chicago Union T. Co. v. Miller, 489.
Chicago Union Tract. Co. v. Sugar, 459.
Chicago & Alton R. R. Co. ads. Brant, 635.
Chicago & A. R. Co. v. Bragonier, 637.
Chicago & A. R. Co. v. Scott, 640.
Chicago & C. R. Co. ads. Walker, 356.
Chicago & Joliet El. R. Co. v. Herbert, 640.
Chicago & J. El. R. Co. v. Spence, 323.
Chicago, etc. R. Co. ads. Baxter, 328.
Chicago, etc., R. Co. ads. Heddles, 544.
Chicago, etc., R. Co. ads. Helgeson, 550.
Chicago, etc., R. Co. ads. Hermes, 278.
Chicago, etc., R. Co. ads. King, 579.
Chicago, etc., R. Co. ads. Materson, 640.
Chicago, etc. R. Co. ads. McMahon, 437.
Chicago, etc., R. Co. ads. Moore, 636.
Chicago, etc. R. Co. ads. Nielson, 396.
Chicago, etc., R. Co. ads. O'Brien, 292, 385.
Chicago, etc., R. Co. ads. Pfeiffer, 288.
Chicago, etc., R. Co. ads. Pronsekvitch, 604.
Chicago, etc., R. Co. ads. Riggins, 638.
Chicago, etc., R. Co. ads. Scagel, 336.
Chicago, etc, R. Co. ads. Uniacke, 477.
Chicago, etc. R. Co. ads. Waterman, 604.
Chicago, etc., R. Co. ads. Weisbrod, 272.
Chicago, etc., R. Co. v. Adler, 200.
Chicago etc, R. Co. v. American McKenna, 638.
Chicago, etc., R. Co. v. Buttolf, 200.
Chicago, etc., R. Co. v. Champion, 285.
Chicago, etc. R. Co. v. Corson, 327.
Chicago, etc., R. Co. v. Fisher, 199, 200.
Chicago, etc., R. Co. v. Holland, 298.
Chicago, etc, R. Co. v. Mayer, 289.
Chicago, etc., R. Co. v. Reyman, 274.
Chicago, etc., R. Co. v. Ryan, 604.
Chicago, etc, R. Co. v. Schmitz, 425.
Chicago, etc., R. Co. v. Smith, 323.
Chicago, etc. R. Co. v. Trayes, 318.
Chicago, etc. R. Co. v. Tuite, 331.
Chick ads. Houston, etc. R. Co., 327.

Chilberg v. Standard Furniture Co., 531.
Chiles ads. Colorado, etc., R. Co., 636.
Chin Mook Sow ads. Peo., 586, 587.
Chisholm v. Beaman Mach. Co., 309.
Choctaw, etc., R. Co. v. True, 199.
Chorley ads. Crawford, 116, 118.
Chotean v. Raitt, 303.
Christianson v. Dunham, etc., 348.
Christy ads. State, 258.
Chronister v. Anderson, 633.
Chrystal ads. Graham, 581.
Church v. Stoldt, 195.
Churchill ads. Old Motor Works, 269.
Churchill ads. Woodman, 581.
Churchill v. Churchill, 196.
Chybowski v. Bucyrus Co., 200.
Cilley v. Preferred, etc., Co., 633.
Cincinnati ads. Neff, 632.
Cincinnati v. Scarborough, 386.
Cincinnati First Nat. Bank v. Kelly, 349.
Cincinnati H. & D. Ry. v. Tafelski, 610.
Cincinnati St. Ry. Co. v. Adams, 214.
Cincinnati Terminal Co. v. Banning, 544.
Cincinnati Tract. Co. v. Harrison, 283.
Cincinnati Traction Co. v. McKim, 636.
Cincinnati, etc., Co. v. Gross, 638.
Cincinnati, etc. R. Co. v. De Onzo, 326.
Citizens' Light, etc. Co. v. Lee, 194.
Citizen's Mut. F. Ins. Co. ads. Barker, 542.
Citizens' Sav. Bank, etc., Co. v. Fitchburg Mut. F. Ins. Co., 194.
Citizens Trust Co. of Utica v. R. Prescott & Son, Inc., 96.
Citizens, etc. Co. v. O'Brien, 384.
City Bank, etc. v. Alcorn, 633.
City of Boston ads. Gray, 204.
City of Charleston v. Newman, 347.
City of Chicago ads. Voche, 642.
City of Chicago ads. Wyman, 348.
City of Chicago ads. Zipkie, 283.
City of E. St. Louis v. Freeds, 334.
City of Ft. Worth v. Lopp, 604.
City of Indianapolis v. Barthal, 283.
City of Joplin ads. Townsend, 517.
City of Medford ads. Bartless, 605.
City of Sedalia ads. Corpenny, 132.
Clark ads. Bride, 331.
Clark ads. Hinchman, 195.
Clark ads. Jones, 342.
Clark ads. Peo., 195, 196.
Clark ads. Pontecorvo, 604, 605.
Clark ads. Rachmel, 275.
Clark v. Baird, 408.
Clark v. Brooklyn Heights R. Co., 285.
Clark v. Dasso, 331, 335.
Clark v. People, 306.
Clark-Rice Corp. v. Waltham, 489.
Clarke ads. Scofield, 638.
Clarke v. Clarke, 116.
Clay v. Aluminum Ore Co., 324.
Clemons ads. Devereaux, 258.
Cleveland, etc., R. Co. ads. Peo., 274.
Cleveland, etc., R. Co. ads. Schweinfurth, 285.
Cleveland, etc., R. Co. ads. Winn, 336.
Cleveland, etc., R. Co v. Pritschan, 638.
Cline ads. Cox, 270.
Clopton v. Clopton, 351.
Close v. Ann Arbor R. Co., 283.
Cobb v. United etc., Co., 462.
Cobb, Bates & Yerxa Co. v. Hills, 604.
Coburn v. Moline, etc. R. Co., 386.
Cochran ads. Peo., 425.
Cochran v. Ward, 331.
Cocke & Co. v. New Era, etc., Co., 549.
Cockrill ads. San Antonio, etc. R. Co., 350, 351.
Coffee ads. Pierce, 384.
Coghlin ads. Prudential Trust Co., 256.
Cogswell v. Dolliver, 309.
Cohen ads. Tabor Coal Co., 270.
Cohen v. Elias, 315, 327.
Cohen v. Long Island R. Co., 288.
Coker ads. Missouri, etc., R. Co., 397.
Colbert v. State, 587.
Colburn ads. Calkins, 580.
Colburn ads. Howes, 459.
Colburn v. Parret, 314.
Cole ads. Peo., 550.
Cole v. Drum, 546, 551.
Coleman ads. Cal. Hirsch, etc., Co., 551.
Collier v. State, 585.
Collins ads. Callen, 385.

Collins v. Gleason Coal Co., 258.
Collins v. Hoehle, 542.
Collins v. State, 198, 200, 284, 289.
Collins v. Wells, 271.
Colonial Knitting Mills, Inc. v. Hosiery Mfr's Corp., 117.
Colorado, etc., R. Co. v. Chiles, 636.
Colrick v. Swinburne, 347.
Columbus R. etc., Co. ads. Gilhooley, 517.
Com. ads. Armistead, 199.
Com. ads. Stone, 636.
Com. ads. Wright, 199.
Com. v. Barber, 590.
Com. v. Borilli, 275.
Com. v. Brelsford, 284.
Com. v. Eagan, 195.
Com. v. Gallo, 488.
Com. v. Hayden, 335.
Com. v. Homer, 569.
Com. v. Hussey, 196.
Com. v. Ingraham, 581.
Com. v. Levine, 256.
Com. v. McDermott, 256.
Com. v. Moore, 195.
Com. v. Mosier, 199.
Com. v. Nefus, 350.
Com. v. O'Neil, 195.
Com. v. Patalano, 602.
Com. v. Rogers, 579.
Com. v. Sacco, 490, 586, 601.
Com. v. Scott, 285.
Com. v. Sturtivant, 476.
Com. v. Turner, 542.
Com. v. Whitman, 273.
Com. Jewelry Co. ads. Inter-State Finance Corp., 383.
Com. Trust Co. v. Coveney, 369.
Coman v. Wunderlich, 425.
Combes v. Maas, 96.
Combs ads. Hermann, 605.
Commerce Trust Co. ads. Haas, 298.
Commercial Coal Co. ads. Woodruff Coal, etc., Co., 282.
Commercial Credit Corp. v. Podhorzer, 149.
Commercial State Bank ads. Metropolitan Nat. Bank, 350.
Commonwealth Bank v. Goodman, 477.
Commonwealth El. Co. v. Rose, 638.
Commonwealth Fuel Co., Inc. v. Powpit Co., Inc., 149.
Compton-Price Piano Co. v. Stewart, 204.
Con Coal Co. v. Schneider, 371.
Condit ads. Dady, 569.
Cone ads. McKivitt, 491.
Conestoga Cigar Co. v. Finka, 279.
Conkey ads. Huntington, 634.
Conkey v. Carpenter, 585.
Conley ads. Eagan, 332.
Conlin v. Ryan, 320.
Conlon v. Osborn, 604.
Conn v. Morgan, 327.
Conn v. Seaboard Air Line Ry. Co., 639.
Connecticut River R. Co. ads. Miner, 531.
Connecticut, etc., Co. ads. Banks, 129.
Connor ads. Majors, 602.
Conrad v. St. Louis, etc., R. Co., 457.
Considine ads. People, 259, 491.
Consolidated Coal Co. of St. Louis v. Scheiber, 639.
Consolidated R. Co. ads. Currie, 459.
Consolidation Coal Co., Inc. ads. Vagaszki, 106, 273.
Continental Bank, etc. v. Greene, 632.
Continental Fire Ass'n v. Bearden, 303.
Continental Life Ins. Co. v. Rogers, 127.
Contoocook Valley R. Co. ads. Page, 194.
Converse v. Langshaw, 371.
Convert v. Bishop, etc., 632.
Conway v. State, 579.
Cooch ads. Mahoney, 601.
Cook ads. Libby, etc., 490.
Cook ads. North Chicago St. R. Co., 292, 385.
Cook ads. State, 326.
Cook ads. Stout, 289.
Cook v. Classheim, 585.
Cook v. Farnum, 362.
Coon Const. Co. ads. Marion, 397.
Cooper ads. U. S. Cement Co., 640.
Copsey ads. Peo., 199, 200.

Corbet v. Union Dime Sav. Inst., 328.
Corgan ads. Hutchins, 289.
Corneau ads. Chicago San. Dist., 477.
Cornelison Motor Co. v. Morris, 634.
Cornell ads. Davidson, 386.
Cornell v. Morrison, 205.
Corpenny v. City of Sedalia, 132.
Corr v. Hoffman, 116.
Corson ads. Chicago, etc., R. Co., 327.
Cotten ads. Miller, 38, 625.
Cotting ads. Cronan, 259.
Coughlin v. Peo., 199.
Counts v. State, 195.
Coveney ads. Com. Trust Co., 369.
Cowen Co. ads. Houk Mfg. Co., 204.
Cox v. Cline, 270.
Crabtree ads. Cadigan, 272.
Craig ads. Omaha St. R. Co., 199.
Craig ads. Williams, 258.
Craig v. State, 579.
Craig v. Trotter, 386.
Crampton ads. Knowles, 373.
Crane ads. Anderson, 350.
Crane Co. ads. Parker, 490.
Crane v. Ross, 373.
Craney v. Schlowman, 350.
Crary ads. Yankee Jim's Union Water Co., 606.
Crate v. Decorah, 293.
Cravens v. Eagle Cotton Mills Co., 371.
Crawford v. Burke, 350.
Crawford v. Chorley, 116, 118.
Crean v. Houmigan, 258.
Creason ads. Missouri, etc., R. Co., 579.
Creedon v. Galvin, 287.
Crew v. Penn R. Co., 361.
Criswell v. Robbins, 283.
Cronan v. Cotting, 259.
Crone v. Jordan Marsh Co., 531.
Cronin v. Fitchburg, etc., R. Co., 385.
Crosby ads. Grand Pass Shooting Club, 334.
Cross ads. Singer, 338.
Crossett v. Owens, 334.
Crouch v. Nat., etc., Co., 346, 349.
Crystal Ice Mfg. Co. v. San Antonio, etc., 256.
Culbertson v. Salinger, 347.
Culver ads. Johnson, 256, 636.
Cuneo-Henneberry ads. Wicks, 324, 397.
Curran ads. Donelly, 605.
Curran ads. Peo., 258, 273, 490.
Curran v. A. H. Stanger Co., 385.
Currelli v. Jackson, 388.
Currie v. Consolidated R. Co., 459.
Curtis ads. Eaton, 218.
Curtis ads. Harding, 334.
Curtis ads. Plumb, 350.
Curtis v. Marfs, 347.
Curtis v. McAuliffe, 364.

D

D. & H. Truck Line v. Lavellee, 640.
Dady v. Condit, 569.
Dakins ads. Benedict, 541.
Dale & Cain ads. Webb, 586.
Dalton v. Smith, 349.
Dalwigh ads. International & G. N. R. Co., 258.
Daly v. Melendy, 258.
Daly v. Whitacre, 387.
Damas v. People, 258.
Dameron v. Ansbro, 349.
Danzey v. State, 195.
Darling v. Grand Rapids, etc., Co., 457.
Darrogh ads. Fuller, 640.
Darrow ads. People, etc., Co., 634.
Darst v. Doom, 315.
Dasso ads. Clark, 331, 335.
Davey v. So. P. Co., 348.
Davidson ads. Shippers, etc., Co., 295.
Davidson ads. Walden, 303.
Davidson v. Cornell, 386.
Davidson v. Wallingford, 195.
Davies ads. Marshall, 606.
Davis ads. Bartholomew, 357.
Davis ads. Estes, 638.
Davis ads. Graham, 606.
Davis ads. International, etc., R. Co., 291.
Davis ads. Kells, 632.
Davis ads. Lessing, 362.
Davis ads. Magnolia, etc., Co., 370.
Davis ads. State, 543.
Davis v. Adrian, 327.
Davis v. E. St. Louis Lodge, 490.

Davis v. Hill, 636.
Davis v. Sanford, 309.
Davis v. State, 195.
Davis v. Willis, 490.
Davis & Co., ads. Graham & Co., 604, 606.
Davis & Co. ads. Novelty Showcase Co., 295.
Dawes ads. Flamion, 640.
Dawson v. Pacific Electric Ry. Co., 606.
Dawson v. Peterson, 331.
Dazey ads. Roberts, 369.
Dean ads. Poole, 457.
De Benavides, ads. Oritz, 127.
De Bolt v. German American Ins. Co., 306.
De Camp ads. Peo., 587.
Decker ads. Peo., 196, 197.
Decorah ads. Crate, 293.
Dedloff ads. West Chicago St. Ry. Co., 641.
Deel v. Heiligenstein, 352.
Deering Southwestern R. Co. ads. Rooker, 199.
De Freitas v. Suisan City, 408.
DeHart ads. Emery Dry Goods Co., 640.
Deigel v. State, 587.
Delancy v. Framingham, etc., R. Co., 457.
De Laveaga's Estate, 551.
Dellapenna ads. F. W. Stock & Sons, 579.
De Lucia v. Kneeland, 638.
Del Visco v. Gen. El. Co., 490.
De Meli v. De Meli, 543.
Deming ads. Scheerer, 605.
De Miranda ads. Govin, 589.
Dempsey v. Goldstein, 437.
Den ads. Manning, 362.
Denham v. Washington Water Power Co., 198.
Dennie v. Williams, 342.
Dennis v. Bolt, 373.
Denton v. English, 335.
De Onzo ads. Cincinnati, etc., R. Co., 326.
Des Moines, etc., R. Co. ads. Stutsman, 457.
Des Noyers Shoe Co. v. Bank, 334.
Detroit ads. Boehm, 386.
Detroit ads. Tattan, 330.
Detroit Iron, etc., Steel Co. ads. Barto, 205.
Detroit R. Co. ads. Selby, 490.
Detroit Taxicab Co. ads. Theisen, 271.
Detroit Taxicab & Transfer Co. ads. Jones, 217.
Detroit United Ry. Co. ads. Hickey, 569.
Detroit, etc., Ins. Co. ads. Rodee, 291.
Deuterman ads. Graham, 384.
DeVault ads. Laub, 256.
Devereaux v. Clemons, 258.
Dexter v. Ivins, 274.
Deyell ads. Skipworth, 309.
Diamond Glue Co. v. Wietzychowski, 256.
Dibble Seedgrower v. Jones, 150.
Dickens ads. Gulf, etc., R. Co., 199.
Dicks v. State, 200.
Dickson ads. Buffalo Structural Steel, 283.
Di Cola ads. Old Colony Trust Co., 543.
Diersson ads. Nathan, 342.
Dilger v. Whitteen, 287.
Dill ads. Eisfield, 404, 406.
Dilleber v. Home L. Ins. Co., 477.
Diller v. No. Cal. Power Co., 328.
Dillie v. Lovell, 634.
Dillman ads. State, 200, 580.
Dillon ads. Graham, 256.
Distler ads. Germania Bank, 370.
Di Tommaso v. Syracuse Univ., 437.
Dittmeier Real Estate Co. v. Southern Surety Co., 205.
Dixon v. Smith-Wallace Shoe Co., 331.
Dobson ads. McCulloch, 541.
Dodez ads. Gishwiller, 606.
Dodwell & Co., Inc. v. Silverman, 150.
Dolan v. Herring, etc., 384.
Dolan v. Meehan, 387, 404, 406.
Doll ads. Metzer, 590.
Dolliver ads. Cogswell, 309.
Donan v. Donan, 362.

Donelly v. Curran, 605.
Donham ads. Labrecque, 544.
Donnelly v. Paramount Organization, 205.
Donohue v. State, 602.
Dooley v. Chicago City R. Co., 397.
Dooley ads. Gulf, etc., R. Co., 475, 640.
Doom ads. Darst, 315.
Doran v. Mullen, 259.
Dore v. Babcock, 579.
Dotterer v. State, 579, 585, 586.
Doty ads. New Castle Bridge Co., 275.
Doubet ads. Pickrel, 351.
Douglas ads. Chicago City Ry., 476.
Douglas & Co. ads. Latman, 348.
Dow v. Bulfinch, 285.
Dowdell v. Wilcox, 640.
Dowie v. Black, 582.
Dowie v. Priddle, 363.
Dowling ads. People, 605.
Downer ads. Sovereign Camp, etc., 271.
Downey ads. Campion, 363.
Downs v. N. Y. C. R. R. Co., 258.
Doyle ads. Farnam, 274.
Doyle ads. Hanselman, 303.
Doyle ads. Pedley, 601.
Doyle v. Singer Sewing Mach. Co., 323.
Drake ads. Legg, 259.
Driscoll ads. Precourt, 256.
Drum ads. Cole, 546, 551.
Dryden ads. Makey, 197.
Dubois v. Baker, 404, 406.
Duffy ads. O'Reilly, 295.
Duffy v. Radke, 580.
Duke Drug Co. ads. Moran, 462.
Duncan ads. Winters, 640.
Duncan v. Seeley, 491.
Dundee v. Chambers, 315.
Dungan ads. Austin, 288.
Dunham ads. Christianson, etc., 348.
Dunham v. Boyd, 293.
Dunham v. Chicago City Ry. Co., 640.
Dunn v. State, 196, 579.
Dunn Oil Mills Co. ads. Murchison Nat. Bank, 194.
Duplanty v. Stokes, 370.
Durbin v. Knox, 275.
Durgin v. Somers, 373.
Durkin ads. Maxwell, 605.
Durrant ads. Peo., 490, 543.
Dwyer v. Rippetoe, 363.
Dyas v. Southern Pacific Co., 637.
Dyckman ads. Peo., 129.
Dyer ads. Rutherford, 315.
Dyer v. Title Guaranty & Surety Co., 219.
Dykstra v. Grand Rapids, etc., Co., 638.

E

Eagan ads. Com., 195.
Eagan v. Conley, 332.
Eagle Cotton Mills Co. ads. Cravens, 371.
Eagle Star, etc., Co. v. Head, 641.
Earl v. Lefler, 283.
East Branch Min. Co. ads. Smith, 362.
Eastern Iowa Tel. Co. ads. Ney, 336.
Eastman v. Boston El. R. Co., 580.
E. St. Louis Lodge ads. Davis, 490.
E. St. L. Ry. Co. ads. Grim, 328.
Eaton v. Curtis, 218.
Eckels v. Bryant, 385.
Eckels v. Halsten, 457.
Eckenfels ads. So. Pac. Co., 326.
Eddy ads. Gage, 295, 348, 349.
Edmandson v. Andrews, 348.
Edwards v. Osman, 541.
Effron, etc., Co. v. American Ry. Express Co., 636.
Ehrich ads. Hanlon, 569.
Eisenman ads. Fraher, 346.
Eisfield v. Dill, 404, 406.
Elias ads. Cohen, 315, 327.
Elias ads. People, 287.
Elkins ads. Bank of Commerce, 363.
Elledge ads. Perry State Bank, 294.
Elliott ads. Texas, etc., R. Co., 195.
Ellis ads. McDavid, 309.
Ellis v. State, 200.
Ellithorpe ads. Harvey, 632, 633.
Elmore ads. Peo., 326.
El Paso El. Co. v. Cannon, 292.
Ellsworth v. Palmtag, 489.
Elston ads. McCormick, 309.
Elston ads. Murray, 129.
Elwood Mfg. Co. ads. Faulkner, 351.

Ely ads. Ashdown, 350, 351.
Ely ads. Harper, 309.
Ely ads. Silvis, 194, 195.
Emery Dry Goods Co. v. DeHart, 640.
Emmett v. Lee, 335.
Empire, etc., Co. ads. Township, etc., 132.
Emry ads. Beaver, 635.
Ende ads. Liverpool, etc., Co., 543.
English ads. Denton, 335.
English ads. Galveston H. El. R. Co., 338.
Enroth ads. Chicago City R. Co., 353.
Ephraims v. Murdock, 289.
Equitable Acc. Co. ads. Shamhan, 334.
Equitable Trust Co. ads. Banca Nazionale di Credito, 116.
Erling ads. Monmouth, 641.
Ertrachter ads. Chicago Union Tract Co., 435.
Essex v. McPherson, 194.
Essex County ads. Peck, 194.
Est. of Ramsey v. Whitbeck, 542.
Estes ads. Mallow, 370.
Estes v. Davis, 638.
Ettelsohn v. Kirkwood, 639.
Ettinger v. Goodyear, 542.
Evans v. Bryant, 542.
Evans v. Rogers, 309.
Everding ads. Supreme, etc., 275.
Everdson v. Mayhew, 347.
Everson v. Casualty Co. of America, 282.
Ewing ads. St. Louis, etc., R. Co., 285.
Ewing v. Hatcher, 373, 387, 414, 425.
Ex Parte Burch, 132.

F

Fain v. Nelms, 633.
Fairfield ads. Stotts, 363.
Fall River ads. Wooley, 326.
Falvai v. Calumet & South Chicago Ry. Co., 605.
Famous, etc., Corp. ads. Guinan, 519.
Farmer v. Norton, 632.
Farmers' Mut. F. Ins. Co. ads. Martin, 195.
Farmers' Mutual Hail, etc., Co. ads. Lee, 282.
Farmers, etc., Bank, In re, 274.
Farnam v. Doyle, 274.
Farnum ads. Cook, 362.
Farrell v. Haze, 459.
Farrell v. Wallace, 369.
Farwell ads. Bartholomew, 336.
Faulkner ads. State, 198.
Faulkner v. I. L. Elwood Mfg. Co., 351.
Faulkner v. Payne, 287.
Fawsett ads. Pittsburgh, etc., R. Co., 309.
Faxon v. Hollis, 309.
Fearing ads. Haack, 256.
Feather ads. Webb, 258.
Featherstone v. Lowell Cotton Mills, 195.
Feld v. Loftis, 345.
Felsenthal v. North Assurance, 489.
Felska v. N. Y. C. R. Co., 387.
Ferguson ads. Arpo, 370.
Ferguson ads. Folts, 348.
Ferguson v. Moore, 636.
Ferguson v. Rochford, 384.
Fetherly v. Waggoner, 127.
Fidelity, etc., Co. ads. Lyman, 634.
Fields ads. Manhattan L. Ins. Co., 331.
Fifield ads. Wiltse, 370.
Fifth Avenue Church ads. Philpot, 637.
Fifth Avenue Coach Co. ads. Pierpont, 292, 385.
Fillingham v. St. Louis Transit Co., 219.
Finch v. Carlton, 338.
Finch v. Weiner, 489.
Fini v. Perry, 204.
Finka ads. Conestoga Cigar Co., 279.
Finley v. West Chicago St. R. Co., 602.
Finnegan Co. ads. Sanford, 373, 374.
Firestone Tire & Rubber Co. ads. Piretti, 350.
First Nat. Bank ads. American Fire Ins. Co., 314.
First Nat. Bank ads. Lefkowitz, 315.
First National Bank ads. Pullin, 637.
First Nat. Bank of Joliet ads. Carpenter, et al., 634.
First Nat. Bank of Tuckahoe ads. Palmison, 95.
Fish v. Glass, 200.

Fisher ads. Chicago, etc., R. Co., 199, 200.
Fisher ads. Peo., 586.
Fishman ads. Mankes, 270, 271.
Fishman v. Brooklyn Jewish Center, Inc., 531.
Fitchburg Mut. F. Ins. Co. ads. Citizens' Sav. Bank, etc., Co., 194.
Fitchburg, etc., R. Co. ads. Cronin, 385.
Fitts v. Southern, 196, 198.
Fitzgerald ads. Peo., 569.
Fitzgerald v. Hedstrom, 328.
Flagler ads. Brill, 295.
Flamion v. Dawes, 640.
Flanigan ads. Mono County, 195.
Fleck ads. Roth, 338.
Fleeson v. Savage Silver Min. Co., 194.
Fleming v. Springfield, 385.
Foley ads. Adams, 363.
Foley v. Cal. Power Co., 282.
Folts v. Ferguson, 348.
Fond du Lac ads. Schoefer, 636.
Fong Ah Sing ads. People, 258.
Foote ads. Hoffman House, 205.
Foote v. Greilick, 306.
Forbes ads. Barney, 371.
Ford ads. Nouman Printer's Supply, 309.
Ford ads. Barker, 579.
Foreman v. State, 579.
Forney ads. Brewster, 457.
Forrestal ads. Frey, 414.
Forsythe ads. Hardin, 272.
Ft. Edward Bk. ads. Streever, 320.
Ft. Howard ads. Wright, 292, 385.
Ft. Worth, etc., Co. ads. Orchin, 639.
Ft. Worth, etc., Co. v. Cabell, 582.
Foster ads. State, 200.
Foster v. Newbrough, 303, 606.
Foster v. Tannenbaum, 491.
Foundation Co. ads. Simpson, 349.
Fouts ads. B. & O. R. Co., 282.
Fowles v. Allen, 373.
Fowles v. Joslyn, 602.
Fox Lake v. Fox Lake, 335.
Foxton v. Moore, 348.
Fraas ads. Reehil, 352.
Fraher v. Eisenman, 346.
Framingham ads. Delaney, 457.
Frank v. Hanly, 275.
Franke v. Kelsheimer, 371.
Frankenthaler ads. Walsh, 641.
Frankfort v. Manhattan R. Co., 457.
Franklin v. State, 196.
Fraternal Banker's Res. Soc. ads Schworm, 298.
Frazer ads. Balsbaugh, 195.
Fredericks v. Judah, 288.
Free ads. Paw Paw Bk., 320.
Freeburg ads. Hageman, 283.
Freeds ads. City of E. St. Louis, 334.
Freeman ads. Burnett, 415.
Freeman ads. Hackett, 585.
Freeman v. Freeman, 489.
Freeman v. United Fruit Co., 639.
Freeman v. Vetter, 638.
Freidrichs ads. Lavene, 282.
French ads. Mayville, 386.
French ads. Southwestern, etc., 637.
Fresno, etc., Co. ads. Balfour, 371.
Frey v. Forrestal, 414.
Frick v. Kabaker, 288.
Friedman ads. State, etc., 542.
Frisby v. St. Louis Transit Co., 218.
Fritch v. State, 585.
Froeming v. Stockton, 542, 550.
Frohlich ads. Wuerth, 129.
Frohman v. Samuel Stores, Inc., 96.
Fruit Dispatch Co. v. Sturgis, 309.
Frye v. State Bank, 579.
Fuchs ads. Tone, 458.
Fuller ads. Morse, 634.
Fuller v. Darrogh, 640.
Fuller Co. ads. Walters, 351.
Fullerton ads. State, 195.
Fulton Bank v. Benedict, 582.
Fultz ads. C. & O. R. Co., 490.
Furnace, etc., Co. v. Heller Bros., 369.

G

Gaar Scott & Co. v. Nichols, 351.
Gaffney v. People, 550.
Gage ads. Pittsburgh, C. C. & St. L. Ry. Co., 604.
Gage v. Chicago, 332, 335.
Gage v. Eddy, 295, 348, 449.
Gagnon v. Sperry, etc., Co., 349.
Gagush v. Hoeft, 636.

Galena, etc., R. Co. v. Haslam, 200.
Gallo ads. Com., 488.
Gallup ads. Pate, 127.
Galveston H. El. R. Co. v. English, 338
Galveston, etc., R. Co. ads. Hanway, 476.
Galveston, etc. ads. Wade, 604.
Galveston, etc., R. Co. v. Kutac, 640.
Galveston, etc., R. Co. v. Manas, 198.
Galveston, etc., R. Co. v. Young, 425.
Galvin ads. Cassen, 258.
Galvin ads. Creedon, 287.
Garber ads. St. Louis, etc., R., 332.
Gardner ads. Atlanta, etc., R. Co., 385.
Gardner v. Barden, 362.
Gardner v. Kiburz, 383.
Gardner v. Meeker, 632, 633.
Garren ads. Sun Oil Co., 204.
Gately v. Irvine, 369.
Gates ads. Prentis, 477.
Gates ads. Troutman, 275.
Gates v. Bowers, 579.
Gates v. Paul, 274.
Geary ads. Trinity, etc., R. Co., 289.
Gehr ads. Peo., 199.
Geidras adv. Peo., 489.
Gelpecke-Winslow & Co. v. Lovell, 349.
General Const. Co. v. Industrial Com., 271.
Gen. El. Co. ads. Del Visco, 490.
Gen. Hospital Soc. v. New Haven, etc., Co., 271.
Geohegan v. Union El. R. R. Co., 284, 408.
George v. St. Joseph, 348.
Geringer v. Novak, 633.
German-American ads. Trainor, 336.
German American Ins. Co. ads. De Bolt, 306.
Germania Bank v. Distler, 370.
Germania Fire Ins. Co. ads. Campbell, 363.
Gesualdi v. Personeni, 637.
Gibbs ads. Hunter, 541.
Gibbs ads. Pendarvis, 468.
Gibson ads. Peo., 126.
Gibson v. Johnson, 606.
Gibson v. Miller, 283.
Gibson v. Milwaukee, etc., Co., 489.
Gifford v. Peo., 581.
Gifford-Wood Co. v. Western Fuel Co., 604.
Gilhooley v. Columbus R., etc., Co., 517.
Gill v. McNamee, 348.
Gillespie v. Murry, 351.
Gillespie Lumber Co. ads. Henri Pelandeau, etc., 274.
Gilliland v. Wallace, 274.
Gilmore v. American Tube, etc., Co., 385.
Gilson v. Boston Realty Co., 370.
Gilvon ads. Gulf, etc., R. Co., 196.
Gishwiller v. Dodez, 606.
Giudice ads. State, 197.
Gladiator Min., etc., Co. ads. Rogers, 194.
Glascoe v. State. 602.
Glass ads. Fish, 200.
Glassheim ads. Cook, 585.
Gleason Coal Co. ads. Collins, 258.
Gleicher ads. Reiche, 351, 605.
Glen Corp. ads. Maxcy-Barton, 126, 303.
Glen Falls Ins. Co. v. Bendy, 346.
Gloag ads. O'Hare, 414.
Globe Brewing Co. v. Amer. Malt Co., 370.
Glos ads. McGraney, 331.
Glover ads. Raymond, 352.
Godair v. Ham Nat. Bank, 271, 543.
Goehringer ads. Peo., 569.
Goldblatt ads. Mohoney, 640.
Golden ads. State, 259.
Goldenson ads. Peo., 476.
Goldfeder v. Greenberg, 132.
Goldman v. Ashkins, 491.
Goldstein ads. Dempsey, 437.
Gollyer ads. Ziedler, 637.
Gonzolis ads. Texas El. Ry., 639.
Good ads. Martin, 256.
Goodfellow ads. Merchants' Bank, 517.
Goodman ads. Commonwealth Bank, 477.
Goodman v. Brooklyn Hebrew Orphan Asylum, 204.
Goodman v. Caledonian Ins. Co., 383.
Goodno v. Hotchkiss, 369.
Goodrich v. Chicago, 362.
Goodyear ads. Ettinger, 542.
Gordon Supply ads. Koban, 379.

Gorgol v. Michigan Cent. R. Co., 604.
Gorman ads. State, 284.
Gorman ads. Western Union Tel. Co., 291.
Gorton ads. Whelan, 126, 303.
Gould ads. Jones, 349.
Gould ads. Ross-Lewin, 345.
Gould v. Norfolk Lead Co., 126.
Govier v. Brechler, 283.
Govin v. De Miranda, 589.
Goyette v. Keenan, 361.
Grade v. Mariposa County, 306.
Grafton v. St. Paul, etc., R. Co., 332.
Graham ads. Krolik, 348.
Graham ads. Stacy, 581.
Graham ads. Texas, etc., R. Co., 285.
Graham ads. Zylstra, 606.
Graham v. Burggraf, 315.
Graham v. Chrystal, 581.
Graham v. Deuterman, 384.
Graham v. Dillon, 256.
Graham v. Plotner, 298.
Graham & Co. v. W. H. Davis & Co., 604, 606.
Grandmaison ads. Moreau, 255.
Grand Pass Shooting Club v. Crosby, 334.
Grand Rapids ads. Williams, 351.
Grand Rapids, etc., Co. ads. Darling, 457.
Grand Rapids, etc., Co. ads. Dykstra, 638.
Grand Traverse, etc., Exch. v. Thomas Canning Co., 370.
Grand Trunk, etc., Ry. Co. ads. Stoddard, 639.
Grant ads. Bradish, 634.
Grant ads. Page, 295.
Grant v. C. & N. W. Ry. Co., 327.
Grant v. Thompson, 387.
Graves v. Merchants' & B. Ins. Co., 254, 259.
Graves v. Rib Lake Lumber Co., 489.
Graves v. Union Oil Co., 457.
Gray ads. McCormick, etc., Co., 459.
Gray ads. Peo., 585.
Gray v. City of Boston, 204.
Gray v. State, 601.
Grayson v. Hays, 551.
Greager v. Blank, 634.
Great Northern Ry. Co. ads. Marron, 258.
Green ads. Continental Bank, etc., 632.
Green ads. Harrison, 326.
Green ads. Peo., 585.
Green v. Ashland Water Co., 332.
Green v. Boston El. R. Co., 477.
Green v. Indianapolis, 332.
Green v. State, 491.
Greenberg ads. Goldfeder, 132.
Greenfield v. Peo., 199.
Greenup v. Stoker, 259.
Greenwich Ins. Co. ads. Adams, 581.
Greenwich Ins. Co. ads. Rademacher, 291.
Greenwood v. State, 196.
Greer ads. Way, 371.
Gregory ads. Chicago City R. Co., 542.
Gregory ads. State, 579.
Gregory v. Rickey, 640.
Greilick ads. Foote, 306.
Greisheimer ads. Snow, 370.
Greisheimer v. Tannesbaum, 309.
Griebel v. Rochestér Printing Co., 636.
Griffin ads. Peo., 579.
Griffin v. State, 580.
Griffith ads. Holloway, 589.
Griffith ads. Mason, 370.
Griffith v. Los Angeles, etc., Co., 475.
Grill v. O'Dell, 458.
Grim v. E. St. L. Ry. Co., 328.
Griswold v. Chicago Rys. Co., 349.
Griswold v. Pitcairn, 341.
Gross ads. Cincinnati, etc., Co., 638.
Gross ads. Hurwitz, 336.
Gross ads. People, 601.
Gross v. Bennington, 205.
Grover, etc., Co. v. Newby, 293.
Groves v. Groves, 371.
Grubb v. Milan, 371.
Guinan v. Famous, etc., Corp., 519.
Gulf, etc., R. Co. v. Abbott, 457.
Gulf, etc., R. Co. v. Dickens, 199.
Gulf, etc., R. Co. v. Dooley, 475, 640.
Gulf, etc., R. Co. v. Gilvin, 196.
Gulf, etc., R. Co. v. Holliday, 604.
Gulf, etc., R. Co. v. McKinnell, 385.
Gully v. Nystel, 258.

Gumberg ads Oshinsky, 96.
Gungrich v. Anderson, 641.
Gunn v. McCabe, 605.
Gustafson ads. Johnson, 285.

H

H. E. Coal Co. ads. Harmon, 491.
Haack v. Fearing, 256.
Haas v. Commerce Trust Co., 298.
Haas v. King, 635.
Haas v. Newberry, 196.
Haber ads. Maxwell, 362, 364.
Hackett v. Freeman, 585.
Hageman v. Freeburg, 283.
Hagenback ads. Chicago City R. Co., 278.
Hale v. San Bernardino, etc., Co., 641.
Haley v. Western Transit Co., 204.
Hall ads. McKiernan, 547.
Hall ads. Mitcheltree School Township, 335.
Hall ads. Overlock, 126.
Hall ads. Phelps, 194.
Hall v. Allemania F. Ins. Co., 489.
Hall v. Murdock, 385, 476.
Halles ads. Peo., 543.
Halley ads. Robinson, 351.
Halliday ads. Shugart, 631.
Halstead ads. Amer. Food Co., 370.
Halsten ads. Eckels, 457.
Ham Nat. Bank ads. Godair, 271, 543.
Hamburg, etc., Bank ads. Butler, 372.
Hamilton ads. People, 635.
Hamilton ads. State, 586.
Hamilton v. Michigan Cent. R. Co., 459.
Hammond ads. N. Y., etc., R. Co., 408.
Hammond v. Bloomington Canning, 460.
Hancock ads. Marshall, 289.
Hand v. Soodeletti, 490.
Handorf ads. Public Utilities Co., 458.
Hangen ads. Walter, 425.
Hanline ads. Beck, 458.
Hanlon v. Ehrich, 569.
Hanly ads. Frank, 275.
Hanna ads. Bowers, 374.
Hanna v. Mitchell, 149.
Hans ads. Bohanan, 347.
Hanscom ads. O'Neil, 386.
Hanselman v. Doyle, 303.
Hanson ads. Larson, 641.
Hanthorn ads. Tuckwood, 602.
Hanton v. Pacific Electric Ry. Co., 605.
Hanway v. Galveston, etc., R. Co., 476.
Harden ads. Tremblay, 640.
Hardin ads. Andre, 425.
Hardin v. Forsythe, 272.
Harding v. Curtis, 334.
Hardy v. Shermer, 642.
Hardy v. Sprowle, 196.
Harlan ads. Houston Ice, etc., Co., 636.
Harmon v. H. E. Coal Co., 491.
Harmon v. Indiana Grove Drainage Dist., 362.
Harper v. Ely, 309.
Harris ads. Ayers, 328.
Harris ads. Putnam, 350, 351.
Harris ads. Simmons, 219.
Harris v. Seattle, etc., R. Co., 282.
Harris v. State, 199.
Harrison ads. Cincinnati Tract Co., 283.
Harrison v. Green, 326.
Harrison v. Trickett, 373.
Harrison Granite Co. v. Penn. Co., 269.
Hart ads. Missouri, etc., R. Co., 414.
Hart v. Automobile Ins. Co. of Hartford, Conn., 119.
Hartford ads. Mauch, 323.
Hartford Inv. Co. ads. Mahoney, 309.
Hartzell ads. Weinberg, 605.
Harvey ads. McKeon, 258.
Harvey v. Ellithorpe, 632, 633.
Harvey v. Osborn, 258.
Hasceig v. Tripp, 195.
Haslam ads. Galena, etc., R. Co., 200.
Hassan ads. State, 256.
Hasty ads. State, 327.
Hatcher ads. Beatty, 632.
Hatcher ads. Ewing, 373, 387, 414, 425.
Hatsfield v. State, 259.
Hausendorf ads. Smith, 327.
Hawes v. People, 640.
Hawkinson v. Valentine, 543.
Hay v. Springfield, etc., 335.
Hayden ads. Commonwealth, 335.
Hayes ads. Lorain Steel Co., 550.

Haynes v. Maybury, 205.
Haynes v. Thomas, 315.
Hays ads. Atchison, etc., R. Co., 491.
Hays ads. Grayson, 551.
Hays v. Johnson, 579.
Haze ads. Farrell, 459.
Heacker ads. Missouri, etc., R. Co., 327.
Head ads. Eagle Star, etc., Co., 641.
Heagy v. State, 634.
Heard v. Heard, 636, 637.
Heath v. Scott, 579.
Heckman ads. Bruno, 585.
Hecla Powder Co. v. Signa Iron Co., 331.
Heddles v. Chicago, etc., R. Co., 544.
Hedstrom ads. Fitzgerald, 328.
Heidenheimer ads. Missouri Pac. R. Co., 271.
Heidler Hardwood Lumber Company v. Wilson & Bennett Mfg. Co., 601.
Heiligenstein ads. Deel, 352.
Helgeson v. Chicago, etc., Co., 550.
Heller Bros. ads. Furnace, etc., Co., 369.
Hellreigel v. Manning, 362.
Heminway, etc., Silk Co. v. Porter, 289.
Hemler v. Hucony Gas. Co., 590.
Hempton v. State, 259.
Hendrix ads. Smith, 352.
Hennessey ads. Carney, 542.
Hennies v. Vogel, 637.
Henninger v. Interocean Cas. Co., 334.
Henry ads. Brannan, 258.
Henry ads. Reynolds & Heitsman, 349.
Henry v. People, 284.
Henwood v. Peo., 199.
Herbert ads. Chicago & Joliet El. R. Co., 640.
Herbert ads. Peo., 328.
Herkel ads. Robbs, 369.
Herman v. Teplitz, 352.
Hermann ads. Caulfield, 370.
Hermann v. Combs, 605.
Hermes v. Chicago, etc., R. Co., 278.
Herrick v. Malin, 301.
Herring ads. Dolan, 384.
Herrington v. Pouley, 635.
Herscovitz ads. Poseil, 214.
Herston ads. Hudspeth, 195.
Hertig v. People, 334.
Hertz ads. Martin, 362.
Hess v. State, 406.
Hester v. Chambers, 196.
Heuscke v. Milwaukee City R. Co., 198.
Hews v. Troiani, 283.
Hibbard Co. ads. Lana, 634.
Hickey v. Detroit United Ry. Co., 569.
Higgins ads. Quin, 457.
Hill ads. Davis, 636.
Hill v. State, 258.
Hill Clutch Co. v. Independent Steel Co., 334.
Hill Co. v. Sommer, 309.
Hiller v. Johnson, 282.
Hilliard ads. Bank of Utica, 129.
Hillis v. Wylie, 580.
Hills ads. Cobb, Bates & Yerxa Co., 604.
Hills v. Ludwig, 606.
Hinchman v. Clark, 195.
Hindenlang v. Mahon, 369.
Hines v. Messer, 353.
Hinkle v. Jas. Smith & Son, 350.
Hinshaw ads. Peo., 200.
Hitchcock ads. Salt Springs Nat. Bank of Syracuse, 150.
Hite v. Keen, 458.
Hoadley ads. Bumsted, 319.
Hoag ads. Bremer, 345.
Hoag ads. Pierson, 476.
Hobart ads. Lake Shore El. Co., 323.
Hoberg v. Sofrancy, 489.
Hock v. Allendale Tp., 350.
Hodge ads. Peo., 254, 259.
Hoeft ads. Gagush, 636.
Hoehle ads. Collins, 542.
Hofacre v. Monticello, 581.
Hoffman ads. Corr, 116.
Hoffman ads. Stephens, 288.
Hoffman v. Metropolitan L. Ins. Co., 335.
Hoffman v. Prussian Nat. Ins. Co., 328.
Hoffman House v. Foote, 205.
Hogle ads. McCloud, 335.
Holland ads. Chicago, etc., R. Co., 298.
Holland v. Riggs, 347.
Holliday ads. Gulf, etc., R. Co., 604.
Hollingshead Co. ads. Sichterman, 551.
Hollis ads. Faxon, 309.

Holloway v. Griffith, 589.
Holmes ads. Carroll, 633.
Holmes ads. Pecos, etc., R. Co., 435.
Holmes v. Jones, 637.
Holmes v. State, 196.
Holt ads. Shaughnessy, 385.
Holzwasser ads. Shelton, 294.
Homberg v. Kekhaffer, 320.
Home Bank & Trust Co. ads. Levinson, 348, 377.
Home Ins. Co. ads. Hoxie, 351.
Home Ins. Co. ads. O'Boyle, 96.
Homer ads. Com, 569.
Homes L. Ins. Co. ads. Dilleber, 477.
Homesteader's Life Ass'n v. Salinger, 542.
Hood ads. Swanson, 458.
Hood v. Bekans, etc., Co., 291.
Hooker ads. Spinney, 195.
Hoopeston First Nat. Bank v. Lake Erie, etc., R. Co., 606.
Hooser ads. St. Louis, etc., R. Co., 196, 197.
Hoover ads. Leedy, 385, 579.
Hoover ads. Suhr, 635.
Hoover v. Patton, 362.
Hopes' Appeal, 350.
Hopkins v. White, 542.
Horn ads. People, 363.
Horry ads. Lynch, 194.
Hosiery Mfr's Corp. ads. Colonial Knitting Mills, Inc., 117.
Hotaling ads. Laver, 350.
Hotaling v. Hotaling, 602.
Hotchkiss ads. Goodno, 369.
Hotel Commercial Co. ads. Schroeder, 282.
Houk Mfg. Co. v. Cowen Co., 204.
Houlka ads. Bugg, 332.
Houmigan ads. Cream, 258.
Housel ads. McGlassen, 310.
Houston v. Maunula, 490.
Houston v. State, 200, 547.
Houston Ice, etc., Co. v. Harlan, 636.
Houston, etc., Co. v. Boone, 638.
Houston, etc., R. Co. v. Chuck, 327.
Houston, etc., R. Co. v. Johnson, 459.
Hovey v. Sandres, 283.
Howard ads. Peninsular Ry. Co., 194.
Howard v. Illinois Trust, etc., 328.
Howard v. McDonough, 258.
Howell ads. Princeton, etc., Co., 325.
Howell v. Huyck, 126.
Howes v. Colburn, 459.
Howland ads. Napa, 351.
Hoxie v. Home Ins. Co., 351.
Hoyle ads. Pullman Co., 386.
Hoyle ads. Truesdale, 126, 303, 633.
Hubb Diggs Co. v. Bell, 636.
Hubbard ads. Stone, 387.
Hubbard v. Allyn, 363.
Hubbs Co. ads. Springfield, etc., Co., 636.
Hucony Gas. Co. ads. Hemler, 590.
Huddle v. Martin, 634.
Hudson ads. Mynatt, 579.
Hudson v. No. Pac. R. Co., 291.
Hudspeth v. Herston, 195.
Huff v. McMichael, 587.
Huffman ads. State, 199, 200.
Hughes v. State, 200.
Hughson ads. Peo., 200.
Hukox v. State, 275.
Huling v. Century Pub. Co., 350.
Hull ads. Weeks, 582.
Hulse ads. Peo., 581.
Humbarger v. Carey, 637.
Hummell ads. Stumm, 196.
Hunt ads. Burdick, 569.
Hunt ads. Pizer, 275.
Hunt v. W. T. Rawleigh Medical Co., 218, 219.
Hunter v. Gibbs, 541.
Hunter v. Lanius, 126.
Hunter v. State, 586.
Huntington v. Conkey, 634.
Huntley v. Whether, 306.
Hupfer v. National Distilling Co., 601.
Hurley ads. Illinois Power & Light Corporation, 204.
Hurley v. O'Sullivan, 632.
Hurwitz v. Gross, 336.
Hussey ads. Com., 196.
Hutchins ads. Veramendi, 195.
Hutchins v. Corgan, 289.
Hutchison v. Kelly, 301.
Hutson v. Wood, 132.
Huyck ads. Howell, 126.

Hyde v. Kloos, 334.
Hyndshaw ads. Chicago City Ry. Co., 351.

I

Ibanez v. Winston, 289.
I. C. R. Co. ads. Althoff, 328.
I. C. C. R. R. Co. v. Berens, 282, 284.
I. C. C. R. R. Co. v. Puckett, 349.
I. C. C. R. R. Co. v. Swisher, 278.
I. C. C. R. R. Co. v. Warriner, 332.
Ill. Cent. R. R. ads. Stephens, 323.
Ill. Cent. R. Co. v. Wade, 550.
Illinois Central R. Co. v. Leiner, 637.
Illinois Power & Light Corporation v. Hurley, 204.
Illinois Power & Light Corp. ads. Thomas, 641.
Illinois Steel Co. ads. Paige, 215, 637.
Illinois Trust, etc., ads. Howard, 328.
Imperial V. F. L. Ass'n. ads. Pallidine, 315.
Independent Breweries Co. ads. Loves, 635.
Independent Steel Co. ads. Hill Cluth Co., 334.
Independent, etc., Co. ads. Interboro Brewing Co., 285.
Indian Grove Drainage Dist. ads. Harmon, 362.
Indiana Union Tract. Co. v. Jacobs, 351.
Indiana, etc., Co. v. Jacobs, 385.
Indiana, etc., Co. v. Scribner, 327.
Indianapolis ads. Green, 332.
Indianapolis & St. L. R. Co. v. Miller, 639.
Indianapolis, etc., R. Co. v. Anthony, 579.
Indianapolis, etc., R. Co. v. Pugh, 636.
Industrial ads. McFeeley, 347.
Industrial Com. ads. General Const. Co., 271.
Ingalls ads. Berry, 291.
Ingebretsen v. Minneapolis, etc., R. Co., 323, 327.
Ingle v. Ingle, 490.
Inglin ads. Reclamation, etc., 386, 425, 462.
Ingraham ads. Com., 581.
Ingwerson v. Carr & Brannon, 258.
In re Baker, 335.
In re Campbell, 387.
In re Champion's Est., 549.
In re Chismore, 315.
In re Cullberg's Estate, 488.
In re Curtis, 387.
In re Du Bois, 476.
In re Dunahugh's Will, 366.
In re Durant, 288.
In re Girds Est., 635.
In re Henry, 459.
In re Hoyt's Estate, 366.
In re Huston's Est., 350.
In re Jessup, 327.
In re Klink's Estate, 489.
In re Littleton's Estate, 151.
In re Loveland, 386.
In re Makames, 129.
In re Martin, 387.
In re Martin's Est., 590.
In re Merrill's Est., 347.
In re Murray, 632.
In re Olson's Est., 518.
In re Osborn's Estate, 585.
In re Relph's Est., 542.
In re Riggs, 350.
In re Snowball, 386.
In re Sparks, 386.
In re Strong's Est., 489.
In re Swain's Estate, 606.
Ins. Co. of America ads. McInturff, 288.
Interboro Brewing Co. v. Independent, etc., Co., 285.
International Harvester Co. ads. Wilcox, 435, 475, 476.
International Ry. Co. ads. Caskie, 97.
International Text Book Co. v. Mackhorn, 363.
International & G. N. R. Co. v. Dalwigh, 258.
International, etc., R. Co. v. Biles & Ruby, 489.
International, etc., R. Co. v. Boykin, 541, 547.
International, etc., R. Co. v. Davis, 291.
International, etc., R. Co. v. Jones, 641.
International, etc., R. Co. v. Ragsdale, 373.

International, etc., R. Co. v. Williams, 385, 386.
Interocean Cas. Co. v. Henninger, 334.
Inter-State Finance Corp. v. Com. Jewelry Co., 383.
Interurban St. R. Co. ads. Perine, 551.
Iowa Falls ads. Riley, 637.
Irvine ads. Gately, 369.
Isenhour v. State, 388.
Itzel ads. Winn, 634.
Ivins ads. Dexter, 274.

J

Jack v. Rowland, 303.
Jackson ads. Currelli, 388.
Jackson ads. McDermott, 258.
Jackson ads. Prussing, 320.
Jackson ads. Smith, 298.
Jackson ads. Sovereign, etc., 590.
Jackson v. Sandman, 195.
Jackson & Sons v. N. Y. C. R. R., 291.
Jacobs ads. Bonnell, 633.
Jacobs ads. Indiana Union Tract Co., 350, 351, 385.
Jacobs v. State, 196.
Jamison v. People, 386.
Janesville ads. Sellack, 459.
Jannottà v. Bestmor Realty Corporation, 96.
Jarvis v. Metropolitan St. R. Co., 457.
Jascula ads. Stein, 269.
Jeffrey ads. State, 518.
Jeffrey v. Keokuk, etc., R. Co., 601.
Jeffrey v. Osborn, 408.
Jennings ads. Peo., 388.
Jennings ads. Smith, 641.
Jerboe v. Kepler, 541.
Jesma ads. O'Mara, 363.
Jewell v. Wisconsin, etc., Co., 635.
Johnsey ads. Western Union Tel. Co., 348.
Johnson ads. Gibson, 606.
Johnson ads. Hays, 579.
Johnson ads. Hiller, 282.
Johnson ads. Houston, etc., R. Co., 459.
Johnson ads. McCarty, 347.
Johnson ads. Moir, 150.
Johnson ads. People, 459.
Johnson ads. State, 585.
Johnson v. Bay State, etc., R. Co., 425.
Johnson v. Brown, 334, 544.
Johnson v. Culver, 256, 636.
Johnson v. Gustafson, 285.
Johnson v. Park City, 199.
Johnson v. Peterson, 541.
Joliet, etc., Co. ads. Locander, 637.
Jones ads. Beville, 638.
Jones ads. Dibble Seedgrower, 150.
Jones ads. Holmer, 637.
Jones ads. International, etc., Ry. Co., 641.
Jones ads. Maxfield, 215.
Jones v. Boston, etc., Ry., 638.
Jones v. Clark, 342.
Jones v. Detroit Taxicab & Transfer Co., 217.
Jones v. Gould, 349.
Jones v. Niagara Junction R. Co., 386.
Jones v. Portland, 458.
Jones, etc., Co. ads. Chicago City R. Co., 291.
Jordan ads. Latham, 543.
Jordan ads. Whidden, 371.
Jordan Marsh Co. ads. Crone, 531.
Joselyn ads. Fowles, 602.
Joyce ads. Peo., 585.
Judah ads. Fredericks, 288.

K

Kabaker ads. Frick, 288.
Kaeding ads. Spitler, 298.
Kahn v. Reedy, 196.
Kalamazoo, etc., Co. ads. Muir, 126, 303.
Kaler v. Builders' Mut. F. Ins. Co., 543.
Kamradt ads. Wabash R. Co., 348.
Kansas City Light, etc., Co. ads. Vessels, 194.
Kansas City R. Co. ads. Pietzuk, 198.
Kansas City Southern R. Co. v. Murphy, 215.
Karpeles ads. Zucker, 205.
Karwick v. Pickards, 289.
Kassing v. Walter, 633.
Kath v. Wisconsin Cent. R. Co., 385.
Kator v. Peo., 579.
Keating v. U. S. Light, etc., Co., 541.
Keaton v. State, 586.
Keeler ads. Laclede Bank, 580.

Keen ads. Hite, 458.
Keenan ads. Board of Ed., 363.
Keenan ads. Goyette, 361.
Keeseville ads. Callanan, 371.
Kekhaffer ads. Homberg, 320.
Kelley ads. Pennsylvania Coal Co., 285.
Kelley v. N. Y. Central R. Co., 530.
Kellogg v. Berkshire Bldg. Corp., 151.
Kells v. Davis, 632.
Kelly ads. Cincinnati First Nat. Bank, 349.
Kelly ads. Hutchison, 301.
Kelly ads. Penn, 284.
Kelly ads. Roger, 371.
Kelsheimer ads. Franke, 371.
Kemble v. Lyons, 289.
Kemper ads. Zeiverink, 301.
Kendall v. Luther, 489.
Kenefick ads. McGuire, 579.
Kenna v. Calumet, etc., R. Co., 477, 636, 642.
Kennedy v. Cherry & Webb Co., 530.
Kennedy v. Lee, 585.
Kennedy v. Rochester, etc., R. Co., 385, 579.
Kennedy-Cahill ads. West Chicago St. R. Co., 387.
Kent v. Mason, 633.
Kent v. Thelin, 348.
Kenyon ads. Wosoba, 323.
Keokuk, etc., R. Co. ads. Jeffrey, 601.
Kepler ads. Jerboe, 541.
Kerns v. McKean, 309.
Keuka College v. Ray, 371.
Key, etc., Co. ads. Aydlott, 640.
Keys ads. Peo., 490.
Kezer ads. S. W. Portland Cement Co., 425.
Khan v. Zemansky, 579.
Kibbe v. Bancroft, 309.
Kiburz ads. Gardner, 383.
Kidman ads. Quaker Oats Co., 346.
Kilbourn v. Muller, 361.
Kimball v. John Budd Co., 96.
Kimball v. Northern El. Co., 323.
King ads. Haas, 635.
King ads. Self, 370.
King ads. Smith, 527.
King ads. Wolf, 341.
King v. Chicago, etc., R. Co., 579.
King County ads. Carter, 205.
King Motor Sales Corp. v. Allen, 150.
Kinlock-Bloomington Telephone Co. ads. Presley, 604.
Kinney ads. Peo., 284.
Kinsella ads. Chance, 543.
Kircheimer v. Barrett, 272.
Kirkwood ads. Ettelsohn, 639.
Kirschner v. State, 587.
Kitchen v. Women's City Club of Boston, 531.
Kleiner v. Third Ave. R. Co., 350.
Kleinman ads. Pleason Realty, etc., Co., 350.
Kloos ads. Hyde, 334.
Klopfer ads. People, 601.
Knapp v. Schneider, 349.
Kneeland ads. De Lucias, 638.
Knickerbocker Ice Co. ads. Novitsky, 569.
Knight ads. State, 581.
Knight v. Overman Wheel Co., 459.
Knight v. Seney, 582.
Knisley ads. Bechat, 272.
Knoll v. State, 476.
Knowles v. Crampton, 373.
Knox ads. Durbin, 275.
Knox v. Sandquist, 519.
Koban v. Gordon Supply, 379.
Koch ads. Manufacturers', etc., Bank, 602.
Kohler v. West Side R. Co., 258.
Kolescheski ads. Carmody, 633.
Koons v. State, 388.
Koppel Industrial Car & Equipment Co. v. Portalis & Co., 114.
Kossuth County St. Bank v. Richardson, 309.
Kotlowitz v. Selberstein, 632.
Krakowski v. Aurora, etc., R. Co., 386.
Kramer ads. Peo., 569.
Kraus ads. Lamb, 279.
Krauser ads. Peo., 258.
Kreigh v. Sherman, 347.
Kreutzer & Wasem v. Reese, 601.
Kreuziger v. C. & N. W. R. Co., 350, 351.
Krolik v. Graham, 348.
Kuhns v. Wisconsin, etc., R. Co., 459.
Kutac ads. Galveston, etc., R. Co., 640.
Kuznik v. Orient Ins. Co., 606.
Kyle v. Miller, 258.

L

La Barre ads. State, 489.
Labrecque v. Donham, 544.
Labrie v. Midwood, 542.
Lacang ads. Peo., 276.
Laclede Bank v. Keeler, 580.
Ladany v. Assad, 632.
Lafferty v. State, 517.
Lagerfelt ads. Wehner, 388.
Laine v. Brainerd, 289.
Lake ads. Peo., 458.
Lake Erie, etc., R. Co. ads. Hoopeston First Nat. Bank, 606.
Lake Shore El. Co. v. Hobard, 323.
Lake Shore El. R. Co. v. Lathrop, 327.
Lake Shore, etc., R. Co. v. Whidden, 477.
Lake Shore & M. S. Ry. Co. ads. Rodeff, 205.
Lamb v. Kraus, 279.
Lambe v. Manning, 369.
Lambert ads. Bullard, 582.
Lamperle ads. Peo., 388.
Lamprecht ads. Lese, 369.
Lamsden ads. Poole, 639.
Lana v. Hibbard Co., 634.
Lancaster R. Co. ads. Rich, 335.
Landis v. Turner, 309.
Lane ads. McKinnie, 372.
Lane v. Butler, 604.
Lane v. Portland Ry., Light & Power Co., 205.
Langdon v. Ahrends, 386.
Lange ads. Mastrobuono, 274.
Langshaw ads. Converse, 371.
Lanius ads. Hunter, 126.
LaPlante v. Warren Cotton Mills, 386.
Lapp ads. Stanton, 605.
Larivee Lumber Co. ads. Lynch, 327.
Larkin v. Nassau El. R. Co., 550.
Larkin Cary Co. ads. O'Neill, 635.
Larson v. Hanson, 641.
Laserowitch v. Reiman, 298.
Latham v. Jordan, 543.
Lathrop ads. Lake Shore El. R. Co., 327.
Latman v. Douglas & Co., 348.
Lavellee ads. D. & H. Truck Line, 640.
Laver v. Hotaling, 350.
La Verne ads. Peo., 585.
Lavitt ads. Wells, 542.
Laub v. DeVault, 256.
Laudano ads. State, 284.
Lauth v. Chi. Union Trac. Co., 386.
Lavene v. Freidrichs, 282.
Lawler ads. Wheeler, 636.
Lawrence ads. Chicago Union Trac. Co., 637.
Lawton v. Oglesby Coal Co., 642.
Lazarus ads. Manuta, 283.
Leadley Co. ads. Butler, 551.
Lebline ads. Seymour Water Co., 259.
Ledford v. State, 195.
Ledwell v. Chicago City Ry. Co., 641.
Lee ads. Abbott, 272.
Lee ads. Citizens' Light, etc., Co., 194.
Lee ads. Emmett, 335.
Lee ads. Kennedy, 585.
Lee ads. State, 517.
Lee v. Andrews, 581.
Lee v. Campbell, 217.
Lee v. Farmers Mutual Rail, etc., Co., 282.
Lee Ah Yute ads. Peo., 549.
Leedy v. Hoover, 385, 579.
Lefkowitz v. First Nat. Bank, 315.
Lefler ads. Earl, 283.
Legg v. Drake, 259.
Lehigh Valley R. Co. v. McGranahan, 218.
Lehner ads. Peo., 579.
Leigh v. Terr, 199.
Leiner ads. Illinois Central R. Co., 637.
Lenhart ads. Peo., 547.
Leonard ads. Waller, 348, 349.
Lese v. Lamprecht, 369.
Leseur v. State, 580.
Lessing v. Davis, 362.
Levant, etc., Co. v. Wells, 425.
Levin v. Spero, 519.
Levine ads. Com., 256.
Levine ads. Peo., 285.
Levinson v. Home Bank & Trust Co., 348, 377.
Lewandowski v. Zuzak, 334.
Lexington, etc., Co. v. Paver, 632.
Libby, etc. v. Cook, 490.
Lichkoff ads. Little, 491.

Lichtenstein Millinery v. Peck, 363.
Light v. Toledo, St. L. & W. R. Co., 606.
Limeberry ads. People, 259.
Linch v. Nebraska, etc., Co., 256.
Lincoln v. Battelle, 341.
Lincoln Furniture Mfg. Co. ads. Baker Matthews Lumber Co., 205.
Lingafelter v. Moore, 196.
Lingle v. Bulfer, 585.
Link v. Sheldon, 347.
Little ads. Bounds, 604.
Little ads. Taft, 289.
Little v. Lichkoff, 491.
Little v. Los Angeles Ry. Corp., 519.
Litzinger v. Panhandle & S. F. R. Co., 364.
Liverpool, etc., Co. v. Ende, 543.
Lizzo ads. Venuto, 386.
Lloyd v. Sandusky, 371.
Loban v. Boston El. R. Co., 386.
Locander v. Joliet, etc., Co., 637.
Loerch ads. Zabowski, 218.
Loftis ads. Feld, 345.
Logan ads. The Clipper, 459.
Logansport ads. Spry, 635.
Lohr ads. Mizner, 610.
Lombardi v. California St. R. Co., 198.
London, etc., Co. v. American Cereal Co., 289.
Long ads. Burt, 582.
Long Island R. Co. ads. Cohen, 288.
Long, etc., Co. v. Barnes, 632.
Look ads. Bailey, 543.
Looney ads. People, 350.
Loose ads. Somers, 362.
Loper ads. People, 326.
Lopp ads. City of Ft. Worth, 604.
Lorain Steel Co. v. Hayes, 550.
Lord El. Co. v. Morrill, 269.
Los Angeles ads. Bidwell, 387.
Los Angeles, etc., Bank ads. Whittier, 370.
Los Angeles, etc., Co. ads. Griffith, 475.
Los Angeles Ry. Corp. ads. Little, 519.
Lotz ads. Bond, 590.
Loughlin v. Brassel, 547.
Louis Storage & Transfer Co. ads. Barker, 458.
Louisville, etc., R. Co. v. Wright,
Lovas v. Independent Breweries Co., 635.
Love v. Anchor, etc., Co., 349.
Lovell ads. Dillie, 634.
Lovell ads. Gelpecke-Winslow & Co., 349.
Lowe ads. St. Louis & S. W. R. Co., 387.
Lowe v. Bliss, 351.
Lowell Cotton Mills ads. Featherstone, 195.
Lowen ads. Peo., 385.
Lowenstein ads. Warth, 489.
Lowenthal ads. Chamberlain, 275.
Ludwig ads. Hills, 606.
Luginbyhl v. Thompson, 637.
Luin v. Chicago Grill Co., 601.
Lurie ads. Peo., 490.
Lush v. Parkersburg, 282.
Luther ads. Kendall, 489.
Luthy & Co. v. Paradise, 542.
Lycan v. People, 517.
Lyman v. Fidelity, etc., Co., 634.
Lynch v. Horry, 194.
Lynch v. Larivee Lumber Co., 327.
Lyons ads. Kemble, 289.
Lyons ads. Peo., 579.

M

MacBard Coal v. Wyatt Coal Co., 298.
Mackay ads. Peo., 586.
Mackhorn ads. International Text Book Co., 363.
Maddox ads. Peo., 256.
Magnolia, etc., Co. v. Davis, 370.
Maguire v. Pan American Amusement Co., 291.
Mahar v. Montello Granite Co., 326.
Maher v. Orange & Rockland Elec. Co., 96.
Mahon ads. Hindenlang, 369.
Mahoney v. Cooch, 601.
Mahoney v. Hartford Inv. Co., 309.
Mahutga v. Minneapolis, St. P. & S. S. M. Ry. Co., 205.
Mainville v. State, 200.
Majoine ads. People, 601.
Majors ads. Peo., 256.
Majors v. Connor, 602.

Makey v. Dryden, 197.
Malcolm v. Thomas, 205.
Malin ads. Herrick, 301.
Malkin ads. Peo., 490, 585.
Malleable Iron Co. v. Brennan, 518.
Mallow v. Estes, 370.
Malmin ads. Thompson, 132.
Manchester St. R. Co. ads. Reagan, 366.
Mandis ads. Young, 275.
Mangano v. State, 199.
Manhattan, etc., Co. v. White Co., 373.
Manhattan L. Ins. Co. v. Fields, 331.
Manhattan R. Co. ads. Boyce, 360.
Manhattan R. Co. ads. Frankfort, 457.
Manhattan R. Co. ads. Mortimer, 349.
Mankes v. Fishman, 270, 271.
Mankus ads. People, 286.
Mann v. Blair, 476.
Manning ads. Hellreigel, 362.
Manning ads. Lambe, 369.
Manning v. Burlington, etc., R. Co., 606.
Manning v. Den, 362.
Manns ads. Galveston, etc., R. Co., 198.
Manol v. Moskin, etc., 638.
Manufacturers Nat. Bank ads. Rosengren, 350.
Manufacturers', etc., Bank v. Koch, 602.
Manuta v. Lazarus, 283.
Manzner's Est., 350.
Marande v. Texas, etc., R. Co., 197.
Marine Trust Co. of Buffalo v. Nuway Devices, Inc., 97.
Marion v. B. G. Coon Const. Co., 397.
Mariposa County ads. Grade, 306.
Market St. Ry. Co. ads. Wallden, 642.
Markham ads. Carpenter, 372.
Marne, etc., Tel. Co. ads. Chicago Tel. Supply Co., 285.
Marriam ads. Barber, 385.
Marron v. Great Northern Ry. Co., 258.
Marrs ads. Curtis, 347.
Mars v. Morris, 370.
Marsh v. Burnham, 353.
Marshall v. Brown, 476.
Marshall v. Davies, 606.
Marshall v. Hancock, 289.
Marshall v. Marshall, 336.
Marshall v. Partyka, 605.
Marston Coal Co. ads. Murphy, 458.
Martin ads. Cadwaller, 363.
Martin ads. Pittsburgh, etc., Railroad Co., 635.
Martin v. Farmers' Mut. F. Ins. Co., 195.
Martin v. Good, 256.
Martin v. Hertz, 362.
Martin v. N. Y. Life Ins. Co., 317.
Martin v. Sherwood, 292, 349, 385.
Martin Emerich Outfitting Co. v. Siegel, 204.
Martlock v. Williams, 303.
Mason ads. Kent, 633.
Mason v. Griffith, 370.
Mason v. Seitz, 632.
Mass ads. Combes, 96.
Massachusetts Bonding & Insurance Co. ads. McAleenan, 604.
Massey v. Bank, 579.
Massman v. Thorson, 287.
Masterson v. Chicago, etc., R. Co., 640.
Mastrobuono v. Lange, 274.
Matalone ads. Yohalem, 286.
Math v. Chicago City Ry. Co., 348, 569.
Mather ads. People, 258, 259, 273.
Matheson ads. Byalos, 338.
Matheson ads. State, 397.
Matlack ads. State, 315.
Matson v. Mitchell, 370.
Matter of East 161st St., etc., 435.
Matter of Higgins, 414.
Matter of Hock, 435, 476.
Matteson v. N. Y. C. R. Co., 459.
Matthews ads. Thede, 269.
Matthews v. State, 582.
Matthieson ads. Chicago City Ry. Co., 546, 551.
Mattoon ads. McRae, 331.
Mauch v. Hartford, 323.
Maunula ads. Houston, 490.
Maxcy-Barton v. Glen Corp., 126, 303.
Maxfield v. Jones, 215.
Maxwell ads. Saintman, 457.
Maxwell v. Durkin, 605.
Maxwell v. Habel, 362, 364.
Maybury ads. Haynes, 205.
Mayer ads. Chicago, etc., R. Co., 289.
Mayer v. Brensinger, 601.

Mayer v. Swygart, 351.
Mayfield ads. Bonner, 459.
Mayhew ads. Everdson, 347.
Maynahan ads. American, etc., Co., 642.
Mayville v. French, 386.
McAfee ads. State, 197.
McAleenan v. Massachusetts Bonding & Insurance Co., 604.
McAnsh v. Blauner, 149.
McArron ads. People, 601.
McAuliffe ads. Curtis, 364.
McBride v. McBride, 491.
McBride v. Wallace, 258.
McCabe ads. Gunn, 605.
McCabe v. Swift, 346, 386.
McCann ads. People, 636.
McCann v. California, etc., 477.
McCardell ads. E. Alkemeyer Co., 551.
McCarin v. Randall, 320.
McCarthy v. Spring Valley Coal Co., 641.
McCarty v. Johnson, 347.
McCarty v. Waterman, 351.
McChesney v. Chicago, 301.
McClintock ads. Taylor, 362.
McCloud v. Hogle, 335.
McCollister ads. Peo., 194.
McComb v. Atchison T. & S. F. Ry. Co., 278.
McCook ads. State, 541.
McCormick v. Elston, 309.
McCormick, etc., Co. v. Gray, 459.
McCort ads. Mullens, 321.
McCourt v. Peppard, 256.
McCoy v. People, 284.
McCulloch v. Dobson, 541.
McCune ads. Trinity, etc., R. Co., 458.
McDaneld v. McDaneld, 348.
McDavid ads. Western Union Tel. Co., 306.
McDavid v. Ellis, 309.
McDermott ads. Com., 256.
McDermott v. Jackson, 258.
McDonald ads. Bradley, 373.
McDonald ads. Ruddy, 347.
McDonald v. McDonald, 387.
McDonald v. Smith, 348.
McDonough ads. Howard, 258.
McDonough v. McGovern, 606.
McDougall ads. Parmenter, 274.
McDowell v. Aetna Ins. Co., 303.
McFarlane ads. People, 349.
McFeeley v. Industrial, etc., 347.
McGann ads. Stale, 275.
McGarrity v. Byington, 293.
McGinnis v. 3rd Ave., R. Co., 459.
McGiven ads. Chicago, 636.
McGlassen v. Housel, 310.
McGlasson v. Scott, 331, 335.
McGoldrick v. Wilson, 309.
McGough v. State, 199.
McGovern ads. McDonough, 606.
McGranahan ads. Lehigh Valley R. Co., 218.
McGraney v. Glos, 331.
McGregor v. Wait, 303.
McGuffey v. McLain, 349.
McGuire v. Kenefick, 579.
McHugh ads. Bankcroft-Whitney, 489.
McInturff v. Ins. Co. of America, 288.
McIrvin ads. Taylor, 127.
McKarren v. Boston, etc., R. Co., 326.
McKean ads. Kerns, 309.
McKee ads. McKinsey, 346.
McKeon v. Harvey, 258.
McKeon v. Proctor, etc., Mfg. Co., 282.
McKiernan v. Hall, 547.
McKim ads. Cincinnati Traction Co., 636.
McKinnell ads. Gulf, etc., R. Co., 385.
McKinnie v. Lane, 372.
McKinsey v. McKee, 346.
McKivitt v. Cone, 491.
McKnight ads. Robinson, 604.
McLain ads. McGuffey, 349.
McLaten v. Birdsong, 198.
McLaughlin v. Thomas, 371.
McMahon v. Chicago City R. Co., 414, 437.
McMichael ads. Huff, 587.
McMichael ads. St. Louis, etc., R. Co., 437.
McMurray ads. Carruthers, 635.
McMurray v. State, 585.
McMurrough v. Alberty, 219.
McNamee ads. Gill, 348.

McPherson ads. Essex, 194.
McPherson v. West Coast T. Co., 284.
McQuary v. Quincy, O. & K. C. Ry. Co., 205.
McQuilken ads. Schee, 633.
McRae v. Mattoon, 331.
McReynolds v. Burlington & O. R. Ry. Co., 632.
Mebius, etc., Co. v. Mills, 363.
Mechem ads. Nordman, 283.
Meehan ads. Dolan, 387, 404, 406.
Meeker ads. Gardner, 632, 633.
Megorden ads. State, 259.
Melendy ads. Daly, 258.
Melinsky ads. Northern Assur. Co., 590.
Meloy ads. Rhodes, 605, 606.
Memmler v. State, 198.
Menard v. Boston, etc., R. Co., 636.
Mendenhall v. Banks, 544.
Menella v. Metropolitan St. R. Co., 276.
Menley v. Zeigler, 315.
Merchant ads. Graves, 254.
Merchants' Bank v. Goodfellow, 517.
Merchants Life Ins. Co. v. Treat, 633.
Merchants' & B. Ins. Co. ads. Graves, 259.
Mercier v. Union St. R. Co., 272.
Meridian El. R. Co. ads. Budd, 351.
Merkel v. State, 200.
Merkle v. Bennington, 366.
Merrill ads. Taylor, 371.
Merritt v. State, 196.
Meshow ads. Yore, 408.
Messer ads. Hines, 353.
Methodist, etc., Church ads. Walsh, 303.
Metro. El. R. Co. ads. Remson, 298.
Metropolitan L. Ins. Co. ads. Hoffman, 335.
Metropolitan Nat. Bank v. Commercial State Bank, 350.
Metropolitan St. R. Co. ads. Baughman, 217.
Metropolitan St. R. Co. ads. Jarvis, 457.
Metropolitan St. R. Co. ads. Menella, 276.
Metropolitan St. R. Co. ads. Naylor, 197.
Metz v. Yellow Cab Co., 636.
Metzer v. Doll, 590.
Meyers ads. Morrison, 550.
Michigan, etc., Co. ads. Terrill, 642.
Michigan, etc., Co. v. Wilcox, 414.
Michigan Air Line R. Co. v. Barnes, 194.
Mich. Bonding & Surety Co. ads. Billett, 609.
Michigan Cent. R. Co. ads. Gorgol, 604.
Michigan Cent. R. Co. ads. Hamilton, 459.
Mich. C. R. Co. ads. O'Dea, 386.
Middleton ads. Shearer, 606.
Middleton v. Whitridge, 457, 459.
Midwood ads. Labrie, 542.
Milan ads. Grubb, 371.
Miles v. Strong, 636.
Miller ads. Chicago Union T. Co., 489.
Miller ads. Gibson, 283.
Miller ads. Indianapolis & St. L. R. Co., 639.
Miller ads. Kyle, 258.
Miller ads. Stitzel, 328.
Miller v. Assured's, etc., Co., 579.
Miller v. Cotten, 625.
Miller v. Montgomery, 351.
Miller v. Perlroth, 634.
Miller v. State, 547.
Miller v. Williams, 345.
Milliken v. Barr, 295.
Millison ads. Casteel, 294.
Mills ads. Mebius, etc., Co., 363.
Mills ads. Peo., 551.
Milwaukee, etc., Co. ads. Gibson, 489.
Milwaukee City R. Co. ads. Heuscke, 198.
Miner v. Connecticut River R. Co., 531.
Miner v. Phillips, 547.
Minneapolis ads. Ingebretsen, 323.
Minneapolis, etc., R. Co. ads. Ingebretsen, 327.
Minneapolis, etc., R. Co. ads. Sullivan, 457.
Minneapolis, St. P. & S. S. M. Ry. Co. ads. Mahutga, 205.
Mishkind-Feinberg Realty Co. v. Sidorsky, 306.

Missouri Pac. Ry. Co. ads. Wasmer, 218.
Missouri Pac. Ry. Co. ads. Wolfe, 271.
Missouri Pac. R. Co. v. Heidenheimer, 271.
Missouri Pac. R. Co. v. South Texas Candy Co., 274.
Missouri, etc., R. Co. ads. Buckman, 425.
Missouri, etc., R. Co. v. Coker, 397.
Missouri, etc., R. Co. v. Creason, 579.
Missouri, etc., R. Co. v. Hart, 414.
Missouri, etc., R. Co. v. Heacker, 327.
Missouri, etc., R. Co. v. Ransom, 336.
Mitchell ads. Hanna, 149.
Mitchell ads. Matson, 370.
Mitchell v. Mystic Coal Co., 635, 641.
Mitcheltree School Township v. Hall, 335.
Mizner v. Lohr, 610.
Modern Woodmen, etc., ads. Kennedy, 579.
Moeller ads. Roth, 517.
Moffett v. State, 200.
Moffitt v. Ford Motor Co., 204.
Mofziger Lumber Co. v. Solomon, 335.
Mohoney v. Goldblatt, 640.
Moir v. Johnson, 150.
Mole ads. Peo., 272.
Moline, etc., R. Co. ads. Coburn, 386.
Monaghan ads. C. C. C. & St. Louis Ry. Co., 327.
Monger v. New Era Assoc., 336.
Monmouth v. Erling, 641.
Mono County v. Flanigan, 195.
Montague Tp. ads. Pool, 383.
Montello Granite Co. ads. Mahar, 326.
Montgomery ads. Miller, 351.
Montgomery ads. Sesler, 638.
Monticello ads. Hofacre, 581.
Moody v. Rowell, 258, 259.
Moody & Son ads. Tuttle, 349.
Mooney ads. Peo., 196, 328.
Mooney ads. Simon, 519.
Moore ads. Comm., 195.
Moore ads. Ferguson, 636.
Moore ads. Foxton, 348.
Moore ads. Lingafelter, 196.
Moore ads. Rogers, 581.
Moore ads. State, 195.
Moore v. Chicago, etc., Ry. Co., 636.
Moore v. Murphy, 637.
Moore v. State, 197.
Moore County ads. Warrick, 488.
Moorhead v. Briggs, 275.
Moran v. Duke Drug Co., 462.
Moran v. State, 601.
Mordoff ads. Silvius, 633.
Moreau v. Grandmaison, 255.
Morehouse v. Morehouse, 289.
Morgan ads. Conn, 327.
Morgan ads. Patterson, 219.
Morgan v. Tutt, 301.
Morrill ads. Lord El. Co., 269.
Morris ads. Cornelison Motor Co., 634.
Morris ads. Mars, 370.
Morris v. Murray, 348.
Morrison ads. Cornell, 205.
Morrison v. Carpenter, 640.
Morrison v. Meyers, 550.
Morrow ads. Rushville, 330.
Morse ads. Peo., 284.
Morse v. Fuller, 634.
Mortimer v. Bristol, 352.
Mortimer v. Manhattan R. Co., 349.
Moshiek ads. Peo., 585.
Mosier ads. Com., 199.
Moskin, etc., ads. Manol, 638.
Mossman ads. Security State Bank of Eskridge, 218.
Mt. Pleasant ads. Tracy, 435.
Mousseau v. Mousseau, 348.
Mucci ads. Boerner Fry Co., 282.
Muir v. Kalamazoo, etc., Co., 126, 303.
Mullen ads. Doran, 259.
Mullens v. McCort, 321.
Muller ads. Kilbourn, 361.
Mulligan v. Smith, 215.
Munday ads. Peo., 129, 287.
Munoz & Co. v. Savannah Sugar Refining Corp., 149.
Murchison Nat. Bank v. Dunn Oil Mills Co., 194.
Murdock ads. Ephraims, 289.
Murdock ads. Hall, 385, 476.
Murphy ads. Kansas City Southern R. Co., 215.
Murphy ads. Moore, 637.

Murphy v. Marston Coal Co., 458.
Murphy v. People, 349.
Murrah ads. Sadler, 273.
Murray ads. Morris, 348.
Murray v. Elston, 129.
Murry ads. Gillespie, 351.
Muse v. State, 196, 199.
Mutual L. Ins. Co. v. Anthony, 289.
Myers ads. Baillargeon, 604.
Mynatt v. Hudson, 579.
Mystic Coal Co. ads. Mitchell, 635, 641.

N

Nagle v. Schnadt; 632, 633, 634.
Names v. Union Ins. Co., 291.
Napa v. Howland, 351.
Nappier ads. San Antonio, etc., R. Co., 580.
Nashville, etc., R. ads. Byers, 476.
Nassau El. R. Co. ads. Larkin, 550.
Nassau El. R. Co. ads. Richardson, 256.
Nathan v. Diersson, 342.
Nat. Bank of Decatur v. Board of Education, 362.
Nat. Cash Register Co. v. Blumenthal, 285.
Nat. Liberty Ins. Co. ads. Burke, 632.
Nat. Live Stock, etc., Co. ads. Crouch, 349.
Nat., etc., Co. ads. Crouch, 346.
National Council ads. Atkinson, 633.
National Distilling Co. ads. Hupfer, 601.
National Ice Co. ads. O'Connor, 517.
Nau v. Standard Oil Co., 543.
Naylor v. Metropolitan St. R. Co., 197.
Nebraska, etc., Co. ads. Linch, 256.
Nedlin Realty Co., Inc. v. Bachner, 96.
Neff v. Cincinnati, 632.
Neff v. Neff, 491.
Nefus ads. Com., 350.
Nelms ads. Fain, 633.
Newberry ads. Haas, 196.
Newbrough ads. Foster, 303, 606.
Newby ads. Grover, etc., Co., 293.
New Castle Bridge Co. v. Doty, 275.
Newell v. Baird, 363.
New Era Assoc. ads. Monger, 336.
New Era, etc., Co. ads. Cocke & Co., 549.
New Haven, etc., Co. ads. Gen. Hospital Soc., 271.
New Jersey Zinc Co. v. American Zinc, Lead & Smelting Co., 605.
Newman ads. City of Charleston, 347.
New Rochelle, City of, ads. Ritacco, 640.
New York ads. Stemmler, 272.
New York ads. Young, 606.
New York El. R. Co. ads. Robinson, 602.
Ney v. Eastern Iowa Tel. Co., 336.
Ney v. Rothe, 634.
Niagara Junction R. Co. ads. Jones, 386.
Nichols ads. Gaar Scott & Co., 351.
Nicholson ads. Schlosser, 369.
Nicholson v. Tarpey, 126.
Niell v. Brackett, 543.
Nielson v. Chicago, etc., R. Co., 396.
Nixon ads. Roseberry, 353.
Noah v. Bowery Savings Bank, 279.
Noble ads. Wallace, 373.
Noblett ads. People, 602.
No. Cal. Power Co. ads. Diller, 328.
No. Chi. St. R. Co. v. Cook, 385.
Nofftz v. Nofftz, 321.
No. Pac. R. Co. ads. Hudson, 291.
Nordman v. Mechem, 283.
Norfolk Lead Co. ads. Gould, 126.
Norman ads. State, 579. 580.
Norris ads. Perkins, 352.
North American Life Insurance Co., etc. ads. Bohen, 636.
North Assurance ads. Felsenthal, 489.
North Chicago St. R. Co. v. Cook, 292.
Northern Assur. Co. v. Melinsky, 590.
Northern El. Co. ads. Kimball, 323.
Norton ads. Farmer, 632.
Norton v. Atlantic, etc., Co., 636.
Norwich Pharmacal Co. v. Barrett, 149.
Nouman Printer's Supply v. Ford, 309.
Novak ads. Geringer, 633.
Novak ads. Peo., 587.
Novak ads. State, 631.
Novelty Showcase Co. v. Samuel I. Davis & Co., 295.
Novitsky v. Knickerbocker Ice Co., 569.
N. S. ads. Am. Surety Co., 335.

Nussbaum v. U. S. Brewing Co., 303.
Nute v. Boston & M. R. R., 601.
Nuway Devices, Inc. ads. Marine Trust Co. of Buffalo, 97.
N. V. ads. Rehberg, 634.
N. Y. ads. Stemmler, 342.
N. Y. C. and H. R. R. Co. ads. Buhrmaster, 637.
N. Y. Central R. Co. ads. Kelley, 530.
N. Y. C. R. Co. ads. Felska, 387.
N. Y. C. R. R. Co. ads. Downs, 258.
N. Y. C. R. R. ads. J. J. Jackson & Sons, 291.
N. Y. C. R. Co. ads. Matteson, 459.
N. Y. C. R. R. Co. ads. Sloan, 544.
N. Y. El. R. Co. ads. Shaw, 289, 348.
N. Y. Life Ins. Co. ads. Martin, 317.
N. Y. Mut. L. Ins. Co. v. Baker, 350.
N. Y., etc., R. Co. ads. Alberti, 326.
N. Y., etc., R. Co. ads. Archer, 326.
N. Y., etc., R. Co. ads. Tozer, 346.
N. Y., etc., R. Co. ads. Welch, 303.
N. Y., etc., R. Co. v. Hammond, 408.
N. Y., etc., R. Co. v. Robbins, 326.
Nystel ads. Gully, 258.

O

Oakland v. Adams, 435, 437.
O'Berry v. State, 195.
Oblaser ads. Peo., 546.
O'Boyle v. Home Ins. Co., 96.
O'Brien ads. Citizens, etc., Co., 384.
O'Brien v. Chicago, etc., R. Co., 292, 385.
O'Brien v. Peck, 370.
O'Connor ads. Carroll County, 364.
O'Connor v. National Ice Co., 517.
O'Dea v. Mich. C. R. Co., 386.
O'Dell ads. Grill, 458.
Oden v. Texas & P. Railway Co., 635.
Ogden ads. Shaw, 530.
Oglesby Coal Co. ads. Lawton, 642.
O'Hara ads. Starks, 364.
O'Hare v. Gloag, 414.
Ohio R. Co. v. Walker, 295.
Okopske ads. Peo., 580.
Old Colony Trust Co. v. Di Cola, 543.
Old Dominion S. S. Co. ads. White, 374.
Old Motor Works v. Churchill, 269.
Olson ads. Smith. 345.
Omaha Beverage Co. v. Temp Brew Co., 605.
Omaha St. R. Co. v. Craig, 199.
Omaha, etc., R. Co. ads. Pearl, 336.
O'Mara v. Jesma, 363.
Omberg v. U. S. Mut. Acc. Assoc., 385.
O'Neil ads. Com., 195.
O'Neil v. Hanscom, 386.
O'Neill v. Beland, 386.
O'Neill v. Larkin Cary Co., 635.
O'Neill v. Ross, 635.
Onseyga Realty Co. ads. Schabel, 364
Onsgard ads. Wittenberg, 476.
Orange & Rockland Elec. Co. ads Maher, 96.
Orchin v. Ft. Worth, etc., Co., 639.
Ordway v. Buckingham, 604.
O'Reilly v. Duffy, 295.
Orient Ins. Co. ads. Kuznik, 606.
Oriental Nav. Corp. ads. American Union Line, 633.
Oritz v. De Benavides, 127.
Orosco ads. Peo., 550.
Osborn ads. Conlon, 604.
Osborn ads. Harvey, 258.
Osborn ads. Jeffery, 408.
Osborn ads. Sneed, 349.
Osborne ads. Seeley, 372.
Oscanyan v. Winchester Repeating Arms Co., 205.
Osgood v. Poole, 309.
Oshinsky v. Gumberg, 96.
Osman ads. Edwards, 541.
O'Sullivan ads. Hurley, 632.
Otto ads. State, 199.
Ouimette v. Chicago, 330.
Overlock v. Hall, 126.
Overman Wheel Co. ads. Knight, 459
Owen ads. Paschell, 642.
Owens ads. Crossett, 334.
Owens ads. Sullivan, 279.

P

Pacific Electric Ry. Co. ads. Dawson, 606.
Pacific Electric Ry. Co. ads. Hanton, 605.
Pacific Monthly Co. ads. Putnam, 195.

Paddock v. Wells, 195.
Paepke v. Stadelman, 219.
Page v. Contoocook Valley R. Co., 194.
Page v. Grant, 295.
Page v. Thomas, 489.
Paige v. Illinois Steel Co., 215, 637.
Painter v. People, 282, 284.
Palestine, etc., Co. v. Terminal Warehouse Co., 414.
Pallidine v. Imperial V. F. L. Ass'n, 315.
Palmer v. Parker, 295.
Palmer Mfg. Co. ads. Carroll, 274.
Palmison v. First Nat. Bank of Tuckahoe, 95.
Palmtag ads. Ellsworth, 489.
Pan American Amusement Co. ads. Maguire, 291.
Pana Coal Co. ads. Bentriss, 200.
Panhandle & S. F. R. Co. ads. Litzinger, 364.
Pantelis v. Arsht, 640.
Paparone v. Ader, 95.
Pape v. Wright, 579.
Paradise ads. Luthy & Co., 542.
Paramount Organization ads. Donnelly, 205.
Parchen ads. Peck, 550.
Pardee ads. Potts, 542.
Pardue v. Whitfield, 601.
Parham ads. Southern R. Co., 425.
Park City ads. Johnson, 199.
Parker ads. Palmer, 295.
Parker v. Crane Co., 490.
Parker v. Schrimser, 200, 550.
Parker v. State, 542.
Parkersburg ads. Lush, 282.
Parkin v. Unity Protective Ins. Ass'n, 96.
Parks ads. People, 574.
Parmenter v. McDougall, 274.
Parret ads. Colburn, 314.
Parrish v. State, 195.
Partyka ads. Marshall, 605.
Pasachone Water Co. v. Slandart, 278.
Paschel v. Owen, 642.
Patalano ads. Commonwealth, 602.
Pate v. Gallup, 127.
Pate v. Peo., 315, 404.
Patrons', etc., Home Protective Co. ads. Price, 195.
Patterson v. Morgan, 219.
Patterson v. Patterson, 605.
Patton ads. Hoover, 362.
Patton v. Bank of Lafayett, 315.
Paul ads. Aetna Ins. Co., 350.
Paul ads. Gates, 274.
Paver ads. Lexington, etc., Co., 632.
Paw Paw Bk. v. Free, 320.
Paxton v. Boyce, 542, 543.
Payne ads. Faulkner, 287.
Pearce ads. Steel Furniture Co., 217, 219.
Pearl v. Omaha, etc., R. Co., 336.
Pechner v. Phoenix Ins. Co., 371.
Peck ads. Lichtenstein Millinery, 363.
Peck ads. O'Brien, 370.
Peck ads. Vinton, 406.
Peck v. Essex County, 194.
Peck v. Parchen, 550.
Pecos, etc., R. Co. v. Holmes, 435.
Pedley v. Doyle, 601.
Pelandeau, etc. v. Fred Gillespie Lumber Co., 274.
Pelton v. Schmidt, 373.
Pendarvis v. Gibbs, 468.
Peninsula, etc., Co. ads. Shippy, 634.
Peninsular Ry. Co. v. Howard, 194.
Penland ads. Baldridge, 309.
Penn v. Kelly, 284.
Penn Co. ads. Harrison Granite Co., 269.
Penner ads. West Texas Utility Co., 641.
Penn. R. Co. ads. Crew, 361.
Pennsylvania Coal Co. v. Kelley, 285.
People ads. Alminowicz, 374.
People ads. Annis, 582.
People ads. Babcock, 258.
People ads. Balbo, 197.
People ads. Barclay, 196.
People ads. Bradford, 527.
People ads. Clark, 306.
People ads. Coughlin, 199.

People ads. Damas, 258.
People ads. Gaffney, 550.
People ads. Gifford, 581.
People ads. Greenfield, 199.
People ads. Hawes, 640.
People ads. Henry, 284.
People ads. Henwood, 199.
People ads. Hertig, 334.
People ads. Jamison, 386.
People ads. Kator, 579.
People ads. Lycan, 517.
People ads. McCoy, 284.
People ads. Murphy, 349.
People ads. Painter, 282, 284.
People ads. Pate, 315, 404.
People ads. Roberts, 635.
People ads. Sanders, 639.
People ads. Siebert, 385.
People ads. Tracy, 349.
People ads. Trask, 635.
People ads. Wagner, 602.
People ads. Young, 16, 303.
People v. Allen, 199.
People v. Andrae, 586.
People v. Andrews, 488.
People v. Arnold, 283, 284.
People v. Babcock, 541.
People v. Barone, 602.
People v. Bartley, 582.
People v. Bastian, 580.
People v. Bertini, 601.
People v. Bolton, 489.
People v. Bowen, 457.
People v. Brocamp, 287.
People v. Brotherton, 199.
People v. Buchanan, 601, 602.
People v. Bundy, 631.
People v. Byrne, 284.
People v. Cascone, 586, 587.
People v. Cassidy, 256.
People v. Castree, 286, 287.
People v. Chin Mook Sow, 586, 587.
People v. Clark, 195, 196.
People v. Cleveland, etc., R. Co., 274.
People v. Cochran, 425.
People v. Cole, 550.
People v. Considine, 259, 491.
People v. Copsey, 199, 200.
People v. Curran, 258, 273.
People v. De Camp, 587.
People v. Decker, 196, 197.
People v. Dowling, 605.
People v. Durrant, 490, 543.
People v. Dyckman, 129.
People v. Elias, 287.
People v. Elmore, 326.
People v. Fisher, 586.
People v. Fitzgerald, 569.
People v. Fong Ah Sing, 258.
People v. Gehr, 199.
People v. Geidras, 489.
People v. Gibson, 126.
People v. Goehringer, 569.
People v. Goldenson, 476.
People v. Gray, 585.
People v. Green, 585.
People v. Griffin, 579.
People v. Gross, 601.
People v. Hallas, 543.
People v. Hamilton, 635.
People v. Herbert, 328.
People v. Hinshaw, 200.
People v. Hodge, 254, 259.
People v. Horn, 363.
People v. Hughson, 200.
People v. Hulse, 581.
People v. Jennings, 388.
People v. Johnson, 459.
People v. Joyce, 585.
People v. Keys, 490.
People v. Kinney, 284.
People v. Klopfer, 601.
People v. Kramer, 569.
People v. Krauser, 258.
People v. Lacang, 276.
People v. Lake, 458.
People v. Lamperle, 388.
People v. La Verne, 585.
People v. Lee Ah Yute, 549.
People v. Lehner, 579.
People v. Lenhart, 547.
People v. Levine, 285.
People v. Limeberry, 259.
People v. Looney, 350.
People v. Loper, 326.
People v. Lowen, 385.

People v. Lurie, 490.
People v. Lyons, 579.
People v. Mackay, 586.
People v. Maddox, 256.
People v. Majoine, 601.
People v. Majors, 256.
People v. Malkin, 490, 585.
People v. Mankus, 286.
People v. Mather, 258, 259, 273.
People v. McArron, 601.
People v. McCann, 636.
People v. McCollister, 194.
People v. McFarlane, 349.
People v. Mills, 551.
People v. Mole, 272.
People v. Mooney, 196, 328.
People v. Morse, 284.
People v. Moshiek, 585.
People v. Munday, 129, 287.
People v. Noblett, 602.
People v. Novak, 587.
People v. Oblaser, 546.
People v. Okopske, 580.
People v. Orosco, 550.
People v. Parks, 574.
People v. Perrin, 490.
People v. Powell, 543.
People v. Preston, 544.
People v. Rardin, 276.
People v. Revtor, 580.
People v. Robers, 327.
People v. Robinson, 199, 200, 602.
People v. Rosenbaum, 364.
People v. Rulia Singh, 547.
People v. Ryder, 580.
People v. Saloni, 285.
People v. Savage, 580.
People v. Schaepps, 256.
People v. Schanda, 587.
People v. Schladweiler, 258, 259.
People v. Schuyler, 476.
People v. Sexton, 258, 489.
People v. Smith, 283, 327.
People v. Spain, 585, 587.
People v. Strollo, 269.
People v. Swanson, 489.
People v. Sweeney, 550.
People v. Thorn, 284.
People v. Thurston, 477.
People v. Tiley, 543.
People v. Tubbs, 601.
People v. Turner, 590.
People v. Vanderhoof, 476.
People v. Van Tassel, 543.
People v. Vatek, 544.
People v. Vitelle, 197.
People v. Webster, 327.
People v. Wilkinson, 366.
People v. Wilson, 332.
People v. Youngs, 543.
People, etc., Co. v. Darrow, 634.
Peoples Gas Light Co. v. Amphett, 328.
Peoria Cordage Co. v. State Ind. Board, 385.
Peppard ads. McCourt, 256.
Perez v. Wilson, 641.
Perine v. Interurban St. R. Co., 551.
Perioux ads. State, 200.
Perkins v. Norris, 352.
Perlroth ads. Miller, 634.
Perrin ads. Peo., 490.
Perrotta ads. Williams, 353.
Perry ads. Fini, 204.
Perry ads. State, 195.
Perry v. Simpson Waterproof Mfg. Co., 342.
Perry v. Smith, 370.
Perry State Bank v. Elledge, 294.
Personeni ads. Gesualdi, 637.
Peskind ads. Pickering, 258.
Peters v. Reichenbach, 334.
Peterson ads. Dawson, 331.
Peterson ads. Johnson, 541.
Petro v. State, 585.
Pfeiffer v. Chicago, etc., R. Co., 288.
Phares v. Barber, 259.
Phelps v. Hall, 194.
Phillips ads. Miner, 547.
Phillips ads. Tegarden, 196.
Phillips v. Chase, 638.
Philpot v. Fifth Avenue Church, 637.
Phoenix Ins. Co. ads. Pechner, 371.
Pickards ads. Karwick, 289.
Pickering v. Peskind, 258.
Pickrel v. Doubet, 351.
Piehl v. Albany R. Co., 388.

Pierce ads. American, etc., Co., 641.
Pierce v. Avakian, 369.
Pierce v. Coffee, 384.
Pierpont v. Fifth Avenue Coach Co., 292, 385.
Pierson v. Hoag, 476.
Pietsch v. Pietsch, 203.
Pietzuk v. Kansas City R. Co., 198.
Pinder v. State, 197.
Pine v. Callahan, 199.
Pioneer, etc., Co. v. Washburn, 639.
Pirek v. Scott, 551.
Piretti v. Firestone Tire & Rubber Co., 350.
Pitcairn ads. Griswold, 341.
Pitman ads. Sharp, 275.
Pittsburgh, C. C. & St. L. Ry. Co. v. Gage, 604.
Pittsburgh, etc., R. Co. v. Carlson, 542.
Pittsburgh, etc., Railroad Co. v. Martin, 635.
Pittsburgh, etc., R. Co. v. Fawsett, 309.
Pizer v. Hunt, 275.
Plant ads. Smith, 363.
Platt ads. Shephard, 636.
Pleason Realty, etc., Co. v. Kleinman, 350.
Plotner ads. Graham, 298.
Plumb v. Cutis, 350.
Podhorzer ads. Commercial Credit Corp., 149.
Poetker ads. U. S. Fidelity & Guaranty Co., 642.
Pontecorvo v. Clark, 604, 605.
Pontiac Clothing Co. ads. Boston, etc., Co., 369.
Pool v. Chase, 372.
Pool v. Montague Tp., 383.
Poole ads. Osgood, 309.
Poole v. Boston & M. R. R., 605.
Poole v. Dean, 457.
Poole v. Lamsden, 639.
Pope v. State, 199.
Portalis & Co. ads. Koppel Industrial Car & Equipment Co., 114.
Porter ads. Heminway, etc., Silk Co., 289.
Porter v. Still, 634.
Porter v. Tenant, 348.
Portland ads. Jones, 458.
Portland Ry., Light & Power Co. ads. Lane, 205.
Portland Ry. Light & Power Co. ads. Tonseth, 294.
Posell v. Herscovitz, 214.
Post ads. Tyson, 370.
Potter ads. R. I. & P. R. R., 271.
Potter v. State, 197.
Potts ads. State, 195.
Potts v. Pardee, 542.
Potvin v. West Bay, etc., Co., 328.
Pouley ads. Herrington, 635.
Powell ads. Peo., 543.
Powpit Co., Inc. ads. Commonwealth Fuel Co., Inc., 149.
Prater ads. State, 194.
Pratt v. Tailer, 288.
Pray ads. Berridge, 640.
Precourt v. Driscoll, 256.
Preferred, etc., Co. ads. Cilley, 633.
Prentis v. Gates, 477.
Presbyterian Church, etc. v. Bevan, 457, 458.
Prescott & Sons, Inc., ads. Citizens Trust Co. of Utica, 96.
Presley v. Kinlock-Bloomington Telephone Co., 604.
Preston ads. Peo., 544.
Price ads. Rudolph Hdwe. Co., 331.
Price v. Patrons', etc., Home Protective Co., 195.
Priddle ads. Dowie, 363.
Prince ads. Chandler, 279.
Princeton, etc., Co. v. Howell, 325.
Pritschan ads. Cleveland, etc., R. Co., 638.
Proctor, etc., Mfg. Co. ads. McKeon, 282.
Producer's Oil Co. v. State, 632.
Pronskevitch v. Chicago, etc., R. Co., 604.
Proper v. State, 258.
Prox Co. v. Bryan, 519.
Prudential Trust Co. v. Coghlin, 256.
Pruit ads. St. Louis S. W. R. Co., 396.
Prus ads. Toledo R., etc., 543.

Prussian Nat. Ins. Co. ads. Hoffman, 328.
Prussing v. Jackson, 320.
Public Service Co. ads. Wolezek, 636.
Public Utilities Co. v. Handorf, 458.
Puckett ads. I. C. C. R. R. Co., 349.
Puget Sound Iron, etc., Work ads. Redding, 204.
Pugh ads. Indianapolis, etc., Co., 636.
Pugsley ads. State, 258.
Pullin v. First National Bank, 637.
Pullman Co. v. Hoyle, 386.
Purdy ads. Butts, 334.
Putnam v. Harris, 350, 351.
Putnam v. Pacific Monthly Co., 195.
Putnam v. Wadley, 387.

Q

Quaker Oats Co. v. Kidman, 346.
Quick v. Amer. Can. Co., 542.
Quigley v. Turner, 585.
Quill v. Southern Pac. Co., 197, 198.
Quimby ads. Barrie, 384.
Quincy v. White, 363.
Quincy Gas Co. v. Schmitt, 462.
Quincy G. & E. Co. v. Baumann, 284, 286, 346, 491, 640.
Quincy, O. & K. C. Ry. Co. ads. McQuary, 205.
Quinn v. Higgins, 457.

R

Rachmel v. Clark, 275.
Rademacher v. Greenwich Ins. Co., 291.
Radke ads. Duffy, 580.
Radke v. State, 541, 580.
Ragsdale ads. International, etc., R., 373.
Raitt ads. Chotean, 303.
Ramsey v. State, 579.
Randall ads. McCarin, 320.
Randolph ads. Wallis, 604.
Rankin v. Rankin, 386.
Ransom ads. Missouri, etc., R. Co., 336.
Rardin ads. Peo., 276.
Rashid ads. Central Shoe Co., 271.
Rathbun v. Ross, 579.
Ratshewsky ads. Ayers, 587.
Ravenscroft v. Stull, 638.
Rawleigh Medical Co. ads. Hunt, 218, 219.
Ray ads. Keuka College, 371.
Raymond ads. Burdick, 350.
Raymond v. Glover, 352.
Ray State, etc., R. Co. ads. Johnson, 425.
Razor v. Razor, 349, 632.
Reagan v. Manchester St. R. Co., 366.
Receivers of Kirby Lumber Co. ads. Bass, 606.
Reclamation, etc., v. Inglin, 386, 524, 462.
Redding v. Puget Sound Iron, etc., Work, 204.
Reddington v. Blue, 371.
Redick v. State, 490.
Redke v. State, 547.
Redlich v. Bauerlee, 309.
Reed ads. Bias, 204, 205.
Reed Orchard Co. ads. Vallejo, etc., R. Co., 384.
Reedy ads. Kahn, 196.
Reehil v. Fraas, 352.
Reese ads. Kreutzer & Wasem, 601.
Rehberg v. N. V., 634.
Reiche v. Gleicher, 351, 605.
Reichenbach ads. Peters, 334.
Reilly ads. Scripps, 203.
Reiman ads. Laserowitch, 298.
Reiner ads. Brownlee, 126.
Reinke v. Sanitary District, 283.
Remson v. Metro. El. R. Co., 298.
Respublica v. Richards, 194, 195.
Revtor ads. Peo., 580.
Reyman ads. Chicago, etc., R. Co., 274.
Reynolds v. Struble, 590.
Reynolds & Heitsman v. Henry, 349.
Rhea v. State, 601.
Rhodes v. Meloy, 605, 606.
Rib Lake Lumber Co. ads. Graves, 489.
Rice v. Rice, 273, 346.
Rice v. Taliaferro, 321.
Rich v. Lancaster R. Co., 335.
Rich v. Township, 348.
Richards ads. Caldwell, 605.
Richards ads. Respublica, 194, 195.

Richards v. Robin, 334, 335.
Richardson ads. Kossuth County St. Bank, 309.
Richardson v. Nassau El. R. Co., 256.
Richardson v. State, 601.
Riches ads. Williams, 527.
Richmond Dredging Co. v. Atchison, etc., R. Co., 387.
Rickel v. Stockman, 323.
Rickey ads. Gregory, 640.
Ridgeway Tp. ads. Turner, 459.
Riggins v. Chicago, etc., Ry. Co., 638.
Riggs ads. Holland, 347.
Riley v. Boehm, 309.
Riley v. Iowa Falls, 637.
Ripon v. Bettel, 476.
Rippetoe ads. Dwyer, 363.
Riseman ads. Roselli, 349.
Ritacco v. New Rochelle, City of, 640.
Robbin ads. American Motor Car Co., 287.
Robbins ads. Criswell, 283.
Robbins ads. N. Y., etc., R. Co., 326.
Robbs v. Herkel, 369.
Roberts v. Chan Tin Pen, 351.
Roberts v. Dazey, 369.
Roberts v. People, 635.
Roberts v. State, 590.
Robin ads. Richards, 334, 335.
Robinson ads. Peo., 199, 200, 602.
Robinson ads. San Antonio, etc., R. Co., 606.
Robinson ads. Singmaster, 126, 303.
Robinson v. Halley, 351.
Robinson v. McKnight, 604.
Robinson v. New York El. R. Co., 602.
Robinson v. State, 259, 335.
Robinson v. Yetter, 371.
Robyn ads. Trainor, 309.
Roche v. Baldwin, 457.
Rochester Printing Co. ads. Griebel, 636.
Rochester, etc., R. Co. ads. Kennedy, 385.
Rochford ads. Ferguson, 384.
Rock Island v. Starkey, 606.
R. I. & P. R. R. v. Potter, 271.
Rodee v. Detroit, etc., Ins. Co., 291.
Rodeff v. Lake Shore & M. S. Ry. Co., 205.
Rodger ads. Stevens, 580.
Rodriguez v. State, 259.
Roger v. Kelly, 371.
Rogers ads. Com., 579.
Rogers ads. Cons. Ins. Co., 127.
Rogers ads. Evans, 309.
Rogers ads. People, 327.
Rogers ads. Schlesinger, 254, 258, 259.
Rogers v. Gladiator Min., etc., Co., 194.
Rogers v. Moore, 581.
Roman ads. Urbanowiez, 641.
Romania v. Boston El. R. Co., 383.
Roman Oolitic Stone Co. v. Shields, 385.
Rommel Bros. v. Wenks, 601.
Rooker v. Deering Southwestern R. Co., 199.
Root ads. Ashley, 331.
Root v. Boston El. R., 477.
Rorvick v. Astoria Box & Paper Co., 219.
Roscum ads. State, 543.
Rose ads. Commonwealth El. Co., 638.
Rose ads. Swing, 383.
Rose v. Chicago City R. Co., 642.
Rose v. Rose, 373.
Roseberry ads. Wright, 301.
Roseberry v. Nixon, 353.
Roselli v. Riseman, 349.
Rosenbaum ads. People, 364.
Rosenberg v. Rubin, 198.
Rosengreen v. Manufacturers Nat. Bank, 350.
Rosenheim ads. Strasburger, 150.
Rosen-Steinsitz v. Wanamaker, 531.
Rosenthal v. Bilger, 258.
Ross ads. Calhoun, 341.
Ross ads. Crane, 373.
Ross ads. O'Neill, 635.
Ross ads. Rathbun, 579.
Ross v. State, 199.
Ross-Lewin v. Gould, 345.
Roszczyniala v. State, 284.
Roth v. Fleck, 338.
Roth v. Moeller, 517.
Roth v. Travelers, etc., Co., 258.
Rothe ads. Ney, 634.

Rowe v. Brooklyn Heights R. Co., 271.
Rowell ads. Moody, 258, 259.
Rowland ads. Jack, 303.
Royal Ins. Co. v. Texas, etc., R. Co., 331, 335.
Rubin ads. Rosenberg, 198.
Ruddy v. McDonald, 347.
Rudolph Hdwe. Co. v. Price, 331.
Rulia Singh ads. Peo., 547.
Runge v. Schroeder, 606.
Ruschenberg v. Southern Electric R. Co., 198.
Rush v. Amarillo First Nat. Bk., 371.
Rushville v. Morrow, 330.
Rutherford v. Dyer, 315.
Ryan ads. Chicago, etc., R. Co., 604.
Ryan ads. Conlin, 320.
Ryan v. Schenectady, 330.
Ryder ads. Peo., 580.

S

Sacco ads. Commonwealth, 490, 586, 601.
Sachs ads. Stinson, 198.
Sacramento Lodge, etc., ads. Bisinger, 364, 635.
Sadler v. Murrah, 273.
Saintman v. Maxwell, 457.
Salen v. Webster, 387.
Salinger ads. Culbertson, 347.
Salinger ads. Homesteader's Life Ass'n, 542.
Salisbury ads. Whitaker, 542.
Saloni ads. Peo., 285.
Salt Springs Nat. Bank v. Schlosser, 634.
Salt Springs Nat. Bank of Syracuse v. Hitchcock, 150.
Samuel Stores, Inc., ads. Frohman, 96.
San Antonio, etc., ads. Crystal Ice Mfg. Co., 256.
San Antonio, etc., R. Co. v. Cockrill, 350, 351.
San Antonio, etc., R. Co. v. Nappier, 580.
San Antonio, etc., R. Co. v. Robinson, 606.
San Bernardino, etc., Co. ads. Hale, 641.
Sandberg v. Chicago Rys. Co., 639.
Sanders ads. State, 197.
Sanders v. People, 639.
Sandmand ads. Jackson, 195.
Sando v. Smith, 634.
Sandquist ads. Knox, 519.
Sandra v. Times Co., 569.
Sandres ads. Hovey, 283.
Sandusky ads. Lloyd, 371.
Sanford ads. Davis, 309.
Sanford ads. Stratford, 258.
Sanford v. John Finnegan Co., 373, 374.
Sanitary District ads. Reinke, 283.
San Miguel Consol. Gold Min. Co. v. Bonner, 217.
San Pacific Co. ads. Arakelian, 285.
Santa Clara, etc., Co. ads. Steen, 579.
Sargeant v. Barnes, 458.
Satterlee v. Bliss, 349.
Saunders ads. Woolsey, 331.
Savage ads. Peo., 580.
Savage Silver Min. Co. ads. Fleeson, 194.
Savannah Sugar Refining Corp. ads. L. R. Munoz & Co., 149.
Savich v. Amer. St. Bank, 569.
Sax v. Zanger, 489.
Scagel v. Chicago, etc., R. Co., 336.
Scarborough ads. Cincinnati, 386.
Scarlett ads. Trussell, 301.
Schabel v. Onseyga Realty Co., 364.
Schaeppi v. Slade, 370.
Schaepps ads. Peo., 256.
Schaffer v. State, 489.
Schanda ads. Peo., 587.
Schantes v. State, 388.
Schee v. McQuilken, 633.
Scheerer v. Deming, 605.
Scheiber ads. Consolidated Coal Co. of St. Louis, 639.
Schenectady ads. Ryan, 330.
Schevers v. American Ry. Express Co., 604.
Schladweiler ads. People, 258.
Schlesinger v. Rogers, 254, 258, 259.
Schlodweiler ads. Peo., 259.
Schlosser ads. Salt Springs Nat. Bank v. Schlosser, 634.

Schlosser v. Nicholson, 369.
Schlowman ads. Craney, 350.
Schmidt ads. Pelton, 373.
Schmitt ads. Quincy Gas Co., 462.
Schmitt v. Baptist Temple, Inc., 96.
Schmitz ads. Chicago, etc., R. Co., 425.
Schnadt ads. Nagle, 632, 633, 634.
Schneider ads. Con. Coal Co., 371.
Schneider ads. Knapp, 349.
Schoefer v. Fond du Lac, 636.
Schoening, etc. ads. Village, etc., 350.
Schoff v. Shephard, 477.
Schomer v. State, 289.
Schonhous v. Weiner, 95.
Schrimsher ads. Parker, 200, 550.
Schrock ads. Bloomington, 476.
Schroeder ads. Runge, 606.
Schroeder ads. Sprengel, 457.
Schroeder v. Hotel Commercial Co., 282.
Schueller ads. Winneskeik Ins. Co., 197.
Schultz v. Starr, 373.
Schuster v. State, 259.
Schuyler ads. Peo., 476.
Schweinfurth v. Cleveland, etc., R. Co., 285.
Schweitzer ads. State, 334.
Schworn v. Fraternal Banker's Res. Soc., 298.
Scofield v. Clarke, 638.
Scott ads. Chicago & A. R. Co., 640.
Scott ads. Com., 285.
Scott ads. Heath, 579.
Scott ads. McGlasson, 335.
Scott ads. Pirek, 551.
Scott v. Caldwell, 346.
Scribner ads. Brush, 331.
Scribner ads. Indiana, etc., Co., 327.
Scripps v. Reilly, 203.
Seaboard Air Line Ry. Co. ads. Conn., 639.
Seaman ads. Bowman, 218.
Seattle ads. Beach, 197.
Seattle, etc., R. Co. ads. Harris, 282.
Security State Bank of Eskridge v. Mossman, 218.
Seeherman v. Wilkes-Barre Co., 195.
Seeley ads. Central, etc., Assoc., 274.
Seeley ads. Duncan, 491.
Seeley v. Osborne, 372.
Seitz ads. Mason, 632.
Selberstein ads. Kotlowitz, 632.
Selby v. Detroit R. Co., 490.
Self v. King, 370.
Sellack v. Janesville, 459.
Seney ads. Knight, 582.
Sesler v. Montgomery, 638.
Sexton ads. People, 258, 489.
Seymour Water Co. v. Lebline, 259.
Shamhan v. Equitable Acc. Co., 334.
Sharp v. Pitman, 275.
Shaughnessy v. Holt, 385.
Shaw v. N. Y. El. R. Co., 289, 348.
Shaw v. Ogden, 530.
Shaw v. Shaw, 345.
Shaw v. State, 258.
Shaw v. Waterbury, 330.
Shearer v. Middleton, 606.
Sheer ads. West Chicago Alcohol Works, 279.
Sheldon ads. Link, 347.
Sheldon ads. York, 334.
Sheldon v. Benham, 387.
Shelledy ads. State, 199.
Shelly ads. Atherton, 372.
Shelton v. Holzwasser, 294.
Shepard ads. Stoudt, 258.
Shephard ads. Schoff, 477.
Shephard v. Platt, 636.
Shepley v. Shepley, 321.
Sherman ads. Kreigh, 347.
Sherman v. State, 585.
Shermer ads. Hardy, 642.
Sherwood ads. Martin, 292, 349, 385.
Shields ads. Roman Oolitic Stone Co., 385.
Shields ads. U. S. Gypsum Co., 371.
Shippers, etc., Co. v. Davidson, 295.
Shippy v. Peninsula, etc., Co., 634.
Shrope ads. Albaugh, 489.
Shugart v. Halliday, 631.
Siberry v. State, 284.
Sichterman v. R. M. Hollingshead Co., 551.
Sidorsky ads. Mishkind-Feinberg Realty Co., 306.
Siebert v. Peo., 385.

Siegel ads. Martin Emerich Outfitting Co., 204.
Siegel ads. Stricks, 151.
Signa Iron Co. ads. Hecla Powder Co., 331.
Silverberg ads. Buckley, 604.
Silverman ads. Dodwell & Co., Inc., 150.
Silvis v. Ely, 194, 195.
Silvius v. Mordoff, 633.
Simmons v. Harris, 219.
Simon v. Mooney, 519.
Simpson v. Foundation Co., 349.
Simpson Waterproof Mfg. Co. ads. Perry, 342.
Singer v. Cross, 338.
Singer Sewing Mach. Co. ads. Doyle, 323.
Singmaster v. Robinson, 126, 303.
Sipes v. Barlow, 373.
Skipworth v. Deyell, 309.
Skliris ads. Walker, 313.
Skurnik ads. Strauss, 373.
Slack v. State, 199.
Slade ads. Schaeppi, 370.
Slandart ads. Pasachone Water Co., 278.
Sloan ads. Waller, 519.
Sloan v. Anderson, 334.
Sloan v. N. Y. C. R. R. Co., 544.
Smalley v. Appleton, 386.
Smith ads. Chicago City R. Co., 323.
Smith ads. Chicago, etc., R. Co., 323.
Smith ads. Dalton, 349.
Smith ads. McDonald, 348.
Smith ads. McGlasson, 331.
Smith ads. Mulligan, 215.
Smith ads. People, 283, 327.
Smith ads. Perry, 370.
Smith ads. Sando, 634.
Smith ads. Stedman Fruit Co., 349.
Smith ads. Wallerich, 350.
Smith ads. Washington, 546.
Smith v. East Branch Min. Co., 362.
Smith v. Hausendorf, 327.
Smith v. Hendrix, 352.
Smith v. Jackson, 398.
Smith v. Jennings, 641.
Smith v. King, 527.
Smith v. Olson, 345.
Smith v. Plant, 363.
Smith v. Smith, 314, 349.
Smith v. State, 590.
Smith v. Wetmore, 275.
Smith v. Young, 363.
Smith-Wallace Shoe ads. Dixon, 331.
Smith & Son ads. Hinkle, 350.
Smoky Hollow Coal Co. ads. Thayer, 279, 459.
Sneed v. Osborn, 349.
Snow v. Greisheimer, 370.
Snyder ads. Stockwell, 129.
Snyder Cigar, etc., Co. v. Stutts, 349.
Sobieski v. Chicago, 274.
So. Cal. R. Co. ads. Yaeger, 348.
Sofrancy ads. Hoberg, 489.
Solomon ads. D. I. Mofziger Lumber Co., 335.
Solomon v. Stewart, 371, 640.
Somers ads. Durgin, 373.
Somers v. Loose, 362.
Sommer ads. Hill Co., 309.
Soodeletti ads. Hand, 490.
So. P. Co. ads. Davey, 348.
So. Pac. Co. v. Eckenfels, 326.
Sorell v. State, 256.
Sorenson v. Chi. Rys. Co., 347, 348.
South Texas Candy Co. ads. Missouri Pac. R. Co., 274.
Southern Electric R. Co. ads. Ruschenberg, 198.
Southern Pacific Co. ads. Dyas, 637.
Southern Pac. Co. ads. Fitts, 196, 198.
Southern Pac. R. Co. ads. Guill, 198.
Southern Pac. Co. ads. Quill, 197.
Southern R. Co. v. Parham, 425.
Southern Surety Co. ads. Dittmeier Real Estate Co., 205.
Southwestern, etc. v. French, 637.
Sovereign Camp, etc. v. Downer, 271.
Sovereign, etc. v. Jackson, 590.
Spain ads. Peo., 585, 587.
Spangler ads. Bever, 477.
Spence ads. Chicago & J. El. R. Co., 323.
Spero ads. Levin, 519.
Sperry, etc., Co. ads. Gagnon, 349.
Speyer v. Stern, 606.

Spicer v. Bonker, 205.
Spillman ads. Amer. Express Co., 285.
Spinney v. Hooker, 195.
Spitler v. Kaeding, 298.
Spooner ads. Teter, 387.
Spreckels ads. Worley, 543.
Sprengel v. Schroeder, 457.
Springer v. Chicago, 284.
Springfield ads. Fleming, 385.
Springfield, etc. ads. Hay, 335.
Springfield, etc., Co. v. Hubbs Co., 636.
Spring Valley Coal Co. ads. McCarthy, 641.
Sprowle ads. Hardy, 196.
Spry v. Logansport, etc., Co., 635.
Stacy v. Graham, 581.
Stadelman ads. Paepke, 219.
Stadler v. Chicago City Railway, 635.
Stale v. McGann, 275.
Standard Furniture Co. ads. Chilberg, 531.
Standard Oil Co. ads. Nau, 543.
Standard Oil Co. ads. Stowell, 458.
Stanger Co. ads. Curran, 385.
Stanton v. Lapp, 605.
Star F. Ins. Co. ads. Bistritz, 491.
Starkey ads. Rock Island, 606.
Starks v. O'Hara, 364.
Starr ads. Schultz, 373.
State ads. Anderson, 194.
State ads. Andrews, 282, 586.
State ads. Bass, 197.
State ads. Bassham, 602.
State ads. Baum, 551.
State ads. Beeson, 581.
State ads. Bell, 489.
State ads. Bennet, 196.
State ads. Bills, 580.
State ads. Blackwell, 195.
State ads. Blume, 458.
State ads. Bolden, 569.
State ads. Brazleton, 194.
State ads. Colbert, 587.
State ads. Collier, 585.
State ads. Collins, 198, 200, 284, 289.
State ads. Conway, 579.
State ads. Counts, 195.
State ads. Craig, 579.
State ads. Danzey, 195.
State ads. Davis, 195.
State ads. Deigel, 587.
State ads. Dicks, 200.
State ads. Donohue, 602.
State ads. Dotterer, 579, 585, 586.
State ads. Dunn, 196, 579.
State ads. Ellis, 200.
State ads. Franklin, 196.
State ads. Fritch, 585.
State ads. Glascoe, 602.
State ads. Gray, 601.
State ads. Green, 491.
State ads. Greenwood, 196.
State ads. Griffin, 580.
State ads. Harris, 199.
State ads. Hatsfield, 259.
State ads. Heagy, 634.
State ads. Hempton, 259.
State ads. Hess, 406.
State ads. Hill, 258.
State ads. Holmes, 196.
State ads. Houston, 200, 547.
State ads. Hughes, 200.
State ads. Hukox, 275.
State ads. Hunter, 586.
State ads. Isenhour, 388.
State ads. Jacobs, 196.
State ads. Keaton, 586.
State ads. Kirschner, 587.
State ads. Knoll, 476.
State ads. Koons, 388.
State ads. Lafferty, 517.
State ads. Ledford, 195.
State ads. Leseur, 580.
State ads. Mainville, 200.
State ads. Mangano, 199.
State ads. Matthews, 582.
State ads. Merritt, 196.
State ads. McGough, 199.
State ads. McMurray, 585.
State ads. Memmler, 198.
State ads. Merkel, 200.
State ads. Miller, 547.
State ads. Moffett, 200.
State ads. Moore, 197.
State ads. Moran, 601.
State ads. Muse, 196, 199.
State ads. O'Berry, 195.
State ads. Parker, 542.

State ads. Parrish, 195.
State ads. Petro, 585.
State ads. Pinder, 197.
State ads. Pope, 199.
State ads. Potter, 197.
State ads. Producers' Oil Co., 632.
State ads. Proper, 258.
State ads. Radke, 541.
State ads. Ramsey, 579.
State ads. Redick, 490.
State ads. Redke, 547.
State ads. Rhea, 601.
State ads. Richardson, 601.
State ads. Roberts, 590.
State ads. Robinson, 259, 335.
State ads. Rodriguez, 259.
State ads. Ross, 199.
State ads. Roszczyniala, 284.
State ads. Schaffer, 489.
State ads. Schantes, 388.
State ads. Schomer, 289.
State ads. Schuster, 259.
State ads. Shaw, 258.
State ads. Sherman, 585.
State ads. Siberry, 284.
State ads. Slack, 199.
State ads. Smith, 590.
State ads. Sorell, 256.
State ads. Stover, 601.
State ads. Stratton, 581.
State ads. Stringfellow, 195.
State ads. Thomas, 195.
State ads. Tosser, 590.
State ads. Turney, 259.
State ads. Ward, 199.
State ads. Washington, 602.
State ads. Weldon, 580.
State ads. Willis, 196, 585.
State ads. Withers, 196.
State ads. Wood, 347.
State ads. Vines, 631.
State ads. Zimmerman, 194.
State ads. Zoldoske, 477.
State v. Alberts, 590.
State v. Ampt, 279.
State v. Beeson, 602.
State v. Behrman, 334.
State v. Blackburn, 579.
State v. Blydenburg, 385.
State v. Brooks, 197.
State v. Buchanan, 272.
State v. Buford, 197.
State v. Castelli, 259.
State v. Christy, 258.
State v. Cook, 326.
State v. Curran, 490.
State v. Davis, 543.
State v. Dillman, 200, 580.
State v. Faulkner, 198.
State v. Foreman, 579.
State v. Foster, 200.
State v. Fullerton, 195.
State v. Giudice, 197.
State v. Golden, 259.
State v. Gorman, 284.
State v. Gregory, 579.
State v. Hamilton, 586.
State v. Hassan, 256.
State v. Hasty, 327.
State v. Huffman, 199, 200.
State v. Jeffrey, 518.
State v. Johnson, 585.
State v. Knight, 581.
State v. La Barre, 489.
State v. Laudano, 284.
State v. Lee, 517.
State v. Matheson, 397.
State v. Matlack, 315.
State v. McAfee, 197.
State v. McCook, 541.
State v. Megorden, 259.
State v. Moore, 195.
State v. Norman, 579, 580.
State v. Novak, 631.
State v. Otto, 199.
State v. Perioux, 200.
State v. Perry, 195.
State v. Potts, 195.
State v. Prater, 194.
State v. Pugsly, 258.
State v. Radke, 580.
State v. Roscum, 543.
State v. Sanders, 197.
State v. Schweitzer, 334.
State v. Shelledy, 199.
State v. Steber, 369.
State v. Tomblin, 199.
State v. Turley, 200.

State v. Twitty, 331.
State v. Walton, 195.
State v. Wood, 477.
State v. Wright, 386.
State Bank ads. Frye, 579.
State, etc. v. Friedman, 542.
State Ind. Board ads. Peoria Cordage Co., 385.
St. Clair v. United States, 258.
Steber ads. State, 369.
Stedman Fruit Co. v. Smith, 349.
Steel Co. ads. Ward, 275.
Steel Furniture Co. v. Pearce, 217, 219.
Steen v. Santa Clara, etc., Co., 579.
Steers ads. Wilson, 295.
Stein v. Jascula, 269.
Stemmler v. New York, 272, 342.
Stephens v. Hoffman, 288.
Stephens v. Ill. Cent. R. R., 323.
Stephens v. Williams, 334.
Stern ads. Speyer, 606.
Stetson ads. Vergie, 294.
Stevens ads. Wright, 132.
Stevens v. Rodger, 580.
Stevenson ads. Toledo, etc., R. Co., 347.
Stewart ads. Belknap, 259.
Stewart ads. Compton-Price Piano Co., 204.
Stewart ads. Solomon, 371, 640.
Still ads. Porter, 634.
Stillman v. Chicago R. I. & P. Ry. Co., 256.
Stinson v. Sachs, 198.
Stitzel v. Miller, 328.
St. Joseph ads. George, 348.
St. Louis S. W. R. Co. v. Pruit, 386.
St. Louis Transit Co. ads. Billmeyer, 198.
St. Louis Transit Co. ads. Fillingham, 219.
St. Louis Transit Co. ads. Frisby, 218.
St. Louis W. R. Co. v. Bishop, 550.
St. Louis & S. W. R. Co. v. Lowe, 387.
St. Louis, etc., R. Co. ads. Blackwell, 384.
St. Louis, etc., R. Co. v. Brown, 278.
St. Louis, etc., R. Co. ads. Conrad, 457.
St. Louis, etc., R. Co. v. Ewing, 285.
St. Louis, etc., R. Co. v. Garber, 332.
St. Louis, etc., R. Co. v. Hooser, 196, 197.
St. Louis, etc., R. Co. v. McMichael, 437.
Stock ads. Ahart, 585.
Stock & Sons v. Dellapenna, 579.
Stockman ads. Rickel, 323.
Stockton ads. Froeming, 542, 550.
Stockwell v. Snyder, 129.
Stoddard v. Grand Trunk, etc., Ry. Co., 639.
Stoker ads. Greenup, 259.
Stokes ads. Duplanty, 370.
Stoldt ads. Church, 195.
Stone v. Com., 636.
Stone v. Hubbard, 387.
Stone Land, etc., Co. v. Boon, 335.
Stotts v. Fairfield, 363.
Stotts v. Stotts, 371.
Stoudt v. Shepard, 258.
Stout v. Cook, 289.
Stover v. State, 601.
Stover Carriage Co. v. American & British Mfg. Co., 286.
Stowell v. Standard Oil Co., 458.
St. Paul, etc., R. Co. ads. Grafton, 332.
Strasburger v. Rosenheim, 150.
Stratford v. Sanford, 258.
Stratton v. State, 581.
Strauss v. Skurnik, 373.
Streblow v. Sylvester, 541.
Streever v. Ft. Edward Bk., 320.
Stretch v. Stretch, 387.
Stricks v. Siegel, 151.
Stringfellow v. State, 195.
Strollo ads. Peo., 269.
Strong ads. Chapman, 489.
Strong ads. Miles, 636.
Struble ads. Reynolds, 590.
Struwe ads. American Automobile Ins. Co., 604.
St. Stanislaus Church v. Verien, 336.
Studwell v. Bush, 370.
Stull ads. Ravenscroft, 638.
Stumm v. Hummell, 196.
Sturgis ads. Fruit Dispatch Co., 309.
Sturtivant ads. Com., 476.

Stutsman v. Des Moines, etc., R. Co., 457.
Stutts ads. C. C. Snyder Cigar, etc., Co., 349.
Sugar ads. Chicago Union Tract. Co., 459.
Suhr v. Hoover, 635.
Suisan City ads. De Freitas, 408.
Sullivan ads. Adams, 425.
Sullivan ads. Boltz, 636.
Sullivan ads. West Chicago St. Ry. Co., 635.
Sullivan v. Minneapolis, etc., R. Co., 457.
Sullivan v. Owens, 279.
Sun Co. ads. Byerley, 294.
Sun Oil Co. v. Garren, 204.
Superior Mfg. Co. ads. Benson, 285.
Supreme, etc. v. Everding, 275.
Susman ads. Bay, etc., Co., 127.
Swanson ads. Peo., 489.
Swanson v. Hood, 458.
Sweeney ads. Peo., 550.
Sweeney ads. Webb, 351.
Swensen v. Brooklyn Heights R. Co., 462.
Swift ads. McCabe, 346, 386.
Swift v. Yanoway, 371.
Swinburn ads. Colrick, 347.
Swing v. Rose, 383.
Swisher ads. I. C. C. R. R. Co., 278.
S. W. Portland Cement Co. v. Kezer, 425.
Swygart ads. Mayer, 351.
Sylvester ads. Streblow, 541.
Syracuse Univ. ads. Di Tommaso, 437.

T

Tabor Coal Co. v. Cohen, 270.
Tabor State Bank v. Brewer, 256.
Tafelski ads. Cincinnati H. & D. Ry., 610.
Taft v. Little, 289.
Tailer ads. Pratt, 288.
Talburt v. Berkshire Life Ins., 543.
Taliaferro ads. Rice, 321.
Tannenbaum ads. Foster, 491.
Tannesbaum ads. Greishheimer, 309.
Tarpey ads. Nicholson, 126.
Tattan v. Detroit, 330.
Taylor v. Adams, 346.
Taylor v. McClintock, 362.
Taylor v. McIrvin, 127.
Taylor v. Merrill, 371.
Taylor v. Taylor, 477.
Tebo v. Augusta, 457.
Teegarden v. Caledonia, 348.
Tegarden v. Phillips, 196.
Temp. Brew Co. ads. Omaha Beverage Co., 605.
Tenant ads. Porter, 348.
Teplitz ads. Herman, 352.
Terminal Warehouse Co. ads. Palestine, etc., Co., 414.
Terr ads. Leigh, 199.
Terrill v. Michigan, etc., Co., 642.
Terwilliger ads. Bender, 632.
Teter v. Spooner, 387.
Teutonia Ins. Co. v. Tobias, 255.
Teutonic Ins. Co. ads. Westfield Cigar Co., 349.
Texas Cent. R. Co. v. Blanton, 199.
Texas El. Ry. v. Gonzolis, 639.
Texas Employers Ins. Ass'n v. Birdwell, 256.
Texas & P. Railway Co. ads. Oden, 635.
Texas, etc., Co. v. Webster, 491.
Texas, etc., R. Co. ads. Marande, 197.
Texas, etc., R. Co. ads. Royal Ins. Co., 331, 335.
Texas, etc., R. Co. v. Elliott, 195.
Texas, etc., R. Co. v. Graham, 285.
Texas Mach., etc., Co. v. Ayers Ice Cream Co., 282.
Thayer v. Smoky Hollow Coal Co., 279, 459.
Thayer v. Tyler, 384.
The Clipper v. Logan, 459.
Thede v. Matthews, 269.
Theisen v. Detroit Taxicab Co., 271.
The Kawailani, 517.
Thelin ads. Kent, 348.
Theurer ads. Baretti, 309.
Third Ave. R. Co. ads. Kleiner, 350.
Third Ave. R. Co. ads. McGinnis, 459
Thomas ads. Haynes, 315.
Thomas ads. Malcolm, 205.

Thomas ads. McLaughlin, 371.
Thomas ads. Page, 489.
Thomas v. Byron, 543.
Thomas v. Illinois Power & Lite Corp., 641.
Thomas v. State, 195.
Thomas v. Winthrop, etc., 489.
Thomas Canning Co. ads. Grand, etc., Exch. 370.
Thomasson v. Wilson, 350.
Thompson ads. Grant, 387.
Thompson ads. Luginbyhl, 637.
Thompson ads. Ward, 489.
Thompson v. Malmin, 132.
Thorn ads. People, 284.
Thornhill v. Carpenter-Morton Co., 282.
Thorson ads. Massman, 287.
Thurston ads. Peo., 477.
Tiley ads. Peo., 543.
Times Co. ads. Sandra, 569.
Title Guaranty & Surety Co. ads. Dyer, 219.
Tobias ads. Teutonia Ins. Co., 255.
Toledo, St. L. & W. R. Co. ads. Light, 606.
Toledo, etc., R. Co. v. Stevenson, 347.
Toledo, etc., R. Co. v. Wales, 606.
Toledo R., etc. v. Prus, 543.
Toluca Coal Co. ads. Bell, 274.
Tomblin ads. State, 199.
Tonn ads. Typer, 334.
Tonseth v. Portland Ry. Light & Power Co., 294.
Tooley v. Bacon, 349.
Tosser v. State, 590.
Townsend v. City of Joplin, 517.
Township ads. Rich, 348.
Township, etc. v. Empire, etc., Co., 132.
Tozer v. N. Y., etc., R. Co., 346.
Tracy v. Mt. Pleasant, 435.
Tracy v. People, 349.
Traders Ins. Co. ads. Catlin, 342, 459.
Trainor v. B. A. Building Ass'n, 310.
Trainor v. German-American, etc., 336.
Trainor v. Robyn, 309.
Trask v. People, 635.
Travelers, etc., Co. ads. Roth, 258.
Trayes ads. Chicago, etc., R. Co., 318.
Treat ads. Arnstine, 303.
Treat ads. Merchants Life Ins. Co., 633.
Tremblay v. Harden, 640.
Trickett ads. Harrison, 373.
Trinity, etc., R. Co. v. Geary, 289.
Trinity, etc., R. Co. v. McCune, 458.
Tripp ads. Hasceig, 195.
Troiani ads. Hews, 283.
Trotter ads. Craig, 386.
Troutman v. Gates, 275.
True ads. Choctaw, etc., R. Co., 199.
Truesdale v. Hoyle, 126, 303, 633.
Trussell v. Scarlett, 301.
Tubbs ads. People, 601.
Tuch ads. Ankersmit, 604, 606.
Tuckowska ads. United States Trust Co., 219.
Tuckwood v. Hanthorn, 602.
Tudor Iron Works v. Weber, 284.
Tuite ads. Chicago, etc., R. Co., 331.
Turley ads. State, 200.
Turner ads. Bailey, 195, 196.
Turner ads. Com., 542.
Turner ads. Landis, 309.
Turner ads. Peo., 590.
Turner ads. Quigley, 585.
Turner ads. Willis & Conner, 632.
Turner v. Ridgeway Tp., 459.
Turney v. State, 259.
Tutt ads. Morgan, 301.
Tuttle v. Robert Moody & Son, 349.
Tweed v. Western Union Tel. Co., 383.
Twitty ads. State, 331.
Tyler ads. Thayer, 384.
Tyler S. E. R. Co. ads. Wheeler, 385.
Typer v. Tonn, 334.
Tyson v. Post, 370.

U

Ullrich v. Chicago City R. Co., 475, 476.
Underhill ads. Yick Wo, 309.
Uniacke v. Chicago, etc., R. Co., 477.
Union Dime Sav. Inst. ads. Corbet, 328.
Union El. R. R. Co. ads. Geohegan, 284, 408.
Union Ins. Co. ads. Names, 291.
Union Oil Co. ads. Graves, 457.
Union St. R. Co. ads. Mercier, 272.
Union Trust Co. v. Best, 370.

United Eng., etc., Co. ads. Bertolami, 345.
United Fruit Co. ads. Freemand, 639.
United States ads. St. Clair, 258.
United States Trust Co. v. Tuckowska, 219.
United, etc., Cô. ads. Cobb, 462.
Unity Protective Ins. Ass'n ads. Parkin, 96.
Upthegrove v. Chicago Great Western R. Co., 285.
Urbanowiez v. Roman, 641.
U. S. ads. Chadwick, 126.
U. S. v. Watson, 129.
U. S. Brewing Co. ads. Nussbaum, 303.
U. S. Casualty Co. ads. Andres, 636.
U. S. Casualty Co. ads. Max L. Bloom Co., 284.
U. S. Cement Co. v. Cooper, 640.
U. S. Fidelity & Guaranty Co. v. Poetker, 642.
U. S. Gypsum Co. v. Shields, 371.
U. S. Light, etc., Co. ads. Keating, 541.
U. S. Mut. Acc. Assoc. ads. Omberg, 385.

V

Vagaszki v. Consolidation Coal Co., Inc., 106, 273.
Valdez ads. Vickery, 271.
Valentine ads. Hawkinson, 543.
Vallejo, etc., R. Co. v. Reed Orchard Co., 384.
Vanderhoof ads. Peo., 476.
Van Norman v. Young, 371.
Van Tassel ads. Peo., 543.
Van Wycklen v. Brooklyn, 458.
Vateck ads. Peo., 544.
Vaughan Corp. ads. Weinberg, 274.
Ventriss v. Pana Coal Co., 200.
Venture, etc., Co. v. Warfield, 371.
Venuto v. Lizzo, 386.
Veramendi v. Hutchins, 195.
Vergie v. Stetson, 294.
Verien ads. St. Stanislaus Church, 336.
Vessels v. Kansas City Light, etc., Co., 194.
Vetter ads. Freeman, 638.
Vickery v. Valdez, 271.
Village, etc. v. Schoening, etc., 350.
Vines v. State, 631.
Vinton v. Peck, 406.
Vitelle ads. Peo., 197.
Vivian's Appeal, 386.
Voche v. City of Chicago, 642.
Vogel ads. Hennies, 637.

W

Wabash R. Co. v. Kamradt, 348.
Wade ads. Ill. Cent. R. Co., 550.
Wade v. Galveston, etc., 604.
Wadley ads. Putnam, 387.
Waggoner ads. Fetherly, 127.
Wagner v. People, 602.
Wait ads. McGregor, 303.
Wait v. Wenks, 256.
Wakefield ads. Wise, 349, 580.
Wakeman ads. Brown, 346.
Walden v. Davidson, 303.
Wales ads. Toledo, etc., R. Co., 606.
Walker ads. Ohio R. Co., 295.
Walker ads. Woodard, 370.
Walker v. Chicago & C. R. Co., 356.
Walker v. Skliris, 313.
Wallace ads. Botsford, 274.
Wallace ads. C. & E. I. R. Co., 457, 458, 477.
Wallace ads. Farrell, 369.
Wallace ads. Gilliland, 274.
Wallace ads. McBride, 258.
Wallace v. Noble, 373.
Wallden v. Market St. Ry. Co., 642.
Waller v. Leonard, 348, 349.
Waller v. Sloan, 519.
Wallerich v. Smith, 350.
Wallingford ads. Davidson, 195.
Wallis v. Randolph, 604.
Walsh v. Chicago Rys. Co., 256.
Walsh v. Frankenthaler, 641.
Walsh v. Methodist, etc., Church, 303.
Walsh v. West Baden Springs Co., 632.
Walter ads. Kassing, 633.
Walter v. Hangen, 425.
Walters v. Geo. A. Fuller Co., 351.
Waltham ads. Clark-Rice Corp., 489.
Walton ads. State, 195.
Wanamaker ads. Rosen-Steinsit, 531.
Ward ads. Cochran, 331.
Ward v. Chicago City R. Co., 387.

Ward v. State, 199.
Ward v. Steel Co., 275.
Ward v. Thompson, 489.
Warfield ads. Venture, etc., Co., 371.
Warren Cotton Mills ads. LaPlante, 386.
Warrick v. Moore County, 488.
Warriner ads. I. C. C. R. Co., 332.
Warth v. Lowenstein, 489.
Washburn ads. Pioneer, etc., Co., 639.
Washington v. Smith, 546.
Washington v. State, 602.
Washington Water Power Co. ads. Denham, 198.
Wasmer v. Missouri Pac. Ry. Co., 218.
Waterbury ads. Shaw, 330.
Waterman ads. McCarty, 351.
Waterman v. Chicago, etc., R. Co., 604.
Watford ads. Carville, 547.
Watkins, etc., Co. v. Campbell, 408.
Watson ads. U. S., 129.
Way v. Greer, 371.
Weathered's Admr. ads. Boon, 579.
Webb v. Dale & Cain, 586.
Webb v. Feather, 258.
Webb v. Sweeney, 351.
Weber ads. Tudor Iron Works, 284.
Webster ads. People, 327.
Webster ads. Salen, 387.
Webster ads. Texas, etc., Co., 491.
Weeks v. Hull, 582.
Wehner v. Lagerfelt, 388.
Weinberg v. Hartzell, 605.
Weinberg v. Vaughan Corp., 274.
Weiner ads. Finch, 489.
Weiner ads. Schonhous, 95.
Weisbrod v. Chicago, etc., R. Co., 272.
Weitzel v. Brown, 334.
Welch v. N. Y., etc., R. Co., 303.
Weldon v. State, 580.
Wells ads. Collins, 271.
Wells ads. Levant, etc., Co., 425.
Wells ads. Paddock, 195.
Wells v. Ann Arbor R. Co., 214.
Wells v. Lavitt, 542.
Wenks ads. Rommel Bros., 601.
Wenks ads. Wait, 256.
West Baden Springs Co. ads. Walsh, 632.
West Bay, etc., Co. ads. Potvin, 328.
West Chicago Alcohol Works v. Sheer, 279.
West Chicago St. R. Co. ads. Finley, 602.
West Chicago St. R. Co. v. Carr, 385.
West Chicago St. R. Co. v. Dedloff, 641.
West Chicago St. R. Co. v. Kennedy-Cahill, 387.
West Chicago St. R. Co. v. Sullivan, 635.
West Coast T. Co. ads. McPherson, 284.
Western Fuel Co. ads. Gifford-Wood Co., 604.
Western Pipe, etc., Co. ads. Bruce, 323.
Western Transit Co. ads. Haley, 204.
Western Union Tel. Co. ads. Tweed, 383.
Western Union Tel. Co. ads. Wolff, 581.
Western Union Tel. Co. v. Gorman, 291.
Western Union Tel. Co. v. Johnsey, 348.
Western Union Tel. Co. v. McDavid, 306.
Western, etc., R. Co. v. York, 639.
Westfield Cigar Co. v. Teutonic Ins. Co., 349.
West Side R. Co. ads. Kohler, 258.
West Texas Utility Co. v. Penner, 641.
Wetmore ads. Smith, 275.
Wharton's Will, 602.
Wheeler v. Lawler, 636.
Wheeler v. Tyler S. E. R. Co., 385.
Whelan v. Gorton, 126, 303.
Whether ads. Huntley, 306.
Whidden ads. Lake Shore, etc., R. Co., 477.
Whidden v. Jordan, 371.
Whitacre ads. Daly, 387.
Whitaker v. Salisbury, 542.
Whitbeck ads. Est. of Ramsey, 542.
White ads. Chang Sim, 298.
White ads. Hopkins, 542.
White ads. Quincy, 363.
White v. Old Dominion S. S. Co., 374.
White Co. ads. Manhattan, etc., Co., 373.
Whitfield ads. Pardue, 601.
Whitman ads. Com., 273.

Whitridge ads. Middleton, 457, 459.
Whitteen ads. Dilger, 287.
Whittier v. Los Angeles, etc., Bank, 370.
Wickenkamp v. Wickenkamp, 605.
Wicks v. Cuneo-Henneberry Co., 324, 397, 398.
Wietzychowski ads. Diamond Glue Co., 256.
Wightman v. Campbell, 283, 347.
Wilcox ads. Dowdell, 640.
Wilcox ads. Michigan, etc., Co., 414.
Wilcox v. International Harvester Co., 435, 475, 476.
Wilkes-Barre Co. ads. Seeherman, 195.
Wilkinson ads. People, 366.
Williams ads. Dennie, 342.
Williams ads. International, etc., R. Co., 385, 386.
Williams ads. Martlock, 303.
Williams ads. Miller, 345.
Williams ads. Stephens, 334.
Williams v. Brooklyn, etc., R. Co., 636.
Williams v. Brown, 458.
Williams v. Craig, 258.
Williams v. Grand Rapids, 351.
Williams v. Perrotta, 353.
Williams v. Riches, 527.
Willis ads. Davis, 490.
Willis v. State, 196, 585.
Willis & Conner v. Turner, 632.
Wilmarth v. Cal. Mut. L. Ins. Co., 279.
Wilson ads. British, etc., Co., 126.
Wilson ads. McGoldrick, 309.
Wilson ads. Peo., 332.
Wilson ads. Perez, 641.
Wilson ads. Thomasson, 350.
Wilson v. Bauman, 279.
Wilson v. Steers, 295.
Wilson & Bennett Mfg. Co. ads. Heidler Hardwood Lumber Co., 601.
Wilson & Co. ads. Boston Food Co., 349.
Wilson, etc., Co. ads. H. F. Cady Lumber Co., 349.
Wiltse ads. Broadhead, 476.
Wiltse v. Fifield, 370.
Winchester Repeating Arms Co. ads. Oscanyan, 205.
Winn v. Cleveland, etc., R. Co., 336.
Winn v. Itzel, 634.
Winnesheik Ins. Co. v. Schueller, 197.
Winston ads. Ibanez, 289.
Winters v. Duncan, 640.
Winterson ads. Carlson, 579.
Winthrop ads. Thomas, 489.
Wisconsin Cent. R. Co. ads. Kath, 385.
Wisconsin Power & Light Co. ads. Brockman, 606.
Wisconsin, etc., Co. ads. Jewell, 635.
Wisconsin, etc., R. Co. ads. Kuhns, 459.
Wise v. Wakefield, 349, 580.
Withers v. State, 196.
Wittenberg v. Onsgard, 476.
Wolezek v. Public Service Co., etc., 636.
Wolf v. King, 341.
Wolfe v. Missouri, etc., Co., 271.
Wolff v. Western Union Tel. Co., 581.
Women's City Club of Boston ads. Kitchen, 531.
Wood ads. Hutson, 132.
Wood ads. State, 477.
Wood v. State, 347.
Woodard v. Walker, 370.
Woodman v. Churchill, 581.
Woodruff Coal, etc., Co. v. Commercial Coal Co., 282.
Woodrum Trunk Lines ads. Bailey, 283.
Woodworth v. Brooklyn El. R. Co., 458.
Wooley v. Fall River, 326.
Woolsey v. Saunders, 331.
Worley v. Spreckels, etc., 543.
Worsham ads. Cauble, 369.
Wosoba v. Kenyon, 323.
Wright ads. Bowe, 204.
Wright ads. Louisville, etc., R. Co., 373.
Wright ads. Pape, 579.
Wright ads. State, 386.
Wright v. Com., 199.
Wright v. Ft. Howard, 292, 385.
Wright v. Roseberry, 301.
Wright v. Stevens, 132.
Wrisley Co. v. Burke, 349.
Wrobel v. Call, 149.
Wuerth v. Frohlich, 129.
Wunderlich ads. Coman, 425.
Wunderlich v. Buerger, 606.
Wyatt Coal Co. ads. MacBard Coal, 298.

Wylie ads. Hillis, 580.
Wyman v. City of Chicago, 348.

Y

Yaeger v. So. Cal. R. Co., 348.
Yankee Jim's Union Water Co. v. Crary, 606.
Yanoway ads. Swift, 371.
Yellow Cab Co. ads. Metz, 636.
Yetter ads. Robinson, 371.
Yick Wo v. Underhill, 309.
Yohalem v. Matalone, 286.
Yore v. Meshow, 408.
York ads. Western, etc., R. Co., 639.
York v. Sheldon, 334.
Young ads. Galveston, etc., R. Co., 425.
Young ads. Smith, 363.
Young ads. Van Norman, 371.
Young v. Brady, 606.
Young v. Bridges, 198.
Young v. Mandis, 275.
Young v. New York, 606.
Young v. People, 126, 303.
Youngblood v. Youngblood, 349.
Youngs ads. Peo., 543.

Z

Zabowski v. Loerch, 218.
Zanger ads. Sax, 489.
Zeigler ads. Menley, 315.
Zeiverink v. Kemper, 301.
Zemansky ads. Khan, 579.
Zerwick ads. C. M. Ass'n, 639.
Ziedler v. Gollyer, 637.
Zimmerman v. State, 194.
Zipkie v. City of Chicago, 283.
Zoldoske v. State, 477.
Zucker v. Karpeles, 205.
Zuzak ads. Lewandowski, 334.
Zylstra v. Graham, 606.

INDEX

[REFERENCES ARE TO PAGES]

A

Absent witness
- as ground for continuance, see CONTINUANCES.
- making fact known to jury, 277–278.

Abstracts of records and briefs
- use of in preparation of facts, 32.

Accident investigators
- as impeaching witnesses, 556–559.
  - cross-examination of, 559–564.

Account books
  - see BOOKS OF ACCOUNT.

Admissions
- before trial, 111–120.
  - documents, genuineness of, 111.
    - failure to admit, 111.
  - facts, 111–112.
    - amending admission, 112.
    - failure to admit, 112.
      - reasonableness of, 112.
    - qualified admission, 112.
    - withdrawal of admission, 112.
  - forms
    - admission in writing of
      - facts, 120.
      - genuineness of documents, 120.
    - notices for admission of
      - facts, 113.
      - genuineness of paper or writing, 113.
      - public records, 119–120.
  - limitations upon right, 114–119.
  - public records, 112.
    - introduction in evidence as admitted fact, 112.

Admissions by attorneys during trial
- binding effect, 272.

INDEX

[REFERENCES ARE TO PAGES]

Admissions in opening statements, 218–219.

Adverse party
cross-examination of, 517–526.
illustration, 521–526.
examination of, before trial, 81–83.
injury cases, 81–83.
stipulations, 83.
impeachment of, 542–543.

Aged witnesses, 49.

Alibi witnesses
cross-examination of
illustration, 516–517.

Alienist and psychiatrist
illustration of proof of qualifications, 399–401.

Alterations and erasures
detection of by ultra-violet light, 6–7.

Alternative questions
objection to
illustration, 378.

Amendments of pleadings, 140–143.
affidavit of, form, 142–143.
during trial, 274–275.
objections, 142.
statute of limitations, 140–141.
time of, 140.
to conform to proof, 141.

Answer not responsive
objection when, 348.
illustration, 366.

Answer permitted subject to objection, 358.
promise to connect, 358–359.

Anticipating and preparing for opponent's proof, 46–47.

Anticipating objections
to method of proof, 60–61.

Anticipation of all propositions of law relied on by opponent, 68–69.

Appeals to passion and prejudice
see ARGUMENTS TO THE JURY, subhead PARTICULAR COMMENTS AND CONDUCT.

[REFERENCES ARE TO PAGES]

Arguing the law, 74–76.
tabulation of legal authorities, 74–75.

Arguments to the jury, 607–691.
addressing juror by name, 639.
appeal and conclusion, 625–626.
appeals to passion and prejudice, 639–641.
appeals to sympathy, 641.
attitude and demeanor of counsel, 612–613.
authorities, reading of, 636.
comments
see subhead PARTICULAR COMMENTS AND CONDUCT.
conduct of parties
comment upon, 638.
corroboration and cumulation, 624–625.
damages
comment as to amount of, 619–620, 641.
exaggerated opening statement
comment upon, 622.
excluded evidence
comment upon, 638.
exhibits
reading of, 612.
failure to produce evidence
comment upon, 639.
failure to produce witnesses
comment upon, 638–639.
framing the argument, 622.
appeal and conclusion, 625–626.
corroboration and cumulation, 624–625.
by documentary evidence, 625.
by parties, 624.
by witnesses, 624–625.
general suggestions, 626–631.
introduction, 622–623.
issues, 623.
opponent's contentions, 625.
picture of cause of action, 623–624.
refutation, 625.
full or incomplete argument, 617–619.
general suggestions, 626–631.
history and well known facts
comment upon, 639.

Arguments to the jury—Continued.
illustrations of, in
disputed document cases, 663–669.
insurance policy, suit upon, 642–656.
necessaries, suit against husband for, 656–663.
personal injury case, 669–691.
improbabilities, 616.
instructions
argument based upon, 620.
right to comment upon, 637.
unfavorable instructions, 621.
insurance
comment upon, 640.
latitude of argument, 635–636.
law, comments as to, 642.
limitation on number of attorneys, 635.
misstating evidence, 617.
objections to improper argument, 617.
right to interrupt, 635.
open and close, right to, 631–634.
criminal cases, 631–632.
defendants' right, 632–633.
determination of right, 632.
discretion of court, 633–634.
waiver, 633.
particular comments and conduct
addressing juror by name, 639.
appeals to passion and prejudice, 639–641.
against corporations, 640.
personal animosity, 640.
reference to insurance, 640.
sympathy, 641.
wealth or poverty, 641.
conduct of parties, 638.
damages, amount of, 619–620, 641.
excluded evidence, 638.
failure to produce evidence, 639.
failure to produce witnesses, 638–639.
history and well known facts, 639.
instructions, 637.
law, 642.
matters within counsel's personal knowledge, 636.
personal animosity, 640.
pleadings, reading of, 637.

Arguments to the jury—Continued.
particular comments and conduct—continued.
poverty or wealth, 641.
prejudice, 639–640.
against corporations, 640.
patriotic, 640.
religious, 640.
previous trial, 637.
reading authorities, 636.
reading of pleadings, 637.
reference to jurors by name, 639.
requesting jurors to make notes, 639.
requesting jurors to put selves in plaintiff's place, 641.
retaliatory remarks, 642.
sympathy, 641.
violent language, 639–640.
vouching for witnesses, 638.
wealth or poverty, 641.
well known facts and history, 639.
pleadings, reading of, 637.
preparation of argument, 608–609.
previous trial
reference to, 637.
questions for counsel to answer, 620–621.
reference to jurors by name, 639.
reference to opening statement, 622.
reference to parties by name, 622.
reply argument, purpose of, 634.
retaliatory remarks, 642.
right to make argument, 634.
right to open and close
see subhead OPEN AND CLOSE.
scope of argument, 635–636.
time limit, 634.
violent language, 639–640.
vouching for witnesses, 638.
waiver of right, 635.

Assuming facts in question
objection to
illustration, 365.
on cross-examination, 490, 508.

Assuming witness alone knows true fact
objections to, illustration, 382.

Index

[REFERENCES ARE TO PAGES]

Attending physician
testimony as to subjective symptoms, 385.

Attorneys' liens, 51.
contingent fee cases, 51.

Authorities
finding of favorable, 61–67.
reading of, in arguments to the jury, 636.
to show opponent's contentions not tenable in law, 69.

Automobiles
determining ownership of, 32.
market value and price
illustration of proving, 291.
questionnaire for use in accident cases, 41–45.
repair bills, 338–341.
admissibility in evidence, 338.
illustration of proving
where bill is paid, 338–339.
where bill not paid, 339–341.
speed
illustration of proving, 288.
sworn applications
use of, to disprove denial of ownership
illustration, 568–569.

B

Best evidence
objection when not, 348.
illustration, 369.

Bias
see IMPEACHMENT, subhead BIAS AND INTEREST OF WITNESS.

Bills of particulars, 120–126.
code provisions, 121–122.
forms
affidavit in opposition to demand, 122.
bill of particulars
fraudulent sale of stock, 125.
motion that demand be denied, 125.
notices
to furnish
goods sold, 122.
labor and materials, 123.

Bills of particulars—Continued.
forms—continued.
notices—continued.
to make pleading fuller, etc., 123–124.
to strike pleading because no bill filed, 124.
with bill of particulars furnished on demand, 124.
value of, 121.
when indicated, 121.

Blood tests
determining parentage by use of, 14–16.

Bone injuries
determining age of, by use of X-rays, 30–31.

Books of account, 308–315.
illustration laying foundation for admission, 310–312.
ledger sheets, 312–313.
testimony of customer, 314–315.
ledger, 309–310.
records made by others, 310.
statutory provisions relating to proof, 308.

C

Carbon copies
illustration of proving contents of lost instrument by, 321–322.

Carbon copies of letters, 302–308.
foundation for proof of, 304.
illustration of proof of
mailing, 306–308.
preparation of original and copy, 305–306.
notice to produce original
form of, 303.
necessity, 303n.
time for serving of, 303n.

Cardio-pneumo-psychograph, 10.
see LIE DETECTOR.

Certificates
admissibility
birth, 334.
death, 334.
marriage, 334n.
of magistracy
when necessary, 334.

Index

[REFERENCES ARE TO PAGES]

Certified and photostatic copies of exhibits
offer in lieu of original, 367.

Certified copies
illustration of proof of, 335–336.

Changes, alterations and interlineations
explanation of, before offering exhibit, 301.

Character and reputation
see IMPEACHMENT, subhead REPUTATION.

Character witnesses
see IMPEACHMENT, subhead REPUTATION.

Check
proof of execution of
illustration, 316–317.

Chemical and medical cases
questionnaire for use in preparation of facts, 39–40.

Chemist
illustration of proof of qualifications, 410–411.

Child witnesses
cross-examination of, 506–507.
qualifying, method of
illustration, 292.

Chiropractor
illustration of proof of qualifications, 403–404.

Cities, records of foreign
statutory provisions relating to proof, 331–332.

City, notice to, before suit, in personal injury cases
form of, 50–51.
illustration of proving, 330.
statutory requirements, 330n.

Closing arguments
see ARGUMENTS TO THE JURY.

Conclusion, of witness
objections, 349.
illustration, 368.

Confessions
signed confessions in criminal cases, 37.

Conjectural questions
objections
illustration, 375.

Connectives, 253–255.
forgetting facts, by witness, 254.
leading of witness through use of, 255.

Continuances, 136–140.
grounds for motion, 138.
absence of material evidence, 138.
amendment of pleadings, 138–139.
see also AMENDMENTS, subhead OBJECTIONS.
court's motion, 139.
witness in military service, 138.
witness member of legislature, 138.
payment of costs, 139.
petition, form of
absent witness, 139–140.

Contracts
proof of execution and foundation for admission
illustration, 316.

Contradictory statements
see IMPEACHMENT, subheads ORAL CONTRADICTORY STATEMENTS, SWORN CONTRADICTORY STATEMENTS, and WRITTEN CONTRADICTORY STATEMENTS.

Contributory negligence
cross-examination to show, 527–533.
illustrations, 528–529, 531–533.

Conversations
foundation for proof of, 269.
illustration of proving, 269.
objections where no foundation laid, 366.
telephone conversations, 269–271.
business calls, 271.
foundation for proof, 269–270.
illustration of proving, 270.
time, fixing of, 271.

Conviction of felony
see IMPEACHMENT, subhead CONVICTION OF INFAMOUS CRIME.

Conviction of infamous crime
see IMPEACHMENT, subhead same.

Corporate minutes
foundation for admission, 336.
illustration of proving, 337.

Court records, foreign
statutory provisions relating to proof, 331.

Court reporters
as impeaching witness
illustration of proof of qualifications, 574–577.
necessity of, in trial, 51.

Courts, reports of foreign
statutory provisions relating to proof, 331.

Credit agency reports
use of, in determining proper parties to sue, 32.

Crime, instruments of
admissibility of, in evidence, 284.

Cross-examination, 487–540.
adverse party, 517–526.
illustration, 521–526.
alibi witnesses
illustration, 516–517.
assuming facts in question, 490, 508.
bias
see BIAS.
character witnesses
illustration, 582–584.
children and women, 506–507.
contradiction on immaterial fact, 490.
contributory negligence, 527–533.
illustrations, 528–529, 531–533.
court, examination by, 490.
court's witness, 517.
demeanor of counsel, 495–496.
discrediting witnesses
see also IMPEACHMENT.
by cross-examination of another witness
illustration, 536–539.
"I don't remember," 508–509.
length of time injured person confined to bed, 533–535.
illustration, 534–535.
"To whom have you talked about this case?" 507–508.

Cross-examination—Continued.
discrediting witnesses—continued.
when case given to attorney, 535–536.
"When did you first know you were to be a witness?" 508.
evasive witnesses, 506.
exhibits, offer on, 298–299, 382.
expert witnesses
see EXPERT WITNESSES, subhead CROSS-EXAMINATION.
hypothetical questions
see HYPOTHETICAL QUESTIONS, subhead CROSS-EXAMINATION.
"I don't remember," 508–509.
impeachment
see IMPEACHMENT.
improbability of direct testimony, 509–512.
illustrations, 492–494, 512–516.
interruptions by opposing counsel, 507.
introduction of exhibits on, 298–299.
investigators of personal injury cases
illustration, 559–564.
leading questions on, 259n.
length of time injured person confined to bed, 533–535.
object of, 487–488.
objections to
when beyond scope, 349.
when of own witness
illustration, 381.
over cross-examination, 504–505.
planning in advance, 491–494.
questions
assuming facts in, 490, 508.
insulting, etc., 490.
right of court to ask questions, 490.
refreshing memory, 491.
repetition of direct testimony, 491, 498–499.
right to cross-examine, 488.
scope of, 489.
signature, where denied
illustration, 526–527.
slipping on rugs, etc., 530–533.
cross-examination to show contributory negligence
illustrations, 528–529, 531–533.
testing recollection
illustration, 429–433, 512.
"To whom have you talked about this case?" 507–508.

Cross-examination—Continued.
truthful witnesses, 498.
when case given to attorney, 535–536.
"When did you first know you were to be a witness?" 508.
women and children, 506–507.

Custom, 279–282.
illustration of proof of, 279–281.
where custom denied, 281–282.

Customary method
objection to question calling for
illustration, 374.

D

Debtor, who claims another person is obligated
suit against all parties involved, 50.

Deceased, transaction with
objection to question pertaining to, 348.

Decisions, courts, of foreign states
statutory provisions relating to proof, 331.

Dedimus
see DEPOSITIONS.

Delivery receipts
illustration of proving, 319–320.

Demonstrations and experiments, 282–287.
admissibility of evidence in general, 282–283.
civil cases, 282–283.
criminal cases, 283.
illegally obtained evidence, 286–287.
instruments of crime, 284.
models of machinery, 284.
physical objects, 284.
preliminary proof, 354–355.
similarity of conditions, 353.
view of locus in quo by jury, 283–284.

Demonstrative evidence
see DEMONSTRATIONS AND EXPERIMENTS.

Demurrers, 80–81.

[REFERENCES ARE TO PAGES]

Depositions, 97–106.
as a means of discovery, 97–99.
commissioner, 98.
compelling attendance of witnesses, 99.
conclusiveness of disclosure, 97.
officers of corporations, etc., 97.
right to take, 97.
statutory provisions, 97.
unjustified taking, penalty for, 97.
when use indicated, 98.
to ascertain proper parties, 98.
as a method of proof, 99–102.
procedure, 100.
statutory provisions, 100.
chancery cases, 100.
law cases, 101.
oral examination, 101.
costs for failure to take, 102.
motions to suppress, 106.
objections during taking, 106.
oral interrogatories, 105.
advantages of, 105.
reading depositions, 106, 272–273.
stipulations for issuance of dedimus, 102.
form of, 102–105.
value of procedure, 112–113.

Detectives, private
acquisition of facts by, 33.

Diagrams
admissibility in evidence, 282–283.
preparation of for trial purposes, 28.
use in opening statements, 223–224.

Dictograph
admissibility of evidence secured by, 24–25.

Direct examination, 247–292.
what is included, 247.
picture of cause of action, 248–251.
presentation of story by proper questioning, 252.
presentation of witnesses, 251.
proof of necessary elements, 248.

Directed verdict on opening statement, 204.

Index

[REFERENCES ARE TO PAGES]

Discovery before trial, 83–97.
see also ADMISSIONS; ADVERSE PARTY, EXAMINATION OF; DEPOSITIONS; INTERROGATORIES.
application for, 83.
failure to produce, 84.
penalties, 84.
forms, 87–95.
list of documents under discovery order, 90–92.
schedule 1, 90.
schedule 2, 91.
supplemental list, 91–92.
motions, 87–90.
discovery of documents, 87.
for order requiring affidavit as to possession, 88.
on refusal to produce or allow inspection, 88–90.
by defendant to dismiss complaint for refusal
to allow inspection, 88.
to produce document, 89.
by plaintiff to strike answer for refusal
to allow inspection, 89.
to produce document, 90.
to produce listed documents for inspection, 87.
to show cause why document should not be produced, 88.
notices of motion, 92–95.
for discovery, 92.
for order requiring affidavit as to possession of documents, 95.
on refusal to produce or allow inspection, 93–94.
by defendant to dismiss complaint for refusal
to allow inspection, 93.
to produce document, 94.
by plaintiff to strike answer for refusal
to allow inspection, 93.
to produce document, 94.
to produce listed document for inspection, 92–93.
to show cause why document should not be produced, 94–95.
introduction of books and documents in evidence
by party demanding, 85.
by party producing, 85.
by party refusing to produce, 85.
legal authorities, 95–97.
statutory provisions, 83–86.
when use indicated, 86–87.

Disputed documents, 16–21.
enlarged photographs, 17.
equipment, 18.
erasures and alterations, 6.
examination by experts, 17–18.
fields of investigation, 18.
ink writing, 18.
paper, 18.
pencil writing, 18.
typewritten documents, 18.
general suggestions, 20.
infra-red rays, 19.
legal citations may be obtained from expert, 18.
standards of comparison, 19.
ultra violet rays, 6.

Distance
illustration of proof, 278.

Distortion
in photography, 26.
in X-rays, 29–30.

Doctors
see PHYSICIANS.

Document speaks for itself, 313.
objections when
illustration, 368–369.

Documentary evidence
see EXHIBITS.

Documents, genuineness of
see ADMISSIONS, subhead BEFORE TRIAL.

Documents, production of
see DISCOVERY BEFORE TRIAL.

Double questions
objections to
illustration, 367.

E

Elements to be proved
outlining of, 47–49.

Encyclopedias
use in preparation of facts, 33.

[REFERENCES ARE TO PAGES]

Engineer
illustration of proof of qualifications, 406–408.

Erasures and alterations
detection of by ultra-violet light, 6–7.

Evasive witnesses
cross-examination of, 506.
leading questions, 258n.

Evidence
illegally obtained, 286–287.
offer of harmful, 267.

Examination of adverse party before trial, 81–83.

Exemplified statutes
statutory provisions relating to proof, 331.

Exhausting recollection
see REFRESHING MEMORY.

Exhibits, 293–344.
account books, see BOOKS OF ACCOUNT.
agreements, 316.
alterations, etc.
explanation of before offering exhibit, 370.
automobile repair bills, 338–341.
admissibility in evidence, 338.
illustration of proving
where bill is paid, 338–339.
where bill not paid, 339–341.
books of account, 308–315.
illustration of proving
books, 310–312.
ledger sheets, 312–313.
testimony of customers, 314–315.
ledger, 309–310.
records made by others, 310.
statutory provisions relating to proof, 308.
both sides, offering of, 300.
carbon copies
illustration of proving lost instrument by, 321–322.
carbon copies of letters, 302–308.
foundation for proof, 304.
illustration of proof of
mailing, 306–308.
preparation of original and copy, 305–306.

Exhibits—Continued.
carbon copies of letters—continued.
notice to produce original
form of, 303.
necessity, 303n.
time for serving of, 303n.
certificate of magistracy
when necessary, 334.
certificates
admissibility
birth, 334.
death, 334.
marriage, 334n.
certified and photostatic copies of exhibits
offered in lieu of original, 367.
certified copies
illustration of proof of, 335–336.
changes, etc.
explanation of before offering exhibit, 301.
check
illustration of proving, 316–317.
cities, records of foreign
statutory provisions relating to proof, 331–332.
city, notice to before suit, in personal injury cases
illustration of proving, 330.
statutory requirements, 330n.
contracts
illustration of proving, 316.
corporate minutes
foundation for admission, 336.
illustration of proving, 337.
court records, foreign
statutory provisions relating to proof, 331.
courts, reports of foreign
statutory provisions relating to proof, 331.
cross-examination
offer of exhibit on, 298–299.
objection, illustration of, 382.
delivery receipts
illustration of proving, 319–320.
document speaks for itself, 313.
exemplified statutes
statutory provisions relating to proof, 331.

Exhibits—Continued.
foreign judgments
illustration of proving, 341–342.
foreign statutes and laws
statutory provisions relating to proof of
court records, 331.
exemplified statutes, 331.
printed statutes, 331.
records of cities, 331.
reports of courts, 331.
foundation for proof, 294–295, 302.
identifying of
illustration of method, 296–297.
interlineations, etc.
explanation of, before offering exhibit, 301.
lease
illustration of proving, 317–318.
letters, see CARBON COPIES OF LETTERS.
limiting purpose of offer, 302.
lost instruments, 320–323.
defined, 320.
illustration of proving
by copy, 321–322.
where no copy available, 322–323.
materiality, 293–294.
mortality tables
illustration of proving, 336.
judicial notice of correctness, 336 and n.
mortgage
illustration of proving, 320.
notary
admissibility of certificate of foreign notary, 334.
certificate of magistracy, 334n.
note
illustration of proving, 315–316.
notice to city before suit
illustration of proving, 330.
statutory requirements, 330n.
notice to produce, 303.
form of, 303.
necessity, 303n.
time for serving of, 303n.
objections to exhibits, 295.
offering both sides, 300.

Exhibits—Continued.
offering exhibits identified by opponent, 299.
ordinances
foreign, 333.
illustration of proving, 333.
judicial notice, 332.
statutory provisions relating to proof, 332.
photographs, 326–330.
admissibility, 327.
amateur photographer, when taken by, 327.
changes in conditions, 327–328.
documents, 328.
enlarged photographs of, 328.
foundation for proof, 327.
illustration of proving, 329–330.
injured persons, 328.
purposes for which admissible, 326–327.
photostatic and certified copies of exhibits
offered in lieu of original, 367.
preliminary foundation, 294–295, 302.
printed statutes, foreign
statutory provisions relating to proof, 331.
promissory note
illustration of proving, 315–316.
reading to jury, 295.
during arguments to jury, 612.
reoffering, 300–301.
repair bills, 338–341.
automobiles
admissibility in evidence, 338.
where bill is paid, 338–339.
where bill not paid, 339–341.
skiagraphs, see X-RAYS.
stipulations of facts, 342–344.
binding effect, 342.
form, 342–344.
weather reports
illustration of proof, 318–319.
when offered, 298–299.
when permitted to offer on cross-examination, 298–299.
X-rays
admissibility in evidence, 323–324.
foundation for proof, 394.
illustration of proving, 324–326.

Index

[REFERENCES ARE TO PAGES]

Experiments, 285–287.
see also DEMONSTRATIONS AND EXPERIMENTS.
preliminary proof, 286–287.
similarity of conditions, 285.

Expert witnesses, 383–451.
admitting qualifications, 389.
alienist and psychiatrist
illustration of proof of qualifications, 399–401.
answer beyond scope of question
illustration, 412–414.
attending physician
testimony as to subjective symptoms, 385.
chemist
illustration of proof of qualifications, 410–411.
chiropractor
illustration of proof of qualifications, 403–404.
compensation of own expert
eliciting fact on direct examination, 390.
contingent fee contracts, 415.
cross-examination, 414–451.
amount of witness fee
illustration, 437–438.
authorities, where witness relies on
illustration, 433–437.
contingent fee contracts, 415.
handwriting witnesses
illustrations, 445–451.
hypothetical questions, see HYPOTHETICAL QUESTIONS, subhead CROSS-EXAMINATION.
latitude of inquiry, 414.
medical books, use of, 475–476.
mental conditions
illustration, 438–445.
qualifications, 425n.
illustration, 425–427.
relationship with parties and lawyers, 437n.
illustration, 437–438.
signaling questions for redirect examination, 414.
testing recollection
illustration, 429–433.
when opinion based on subjective symptoms
illustration, 427–429.

Expert witnesses—Continued.
engineer
illustration of proof of qualifications, 406–408.
examination solely for purpose of testifying, 385–386.
handwriting experts
illustration of proof of qualifications, 404–406.
handwriting witnesses
cross-examination of
illustration, 445–451.
jeweler
illustration of proof of qualifications, 411–412.
layman, opinion of, 386–387.
opinion evidence, 383–384.
facts upon which based, 387.
layman witness, 386–387.
health and physical condition, 386–387.
reasons, 386.
sciences and trades, 384.
physicians
attending physician
testimony as to subjective symptoms, 385.
examination solely for purpose of testifying, 385–386.
qualifications
illustration of proof, 391–398.
psychiatrist and alienist
illustration of proof of qualifications, 399–401.
qualifications, 388–389.
admitting of, 389.
cross-examination as to, 425n.
illustration, 425–427.
illustrations of proof
alienist and psychiatrist, 399–401.
chemist, 410–411.
chiropractor, 403–404.
engineer, 406–408.
handwriting expert, 404–406.
jeweler, 411–412.
physician, 391–398.
real estate appraiser and broker, 408–410.
toxicologist, 401–403.
X-ray experts, 324–326, 391–398.
qualifying by cross-examination of opponent's expert, 389–390.
illustration, 390.

Expert witnesses—Continued.
qualifications—continued.
questions for court, 384.
study as basis for qualification, 384–385.
real estate appraiser and broker
illustration of proof of qualifications, 408–410.
reasons for opinion, 386.
selection of expert, 387–388.
study as basis for qualification, 384–385.
subjective symptoms
who may testify as to, 385.
toxicologist
illustration of proof of qualifications, 401–403.
withdrawing witnesses, 390–391.
X-rays
illustration of proof of, 324–326, 391–398.

F

Facts, admission of, before trial
see ADMISSIONS, subhead BEFORE TRIAL.

Failure of witness to remember, 253–254.

Felony, conviction of
see IMPEACHMENT, subhead CONVICTION OF INFAMOUS CRIME.

Final arguments
see ARGUMENTS TO THE JURY.

Fluorescence, 8–9.
photography of, 8–9.

Fluoroscope, 29.
see X-RAYS.

Foreign judgments
illustration of proving, 341–342.

Foreign statutes and laws
statutory provisions relating to proof of
court records, 331.
exemplified statutes, 331.
printed statutes, 331.
records of cities, 331.
reports of courts, 331.

Forgotten questions
on direct examination, 348.
on redirect examination, 600.

Former contradictory testimony
see IMPEACHMENT, subhead SWORN CONTRADICTORY STATEMENTS.

Former conviction
see IMPEACHMENT, subhead CONVICTION OF INFAMOUS CRIME.

Fractures, 30.
see X-RAYS.

G

General objections
see OBJECTIONS.

Genuineness of documents
see ADMISSIONS, subhead BEFORE TRIAL; DISPUTED DOCUMENTS.

Gunpowder tests, 16.

H

Handwriting
see DISPUTED DOCUMENTS; EXPERT WITNESSES; STANDARDS OF COMPARISON.

Harmful evidence
disclosure of, in opening statement, 217.
offer of, on direct examination, 267.

Household furnishings
market price and value of, 291.
testimony of layman, 386.

Husband and wife
competency as witnesses, 375–376.

Hypothetical questions, 452–486.
amending and correcting upon objection, 460, 471–475.
answers to, 462–463.
illustrations of, as to
basis of opinion, 463.
causal connection, 463.
temporary or permanent, 463.
motion to strike, 463.
objections, 462.
scope, 462.
body of question, 454.

Hypothetical questions—Continued.
coloring and exaggeration of facts, 458.
commencement, 454.
improper form, 460.
conclusion, 455–456.
illustrations of
causal connection, 455–457.
future medical treatment, 457.
permanency of condition, 456.
temporary or permanent, 456.
cross-examination
additional facts, assuming of, 478–479.
admissions, 478.
anticipating of, 461–462.
authorities relied upon, 476.
breaking up question into parts, 476–477.
disproved facts, 479–480.
emphasizing hypothetical nature of question, 478.
medical books, 475–476.
mind and memory, 482–486.
illustrations, 484–486.
requesting opponent's hypothetical question, 478.
sanity and testamentary capacity, 482.
testing recollection, 477, 481–482.
unnecessary elements in question, 480.
where witness has not examined injured person, 480–481.
where witness has prepared question, 477.
death case
illustration, 468.
defendant's hypothetical question
illustration, 466–467.
length of question, 458.
modifying question, 460.
objections
grounds, 459.
modifying question, 460.
re-reading question, 461.
specific objections, 458, 471–475.
to answers, 462.
personal injury case
illustration, 464–466.
preparation of question, 452–453.
method of, 453.
using opponent's question, 463–464.

Index

[REFERENCES ARE TO PAGES]

I

Identifying exhibits
illustration of method of, 296–297.

Identifying persons
by witness during trial, 273.
illustrations, 273–274.

Illegally obtained evidence
admissibility of, 286–287.

Impeachment, 541–592.
admission by witness of contrary statement
effect when witness does not admit, 544.
adverse party, 542–543.
bias and interest of witness, 589–592.
cross-examination to show
illustrations
financial interest, 591–592.
relationship to party, 590–591.
character, see subhead REPUTATION.
conviction of infamous crime, 584–589.
admission as to conviction
effect of, 586.
arrests, etc.
admissibility of evidence of, 585.
felony, conviction of, 585.
foundation, laying of
illustration, 586–587.
indictments, etc.
admissibility of evidence of, 585.
old convictions, 588–589.
probation, effect of, 585–586.
proof of former conviction
illustration, 587–588.
statutory provisions, 584–585.
immaterial issues
impeachment not permitted on, 543.
impeaching evidence
nature of, 543–544.
necessity of producing, 546.
objections to laying foundation, 546.
oral contradictory statements, 546–550.
foundation, laying of
illustration, 547–549.
impeaching testimony
illustration, 549–550.

Impeachment—Continued.
- own witness, 542.
  - objections to
    - illustration, 381.
- public records, use of, 592.
- refreshing memory, 543.
- reputation, 577–584.
  - character witnesses
    - cross-examination of
      - illustration, 582–584.
    - preparation of, 580.
    - selection of, 578.
  - discussing of reputation by witness, 580.
  - good reputation, 577.
  - proving reputation, 578–582.
    - foundation, laying of, 578–579.
    - illustration, 581–582.
  - using opponent's witness as own, 584.
  - "Would you believe him under oath?" 580–581.
- sworn contradictory statements, 565–577.
  - former testimony, 569.
    - laying foundation, 569.
      - illustration, 570–574.
    - proof of contradictory statement, 574–577.
      - impeaching witness—court reporter, 574.
        - illustration, 574–577.
  - written statements
    - foundation, laying of, 567.
    - illustration, 568–569.
- when impeachment available, 545.
- written contradictory statements, 550–565.
  - foundation, laying of
    - illustration, 552–556.
  - impeaching evidence
    - illustration, 556–559.
      - cross-examination of impeaching witness, 559–564.

Improper remarks
- objections to
  - of counsel, 352.
    - illustration, 352.
  - of court, 353.
    - illustration, 353.

INDEX

[REFERENCES ARE TO PAGES]

Indefinite term
    objection to question
        illustration, 367.

Indicating by witness during trial
    illustration, 275–276.

Infra-red rays
    use of in document investigation, 19.

Ink writings, 18.
        see DISPUTED DOCUMENTS.

Instruments of crime
    admissibility of, 284.

Insurance, informing jury of
    during arguments to jury, 640.
    while examining witness
        motion to withdraw juror
            illustration, 380–381.

Interest
    illustration of proof of, 279.

Interlineations, alterations and changes
    explanation of, before offering exhibit, 301.

Interpreters, 276.

Interrogatories, 106–111.
    general reference, 106–107.
    form, 107–111.

Interview of client and witnesses
    preparation for examination, 266.
    preparation of facts, 33–46.
        corroboration of client's story, 37–38.
            by documentary evidence, 38.
        intimate details, 35.
        investigating client and his story, 38–40.
        questionnaire for use in
            automobile accident cases, 41–45.
            medical and chemical cases, 39–40.
        signed statements, 34–37.
            forms of
                narrative, 34.
                question and answer, 35–36.

Interview of client and witnesses—Continued.
preparation of facts—continued.
signed statements—continued.
general suggestions, 36–37.
in handwriting of witness, 35.
"O. K.'d" statements, 45–46.
writing out of story by witnesses, 35–36.

Investigators
see Accident Investigator.

J

Jeweler
illustration of proof of qualifications, 411–412.

Judicial admissions
during trial, 272.
in opening statement, 218–219.
stipulations of facts, 342.

Jury
selecting the jury, 152–200.
accepting without questioning, 168–169.
admission of prejudice by juror, 196–197.
bias against class of action, 197–198.
business relationship with party, 196.
challenges
after tender or acceptance, 179.
causes for, 193.
kinds of, 191.
watch number of, 175–176.
client, consult with, during impanelling, 165–166.
competency and qualifications of jurors, 194–200.
corporations, prejudice against, 197.
diagrams, 155.
embarrassing prospective juror, 161–162.
examining in panels of four or twelve, 154–155.
excusing jurors, 166–167.
exemption from service, 191–192.
fairness, 161.
financial interest in case, 194.
friendship toward party, 198–199.
hostility toward party, 198.
hypothetical questions, 199–200.

Jury—Continued.
selecting the jury—continued.
impanelling petit jurors, 193–194.
drawing by lot, 193.
passing upon jurors, 194.
importance of proper selection, 152.
investigating jury, 165.
judge, examination by, 178–179.
law, preventing statements on the, 174.
law, when to stress, 172–174.
legal qualifications, 191.
manner of counsel, 163–164.
manner of juror, 177.
mutual insurance company a party, member of, 195.
new jury, 153.
objections, explaining purpose of, 180–181.
one-man jury, 159–160.
opening remarks and conclusion, 181.
opinion fixed, 199.
"please," use of word, 171–172.
prejudice of juror
class, 197.
corporations, 197.
race or nationality, 197.
recognition of natural sympathies, 167–168.
where juror admits, 196–197.
preparation of questions in advance, 176.
prior accidents, examining in reference to, 158.
prior trial, where juror has served at, 196.
public officials, 194.
qualifications, and competency, 194–200.
questions, list of, 182–191.
when representing defendant, 186–190.
when representing plaintiff, 182–186.
automobile accident cases, 184.
women drivers, 185.
where juror has no prior service, 185.
where juror has served only in criminal court, 184.
recognizing prejudices and natural sympathies, 167–168.
relationship to party, 195.
six or twelve-man jury, 153–154.
society organized to prosecute crime, member of, 195.
statutory provisions, 191–194.
stockholder of corporation a party to suit, 194.

Jury—Continued.
selecting the jury—continued.
street-car motormen, as jurors, 177.
study of law or medicine by juror, 160–161.
technical terms, 163.
testing jurors' knowledge and education, 162–163.
types of jurors, 156–157.
women jurors, 158.
view of locus in quo by, 352–353.
when to demand jury, 152–153.

K

Keeler polygraph
see LIE DETECTOR.

L

Law
recognition of propositions of, 52–59.
in personal injury cases, 53–56.
method followed, 56–59.

Law books
their use, 62.

Layman
opinion of
admissibility of evidence, 386–387.

Leading questions
connectives, 253–255.
defined, 258 and n.
objections to
illustrations, 364–365.
on rebuttal, 603.
on redirect examination, 596.
when permitted, 258n, 259n.

Lease
proof of execution
illustration, 317–318.

Letters
proof of carbon copy and mailing
see CARBON COPIES OF LETTERS.

Lie detector, 10–14.
cooperation of subject, 12.
criminal cases, 13–14.
divorce cases, 10–11.

Lie detector—Continued.
missing merchandise, 11–12.
objections to, 12–13.
personal injury cases, 11.
personnel work, 12.

Lost instruments, 320–323.
defined, 320.
illustration of proving
by copy, 321–322.
where no copy available, 322–323.

M

Mailing of letter
proof of
see CARBON COPIES OF LETTERS.

Maps
admissibility in evidence, 282–283.
preparation of, for trial purposes, 28.

Market price and value, 291.
illustration of proving, 291.

Medical and chemical cases
questionnaire for use in preparation of facts, 39–40.

Medical facts
preparation of, 31–32.

Memory
see REFRESHING MEMORY.

Models of machinery
purpose for which admissible, 284.

Mortality tables
illustration of proving, 336.
judicial notice of correctness, 336 and n.

Mortgage
proof of execution
illustration, 320.

Motion to exclude witnesses, 209–210.
corporation a party, 210.
expert witnesses, 210.
parties, 210.

Motion to exclude witnesses—Continued.
purpose of motion, 209.
violation of order, 210.

Motions to strike and demurrers, 79–81.
harmful effect of improper use, 80.
when to make, 81.

Moving pictures
admissibility of evidence secured by, 24–25.

Municipal corporations, notice to, before suit
form of, 50–51.
illustration of proving, 330.
statutory requirements, 330n.

N

Notary
admissibility of certificate of foreign notary, 334.
certificate of magistracy, 334n.

Note
proof of execution
illustration, 315–316.

Notice to city before suit
form of, 50–51.
illustration of proving, 330.
statutory requirements, 330n.

Notice to produce
as condition precedent to introduction of secondary evidence, 126.
failure to serve notice, 126.
form of, 128, 303.
necessity of, 303n.
sufficiency of, 128.
time for serving, 303n.
when notice not necessary, 126–127.

O

Objections, 345–382.
general objections
defined, 346.
waiver of specific objection by, 350.
illustration, 377.
when used, 346.

Objections—Continued.
how should be made, 345–346.
offers of proof, see OFFERS OF PROOF.
preserving record for appeal on, 345, 351–352.
promise to connect, 358–359.
renewal of, 358.
ruling of court, 351–352.
specific objections
defined, 347.
form of, 347–348.
when necessary
alterative questions
illustration, 378.
answer not responsive, 348.
illustration, 366.
arguing with witness
illustration, 381–382.
assuming facts in question
illustration, 365.
assuming witness alone knows true fact
illustration, 382.
best evidence, when not, 348.
illustration, 369.
characterizing conclusion
illustration, 368.
conclusions, 349.
illustration, 368.
conjectural question
illustration, 375.
conversation, no foundation
illustration, 366.
cross-examination
beyond scope, 349.
of own witness, illustration, 381.
customary method
illustration, 374.
deceased, transaction with, 348.
depositions, when irregular, 349.
document speaks for itself
illustration, 368–369.
double questions
illustration, 367.

Objections—Continued.
specific objections—continued.
when necessary—continued.
exhibits, 295–296.
improper foundation, 348.
introduction on cross-examination
illustration, 382.
form of question, 349.
hearsay evidence, 349.
illustration, 367.
immaterial evidence, 378.
impeaching own witness
illustration, 381.
improper remarks, exception to
of counsel, 352.
illustration, 352.
of court, 353.
illustration, 353.
incompetent witness, 350.
illustration, 375.
indefinite term
illustration, 367.
insurance, informing jury of
illustration, 380–381.
introduction of exhibit on cross-examination, 382.
leading questions, 348.
illustration when improper, 364–365.
illustration when proper, 365.
method of proving fact improper, 349.
not bearing on issue
illustration, 378.
offers of compromise, 372–374.
illustration, 373.
ordinances, validity questioned, 348.
parol evidence rule violated, 350.
illustration, 372.
merged in contract, 372.
photographs, improper foundation, 348.
privileged communications, 379.
question previously answered, 349.
re-cross examination improper, 349.
re-direct examination improper, 349.
secondary evidence, 348.
illustration, 369.

Objections—Continued.
specific objections—continued.
when necessary—continued.
self-serving document, 350.
illustration, 379–380.
statute, validity questioned, 348.
variance, 348, 377.
witnesses
cross-examination or impeachment of own
illustration, 381.
incompetent, 350.
illustration, 378.
X-rays, 348.
time objection should be made, 347.
illustration, 376–377.
waiver of objections, 350–351.
cross-examination of witness on matter objected to, 350.
examining other witness on matter objected to, 350.
express waiver, 350.
failure to object, 351.
failure to renew objection, 351, 358.
general objection as waiver of specific objection, 350.
illustration, 377.
implied waiver, 350.
introduction of evidence objected to, 351.
specific objection as waiver of other objections, 350.
illustration, 374.
withdrawal of objection, 350.
withdrawal of question upon objection, 359.

Offers of compromise, 372–374.
admissibility of evidence of, 372–373.
letters containing offer, 373.
objections to, illustration, 373.
voluntary admissions, 373–374.
without prejudice, 374.

Offers of proof, 359–364.
illustration, 359–361.
requisites and sufficiency
conclusions, 362.
documentary evidence, 363.
offer en masse, 363.
limiting proposal, 362–363.

Offers of proof—Continued.
requisites and sufficiency—continued.
part competent, 362.
presence of jury, 364.
re-offer, 364–365.
right to make offer, 361–362.
ruling on offer, 363.
specific offer, 362.
time for making, 362.
what constitutes, 361.

Open and close
right to, 631–634.
criminal cases, 631–632.
defendant's right, 632–633.
determination of right, 632.
discretion of court, 633–634.
waiver, 633.

Opening statements, 201–246.
admissions in, 218–219.
anticipating defense, 215–216.
argument, propriety of, 214–215.
"As you know," 212–213.
to court, 213.
to jury, 213.
calling attention to adverse witness' idiosyncrasies, 220–221.
citing the law, 217.
contract case
framing opening statement, 232–235.
demeanor of counsel, 214.
detailed or short opening statement, 202–204.
where case complicated, 203.
witnesses illiterate, 203–204.
diagrams and photographs, 223–224.
directed verdict on opening statement, 204.
failure to make good opening statement, 201.
forcing defendant to make, 207–208.
framing opening statement, 221–235.
contract case, 232–235.
defendant's opening statement, 235.
plaintiff's opening statement, 235.
conclusion, 235.
damages, 234.

Index

[REFERENCES ARE TO PAGES]

Opening statements—Continued.
- framing opening statement—continued.
  - contract case—continued.
    - plaintiff's opening statement—continued.
      - introduction, 233.
      - parties, 233.
      - picture of cause of action, 233–234.
      - theory of case, 233.
  - personal injury case, 221–232.
    - defendant's opening statement, 228–232.
      - conclusion, 232.
      - establishing issue, 229–230.
        - contributory negligence, 229.
      - introduction, 229.
      - party defendant and his agents, 230.
      - picture of accident, 231.
      - theory of defendant, 231–232.
    - plaintiff's opening statement, 221–228.
      - conclusion, 228.
      - extent of injuries, 227.
      - injuries sustained, 226–227.
      - introduction, 221–222.
      - medical, surgical, etc., care, 227.
      - monetary loss, 227.
      - parties, 222–223.
      - scene of accident, 223–225.
      - theory of case, 223.
      - word picture of accident, 225–226.
- harmful evidence
  - disclosure of, 217.
- judicial admissions, 218–219.
- law, citing of, 217.
- logical sequence, 212.
- motion to exclude witnesses, 209–210.
  - corporation a party, 210.
  - expert witnesses, 210.
  - parties, 210.
  - purpose of motion, 209.
  - violation of order, 210.
- objections, 216.
- overstating and exaggeration, 211.
- parties
  - explanation of representative capacity of, 205.
  - manner of reference to, 217–218.

Opening statements—Continued.
photographs and diagrams, 223–224.
pictures, 212.
purpose of opening statement, 201.
real estate commission case
illustration of opening statement
for defendant, 238–240.
for plaintiff, 235–238.
representative capacity of party, explanation of, 205.
reserving or waiving, 206–207.
secret defense, 208–209.
testing opening statement, 202.
waiving or reserving, 206–207.
criminal cases, 206.
personal injury cases, 206.
secret defense, 206.
"We," use of word, 219–220.
"We expect to prove," use of phrase, 211–212.
witnesses, motion to exclude, 209–210.
wrongful death case
illustration of opening statement
for defendant, 245–246.
for plaintiff, 242–245.

Opinion evidence, 383–384.
facts upon which opinion based, 387.
layman witness, 386–387.
reasons, 386.

Opponent's proof
anticipating and preparing for, 46.

Oral contradictory statements
see IMPEACHMENT, subhead ORAL CONTRADICTORY STATEMENTS.

Ordinances
foreign, proof of, 332.
illustration of proving, 333.
judicial notice, 332.
objection to introduction, 348.
statutory provisions relating to proof, 332.

Outline of all propositions of law involved, 69–70.

Outlining of elements to be proved, 47.
diagram of case, 47–49.

P

Pain and suffering
who may testify as to, 291–292, 385.

Parol evidence, 369–372.
exceptions to rule
consideration, 371.
construction of parties, 371.
contract not intended binding, 369.
date, 369.
fraud and deceit, 371.
part in writing, 370.
receipts, 371–372.
subsequent agreements, 370.
waiver, 370.
objections to violation of rule, 350.
illustration, 372.
merged in contract, 372.

Parties
debtor who claims another person obligated
suit against all parties involved, 50.
determining proper, to sue
automobile owners, 32.
credit agency reports, 32.
telephone, gas and electric records, 32.

Pencil writings
see DISPUTED DOCUMENTS.

Personal injury cases
questionnaire for use in preparation of facts, 41–45.
recognition of propositions of law involved in, 53–59.

Phonograph records
admissibility of evidence secured by, 24.

Photographs, 326–330.
admissibility, 327.
amateur photographer, when taken by, 327.
changes in condition, 327–328.
documents, 328.
enlarged photographs of, 328.
foundation for proof of, 327.
illustration of proving, 329–330.
injured persons, 328.
purposes for which admissible, 326–327.

Photographs—Continued.
legal use, 25–28.
color filters, 27.
distortion, 26.
filing of data, 27.
films, 26.
fluorescence, 24.
lighting, 27.
perspective, 27.
photographs in dark, 24.
retouching, 27.
use of, in opening statements, 223–224.

Photostatic and certified copies of exhibits
offered in lieu of originals, 299.

Physical examination
of plaintiff in personal injury cases, 81–83.
stipulations, 83.

Physicians
attending physician
testimony as to subjective symptoms, 385.
examination solely for purpose of testifying, 385–386.
qualifications
illustration of proof, 391–398.

Pleadings
amendment of, during trial, 274–275.
preparation of, 77–78.
reading of, during arguments to jury, 637.

Powder nitrate tests, 16.

Preliminary motions, 79–151.
admissions, 111–120.
adverse party, examination of, 81–83.
amendments, 140–143.
bill of particulars, 120–126.
continuances, 136–140.
depositions, 97–106.
discovery before trial, 83–97.
interrogatories, 106–111.
motions to strike and demurrer, 79–81.
notices to produce, 126–128.
subpoena duces tecum, 128–131.

Preliminary motions—Continued.
- summary judgments, 143–151.
- venue, change of, 131–136.

Preparation of facts, 1–51.
- what it includes, 4.
  - acquisition of knowledge, 4–33.
  - anticipating and preparing for opponents' proof, 46–47.
  - interviewing client and witnesses, 33–46.
  - outlining elements to be proved, 47–49.

Preparation of the law, 52–78.
- anticipation of all propositions of law relied on by opponent, 68–69.
- finding favorable authorities, 61–67.
- outline of all propositions of law involved, 69–70.
- recognition of propositions of law involved, 52–59.
- recognition of questions involving method of proof, 59–61.
- securing authorities to show opponent's contentions not tenable in law, 69.
- trial brief, 70–74.

Previous trial
- see IMPEACHMENT, subhead SWORN CONTRADICTORY STATEMENTS.
- reference to, in argument to jury, 637.

Printed statutes, foreign
- statutory provisions relating to proof, 331.

Privileged communications
- objections to
  - illustration, 379.

Production of documents
- see DISCOVERY BEFORE TRIAL.

Promissory note
- proof of execution
  - illustration, 315–316.

Proof, method of
- recognition of questions involving, 59–61.
  - anticipating objections, 60.
  - method, 60–61.

Psychiatrist and alienist
- illustration of proof of qualifications, 399–401.

[REFERENCES ARE TO PAGES]

Public records
introduction in evidence as admitted fact, 112.

Public utility company records
use of in determining proper parties to sue, 32.

Q

Questions
cross-examination, on
assuming facts in, 490, 508.
court, right of, 490.
insulting, etc., 490.
objections
alternative, 378.
assuming facts in, 365.
assuming witness alone knows true fact, 382.
conclusion, calling for, 349.
conjectural, 375.
customary method, 374.
double, 367.
form, 349.
indefinite term, 367.
leading questions, see LEADING QUESTIONS PREVIOUSLY ANSWERED, 349.
privileged communication, calling for, 379.
withdrawal upon objection, 359.

R

Radiograph
see X-RAYS.

Reading of testimony given at previous trial, 288–290.
illustration of method, 289–290.
when permitted, 288n, 289n.

Real estate appraiser and broker
illustration of proof of qualifications, 408–410.

Rebuttal, 602–606.
direct questions, 603.
evidence in chief, 606.
purpose of, 604.
reply or surrebuttal, 606.
scope
admissibility of evidence, 604–605.
witnesses, 603–604.

[REFERENCES ARE TO PAGES]

Recollection
see REFRESHING MEMORY.

Record
preserving, on objection, 351–352.

Re-cross examination
objection when improper, 349.

Redirect examination, 593–602.
admissibility of evidence, 601–602.
forgotten questions, 600.
leading questions, 596.
opening the door, 599.
refreshing recollection, 597–599.
scope, 601–602.
signals on cross-examination, 595–596.

Refreshing memory
before trial, 598–599.
cross-examination as to, 491.
exhausting recollection as foundation to, 365, 259n.
illustration of method, 256–258.
leading questions permitted, 365.
memorandum, 256n.
by whom prepared, 256n.
independent recollection, 256n.
right of opposing counsel to examine, 256n.
when prepared, 256n.
own witness, 543.
redirect examination as to, 597–599.
testing memory of witness
illustrations of cross-examination, 429–433, 512.

Repair bills, 338–341.
automobile
admissibility in evidence, 338.
illustration of proving
where bill is paid, 338–339.
where bill not paid, 339–341.

Reputation
see IMPEACHMENT, subhead same.

Right to correct testimony, 255.

Right to open and close
    see Op. and Close.

Roentgenogram
    see X-R. s.

S

Scientific aids in preparation of facts, 5–6.

Scientific crime detection laboratory, 21–24.

Secondary evidence
    see also Notice to Produce.
  objection to
    illustration, 369.

Selecting the jury, 152–200.
    see Jury.

Self-serving document
  objection to, 350.
    illustration, 379–380.

Signature
  cross-examination where denied
    illustration, 526–527.

Signed statements by witnesses
  for use in preparation of facts, 34–37, 45–46.
  impeachment purposes, 550–564.

Skiagraphs
    see X-rays.

Speed, 287–288.
  illustration of proving, 288.

Standards of comparison, 19–20.

Statutes
  objection to introduction in evidence, 348.
  their use, 62.

Stereoscopic films
    see X-rays.

Stipulations
  dedimus, for issuance of, 102–104.
  facts, 342–344.
    binding effect, 342.
    form, 342–344.

Stipulations—Continued.
importance of record showing, 271–272.
legal effect, 271n.
of facts, 342–344.

Subjective symptoms
who may testify as to, 291–292, 385.

Subpoena duces tecum, 128–131.
form of petition, 130.
improper issuance of, 129.
persons subject to process, 129n6.
petition, necessity of, 129.
when use indicated, 128–129.

Summary judgments, 143–151.
affidavit for, 144.
affidavit of merits, 144.
facts known to hostile person, 144.
counterclaim, 144–145.
forms, 146–149.
affidavit for summary judgment, 146–147.
recovery of land, 146.
recovery of money, 146.
affidavit of defense, 147–148.
facts known to hostile person, 148.
to all of claim, 147.
to part of claim, 147.
motion, 149.
notice, 148.
New York authorities, 149–151.
value, 145.

Surrebuttal, 606.

Sworn applications
use of to disprove denial of ownership
illustration, 568–569.

Sworn contradictory statements
see IMPEACHMENT, subhead same.

T

Tabulating and arranging
documentary evidence for trial purposes, 49.
legal authorities, 49, 74–75.

Telephone conversations, 269–271.
business houses and offices, 271.
foundation for proof of, 269–270.
illustration of proving, 270.

Testimony
reading of, given at previous trial, 288–290.
illustration of method, 289–290.
when permitted, 288n, 289n.
right to correct, 255.

Testimony, former contradictory
see IMPEACHMENT, subhead SWORN CONTRADICTORY STATEMENTS.

Toxicologist
illustration of proof of qualifications, 401–403.

Trial brief, 70–74.
abstract of each witness' story in narrative form, 72.
abstract of pleadings, 72–73.
brief on law, 73.
detailed signed statement from each witness, 72.
diagram of the case, 47–49, 71.
instructions, 73.
list of witnesses, 72.
presenting to court, 73–74.
resumé of facts in narrative form, 71–72.
what it should contain, 71.

Truthful witnesses
cross-examination of, 498.

Typewritten documents, 18.
see DISPUTED DOCUMENTS.

U

Ultra violet rays, 6–9.
criminal cases, use in, 7.
erasures and alteration of documents, 6.
fluorescence and photography, 8.

V

Value
see MARKET PRICE AND VALUE.

Variance
objection when, 348, 377.

Venue, change of, 131–136.
application, when may be made, 135.
forms
affidavit in opposition, 135.
affidavit or verification, 135.
petition
prejudice of judge, 136.
prejudice of people, 136.
statutory provisions, 132–135.

View of locus in quo by jury, 283–284.

W

Weather reports
as aid in preparation of facts, 33.
proof of
illustration, 318–319.

Wills
illustration of proving execution of, 289–290.

Witnesses
absent
as ground for continuance, 138.
making fact known to jury, 277–278.
aged, 49, 259n.
alibi, 516–517.
arguing with, 381–382.
biased, 589–592.
child
cross-examination of, 506–507.
leading questions, 259n.
qualifying, method of, 292.
court's, 517.
cross-examination, see CROSS-EXAMINATION.
discrediting of
see CROSS-EXAMINATION; IMPEACHMENT.
evasive, 506.
experts, see EXPERT WITNESSES; HYPOTHETICAL QUESTIONS.
handling of, 258n, 277–278.
hostile, 258n.
identifying persons in courtroom, 273–274.
ignorant, 259n.
impeachment, see IMPEACHMENT.